The JLC Guide to

Energy Efficiency

Best Practices for Builders and Remodelers

From the Editors of

The Journal of Light Construction

A Journal of Light Construction Book

www.jlconline.com

hanley▲wood

First printing: October 2011

Cover Design: Jennifer Griffiths
Cover Photo: Paul Huijing

Project Editor: Steven Bliss
Editorial Direction: Sal Alfano, Don Jackson
Managing Editor: Leslie Ensor

Graphic Designer: Jennifer Griffiths
Illustrator: Tim Healey, except where noted
Production Director: Theresa Emerson

International Standard Book Number: 978-1-928580-46-1

Printed in the United States of America

A Journal of Light Construction Book
The *Journal of Light Construction* is a trade name of Hanley Wood, LLC.

The Journal of Light Construction
186 Allen Brook Lane
Williston, VT 05495

Acknowledgments

We wish to thank the many JLC authors who contributed to this book, drawn largely from the pages of the *Journal of Light Construction*, with material updated by JLC staff and contributors. *JLC*'s strength lies in its authors who have pioneered and fine-tuned many of the energy-efficient building concepts and techniques covered in this book. With an emphasis on practical solutions, they have been generous in sharing their hard-won knowledge with the larger building community to the benefit of all. For their contributions, we wish to thank the following: Dwayne Akers, Steve Andrews, Gary Bailey, William Baldwin, Joel Boucher, Paul Bourke, Terry Brennan, Thorsten Chlupp, Ted Cushman, David Damroth, Jeri Donadee, Bob Dwyer, Steve Easley, Bill Eich, Paul Eldrenkamp, Paul Fisette, David Frane, Don Fugler, Gary Gerber, Jerry Germer, Alan Gibson, Matt Golden, Rick Groff, Mark Gronley, David Grubb, John Gulland, David Hansen, Bruce Harley, Martin Holladay, David Joyce, David Keefe, Mason Knowles, Don Kolbert, Jim Larson (of Cardinal Glass Industries), Joe Lstiburek, Jim Lunt, Rich McNally, Malcolm Meldahl, James Morshead, Doug Mossbrook, Terry Nordbye, Danny Parker, Dan Perkins, Robert Post, Gary Pugh, John Raabe, Victor Rasilla, Mike Rogers, Carl Saunders, Andrew Shapiro, John Siegenthaler, Chuck Silver, Mike Sloggatt, Steven Smulski, Rick Stacy, Bruce Sullivan, Bruce Torrey, Gordon Tully, Michael Uniacke, John Vastyan, Doug Walter, Cary White, Adam Winter, Ralph Woodard, and Harvey Youker.

Our apologies to anyone inadvertently left off the list.

Contents

Chapter 12: Combustion Air 277

Chapter 13: Mechanical Ventilation 293

Chapter 14: Energy Retrofits 307

Chapter 15: Building Innovations 331

Chapter 16: Solar and Alternative Energy 359

Index 393

Introduction

With oil prices over $100 a barrel at the time of this writing, the Japanese nuclear crisis barely contained, and the Mideast in political turmoil, we are reminded once again that our energy supply is anything but secure and that energy prices are largely beyond our control. What we can control, however, is the amount of energy we consume.

Energy-efficient construction plays a critical role here. In addition to shrinking homeowners' heating and cooling bills and protecting them from future rate shocks, buyers of well-built, low-energy homes enjoy greater comfort, a healthier indoor environment, and superior building durability. The country as a whole benefits, too, since buildings account for an estimated 40 percent of our nation's total energy consumption.

Achieving the goal of cutting home energy use has been a long and bumpy road, however. Since the late 1970s, advocates of low-energy housing have experimented with a wide range of materials, techniques, and building systems, some more successful than others. Solutions to one problem often led to other problems. For example, adding more insulation and building tighter cut energy bills but, in some cases, led to moisture and air-quality problems. Raising the efficiency of "condensing" furnaces to over 90 percent often led to corrosion and product failure. Early passive solar homes were often too hot when the sun shone and too cold at night. And debates over the proper application of air and vapor barriers continue to this day.

Overcoming these problems has taken hard work and a commitment to innovation throughout the building industry. It has required a new understanding of how buildings work and how the many systems that make up a house interact in complex ways. Builders and designers have had to master new materials, new knowledge, and new skills. With time and effort, builders have learned how to achieve the sometimes conflicting goals of low energy use, occupant comfort, a healthy indoor environment, and building durability.

Many of the authors in this book have played key roles in this effort. In this volume, they share the practical, hands-on techniques they've pioneered to build comfortable, healthy, and durable low-energy homes. We hope that their hard-won knowledge will help make your job a little easier and help you succeed in building homes that are pleasing to customers, easy on their wallets, and kind to the environment.

Steve Bliss
Project Editor

Chapter 1

BUILDING ENERGY BASICS

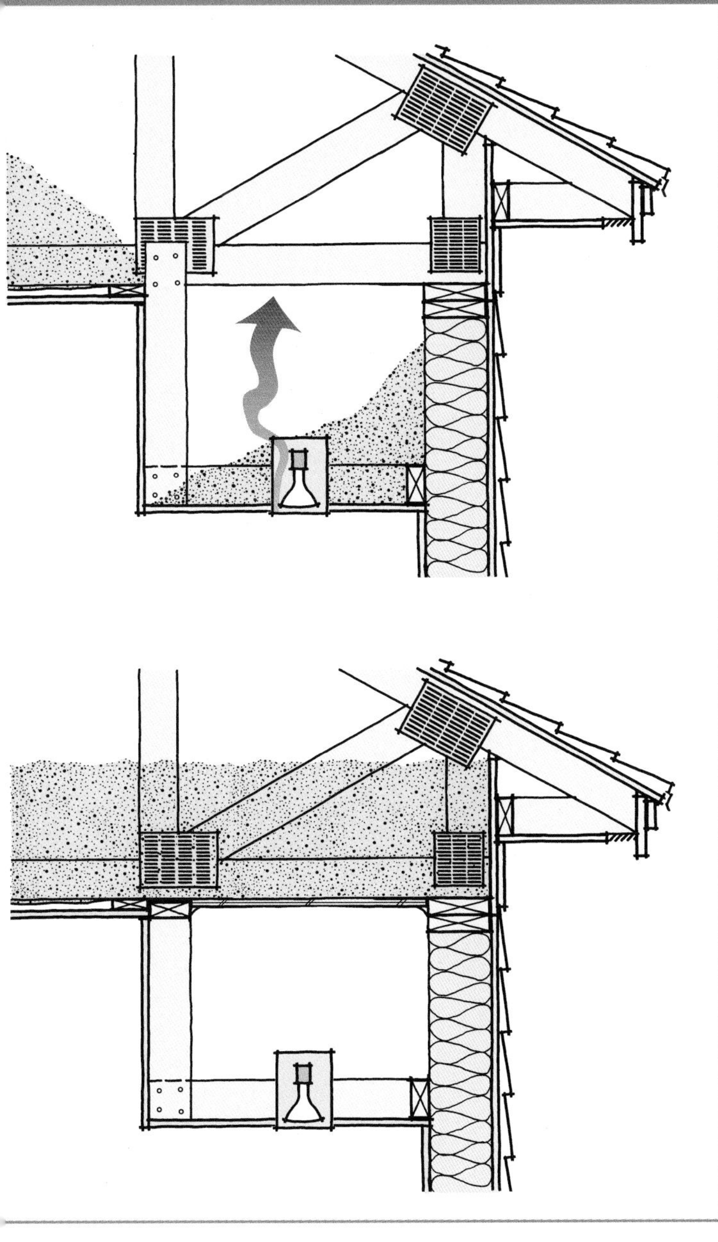

- Best-Practice Energy Upgrades
- Common Energy Claims: Fact or Fiction?
- Energy & Moisture Matters
- Guide to the Energy Codes

Best-Practice Energy Upgrades

by Steve Andrews

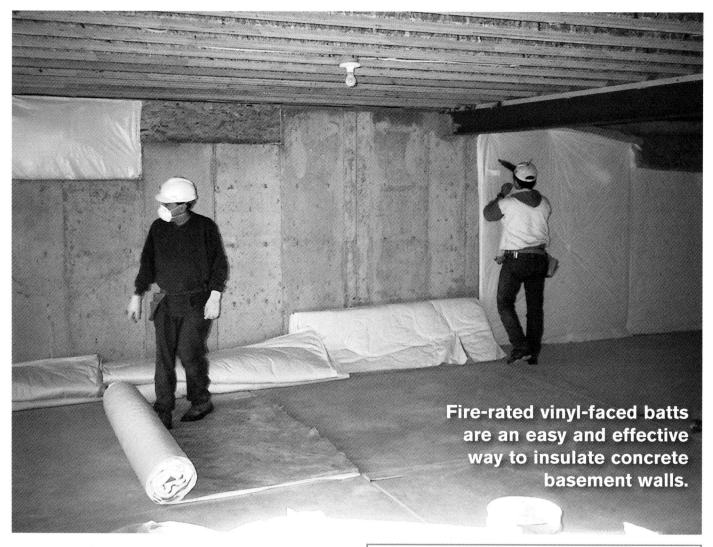

Fire-rated vinyl-faced batts are an easy and effective way to insulate concrete basement walls.

I've been an energy consultant to Colorado builders for more than 20 years, and I've done detailed performance tests on nearly 200 homes in the state. Based on that experience, here are the energy-saving features I most strongly recommend to both production and custom builders in my home state. All five measures are proven and widely accepted, which should make them equally useful to builders in other cold-climate areas.

Build Tight, Vent Right

Tests indicate that attics account for about 40 percent of the air leakage in a typical two-story home. The crawl space, rim joist, and garage account for 30 percent, with another 10 percent issuing from the pair of six-inch combustion air ducts in the basement. Air leaks through windows, doors, and exterior walls kick in another 10 to 15 percent, and 5 to 10 percent comes from cantilevers close to ground level.

Figure 1. Use a smoke pencil to check the seal between the garage foundation wall and drywall. This joint must be sealed with urethane caulk, an EPDM gasket, or expanding foam to prevent negative pressure from drawing toxic fumes into the basement.

Shell Tightening Dos and Don'ts

by Martin Holladay

Do Address the Basics First

The design of an energy-efficient house begins with a well-insulated, air-sealed shell and very efficient hvac equipment. Anyone intending to build an energy-efficient house needs to be sure these basic requirements are met before considering exotic (and expensive) components, like photovoltaic modules.

Also, specifications for an energy-efficient house depend greatly upon local climate. Before settling on any construction details, you should always investigate methods used by other energy-efficient builders in your region.

Do Install Rigid Foam Wall Sheathing

Many cold-climate builders still cling to the belief that foam sheathing creates a wrong-side vapor retarder and, therefore, contributes to wall rot. In fact, the inside surface of foam sheathing will be much warmer than the inside surface of OSB or plywood sheathing and will, therefore, be less likely to support condensation. Foam-sheathed walls, if built correctly, are less likely to have moisture problems than walls sheathed with OSB or plywood.

Foam sheathing wraps a home's walls in a warm jacket, keeping the framing warm and dry and greatly reducing thermal bridging through studs. Furthermore, if foam sheathing is held in place with vertical strapping, a rain screen is created behind the siding.

Builders making the switch to foam sheathing must choose one of three strategies for bracing walls against racking. They can install traditional 1x4 let-in braces, diagonal steel strapping (for example, Simpson TWB straps), or sheets of well-nailed 1/2-inch plywood at the corners. The plywood can then be covered with 1/2-inch rigid foam to match the thickness of the 1-inch foam installed everywhere else. Of course, before settling on a bracing method you should make sure your local building inspector approves of your plan.

Don't Insulate Rim Joists With Unfaced Fiberglass

Although fiberglass insulation is a thermal barrier, it is not an air barrier. If unfaced fiberglass is used to insulate a rim joist, moist indoor air can filter through the batt, leading to condensation at the cold rim joist. The result, eventually, is mold and rot.

There are several acceptable ways to insulate a rim joist. Rigid foam insulation can be installed on the exterior of a recessed rim joist, small pieces of rigid foam can be inserted in each joist bay from the inside, or spray polyurethane foam can be used to seal the entire rim-joist area.

Do Arrange for Blower-Door Testing

Do you know how much air leaks under your rim joists or bottom plates? If you've never used a blower door, you haven't yet earned the right to brag to customers about construction quality. Most blower-door contractors can recount stories of proud builders humbled by the revelations of a door-mounted fan.

Once you're familiar with the lessons taught by whole-house depressurization, you'll probably be more conscientious with gaskets and spray foam on your next house.

Martin Holladay *is senior editor of www.GreenBuildingAdvisor.com and was formerly the editor of Energy Design Update.*

Start with the garage. But the single biggest concern is leaks around the garage door bringing air into the house through penetrations in the drywall or between the drywall and concrete (Figure 1). That air carries with it a toxic soup: carbon monoxide after a car starts up, plus effluents and off-gassing from turpentine, paints, gas cans, power equipment, and cleaning products.

The solutions are straightforward: After drywall is installed, seal all joints between drywall and concrete, then caulk all penetrations and seal any cantilevered chases that run up into a second floor. On average, this should take one person about 20 minutes. We're not talking about a big hole here, just a really bad one.

The largest leaks into attics are generally chases tied to entertainment centers, fireplaces, flues, and decorative or architectural support columns. Seal flues with sheet metal and caulk (Figure 2). Seal the open tops of interior soffits with any suitable rigid or sheet material, such as pieces of Thermoply or foil-faced bubble-pack insulation (Figure 3). A surprising amount of air leaks up through partition walls. Have your insulator seal these from the attic after drywall is installed, using a hand-held canister and spraying a thin coat of foam over the plate/drywall connections.

Sealing a partial at-grade crawlspace from the house is often impractical and always time consuming. The better strategy is to make it an unvented crawlspace, then seal the crawlspace from the exterior, placing a carefully sealed vapor barrier down on the ground, and heat the space.

Ventilation made simple. The "ventilate right" part of this equation can be accomplished in two ways. First, you can upgrade your client's existing kitchen and bath fans. A recent market survey by a utility in my area indicates that the cheap little bath fans installed in most homes are so noisy that homeowners hate to use them.

Going to a quiet bath fan costs from $75 to $100 per fan. Upgrade at least one controller with an intermittent timer so the bath fan runs part of every hour of the day, providing limited ventilation year-round. Replace unventilated kitchen fans with a quiet fan that is always ventilated to the outdoors.

The second option is a low-cost approach to whole-house ventilation: Install a fan recycler controller (Aircycler, www.aircycler.com) that enables a furnace blower to provide ventilation thoughout the year. If your furnace or air conditioner hasn't run for an hour, the controller turns the blower on for five minutes. Whenever the blower operates, a small duct on the return-air side of the unit brings fresh air in through a duct to the outside and circulates it throughout the home. Several production builders working with the Building America program have opted for this approach, which costs only about $150 to $200 to install.

Figure 2. The flue is correctly sealed where it enters the sheet-metal covering at the bottom of the chase. But the edges of the plate should also have been sealed.

Insulate the Foundation

Like windows, concrete foundations are a major source of conductive heat loss. In states and localities that use the Model Energy Code, you generally have to insulate every part of your foundation, and it's a cost-effective measure in all cold-climate areas. Don't forget the slab edges, as far too many builders do.

Blankets and ICFs. In unfinished basements, the most common solution is a vinyl-faced R-11 or R-19 blanket attached to the inside of the concrete foundation walls (see photo, page 2). If the basement will be finished, consider using insulated concrete forms (ICFs). You can simply screw the drywall to the facings of the spacers that hold the two walls of foam apart. Most ICFs provide insulation values that fall between R-14 and R-22. Going with ICFs also means that you'll need less concrete.

Crawlspaces and shallow foundations. In crawlspaces, insulate the concrete stem walls with fiberglass batts (go with R-13 or R-19 batts, depending on your climate), securing them as for a full basement wall. In my area, the building codes permit the use of unfaced batts in crawlspaces, rather than the vinyl-faced batts required in basement applications. However, there is evidence that batts covered on all faces perform better. Make sure that the bottom edge of the batt "curtain" extends beyond the base of the footing, not just to the bottom of the wall, and remember to insulate the rim joists.

For an on-grade slab, consider using some form of shallow foundation (Figure 4), which is thermally efficient and far less costly than a conventional slab and

Sealing Interior Soffits

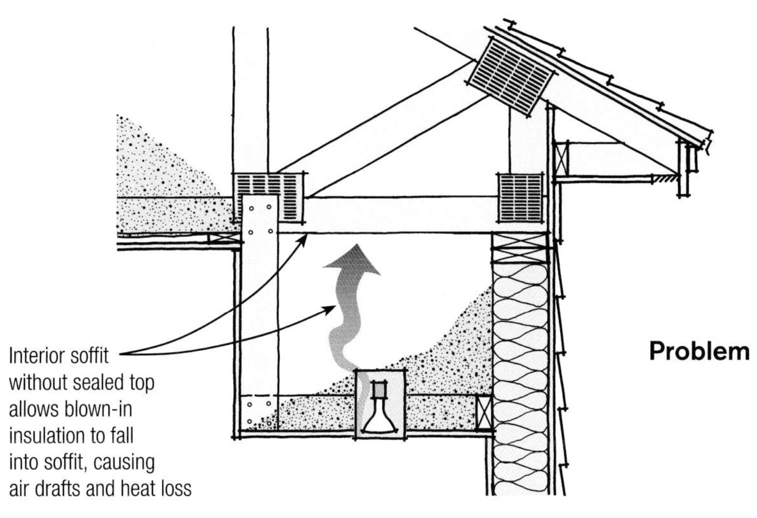
Interior soffit without sealed top allows blown-in insulation to fall into soffit, causing air drafts and heat loss
Problem

Figure 3. Interior soffits are common sources of heat loss. In the top illustration, the cellulose insulation that was blown toward the eaves wall has fallen into the soffit, allowing heat to radiate through its uninsulated vertical wall. The recessed can light compounds the problem by allowing heated air to escape to the attic as well. One solution is to seal the open top of the soffit with plywood as part of the framing process, providing a flat surface that can be easily insulated from the attic (middle). Better yet, first drywall the ceiling above the soffit, then frame and drywall the soffit itself.

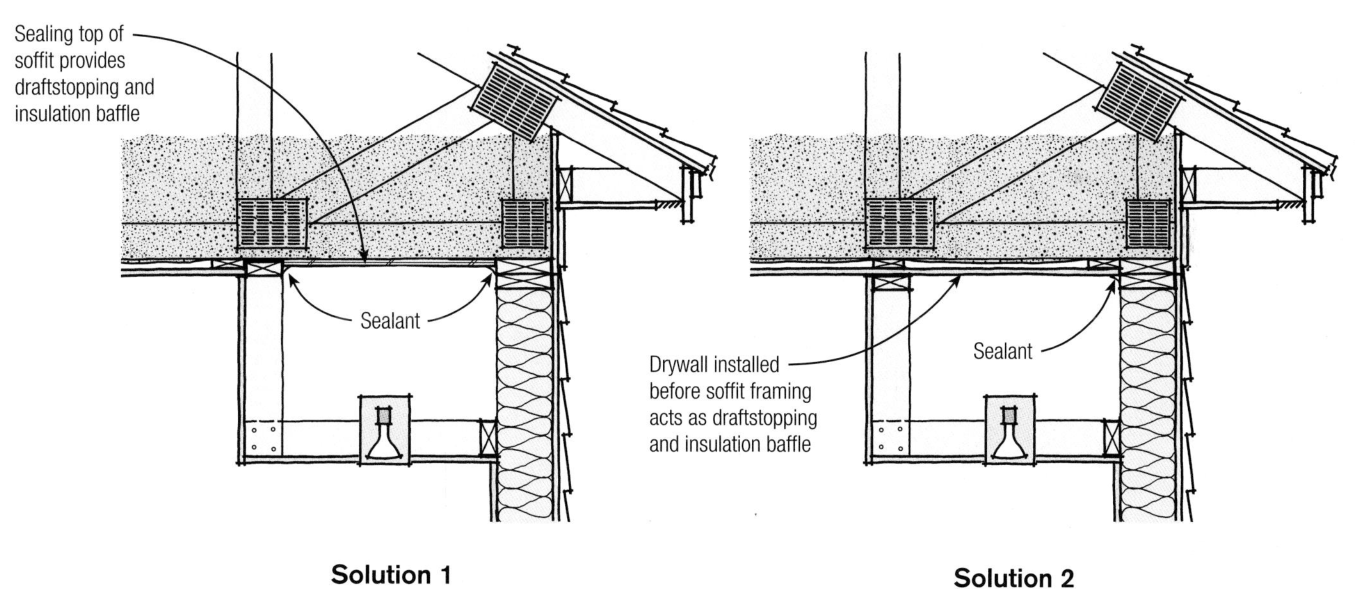
Sealing top of soffit provides draftstopping and insulation baffle
Sealant
Drywall installed before soffit framing acts as draftstopping and insulation baffle
Sealant
Solution 1
Solution 2

stem wall (see "Frost-Protected Shallow Foundations," page 86).

If the slab will be heated directly — either hydronically or from passive solar gain — don't forget to insulate it from beneath with rigid foam. In a cold heating climate of 4,000 degree days or more, I recommend a minimum value of R-5 in this application. In severely cold climates or in a home that will be heated with an expensive fuel, such as propane, R-10 would be a better choice.

Attack the Attic

As I mentioned earlier, most attics have enough insulation. But many attics have little flaws that can eventually cause big problems, such as mold and mildew in uninsulated corners.

If you're building with conventional roof trusses, for example, there are only 2 to 6 inches of insulation covering the first foot and a half of your attic next to exterior walls, except along gable ends. Solution: Use energy trusses (Figure 5), so there's room for at least 6 inches of insulation over the top plates.

Blown cellulose can't be used to insulate above cathedral ceilings, because the loose insulation tends to slide down the slope and pile up at the top of the adjoining wall. Fiberglass batts are the usual choice in

Foundation Dos and Don'ts

Do Install Basement Wall Insulation

According to the prescriptive requirements of the International Energy Conservation Code, basement walls should be insulated in climate zones 4 and higher.

Basement walls can be insulated from the exterior or the interior. Most builders find that installing interior basement insulation is easier and cheaper than installing exterior basement insulation; far too often, however, they get the details wrong.

Interior basement insulation is effective only if the work is properly detailed and meticulously installed. The rim-joist area must be air sealed (either with sprayed polyurethane foam or very careful caulking), and the rim-joist area and walls must be carefully insulated with rigid-foam sheets or sprayed polyurethane foam. Never use fiberglass batts to insulate basement walls.

Exterior basement insulation usually performs better than interior basement insulation. It locates the wall's thermal mass within the building's thermal envelope; if installed properly, it can be used to protect the rim-joist area. Also, by keeping the concrete warm, it prevents the condensation and moisture problems often associated with interior basement insulation.

Don't Build a Poorly Insulated Slab

In a hot climate, an uninsulated slab in contact with cool soil can lower cooling costs. In a cold climate, though, slabs should be well insulated.

Some cold-climate builders, having learned that heat rises, install thick attic insulation while leaving their slabs uninsulated. But heat actually moves from warm to cold in all directions. While it's true that in winter the soil beneath a slab is warmer than the outside air, a slab can still lose a significant amount of heat. In cold climates, a basement slab should be insulated with at least 2 inches of extruded polystyrene (XPS) under the entire slab. For a slab-on-grade home in a cold climate, specify 3 or 4 inches of XPS under the entire slab, with additional vertical foam at the slab's perimeter.

Foil-faced bubble pack (R-1.3) is no substitute for adequate insulation; under a slab, it's virtually useless.
—Martin Holladay

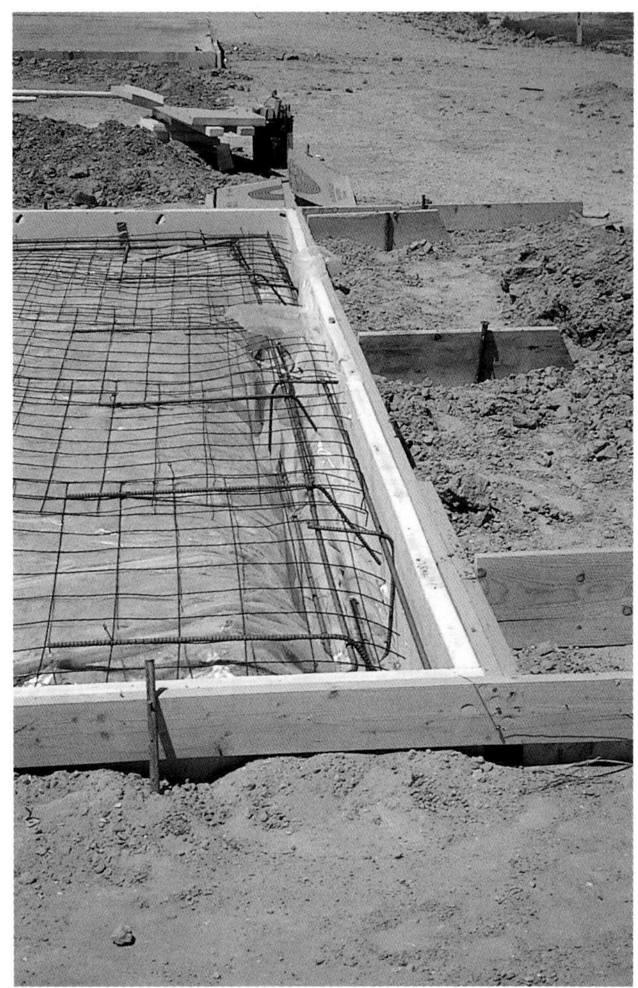

Figure 4. Cost savings associated with an energy-efficient shallow foundation can be used to pay for additional energy upgrades.

Figure 5. Energy trusses provide full insulation depth all the way to the outside face of the wall. The addition of cheap blocking will keep loose-fill insulation from falling into the interior soffit cavity.

this application, even though gaps between batts or compression caused by wiring can significantly reduce the insulation's performance.

If you also have some flat ceiling areas that call for cellulose, though, there's a simple solution to this problem: Blow an R-11 layer of loose-fill cellulose over the fiberglass batts to cover the gaps and other imperfections. On moderate slopes — up to 5/12 or so — the texture of the batts will keep the loose fill from sliding off. The trick here is to make sure that you get enough batt material down at the base of the ceiling, where the lack of clearance between the batts and the roof decking make it awkward to blow in the cellulose.

It's the installation, stupid. Advocates of blown fiberglass like to claim that cellulose settles, thereby losing R-value. The cellulose crowd counters that fiberglass installers often install their product at too low a density ("fluffing"), thereby losing R-value. Though both charges contain some truth, both products, when properly installed, will provide the stated R-value.

What really matters is the quality of the installer's work. Attics I've inspected recently have fallen far short of specified levels (Figure 6).

Ventilation Dos and Don'ts

Do Upgrade the Mechanical Ventilation System

Because an energy-efficient house has a well-defined air barrier and very low air-leakage rates, mechanical ventilation is essential.

Ventilation can be provided with a simple exhaust-only system (a timer-controlled bath exhaust fan, for example) or a passive supply system (such as a passive fresh-air duct controlled by a motorized damper and connected to a furnace's return-air plenum).

But the most efficient way to provide fresh air to every room is with an HRV or an energy-recovery ventilator (ERV).

Do Install Dedicated Ventilation Ductwork

Every HRV deserves dedicated ventilation ductwork. Ducts designed to distribute air for heating or cooling are not optimal for distributing ventilation air, so don't try to use the same ducts for both purposes.

A forced-air heating system usually draws its return air from a big grille in the hallway. An HRV, on the other hand, should draw its exhaust air from bathrooms, utility rooms, and the laundry room. Unlike forced-air heating ducts, ventilation ducts are sized for low airflow; usually they measure only 4 inches or 6 inches in diameter.

Don't Use a Standard Furnace Fan To Distribute Ventilation Air

Most new homes include some type of whole-house mechanical ventilation system — for example, a passive outdoor-air duct connected to a furnace's return-air plenum. Some builders provide ventilation by connecting a heat-recovery ventilator (HRV) to the home's forced-air ductwork.

Both methods have an Achilles heel: They depend on the furnace fan to distribute ventilation air. In homes equipped with air cleaners, homeowners may leave the furnace fan running continuously.

This can carry a substantial energy penalty. Furnace fans are designed to move a lot of air — up to 1,400 cfm — yet most homes require only 50 or 100 cfm for ventilation. In fan-only mode, certain furnaces can draw as much as 700 to 800 watts.

One solution is to specify a furnace with a blower powered by an electronically commutated motor (ECM) that draws 200 to 250 watts in fan-only mode. Another is to choose a different type of ventilation system — a simple exhaust-only system or an HRV with dedicated ventilation ductwork.

Don't Install a Humidifier

Homes with very dry indoor air during the winter are usually leaky. Make the building more airtight, and it won't be as dry.

Installing a humidifier is so risky it should be avoided like the plague. In cold climates, almost all moisture problems are worsened by elevated indoor humidity. High levels of indoor humidity are associated with wet walls and wet roof assemblies.

If homeowners want a humidifier, warn them about the dangers of humidification. If they insist, let them install it themselves after you leave the job.

—M. H.

Figure 6. Note the sloppy batt installation, and a thermal canyon excavated by the electrician. You get what you *inspect*, not what you *expect.*

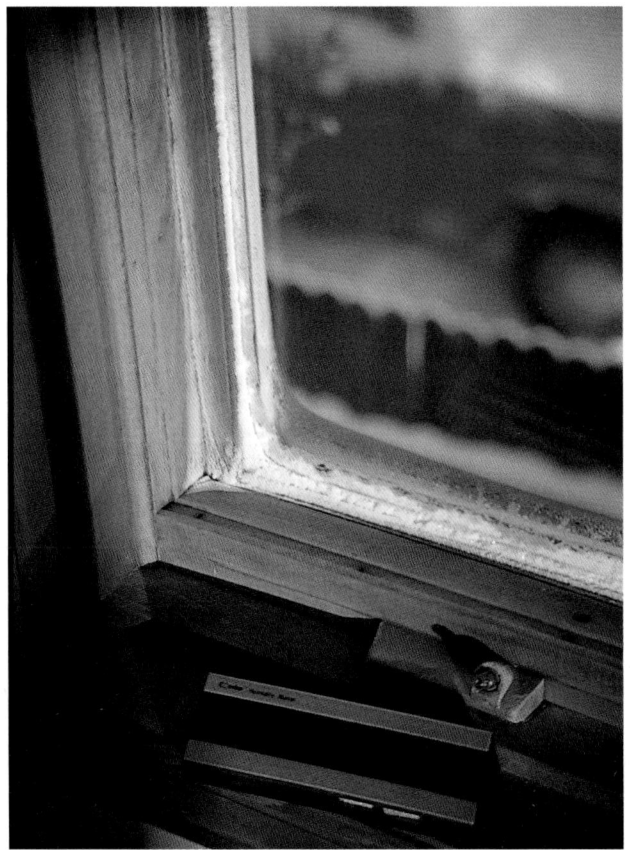

Figure 7. In addition to lowering heating and cooling costs, upgrading to low-E windows will increase homeowner comfort and reduce or eliminate condensation and frost.

Upgrade the Windows

Your best opportunity to reduce conductive heat loss and improve indoor comfort is to add insulating value to the building components that are losing the most heat to begin with. In other words, before you add insulation to the attic, which usually has an insulating value of at least R-30, it makes sense to upgrade your windows.

Switching from metal to vinyl windows, for example, typically increases their insulating value from R-1.5 to R-2. To put that another way, the R-1.5 window loses heat 20 times as fast as a square foot of attic, while the R-2 window loses heat only 15 times as fast. Going to windows with a typical low-E coating increases their R-value to R-2.5 or better, and a low-E coating combined with an insulating gas filling brings it up to R-3 or so.

On a 2,000-square-foot house, the move from R-2 to R-3 windows will bump the overall price of the window package by $250 to $400. Compared with the cost of upgrading to better windows ten years down the road — when energy prices may be much higher than they are today — that has to be seen as a tremendous bargain.

Better windows make a better house. Upgrading windows from R-2 to R-3 does more than just reduce heat loss. On a cold night, the surface of the R-3 glass may be ten degrees warmer, increasing comfort and reducing the chance of condensation forming on the glass (Figure 7). It reduces fabric fading caused by UV radiation and increases long-term resale value. In homes with large expanses of unshaded east and west-

Roof & Attic Dos and Don'ts

Do Design a Roof That's Easy to Insulate

For those who espouse the principle "form follows function," the ideal roof is a simple gable over an unheated attic, much like the roof on the house we all drew in kindergarten. Unfortunately, designers these days are fond of complicated roofs — ones with enough valleys, dormers, and intersecting planes to make the home look from a distance like an entire Tuscan village.

Such roofs are difficult to insulate without resorting to spray polyurethane foam. Though spray foam is effective, it's also expensive. In most cases, simple roofs are easier to insulate, easier to ventilate, and far less prone to ice dams than complicated roofs.

Don't Install Recessed Can Lights on the Top Floor

Despite their tendency to cast strange shadows on people's faces, recessed can lights retain an inexplicable popularity. Ignoring the pleas of lighting experts — who note that it makes more sense to light the ceiling than the floor — many customers still request recessed cans.

When installed in an insulated ceiling, these fixtures are an energy disaster.

Some builders have switched to "airtight" cans. But airtight cans are not completely airtight. The amount of leakage depends on the care exercised when installing the gasketed trim kit, and any future trim changes can affect the fixture's air tightness.

It is much easier to air-seal electrical boxes installed for surface-mounted fixtures than to air-seal a recessed can. Just say no to recessed cans.

Don't Install a Powered Attic Ventilator

Many builders assume that hot attics are a problem. If soffit and ridge vents don't keep an attic cool, they may decide to install an exhaust fan in the attic to improve attic ventilation. This is almost always a mistake.

If an attic has no ductwork or hvac equipment and its floor has a deep layer of insulation, high attic temperatures don't matter much. In fact, high attic temperatures can help lower winter heating bills.

Several studies have shown that a powered attic ventilator often draws its makeup air from air leaks in the attic floor, pulling conditioned air out of the house instead of in from the soffits. This, of course, increases the homeowner's energy bills.

—M. H.

facing windows, upgrading to low-E glass can prevent overheating on sunny days and reduce the cost of air conditioning. In an air-conditioned house with a large heat gain, low-E glass may be cost effective on the basis of cooling alone.

Tighten the Ductwork

Leaky ductwork is common everywhere, and it's a bigger problem than many builders realize. It reduces comfort and wastes energy, but it is also a potential safety problem. During one recent six-year period, there were 352 cases of carbon monoxide poisoning in Colorado alone, including 34 fatalities. The vast majority of the cases involved gas appliances, and although blocked flues were implicated in many of them, negative pressure was another troublesome issue.

When more air is drawn out of the room than is being easily supplied, the result is negative pressure. If the negatively pressurized space is a basement, combustion gases can be drawn back down the flue and into the home. When those gases are reburned, they produce carbon monoxide.

The usual causes of negative pressure, in approximate order of importance, include leaky return-air ducts, fireplaces, down-draft kitchen exhaust fans, undersized cutouts through floor plates for return air drops, dryers, large combustion air ducts located on the sheltered (leeward) side of a home, and normal exhaust fans.

Testing for negative pressure. Fifteen to twenty percent of all new homes have a negative pressure problem, so here's a quick test that will tell you whether your home is one of them. It should be performed on every home with a basement: Close the basement door, turn the furnace blower on, and feel if air is rushing underneath the door from the house into the basement. If there is, the home has negative pressure in the basement, probably caused by leaky return-air ductwork.

A negatively pressurized basement is a potentially serious safety problem, and requires more additional safety testing than I can describe here. Call your heating contractor or local energy specialist for help. (If air is rushing out of the basement and into the house, on the other hand, you have a pressurized basement. That's an energy problem, but not a safety worry.)

Seal for real. Eliminate leaks by sealing ductwork on

Window Dos and Don'ts

Do Orient the House Properly

Passive-solar design does not need to be complicated; a few simple steps can save significant amounts of energy. Yet most new-home builders still pay almost no attention to orientation.

If the lot size permits, a house should always be oriented with its long axis aligned in an east-west direction. In most climates, about half the home's windows should be facing south. In hot climates, it's important to minimize the number and size of west-facing windows.

Do Install Better Windows

Windows represent the weakest thermal link in most building envelopes. Unfortunately, the U.S. Department of Energy has chosen to set a very low bar for Energy Star windows, so Energy Star labels provide little guidance to builders. In most parts of the country, in fact, an Energy Star window is equal to a code-minimum window.

Specifying windows can be complicated, but a few general principles apply. Casement windows usually have less air leakage than double-hung windows. In heating climates, the best windows will have a lower U-factor than windows minimally complying with Energy Star standards (U-0.35). Consider investing in windows with argon-filled triple glazing and two low-E coatings; such windows are available with a whole-window U-factor as low as 0.17.

In south central and southern climate zones, Energy Star specifications call for windows to have a maximum solar heat-gain coefficient (SHGC) rating of 0.40. In these zones, consider purchasing windows that beat this standard — that is, windows with an SHGC below 0.40. Specifying glazing with a very low SHGC is especially important for west-facing windows, since these are the ones most likely to contribute to overheating.

—M. H.

Figure 8. Ideally, return air should be ducted, but well-made panned joist returns also work well. The edges of this tin header are correctly sealed with mastic. The edges of the tin panning that will span the joists on the other side of the supporting steel beam will also need to be carefully sealed to provide a tight return-air cavity. Pipe and wiring penetrations must also be sealed.

Figure 9. Each extra elbow in this run of duct adds the frictional equivalent of 10 feet of straight pipe. The added resistance often means poor airflow, especially when the duct serves a bedroom over the garage, which already has higher-than-average heating and cooling demands.

the outside with mastic. Another alternative is to use the new aero-seal procedure, which pressurizes the ductwork and shoots sealant into all the small holes from the inside. Whatever you do, don't use tape, which deteriorates rapidly with age. Emphasize to your heating contractor that you really want the return air ductwork carefully sealed at potential sources of leakage: headers to floor joists (Figure 8), drops from the floor joists into the return-air plenum, and top takeoffs at the plenum.

Finally, check the tops of plenums to make sure there are no exposed cutouts. In production homes, sealing your ductwork with mastic will typically cost from $200 to $400, depending on house size.

HVAC Dos and Don'ts

Do Install Very Efficient Hvac Equipment

Choose a furnace with a minimum 90 percent AFUE (annual fuel utilization efficiency) and an air conditioner with a minimum 14 SEER (seasonal energy efficiency ratio).

Don't Install Oversized Hvac Equipment

Compared with homes built 30 years ago, today's houses are more airtight and better insulated, so their heating and cooling loads are smaller.

Yet many hvac contractors continue to use old rules of thumb to size furnaces and air conditioners, often throwing in a generous safety factor for good measure.

Oversized furnaces and air conditioners cost more than right-sized units. Oversized equipment frequently operates less efficiently, too, because it suffers from short cycling. An oversized air conditioner often shuts down before it's had a chance to wring much moisture out of the air, compromising comfort.

Although hvac contractors usually claim to have performed detailed load calculations, you should insist on seeing written evidence. Heating and cooling loads should be calculated for each room and must be based on accurate specifications for window sizes, orientation, and U-factor, and for the installed glazing's solar heat coefficient. Don't let your contractor talk you into adding a safety factor to a calculated load.

Experience has shown that builders who want right-sized hvac equipment need to educate themselves on this issue and double-check the work of their hvac sub.

If you don't feel qualified to verify your sub's calculations, at least specify two-stage equipment that can operate at partial load most days of the year.

Don't Install Hvac Equipment or Ducts in an Attic

An attic is almost as cold as the exterior in winter and can be much hotter than the exterior in summer. While attic floors are often insulated to R-38, attic ducts are usually insulated to a measly R-4 or R-6.

During the summer, the difference in temperature between the cool air in the ducts and a hot attic is much greater than the difference in temperature between the indoor and the outdoor air. So why does attic ductwork have so much less insulation than a wall or a ceiling?

Moreover, the air in a supply duct is at a much higher pressure than the air inside a house. Since most duct seams leak, a significant portion of the volume of air passing through attic ducts usually leaks into the attic. Any leaks in return ducts allow the blower to pull hot, humid attic air into the air handler.

Installing a furnace or air handler in an attic causes even more problems than merely installing ductwork there. A recent study found that the leakage of a typical air handler, coupled with the leakage at the air-handler-to-plenum connection, amounts to 4.6 percent of the airflow on the return side. If the air handler is installed in an attic, a 4.6 percent return-air leak can produce a 16 percent reduction in cooling output and a 20 percent increase in cooling energy use. Any duct leakage would make the situation even worse.

In most homes, hvac equipment and ductwork belong in the basement or crawlspace. If it's absolutely necessary to build on a slab, include a utility room for hvac equipment and install ducts in air-sealed interior soffits.

—M. H.

Sealing the ductwork will also reduce comfort problems, especially the annoying "Goldilocks effect" that often plagues air-conditioned homes: too cold in the basement (60 degrees or so), too hot on the second floor (78 degrees), and just right on the main floor (74 degrees.) This is often caused by leaky supply air ducts and supply plenums in the basement.

While the warm air that leaks into a basement during the heating season will keep the floor warm and slowly rise through connections to the upper floors, cool air leaking into the basement during the summer just stays there. Sealing the ductwork increases the pressure in all supply ducts, which improves the chances that heated or cooled air will be delivered to those hard-to-reach bedrooms over the garage.

Plan ahead. Besides leaky ductwork, it's poor ductwork design that prevents conditioned air from reaching its destination. Ninety-nine percent of the new homes I've worked with never had a sheet in the floor plans showing how and where ductwork would run. Drawing an HVAC plan will reveal potential conflicts between ducts and plumbing drains or other systems and will help reduce the tendency to install long duct runs with so many elbows that air resistance will prevent adequate airflow (Figure 9).

Steve Andrews *is an energy consultant based in Denver, Colo.*

Common Energy Claims: Fact or Fiction?

by Martin Holladay

You can't gauge the truth of an energy claim by how often you hear it repeated. Many builders' beliefs concerning energy, insulation, heating, and cooling are derived in part from marketing literature, obsolete recommendations from "experts," and oft-repeated tales heard at lumberyards. Upon closer inspection, many prove to be half-truths or outright misconceptions. Let's examine them one at a time.

Claim: Window replacement is a cost-effective way to save energy.

Fact: Replacing old single-pane windows with new double-pane low-E units certainly saves energy. But the cost is so high — and the amount of energy saved is so low — that window replacement is almost never cost-effective. Depending on the climate and the window cost, the payback period for replacement windows can be as long as 20 or 30 years. (In new construction, however, high-efficiency windows are highly cost-effective.)

According to calculations posted on an Energy Star program Web site, installing new double-pane low-E windows in a typical 2,000-square-foot single-story house that previously had single-pane units will result in annual energy savings of $125 (in a mild climate like California's) to $340 (in a severe climate like New England's). If the old windows had storms, the savings drop to $20 to $70 per year. Exact savings may vary, but anyone who expects that window replacement will have an energy payback needs to be prepared for a very long wait.

The most cost-effective window retrofit measure is the installation of low-E storm windows. Although many storm-window suppliers are unfamiliar with the product, low-E storms can be ordered. Suitable glass with a pyrolitic (hard-coat) low-E coating is available from most glass distributors. According to a recent study, the payback period for installing low-E storm windows on older houses in Chicago averaged just 4.3 years.

Claim: Housewrap is an air barrier.

Fact: When housewrap was first marketed to builders in the 1980s, manufacturers touted its benefits as an air barrier. The marketing campaigns were so successful some builders still believe that "housewrap" and "air barrier" are synonyms.

In fact, the most important function of housewrap is as a water-resistive barrier (WRB). Installed between siding and sheathing, a WRB is designed to stop rain that sneaks past the siding.

Housewrap can reduce air leakage between sheathing panel edges somewhat, especially if the housewrap seams are taped. But the cracks between wall sheathing panels don't account for much of the air leakage in a typical home; the big air leaks are elsewhere.

Air leaks occur in many locations, from the basement to the attic. For example, leaks are common between the top of a concrete foundation and the sill plates, between the subfloor and bottom plates, and around attic access hatches. Significant amounts of air can also leave a house through electrical boxes in partition walls, by traveling up the stud bays and into the attic through cracks between the drywall and the partition top plate. All of these leaks — and many others — need to be addressed before a builder can brag about the tightness of a home's air barrier.

Claim: Interior vapor retarders are a good way to prevent wet-wall problems.

Fact: Northern builders tend to overestimate the importance of vapor retarders. Worries about vapor-retarder placement are often misguided, since wet-wall problems are usually caused by wind-driven rain or deficient air barriers, not by vapor diffusion. Most of these baseless worries concern either the use of foam sheathing (sometimes vilified as a "wrong-side vapor retarder") or the lack of an interior vapor retarder.

By keeping wall cavities warm, properly installed foam sheathing of adequate R-value actually reduces the chance of condensation inside a wall. And interior polyethylene can be safely omitted from walls — even in cold regions of the country — as long as kraft-faced insulation is used. Almost all walls are free of vapor diffusion problems, in part because even painted drywall provides a fair amount of resistance.

According to the 2007 Supplement to the International Energy Conservation Code, polyethylene vapor retarders are not required in any location in the U.S. In northern climates (Marine Zone 4, as well as Zones 5 through 8), the code requires that walls include an interior vapor retarder; either kraft facing or polyethylene is acceptable (see Climate Zone Map, page 16).

Claim: It's good to omit vapor retarders in ceilings, to provide a way for moisture to leave the building.

Fact: Some cold-climate builders believe that, while vapor retarders are useful on walls, they should never be installed on ceilings "because you have to let the ceiling breathe, so that moisture can get out of the house." This interesting misconception contains several wrong-headed notions wrapped up in a single idea.

Most attics include ventilation. In theory (although not always in practice), attic ventilation can help remove high levels of humidity that might otherwise condense on the cold roof sheathing. However, attic moisture problems usually indicate the existence of two flaws: a wet basement or crawlspace, and a ceiling with air leaks.

Ceilings were never intended to be "moisture-relief valves" for homes. Ideally, a ceiling should be as airtight as possible, to keep warm, humid indoor air from reaching the attic. In cold climates, the ceiling should include a vapor retarder (for example, kraft facing or vapor-retarder paint) on the warm-in-winter side, to limit vapor diffusion through the ceiling.

High indoor humidity in homes during the winter — usually indicated by condensation on windows — is not that common. When it occurs, the solution is to reduce the source of moisture (firewood drying in the basement, wet crawlspace or basement, unvented dryer, etc.), and, if necessary, increase the rate of mechanical ventilation. If the home lacks a whole-house ventilation system, a simple remedy for dripping windows is to leave bath exhaust fans on for 24 hours a day until the moisture problems go away.

Claim: In-floor radiant heating systems save energy.

Fact: Proponents of in-floor radiant heating systems often claim that such systems save energy compared with conventional heating systems. The idea is that people living in homes with warm floors are so comfortable they voluntarily lower their thermostats, thereby saving energy.

The only problem with the theory is that no reputable study has ever shown it to be true, while at least one study has disproved it. Canadian researchers visited 75 homes during the winter to note where the homeowners set their thermostats. The 50 houses with in-floor radiant heating systems had thermostats set at an average of 68.7°. This was actually a little bit higher than the thermostats at the 25 homes with other types of heat delivery (either forced air or hydronic baseboard), which averaged 67.6°F. The researchers concluded, "There will generally be no energy savings due to lower thermostat settings with in-floor heating systems."

Other radiant-floor proponents have suggested that homes with radiant floors have lower boiler temperatures compared with homes with baseboard units. This factor, however, would be responsible for only very minor energy savings, if any. It has also been suggested that homes with radiant floors might have reduced infiltration compared with homes with forced-air heat. While this is certainly possible, high infiltration rates are best solved by addressing air-barrier problems at the time of construction.

Finally, it should be noted that a home with a slab-on-grade radiant floor heating system may lose more heat to the ground than a home with a forced-air heating system would — a factor that might lower the radiant heating system's overall efficiency. The best way to counteract this problem would be to increase the thickness of insulation under the slab.

Claim: Caulking the exterior of a house reduces air leakage.

Fact: Newspaper columnists often suggest that leaky walls can be improved by filling cracks on the exterior of a house with caulk. This is bad advice, for two reasons: First, most significant air leaks are located elsewhere; and second, exterior caulk can do more harm than good.

A caulk gun in the hands of an overenthusiastic builder can be a dangerous weapon. It's not unusual to see caulk where it doesn't belong — for example, blocking drainage at the horizontal crack between courses of wood lap siding, or blocking weep holes in windows.

If you want to limit infiltration in a leaky house, put away the caulk gun and ladder. Instead, get a few cans of spray foam and head for the basement and attic.

Claim: Spray polyurethane foam is a vapor retarder.

Fact: This is a half-truth. Closed-cell spray foam — also called "2-pound foam" because it has an average density of 2 pounds per cubic foot — is an effective vapor retarder. Installed at a thickness of 2½ inches, closed-cell spray foam has a permeance of only 0.8 perm.

On the other hand, open-cell spray foam (average density, ½ pound per cubic foot) is not a vapor retarder. Installed at a thickness of 3 inches, open-cell spray foam has a permeance of about 16 perms, making it fairly permeable to water vapor.

When installed directly against wall or roof sheathing in a cold climate, open-cell spray foam needs to be protected on the interior side with a vapor retarder. In most cases, painted drywall provides enough vapor resistance to avoid problems.

However, when open-cell spray foam is installed in a cold climate between rafters to create a so-called "cathedralized" attic, the roof sheathing can accumulate moisture. Though rare, this problem is most likely to occur in homes with elevated indoor humidity. The solution is to cover the attic side of the insulation with a vapor retarder— vapor-retarder paint, for instance.

Claim: Air-conditioned homes don't need a dehumidifier.

Fact: In a hot humid climate, air conditioners make a home more comfortable by lowering the temperature of the air (sensible heat removal) and by dehumidifying the air (latent heat removal). When the thermostat detects that the indoor air temperature is too warm, the air conditioner switches on; when the thermostat is satisfied, the air conditioner switches off. While the equipment is operating, some dehumidification occurs.

However, the ratio of latent heat removal to sensible heat removal is a function of equipment design and weather conditions; it is out of the control of the homeowner. Also some modern, high-efficiency air conditioners sacrifice latent cooling in order to boost the rated efficiency (which is based solely on sensible cooling).

Latent heat removal is lowest at the beginning of the cooling cycle. When an air conditioner runs flat out for hours at a time, it's usually pretty good at dehumidification. But in an energy-efficient house with low-solar-gain windows, the typical air conditioner runs for fewer hours. Although the equipment easily cools the house, it may not lower indoor humidity to comfortable levels.

As reported in *Energy Design Update* (January 2003), researchers in Houston were called to investigate high levels of indoor humidity plaguing a group of energy-efficient homes participating in the U.S. Department of Energy's Building America program. They discovered that "improvements in window performance and envelope tightness ... lowered the buildings' sensible cooling loads to the point that existing air conditioners [were] unable to handle the latent load." The recommended solution: Each house needed a stand-alone dehumidifier in addition to a central air conditioner.

As homes continue to be built to higher energy standards, the need for supplemental dehumidification is likely to increase in hot humid climates along the Gulf Coast and in the Southeast. Stand-alone dehumidifiers are a fairly inexpensive solution to the problem. Unlike an air conditioner, a stand-alone dehumidifier continues to lower indoor humidity until the desired setpoint is reached. The downside: a dehumidifier adds heat to the house. But as long as the house has a properly sized air conditioner, this shouldn't be a problem.

Claim: R-value measures only conductive heat transfer.

Fact: Of the three heat-flow mechanisms — conduction, convection, and radiation — radiation is probably least understood by the average builder. Sensing an opportunity, some marketers of radiant barriers, reflective insulations, and "ceramic coatings" take advantage of this common misconception (that R-value is a measure of conductive heat transfer alone) to promote their products. But in fact, R-values include all three heat-transfer mechanisms.

The most common method of testing a material's R-value is ASTM C518. In this test, a technician measures the thermal resistance (resistance to heat flow) of a specimen of insulation placed between a cold plate and a hot plate.

To understand how all three heat-transfer mechanisms are involved, consider the flow of heat across a fiberglass batt. Heat wants to flow from the hot side of the fiberglass batt to the cold side. Where individual glass fibers touch each other, heat is transferred from fiber to fiber by conduction. Where fibers are separated by an air space, heat is transferred from a hot fiber to a cooler one by radiation and by conduction through the air. In ASTM C518 tests of fiberglass insulation, air movement within the fiberglass batt (that is, a convective loop) is rare, although the test captures the phenomenon when it occurs.

Since R-value measures the resistance of a material to all three heat-flow mechanisms, it remains a useful way to compare insulations and to judge the performance of insulation alternatives.

Once insulation is inserted into a wall, however, the performance of the insulation is affected by additional factors that aren't measured by R-value testing. While R-value testing measures the effects — if any — of convective loops with a tested sample, it can't be expected to account for air leakage through a wall caused by wind or other pressure differences. A leaky wall assembly that is insulated with fiberglass batts will not perform as well as the same wall assembly that is insulated with spray foam with the same R-value; but the difference in wall performance is due to the spray foam's ability to reduce air leakage rather than to a difference in R-value between the two materials. The fact that some insulations are more porous than others does not imply that R-value tests are misleading.

To obtain the best performance from fiberglass insulation, the Energy Star Homes program now requires most fiberglass-insulated framing cavities (including knee walls) to be enclosed by air barriers on all six sides. If builders pay attention to airtightness, fiberglass insulation can (at least in theory) meet the performance expectations that the R-value label promises. Nevertheless, in the real world, builders who use fiberglass are unlikely to reduce air leakage enough for a fiberglass-insulated wall to perform as well as a wall insulated with the same R-value of cellulose or spray-foam insulation.

Claim: Radiant heat passes right through conventional insulation.

Fact: The idea that conventional (mass) insulation products allow radiant heat to pass right through them — that "mass insulation is transparent to radiant heat" — is a scare tactic used by some marketers of radiant barriers. The misleading claim leads some builders to falsely conclude that radiant heat can travel like radio waves right through a deep layer of attic insulation, with the only solution being a layer of aluminum foil.

However, when radiant heat hits one side of an insulation blanket, only a tiny percentage of that radiant heat passes through the insulation as "shine-through" radiation — that is, radiation that manages to miss all of the fibers in the insulation blanket and emerge unscathed on the other side of the blanket. "With insulations like fiberglass or cellulose, radiation can be absorbed by one piece of material and then reradiated," explains David Yarbrough, an insulation expert and research engineer at R&D Services in Cookeville, Tenn. "There is very little shine-through radiation with any of these materials."

The fact that some heat flows through a layer of insulation, usually by a combination of two or three heat-transfer mechanisms, does not mean the insulation isn't working. Although insulation doesn't stop heat flow, it slows it down considerably; the more insulation, the lower the heat flow. How much heat flows through an uninsulated ceiling into a 1,000-square-foot 32°F attic? Assuming that a 72°F house has an uninsulated drywall ceiling — that is, a ceiling assembly with an R-value of 2 — the heat flow across the uninsulated ceiling is 20,000 Btu per hour.

If insulation is added until the ceiling assembly has an R-value of 38, the heat flow is reduced by 95 percent, to 1,052 Btu per hour.

***Martin Holladay** is senior editor of www.GreenBuildingAdvisor.com. He was formerly the editor of Energy Design Update.*

Energy & Moisture Matters

JLC asked a panel of building scientists and builders — all keen, experienced observers of wood-frame building performance — to answer some of the questions about energy and moisture that never seem to go away.

Q. *When and where should I install a vapor retarder?*

A. *Martin Holladay, senior editor of www.GreenBuildingAdvisor.com and former editor of Energy Design Update, responds:* Vapor retarders help slow the diffusion of water vapor through a building assembly, such as a wall or ceiling. During cold weather, a vapor retarder on the interior of a wall will slow down the transfer of water vapor from the humid interior of the home into the cooler stud bays. During the summer, a vapor retarder on the exterior of a wall will slow down the transfer of water vapor from damp siding toward the cool stud bays.

If too much moisture enters the stud bays and contacts a cold enough surface (the back of the sheathing in winter or the back of the vinyl wallpaper, for example, in summer) then it will condense into liquid water, collect as frost, or raise the moisture content of the sheathing, potentially leading to mold or rot. The temperature at which the moisture in the air will condense into liquid water is called its *dew point*.

However, a vapor retarder is a double-edged sword: While under some circumstances it can have the beneficial effect of helping to keep a wall or ceiling dry, under other circumstances it can have the undesirable effect of preventing a damp wall or ceiling from drying out.

It's important to distinguish between a *vapor barrier* — usually defined as a material (like polyethylene) with a permeance of 0.1 perm or less — and a *vapor retarder* — usually defined as a material (like vapor-retarder paint or the kraft facing on a fiberglass batt) with a permeance between 0.1 and 1.0 perm. Some sources (including the 2009 International Residential Code) recognize a third category, the Class III vapor retarder, defined as a material (like a coat of latex paint) with a permeance ranging from 1.0 to 10 perms.

It's also important to distinguish between a vapor barrier/retarder and an air barrier. A vapor barrier can be effective despite having penetrations and unsealed seams, since its job is to reduce the slow diffusion of water vapor through the material. An air barrier, on the other hand, needs to be nearly perfect to be effective at blocking air leakage. In general, air leakage transports much more water vapor into walls than does vapor diffusion. Some materials, including polyethylene, can serve as both a vapor barrier and air barrier as long as seams and penetrations are carefully sealed (see the question below for more on this topic).

General Guidelines. There is a general consensus among building scientists on where to use a vapor barrier or vapor retarder. You should install a vapor barrier like polyethylene:

- under most concrete slabs
- on top of the dirt floor of a crawlspace
- in cold climates, behind drywall installed on insulated walls and ceilings of very damp rooms such as greenhouses and indoor swimming pools, as long as the building has no exterior foam insulation
- if desired, in very cold climates (>8,000 heating

degree days), behind drywall installed on insulated walls and ceilings, as long as the building has no exterior foam insulation and is not air conditioned (if the building will be air conditioned, MemBrain is preferable to polyethylene (see "Membrain: A Smarter Vapor Retarder," page 19)).

Polyethylene should never be installed:

- on any part of a basement wall
- on the interior side of walls or ceilings in air-conditioned buildings (including homes air conditioned for only two or three months a year)
- on the interior side of walls that include exterior rigid foam

You should install a vapor retarder like vapor-retarder paint, kraft facing, or MemBrain:

- on the interior side of insulated walls and ceilings in Climate Zones 5 to 8 and Marine 4
- on the interior side of open-cell spray polyurethane foam installed between attic rafters in Climate Zones 5 to 8 (see U.S. Climate Zone Map)

Buildings in mixed climates, hot dry climates, and hot humid climates (Zones 2, 3, and 4) do not need an interior vapor retarder (see Climate Zone Map, below).

Some wall assemblies are at risk of getting wet during the summer due to inward solar vapor drive. The riskiest wall assemblies include the following components: a "reservoir" cladding that can store water, like stucco, brick, or manufactured stone veneer; a vapor-permeable sheathing like Homosote or Thermo-ply; and interior polyethylene. If the house is air conditioned, such walls can begin to rot in just a few months. This problem has been seen in all parts of the U.S.

To lower the risk of inward solar vapor drive, air-conditioned homes with reservoir claddings should never include interior polyethylene and should always include a ventilated rainscreen gap between the cladding and the sheathing. For walls at risk of inward solar vapor drive, rigid foam sheathing is preferable to OSB.

Code requirements. While building experts may agree on the principles of when and where to use vapor retarders, the building codes have had less success in formulating clear rules that reflect these principles. The latest IRC rules take some time to untangle.

The 2006 International Residential Code (IRC) avoids the use of the term *vapor barrier* and defines a vapor retarder as a material with a permeance of 1.0 perm or less. This definition includes such materials as polyethylene sheeting, aluminum foil, kraft paper facing, and vapor-retarding paint.

In section R318.1, the 2006 IRC requires that "In all

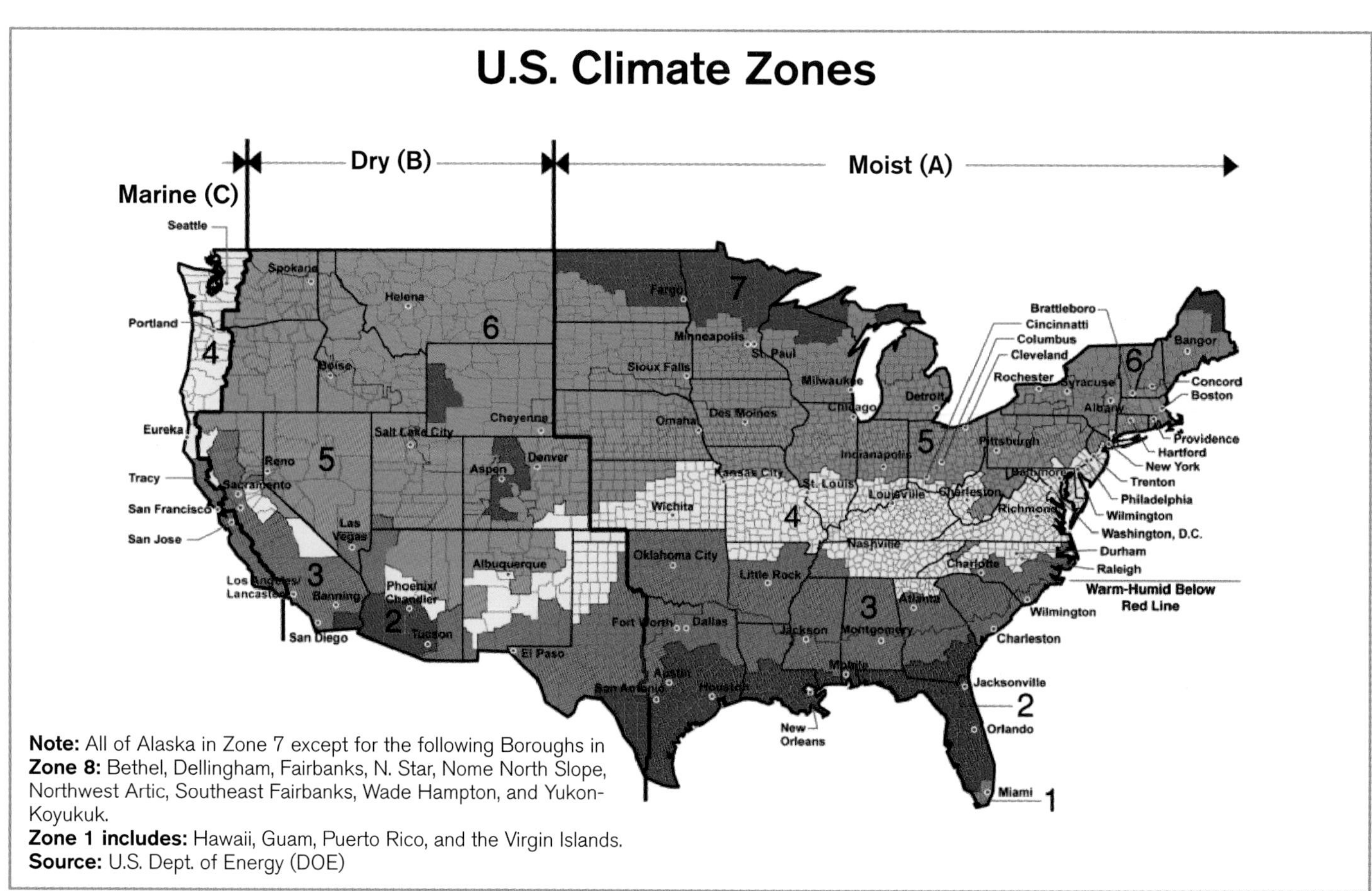

Note: All of Alaska in Zone 7 except for the following Boroughs in **Zone 8:** Bethel, Dellingham, Fairbanks, N. Star, Nome North Slope, Northwest Artic, Southeast Fairbanks, Wade Hampton, and Yukon-Koyukuk.
Zone 1 includes: Hawaii, Guam, Puerto Rico, and the Virgin Islands.
Source: U.S. Dept. of Energy (DOE)

framed walls, floors, and roof/ceilings comprising elements of the building thermal envelope, a vapor retarder shall be installed on the warm-in-winter side of the insulation." It should be emphasized that this code requirement makes no mention of polyethylene; vapor-retarding paint fulfills this code requirement.

The 2006 IRC includes exceptions to the vapor-retarder requirement. It allows a vapor retarder to be omitted:

- in Climate Zones 1 through 4 (an area including most of the West Coast and the South);
- in walls, floors, and ceilings made of materials (like concrete) that cannot be damaged by moisture or freezing
- "where the framed cavity or space is ventilated to allow moisture to escape" — an apparent (although poorly worded) reference to vented attics and walls with rainscreen siding

The requirements of the 2006 International Energy Conservation Code (IECC) differ slightly from those of the 2006 IRC. In Section 402.5, the 2006 IECC requires that "Above-grade frame walls, floors and ceilings not ventilated to allow moisture to escape shall be provided with an approved vapor retarder. The vapor retarder shall be installed on the warm-in-winter side of the thermal insulation."

In the 2006 IECC, the exceptions to the vapor retarder requirement are very similar to the exceptions listed in the 2006 IRC, except for an additional exception: "Where other approved means to avoid condensation are provided." This last exception gives broad latitude to the building official — and places a heavy burden on any builder intent on convincing a local official that a certain building assembly complies with this exception.

The 2007 Supplement to the IECC and the 2007 Supplement to the IRC introduced a new vapor-retarder definition. (Of course, many jurisdictions in the U.S. are still using local codes based on the 2006 — or even earlier versions — of the IRC and IECC.) Vapor retarders are now separated into three classes:

- Class I: Less than or equal to 0.1 perm (e.g., polyethylene or aluminum foil)
- Class II: Greater than 0.1 perm but less than or equal to 1.0 perm (e.g., kraft facing or vapor-retarding paint)
- Class III: Greater than 1.0 perm but less than or equal to 10 perm (e.g., latex paint)

The 2009 IRC incorporates the changes introduced in the 2007 Supplement. The 2009 IRC requires (in section R601.3) that a Class I or Class II vapor retarder (in other words, kraft facing, MemBrain, or polyethylene) be installed on the interior side of frame walls (but not ceilings) in Climate Zones 5 (e.g., Nevada, Ohio, Massachusetts), 6 (e.g., Vermont, Montana), 7 (e.g., northern Minnesota), 8 (e.g., northern Alaska), and Marine Zone 4 (Western Washington and Oregon). Building scientists point out that there is no logic to support different vapor retarder requirements for ceilings than for walls.

Exceptions are allowed in IRC section R601.3.1, which states that in climate zones where a Class I or Class II vapor retarder would normally be required, a less stringent vapor retarder — a Class III retarder like latex paint — can be used under the conditions listed in Table R601.3.1. Only certain types of wall assemblies are worthy of this exception; they must have either an adequate layer of exterior foam sheathing or "vented cladding." The minimum R-value of the foam sheathing varies depending on the thickness of the wall framing and the climate, as explained below.

Foam Sheathing. The use of foam sheathing has gained in popularity because it solves a number of vapor transmission problems by serving as an exterior vapor retarder in hot weather, while acting to warm the wall cavity and minimize condensation in cold weather.

If you're planning to build walls with exterior rigid foam, remember:

- Walls sheathed with rigid foam must be able to dry to the interior and should, therefore, never include interior polyethylene or vinyl wallpaper.
- Exterior rigid foam should always be thick enough to prevent moisture from accumulating in the sheathing or studs during the winter. The thicker the exterior foam insulation, the warmer the inside face of the sheathing or rigid foam will be, helping to prevent condensation within the wall cavity. The minimum foam sheathing R-value required to prevent condensation depends on the climate and insulated wall thickness inside the foam. Recommended foam sheathing levels in the 2009 IRC are shown in the table below.

Minimum R-Value for Foam Sheathing

Climate Zone	R-Value of Foam Sheathing	
	2x4 walls *	2x6 walls*
Marine Zone 4	R-2.5	R-3.75
Zone 5	R-5	R-7.5
Zone 6	R-7.5	R-11.25
Zones 7 and 8	R-10	R-15

Source: Based on IRC Table R601.3.1

*Assumes cavity filled with fiberglass or cellulose insulation.

Builders should remember that some types of insulation and sheathing are effective vapor barriers or vapor retarders.

- One inch of foil-faced polyisocyanurate has a permeance of 0.05 perm.
- One inch of extruded polystyrene (XPS) has a permeance of 0.4 to 1.6 perm.
- One inch of expanded polystyrene (EPS) has a permeance of 2.0 to 5.8 perms.
- One inch of closed-cell spray polyurethane foam has a permeance of 1.9 to 2.5 perms.
- Plywood sheathing has a permeance of 0.5 to 20 perms, depending on moisture content.
- OSB sheathing has a permeance of 0.7 to 2 perms, depending on moisture content.

Q. *What exactly is the difference between an air barrier and a vapor retarder?*

A. *Joe Lstiburek, PE, principal of Building Science Corporation in Somerville, Mass., responds:* Air barriers control airflow, and vapor retarders control vapor flow. Vapor retarders are not typically intended to slow the migration of air; that's the function of air barriers.

Confusion between the two arises because air often holds a great deal of moisture in the vapor form. When this air moves from location to location due to an air-pressure difference, the vapor moves with it. In the strictest sense, air barriers are also vapor barriers when they control the transport of moisture-laden air.

Part of the problem is that we struggle with names and terms: vapor retarders, vapor barriers, vapor permeable, vapor impermeable. In an attempt to clear up some of the confusion, here are the definitions that I use.

Vapor Retarder: An element designed and installed in an assembly to retard the movement of water by vapor diffusion. The unit of measurement typically used in characterizing the water-vapor permeance of materials is a "perm." There are several classes of vapor retarders:

Class I vapor retarder: 0.1 perm or less
Class II vapor retarder: 1.0 perm or less, and greater than 0.1 perm
Class III vapor retarder: 10 perms or less, and greater than 1.0 perm
Vapor barrier: a Class I vapor retarder

Materials can also be separated into four general classes based on their permeance:

Vapor impermeable: 0.1 perm or less
Vapor semi-impermeable: 1.0 perm or less, and greater than 0.1 perm
Vapor semi-permeable: 10 perms or less, and greater than 1.0 perm
Vapor permeable: greater than 10 perms

Air Barrier: A system of materials designed and constructed to control airflow between a conditioned space and an unconditioned space. The air-barrier system is the primary air-enclosure boundary that separates indoor (conditioned) air from outdoor (unconditioned) air.

Air barriers also typically define the building's pressure boundary. In multiunit construction, the air-barrier system also acts as the fire barrier and smoke barrier between units. In such assemblies, the air barrier has to meet the specific fire-resistance rating requirement for the given separation.

Air barriers can be located anywhere in the building enclosure—at the exterior surface, the interior surface, or at any location in between. In heating climates, interior air barriers control the exfiltration of interior, often moisture-laden, air. Exterior air barriers control the infiltration of exterior air and prevent wind-washing through insulation.

Wherever they are, air barriers should be:

- impermeable to airflow
- continuous over the entire building enclosure
- able to withstand the forces that may act on them during and after construction
- durable over the expected lifetime of the building

Air-barrier systems consist of individual materials incorporated into assemblies that are interconnected to create enclosures. Each of these three elements has measurable resistance to airflow (in liters per second per square meter at 75 Pascal pressure). The minimum resistance, or air permeance, for each is:

Material: 0.02 l/(s-m2)@ 75 Pa
Assembly: 0.20 l/(s-m2)@ 75 Pa
Enclosure: 2.00 l/(s-m2)@ 75 Pa

For more information on air barriers and vapor retarders, visit www.buildingscience.com/documents/digests.

Q. *Is installing painted wood siding and trim over an air space — so-called rain-screen siding — really worth the effort?*

A. *Paul Eldrenkamp, owner of Byggmeister, a custom remodeling firm in Newton, Mass., responds:* The first project we did with rain-screen siding was in 1989. It entailed stripping existing shingles, applying rigid foam insulation over the old sheathing, screwing horizontal 1x3 battens through the foam into the sheathing, and then installing cedar shingles that had been prestained on all edges over the strapping.

We have been back to the house several times since, including a recent visit, and the whole installation has held up superbly: The shingles lie flat, the stain is holding up well (the house has been restained once in the intervening years), and the strapping has consistently been bone dry when we've tested it. This is on a house with minimal overhangs along the eaves, no overhangs on the gable ends, and a lot of shading from large trees, so water exposure is significant and drying opportunities are limited.

We also used the rain-screen approach at my own house in 1997. I have clapboards above first-floor window-sill height, but up to the sill height we installed tongue-and-groove fir beadboard for a wainscot effect. All the wood was preprimed and prepainted on all sides prior to installation and installed over strapping, which in turn was installed over rigid foam. I have small overhangs — 6 inches on the gable ends, 12 inches at the eaves.

The 10-year-old paint job shows no sign of failure whatsoever. There are a few mildew spots, which wash off easily with a mild detergent solution when I bother to do it. On several occasions after an extended rainy period I've tested the wood siding for moisture content, and I've found elevated readings (18 percent or so is not unusual), but never any sign of paint failure, which to me indicates a resilient system.

Additionally, we once had occasion to do work on a stucco house built in the 1940s. Felt had been applied to the sheathing, then vertical wood strapping, then metal lath, then three-coat stucco. The lath was a little corroded in places, but overall the stucco was in good condition, and the strapping and felt appeared to have another half-century of life left in them.

These are not the only jobs we've done (or seen done) this way; there have been dozens over the years. They all perform extremely well.

So rain-screen siding clearly works. For me, the question has been, "Is it overkill?" In other words, is the extra benefit really worth the extra work? Actually, I'm so confident it's worth the effort, we don't install siding any other way. But I'm also keenly aware of what I perceive to be still-unanswered questions, such as "If I'm using wood siding, do I need to both prefinish on all sides and create the air space, or can I do one or the other?" And "How big does the air space need to be?"

With wood siding (especially clapboards), back-priming seems to be more important than the air space. We have done some jobs with no air space but with wood siding prefinished on all sides, and the paint's held up very well (10 years without failure, in at least one case). These jobs do seem to have more mildew and cedar bleed, but I don't know if there's a connection (or even if that observation would really hold up if I tried to quantify it).

Some researchers have suggested that a clear preservative on the back of the clapboards would be preferable to primer or paint, creating the best balance of antiabsorption and drying properties. I think that this is over-thinking the problem, and that it fails to acknowledge the realities of the job site. Ordering the claps prefinished on all sides is much easier and faster — and, in my experience, yields an entirely effective end result. Plus, should any problems arise, just imagine your conversation with the paint-manufacturer representative when you tell him you have a different finish on each face of the clapboard.

So if there is absolutely no way to create an air space — a job, for example, where there's no latitude to thicken the wall even by a fraction — at the very least, order your clapboards prefinished on all sides. Our

MemBrain: A Smarter Vapor Barrier

In mixed climates with cold winters and hot summers, vapor-retarding paint is usually adequate to prevent moisture from accumulating in walls. In some cases, however, local building inspectors still insist on the installation of an interior vapor retarder that comes in a roll.

If the problem of inward solar vapor drive scares you away from the use of polyethylene — and it should — you might want to consider using a "smart" vapor retarder from CertainTeed called MemBrain.

Unlike polyethylene, MemBrain has a permeance which varies with the relative humidity (RH). As long as the RH is below 50%, the film is a vapor barrier with a permeance below 1 perm. As the RH rises, so does the film's permeance; at 90% RH, the film has a permeance of 36 perms. In cold and mixed climates, the use of MemBrain instead of poly under drywall should increase the drying ability of wall and ceiling assemblies by allowing the assemblies to dry to the interior during the summer.

A Wisconsin study funded by the U.S. Department of Energy confirmed that during the summer months, walls with interior MemBrain stayed dryer than walls with interior polyethylene. The benefits of MemBrain are particularly apparent on walls facing south (the orientation that is most likely to suffer from inward solar vapor drive).

— Martin Holladay

contracts often include a drop-dead date by which the homeowner has to select an exterior paint color so we have time to have the prefinishing done.

How big an air space to use is a harder question. Some researchers seem to think that only drainage is important — that the depth of the space needs to be just enough to allow water to flow down behind the siding, something on the order of ⅛ inch or even less.

Others seem to think that ventilation is important, too — that there should be clear continuous channels not only for top-to-bottom drainage but also for bottom-to-top airflow. This is the thinking behind Benjamin Obdyke's Home Slicker and the old-fashioned 1x3 (or plywood strip) battens that we use. A few researchers seem to think that the air space itself is what's important — to allow for even drying of the cladding material when it does get wet.

My observation of our projects in our Boston-area climate is that you will have a durable, trouble-free exterior regardless of what products you use and of whether you actually achieve continuous top-to-bottom drainage, as long as the following conditions are met:

- The flashings and building paper guide the water away from the sheathing and to the outside with 100 percent reliability.
- You have an air space of at least ½ inch behind the siding material.
- All wood siding and trim is finished on all sides before installation.

Every new exterior job we do gives us an opportunity to test the durability of rain-screen siding. To complete the experiment, we need to observe its outcome over an extended period. There is no substitute for going back to past projects in a systematic way and seeing first-hand how they've held up.

Q. *Ever since we began building tighter walls and ceilings, it seems we've been getting more moisture and mold problems in houses. Isn't it better to leave our houses a little bit leaky than to make them too tight?*

A. *Martin Holladay responds:* A hundred years ago, most houses had uninsulated walls and numerous air leaks. Now that tighter building practices are standard, any incidental water that gets into a wall dries very slowly, and problems with wall rot and mold have increased. But building a new home to be "a little bit leaky" is more apt to increase than decrease the likelihood of moisture problems.

Filling framing bays with insulation — rather than leaving them empty — makes walls and ceilings less forgiving of moisture intrusion, for three reasons: Insulation can act like a sponge, absorbing water that might otherwise have drained out; it reduces airflow, slowing the rate of drying; and it makes the exterior sheathing colder, introducing a potential condensing surface.

Since building uninsulated houses is no longer an option, builders must learn how to assemble walls and roofs in ways that minimize water intrusion. To keep out exterior water — wind-driven rain — a house needs careful flashing at windows and other penetrations, and the flashing must be properly integrated with a water-resistant barrier. Ideally, a wall should include a free-draining air gap (rain screen) between the siding and the sheathing.

Interior moisture is usually less of a problem for walls and ceilings than exterior moisture. Since recent research has shown that interior polyethylene can do more harm than good in many U.S. climates, knowledgeable builders in all but the coldest areas often omit interior poly. The most common way that interior moisture enters walls and ceilings is by hitching a ride with exfiltrating air; that's why it's important for most homes to have a very good air barrier.

What's wrong with leaving a house "a little bit leaky"? In theory, a certain amount of air exchange is a good thing: Introducing fresh air is good for a home's occupants, and air movement through walls and ceilings can, in some circumstances, help dry out moisture that would otherwise be trapped.

In practice, however, this approach doesn't accomplish either task very well. If interior air enters a wall through one of the "little leaks," moisture in the air can condense on the back of the wall sheathing. In other words, even though air movement through a wall assembly can help dry out moisture in some circumstances, it can deposit moisture in others.

Moreover, infiltration levels vary with the weather. In cold weather, the stack effect increases airflow through a house; in mild weather, infiltration and exfiltration are lower. Similarly, wind increases the rate of air exchange in most homes. But people need a relatively constant supply of fresh air, whether the weather is hot or cold, windy or still.

If you want a house with few mold and moisture problems, you have two choices. The first — to build a house without any insulation at all — is illegal in most locations. The second and more logical choice is to build a tight building envelope — designed to handle incidental moisture — and equip the house with some type of mechanical ventilation.

Q. *Is spray-foam insulation worth the extra expense?*

A. *Paul Eldrenkamp responds:* Often, but not always. For an effective insulation job, you need both good R-value and good air-sealing. Spray foam is an expensive way to get R-value but a relatively cheap way to get good air-sealing — especially in retrofits.

Spray foam is probably not worth the extra expense in the following types of projects:

- Closed-cavity retrofits, like the walls of an older home with no insulation. Here, use cellulose, and try to get it installed to a high density — 3.5 pounds of material per cubic foot of volume. You may have a hard time finding a cellulose insulation contractor who knows how to do this (or has even heard of it), but it's worth trying.

- New construction or large-scale additions where you can cost-effectively wrap the structure (both walls and roof) with a layer of rigid foam before applying the exterior finish. This minimizes thermal bridging and provides good air-sealing (as long as you tape or gasket the joints in the foam boards). And it means that almost anything you use for framing cavity insulation — including fiberglass batts — will be effective.

- New construction or large-scale additions where you can get a quote for cellulose (blown-in/mesh system or damp-spray system) that beats the quote you get for spray-foam. A good cellulose installation is often less costly and just as effective as a spray-foam installation.

- Attics with a simple geometry in which you choose to insulate the floor rather than the rafters. You do need to make sure to seal all of the penetrations in the ceiling plane before you blow in the cellulose, and you should avoid putting mechanical equipment in the attic above the insulation.

- Cast-concrete basements or crawlspaces where the walls and floors are even enough that you can install sheets of rigid foam easily and tightly.

Spray-foam is usually worth the extra expense in these types of projects:

- Relatively small jobs, like small additions or partial gut jobs, where there's a logistical and scheduling advantage to having just one subcontractor and one material to deal with.

- Houses where the attic is wholly or partly finished. Once the attic starts becoming living space, the most effective approach is almost always to insulate and air-seal the outermost plane of the roof structure (rafters rather than knee walls, for instance). This is where spray foam shines. Install it from the top plate of the wall up to the ridge all around the attic, like putting a cap on the house.

  Don't worry about venting the roof. Most researchers I've spoken with (Joe Lstiburek, William Rose, Terry Brennan) advocate applying one or two coats of latex paint to open-cell foam insulation to minimize vapor diffusion. There's uncertainty as to whether this is a necessary precaution, but it's cheap and easy enough to do. Closed-cell foams have a low enough perm rating that they do not need the vapor diffusion retarder.

- Any house where it's difficult to define a simple, continuous boundary between tempered and untempered space. Houses with lots of angles, plane changes, split levels, dormers, bays, and so on are often going to be easier to insulate and air-seal with foam than with other methods.

- Old, uneven basement walls and floors. We use a closed-cell foam on old basement walls and then spray it with shotcrete to get the flame-spread rating required by code. We've even sprayed the higher-density closed-cell foam on basement floors, then poured lightweight concrete over the foam to create a level, insulated floor slab.

Ultimately, you need to figure out for yourself when one material or technique is more appropriate than another. A lot depends on the relative skills of your crew, on which insulation subcontractors in your area are most reliable and knowledgeable, and on what types of houses you work on.

One unavoidable fact, though, is that you will never know for sure which materials and techniques are working best unless you regularly test your jobs with a blower door and infrared camera; otherwise, you'll just be guessing.

Q. *My insulation contractor installed dense-pack cellulose in the walls of a 100-year-old house. Two years later, the exterior paint began to peel, even though the paint job was only four years old. Did the insulation cause the paint to fail?*

A. *Martin Holladay responds:* Indeed, adding insulation to the walls of an older home can shorten the life of the exterior paint. The phenomenon has been observed for decades; when conducting research on vapor retarders, William Rose, a building researcher at the University of Illinois at Urbana-Champaign, unearthed evidence of failing-paint disputes between insulation contractors and exterior painters dating back to the 1940s.

The failing paint has often been blamed on the fact that the walls of most old houses lack interior polyethylene. With little to slow vapor diffusion, interior moisture is said to travel through the walls until it reaches the sheathing, the siding, or the back of the paint film, causing the exterior paint to fail.

As it turns out, this explanation is incomplete and misleading. Although vapor diffusion can occur through exterior walls, the effect of vapor diffusion on exterior paint performance has been greatly exaggerated. Moreover, since most old houses have several layers of interior paint, the walls in question usually do include a vapor retarder; even two coats of paint have a relatively low permeance (1.5 to 5 perms), and each additional layer of paint will improve the paint's performance as a vapor retarder.

In fact, adding insulation to a wall does make the siding more humid, but not because of the lack of a vapor retarder. Adding a thermal barrier between the siding and the warm interior makes the siding colder; under the same conditions of vapor pressure, colder materials are wetter than warmer materials. In other words, before the insulation was installed, the relatively warm stud bays helped keep the siding dry.

Of course, damp siding doesn't hold paint as well as dry siding. The source of the moisture absorbed by cold siding under these circumstances — called "regained moisture" by building scientists — is the exterior environment, not the interior.

On a new home, several measures can lengthen the life of a paint job, among them specifying siding that has been factory primed on all sides and installing the siding over rain-screen strapping. On an existing house, such measures are not usually possible; in many cases, homeowners who choose to insulate the exterior walls of an older home may have to get used to more frequent exterior-paint jobs.

Despite evidence that it's harder to keep paint on an insulated wall than an uninsulated wall, a good painting contractor should not hesitate to stand behind an exterior paint job on an old, recently insulated house. Exterior paint will last longer when the siding is carefully prepped; ideally, this work should include the complete removal of all the old paint, down to bare wood. If quality paint is specified and the paint is applied in good weather, the paint job should last for many years.

Q. *Mold has been around forever; many of us grew up in houses that had the occasional mildew spots in the corner of the ceiling, or mold-stained lumber in the basement or attic. But in recent years it seems like mold has become a big issue. Is this a justifiable concern? Is mold in houses a worse health problem today than in the past?*

A. *Terry Brennan, a principal of Camroden Associates in Westmoreland, N.Y., who served as a moisture consultant on the Institute of Medicine's Committee on Damp Indoor Spaces, responds:*
Mold has indeed been here much longer than we have and will no doubt still be here in the distant future.

While we don't have statistics on the changing mold levels in homes, I do believe the amount of mold in buildings has increased as changes in construction have occurred. Some construction changes made walls stay wet longer — filling the cavities with porous insulation, replacing diagonal board sheathing with sheets of plywood and OSB, and adding poly vapor retarders (or unintentional vapor barriers, like vinyl wallpaper) to the inside of walls.

We also gradually replaced relatively mold-resistant materials — such as brick, plaster, and old-growth heartwood — with materials containing sugars and starches that many molds can use as food, like paper-faced gypsum board, wood-based composites, and wood species with little resistance to mold growth.

During the same period, we also began air conditioning more buildings, which cools indoor walls, ceilings, and floors below the outdoor air temperature. When the outdoor dewpoint is higher than the indoor air temperature, the ventilating air no longer dries out the house, but wets it. Any surfaces in the air-conditioned house that are colder than the room temperature — for example, the supply ducts, the supply diffusers, or anything the supply air blows on — will be the first to collect moisture and grow mold.

So in general, there's more humidity in the house, better food, and, yes, more mold. But is it harmful?

The Institute of Medicine of the National Academy of Sciences convened the Committee on Damp Indoor Spaces to examine the medical literature for evidence of health effects linked to occupying damp buildings. In 2004, the committee published its findings in a book, "Damp Indoor Spaces and Health," which reported evidence of an association between living in damp spaces and upper-respiratory (nose and throat) symptoms, wheezing, and coughing. There was also an association between living in dampness and asthma symptoms in sensitized asthmatics, coughing, and hypersensitivity in susceptible persons, as well as limited evidence connecting damp living spaces with lower-respiratory illness in otherwise healthy children.

Q. *What's the best way to insulate a basement foundation?*

A. *Paul Fisette, director of Building Materials and Wood Technology at the University of Massachusetts Amherst and a JLC contributing editor, responds:* The answer depends on the budget, the R-value you're trying to achieve, how the space will be used, and whether you're simply housing mechanicals or creating a living space in the basement.

Assuming you don't need a tempered basement space, the best and most economical approach is to insulate the floor that separates the living space from the basement. This will minimize the volume of the home's thermal envelope and the amount of energy required to condition the living space. Also, it's easier to install insulation with higher R-values in the basement ceiling. This is the design that will have the greatest payback in reduced energy costs.

The cheapest way to insulate the basement ceiling is to install unfaced fiberglass insulation. A better method is to cover the ceiling with drywall, then blow in cellulose — a comparatively inexpensive upgrade, considering the benefits. Not only does this method provide superior R-value, but — if detailed well — it stops air leakage at one of the most critical places in the house. (Most of the inward air leakage caused by the wintertime stack effect happens at the bottom of a house.)

If the goal is to provide basement living space, then of course you'll have to insulate the basement walls. Wrapping the outside of the foundation with rigid polystyrene is a common approach; the materials aren't expensive, and the foam board needs protection only above grade.

However, the space between the concrete foundation and the back of the foam board can become a termite highway — a hidden path connecting the soil directly to the framing — unless you add the cost of a carefully installed termite shield. Also, consider that a 1-inch layer of polystyrene provides a meager R-5 of thermal protection; if you increase the thickness to 2 inches or more, the project gets even pricier — plus it's tricky to integrate the foam with the frame wall above.

A simpler, better approach is to insulate the inside of the foundation. First, though, make sure the basement doesn't leak and is protected by a good drainage system. In a retrofit situation, applying a layer of dampproofing on the interior surface of the foundation wall is cheap insurance. I've had good luck using Sto Watertight Coat, a two-component cementitious compound with a low perm rating.

On top of the waterproofing, I attach rigid foam insulation directly to the inside surface of the foundation walls with construction adhesive, then caulk or tape the seams so that warm interior air can't reach the cold foundation. Finally, I build an uninsulated wood frame, spaced away from the foundation to make room for plumbing and wiring. The foam insulation keeps the surface of the wall above dewpoint temperature, reducing the likelihood that condensation will form in the wall.

Q. *Even though I installed R-38 fiberglass batts on the attic floor, a house I recently built has suffered from roof leaks caused by ice dams. What's the solution?*

A. *Martin Holladay responds:* If the attic floor has adequate insulation, the most likely cause of an ice-dam problem is that warm interior air is leaking into the attic through cracks in the ceiling.

Ice dams begin when warm attic temperatures melt the lowest layer of snow on a roof. The water flows downhill and refreezes when it reaches the colder roofing at the eaves, gradually thickening until an ice dam is formed. Such dams can become thick enough to trap upslope meltwater; in some cases, the water can be forced under the roof shingles and can wet the ceilings below.

In sunny, cold weather, icicles can appear on any roof. As long as the ice doesn't lead to a wet ceiling, it isn't really a problem. Heavy ice at a building's eaves, however — with or without wet ceilings — is usually a sign that too much heat is escaping through the ceiling.

To some extent, ice-dam problems can be reduced by the installation of a rubberized roof membrane like Grace Ice & Water Shield. While a 6-foot-wide band of rubberized membrane at the eaves is always a good idea, rubberizing the entire roof is a crude defense against roof ice. If the roof sheathing is warm enough to melt snow, the solution is not to install wider and wider bands of rubber, but to prevent the heat from escaping the house.

Many builders try to solve ice-dam problems by increasing the size of soffit and ridge vents, but this strategy rarely works. In fact, since air leakage is a more common cause of ice-dam problems than insufficient insulation, increasing attic ventilation can actually make things worse. A larger ridge vent tends to increase the flow of air into the attic; the source of that air might be the soffit vents, but if the ceiling is peppered with holes and cracks, it might also be the home's interior. In other words, a better ridge vent can actually increase the flow of heated air into the attic.

The first step in any ice-dam investigation should be to crawl up in the attic and look for ceiling air leaks. (If the house has a cathedral ceiling, air leaks should be sealed from the interior.) Common leak areas include attic access hatches, recessed can lights, plumbing and electrical penetrations, chimneys, bathroom exhaust fans, poorly sealed bathroom and kitchen soffits, and cracks between drywall and partition top plates (see "Effective Air Sealing in Existing Homes," page 308).

Once the ceiling is relatively airtight, the next step is to verify that the attic insulation is thick enough, especially near the eaves, and that its R-value is not being degraded by wind-washing.

The use of fiberglass batts near the eaves, if not properly detailed, can actually increase the likelihood of ice-dam problems. Since fiberglass insulation does little to slow airflow, it can't stop warm air from escaping upward through a ceiling leak. Moreover, its effectiveness can be degraded by the flow of cold air entering the soffit vents. Fiberglass batts also have a lower R-value per inch than rigid foam and sprayed urethane foam.

In some houses, the space between the exterior wall plates and the roof sheathing is too cramped for adequate levels of fiberglass insulation, especially if a vent channel is required. If the roof is framed with raised-heel trusses, fiberglass batts may work well, as long as the ceiling is relatively airtight and as long as the builder includes a wind-washing dam above the top plate (see "Attic Ventilation Details," page 166). In many attics, however, the problematic area under the eaves is best insulated with sprayed polyurethane foam or several layers of rigid foam.

Once a leak-free air barrier is installed, the next line of defense is an uninterrupted layer of thick insulation. With these in place, the amount of attic ventilation is a relatively minor concern.

Guide to the Energy Codes

by Martin Holladay

Many states have recently increased the strictness of their residential energy codes, forcing builders to rethink long-established construction practices. In some areas, contractors who have always built houses with 2x4 walls and uninsulated basements are waking up to new regulations requiring basement wall insulation and much higher R-values for above-grade walls. Elsewhere, building officials have begun checking the U-factors on window labels for the first time.

Energy codes vary widely from state to state. While many states require residential builders to comply with the International Energy Conservation Code (IECC), the successor to the old Model Energy Code (MEC), other states — including Alabama, Arizona, Colorado, Illinois, Mississippi, Missouri, and South Dakota — have no statewide residential energy code.

Even when a state decides to adopt the IECC, however, plenty of opportunities for confusion remain. At least five different versions of the IECC are currently being enforced in the United States. The most recent version, the 2006 IECC (adopted by Iowa, Louisiana, Pennsylvania, and Utah), is radically different from earlier versions of the IECC enforced in several other states.

Moreover, a number of states have adopted the IECC with state-specific modifications. For example, New Jersey's code permits builders to omit basement wall insulation in any home equipped with a 90 percent AFUE (or better) furnace; New York, on the other hand, specifically prohibits any design with a trade-off that eliminates basement wall insulation.

Several model residential energy codes are currently in print, including the 1992 and 1995 MECs, and the 2000, 2003, and 2006 IECCs; code books are available at prices from \$11 to \$31 from the International Code Council (www.iccsafe.org).

Forty-four states now enforce an energy code based on either the old MEC or a pre-2004 version of the IECC (see "Residential Energy Codes by State," below). These codes allow builders to choose from three compliance options: a prescriptive path, a component trade-off path, and a systems analysis path.

The Prescriptive Path

Dubbed the "cookbook" path in Minnesota, the prescriptive path is the simplest — though not necessarily the most cost-effective — way for builders to meet energy-code requirements. Prescriptive-path requirements usually include minimum R-values for insulation, with different R-values specified for walls, ceilings, floors, basement walls, and slab edges. Some prescriptive codes also specify a maximum U-factor or a maximum solar heat-gain coefficient (SHGC) for windows.

Prescriptive-code requirements are usually shown in a table, for example, Table 602.1 in the 2000 IECC (Figure 10), that specifies minimum R-values, maximum U-factors, and maximum SHGC values. These prescribed values typically vary by climate zone or by the number of heating degree days at the building site.

Windows from major manufacturers are labeled with U-factor and SHGC values calculated according to procedures established by the National Fenestration Rating Council (NFRC). If a window lacks an NFRC label, builders must use code-specified "default val-

ues" when demonstrating code compliance; for example, a vinyl window with double glazing is assigned a default U-factor of 0.55.

In some regions of the country, the best available default window U-factors or SHGC values aren't low enough to satisfy the prescriptive code, so NFRC-labeled windows are the only option open to builders following the prescriptive path.

In pre-2004 versions of the IECC, builders following the prescriptive path need to calculate the home's window-to-wall ratio (WWR). Homes with a WWR of 15 percent or less should follow the prescriptive tables in Chapter 6 of the code, and homes with a WWR of more than 15 percent need to follow the prescriptive tables in Chapter 5. Builders must include rim joist areas in wall-area calculations; window areas are based on rough-opening areas. The idea of the WWR originated in the original 1992 MEC. In pre-2004 versions of the IECC, all three compliance paths require builders to calculate the WWR. (In Washington state, the residential energy code requires builders to calculate the window-to-floor-area ratio.)

The Component Trade-Off Path

Because the prescriptive path is inflexible, its use often results in a house that costs more to build than a house that follows the component trade-off path. Builders who choose the component trade-off path are able to adjust several variables — such as insulation thickness, window area, or furnace efficiency — in search of the most cost-effective way to comply with energy-code requirements. In pre-2004 versions of the IECC, the component trade-off path is found in Chapter 5.

In some states, the component trade-off path is called the component performance path or — somewhat confusingly — the performance calculation path. However, this path does not involve a full-fledged calculation of a home's energy performance; rather, it involves a simplified performance calculation based on a limited number of trade-offs.

For example, many state energy codes allow a house equipped with a high-efficiency furnace to skimp on wall or ceiling insulation. The rationale behind such a trade-off is simple: Although the resulting house has different specifications than a house following the prescriptive path, the two houses cost about the same to heat.

"The energy codes don't really require minimum levels of insulation," says Joe Nagan, technical direc-

Figure 10. Prescriptive tables, like this one in the 2000 IECC, provide a cookbook approach to energy design but may not result in the least expensive building.

Residential Energy Codes by State

Model Code State Code Is Based on	States
2006 IECC	Iowa, Louisiana, New Jersey, Pennsylvania, Utah
2003 IECC	Alaska, Arkansas, California, Connecticut, Idaho, Kansas, Maine, Maryland, Montana, Nebraska, Nevada, New Mexico, Ohio, Oregon, Rhode Island, Virginia, Washington, West Virginia
2003 IRC	Oklahoma, South Carolina
2001 IECC	New York, Texas
2000 IECC	Alabama, Arizona, Delaware, District of Columbia, Florida, Georgia, Kentucky, New Hampshire, North Carolina, Vermont
1995 MEC	Hawaii, Massachusetts, Minnesota, Wisconsin
1993 MEC	Colorado, North Dakota
1992 MEC	Indiana, Michigan, Tennessee
Code older than 1992 MEC	Wyoming
No energy code	Illinois, Missouri, Mississippi, South Dakota

In six states — Alabama, Arizona, Colorado, Hawaii, North Dakota, and Wyoming — code implementation depends upon voluntary adoption by local jurisdictions. The information in this table comes from the Building Codes Assistance Project Web site.

tor for Wisconsin Energy Star Homes. "For example, in their prescriptive insulation tables, the codes generally assume that you have a 78 percent AFUE furnace. But as long as your trade-off gives you a heat loss that is less than the maximum allowable heat loss, you pass. If you don't pass, you can either beef up the walls or you can go to a more efficient furnace."

In states with an energy code based on the 2004 IECC or earlier model codes, adjustments in window area can be used as a trade-off. For instance, thicker attic insulation or better-performing windows can be used as a trade-off for a high window-to-wall ratio; conversely, a low WWR may allow builders to use less insulation.

The easiest way to follow the component trade-off path is to use computer software — for example, a free program called REScheck — to fine-tune a home's specifications. Although first-time users of REScheck may be intimidated by the software, most builders soon navigate the program with ease (see "Using REScheck," page 28).

While the component trade-off path is popular in northern states, southern builders often stick with the prescriptive path. "Where the prescriptive codes most align with current building practice, builders tend to use the prescriptive codes," says Mike DeWein, technical director for the Building Codes Assistance Project in Washington, D.C. "That tends to be in the warmer climate zones. Where current practice varies from the prescriptive requirements, builders usually want to use the trade-off or the performance method. In a good chunk of the northern half of the country, builders and design professionals are very comfortable with REScheck."

Builders should remember that some trade-off strategies, though code-compliant, may result in an uncomfortable building. For example, many state energy codes allow builders to trade thicker attic insulation for cheaper windows. While the resulting house may satisfy the energy code, high U-factor windows may lead to comfort complaints.

Energy-Code Resources

Every builder needs to know what documents are required by the local building official to demonstrate compliance with local energy codes. A wealth of resources is available to builders looking to learn more, including the following:

- The local code authority
- The Web site of the state energy office
- A useful Web page maintained by the Pacific Northwest National Laboratory at www.pnl.gov
- The Web site of the Building Codes Assistance Project at www.bcap-energy.org
- Model residential energy code books available from the International Code Council at www.iccsafe.org
- The Code Notes Web page maintained by the DOE's Building Energy Codes Program at www.energycodes.gov/support/code_notes.stm
- Free online training (Webcasts) for REScheck users available through www.energycodes.gov
- A very useful book, *Field Guide to Residential Construction*, produced by the Conservation Services Group; state-specific versions of the book (available for Connecticut, Idaho, Maryland, Massachusetts, Montana, New Hampshire, New Jersey, New York, Oregon, Rhode Island, Vermont, and Washington) are distributed through each state's Energy Star Homes program.

The Systems Analysis Path

Sophisticated energy modeling software is needed for the systems analysis path. Depending on the state, the systems analysis path may be called the systems performance path, the simulated performance alternative, or whole-house performance analysis. It's found in Chapter 4 of pre-2004 versions of the IECC. In general, builders following this path must show that a proposed house design has an annual energy budget less than or equal to a similar house that complies with the code's prescriptive requirements.

While REScheck is perfectly adapted to calculating the effects of component trade-offs, it cannot be used for the systems analysis path. Builders following the systems analysis path need to use a program like DOE-2 or REM/Rate, the software used by consultants who rate a home using the Home Energy Rating System (HERS) index. Whereas the REScheck program has no way for a builder to input a home's air infiltration rate, REM/Rate does — so that a very tight home can obtain credit for its superior performance compared with a typical, somewhat leaky home.

If a builder follows the systems analysis path for code compliance using an air-infiltration rate that is lower than the code-specified default value, the code stipulates that a blower-door test must be performed to verify that the home meets its tightness goal. In theory, a builder who cannot provide blower-door results under these circumstances can be denied a certificate of occupancy.

Systems analyses are usually performed by an energy consultant, HERS rater, architect, or engineer. A systems analysis is the only way a builder can get full credit for certain energy-efficiency features that are not otherwise required by code — window orientation optimized for passive solar heating, for example, or a sealed and tested duct system.

Following the systems analysis path makes sense for homes that have unusual design or energy-efficiency features. Because the systems analysis path usually requires the assistance of an energy consultant, it is rarely used for residential construction.

Mandatory Requirements

In addition to offering three compliance paths, residential energy codes impose additional mandatory requirements. For example, pre-2004 versions of the IECC require attics to be equipped with permanent insulation depth markers.

Mandatory requirements also vary from state to state; for instance, Washington state requires all homes, regardless of which path is used for code compliance, to be equipped with a whole-house ventila-

Big Changes to the IECC

Besides being 150 pages shorter than the previous edition, the 2006 IECC incorporates radical code revisions. The changes were promoted by the U.S. Department of Energy in response to critics who complained of code complexity.

The rewriting of the IECC was intended to be "stringency neutral" — that is, to result in houses that are just as efficient as houses built to earlier versions of the code.

Among the most important changes to the 2006 IECC are the following:

- The number of climate zones has been reduced from 19 to eight, and all references to heating degree days have been eliminated.
- All references to the window-to-wall ratio have been eliminated.

With the elimination of window-to-wall area restrictions, the 2006 IECC no longer penalizes a house with a lot of windows. Although builders will probably welcome the chance to jettison WWR calculations, anyone accustomed to building houses with few windows may be surprised to learn that some house designs that formerly met code may no longer comply. The reason is that the 2006 IECC no longer allows builders to get credit for a low WWR as a trade-off for lower insulation levels in 2x4 walls.

"The intent of the code was never to create caves with no windows," says DeWein. "The intent was to try to do a static heat-loss analysis and to compare the home with some baseline. With the older versions of the IECC, when you had designs with low window areas, they scored a little better overall. With the new code, that's no longer the case."

Like the earlier versions of the code, the 2006 IECC has three compliance paths. Builders who choose the prescriptive path must follow the requirements of Table 402.1, which specifies the maximum window U-factor, maximum skylight U-factor, maximum window SHGC, and minimum R-values for ceilings, walls, floors, basement walls, crawlspace walls, and slabs. These specifications vary by climate zone. Table 402.1 allows lower R-values in walls with high thermal mass — ICF walls, for example — than in wood-frame walls.

Builders who choose the component trade-off path (which the 2006 IECC calls "the U-factor alternative") must follow the requirements of Section 402.1.2. The easiest way to comply with this path is to use REScheck software.

The requirements for the systems analysis path (which the 2006 IECC calls "the simulated performance alternative") can be found in Section 404 of the 2006 IECC. While earlier versions of the IECC base systems analysis comparisons on a home's annual energy budget as measured in Btus or kilowatt-hours, the 2006 IECC requires that the comparison be based on the dollar cost of the energy used.

The 2006 IECC includes several new mandatory provisions, including a requirement (403.2.2) for R-8 insulation on ducts located outside the thermal envelope and a requirement (401.3) for posting a "panel certificate." This document — which must be permanently affixed to the electrical distribution panel — must list the home's insulation R-values, window U-factors, window SHGC values, water-heater efficiency, and furnace or boiler efficiency.

The latest version of REScheck includes a new clickable button that automatically generates and prints a panel certificate.

Here are a few more noteworthy provisions of the 2006 IECC:

- The Code waives SHGC requirements for windows in the special marine zone along the Pacific coast, where cooling loads (and therefore solar-gain concerns) are low.
- The Code (402.2.1) allows builders who use raised-heel trusses to reduce the thickness of attic insulation, as long as the insulation covers wall plates at the eaves.
- The Code (402.2.2) allows builders in climate zones where R-38 ceiling insulation is normally required to install R-30 insulation in a cathedral ceiling if that's all that will fit, as long as the area of the cathedral ceiling doesn't exceed 500 square feet.

Using REScheck

REScheck is a software tool used to demonstrate that a house design complies with residential energy codes. The program was developed by the U.S. Department of Energy, and can be downloaded at no charge from www.energycodes.gov.

Not all states allow the use of REScheck for demonstrating energy-code compliance, so it's important to check local code requirements before deciding to use REScheck. Florida builders usually show code compliance with EnergyGauge software, while California energy consultants use one of several California-specific software tools to meet the state's Title 24 requirements. Among the states that do allow the use of REScheck are Arkansas, Georgia, Massachusetts, Minnesota, New Hampshire, New Jersey, New York, Vermont, and Wisconsin.

Once you have REScheck loaded on your computer, you're ready to see if your house design meets code. At the "Code" tab, choose the code you will be complying with — for example, MEC or a particular version of the IECC. If you live in a state with a state-specific code, it's important to indicate (at the "Code" tab) the state where the house is being built.

The program has five main tabs to click: "Project," "Envelope," "Mechanical," "Loads," and "Energy Star." Under each tab are boxes where the user enters information about the house in question. Probably the most time-consuming step is calculating the area of the home's components, including floor areas, wall areas, ceiling areas, and window areas.

In this example, a simple 30-foot-by-40-foot ranch house has R-19 wall insulation, R-38 ceiling insulation, R-5 basement wall insulation, and windows with a U-factor of 0.34. If the house is equipped with a 78 percent AFUE furnace, it does not pass Wisconsin code (see Figure A). On the REScheck program, the line at the bottom of the screen indicates code compliance or failure; in this case, it indicates "Fails" and "9.2% Worse Than Code."

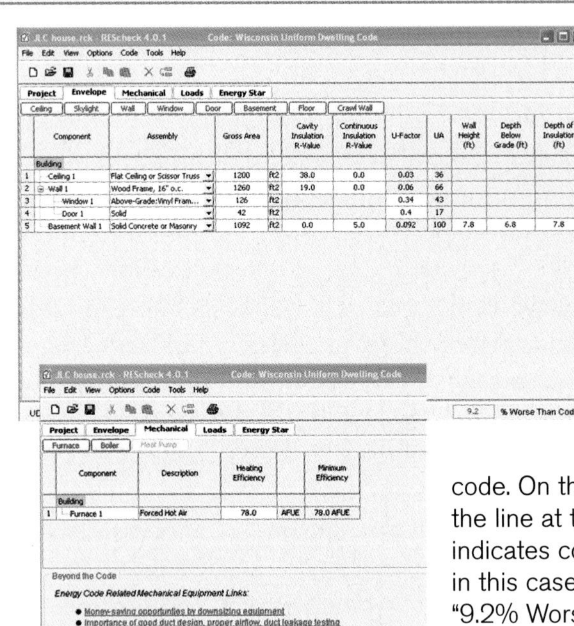

Figure A. In this example, a simple 30-foot-by-40-foot ranch house has R-19 wall insulation, R-38 ceiling insulation, R-5 basement wall insulation, and windows with a U-factor of 0.34. If the house is equipped with a 78 percent AFUE furnace, it does not pass Wisconsin code. On the REScheck program, the line at the bottom of the screen indicates code compliance or failure; in this case, it indicates "Fails" and "9.2% Worse Than Code."

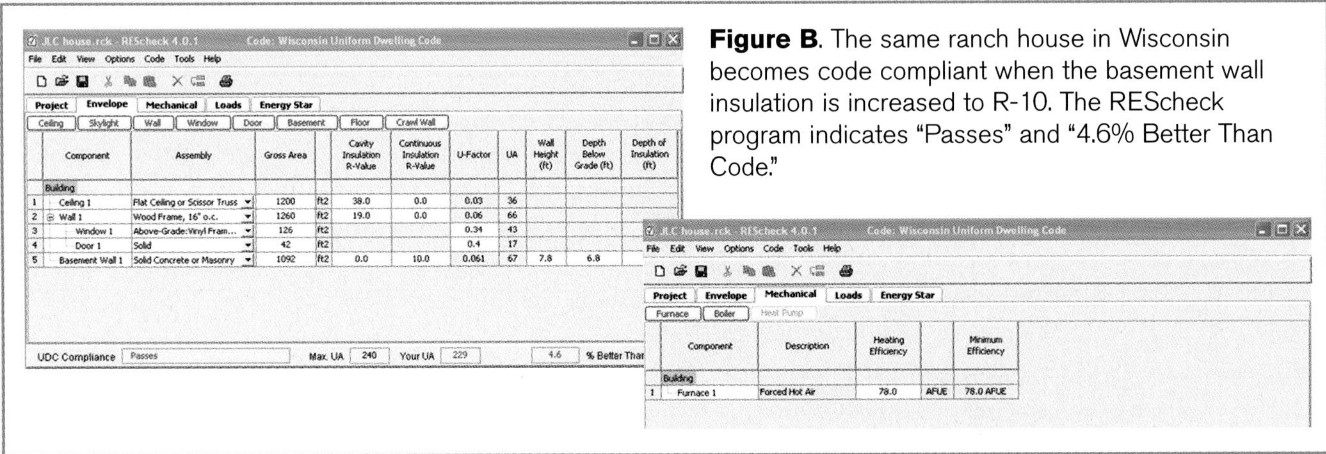

Figure B. The same ranch house in Wisconsin becomes code compliant when the basement wall insulation is increased to R-10. The REScheck program indicates "Passes" and "4.6% Better Than Code."

After entering the required information, including the insulation R-values, it's time to click the "Check compliance" button in the lower left-hand corner. The program then indicates whether your design "Passes" or "Fails," and displays the percentage by which it either exceeds or falls short of your energy code (for example, "Your UA is 2.6% better than code," or "Your UA is 16.2% worse than code"). By changing the home's insulation values or window sizes, an out-of-compliance home can be brought into compliance.

The same ranch house in Wisconsin becomes code-compliant when the basement wall insulation is increased to R-10. The REScheck program indicates "Passes" and "4.6% Better Than Code" (see Figure B).

Instead of increasing the thickness of the attic and basement wall insulation, a builder could swap the 78 percent AFUE furnace for a 92 percent AFUE furnace. That upgrade results in a house that is 7.4 percent better than code — even with the original R-5 basement wall insulation (see Figure C).

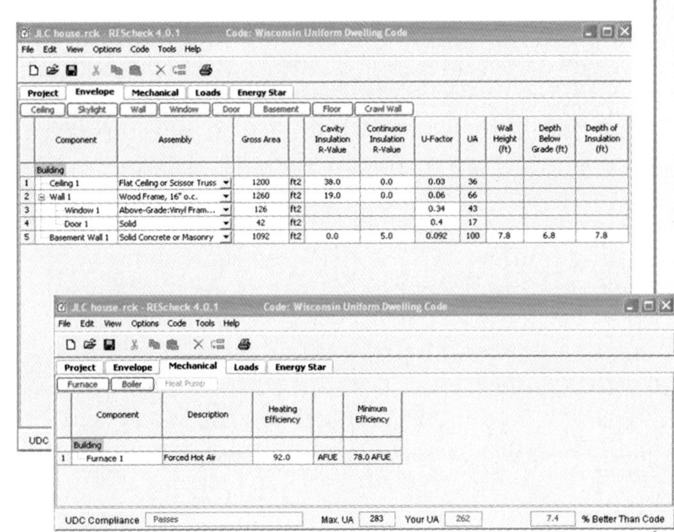

	Component	Assembly	Gross Area		Cavity Insulation R-Value	Continuous Insulation R-Value	U-Factor	UA	Wall Height (ft)	Depth Below Grade (ft)	Depth of Insulation (ft)
	Building										
1	Ceiling 1	Flat Ceiling or Scissor Truss	1200	ft2	38.0	0.0	0.03	36			
2	Wall 1	Wood Frame, 16" o.c.	1260	ft2	19.0	0.0	0.06	66			
3	Window 1	Above-Grade:Vinyl Fram...	126	ft2			0.34	43			
4	Door 1	Solid	42	ft2			0.4	17			
5	Basement Wall 1	Solid Concrete or Masonry	1092	ft2	0.0	5.0	0.092	100	7.8	6.8	7.8

	Component	Description	Heating Efficiency		Minimum Efficiency
	Building				
1	Furnace 1	Forced Hot Air	92.0	AFUE	78.0 AFUE

Figure C. Instead of increasing the thickness of the attic and basement wall insulation, a builder could swap the 78 percent AFUE furnace for a 92 percent AFUE furnace. That upgrade results in a house that is 7.4 percent better than code — even with the original R-5 basement wall insulation.

In most cases, REScheck determines code compliance by calculating the home's UA. (UA is the overall average heat transmission of the area of a building's exterior envelope; that is, the average U-factor of the envelope times the area of the entire envelope.)

If the home includes high-efficiency hvac equipment, REScheck can (in certain states or for some model codes) perform a limited-scope performance analysis. However, use of the performance path is not always advantageous to a builder. Under the 2006 IECC, the performance path calculation considers glazing area and orientation, so a home that is not advantageously oriented (from a solar perspective) may fail worse when following the performance path than it did using the prescriptive path.

Here, then, are a few facts to remember:

- When entering wall areas into REScheck, use gross wall areas (including band-joist areas), not net wall areas. REScheck automatically subtracts the area of the windows and doors to calculate net wall areas.
- When entering window areas, enter either the rough opening area or the window frame area, not the sash area or the glass area.
- REScheck automatically adjusts R-values as required to account for drywall, air films, and the like, so enter only the R-value shown on the insulation label.
- If you are passing code by means of the UA calculation method, you don't need to enter information on the home's hvac system.
- If you are complying with the 2006 version of the IECC, some compliance paths require specifying the orientation (north, south, east, or west) of the windows and walls.
- REScheck has certain inherent limitations; for example, it is unable to handle a house with more than one heating system.

Anyone with questions about REScheck should explore the resources available online at www.energycodes.gov. They include the REScheck Software User's Guide, posted at www.energycodes.gov/rescheck/download.stm (click on "Support Documents").

tion system and equipment to provide combustion air for solid-fuel appliances.

Getting Your Permit

In most jurisdictions, a building permit will not be issued until the builder has submitted documentation — such as a REScheck report — showing that the design complies with the local energy code. Energy code documents are prepared by a range of service providers, including builders, engineers, architects, energy consultants, lumberyards, and heating contractors.

Although REScheck reports are routinely prepared by

builders in many areas, a few jurisdictions — including some New Jersey municipalities — require REScheck calculations to be submitted by a licensed engineer. California's energy code, called Title 24, is unique. Because of the code's complexity, California builders usually demonstrate code compliance by hiring an energy consultant familiar with the use of Title 24 software.

Many builders are happy to hand off responsibility for code-compliance paperwork. "In Wisconsin, the overwhelming number of REScheck reports are done by the lumberyard or the heating contractor," reports Nagan.

What About Airtightness?

Since many attributes of home performance are not regulated by code, complying with the energy code, though necessary, is not sufficient to guarantee that a house will be energy efficient. For example, the prescriptive and component trade-off paths do not directly address a home's air-leakage rate. As Nagan notes, "REScheck can perform trade-offs between heating equipment and insulation levels, but REScheck knows nothing about infiltration."

In some countries, such as Sweden, a new home must pass a blower-door test before it can be issued an occupancy permit. U.S. codes, however, show no sign of following Sweden's lead. "The 2006 IECC is better at calling out how one deals with air leakage and duct sealing," notes DeWein. "But there is still no performance metric for it, unless you go to the full-performance methodology."

The 2006 IECC requires submitted plans to indicate air sealing details (104.2); it also specifies that "the building thermal envelope shall be durably sealed to limit infiltration" (402.4.1). Some state codes, including the Minnesota, New York, and Oregon residential energy codes, have similar mandatory requirements intended to improve the airtightness of a home's envelope. Oregon's provisions are subject to interpretation by local building officials: "All exterior joints around windows, around door frames, between wall cavities and window or door frames, between wall and foundation, between wall and roof, and other openings in the exterior envelope shall be sealed in a manner approved by the building official."

A house that complies with the energy code does not necessarily include all cost-effective efficiency measures.

"Most Wisconsin builders install one inch of foam on the exterior of their basement walls," says Nagan. "When we do our REM/Rate action reports to evaluate a house for an Energy Star builder, overwhelmingly the reports show that the foundation is the largest contributor to the heating cost. Even Energy Star builders are using just one inch of foam, so these buildings still have a very weak link. These homes could be cost-effectively upgraded, with no more labor, just by going from one inch of foam to two."

Code Compliance Varies

Several studies have documented the fact that in many areas of the country, energy code provisions remain largely unenforced. For example, a 2001 study in Fort Collins, Colo., investigated duct tightness in new homes. In spite of a local code provision that required ducts to be "substantially airtight," performance testing in new homes revealed that hvac systems had duct leakage averaging 75 percent of system airflow.

Similarly, a 2001 study of 186 new Massachusetts homes found that only 46 percent of the homes met minimum code requirements for UA (building envelope U-factor), and only 19 percent met code duct-sealing requirements.

Building officials rarely bring along a home's REScheck report during site inspections. Although all residential energy codes, except the 2006 IECC, impose window-area limits, "there is not a single jurisdiction in the country that goes out and measures window areas on site," says Craig Conner, a former engineer at the Pacific Northwest National Laboratory in Richland, Wash.

Some states, including Vermont, have a mandatory energy code but no system of enforcement. "In Vermont, compliance with the energy code requires filing a copy of the documentation report with the local town clerk," says Richard Faesy, a senior energy analyst for Vermont Energy Investment Corp. in Burlington. "As far as I know, fewer than 10 percent of new houses are in compliance with the code. There's no enforcement infrastructure."

Many builders see lax code enforcement as a blessing. The trouble with uneven enforcement, however, is that a builder can never be sure when a new building official will begin enforcing long-ignored regulations. Builders intent on following the code as written should be aware of the following rarely enforced provisions:

- Some codes (for example, in Massachusetts and California) include duct-tightness requirements.

- Many codes (IECC 102.2, for instance) include a provision requiring all materials, systems, and equipment to be installed according to manufacturers' installation instructions. According to this provision, fiberglass batt insulation must be installed without voids or compression. Moreover, housewrap must be carefully lapped at horizontal seams, and some brands of housewrap must have taped seams.

- Many energy codes (such as IECC 803.2.1.1) require "right sizing" of hvac equipment; according to this requirement, oversized furnaces, boilers, and air conditioners violate the code.

Martin Holladay *is senior editor of www.GreenBuildingAdvisor.com and was formerly the editor of Energy Design Update.*

Chapter 2

ENERGY RATING & DIAGNOSTICS

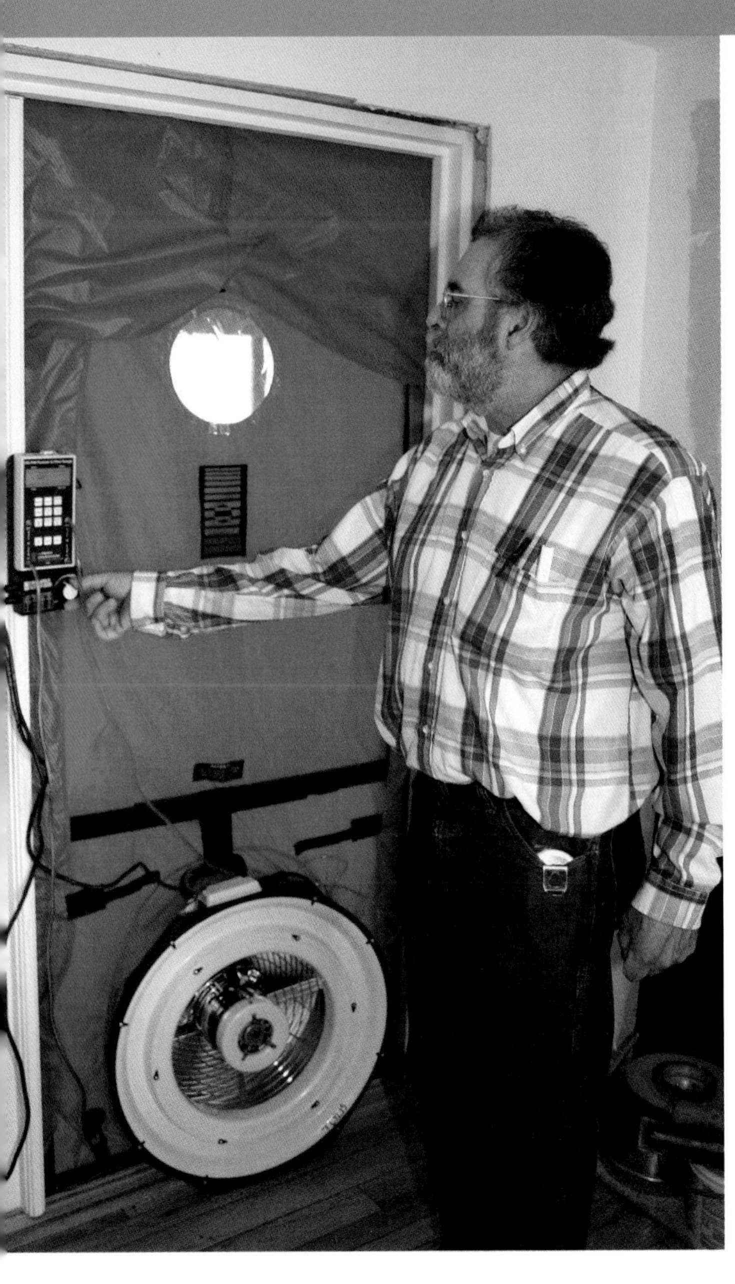

- Home Performance Contracting
- Blower-Door Testing
- Pressure-Testing Ductwork

Home Performance Contracting

by Mike Rogers

If you were to ask the average American to define "home performance contracting," you'd probably get a blank look. In fact, I doubt that most professional remodelers really know what it is. In coming years, though, I believe we're going to see home performance contracting become a household term. My own company, GreenHomes America, is betting on it: After fine-tuning our business model in Syracuse, N.Y., we went nationwide with company-owned branches and franchises in 2009. We're active in five states and plan to repeat throughout the country what we proved in Syracuse.

Home performance contractors use a comprehensive "house as a system" approach to upgrading the energy systems in existing homes. We start with a complete battery of diagnostic tests and a careful analysis of the house's energy efficiency, comfort, and indoor environment. We call this "testing in." Then we apply the upgrades that make sense. After the work is done, we test the house again — "testing out" — to make sure that the measures we have installed are going to perform the way we intended and that we're leaving the home in a safe condition.

We're not consultants — we do most of the work ourselves. Our crews blow insulation, seal attics, put in doors and windows, and install furnaces and water heaters. We even put up solar water heaters and, occasionally, photovoltaic solar panels.

The way we work, homeowners get the benefit of "one-stop shopping" for the whole package of energy and comfort upgrades. More important, we take one-point responsibility for the way all the systems in the house will interact. It's not the usual situation, where one trade contractor rarely thinks about how his work may affect the work of other trades. In home performance contracting, we treat all the home's elements, from building shell to mechanical systems, as related pieces of one big puzzle. We systematically apply our upgrades in ways that take into account how all those sub-systems interact.

In this article, I'll describe the business methods we use and the technology we employ to make existing houses function better.

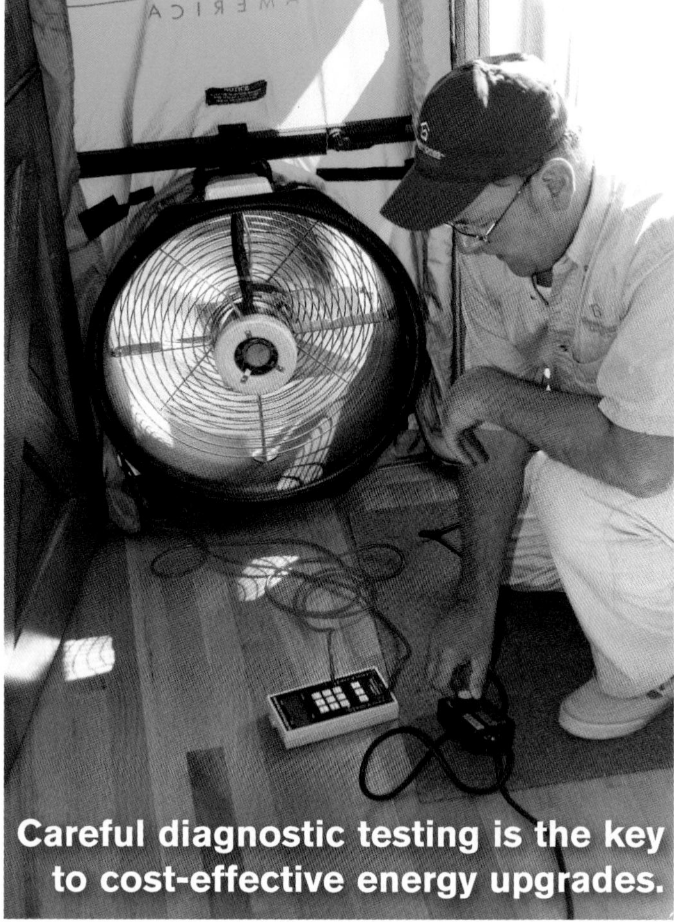

Careful diagnostic testing is the key to cost-effective energy upgrades.

Marketing and Sales

Our comprehensive approach is new in the local home-improvement market. For example, there's no section in the Yellow Pages for "Home Performance Contractors." So in Syracuse, we have ads under Replacement Windows, Insulation Contractors, and Heating and Cooling Contractors. And yet we're not a window company, or an insulation company, or an hvac contractor — instead, we're all three, but we're also more than that. So when we get sales leads from various sources — TV and radio advertising, print ads, the Yellow Pages, our Web site, or people who have noticed our phone number on our fleet of trucks — our first challenge is to explain to the caller what it is that we really do.

Energy efficiency is our focus, and we deliver energy savings every day. However, many people who call us are not necessarily looking for savings on their energy bill. Most Americans don't even know that a typical house can easily save 25 percent or more on its energy bills with a modest investment. So our typical customer is calling about something else — usually a comfort or performance issue, like a chilly draft or a room that's too hot or too cold all the time, or some durability problem like ice on the roof or moisture-related paint failure.

No matter what the reason for the call, we always provide the same service first: One of our advisors (we don't call them "salesmen") visits the house for a comprehensive inspection. We visually inspect the building, inside and out. We check airtightness with a blower door, we test the furnace and water heater for

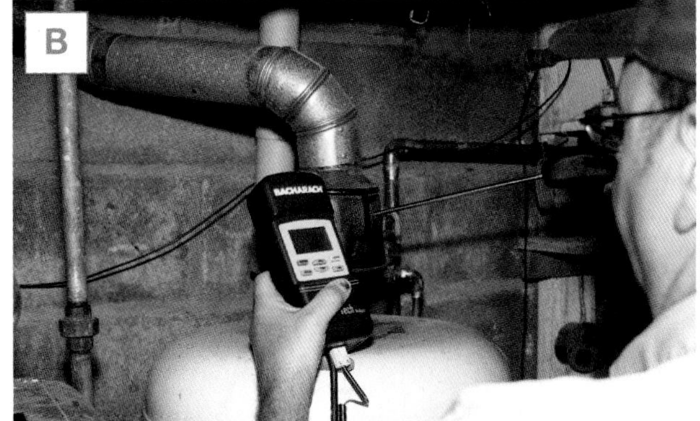

Figure 1. After drilling holes to insert sensor probes in the appliance flues (A), the advisor uses a combustion analyzer to check for complete combustion in the furnace and water heater (B). With doors and windows shut and all exhaust fans in the building operating, he uses a manometer to check the draft (C); he is also required to check gas piping for leaks (D).

combustion efficiency and safe operation, we use infrared imaging cameras to find insulation voids or thermal bypasses, and we use smoke pencils to locate air leaks. We "sniff" the gas piping for leaks. Depending on the situation, we may measure duct system airtightness and airflows. Then, once we know exactly what's going on and how the house works, we recommend the upgrades that we predict will save the most energy most cost-effectively while also improving the safety and durability of the building.

Safety is one of the critical reasons for testing. We can't come in and tighten up a house that already has a carbon monoxide problem or a gas leak — we don't want to expose our crews to the hazard, and we clearly don't want to risk the homeowners' safety or incur legal liability. So without combustion testing and air-quality testing, we won't touch the house.

We also never quote prices before we've determined what the house needs. Ultimately, of course, it's the homeowners who will decide what to buy. After all, it's their investment and their budget. We might recommend insulating and air-sealing the attic as a first step, and they might decide they want new windows instead. But they don't have to make that choice blindly, because we give them good information to work from.

We occasionally lose customers. There are those who say, "I just want new windows, I don't want you going down into my basement," or "Joe said he would put in a new 95,000-Btu furnace for X dollars; I just want to know what your price is." But most of the time, customers appreciate our need to know what we're looking at before we start trying to sell them a product. And our goal is to have a lifetime relationship with every customer (in fact, one good reason to install the hvac systems ourselves is that it means we will visit that house again every year for routine maintenance).

Testing In

Our advisors are the primary point of contact with the homeowner. They need a lot of training to be ready for this work because they do a lot: Each advisor is a diagnostician and a salesperson rolled into one. It's quite technical — the advisor has to know how to operate the blower door, use the combustion testers, run the duct blaster, operate the infrared camera, visually inspect the house, and interpret all the results. But he also needs good sales and communication skills because he has to make our analysis of the house understandable to a layperson — and at the end of the day, he has to put together a scope of work, sign the agreement with the customer, and get that deposit check.

Combustion testing. Furnace and water-heater efficiency are key elements of a home's energy efficiency, and their safe operation (and that of the gas range in the kitchen) is important for the safety of the home. So our advisor checks flue gases with a combustion analyzer to measure the system's baseline performance (Figure 1).

Appliance vent draft. The advisor also assesses the ability of heating appliances to draft properly. Flue draft and room air pressures are related: If the draft is weak, and there's also negative pressure in the basement, the unit could backdraft and send combustion products into the living space. We need to know what might happen in the worst case. So the advisor closes all the windows and doors, turns on all the exhaust fans in the house — the range hood, bath vent fans, the clothes dryer — and checks the pressure difference between indoors and outdoors. He compares his reading with a standard set by BPI, the Building Performance Institute (www.bpi.org). Whatever change we make to the home must correct any pressures that fall outside recommended levels.

Sniffing for gas leaks. GreenHomes is "accredited" by the Building Performance Institute — a contractual relationship that means all our personnel must earn BPI certification (see "Getting Certified for Home Energy Audits," page 40). It also means we agree to correct certain deficiencies in any house we work on: We're required to test for leaks on any accessible gas piping and to repair any leaks we find (or, if they are on the gas company's side of the meter, call the utility in to fix them).

Blower-door testing. We use the blower door to measure the total air leakage of the house. If the house leaks too much, it costs too much to heat and cool. On the other hand, if it's too tight, it may need mechanical ventilation for fresh air and will require direct-vented combustion equipment. Most houses we work on start out too leaky, so the "test-in" blower-door values provide us with a baseline. After we do our work, we'll test again to make sure we accomplished the air-tightening we set out to achieve.

To run the test, the advisor shuts all the windows and doors, blocks off the fireplace, and installs his equipment in the door. He runs an air line from his manometer to the outside, then runs the blower-door fan and records the airflow required to bring the house to –50 pascals of pressure compared with outdoors. That number can be used to estimate the air-leakage area of the house envelope, which gives us an idea of how much air-sealing work will be needed.

The blower door gives you an aggregate airtightness number, but you still need to run around and locate the leaks using smoke pencils. (The attic, by the way, is typically where most of the leaks are.)

Infrared imaging. The infrared (IR) camera lets us locate areas where there are voids or not enough insulation — where somebody missed a spot, the batts are compressed, or blown insulation has settled.

The IR camera is also helpful for educating the homeowners. Rather than try to explain all the science, we can bring the homeowners along as we inspect and show them the cold or hot spots on the screen. When the blower door is operating, those spots show up even better on the camera display, as the suction pulls outdoor air in through leaky uninsulated spaces.

Infrared cameras are getting better and cheaper as technology advances. The best new equipment will reveal insulation defects when there's just a 5°F difference from inside to outside (it doesn't matter whether the outside is warmer or colder than the inside, as long as they're different). And prices for the equipment have come down, too: Ten years ago a good camera might have cost more than $20,000, while today you can get a camera with better resolution, a better sensor, and many more functions for around $5,000.

Testing ductwork. We test ductwork when we need to. Purists may insist that you should do a duct-blaster test on every house you work on. But if the ducts are all inside the conditioned space, testing them is a low priority for us. We're more concerned that the pressures and airflows are balanced.

In predominantly heating climates, where the ducts are in the basement, research and our own experience both show that duct leakage is not very important — it's all within the conditioned space anyway. So we focus our efforts on the envelope instead.

In the South, on the other hand, where air-conditioning ducts typically run through an unconditioned hot attic, it's critical that you take a close look at duct leakage and do a very thorough job of sealing any leaks you find. But even then, duct blasting when you're testing in may be superfluous. If you can see at a glance that the ductwork needs to be torn out and redone, you shouldn't spend hours on a duct-blaster test first — moving the furniture around, sealing registers, and so forth. The important thing is to test after the work is done, to verify the performance of the new ducts. (For more on duct testing, see "Pressure-Testing Ductwork," page 48.)

Evaluating the Data

We always give the homeowner an estimate of how our upgrades will affect the home's energy bills. We offer a 25 percent energy-savings guarantee, whether there's a government program involved or not, if the customer chooses to install the entire package of measures we recommend. In our experience, you can achieve that degree of improvement in almost any house. Even a brand-new code-compliant house can usually cut its energy bills 25 percent — after all, code is the legal minimum, not some kind of high-performance ideal.

We don't rely on computer models; among energy practitioners, they're notorious for overestimating the savings. If we're working in a local or state program that requires us to model the house, we'll do it — but I'd be terrified to use a computer model as the basis for our own energy-savings guarantees. Instead, we use our own in-house methods, based on experience, to predict energy savings. However, you can get pretty close with publicly available methods that anyone can use. The EPA has a useful tool for analyzing utility bills posted on its Energy Star Web site (click on "Home Performance With Energy" at www.energystar.gov). BPI also has a statistical database of before-and-after home energy bills that you can use to make a fair estimate of how an upgrade will change a house's performance.

Assessing utility bills. We start by taking a careful look at the utility bills. We "dis-aggregate" the utility bill, breaking it down to figure out where the major loads are and how the energy is being used. And based on the improvements we recommend, we do a very conservative estimate of the savings we want to see.

Here's a simplified example. Let's say you have all the gas bills for a house that is heated with gas. You can track the usage month by month for the past year. July 1 is a good starting point, because we know the house isn't being heated. So the gas bill that month reflects what the occupants use for everything else: cooking, water heating, and maybe a gas clothes dryer. When fall comes, that number starts to rise. It climbs through November and December and on into the dead of winter. Then in February or March it starts to decline again. If you graph it, you get a bell-shaped curve.

From the summer bills, we know the home's baseline usage for nonheating needs. Now we can figure out what portion of the midwinter bill goes for space heating. With that, we can pretty well figure out how much we stand to save if we improve the insulation by so much, if we reduce the building air leakage by so much, or if we change from an 80 percent efficient furnace to a 94 percent efficient furnace.

In the same way, we can pick apart the electric bill. We figure out how much each appliance is responsible for: the refrigerator, the air conditioner, the blower motor on the furnace, lighting, and so on. And we can guess pretty accurately how much the owners will save if we improve each of those elements.

It takes experience to make accurate estimates. But once that experience is acquired, a careful house-by-house analysis is more reliable than any software on the market today.

Of course, the homeowners make the final call on what we do — it's their money, and they get to decide. Naturally, they often make their decisions based on things other than energy savings. They may choose a furnace because they like the easy controls, or buy insulation and air-sealing to make their home office more comfortable. Still, the energy savings are always a plus. We like to show customers that with the financing we can help them get and with other available incentives — plus the reduction in energy use they'll achieve — they could end up with extra cash in their pocket every month.

Upgrading the House

Once we've reported our assessment and the homeowners have made their choices, we move to the next phase of the job, implementation. As I mentioned above, energy efficiency is not always the customer's only objective. But when reduction in energy use is in fact the main goal, the most cost-effective upgrade is almost always air-sealing and insulation.

I'm continually amazed at how many houses in the cold Northeast are under-insulated. Many old houses still have no wall insulation and just a few inches of attic insulation. Even houses built in the last three years typically offer major opportunities to improve the air-sealing and insulation. Crews may miss spots when they insulate, and most builders still pretty much ignore air-sealing in the attic, so a good air-sealing job is usually our top recommendation.

Air-sealing and insulating. The attic is usually the gold mine of opportunity (Figure 2). Even today, builders rarely give it the attention it deserves. The stack effect places the boundary between the living space and the attic under a lot of pressure, and the ceiling is a large area. In most houses, air constantly flows across that plane.

The goal is to keep the indoor air that you've paid to heat or cool down in the living space where it belongs. So our crew goes through the attic and finds every hole that connects to downstairs (Figure 3) — plumbing chases, chimneys, vent pipes, electric wiring, duct penetrations, whatever — and seals them. They also look for joints where dissimilar materials meet. Partition walls often communicate with the attic at cracks and gaps between the drywall and framing.

In a one-story home, kitchen cabinet soffits are a major point of leakage. In new construction, a good approach is to install drywall on the ceiling before you build the soffit, creating a continuous air barrier at the ceiling level. But in most existing houses, those soffits were framed before the drywall was installed, leaving the dead space above on the attic side of the ceiling. That often creates an air leak, and it also makes it hard to keep the insulation in contact with the drywall air barrier. We fix those situations by installing rigid foam or drywall at the attic floor level and air-sealing the joints before blowing insulation.

Once the air-pressure boundary is sealed, insulation

can be blown into the space. The key is to keep the insulation aligned with the air-pressure boundary and in contact with it. That way, the insulation can perform at its full rated value.

Houses with complicated rooflines and tight attic spaces offer the greatest challenge. On the cape shown in Figure 4, we lined the knee-wall crawlspace with Typar, then blew the walls and the sloped portion of the ceiling with dense-pack cellulose. Above, in the attic, we sealed the air leaks individually, then installed loose-blown cellulose over the floor. The result is a continuous insulated boundary and a continuous air-sealed plane, both in contact with each other.

In houses that lack wall insulation, we blow dense-pack cellulose into the walls (Figure 5). This improves airtightness and boosts the wall's R-value.

Hvac upgrade. The next step is typically to upgrade the heating and cooling system. There are lots of 80 percent efficient furnaces out there, but in heating climates it's usually worthwhile to upgrade to a 95 percent efficient unit or better and to replace old air handler motors with new variable-speed ECM (electronically commutated) motors.

When it comes to cooling systems, our recommendation depends on the climate. In Syracuse, where most houses don't even have air conditioning, installing anything higher than SEER 14 or 15 doesn't make much sense. But in Houston or Dallas, you'd want to consider a SEER in the high teens or twenties.

Windows. Windows, typically, are not high on our list. Almost all homeowners think they can get big improvements from high-performance windows — the window industry has done a great job of selling that idea. But in reality, windows are usually the least cost-effective energy upgrade.

Homeowners may have good reasons to get new windows — the old ones may be in bad condition or painted shut. And if they're getting new windows anyway, it always makes sense to choose energy-efficient units, because the cost difference trivial. But getting new windows just for energy-performance doesn't usually pay. We're careful to be clear with homeowners about that. (This doesn't hurt us, by the way. We still sell and install a lot of replacement windows.)

Although they seldom accept our entire package of recommendations, homeowners usually decide to adopt several measures. Sometimes it makes more economic sense to upgrade the furnace and air conditioner than to buy new windows. But if the plan is to do both, we upgrade the windows before replacing the hvac equipment. Shell upgrades — like windows and insulation — let you reduce the size of the hvac system, which saves up-front cost as well as the expense to operate the equipment.

Solar hot water. In our experience, solar thermal panels — rooftop water heaters — typically turn out to

Figure 2. Crews seal spaces over cabinet soffits by installing rigid insulation across the opening at attic floor level and sealing the joints with foam (left). Gaps where wall plates meet the attic floor must also be sealed (right).

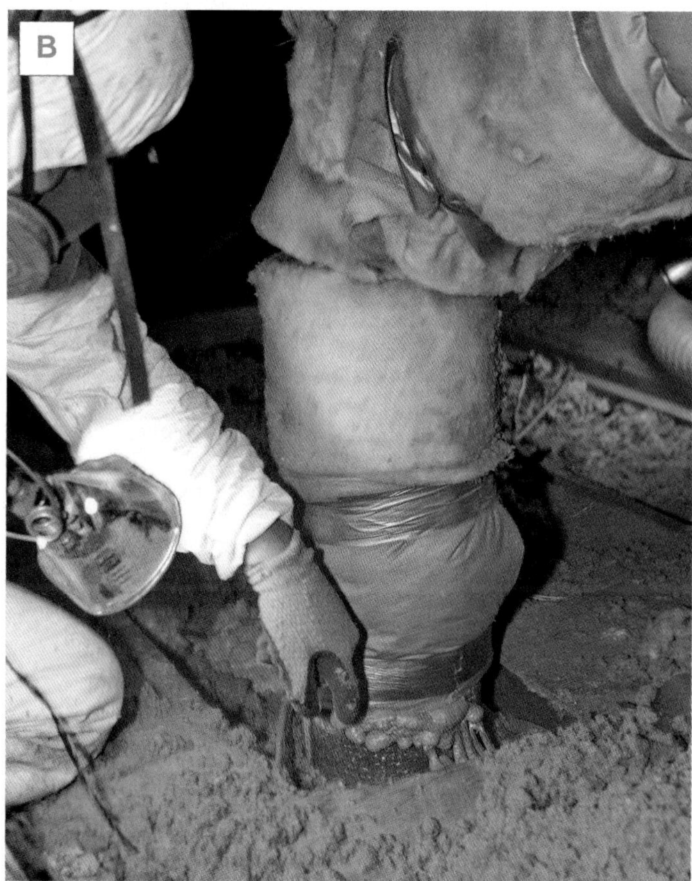

Figure 3. Can lights are covered with boxes made from duct board, which are foamed in place (A); hvac boots are also sealed (B). This chimney (C) was decommissioned when a direct-vent furnace was installed, so the crew has sealed around it with foam; air gaps around active chimneys are sealed using sheet metal and high-temperature silicone caulk.

Figure 4. Here, a crew has applied housewrap to the inside face of a knee wall and low roof and is dense-blowing cellulose into the wall cavities (right) and the short sloped section of ceiling (above).

be a smarter investment than new windows when considered individually. This is true even in a northern market like Syracuse. We're very excited about the potential market for solar water heating. The new systems are much simpler and more reliable than those of the 1970s or 1980s, when you had to be a master plumber, a mechanical engineer, and build the whole thing from scratch yourself. These days, a solar thermal installation is essentially an appliance that you mount on the roof. You may still need a licensed plumber to tie it in, but it's no more complicated than tying in a standard water heater or any other appliance.

Upgrading the lighting is also usually cost-effective. On most houses, we offer a basic lighting upgrade for free — we just walk around with a 12-pack of compact fluorescent bulbs and replace every incandescent bulb we see. For a few important high-use fixtures, we may recommend replacing the whole fixture with an advanced unit.

Testing Out

I don't have space in this article to go into the details of window replacements or hvac upgrades. Instead, I want to emphasize the crucial quality-control process — testing out after the work is done (Figure 6). The final tests are always performed by different technicians than the advisors who test in; that way, there's no unconscious bias in favor of fudging the numbers.

At the end of the test, our technicians hand the homeowners a certificate documenting the work that was done and the energy savings predicted — including the reduction in their "carbon footprint" in tons of carbon dioxide per year that their house will no longer contribute to the atmosphere. We want to

continued on page 42

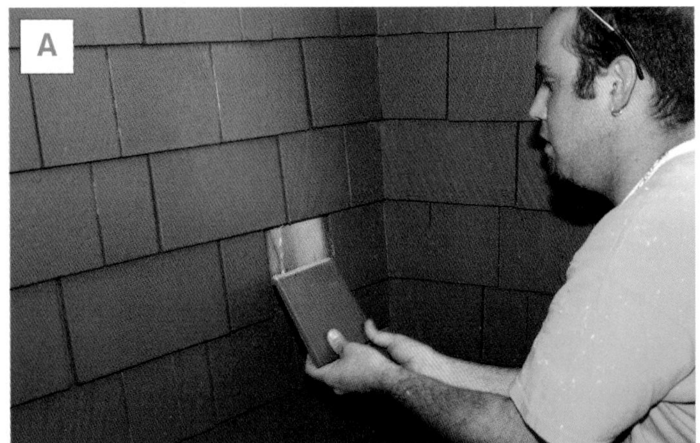

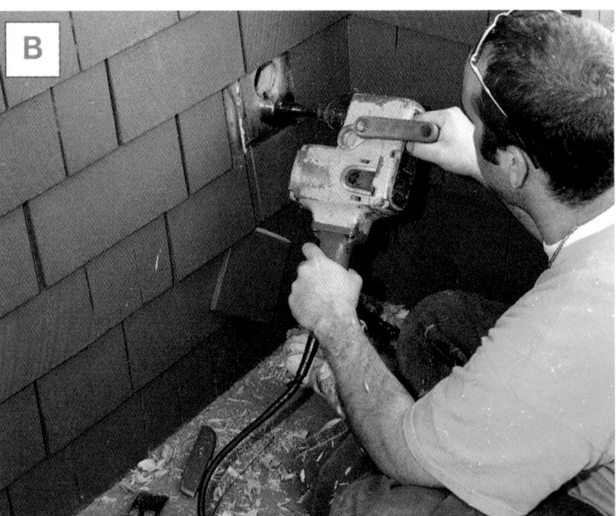

Figure 5. A GreenHomes wall-insulation crew carefully cuts off wood shingle siding to expose the sheathing (A), then drills holes for the insulation blower hose (B). After blowing in the cellulose (C), they seal the holes in the sheathing with closed-cell expanding foam (D), then carefully re-nail the shingles.

Figure 6. "Testing out" is a key element in quality assurance and customer service. In the house shown here, the technician saw the need to touch up the mastic on the basement ducts (left). More important, he discovered a previously unnoticed gas leak (above) — a leak that probably became evident after other fittings in the piping were tightened.

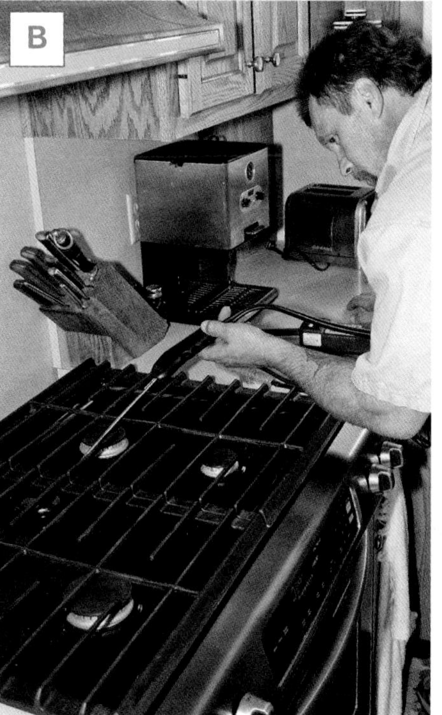

Figure 7. The technician verifies the correct operation of a new furnace and water heater (A) and documents the safety of the new kitchen range (B). A final blower-door test (C) indicates the increase in house airtightness from 3,600 CFM-50 to just over 1,900 CFM-50.

Getting Certified for Home Energy Audits

by Robert Post

As the owner of a small remodeling and handyman company (nearly $1 million annual sales before the downturn), I've always been careful to stay focused on our core offerings — bathrooms, kitchens, basements, and small jobs ranging from two-hour service calls to week-long "honey do" lists.

Over the years, we've resisted the temptation to take on larger projects like additions and new homes. We've also resisted various opportunities to offer specialty products and services, like replacement windows, siding, and garage systems. One area that did make sense for us was the remediation work resulting from residential energy audits. I've always been interested in energy efficiency and the various problems that stem from air and moisture movement in homes. And like many others, I've also come to believe that the shift to sustainable building practices is inevitable.

So recently, prompted by the economic downturn, I decided to pursue Building Analyst certification from the Building Performance Institute (www.bpi.org) and begin offering energy audits and home-performance contracting. For us, entering this niche was a natural move. I already had many years of experience working with home-energy auditors and performing the follow-up work needed. As a result, our small field staff has developed a good basic understanding of the common flaws in residential structures and how to fix them. We are already accustomed to working in crawlspaces and attics and are familiar with the steps needed to assess a home's insulation levels and airtightness.

For the most part, remediation projects are similar in size and scope to the remodeling jobs that make up much of our sales. They require the same logistical procedures and cost accounting, so we didn't need to change our business systems to accommodate home-performance contracting.

Back to School

Gaining certification required a considerable amount of time. The BPI coursework is offered in various places and formats; I started by enrolling in a two-month Web-based program from Saturn Online, which offers "guaranteed test prep" for the BPI exam. I spent approximately four to six hours a week working through the material and taking a weekly quiz. The time you spend will vary depending on how much you already know about building science. The course is based on a textbook and manual, which Saturn sells. This was a valuable program, and I would recommend it to anyone on this path.

After completing the online course, I took a week-long BPI class, which met for eight hours a day in a classroom setting, with two field trips — one to observe a building audit and one to run practice tests on several different systems at an hvac demonstration facility. The class was fairly intense and conveyed a lot of information. The instructor showed a real mastery of the subject and presented the material with enthusiasm. The week culminated with a two-hour, 100-question test, which required a score of 70 percent or higher to pass. This was followed with a proctored field exam, in which I performed an energy audit on an actual residence. The field exam was graded pass/fail; you have to pass both the written and the field exams to get your certification. Also, you're required to be recertified every three years. There are a variety of ways to satisfy this, one of which is 30 hours of qualified continuing education.

The Financial Investment

I chose a BPI training package that covered the cost of the online course, the week-long class, and both tests. It cost around $1,200; the textbooks added about $95. As a business owner who spends roughly half his time in the field — hours that are directly billable — I also needed to count the lost revenue.

The equipment you'll need to perform audits using the BPI protocol starts at about $7,000 (I split the investment with another business owner who also performs audits). Here's a breakdown:

- Blower-door kit, used to measure and locate air leakage
- Combustion analyzer, to measure steady-state efficiency of combustion appliances
- Gas-leak detector, to check all accessible gas lines for leaks
- Moisture meter, either a pin type or noninvasive, suitable for various materials
- Smoke stick, to locate air leaks and assess draft of atmospherically vented combustion appliances
- Personal CO detector

- There are also some tools you may want to consider after you're comfortable with the basic kit, though they're not necessary for meeting BPI standards:
- Digital camera
- Laptop
- Infrared camera, used to scan buildings for thermal quality, air leaks, and other issues
- Pressure pan, used to block a duct register while measuring the static pressure behind it during a blower-door test
- Anemometer, for measuring wind speed and diagnosing comfort issues relating to duct airflow
- Duct blaster, like a small blower door, used to test for duct leaks
- Boroscope, for inspecting inside wall cavities or other concealed areas
- Reporting and analysis software such as Treat or REM/Rate, for home energy modeling

Your home measured 2.26 times more leaky than the high range of the goal, 3.25 times leakier than the low range of the goal.

The ASHRAE 62-89 ventilation standard range for your home is 1332 cfm50 (70%) to 1903 cfm50 (100%). If sealed below the 70% number, we would have to introduce mechanical ventilation in order to provide enough fresh air. This shouldn't be a problem in your home. Our challenge will be getting near that 100% number. All of the excess air represents energy lost and an increased load on your heating and cooling system.

Observations:

➢ Basement
- Air leakage at old windows
- Air leak
- Air leak band joi

Type:	Residential Boiler
Construction:	Cast Iron
Fuel:	Gas-Fired
Input:	70 to 260 MBH
Output:	58 to 211 MBH
Venting:	Natural Draft
Trim:	Water
Ignition:	Intermittent Ignition
Model #:	MI-04
Serial #:	339150-200012
AFLUE	82.1%

➢ 1st Floor
- HVAC
- Air leak
- Air leak
- Air leak
- Air leak
- Air leak
- Windov
- Weathe
- Air leak
- Air leak

- The AFUE is the most widely used measure of a furnace's heating efficiency. It measures the amount of heat actually delivered to your house compared to the amount of fuel that you must supply to the furnace. Thus, a furnace that has an 80% AFUE rating converts 80% of the fuel that you supply to heat -- the other 20% is lost out of the chimney.
- Distribution: 1 radiant floor heat zone (1st fl.), 2 hydronic baseboard zones (2nd and basement) and 1 water heating loop

➢ The testing results
- Peerless Boiler
  - Flue Gas Analysis-**GOOD**
    - T stack- 222 F
    - C02- 3.27%
    - EFF- 81.9%
    - ExAir- 228.8 %
    - O2- 15.1%
    - C0- 1ppm
    - C0 Airfree- 3ppm
    - Draft- -7.9 pa
    - Ambient Temp- 73.3 F

➢ Air Conditioner
- Age: Manufactured 5/2006
- Manufacturer: Trane
- 14 Seer (see text box→)

➢ Ductwork is located inside the attic space and closets of your home.

➢ Thermostats
- Basement: heat only; older non-programmable mercury type
- 1st: heat only; programmable
- 2nd:
  - ➢ Heat only; programmable
  - ➢ AC only programmable

SEER
Seasonal Energy Efficiency Ratio: This is the standard efficiency measurement for air conditioners. In 2006 when yours was made, 14 Seer was the minimum allowed and the entry level Energy Star efficiency. Today, state of the art units rate as high as 24.5 SEER.

The author provides clients with a comprehensive report after completing an audit. These two pages are from a 22-page report.

Good Subs Are a Must

Home-performance work requires excellent insulation and hvac contractors. Fortunately, we had already developed relationships with high-quality subs accustomed to delivering on best-practice specifications — extensive air sealing, high R-value insulation, efficient hvac equipment, and insulated and sealed ductwork.

Attention to detail and quality control are critical at every step of the process. With home-performance work, the results are quantified during "test-out," which includes, for example, a final blower-door measurement and combustion tests on the heating equipment. This means the client knows immediately how well we've performed. Therefore, having subs who understand the goals and methods of home-performance remediation is essential.

A Tough Sell

Despite the recent national emphasis on a "green" economy, in our area the demand for energy audits and home-performance work is not great. One reason is that the cost of bringing older homes up to current energy standards can be substantial, yet the projects lack the emotional appeal of a new kitchen or a finished basement. Frankly, energy audits can be a really tough sell, especially in the current economic downturn.

But already I've seen that having the BPI certification has helped me distinguish myself from the competition and win projects with good profit margins. On one occasion, I closed on a substantial sale by offering a complimentary energy audit.

While I don't expect any short-term windfalls, the investment in training and equipment seems to be a good long-term strategy for our company and should position us well when energy prices spike again.

***Robert Post** is a Philadelphia-based BPI-certified Building Analyst. He owns Post Remodeling and Handyman Services.*

continued from page 38

make clear in the homeowners' minds the link between the improved comfort they'll be noticing, the money they're saving on their energy bills, and the good they are doing for the planet (Figure 7, page 39).

I believe that if you're going to sell this kind of service to homeowners, you ought to be willing to buy it yourself. I recently bought a 1920s-vintage house in Burlington, Vt., that had no insulation in the walls and just 3½ inches of insulation in the attic; my plan was to make it into a net zero-energy home. What I discovered with these upgrades is that, completely apart from the money you save and the good you're doing, once you've experienced the comfort of that well-lit, comfortable, healthy indoor environment, you never want to go back.

***Mike Rogers** is senior vice president for business development at GreenHomes America; he's based in Burlington, Vt.*

Blower Door Testing

by David Keefe

Air flowing in and out of a building can cause lots of problems; in fact, air leakage can account for 30 to 50 percent of the heat loss in some homes. But air flowing through a building can help solve lots of problems, too — as long as it's the result of a blower-door test. With a blower door, builders can quantify airflow and the resulting heat (or cooling) loss, pinpoint specific leaks, and determine when a home needs additional mechanical ventilation.

First developed in the 1970s as a research tool, a blower door typically consists of a powerful variable-speed fan mounted in an adjustable panel temporarily set up in a doorway (Figure 8). The fan moves air through the building in a controlled fashion, while a pressure gauge — connected to the fan and to the outdoors by small-diameter pressure tubes — measures the rate of airflow required to maintain the building at a certain pressure. The blower creates exaggerated air leaks, which can then be found with the help of tools, like smoke puffers or infrared cameras, or even just by feeling with the face or the back of the hand.

Blower doors for residential work now weigh less than 50 pounds and can be easily carried in a small trunk. A basic kit costs between \$2,500 and \$3,500 and can be set up, used, and repacked in a half-hour (see "Blower-Door Manufacturers" page 48).

Pressure, Airflow, and Holes

The amount of air that flows through a hole depends on the characteristics of the hole and the pressure driving the flow. Since the three variables — hole, pressure, and flow — interact, a change in any one also changes at least one other. This behavior can be measured fairly reliably, so given any two of these variables, we can calculate the third.

If we know nothing about the hole, but can measure the pressure and the flow, we can figure out what the hole must be like. That's what a blower door does: It generates and measures airflow and pressure. We then use that information to describe the size and shape of the hole in the building shell.

Diagnose problems in the building shell with this simple, reliable tool.

About natural infiltration. Once we have used flow and pressure to determine what the leaks are like, we can use that hole description, along with weather and site data (the test pressure), to estimate the airflow that can be expected under normal conditions. But estimates of "natural airflow" are inherently inaccurate because it's difficult to know how the wind blows

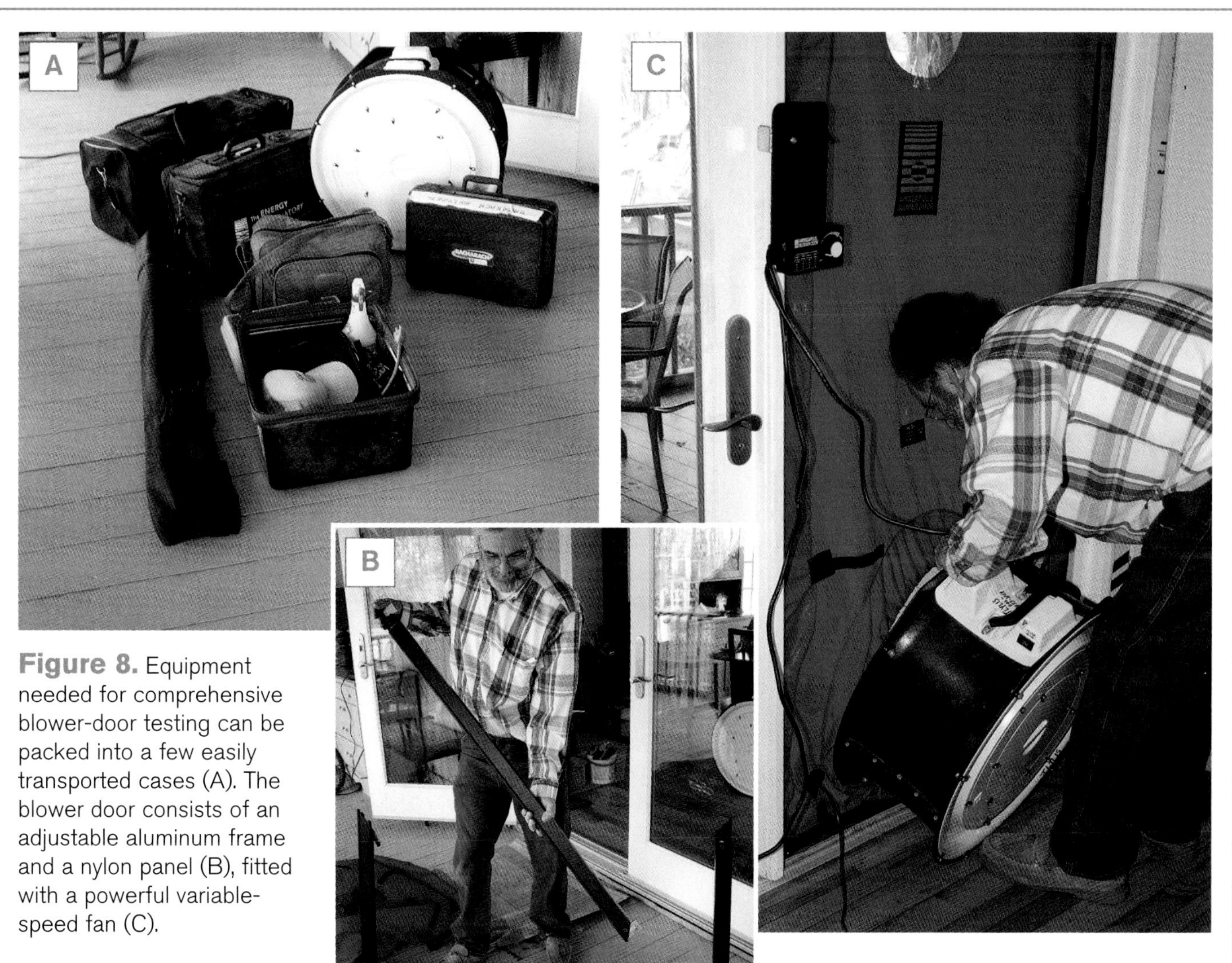

Figure 8. Equipment needed for comprehensive blower-door testing can be packed into a few easily transported cases (A). The blower door consists of an adjustable aluminum frame and a nylon panel (B), fitted with a powerful variable-speed fan (C).

on a particular site, what the occupant behavior is like, or how the mechanical equipment interacts with the building. So it's important to know whether airflow descriptions are measurements of leakage under specified conditions or estimates of airflow under normal conditions.

To measure airflow, a closed-up house is depressurized with the blower-door fan to a constant pressure differential as compared with outside conditions, typically 50 pascals (Pa). A pressure gauge attached to the blower-door assembly measures the rate of airflow required to maintain that pressure differential in cfm (cubic feet per minute).

Sometimes several readings are taken at different pressures, then averaged and adjusted for temperature using a simple computer program. This provides the most accurate picture of airflow, including *leakage ratios, correlation coefficients,* and *effective leakage area* (Figure 9).

Most of the time, though, this detailed output isn't needed, and all we want to know is how much the building leaks at the specified reference pressure of 50 Pa. So-called single-point testing is popular with crews who do retrofit work because once the door is set up, it takes only about a minute to measure the effectiveness of their air-sealing strategies (Figure 10).

The pressures exerted on a building are quite small (50 Pa is the suction pressure required to lift a column of water up a soda straw less than a quarter inch), so test results can be affected by wind gusts. There are some tricks for moderating wind effects and increasing accuracy: For example, multiple tubes protected with wind dampers can be run outdoors to sample air pressure on different sides of the building, and several measurements can be taken and averaged. Using these techniques, blower-door testing can be done in all but the windiest weather. An experienced operator can tell whether reasonable measurements are possible by the behavior of the gauges. Computer analysis of the data — if it's done — also includes a check for accuracy.

Cfm and ACH. While airflow can be measured in cfm, it can also be expressed as airflow compared with volume, or air changes per hour (ACH). ACH50 indicates air changes per hour at a 50 Pa pressure differ-

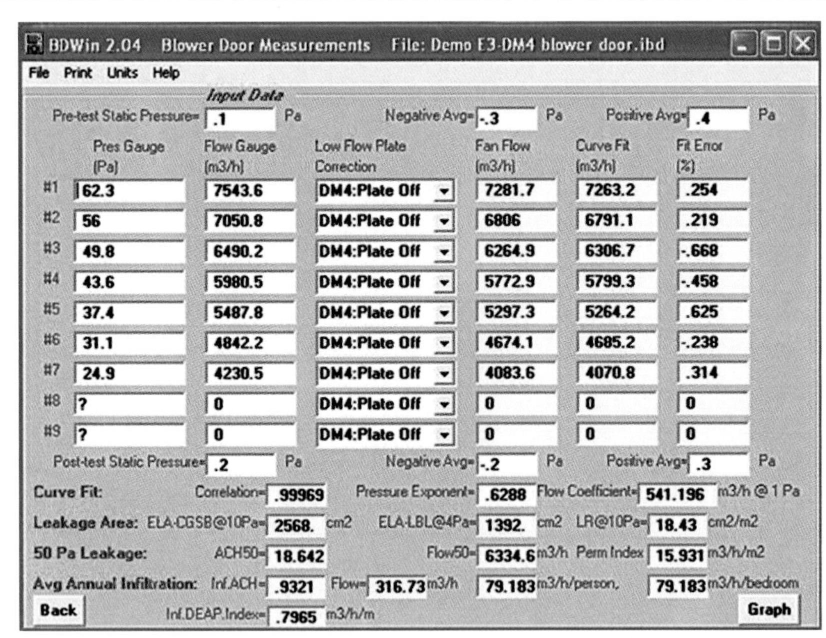

Figure 9. Blower-door testing can generate a detailed summary of a building's airflow characteristics. Leakage can be expressed either as an equivalent hole size — called ***effective leakage area***, or ELA — or as a ratio of leakage to shell area, or ***leakage ratio*** (LR), a useful unit for comparing the tightness of different building shells.

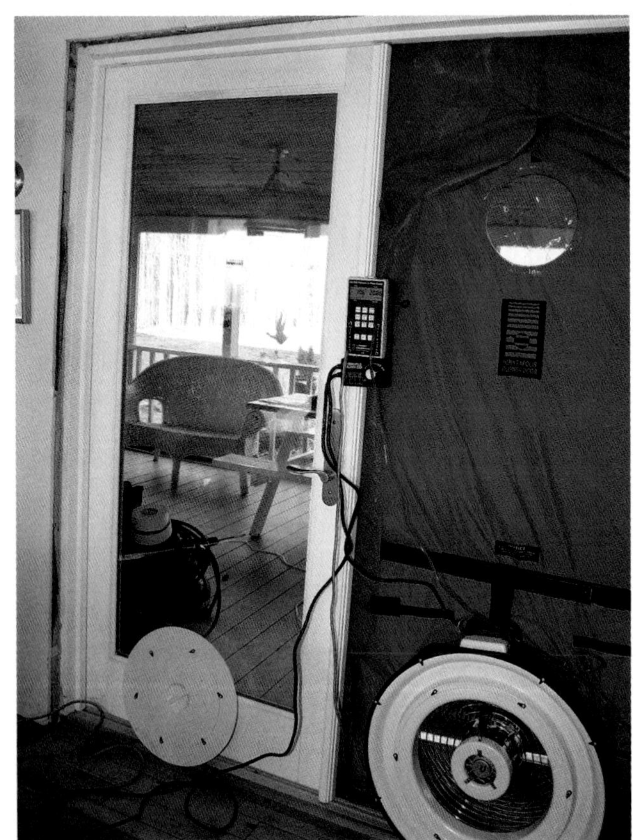

Figure 10. Heated air is less dense than cold air, so houses tested in cold weather appear leakier than they really are (by about 1 percent for each 10°F difference between indoor and outdoor temperature) unless an adjustment for temperature has been made. Otherwise, testing will indicate the amount of less dense, warm air flowing through the blower door and not the amount of colder, denser air flowing through the holes.

ence (not to be confused with natural ACH). Generally speaking, houses with less than 5 to 6 ACH50 are considered tight and those over 20 quite leaky, though these numbers can be misleading without considering other variables such as climate, house size, and old versus new construction.

While the airtightness and ventilation requirements of a space have traditionally been expressed in ACH, many blower-door professionals routinely use cfm as their primary unit of measure. Cfm is easier to obtain because it doesn't require calculations of volume. More important, it's a more direct expression of the main variable with which we are concerned — namely, air leakage.

If we're considering ventilation levels, we can more easily deal with cfm than ACH and are probably more concerned with absolute flow than the flow as compared with volume. If we're dealing with large spaces with few occupants — or small, heavily occupied spaces like trailers and apartments — ACH can be misleading because it can make a large space look tighter and a small space look leakier. For these and other reasons, cfm is being used more often and ACH less. Because cfm50 (the cubic-feet-per-minute airflow with a 50 Pascal indoor-outdoor pressure difference) is easily obtained with single-point tests — and is low enough to be consistently reached yet high enough to be resistant to the effects of wind — it has become the main unit of measure for the description of airtightness. Tight houses tend to measure less than 1,200 cfm50, and moderately leaky homes measure between 1,500 and 2,500 cfm50. Homes that measure over 3,000 cfm50 are considered leaky.

Testing a Home

Blower-door tests are performed with doors and win-

Blower-Door Testing Equipment and Basic Procedure

Recommended Tools

- Blower door with accessories
- Extra tubing, wind dampers
- Thermometers
- Computer (best if portable)
- Calculator, clipboard, and paperwork
- Duct tape, masking tape, scrap poly
- Stepladder, flashlight, measuring tape
- Smoke bottle

Procedure

1. Measure building, calculate area and volume (not needed for cfm, only for ACH and leakage ratio).
2. Measure temperature inside and out.
3. Shut off combustion appliances.
   - Customers burning wood or coal need prior notification.
   - Close fireplace damper, cover ashes if damper not tight.
4. Verify condition of intentional openings.
   - Doors and windows closed, interior doors open.
   - Seal mechanical ventilation, clothes dryer if desired.
   - Fill plumbing traps if house not occupied.
5. Decide on configuration of doors to semiconditioned spaces.
   - In general, include partially heated spaces.
   - When in doubt, test both ways.
6. Set up blower door, following manufacturer's instructions.
   - When possible, use doorway directly to outside. If not, make sure end of tubing is all the way outside.
7. Record the baseline pressure between the house and outside, following the manufacturer's instructions.
8. Take measurements.
   - Turn the fan up enough to change the house pressure by 50 Pa and record the flow.
   - For multipoint tests, take several readings at pressures between 10 and 60 Pa, instead of just one at 50 Pa.
   - If gauges move too much, use multiple outside ports, wind dampers, or time averaging.
9. Look for leaks.
   - 20 to 30 Pa depressurization, depending upon temperature outside
   - Focus on:
     - Areas that experience higher pressures (top and bottom)
     - Areas where moisture escapes (upper stories, humid rooms)
     - Areas where pipes freeze
     - Areas with specific comfort problems (cold drafts)
     - Problems that are cheap (quick) to fix
     - Rough holes, often not accessible from living space
   - Compartmentalize: Check individual rooms by cracking open door.
10. If heated by combustion equipment, perform combustion safety tests.
11. If the house has a forced-air system, perform a room-to-room pressure test to evaluate whether interior door closing affects the distribution of conditioned air.
12. Turn combustion appliances back on (check pilot lights).
    - Remove temporary seals, if used.

dows closed, and often decisions have to be made concerning doors to semiconditioned spaces. The rule of thumb for basements and similar spaces is to include any area that is at least semiheated (even if unintentionally, as in an unfinished basement with a furnace). Often, it makes sense to test both ways, which is simple once the blower door is set up.

Whether or not intentional openings like ventilation ports are temporarily sealed depends on the test being performed. For a description of how an existing house normally behaves, such openings are usually left uncovered. On the other hand, if a new house is being tested for sufficiently tight construction, it may make sense to seal intentional openings, removing them from the measurement.

Since the test depressurizes the house, sucking air in through all the openings (including flues), combustion devices must be disabled. Heating systems and gas water heaters must be shut off. All wood-burning appliances in the house need to be out, which requires prior notification for occupied houses during the heating season (Figure 11).

Checking for backdrafting. An analysis of a house's airflow should include a check of all combustion equipment. Any device that uses indoor air for combustion must have an adequate air supply. The greatest occupant safety hazard — backdrafting — tends to be the result of excessive negative pressure caused by air-moving appliances. This works the same way as the blower door: A fan moves air out of a space, which produces a pressure difference relative to the outside. This fan can be one that is intended to remove air from the building — like a bathroom exhaust fan, range hood, clothes dryer, or central vacuum system — or it can be a fan that moves air within the building, such as a furnace fan. It can also be a combination of several fans or an exhaust force other than a fan, such as the heat-driven force of a chimney. If the negative pressure in a combustion appliance's space is greater than the chimney draft (often only 3 to 5 Pa), the airflow in the flue will be reversed and flue gases will be dumped inside (Figure 12).

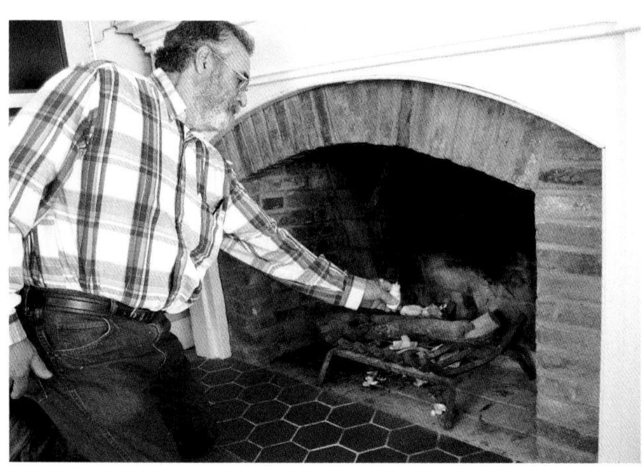

Figure 11. In a depressurized house, air will rush in through any available opening, so combustion appliances need to be shut down during a blower-door test to prevent backdrafting. Here, a smoke puffer indicates that the chimney flue is leaky even with its damper fully closed.

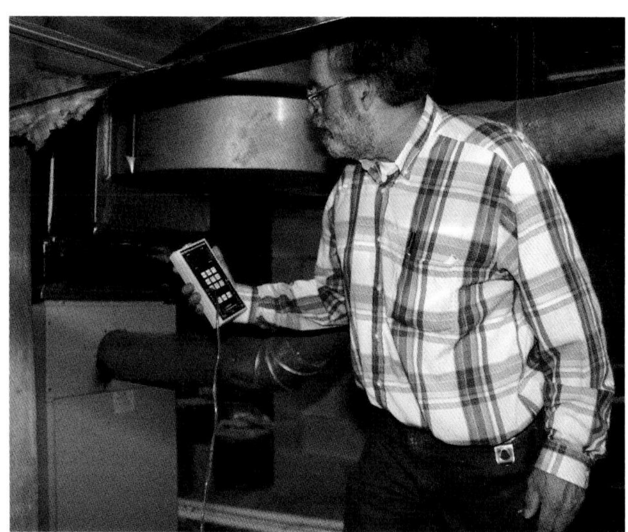

Figure 12. A digital manometer is used to measure the oil-fired furnace's draft, or ability to vent combustion gases.

Although backdrafting tends to be more common in tight houses, it is also affected by the specific appliances involved and where they are located. Compartmentalization created by interior doors can contribute to the problem as well.

To check for the likelihood of backdrafting, I place the house in a worst-case condition, turn on the air-moving equipment, and either measure the resulting indoor-outdoor pressure or fire up the combustion device. Many testing protocols (such as the Building Performance Institute's) specify a maximum allowed depressurization. If this maximum is exceeded, or if the appliance does not establish draft under the worst-case condition, some action must be taken to either improve the draft or reduce the depressurization so that flue gases are reliably exhausted outside.

Air-Sealing

In addition to measuring total airflow, a blower-door test is useful for identifying specific leaks, since it can force the leaks to become more apparent. Larger leaks directly into the living space can be felt with the back of the hand from inside the house when the house is depressurized, typically to between 20 and 30 Pa. A smoke bottle or pencil is handy for finding smaller leaks and leaks from unconditioned spaces. Sometimes it's more effective to reverse the airflow and pressurize the house. In general, airflow toward a person can be felt; airflow away is more easily found with smoke.

This demonstration can have a powerful impact on customers. When told that their main problem is not windows and doors but plumbing penetrations and attic bypasses, customers are often skeptical, but they become convinced when they actually feel the air pushing out from under their kitchen sink. Even people who understand almost nothing about their home's thermal performance can easily tell the difference between small and large leaks when they feel them with their own hands or see them with their own eyes (Figure 13).

To get a sense of where the major leaks are, I depressurize the house with the blower door. I close the interior doors most of the way (one at a time) and feel for airflow around the doors. If major leaks exist on the other side of the door, I can feel the airflow at the door. If little or no flow is felt, the area behind the door is reasonably tight. This way, I can tell whether further investigation of an area is needed without even entering the room.

Crews who do retrofit work often leave the blower running for extended periods while they work, allowing instant diagnosis and feedback. Instead of sealing every hole that looks like it may leak, specific locations can be checked, sealed only if necessary, and rechecked to verify success.

It's always more efficient to air-seal while the blower door is running than to conduct a blower-door test and then come back later. Attempting to itemize leaks in advance wastes time, since each leak has to be described on paper, understood by the crew, and found a second time. Many leaks take less time to seal than they require for access. In addition, crews without blower doors have no way to verify that their first attempt at sealing a given area has been successful (often it hasn't been), nor can they determine whether a leak found by an auditor has already been sealed by other work done in the building (often it has).

Because crews measure results as they go along, blower-door-directed air-sealing makes it possible to determine how much effect a particular measure has had, or how much reduction has been accomplished in a given period of time. Workers become more productive because they can focus on areas where the best results are likely to be obtained. By establishing simple rules of thumb for cost-effectiveness, crews can determine when to stop retrofit work and move on to the next building, rather than continuing work with diminishing returns. In fact, a common worry for those who consider using blower doors is that too much time will be spent sealing leaks that are not important. But usually the opposite happens: Crews discover that some leaks they would have thought deserving of treatment are not, and they don't waste time on them.

Building-Tightness Guidelines

Many organizations involved with blower-door air-sealing have established program guidelines that specify a minimum leakiness and advise stopping air-sealing work when the building's estimated average infiltration equals a recommended ventilation rate. Building-tightness guidelines are thought to be helpful for weatherization crews who need to be concerned about providing adequate fresh air for occupants in situations where there is little or no mechanical ventilation (the issues of combustion safety and makeup air for exhaust fans are supposed to be dealt with separately).

However, I believe that this approach is fundamentally flawed and agree with the many experts who think that buildings should be sealed as tightly as economically sensible. Tightness guidelines have serious limitations, because blower-door numbers indicate nothing about the sources of pollutants or the use of mechanical ventilation, and estimates of natural infiltration (which determine the building tightness limit) can easily be off by 50 percent or more.

Indoor air quality is affected by many factors, not just the tightness of the building. Establishing minimum leakiness standards on a program-wide basis without also addressing source control, ventilation,

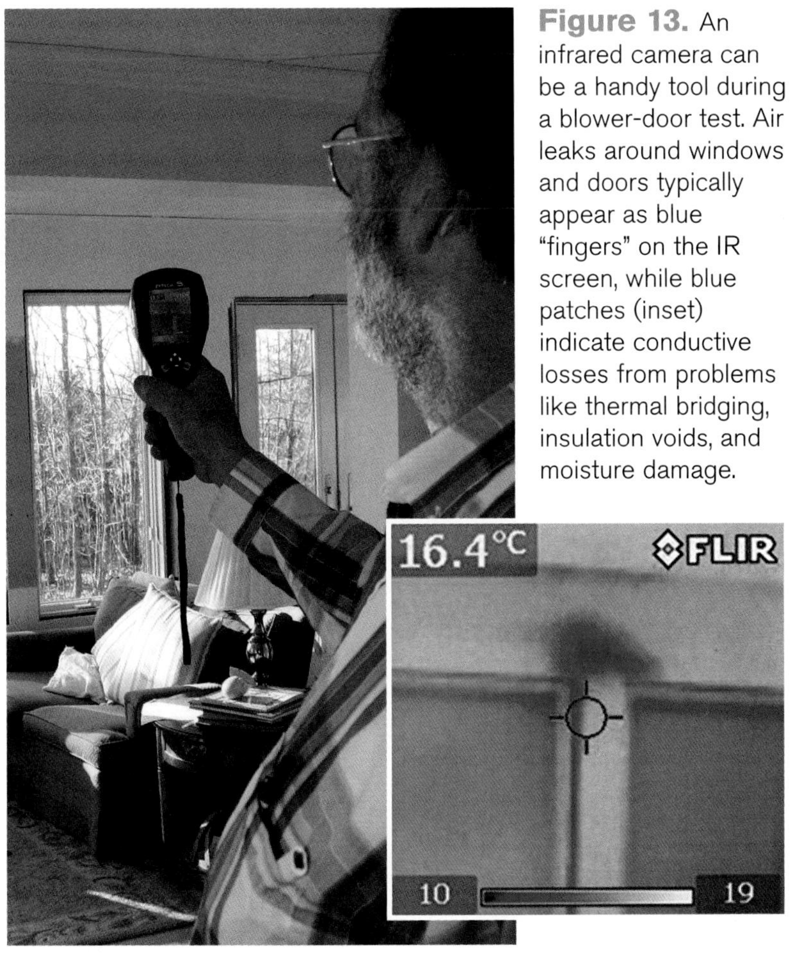

Figure 13. An infrared camera can be a handy tool during a blower-door test. Air leaks around windows and doors typically appear as blue "fingers" on the IR screen, while blue patches (inset) indicate conductive losses from problems like thermal bridging, insulation voids, and moisture damage.

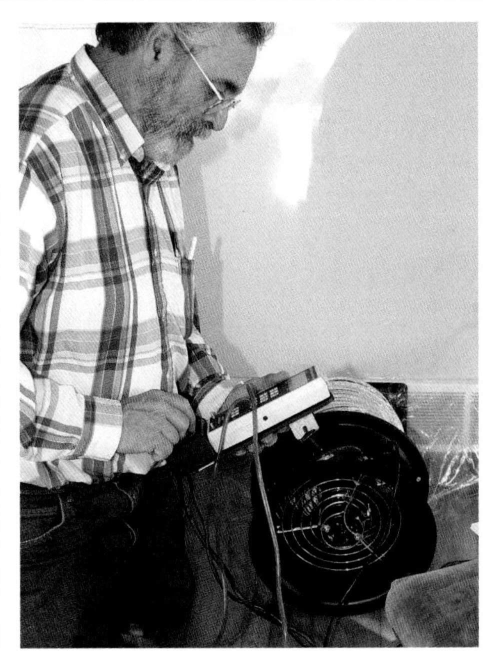

Figure 14. Duct system leakage can be estimated using the "blower-door subtraction method," but a Duct Blaster test is more accurate. After the supply and return registers are sealed with tape, airflow is directed into the supply plenum, measured at a reference pressure of 25 Pa, and compared with accepted leakage rates.

Blower-Door Manufacturers

The Energy Conservatory

www.energyconservatory.com

Minneapolis Blower Door Model 3 system includes DG-700 digital micro-manometer and calibrated 300- to 6,300-cfm fan. Includes tubes, door case, and padded accessory case. Fan weighs 33 pounds.

Infiltec

www.infiltec.com

Model E3-A-DM4-110 system includes DM4 digital micro-manometer and calibrated 42- to 5,450-cfm fan. Includes tubes, door case, and padded accessory case. Fan weighs 36 pounds.

Retrotec

www.retrotec.com

Model Q46 system includes DM-2A digital micro-manometer and calibrated 38- to 6,300-cfm fan. Includes case for gauge and hard cases for fan and for frame and cloth. Fan weighs 34 pounds.

and indoor combustion is an ineffective and risky health and safety strategy.

Advanced Blower-Door Techniques

Once you start using a blower door for basic diagnostics, you'll likely start discovering other ways to use the hole/flow/pressure relationship. For example, diagnosing ductwork problems involves the same principles and much of the same equipment as evaluating building shells (Figure 14). Ensuring that combustion products end up outside rather than inside a house comes with understanding and controlling airflows and pressures. So does radon mitigation. Advanced pressure diagnostics — like evaluating airflow through multiple barriers or between zones — requires knowledge of blower-door testing. Effective ventilation strategies are dependent upon holes and pressures, in addition to flows.

The blower door has greatly increased our collective understanding of the ways in which air movement in buildings influences comfort, durability, health, and safety. It's a practical, cost-effective tool for anyone working to improve home performance and safety.

***Former contractor David Keefe** is manager of training services for the Vermont Energy Investment Corp. This article is adapted with permission from Home Energy magazine. Thanks to Ted Lylis for his assistance with photos.*

Pressure-Testing Ductwork

by Michael Uniacke

Airtight ductwork is one of the keys to a quality heating and cooling system. It helps to make a home more healthful, more comfortable, and more energy efficient. By reducing the load on the equipment, it also reduces wear and tear.

There is only one way to make sure that the ductwork has been thoroughly sealed: Test it. A simple pressure test can measure the airtightness of the air distribution system and helps you hold your installers to a high standard of quality.

Of course, airtight ductwork is only one of the keys to quality hvac. A Manual J load analysis and Manual D duct design, proper refrigerant charge, and correct airflow over the evaporative coil are all just as vital. But poorly sealed ductwork can undermine the good work in all those other areas: You can properly size the unit, lay out the distribution system correctly, tune the compressor perfectly, and set the fan just right, but if leaky ductwork blows most of your conditioned air into the attic, or pulls most of the system's return air

Pressure testing of ductwork leads to greater comfort and substantial energy savings.

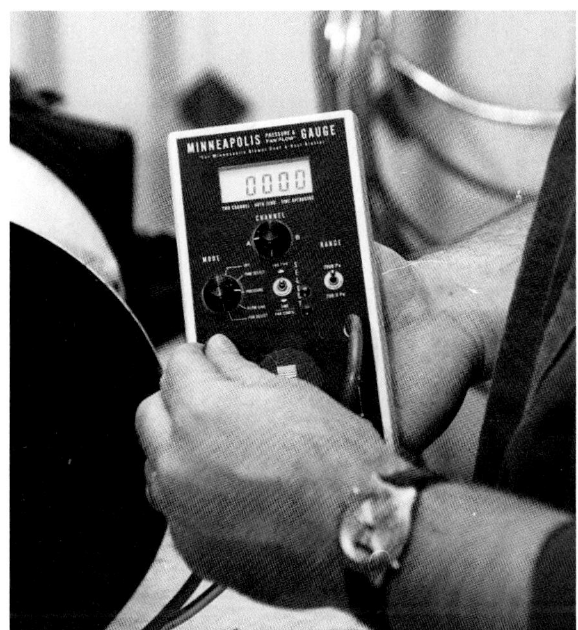

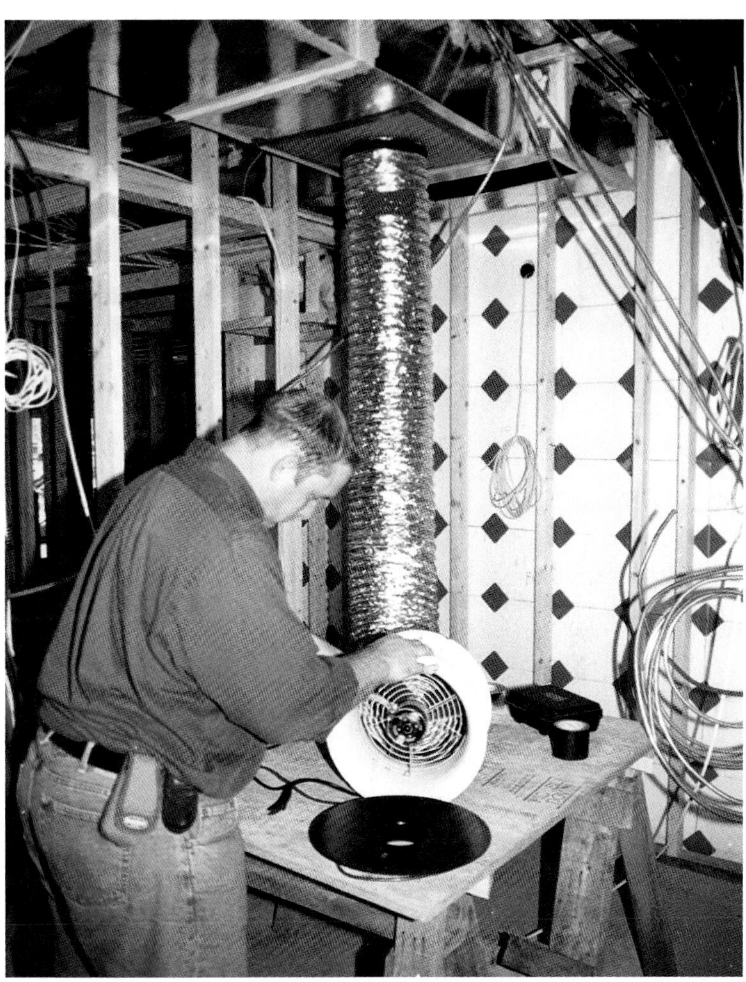

Figure 15. The Minneapolis Duct Blaster is a calibrated variable-speed fan that's tied into the heating or cooling air distribution system at a supply plenum, return grille, or air handler compartment (right). The digital pressure gauge (above) calculates air leakage rates from pressure and fan speed data.

from the crawlspace, you'll have a system that costs too much to run and doesn't do its job.

Pressure testing is not a new concept in home construction. Plumbers have their work pressure tested on every job, and the test forces them to get it right — meaning no leaks, period. But when plumbing leaks, there is an immediate consequence: Things get wet. Air leakage, on the other hand, is invisible and seldom causes immediate trouble. Instead, homeowners gradually become aware of comfort problems, high utility bills, and decreasing indoor air quality over time. Testing is the only way to identify the defects in advance.

In more than ten years of testing ductwork before drywall is hung, I've seen some excellent ductwork installations and some atrocious ones. I've learned that if you want consistently good results, you have to test consistently. All tradespeople do better work when they know they face inspections. As one local mechanical contractor's lead man put it to me, "There are three kinds of air distribution systems: regular, sealed, and sealed and tested." If you test your installer's work, it will get better. And realistically, until you start testing, and showing your installers the results, they won't even know that their system leaks. They certainly won't know where it leaks. The test makes them face reality, but it also helps them learn.

The duct airtightness testing system I use is called Minneapolis Duct Blaster, from the Energy Conservatory (www.energyconservatory.com). It consists of a calibrated variable-speed fan, a fan speed control, and a digital pressure-reading gauge called a digital manometer (Figure 15). The test itself is pretty simple: We attach the Duct Blaster fan to the air distribution system at a return grille, a supply plenum, or the blower compartment on the air handling unit. We temporarily seal off all the registers and grilles. Then we turn on the Duct Blaster fan and apply pressure. The Duct Blaster system measures the airflow needed to create a test pressure of 25 pascals (a 0.10-inch water column) in the duct system. This airflow rate is our duct leakage measurement. We compare the duct leakage reading with a recognized standard, and we give the system either a pass or a fail. The whole process takes less than two hours (mostly for setup and takedown) and typically costs around $220.

Over the years, my company has headed off a lot of potential problems by testing ductwork before the drywall is hung. When the drywall is up, we can still gain access to the ducts, but the problems are harder to locate and assess.

Why Airtight Ductwork Matters

Good duct sealing makes a major contribution to the healthfulness, safety, comfort, and efficiency of a new home. Sealing the ducts is even more important than sealing the building envelope, because when the air handler is running, the pressures in the air distribution system are much greater than in the building or the outside air. Pressure differences are what drive infiltration; a hole or crack in the building envelope is not an air leakage point unless it sees a pressure. Ducts always operate under pressure, so a hole in the ductwork is always a leak.

To clarify the importance of pressure, let's look at some numbers. Wind, stack effect, exhaust fans, and the like generate air pressures across the building shell that range from 0.5 to 10 pascals. On average, a house is usually in the low end of this range. (A pascal is a very small metric unit of pressure. There are 25 pascals in 0.10 inch of water column. If you were to put a straw into a glass of water and suck the water up the straw 1 inch, you'd create an inch of water column pressure, or 250 pascals.)

Pressures created in air distribution systems when the air handler is running range from 10 to 125 pascals, tens of times greater than the ordinary pressures acting on the house envelope. And these pressures, unlike the wind, are continuous when the air handler is running. That is why house infiltration rates can double or triple when the equipment is active.

Temperatures. Remember, too, that leaks in supply ductwork involve conditioned air, not room air. The air that escapes from supply ductwork has been heated to 140°F or cooled to 58°F, and it is not getting to the room it was meant for. If most of the ductwork is in the attic or crawlspace (which is often the case), all this heated or chilled air is now leaking straight to the outdoors. The resulting energy loss is much greater than the loss that occurs when 70°F room air leaks out around a window, for example. That's why simple duct tightening may cut heating and cooling costs by 15 to 30 percent in many homes.

Duct leaks also typically affect comfort, because the system doesn't deliver the intended amount of conditioned air to satisfy the design load for a room. Rooms at the end of long duct runs suffer the most: The farther away from the fan a room is, the greater the likelihood that air will find its way out of a leak instead of going where it's meant to.

On the return side of the air distribution system, leaks pull ambient air or even hot attic air into the system, further compromising efficiency. Leaks also threaten indoor air quality: Air from a crawlspace may carry pesticides, moisture, radon, and mold spores, all of which can get sucked into the return leak, then sent through the supply side to every room in the house.

Energy penalty. How much do these leaks affect energy consumption? A 1999 summary report of 19 separate studies from around the country (www.aceee.org/pubs/a992.htm) suggests that the average annual energy savings potential in a typical house from sealing the ductwork is around 17 percent. These studies include both heating and cooling climates. Anywhere ductwork can leak outside of the house, there is the potential for a large energy penalty. In one study, researchers at the Florida Solar Energy Center found that sealing ductwork in existing homes cut cooling bills by about a third.

Locating the Leaks

Where are these leaks happening? Basically, leaks are possible at any joint or seam in the system, from the air handlers supplied by manufacturers right on through to the sheet-metal supply boots your installer brings to the job. If you look at all the joints, you'll find the leaks.

There are leaks on sheet-metal trunk ducts every 48 inches, where the trunk sections connect. Every collar attached to the trunk, where flex duct branches take off, represents a possible leak. So does every adjustable elbow. We also find leaks where flex duct connects to supply boots, in the boots themselves, and around the plaster grounds. I'm often surprised by how leaky some of the manufacturers' mechanical units are. I've tested units that leaked 40 to 45 cfm right out of the box.

I used to commonly find flex ducts that either had never been connected or had been accidentally disconnected by another trade. During the early to mid 1990s, most framed return cavities were major leakage sites. Disconnected ducts and framed cavities still tend to be the biggest culprits, but practices have improved significantly.

Stud and joist bays used as returns are still common in my part of the country and often present a lot of problems. All framed cavities should be lined with OSB, plywood, duct board, drywall, or sheet metal and then sealed with mastic at every joint. Hvac contractors sometimes blame the framers for not lining the cavities, but we don't accept that excuse — if it leaks, you fail.

The most frustrating leaks are where the hvac installer tried to seal the system and failed — where someone did the sealing but didn't get it right. For example, it hasn't yet dawned on everyone that each joint and seam have to be sealed on four sides, not just three. If a crew hasn't had the benefit of some training, and has never seen a system tested and fogged, it's a good bet the system won't pass. Installers just can't picture the consequences of an average duct sealing job.

Running the Test

A Duct Blaster test on a single air distribution system takes about 45 minutes to 1½ hours to perform. Most of that time is spent sealing off registers and grilles and setting up the equipment. Once a system is prepared, it takes only about 2 minutes to perform the test.

The first step is to attach the Duct Blaster fan to the air distribution system (Figure 16). We can attach it to the blower compartment on the air handler or to a return grille. If the air handler is not set when I arrive to test, I connect the Duct Blaster directly to the trunk lines in the mechanical room where the air handler will eventually be set. But we prefer to test with the air handler installed, because of the leakage we've seen in even brand-new units.

The second step is to seal off the air distribution registers with a poly product called Duct Mask (also available from Energy Conservatory) (Figure 17). It comes on a roll, so I simply run a belt through the roll and wear it around my waist. Duct Mask is perforated every 4 inches and has adhesive on one side. It makes sealing up the system such a simple task that I consider it essential. But I now have some mechanical contractors who seal all the supply registers that are installed in floors with sheet metal and mastic. This keeps construction debris and rain out of the ductwork and also prepares the system for testing.

The last piece of equipment to hook up is the digital manometer, which is simple to set up and operate. The digital manometer I use measures the pressure in the duct system and also directly displays air flow

Figure 16. The author tapes a plastic transition fitting to a piece of cardboard cut to fit the opening in the air distribution system (A), then places the assembly in the opening (B) and connects the fan to the opening with a length of flex duct (C). It's best to test the system with the air handler installed, because the air handlers are often a leakage point. If the air handler has not been set, the author hooks up the Duct Blaster to the trunk line where the air handler will go. The equipment can also be attached to a return grille (D).

through the Duct Blaster fan in cubic feet per minute, which is convenient and cuts down on errors.

I can often tell how leaky a duct system is simply by turning on the Duct Blaster and seeing how quickly or slowly the duct reference pressures respond. A leaky system will require that I ramp up my Duct Blaster fan speed to overcome the numerous leaks in the system. In fact, in some homes the ducts are so leaky that I can't pressurize the air distribution system at all. In a system with a return that leaky, it's very possible that more air is being drawn into the system from the crawlspace or attic than is being pulled from the house.

Once the air distribution system is pressurized to 25 pascals, I read the air flow through the Duct Blaster fan from my digital manometer.

It's important to recognize that the Duct Blaster measures the air leakage at a test pressure of 25 pascals, not the actual duct leakage when the system is running. The actual duct leakage under normal use depends on where the leaks are located and what pressures they see. The closer the duct leaks are to the air handler fan, the higher the pressures. The typical leaks where refrigerant lines enter the coil, for example, will see much higher pressures than the leaks around the supply boots at the end of branch runs, and thus will leak more air.

The tests are performed at a uniform pressure of 25 pascals because that represents a typical average operating pressure in residential systems and gives us a quick way to compare the measured leakage rate to accepted standards.

The Fog Machine

The shortcoming of a digital manometer readout is that tradespeople can't picture the leakage; in their minds that number is not associated with anything. Also, we still don't know just where the leaks are. By introducing theatrical fog into the system through the Duct Blaster, we can make most of the leaks visible (Figure 18).

The fog pouring out of duct leaks is a real eye opener. No one argues with this part of the test. Even after ten years of using a fog machine out in the field, I'm shocked sometimes that so much fog can leak out so fast. It is truly telling.

In my experience, installers really appreciate being on hand when their work is tested and fogged. It's often the first time they've seen their work tested, and the fog drives home the importance of paying attention.

Sealing the system. Fortunately, duct leakage problems are simple to eliminate during new construction if you know where to look for leaks and how to seal them. The cost varies depending on the system's size and complexity, but most systems can be sealed for somewhere between $150 and $600. Research has shown that the cost is recovered within one to five years; after that, the savings go to the homeowner's bottom line. And of course, the greatest benefit is a more healthful and comfortable home.

The products of choice are water-based mastic accompanied by a fiberglass mesh on larger holes. The mastic has the consistency of mashed potatoes. It is easily spread over joints in the ductwork with an inexpensive paintbrush or one's hand. On cracks and gaps wider than ¼ inch, a 2-inch fiberglass mesh tape is placed in a bed of mastic to reinforce the seal. The advantage of mastic over duct tape is that it provides a long-term durable seal. The water-based mastic cleans up easily with water.

Duct Tightness Standards

The goal of duct sealing is to ensure that the system is sufficiently airtight. That does not mean submarine airtight or hermetically sealed. We aim not to eliminate leakage entirely (although some contractors

Figure 17. The author carries a roll of adhesive poly Duct Mask on his belt (left) and uses the material to seal registers and grilles (above).

come close) but to reduce the leakage to an acceptable threshold. I use one of two standards for duct system airtightness, and each generates a "not to exceed" duct leakage number.

One standard is 3 percent of the livable square footage. For example, a 2,000-square-foot home should have no more than 60 cfm of leakage in the air distribution system. The other common standard is based on the size of the air-conditioning unit, which you can read off the unit's label (or the installer can tell you). It's common practice to assume 400 cfm per ton, so a 4-ton unit would be rated at 1,600 cfm; the air leakage should not exceed 5 percent of the total airflow capacity, or in this example, 80 cfm.

These levels are realistic on the job; conscientious workers can easily satisfy them. In my experience, if a crew can't meet these criteria routinely, either they don't have enough training and experience, or they aren't trying hard enough.

Who Should Test?

There are a growing number of third-party testing companies like mine. A list of testing contractors by state is available on the Energy Conservatory website (www.energyconservatory.com).

I believe that hvac companies should conduct in-house testing of air distribution systems. If your hvac contractor already owns a Duct Blaster and other diagnostic tools, that tells you that the company truly wants to do quality work. Companies that don't own a Duct Blaster have to ask someone else to test their work, as well as show them their mistakes.

I've worked with architects who make the builder pay for the first test and the hvac contractor pay for

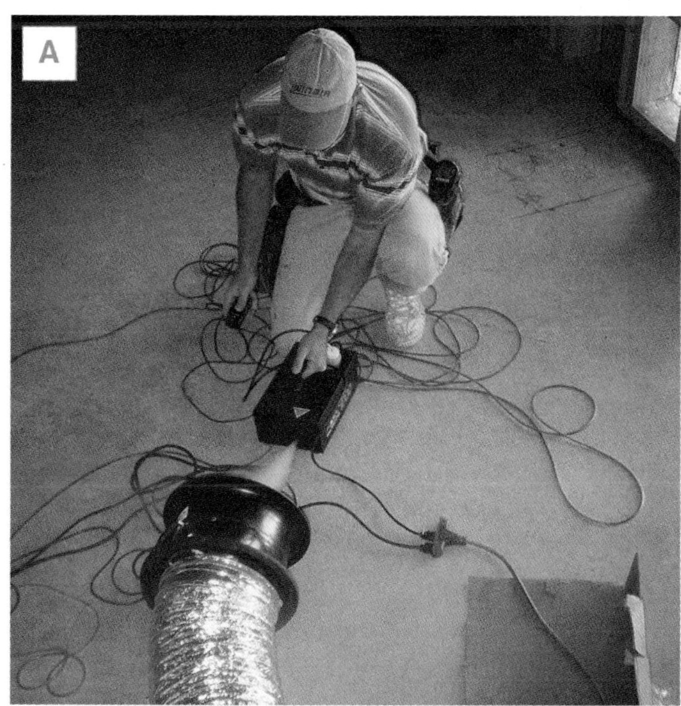

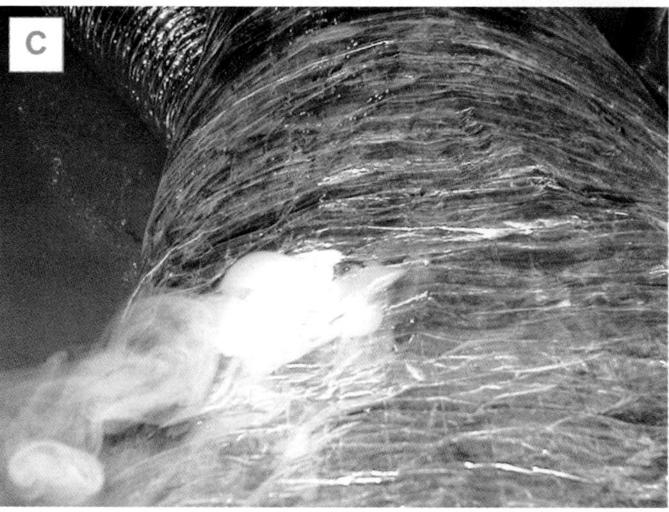

Figure 18. When a system exceeds the allowable air leakage standard, the author uses a theatrical fog generator to introduce visible vapor into the Duct Blaster fan intake. The fog makes it easy to find the leak locations.

Low-Tech Airflow Test: The Calibrated Garbage Bag

by Don Fugler

Do the phrases "This room is always too cold" and "My bathroom fan doesn't do anything" ring a bell? Whenever a homeowner complains about the performance of some heating or ventilating equipment, it's handy to have a flow-measuring device available to check out the complaint.

The Research Division of Canada Mortgage and Housing Corporation (CMHC) has tested ventilation system performance for years, sometimes with specially built equipment. While this equipment can accurately measure flows, it's too bulky, expensive, and fragile to be of real use in day-to-day inspections. So an inexpensive alternative was developed — the calibrated garbage bag.

To make the bag tester, open up a wire coat hanger until you have a rough rectangle. Now tape the open end of a garbage bag around the wire (make sure the bag has no holes in it). The result should look like a big green butterfly net (see photo, right).

To use the bag tester, crush the bag gently to deflate it, hold it over a supply duct, and time how long it takes to inflate. Don't worry about full inflation, just get the bag up and wrinkly. Since the bag has a fixed volume, the bigger the airflow, the faster it fills up. To estimate airflow, use the graph below, which calibrates a standard bag (Glad 66x91 cm) to CMHC's expensive machine. For times when the graph isn't handy, remember these simple numbers:

Time to Inflate	Airflow
3 seconds	50 cfm
5 seconds	30 cfm
12 seconds	10 cfm

You can also use the test for exhaust fans: Swing the tester up to a bathroom exhaust grille (this will fill the bag with air), then time how long it takes to almost completely deflate the bag.

The accuracy of the bag tester is nothing to write home about, but the test will certainly distinguish between a good duct and one that's not working. In one case I know of, for example, a householder grumbled about a cold second floor, despite several visits by his heating contractor. A 15-minute check with the bag tester showed that only two of his 18 supply ducts had flows over 10 cfm, compared with a healthy supply-duct flow of 40 to 80 cfm. Somehow, the furnace installer or service person hadn't noticed this critical lack of flow, even after four years of complaints. In another case, a woman phoned about a cold bedroom on the last day of her new home

Calibrated airflow graph: On the left side of the graph, find the number of seconds it took to inflate or deflate the bag. Follow the grid horizontally until it intersects with the plotted line, then read down to the cfm scale at the bottom. Normal flow is between 40 and 80 cfm.

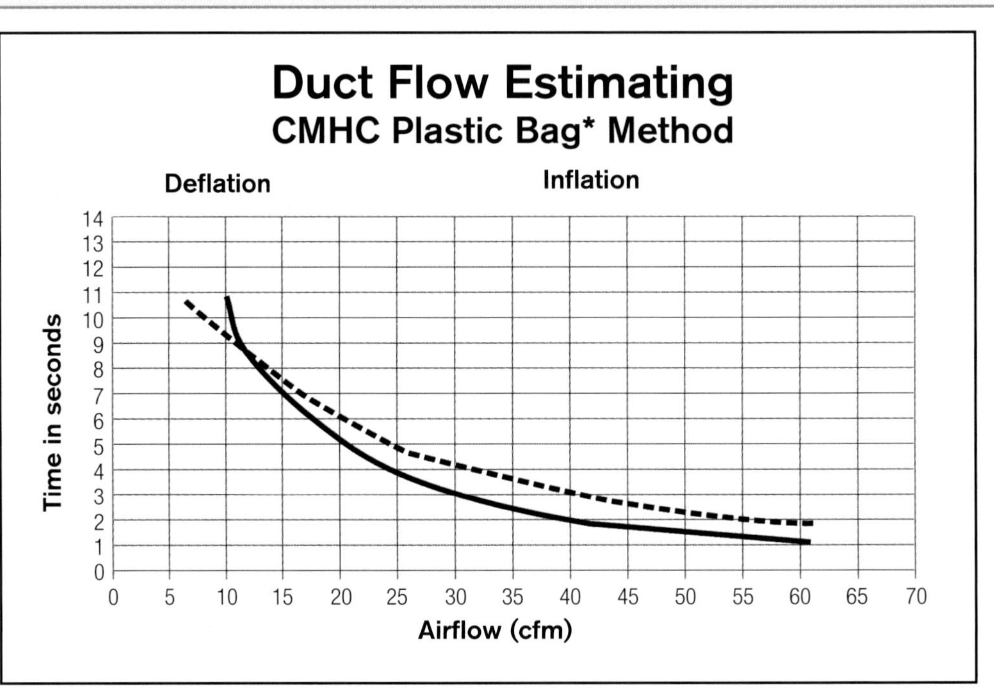

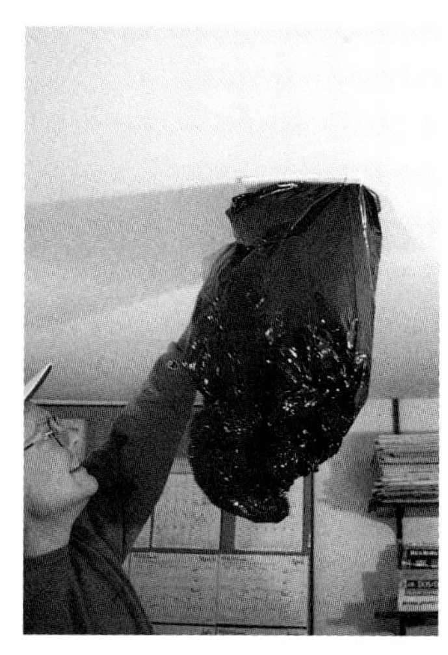

A simple airflow tester: By counting the number of seconds it takes to inflate (or deflate) an ordinary plastic garbage bag, you can get a rough measurement of airflow in heating, cooling, and exhaust systems.

warranty period. She wanted duct improvements to fix the problem. She was told over the phone how to test her duct and discovered she had lots of airflow. Her cold room was due to other factors.

So give the bag tester a try. It works well, it works fast, and the results are immediately obvious, both to you and to your client. And if you don't like the system after trying it out, just put the coat hanger in the bag, top it off with household waste, and toss the whole works. What do you have to lose?

Don Fugler *works for the Research Division of Canada Mortgage and Housing Corporation of Ottawa. This article was adapted with permission from the July 1995 issue of Solplan Review.*

Sources of Supply for Duct-Sealing Mastic

AM Conservation Group, Inc.
www.amconservationgroup.com

Schnee-Morehead Products
www.trustsm.com

Carlisle Coatings & Waterproofing, Inc.
www.hardcast.com

Aeroseal, LLC
www.aeroseal.com
(aerosol duct sealing franchiser)

Ductmate Industries
www.ductmate.com

Duro Dyne Corporation
www.durodyne.com

Foster Products Corporation
www.fosterproducts.com

McGill AirSeal Corporation
www.unitedmcgill.com

Mon-Eco Industries, Inc.
www.mon-ecoindustries.com

RCD Corporation
www.rcdmastics.com

Rectorseal Corporation
www.rectorseal.com

Shelter Supply
www.sheltersupply.com

the second test if he fails the first one. If a system fails, as a part of my fee, I'll spend up to an hour on the job helping the crew find the leaks with my Duct Blaster and fog machine.

Reaping the Benefit

On most jobs, there is a tug of war between quality and profit, and profit routinely wins. This means that ductwork is often not sealed or it's sealed but not tested. When customers have a comfort, air quality, or utility bill problem, it adds to their distress to learn that no one bothered to implement a simple quality-control step. They begin to wonder what other corners the builder cut.

I always advise my builder and hvac customers to at least offer sealed ductwork and testing. If you offer it and the customer turns you down, there's a record, in case of later complaints, that the customer chose low price over quality.

For builders who do test, we file a test report, which becomes a record for the house. I encourage my builder customers to use this report as evidence that they are truly committed to quality behind the drywall. If you seal and test ductwork and the contractor across the street doesn't, you have a better product, and you can use our documentation to build your reputation.

Satisfied customers also provide a marketing advantage. A customer who moves into a new home that is more healthful, comfortable, and energy efficient is more likely to tell friends that you are someone who builds a home that works.

Michael Uniacke *is principle owner of Advanced Insulation, Inc., a Prescott, Ariz.-based company that supplies insulation, energy auditing, diagnostics, testing, and consulting services.*

Chapter 3

INSULATION OPTIONS

Getting Quality From Fiberglass Batts

by Michael Uniacke

My company specializes in high-quality insulation work, in both new construction and retrofit applications. We also provide energy consulting and energy audits that include testing with a blower door, duct blaster, infrared camera, and other diagnostic tools.

Experience has convinced us that blown-in insulation is the way to go if quality is the top priority. Correctly done, a blown-in job has inherent quality control, making it the simplest and best way to eliminate heat-wasting gaps or voids in exterior walls. But blown-in insulation products cost more than fiberglass batts, so most walls today are insulated with batts.

Unfortunately, most fiberglass installers don't give much thought to quality. That's not surprising — batts are the budget choice to begin with, and when the job goes to the lowest bidder, the only way the installer can make money is to rush through the work. But the results are bad news for the home's thermal performance. The more complicated the wall assembly, the harder it is to get a good fit (Figure 1). A 6-inch batt may have a measured R-value of 19 at the factory, but a poor installation in an exterior 2x6 wall can degrade the R-value by as much as 40 percent.

It doesn't have to be that way. Given a realistic budget to work with, we've found that we can do high-quality work with fiberglass and still make a profit. The keys are coordination between trades, quality control, and knowing the right details.

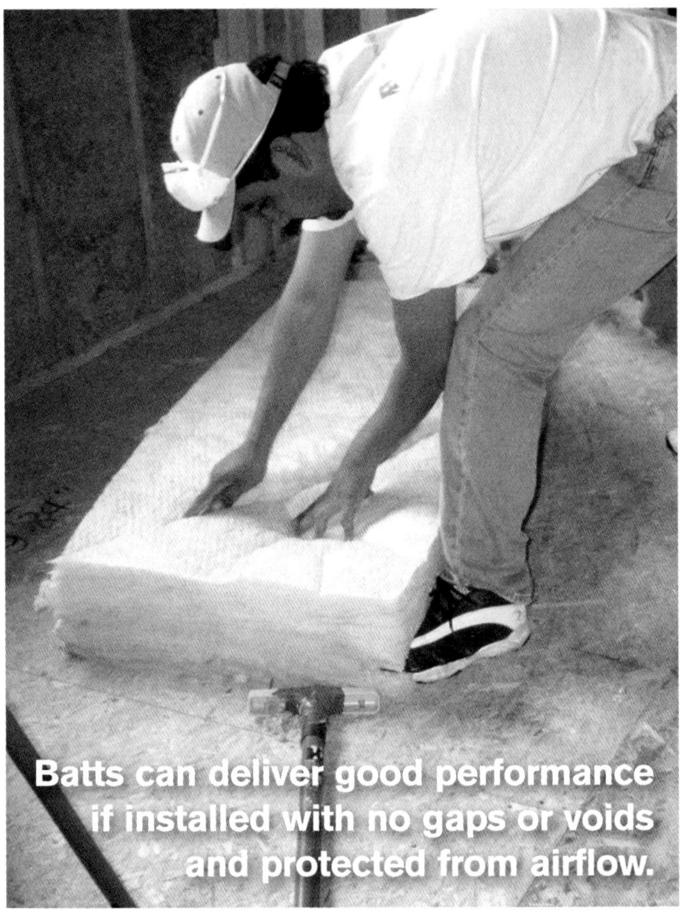
Batts can deliver good performance if installed with no gaps or voids and protected from airflow.

How Insulation Works

Fiberglass itself has little resistance to heat flow. The actual insulator is the air trapped in the tiny spaces between glass fibers. The tiny air voids slow conductive heat movement, while the glass fibers reduce radiant losses and impede air movement to block convective heat flow.

Don't be fooled by so-called dead air spaces. Small air voids slow heat flow, but large voids don't. A dead air space is one in which air does not move — once a gap gets larger than 3/4 inch, convection kicks in and overrides the insulating effect. Even though they contain air, uninsulated framing cavities have little or no R-value.

Making contact. That understanding should govern the way batts are installed in the field. To be effective, at least one face of the batt must be in full contact with the wall, ceiling, or subfloor, and the tops and sides of the batt must also fit snugly in the cavity with no gaps. If the batts don't touch the inside face of the drywall or subfloor, convection coupled with air leakage will seriously undermine their thermal performance. We use only unfaced batts in exterior walls, because we've found that inset-stapled kraft-faced batts tend to create gaps between the insulation and the drywall. (Using unfaced batts also prevents the drywallers from complaining about the presence of stapling flanges on the surface of the framing.)

In other words, even though shoving batts into a stud cavity may seem like a no-brainer, doing it right takes some care. If a batt is simply jammed into place, its edges tend to drag along the sides of the studs on either side, which often prevents the rear corners of the batt from coming into contact with the exterior sheathing. To avoid this problem, I teach my crews to push each batt into its cavity, then pull it out flush with the face of the framing (Figure 2).

Fiberglass needs protection. Fiberglass batts insulate properly only if they can trap still air; they aren't an air barrier material themselves. Wind or even stack pressure in a heated house can readily push air through unprotected batts. So framing cavities need to be closed in with cardboard or plastic baffles, rigid foam, caulking, and the like, and walls should be protected with housewrap or something similar. I recommend an inch of rigid insulation on the exterior of buildings in addition to the fiberglass in the wall cavities.

In addition to keeping wind pressure from pushing air through or around the batts themselves, the rigid foam also cuts conductive heat loss. Fiberglass batts have an R-value of R-3 to R-4 per inch, but wood framing — which makes up at least 20 to 30 percent of an exterior wall — has an R-value of 1 per inch, allowing heat to bypass the insulation by flowing through studs, plates, and headers. The added inch of rigid foam can reduce this bypass heat loss by half, significantly boosting the performance of the whole assembly. You'll see the difference in equipment sizing and utility bills.

Quality Control

The market seldom rewards or demands much in the way of professionalism from insulation contractors. Bad work gets rocked over within days or hours, and unlike plumbing, roofing, and electrical defects, sloppy insulation rarely comes back to haunt a builder.

Most installers get paid by the piece at a rate of pennies per square foot, which rewards quantity, not

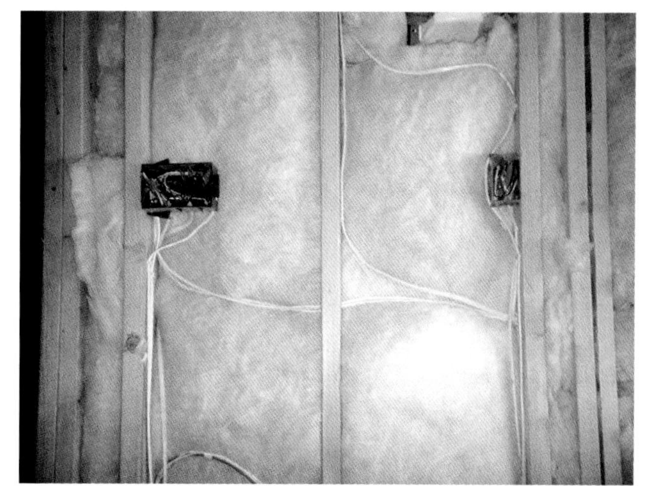

Figure 1. Irregular stud cavities, wiring, and other obstructions in a wall like this make it harder to cut and fit fiberglass accurately. Dark lines and visible stud shoulders in this wall indicate a hurried job.

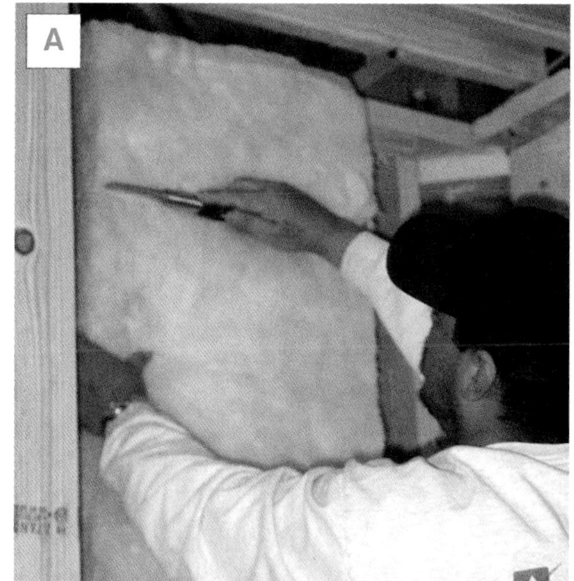

Figure 2. To achieve the required tight fit, batts are trimmed to the required height and width in place (A). Each batt is pushed tight to the sheathing, then pulled forward until it's flush with the stud faces (B). On inspection tours, the author checks for exposed stud shoulders and makes sure batts have been split around wires as needed (C).

quality. Can you blame them for blasting through a job to get a bigger check? With piecework, it's practically impossible to see that the job is done right. I pay my men hourly, and even then it's essential to inspect the work and make sure that any errors are fixed before the walls are closed in.

Seams and shoulders. When I walk onto a fiberglass job, I immediately begin looking for dark seams or shadow lines that indicate where an improperly cut batt stops short of the framing. Another detail I look for is the shoulder or side of the stud. I want to see only the edge or the face of the framing, not the side. If I see a lot of shoulder, I know the batts have been compressed from hasty installation. I also lift up batts adjacent to electrical receptacles and plumbing fixtures to make sure they have been split around wires and pipes.

Working with subs. Good batt installation requires the cooperation of the builder, framers, plumbers, and other subs, because framing, plumbing, and other details can create large inaccessible areas that often don't get insulated during assembly.

In infrared camera images, those empty voids show up clearly as hot spots or cold spots on a wall. It's common to find inaccessible voids framed into arched window headers, outside corners, wall intersections, and rim joist areas (Figure 3). Draft stops are often missed, and many builders mistakenly think that simply laying a batt over a chase will be adequate.

When a house has big built-in voids that the insulators can't reach, it doesn't much matter how careful you are everywhere else. Ideally, the plans should call out good framing and insulation details to ensure that no major thermal defects will be built into the structure.

I advise builders to let us come out to a job and insulate before they seal up cantilevers, install metal fireplaces, set fiberglass tub enclosures, run ductwork, or do anything else that will make the installation of batts more complicated later. When we insulate behind metal fireplaces, for example, we strap up the batts so they are supported for the life of the building (Figure 4). Unfaced batts that are not strapped or wired off might slip or sag over time. For the sake of fire safety, we don't use kraft-faced batts in those areas. If timing is an issue, we encourage our GCs to take

Figure 3. Framers often leave spaces blocked off that are hard or impossible to insulate. The intersection between an interior and an exterior wall (top) can be reached only through a small gap. A wood I-joist has been hung out over the top plate to serve as a nailer for the ceiling drywall (above), completely blocking access to the band joist. (For the correct detail in this area, see Figure 5.) In both photos, the kraft-faced batts have been jammed into place with no effort to achieve a proper fit.

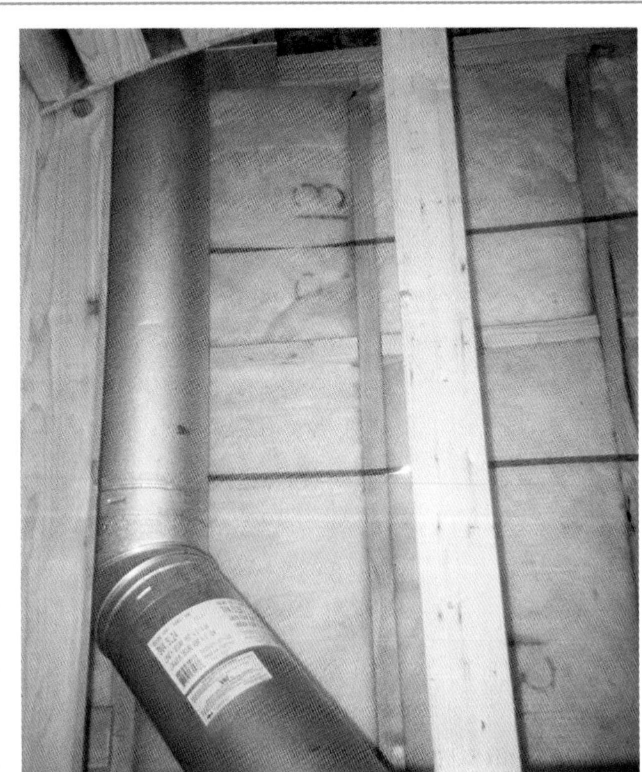

Figure 4. Batts behind manufactured fireplaces are strapped in place so they won't sag or droop. Kraft-faced batts aren't used because the facings are combustible.

some fiberglass from our warehouse so they can insulate special details themselves.

Rim Joists and Cantilevers

A quality fiberglass job in an exterior wall is straightforward, and everyone can see it until the drywall is hung. Miss a stud bay, and someone will likely say something, but rim joists and cantilevers are easy to overlook. A small cantilever may need to be insulated before my crew arrives in order to keep the stucco contractor on schedule. These little details are important, because even a small uninsulated area can have a huge impact on overall R-value.

Framers often create big problems at rim joists. They place a truss joist on the exterior of a top plate and then hang another out over the edge of the top plate on the inside for a nailer (Figure 5). This is a disheartening detail to deal with. It would be better to nail a piece of one-by stock flat as a drywall backer, leaving us access for insulation. When the rim joist is open, I cut pieces to fit and install them separately.

Where batts are placed between conditioned floors for sound control, I don't let my men curl down the batt end when they come to the end of the joist bay, even though it's fast. At the wall, a tight fit is required for effective R-value, so the crew must cut small pieces to fit.

In extremely cold climates, I recommend that builders inset the rim joist an inch so they can get an inch of rigid insulation over the exterior side of the band joist. Details like this will reduce the potential for condensation.

Attics

We install batts in attics only if access problems make

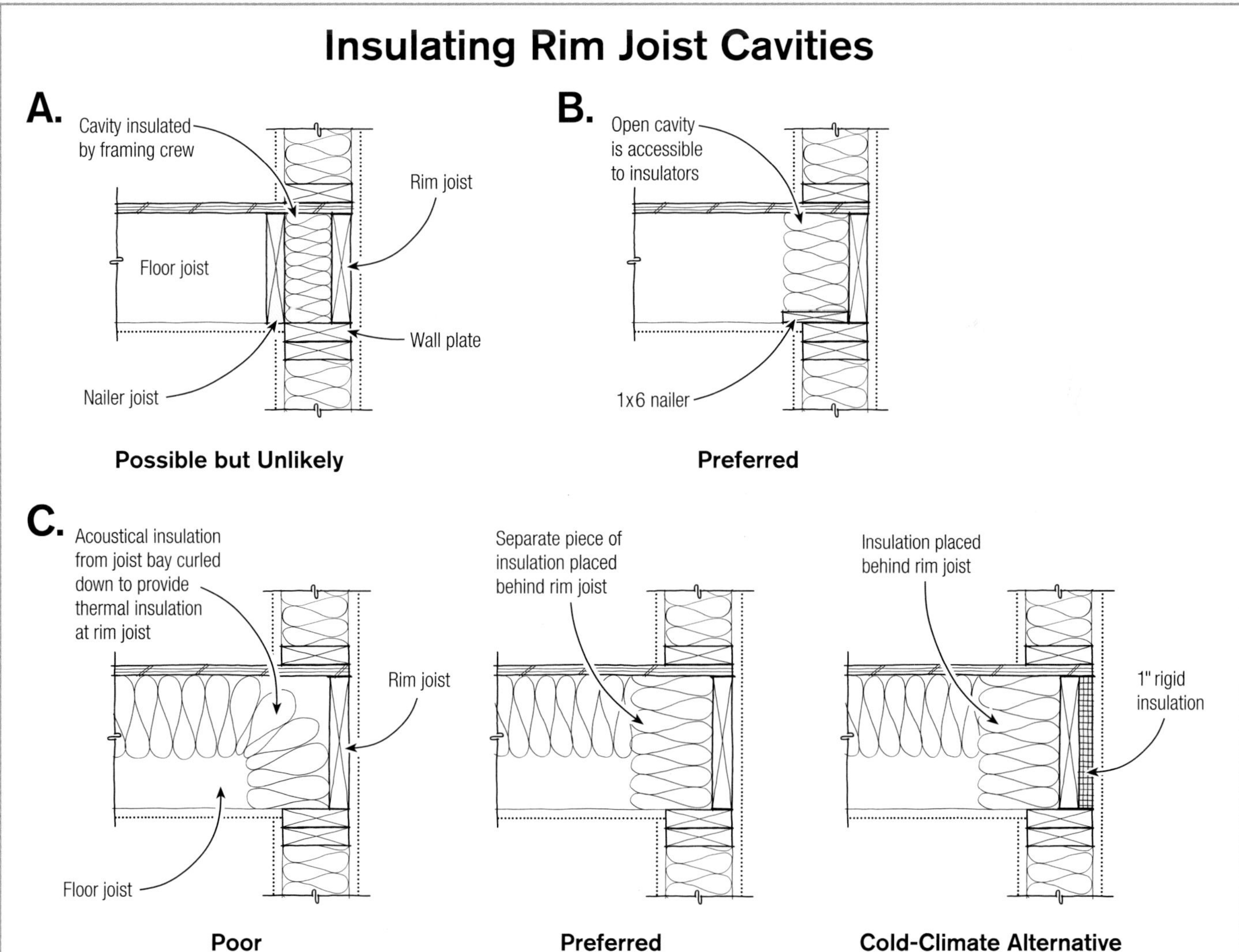

Figure 5. Because band joist cavities are often framed in a way that makes them inaccessible to insulation crews, the author makes insulation available to the GC so his crew can insulate those areas during the framing phase of the job (A). A better option is to nail a one-by board flat on top of the wall plate to provide a drywall nailer that leaves the floor cavity accessible (B). Where batts are placed in a conditioned floor for sound control, a separate piece of insulation should be cut and fitted at the band joist (C).

it impossible to blow in insulation (Figure 6). For one thing, it costs much less to blow in attic insulation than to install batts. We can also do a better job blowing in loose fill, because the blown-in fibers conform closely to elements like recessed cans, ductwork, truss ties, and plumbing, electrical, sprinkler, security, and audio systems, all of which create trouble when you're trying to fit a batt.

Like most installers, we use "toros" — telescoping poles with pronged heads — to manipulate batts overhead (Figure 7). These tools are a real convenience, but because they require you to work at a distance, they can lead to sloppiness if you're not careful, especially if you have to split batts around wires and other obstructions.

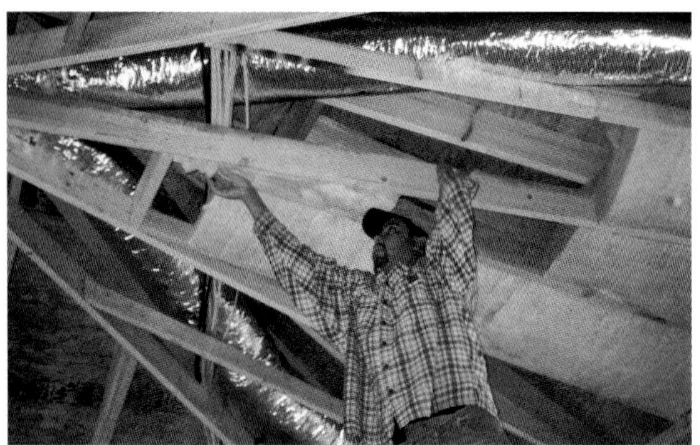

Figure 6. Low "Santa Fe" attics like this one don't leave room for blown-in products. Instead, carefully fitted batts are installed between the bottom truss chords.

I expect my men to climb up on ladders where needed to get the difficult details by hand.

Soffits and dropped ceilings. On our jobs, we place the batt in contact with the drywall if at all possible. In many higher-end custom homes, however, we see dropped ceilings and soffits with ductwork running through them, which forces us to run the batts at the level of the trusses.

In that situation, we support the batts with plastic strapping or wire (Figure 8). We don't want the batt to drop or get knocked down, because that would expose the uninsulated kneewalls and ceiling to ambient air.

Cathedralized attics. Unvented "cathedralized" attics are catching on in our area as a way to deal with halogen lights, wires, truss ties, and other systems that run through attics. The insulation is installed underneath the roof sheathing, and the attic is not vented, making this approach well suited to low-profile attics.

The advantage is apparent in a lot of the Santa Fe–style houses we insulate, where the roof plane is only 3 to 4 feet above the drywall. Besides eliminating conflicts with recessed cans, wires, and plumbing, this technique brings the ductwork inside the thermal and pressure envelope, which makes a huge increase in energy efficiency (Figure 9).

The 10-inch or 13-inch batts we use for cathedralized roofs tend to slip out from the truss bays formed by the 2x6 top chords. To hold the batts tight to the roof sheathing, we drive nails into the flat faces of the truss webs at the proper distance below the roof sheathing, then run wires from nail to nail parallel to the bays to support the batts. We run additional wires

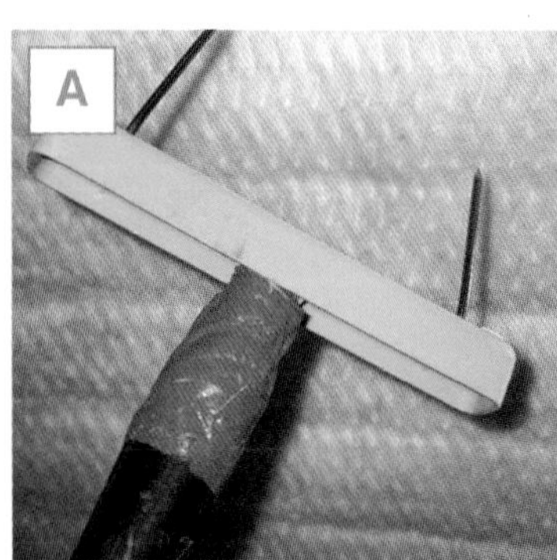

Figure 7. The author's crew uses toro poles (B) with pronged ends (A) to place batts in high ceilings. To reduce convection and infiltration losses, batts should be pulled down to make contact with the ceiling drywall (C).

at right angles to the trusses for extra support.

This doubles our labor cost for the job and compresses the batts slightly, but the benefits outweigh the disadvantages. In Phoenix, where attic temperatures can be as high as 140°F, we think it's worth it. In other climates, it may not be appropriate or may need to be modified. Before you use this detail, consult local code officials and study the Builder's Guide for your climate, which you can purchase from the Energy & Environmental Building Association website (www.eeba.org).

Conventional Cathedral Ceilings

Cathedral ceilings framed with lumber or wood I-joists are subject to a serious thermal defect at the ridge.

Figure 8. When a dropped ceiling or soffit sits lower than the trusses, the author's crew runs straps between the bottom truss chords to hold the batts in place. This is preferable to a foil or paper support that could fail and let the batts sag, exposing the dropped ceiling to hot or cold air from the unconditioned attic.

Figure 9. This example of a low-pitch cathedralized attic roof shows how the ductwork is brought within the conditioned space. Batts fit neatly into the roof-plane cavities, avoiding the need to make complicated cuts and fits around the can lights and other ceiling penetrations.

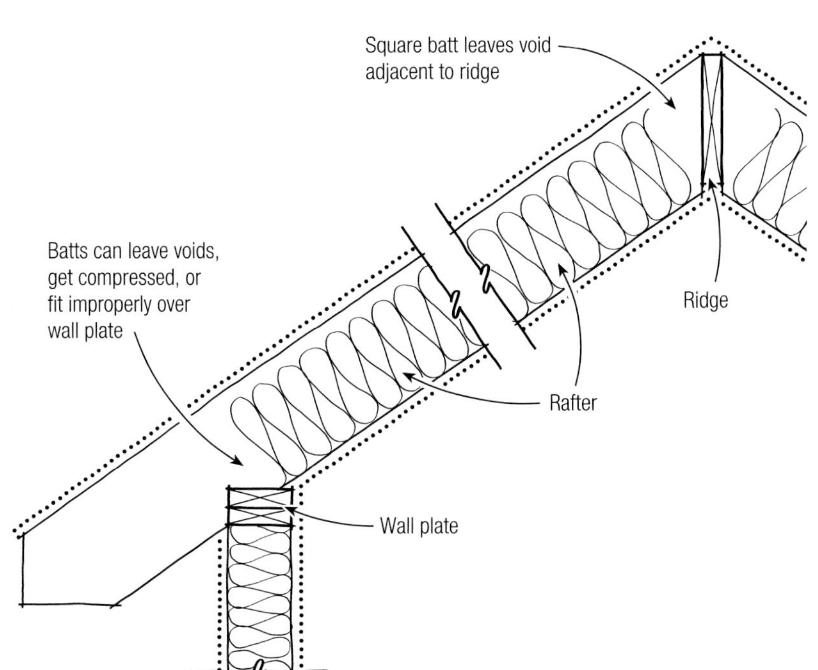
Insulating Cathedral Roofs
Square batt leaves void adjacent to ridge
Batts can leave voids, get compressed, or fit improperly over wall plate
Ridge
Rafter
Wall plate

Figure 10. In rafter-framed cathedral roofs, batts often fit poorly at the ridge and plate, leaving voids that may cause thermal losses and condensation. Trimming the batts at the required angle makes for a better job.

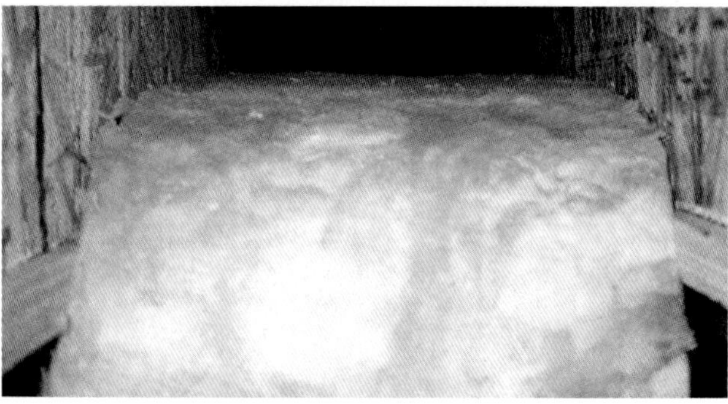

Figure 11. The author uses 16-inch-wide commercial batts to insulate engineered floors. He recommends wire batt hangers (top) to hold the batts tight to the floor sheathing. Standard-width batts don't fit snugly between the thin webs of wood I-joists (above).

Unless the ends of the batts are plumb-cut to match the rafters, a big gap is created where the square-cut batts meet the ridge board (Figure 10). This is an area that's difficult to inspect without a ladder or scaffold, so we make sure to cut the batt at the plumb angle or else install a piece of scrap fiberglass in that spot in advance.

Tall recessed-can lights are another common problem in cathedral ceilings, especially where the roof is framed with 2x8 or 2x10 rafters. That leaves little room for insulation between the roof sheathing and top of the can. About all you can do there is install rigid insulation in the gap and hope for the best. It's better to design the detail differently to begin with.

Crawlspaces

Building science supports the idea that crawlspaces should remain unvented and insulated at the exterior walls. But because the codes haven't caught up with current research, we still have to insulate floors over vented crawlspaces. As in other areas, it's important to make sure the batts make good contact with the adjoining sheet material — in this case, the underside of the subfloor.

A lot of new homes have floors framed with engineered lumber. Because of the wider distance between the webs of engineered lumber (15 3⁄8 inches compared with 14 1⁄2 inches between sawn lumber joists), we use commercial batts that are a full 16 inches wide (Figure 11). This is a simple detail, but some insulation contractors still use 15-inch-wide batts on the bottom web of a wood I-joist, which is a major installation flaw.

We also use a larger wire batt hanger on I-joist floors. Wire batt hangers are pieces of wire with sharpened ends that wedge in between floor joists to hold the batt in place. They compress the batts slightly and some R-value is lost, but I think the benefit of supporting the batt firmly against the floor sheathing outweighs the loss in R-value from compression.

__Michael Uniacke__ is owner of Advanced Insulation, Inc., in Prescott, Ariz.

Insulating With Spray Cellulose

by Michael Uniacke

In the hierarchy of the building trades, insulation contractors are often considered about half a step above the portable toilet guys. That's because insulation is one of the most taken-for-granted systems in a house. It's installed in exterior walls one day and covered up with drywall the next, and few municipalities require substantive insulation inspections. The result is little accountability or quality control on the majority of jobs I inspect.

In spite of all that, insulation can and should be done right. My company, Advanced Insulation in Prescott, Ariz., works with several types of insulation, but our workhorse product for wall applications is damp-spray cellulose (formerly known as wet-spray cellulose).

That preference is based on years of experience in

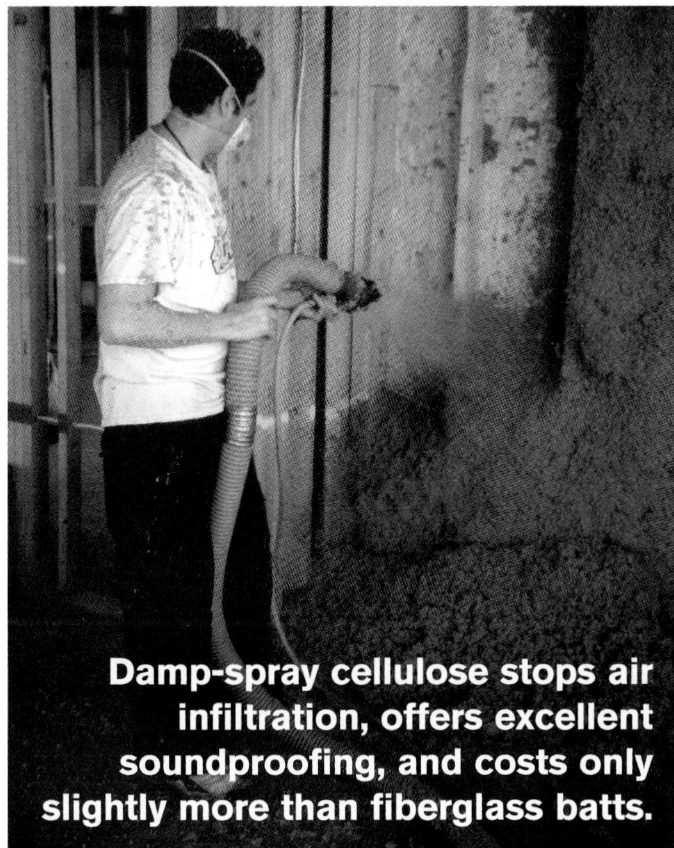
Damp-spray cellulose stops air infiltration, offers excellent soundproofing, and costs only slightly more than fiberglass batts.

our marketplace, which is at 5,000 feet elevation and has a climate similar to that of Denver. We've found that walls insulated with spray cellulose are more thermally efficient than those with fiberglass batts. In our 5,000 heating-degree-day climate, we are seeing 1,600-square-foot homes that don't require conventional forced-air heating systems. In some cases, the actual heating load is so small that it can be handled by a heater-rated gas log fireplace. Equally important, our customers tell us that spray cellulose provides a much more comfortable house.

Spray cellulose does cost a little more than batts — in our market, it's about 50 percent more than fiberglass, or an additional few hundred dollars for the walls of a typical 2,000-square-foot house — but the gain in energy efficiency and overall comfort makes the investment well worth it.

Cellulose Basics

Cellulose fiber is produced from paper, which in turn is derived from wood. However the insulation is installed — blown into the attic or damp-sprayed into wall cavities — the material is the same. It comes packed in bags that weigh from 25 to 35 pounds apiece (see Figure 12). By weight, about 82 to 85 percent of the material is cellulose fiber — most of which is reprocessed from old newspaper — with the remainder consisting of chemical fire retardant. The fire retardants are added in the form of a dry powder. The borate chemicals used — often in combination with ammonium sulfate — also add mold, insect, and rodent resistance. We often use an all-borate insulation called Incide (www.hmi-mfg.com) that is designed to prevent infestation by termites and other insects throughout the life of the structure.

Cellulose and fire. Although pure cellulose is flammable, the added fire retardants make cellulose insulation a safe material. The cellulose manufacturing industry adheres to strict standards set by ASTM and the Consumer Product Safety Commission, and at least three of the ten material attributes considered by ASTM (thermal resistance, surface burning characteristics, adhesive and cohesive strength, smoldering combustion, fungi resistance, corrosiveness, moisture vapor absorption, odor, and flame resistance permanency) relate directly to fire safety.

Test data consistently show that the fire resistance of cellulose is as good as or better than that of most insulating materials. According to Canada's National Research Council, for example, cellulose-insulated walls are from 22 percent to 55 percent more fire resistant than uninsulated walls. Walls insulated with fiberglass were found to be slightly less fire resistant than uninsulated walls.

My own experience has led me to the conclusion that cellulose insulation simply does not burn, partly because of the added fire retardants but also because cellulose contains few voids, excluding the air necessary for combustion. Not long ago a plumber working in a house that we had recently insulated got careless

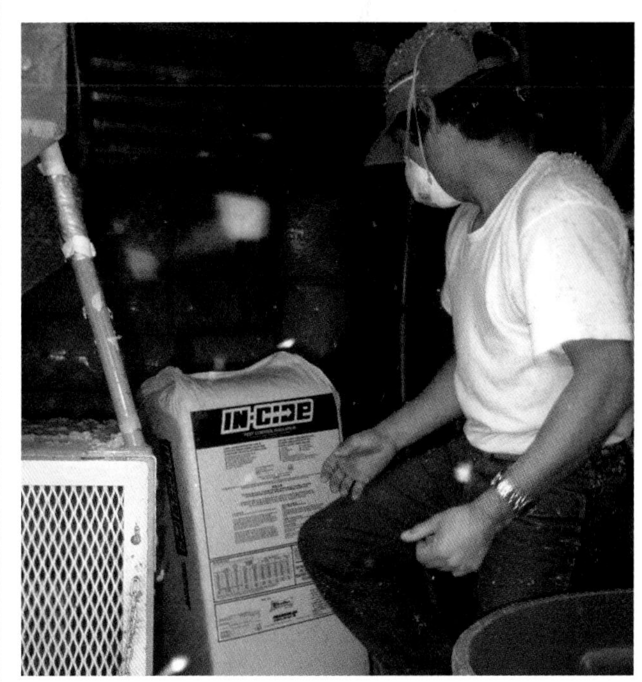
IN-CIDE

Figure 12. The same cellulose material is used for both wall-spray and loose-fill applications. A typical whole-house wall-spray application requires 60 to 120 bags.

with a torch and set fire to a stud. The stud and adjacent insulation smoldered all night and filled the crawlspace with smoke, but the fire never spread.

I've also inspected hundreds of attics insulated by others in which cellulose was carelessly blown against B-vent chimneys, on top of metal fireplaces, and against recessed cans and other hot points, and although I've occasionally seen slight charring, I've never seen evidence of fire. (I've also seen charring of the kraft facing of improperly placed fiberglass batts.) It goes without saying that such practices should be avoided, but it's reassuring to know that even under such worst-case conditions, the material appears not to burn.

Why Damp Spray?

In a blown cellulose installation, the material is simply blown into place in a loose, unconsolidated state. This is commonly done in attics, where the cellulose is supported by the ceiling beneath. Loose-fill cellulose can also be blown into enclosed walls in remodeling applications — an application known as dense-pack cellulose — although it can be tricky to do that without leaving hidden voids.

Damp spray, on the other hand, is self-sticking, so it can be placed in open wall cavities that are backed by sheathing or spray mesh.

Blown and damp-spray cellulose use the same basic equipment — typically, a truck-mounted insulation-blowing machine that delivers the material through a 2½-inch hose — but with one important difference: The nozzle of a damp-spray hose contains a separate water nozzle that mixes the cellulose with a fine water spray as it emerges (Figure 13). The water, which is delivered at 200 to 300 psi, comes from a truck-mounted tank through a hose like those used on pressure washers. The 200-gallon tanks on our trucks contain enough water to complete a typical house.

Fiber and water. When the spray nozzle is properly adjusted, it delivers a fine spray that simultaneously moistens the studs and sheathing as well as the insulation itself. The moistened fibers then adhere strongly to both the substrate and one another.

This bond gets even stronger as it dries, which makes correctly installed spray cellulose very resistant to settling. At the recommended density of 3 pounds per cubic foot, it's reliably self-supporting. (For comparison, loose-fill attic insulation is typically installed at about 1.6 pounds per cubic foot.) Some cellulose manufacturers regularly test their products in a machine that vibrates an 8-foot-tall wall cavity for 24 hours to simulate 20 years of normal vibration. For a product to meet the standard, no more than a quarter-inch gap can appear at the top of the cavity.

Some damp-spray cellulose used in commercial construction — for coating gym ceilings, for example, where the insulation will be left exposed — contains adhesives that provide an even stronger bond. A similar technique is used for blowing insulation against the masonry walls of unvented crawlspaces. But this is overkill in residential wall cavities and complicates cleanup, so we don't use added adhesives there.

Spraying and Cleanup

When we arrive on a job site, we park our 24-foot box truck in a convenient spot and run a power cord, water hose, cellulose hose, and vacuum hose into the house (Figure 14). The truck has its own generator and water tank, so we're not dependent on the job for

Figure 13. A high-pressure water nozzle moistens both the surface to be sprayed and the insulation as it is blown from the hose. The water flow can be adjusted by the operator, who must supply enough moisture to get the insulation to adhere properly but not so much that excess moisture leads to nail pops and other problems. Freshly applied spray cellulose should contain between 30 percent and 40 percent moisture by weight.

Figure 14. A 24-foot box truck holds up to 200 bags of insulation, as well as the blower, water supply, and other equipment. We try to get as close to the job as possible, but our equipment is powerful enough to push material up to 250 feet if necessary.

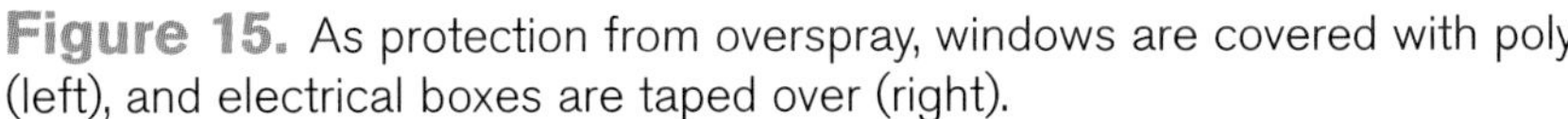

Figure 15. As protection from overspray, windows are covered with poly (left), and electrical boxes are taped over (right).

power or water.

A wall-spray job begins by prepping the house. The combination of moisture and cellulose can leave quite a mess, so all windows and electrical outlets are covered with polyethylene, and electrical boxes are protected with tape (Figure 15).

Add water. The key to a good spray job is achieving a proper blend of air, fiber, and water. We've seen and heard about installations in which the product was sprayed so wet that the water literally started to seep out of the bottom of the cavity just as it would from a saturated sponge. That is unacceptable. Normally, the liquid-to-fiber ratio should be .3 to .4 pounds of water per pound of fiber, or about a gallon of water per bag of insulation. In simple terms, this means that the applied material should be damp but not wet. A basic test we often use is to grab a handful of wall-spray cellulose right after it is sprayed and squeeze it. If any water can be squeezed out, the mix is too wet.

Scrubbing and scraping. The spraying itself goes pretty quickly. It takes about 30 to 45 seconds to fill an 8-foot wall cavity, and a three- or four-person crew can spray a 3,000- to 4,000-square-foot house in a day. Spraying well takes some experience. If you spray at too oblique an angle or don't get close enough, gaps may appear between the cellulose and the framing. This happens most often in the last three to five inches below a plate or sill, resulting in a horizontal defect we call a "smile" (Figure 16).

When a cavity is sprayed, it is filled past the face of the studs. This fills the cavity completely but also creates another step. We use a tool called a scrubber — a rotating brush that rides on the face of the studs — to

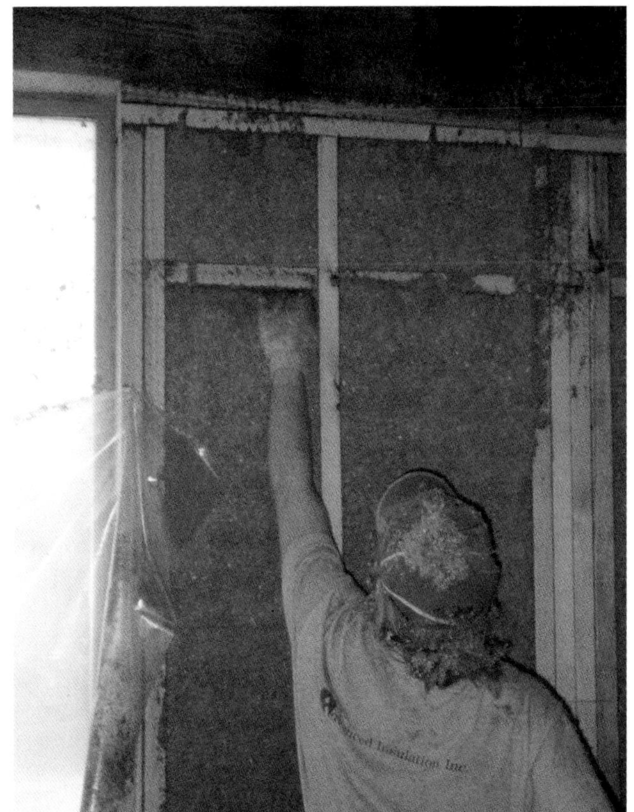

Figure 16. "Smiles" are horizontal gaps that result from poor technique when spraying below window sills, plates, or blocking. To correct the problem, the worker is compressing the insulation by hand before re-spraying the affected area.

cut or shave the cellulose flush with the face of the studs (Figure 17). Our usual crew consists of one worker to spray, one or two to move material and keep the hopper filled, and one to run the scrubber and keep the job clean.

The scrubber works well on open expanses of wall, but it can't get all the way into inside corners, so there's always some hand work as well. To clean out corners and other obstructed areas, we use a wide-bladed paint scraper with a threaded socket on the handle. This accepts an extension handle like those used with paint rollers, making it possible to reach the angle between wall and ceiling (Figure 18). To allow the blade to slide easily over the framing rather than digging in, we often cover the metal edge with a strip of duct tape.

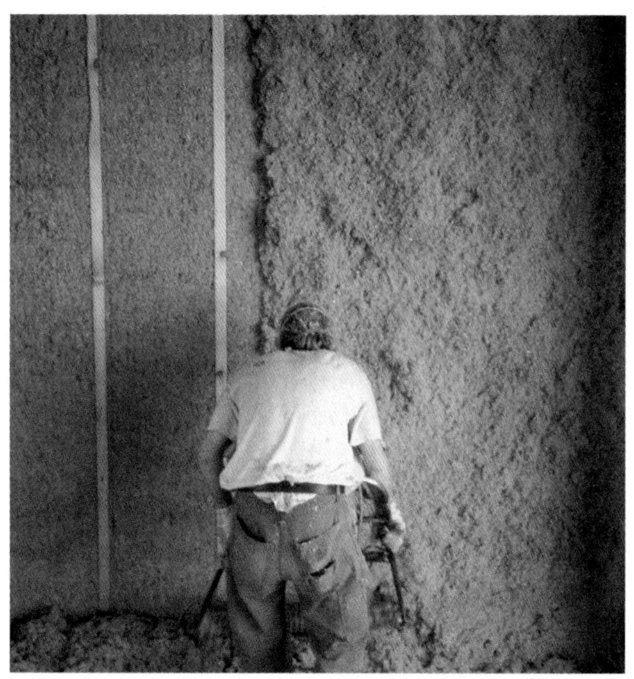

Figure 17. The area at left in this photo has already been scrubbed, leaving the faces of the studs flush with the surface of the cellulose. The scrubbed-off material accumulating on the floor will later be collected, combined with fresh material, and reapplied elsewhere.

Figure 18. Damp, freshly sprayed cellulose comes off easily, but the material sticks firmly when dry. Corners and other areas too tight for the scrubber to handle are cleaned with a paint scraper fitted to a pole extension.

The excess cellulose comes off readily while it's still damp, but if it's left for the drywallers to deal with, it dries to something like paper-mâché. That makes their job much more difficult, so we make a point of cleaning up thoroughly as we go.

Drying time. Unless the cellulose is installed too wet, there's no need to worry about nail pops or other drywall problems. In our climate, we find that insulated walls can be closed in within 24 hours of spraying. This seems to hold true for us even during the occasional spell of damp rainy weather. The residual moisture will migrate out through the wall through vapor diffusion, and the cavity will dry completely over the next month or two. The borate content of the cellulose prevents any mold growth during that time.

Filling in With Fiberglass

Cellulose is difficult to use in some areas. Kneewall framing, for example, is often left open on the back side, leaving nothing to spray against. In such cases, we resort to carefully fitted kraft-faced fiberglass. We also make limited use of batts around rim joists, blocking, and some difficult-to-spray corners.

This approach might upset cellulose purists, but it's a necessary compromise in our competitive marketplace. In our market, many customers are unwilling to

Figure 19. Spray cellulose is ideal for sound insulation in partition walls containing plumbing and wiring. Because it contains few voids and seals small openings, it allows little sound to pass from room to room.

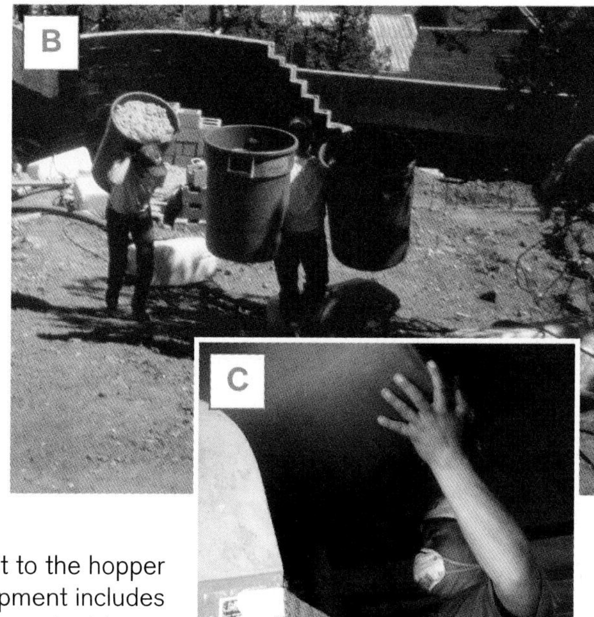

Figure 20. The low-tech method of dealing with excess cellulose is to collect it in clean garbage cans (A) and hand carry it to the hopper (B), where it's mixed with virgin material for reuse (C). Newer equipment includes a vacuum system that eliminates most hand work. Either way, it's important to start with a clean, well-swept floor to keep sawdust and other debris from contaminating the insulation.

bear the cost of installing the mesh or rigid-foam backing needed to make spraying possible in that situation. Even though sprayed kneewalls are thermally superior, we'd rather see a customer invest in airtight ductwork and a duct blaster test instead if there's no room in the budget for both.

Air and vapor barriers. Except in kneewall areas, where the batt facing provides a localized vapor barrier, we don't use a vapor retarder or additional air barrier. We feel that spray cellulose contains so few voids that there's little convective movement to allow moisture-laden air into the wall. The combination of an outer layer of housewrap and sheathing and an inner layer of drywall is enough to control air penetration.

Interior Partitions

Where interior soundproofing is called for, we often spray interior partitions as well. Many of the general contractors we work with tell us that cellulose performs much better than fiberglass batts in this application. In addition to being three times as dense as the batts, spray cellulose leaves fewer voids, which helps resist sound transmission at electric boxes and other small openings (Figure 19).

Mesh and drywall. Many of the contractors we work with install drywall on one side of interior walls to provide backing for us to spray against, and we've never had any problems with excess moisture soaking the drywall. That approach does require the drywall sub to make an extra trip to the job site, though. If that's too much trouble, we can staple spray mesh to the studs instead. The key to using spray mesh — which is actually not a mesh but a porous, nonwoven material something like the filter fabric used in footing drains — is to get the material taut, so it won't belly out beyond the studs and complicate life for the drywall crew.

Recycling

The excess material that the scrubber shaves off the wall is referred to as "recycle." The traditional method of dealing with it is to shovel it into clean garbage cans and dump it back into the hopper on the truck (Figure 20). This works well, although it can be a lot of work if the truck is some distance from the house; if that's the case, we'll often assign a fourth member to the crew.

The easy way — which we're able to use with the newer of our two truck-mounted spray rigs — is to suck up the recycle with a powerful vacuum hose that sends it back to a dedicated recycle hopper. This pre-dampened cellulose is automatically blended with the virgin material in a separate dry hopper. In addition to saving a lot of labor, this makes it easier to maintain a consistent moisture content, which improves quality control and keeps dust down. The only disadvantage is higher cost: Not counting the trucks, our older rig, without the vacuum system, cost us about $18,000, while the newer one set us back $40,000 (in 2001). That's a big investment, but we — and our customers — are convinced that the results are worth it.

***Michael Uniacke** is principal owner of Advanced Insulation Incorporated in Prescott, Ariz.*

Rigid Foam Options

by Rick Stacy

Over the past three decades, the use of rigid foam insulation in residential construction has grown enormously. From below-grade foundation insulation to structural insulated panel systems, from vinyl siding backers to cathedral ceiling insulation, rigid foam has proved to be an effective means of reducing air infiltration, adding R-value, and eliminating conductive heat loss, particularly where conditions limit the allowable thickness of the insulation.

Although several foam recipes have come and gone, three main types of rigid foam boards are still readily available today: expanded and extruded polystyrene, and polyisocyanurate (Figure 21).

Expanded polystyrene (EPS), commonly referred to as "beadboard," is a closed-cell foam made of dense polystyrene crystals that are steam-expanded to 40 times their original volume. Although the resulting beads can be used as loose-fill insulation, EPS beads are commonly steam-molded into rigid blocks or sheets. Densities range from .9 pcf (pounds per cubic foot) to around 1.8 pcf, with corresponding compressive strength from 10 psi to 25 psi. Higher densities are available by special order. EPS has an insulating value of R-4 per inch and a perm rating of 5 per inch.

Foam board is a great problem solver, but you have to match the type to the application.

There are at least 60 manufacturers listed with the EPS Molders Association. Foam quality, density, and compressive strength can vary substantially among them, because of varying amounts of recycled polystyrene, known as re-grind, mixed with virgin polystyrene beads during manufacture. Because re-grind content may compromise panel quality, it's best to use only EPS products with a grade stamp or third-party certification of conformance to ASTM-C578.

Figure 21. The individual "beads" of foam in expanded polystyrene (EPS) are visible in the rigid blocks or sheets, commonly called "beadboard" (top). Extruded polystyrene (XPS) is uniform throughout its thickness and forms a "skin" while curing, making it nearly impervious to moisture penetration (middle). Polyisocyanurate (bottom) is most susceptible to moisture damage, but has the highest R-value of the three types of foam.

Extruded polystyrene (XPS) is made by mixing polystyrene crystals, additives, and a blowing agent under high heat and pressure. As the liquified material emerges from an extrusion die, it expands and is shaped and cooled. The extrusion process produces a closed-cell foam panel with a natural "skin" that makes the board more resistant to moisture than EPS, with a perm rating of about 1.2 per inch and an R-value of 5 per inch. Residential XPS has a density of about 2 pcf and an average compressive strength of 30 psi. (Higher density XPS, with compressive strength from 40 to 100 psi, is available for heavy construction.) Re-grind content in XPS is limited to the reintroduction of manufacturing waste and has no adverse effect on the quality of the foam.

There are only four manufacturers of XPS, identifiable by their products' color: blue (Dow), pink (Owens Corning), green (Tenneco), and yellow (DiversiFoam).

Polyisocyanurate (PIR) is a member of the urethane family of chemical compounds. PIR, or "polyiso," boards are formed by a chemical reaction in a laminator that controls the temperature and thickness. The resulting closed-cell foam cures almost instantaneously, and the density is controlled by the amount of HCFC blowing-agent introduced into the mixture — the less blowing-agent, the denser the foam. Compressive strength is between 16 and 25 psi. HCFC gas trapped in the closed-cell structure gives polyiso the highest initial per-inch R-value (about 7.4) among rigid foams. Although the R-value of polyiso degrades somewhat over time, as explained below, the use of foil and other facing materials slows the process. Perm rating is also affected, ranging from .4 to 1.6 per inch, depending on the facing material.

Common Characteristics

While the benefits of using rigid foam seem clear, determining which one is best for a given application can be confusing. No single type of foam is categorically better than the rest; each type has advantages and disadvantages.

R-value. While both strength and R-value increase with density, thermal performance is most improved by increasing the thickness of the foam. In EPS, for example, doubling the density from 1 pcf to 2 pcf more than doubles the compressive strength, but the R-value increases by only about 12 percent. However, doubling the thickness of any rigid foam doubles the R-value.

The R-values of EPS and XPS are close to that of dead air, so the value remains stable over the life of the product. In polyiso, however, R-value deteriorates over time. The HCFC trapped in the cellular structure is a better insulator than air, so polyiso has a high initial R-value. But as the gas gradually migrates through the cell walls, it is replaced by air — called "thermal aging" or "thermal drift." This puts the long-term R-value of polyiso closer to between R-5 and R-5.6, although due to disparate testing methods, manufacturers may publish higher aged values.

Permeability. With regard to moisture penetration, polyiso is least resistant — the facing material protects the face, but board edges are still exposed. Since moisture reduces R-value, polyiso is best confined to above-ground, indoor applications. XPS, however, is virtually impervious to moisture, making it a good choice for wet locations, such as in contact with the ground (Figure 22).

Moisture penetration in EPS has long been a subject of debate. In below-grade applications, for example, the concern has been that while moisture can't penetrate the foam beads themselves, the voids between the beads will absorb moisture and permit water to pass through the molded boards. However, an extensive field-test study of EPS foundation insulation, conducted over a three-year span in Canada by the National Research Council, has concluded that EPS performs on an equal footing with extruded polystyrene, showing no ill effects from moisture or freeze/thaw cycles, and no appreciable loss in R-value. As a result of this testing, Canada lifted its restriction

Figure 22. Because of its high resistance to moisture, XPS is the best material to use in wet locations or in contact with the ground. At foundations, a waterproofing membrane is still required, however, since water can still migrate through joints between sheets.

(National Building Code, Part 9) against the use of EPS in ground contact.

Insect infestation. Termites and other wood-boring insects find easy nesting in rigid foam, particularly in below-grade applications (see "Insect Infestations in Buried Foam," page 104). In response to this problem, AFM Corp. developed Perform Guard, a line of borate-treated EPS that has shown success in resisting insect infestation (Figure 23). The company's Vanguard fan-fold siding underlayment is also borate treated. Insects can avoid or circumvent the foam board, however, so borate treatment should not be considered a deterrent to infestation of a structure, but only to nesting in the foam itself.

XPS and polyiso manufacturers have yet to find a practical means of incorporating insecticide into their products.

UV exposure. If left exposed to direct sunlight, rigid foam will become dusty, eventually losing thickness and R-value. The facing on polyiso blocks ultraviolet light, but board edges are unprotected. It's important to keep all three types of foam covered when stored and protected from exposure after installation.

Facings. All three foam types are available with foil, polyethylene, or kraft-paper facings (Figure 24). Polyiso is also made with fiberglass-mat facing for EIFS or stucco underlayment and organic asphalt facing for roofing applications. Facings serve several purposes: They reduce breakage from handling, improve surface cohesion for nailing, retard thermal drift, increase perm rating, provide a bonding surface for adhesives and coatings, and protect the board from ultraviolet degradation. Polyiso products all have facings to prevent outgassing, while XPS is typically installed unfaced. EPS is often used unfaced, but may have various facings for special applications.

Foil- or poly-faced foam performs as a vapor barrier when installed on interior wall surfaces. Foil has the better perm rating, but is more easily damaged during installation. Use adhesive-foil tape to repair tears and punctures and to seal all seams.

Reflective foil facing also serves as a radiant barrier when used in conjunction with a minimum ¾-inch air space. Concern over the potential for heat buildup has led some vinyl siding manufacturers to void their warranties if their products are installed over reflective-foil-faced foam sheathing. One solution is to use foam board with non-reflective facing on one side and a reflective facing on the other.

Adhesive compatibility. Petroleum-based solvents found in many adhesives and bituminous coatings will dissolve polystyrene foam on contact (Figure 25). Even polystyrene faced with polyethylene is susceptible to damage because vapor emissions from petro-

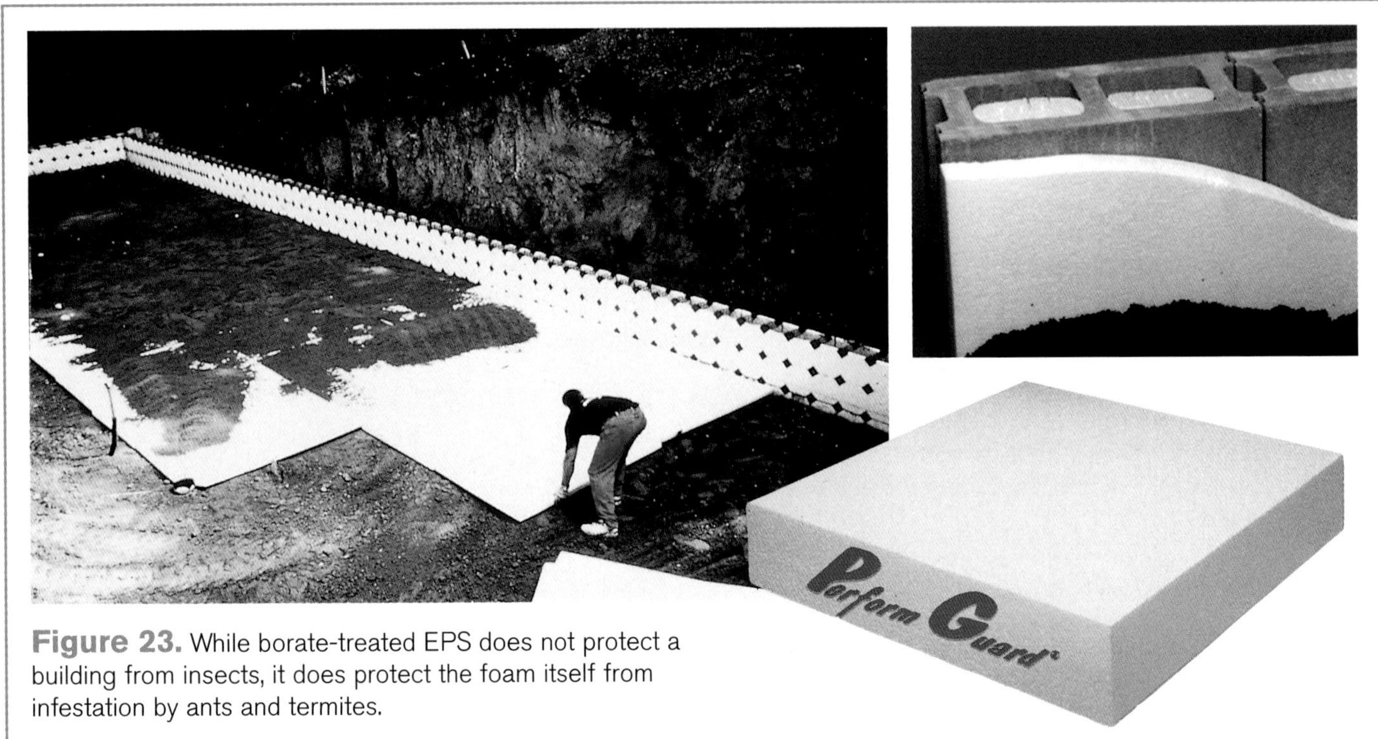

Figure 23. While borate-treated EPS does not protect a building from insects, it does protect the foam itself from infestation by ants and termites.

Figure 24. A polyethylene skin, whether plain or reinforced, protects some foam sheathing products from damage during installation and can be peeled off to increase permeability. Foil or plastic facings on polyiso board also help slow the escape of gas, which lowers the board's R-value. A foil facing also adds a radiant barrier, effective if facing an air space. Other specialty facings on rigid foam are available for various applications.

leum-based compounds can penetrate the facing. Polyiso isn't affected by petroleum-based solvents, but a polystyrene-compatible adhesive may not bond to polyisocyanurate.

Fasteners. To secure rigid foam sheathing, manufacturers recommend using ¾-inch crown staples, asphalt-roofing nails, or plastic or metal cap nails. Fasteners should be long enough to penetrate ¾ inch into studs. Foundation insulation can be secured to concrete or block with powder-actuated fasteners, concrete screws such as Tapcons, or a compatible adhesive.

Fire resistance. EPS and XPS are classified as "thermoplastic" materials, which means that they will soften at 165°F and melt at just over 200°F. Polystyrenes also fail to meet the standard as a Class 1 roofing material, according to the *Factory Mutual Approval Guide*. Without a thermal barrier between the foam and a roof deck, flaming droplets of molten polystyrene can run ahead of a fire through seams in the deck, spreading the fire.

Polyiso, on the other hand, is a "thermo-set" material, which while it does burn, retains its shape and some structural integrity at its recommended maximum service temperature of 250°F. For this reason, polyiso is commonly chosen for roof insulation in areas where roof-surface temperatures reach the limits of polystyrene.

When burned, EPS and XPS produce the same combustion gases as wood — carbon monoxide and carbon dioxide. Burning polyisocyanurate, however, also produces hydrogen cyanide and nitrogen oxides, both chemical asphyxiants. Most manufacturers and building codes call for a minimum ½-inch drywall to be installed over rigid foam when used on the interior side of a living space. For safety, rigid foam insulation should be left exposed only if it has a flame-spread index at or below 25 (the label should say FS-25), but check your local codes.

Foam and the environment. Of the three foam types, EPS probably is the least threatening to the environment, because it's considered to be recyclable and uses pentane as a blowing agent (5 to 8 percent by volume). Although classified as a pollutant, pentane has little effect on global warming and isn't considered harmful to the ozone layer. XPS and polyiso were originally manufactured using CFCs, which are "greenhouse" gases that contribute significantly to global warming and are also harmful to the earth's stratospheric ozone layer, according to many scientists. Under pressure from environmental legislation, polyiso manufacturers have switched to pentane, with no measurable effect on performance. XPS, however, as well as most closed-cell spray polyurethane foams (SPF) are still made with HFC (hydrofluorocarbon) blowing agents, which are potent contributors to global warming to the extent that the gases leak out of the foam. How rapidly this occurs has not been well studied, but experts estimate that half the chemical may leak out over the service life of the foam board. XPS products in Europe have switched over to more environmental blowing agents with a slight loss of R-value, and some U.S. manufacturers may do the same in the future. For the time being, however, environmentally conscious builders may be better off using EPS or polyiso foam board.

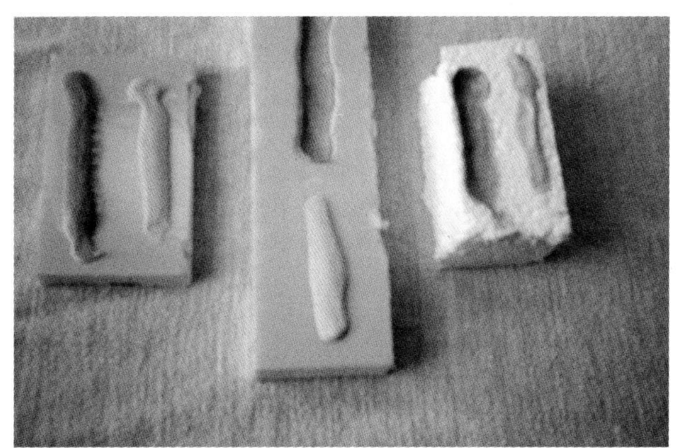

Figure 25. An incompatible construction adhesive (darker bead in photo) will dissolve rigid foam — including poly-faced XPS (on left in photo).

Common Applications

All three types of foam are available for use under exterior stucco finishes. Some products, such as Atlas roofing's Stucco-Shield (www.atlasroofing.com), are coated with a reinforced fiberglass facing for use with polymer-based and modified stucco finishes. Others, such as Johns Manville's AP Foil-Faced polyiso board (www.jm.com), are bonded on each side to a laminated foil facer and are recommended for use behind all siding types, including brick veneer and stucco. One face is non-reflective for sidings that are not compatible with reflective foil.

Foundations. Because of its superior moisture resistance, polystyrene is the best choice for below-grade and buried insulation (Figure 26). It's available in 2x8- and 4x8-foot boards, from ¾ to 4 inches thick, with square, tongue-and-groove, and shiplap edge treatments. Make sure solvents in bituminous foundation coatings are completely evaporated before installing EPS or XPS and note regional code bans on below-grade applications in insect-prone areas.

Finished basements. For interior basement walls, some foam boards are grooved to accommodate 1x3 or 2x3 furring strips. Panels sized to fit between conventional framing centers are also available.

Roof insulation. Polyiso is common in roofing applications, partly because of the reflective foil facing, and partly because of its stability in high temperatures. For flat roofs (typically commercial), a tapered polyiso is available in ⅛-, ¼-, and ½-inch-

Figure 26. For interior basement insulation, wide shiplaps on some XPS boards accept furring strips, which can be fastened through the foam to poured concrete or masonry (left). DiversiFoam's "CertiStud" EPS board has plywood furring strips bonded to the foam (right).

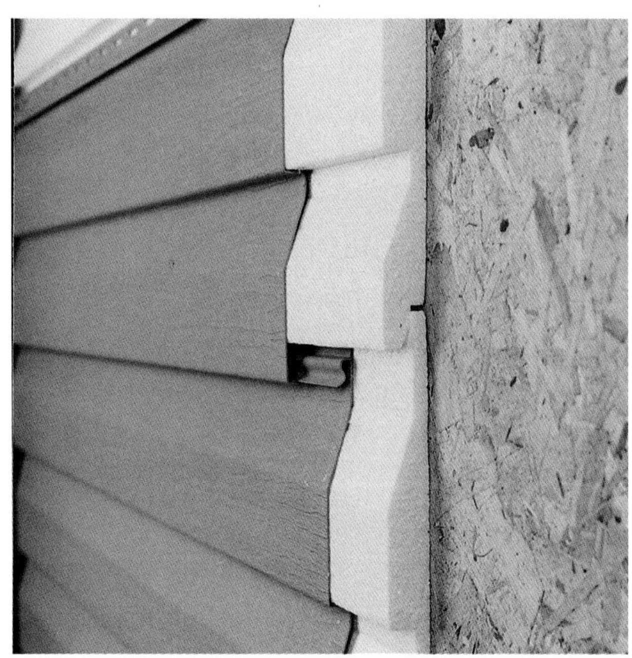

Figure 27. Some foam producers, such as Progressive Foam Products, mold EPS to match common vinyl siding profiles and accessories. However, not all such EPS moldings are approved by all siding manufacturers, and some siding companies will not warrant their products when installed over EPS.

per-foot slopes to introduce positive drainage to a level surface.

EPS and XPS can be successfully installed over residential wood roof decks, if covered with a layer of plywood or OSB, which not only provides a nail base, but also serves as a buffer against damage following installation and reduces heat buildup in roofing material.

Sheathing. Rigid foam sheathing is commonly available in 2x8-, 4x8-, and 4x9-foot sheets, and in thicknesses of ½ inch to 4 inches. Applied over wood sheathing or directly to diagonally reinforced framing, an inch of foam adds between R-4 and R-6 to a standard wall system, and reduces conductive heat loss through studs and headers. Proper installation can also eliminate the need for an air-barrier house wrap, especially when seams are taped to block air infiltration between panels.

Rigid foam sheathing can also help solve a number of moisture problems. In cold climates, if a sufficient thickness of foam sheathing is used, the interior side of the sheathing is warm enough to eliminate condensation within the wall (see "Foam Thickness and Dew Points," page 138). Many designers also consider foam sheathing to be an ideal insulation for mixed climates, where the vapor retarder should go on the interior in the winter and the exterior in the summer. The foam sheathing acts as an exterior vapor retarder during the cooling season and warms the wall cavity to prevent moisture problems in winter.

Siding underlayment. Available in 4x8 sheets and in 4x50 fanfold panels, siding underlayment is designed to bridge irregularities when applying new siding over existing, or to reduce air infiltration of the building envelope. At ¼- to ⅜-inch thick, however, the underlayment doesn't add much R-value.

Some EPS fabricators have gained widespread industry approval for foam drop-ins or backers made to match the profiles of many vinyl siding manufacturers (Figure 27). However, some vinyl siding manufacturers won't honor warranties if an unapproved backer is used with their siding.

Under-floor insulation. Both wood and concrete floors are commonly insulated with rigid foam. Compressive strength of all three foam types is adequate for under-slab duty, but polyiso's tendency to absorb moisture makes it less suitable for ground-contact application. Rigid foam can also be used to provide a firm, low-profile layer of insulation under "floating" wood or laminate floor installations.

Wall insulation. Because of its higher R-value and moisture resistance, rigid foam can take the place of fiberglass batts, particularly during rough framing in areas that won't be easily accessible later, such as behind partition backers, corner studs, and rim joists, and in built-up headers. Installed on the interior side of exterior walls, rigid foam can serve as a combination thermal and vapor barrier, provided low-perm tape is used at the seams.

***Rick Stacy** is the owner of R.A. Stacy Construction in Bergen, N.Y.*

Spray Foam Basics

by David Frane

Most residential structures are insulated with either fiberglass batts or cellulose because both are cheap sources of added R-value. But there's more to insulation than R-value. For best results, the insulation must be accurately cut to fit the joist or stud cavities, and an effective air barrier is needed to keep unconditioned outdoor air from penetrating the insulation like wind blowing through a sweater. In most climates, a poly or kraft-paper vapor retarder is also needed to limit the flow of moisture-laden air and prevent condensation from forming within the insulation.

None of that is exactly rocket science, but doing the job right does take some care and attention to detail. Unfortunately, because both fiberglass and cellulose installations are typically subbed out to the lowest bidder, vapor retarders, air barriers, and the insulation itself are often thrown into place with little regard to quality.

When quality is a more important consideration than price, spray-applied polyurethane foam (SPF) is emerging as the first choice of a growing number of builders. Although it costs up to several times as much as its competitors, foam eliminates many of the installation headaches associated with fibrous insulating materials.

First, SPF has exceptional air-sealing ability. When sprayed or injected into a framing cavity, it sticks tight to the sheathing and framing and rapidly expands to fill every crack and opening in the exterior shell. This is especially valuable around rim joists and other difficult-to-seal areas. Some types of foam are also effective vapor retarders, so it's often possible to omit the separate poly or kraft-paper vapor retarder.

Finally, going with foam can provide added flexibility in designing a framing package: Because dense varieties of foam offer a lot of insulating value per inch of thickness, it's often possible to size studs and rafters based on structural loads rather than the amount of space needed for insulation.

Spray-in-place polyurethane provides high R-value, an effective air barrier, and vapor control in one application.

Material Characteristics

SPF was developed in Europe. It was first used in North America during the 1960s, first as an insulator for commercial cold-storage buildings and later as a commercial roofing material.

Polyurethane foam has had a harder time penetrating the residential market. During the 1970s and early '80s, a foamed-in-place product known as UFFI — an abbreviation for urea formaldehyde foam insulation — was widely used for retrofitting uninsulated houses but was later found, in some homes, to offgas potentially harmful amounts of formaldehyde into living spaces. The resulting uproar left all foamed-in-place insulating materials with an image problem that they have only recently overcome.

Today's SPF does not contain urea formaldehyde. Current products are made from isocyanate — a material derived from petroleum — and urethane resins, which are often made from sugar cane or soybeans. Potentially toxic vapors may be present while the foam is being applied, but the cured material is non-toxic and will not offgas harmful chemicals.

Density. There are many brands of proprietary foams on the market, and they vary widely in density and insulating power. Commercial flat roofs, for example, are often insulated with a high-density material that weighs about 3 pounds per cubic foot, which makes it hard and strong enough to walk on without damage. But most residential polyurethane foam insulation used today weighs approximately .5 or 2.0 pounds per cubic foot. The low-density half-pound foam has an open-cell structure, allowing vapor transmission, and the medium-density 2-pound foam is typically closed cell.

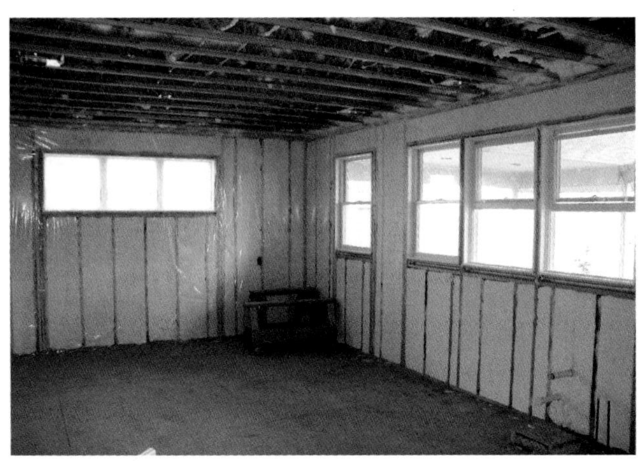

Figure 28. Open-cell foam is more permeable to vapor than closed-cell material. Depending on the climate zone and local code requirements, this kitchen, insulated with ½-pound foam, may need a vapor barrier installed on the winter-warm side of the insulation.

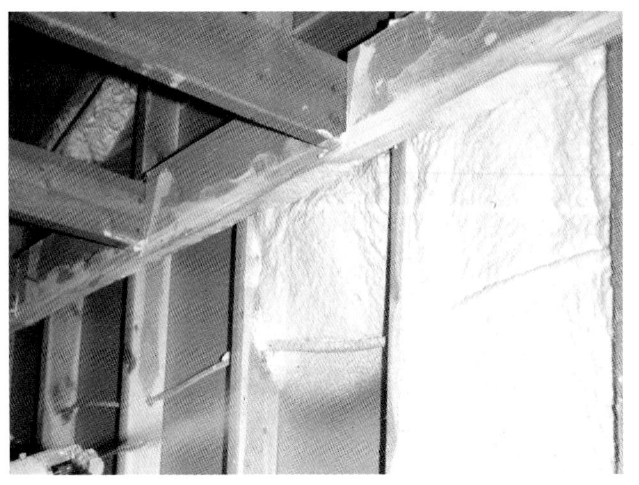

Figure 29. Polyurethane foam expands to between 30 and 100 times its wet volume. Dense, closed-cell material such as this has twice the R-value per inch of light, open-cell material.

With most common building materials, lower density translates into higher insulating value. That's why fiberglass batts insulate better than wood, and wood insulates better than concrete. But the opposite is true of foam. A ½-pound foam such as Icynene (www.icynene.com), for example, has an R-value of about 3.5 per inch — roughly the same as fiberglass batts or loose-fill cellulose.

A denser, 2-pound urethane foam, on the other hand, has an R-value of 6 to 7. But because the 2-pound foam contains nearly four times the amount of chemicals per unit of volume as the ½-pound material, the square-foot cost is substantially higher

Moisture Control. Dense foams have what's known as a closed-cell structure, which means that the gas bubbles that form during the application process remain permanently locked into the cured foam. The result is something like a three-dimensional bubble wrap with extremely tiny bubbles. Because there are no interconnections between individual bubbles, the foam absorbs little water and also resists the passage of water vapor. A 2-pound closed-cell polyurethane foam, applied at least 2 inches thick, has a perm rating less of than 1.0 and usually doesn't require an additional vapor retarder (see "Density, R-Value, and Moisture Control," page 79).

Low-density open-cell foams, on the other hand, have a structure more like a very fine-grained sponge. The cured material consists of a series of tiny interconnected passageways. These open cells are too small to permit the passage of much air, but they are more permeable to water vapor than closed-cell foams. Unless there's an exceptional amount of vapor drive, though, that isn't usually a problem. However, depending on the climate zone and local code requirements, low-density open cell foams may be required to have vapor retarder such as kraft paper or vapor-barrier paint on the winter-warm side (Figure 28).

Equipment and Installation

Application methods vary somewhat depending on the proprietary product used, but most residential foam contractors arrive on the site in a small box truck that contains the necessary drums of chemicals, a pumping machine, and several feet of hose. The pumping machine precisely meters out the two components of the foam and heats them to accelerate the chemical reaction that causes them to foam when combined.

The chemicals pass through separate lines that are combined in a single hose until they mix at the nozzle. The liquid that emerges expands almost instantly from a paint-like consistency to a thick foam that sets up into a durable solid.

Trimming the foam. High-density foams are usually

applied to a total thickness that's significantly less than the depth of the framing. An experienced applicator will take care to avoid getting much foam on the exposed edges of the studs, since any stray drops or spatters have to be scraped off before the drywall goes on. Low-density foams, by contrast, expand much more and usually bulge out beyond the framing. This excess material must be trimmed off with a long, flexible saw blade before the wall or ceiling finish can be applied.

Framing dimensions. With low-density foam, as with fiberglass batts or cellulose, the dimensions of the framing are driven more by the insulation value required than by structural considerations. For example, the 2x6 wall studs used on so many residential jobs are overkill from the standpoint of supporting the weight of the building. The real reason for using them is that they provide stud bays deep enough to accommodate R-19 fiberglass batts. Because the R-value of low-density foam is comparable to that of fiberglass, the framing requirements are also similar.

But when a denser foam is used, it's possible to pack more R-value into a shallower bay. With 1.8-pound foam, you can frame walls with 2x4s and still achieve an R-value of 24 (Figure 29). Another option is to frame with 2x6s and fill the cavities only partially, leaving an open space for running pipes or wires.

Trading places. Proponents of SPF claim that it's an ideal insulating material for mixed climates, where the warm and cold sides of the building envelope reverse during the year. During the heating season, the vapor retarder belongs on the inside of the wall, but when the air conditioning kicks on during the summer, it belongs on the outside. This is a practical impossibility with permeable insulating materials. But because foam is uniformly solid, it resists the passage of vapor equally well in either direction.

Roofs and Attics

Cathedral ceilings are notoriously difficult to insulate effectively. Unlike walls, ceilings don't have air barriers like Tyvek and are usually vented to maintain a cool roof surface and prevent ice dams. But venting makes it easier for cold air to infiltrate batt insulation, which reduces its effective R-value. Ceiling penetrations like recessed lights are also common sources of air leakage.

Cold roofs and foam. One way to deal with these sorts of troublesome leaks is to fill the ceiling with spray foam. According to Matt Momper — whose Indiana-based company, Momper Insulation, is one of the region's largest installers of foam, fiberglass batts, and other materials — foamed cathedral ceilings should be vented if possible.

"Some roofing manufacturers won't warrant their shingles if the roof isn't vented," he says. Before spraying the closed-cell foam, Momper installs polystyrene baffles below the sheathing to create a channel connected to soffit vents and a continuous ridge vent.

Figure 30. Closed-cell foam insulation allows you to build cathedral ceilings without venting or vapor barriers.

But if the rafters aren't deep enough to leave room for a vent channel, or if the design of the roof makes it impractical to install a ridge vent, Momper has found that unvented ceilings also work well.

Unvented attics. SPF is also effective in areas where codes permit unvented attics. This technique is especially popular in parts of the South, where the humidity is high and it's common to put air handlers in the attic. Spraying the underside of the sheathing and the gable-end walls turns the attic into a conditioned space and prevents humid air from entering and condensing on cold ductwork (Figure 30).

Placing the air handler in the relatively cool environment of a sealed attic also decreases the load on the hvac system and may allow you to install smaller, less expensive equipment. Finally, any air that leaks from ductwork located in the attic will help cool the conditioned space rather than escaping uselessly to the outdoors.

Other Applications

Spray foam works well under floors because it won't sag or fall down the way batts sometimes do. This makes it a good choice for rooms over exterior porches or small additions built on elevated piers. Foam is especially useful for insulating truss-framed assemblies and other areas that are difficult or impossible to insulate with batts (Figure 31).

Unvented crawlspaces. Spray foam adheres well to masonry of all kinds, including the irregular stone foundations sometimes encountered in old houses. As a result, it's becoming a popular choice for sealing and insulating the perimeter walls of crawlspaces, especially in areas where unvented crawlspaces are permitted by code.

Figure 31. Rim joists are difficult to insulate and nearly impossible to fully seal with traditional insulation and vapor barriers. Foam allows you to do a much better job of insulating here and in other difficult areas.

Like unvented attics, unvented crawlspaces aim to prevent condensation and moisture problems by keeping humid air outside the conditioned envelope. The air-sealing properties prevent the entry of airborne moisture, but it's also important to seal out moisture in the soil. The usual way of doing this is to cover the dirt floor of the crawlspace with a continuous poly vapor retarder

Foam and batts: hybrid or bastard? Some insulation contractors install foam and batts in the same framing cavity in order to combine the air-sealing and vapor-resistant properties of foam with the economy of fiberglass. Momper uses this technique regularly. The framing cavities are first sprayed with a ½-inch layer of closed-cell foam before the rest of the cavity is filled with batt insulation to beef up the overall R-value.

Momper reports no problems with this approach, but the technique is a controversial one within the spray-foam industry. Opponents of this method refer to it as "flash and dash," the implication being that it's a shoddy way to do the job. They claim that putting foam outside the fiber insulation may result in a wrong-side vapor retarder in heating climates. Proponents say that it's an effective system because the foam will prevent air from infiltrating the wall, and vapor usually gets into walls because of air infiltration, not because of diffusion.

Foam and structural strength. There's both anecdotal and scientific evidence to suggest that SPF also adds strength and stiffness to wood-framed buildings. Builder Joseph Jackson, of Faust Contracting in Little Silver, N.J., recalls framing a house that moved slightly every time the wind blew. Once the walls were sprayed with 2-pound foam, Jackson reports, the structure felt absolutely rigid.

According to Craig DeWitt of RLC Engineering in Clemson, S.C., Clemson University has performed extensive testing to evaluate the structural value of foam. Racking tests showed that walls filled with sprayed-in-place foam were stiffer than walls filled with fiberglass batts. Tests also showed that spray foam significantly strengthened the bond between rafters and sheathing, which is a plus in high-wind areas. DeWitt cautions that building codes do not recognize sprayed foam as a structural component. But he says that engineers can include the strength of this bond in the structural calculations for engineered buildings.

David Frane*, formerly a senior editor of The Journal of Light Construction, is editor of Tools of the Trade.*

Resources

Spray Polyurethane Foam Alliance
www.sprayfoam.org

SprayFoam.Com
www.sprayfoam.com

Troubleshooting Spray-Foam Installation

by Mason Knowles

Most spray-foam insulation is installed correctly, but as an industry consultant I've inspected SPF (spray polyurethane foam) projects that have left me scratching my head in wonder. Sometimes the foam is cracked or delaminated, indicating an improper mix or poor substrate preparation; in other cases, there's too much overspray. Occasionally the foam is properly installed but applied in the wrong place or at the wrong thickness. Sometimes there is a vapor retarder when one isn't required, or a required one is missing (see "Density, R-Value, and Moisture Control").

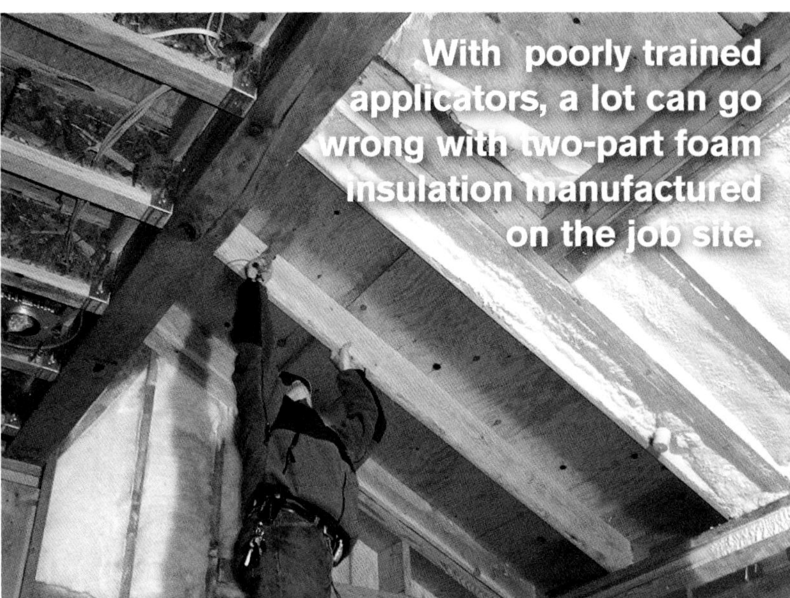

With poorly trained applicators, a lot can go wrong with two-part foam insulation manufactured on the job site.

A decade ago, most SPF problems could be traced back to equipment issues. But with the recent expansion of the spray-foam industry, I'm also seeing a growing number of application defects made by inexperienced or poorly trained installers. Faced with job competition, some installers may be trying to cut costs by taking shortcuts, or they may be trying to extend the window of application into risky climatic conditions in order to squeeze in more jobs.

Since a poor foam installation can sabotage a building envelope's performance, general contractors should know what can go wrong and learn how to

Density, R-Value, and Moisture Control

There are two main types of spray foam used for interior insulation: 1/2-pound open-cell SPF and 2-pound closed-cell SPF. Thanks to ASTM and industry-wide standards, different foams from different manufacturers within these two categories have roughly similar physical properties, such as R-value and the amount of closed- and open-cell content.

A few companies also offer 1.2-pound SPF, a kind of hybrid that shares some of the characteristics of both open-cell and closed-cell foam. But with no current industry standards or general code criteria for this type of foam available, installers will need to consult the manufacturers' literature, case studies, and ICC evaluation reports carefully to compare various products' physical properties and determine which is suitable for the application and meets local code requirements.

Stored in liquid form, SPF insulation consists of a petroleum-based "A" side (primarily methylene diphenyl diisocyanate) and a "B" side consisting of polyols, catalysts, fire retardants, blowing agents, and other chemicals.

Half-pound low-density open-cell SPF. Water is the blowing agent in low-density foam, which weighs between 0.4 and 0.6 pound per cubic foot of reacted material and expands to 100 to 150 times its liquid volume. This foam has an R-value range of 3.5 to 3.8 per inch and a vapor permeance of between 6 and 10 perms at a 3-inch application, which — according to current ICC building codes — qualifies it as a Class III vapor retarder.

Two-pound medium-density closed-cell SPF. Proprietary blends of HFC-245fa and water are the current blowing-agent packages used in medium-density foam, which weighs between 1.5 and 2 pounds per cubic foot of reacted material and expands to about 30 times its original volume. The foam has an R-value range of 5.8 to 6.8 per inch (depending on the blowing-agent formula) and a vapor permeance of less than 1 perm at 2 inches or more, qualifying it as a Class II vapor retarder. Unlike open-cell foam, 2-pound closed-cell foam is water-resistant and accepted by FEMA as a severe-flood-zone approved material.

Vapor retarder. Whether or not foam insulation requires an additional vapor retarder depends on the

continued on next page

continued from previous page

foam being used and its thickness, the climate, and local building codes. Closed-cell foam has a permeance averaging about 1.5 per inch, so as the average temperature goes down, more foam thickness is needed to keep the temperature inside the wall or ceiling cavity above the dewpoint and minimize the potential for condensation inside the assembly. The IRC allows a Class III interior vapor retarder — that is, latex or enamel paint — when at least R-15 of closed-cell foam is used in a 2x6 wall in Climate Zones 7 and 8. (For specific requirements for other climate zones, see 2009 IRC Table R601.3.1.)

With an open-cell content of over 80 percent, which allows liquid water to enter the foam, ½-pound SPF is considered a Class III vapor retarder. So, with a few exceptions, the IRC requires an additional Class II vapor retarder, such as the kraft-paper facing on batt insulation, on the warm-in-winter side of open-cell foam installed in Climate Zones 5, 6, 7, 8, and Marine 4. —M.K.

evaluate the quality of their installer's work.

Equipment

Good foam requires the correct combination of heat, pressure, and spray-gun configuration. Getting just one of these factors wrong can result in poor cell structure and dimensional instability, leading to such problems as shrinking and cracking, voids and fissures, and poor adhesion.

In addition, the liquid "A" and "B" components in SPF systems are designed to be mixed in a 1:1 ratio by volume (within 2 percent). Off-ratio "A"-rich foams tend to be hard, friable, and brittle, while "B"-rich foams tend to be soft and gummy and are more likely to have a high odor. Off-ratio foams can occur when the liquid components haven't been properly stored within the temperature range specified by their manufacturer — typically between 60°F and 80°F in a dry environment — or when the components are contaminated or out of date.

Faulty spray equipment can also lead to off-ratio foam. Sometimes, one of the two transfer pumps that send the "A" and "B" components to the proportioning pump fails, causing a crossover that can fill the spray gun and sometimes the whip hose with off-ratio or even reacted foam. If the proportioning pump fails

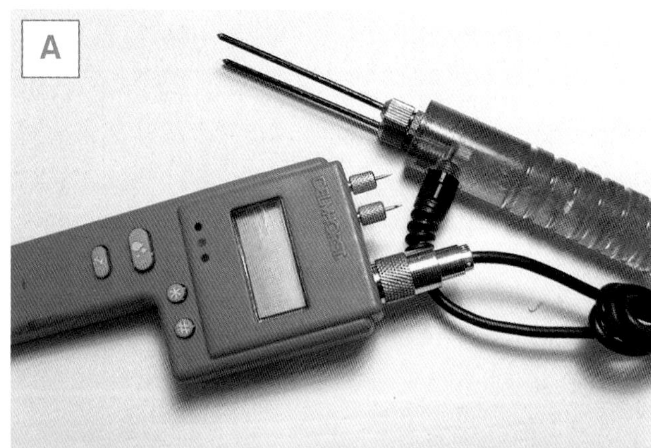

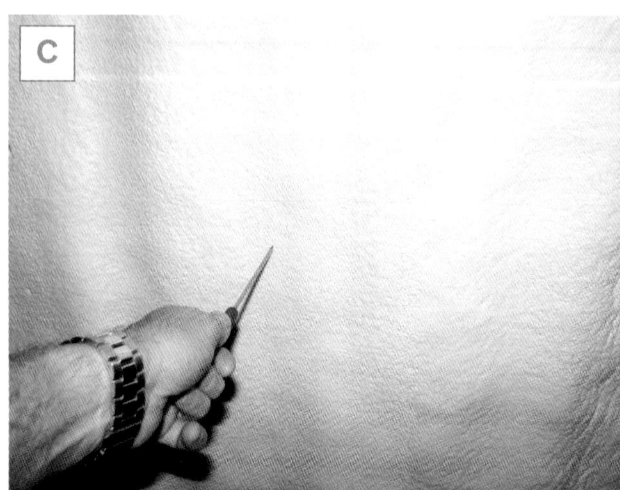

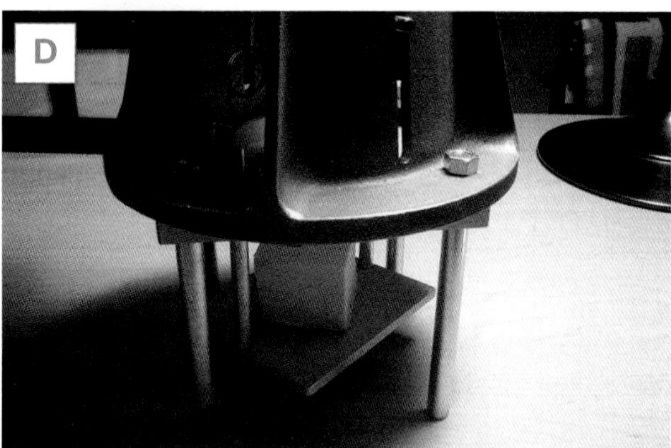

Figure 32. The author uses a Delmhorst moisture meter (A) to measure substrate moisture content; this one (model BD 2100) has separate settings for different materials, including wood and foam insulation, and can be fitted with 6-inch-long contact pins. To calculate dewpoint, he uses a portable Kestrel 3000 temperature and humidity gauge (B). After installation, a simple probe confirms that the foam insulation has been sprayed at the proper thickness (C). Com-Ten's compressive-strength tester (D) is useful if there are concerns about the quality and compressive yield strength of the foam.

to properly heat and pressurize the components to acceptable levels before pumping them in separate hoses to the spray gun, the foam may not get hot enough to react properly. And if the spray gun is dirty or the nozzle too large, the components won't mix well in the gun's mixing chamber when the installer pulls the trigger.

Substrate Preparation

SPF can be sprayed on wood, concrete, metal, asphalt, foam sheathing, and other substrates. But the substrate needs to be clean and dry — "paintable" is a reasonable benchmark — for the foam to adhere well. SPF shouldn't be installed when temperature and humidity levels fall outside the range recommended by the SPF manufacturer.

Moisture. When a surface is wet or damp, the moisture acts as a blowing agent that reacts with the "A" side of the SPF system, resulting in off-ratio foam with poor physical properties and poor adhesion. When foam is sprayed on wet framing or sheathing with greater than 19 percent moisture content, for example, there's a risk that the foam will have poor cell structure and won't bond well when the framing dries, leading to cracks between the foam and framing. For this reason, the spray-foam industry recommends that installers measure substrate moisture content with a moisture probe before applying foam — but many of them don't (Figure 32).

Safe moisture content is relatively easy to determine in wood, but trickier to do in masonry. Concrete may appear to be dry yet still hold quite a bit of moisture that will be brought to the surface during foam's exothermic reaction.

Currently, the SPF industry doesn't have any specific moisture-content recommendations for concrete, beyond allowing for a 28-day curing time if it's green. Some coating manufacturers consider moisture contents as high as 85 percent acceptable for paint, but I think this number is too high for foam. To be safe, tape an 18-inch by 18-inch sheet of clear plastic to the concrete, making sure it's sealed on all four sides. If condensation appears on the plastic or if the surface of the concrete darkens after 16 hours, the concrete is too wet for foam.

An experienced installer will often just spray a small section of concrete to see if the surface becomes damp and reacts with the rising foam. If it does, he'll wait until the concrete dries out before continuing to spray.

Temperature. While there is some variation among manufacturers, most SPF systems are designed to be installed when substrate temperatures are higher than 55°F. A few low-temperature foams can be used in colder conditions, but they're the exception. With most foams, spraying when temperatures dip below 55°F (or below the manufacturer's recommendation) can lead to the formation of a high-density shellac-like coating on the surface of the substrate that reduces the adhesive quality of the foam. In some cases, the foam can actually separate from the substrate, because of the difference in temperature between the two materials.

Humidity. When relative humidity levels are high, moisture can combine with the liquid components of rising foam and affect the foam's cell structure. To avoid problems like low density, low compressive strength, and too many open cells, foam shouldn't be sprayed when the ambient temperature is within 5°F of dewpoint. Since dewpoint is based on relative humidity and air temperature and can vary widely over the course of a day, these conditions should be measured and recorded a few times daily with a humidity and temperature gauge, such as a Kestrel 3000 (www.kestrelmeters.com).

Application

Once spraying begins, it's a good idea to check foam regularly for quality, thickness, and yield, particularly when temperatures are cool or the humidity high. Quality-control samples — taken periodically during the job by either the installer or the GC — can indicate problems with foam thickness, adhesion, and cell structure, and can help document that a foam installation meets specifications.

Lifts for closed-cell. To avoid problems, closed-cell foam should be installed in lifts less than 1½ inches thick, with breaks of about 10 to 15 minutes between lifts to allow exothermic heat to dissipate. A certain amount of exothermic heat is needed to properly cure SPF foam, but excessive heat can result in cracks and shrinkage. Unusually strong odors after foam application can be an indication of this problem.

A good rule of thumb is to size the spray gun's mixing chamber and nozzle so that passes overlap by more than 60 percent. This will allow the foam to grow at a uniform rate from one side to the other during a lift. When spraying studwall and ceiling cavities, for example, the installer should picture-frame the cavity, allow the foam to set a few minutes, and then fill in the middle, spraying parallel to the direction of the studs.

On a masonry wall, an experienced installer should be able to spray 2 or 3 inches of closed-cell foam in two or three lifts within a ¼-inch tolerance. In framing cavities, the variation is typically greater due to the thicker application against rafters or studs.

One shot for open-cell. Half-pound SPF is typically installed in a single lift, starting at the bottom of a studwall or ceiling cavity and working up. To prevent gaps and voids, hard-to-reach areas or spaces behind the studs are usually picture-framed first.

You can expect considerably more thickness variation with open-cell foam due to its greater expansion rate. A ½-inch tolerance when spraying 3½ to 5½ inches of foam would be considered exceptional, while a more

Spray Foam Problems

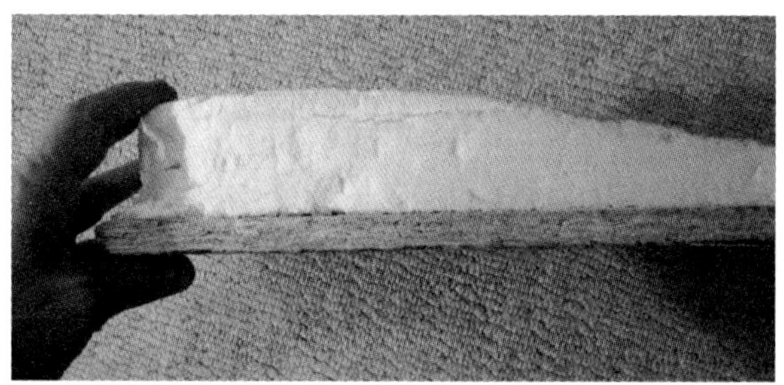

Excessive moisture in the substrate can act as a blowing agent. Here, 2-pound SPF was sprayed on sheathing that was wet on the left side and dry on the right side. The foam on the wet side has increased in volume, compromising cell structure and substrate adhesion.

The large void and delaminated area on this core sample indicate that the low-density foam was sprayed on a substrate that was too cold.

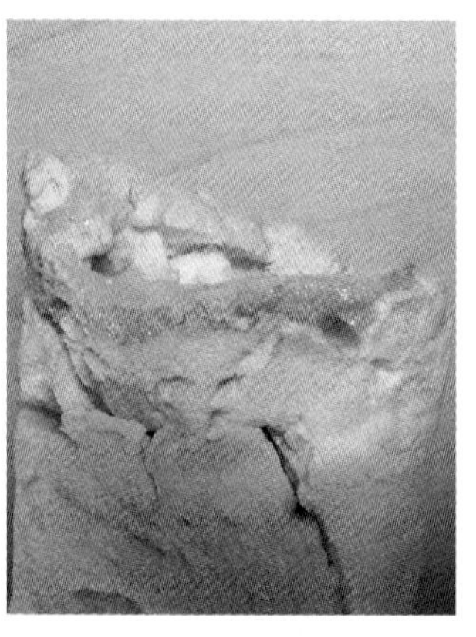

In this example of off-ratio foam, the darkened layer at the top has very high compressive strength, an indication of an "A"-rich foam caused by a cold "B"-side component. Equipment malfunctions can also lead to off-ratio foam.

Excessive exothermic heat can actually scorch foam, as shown here, and in extreme cases cause it to catch on fire.

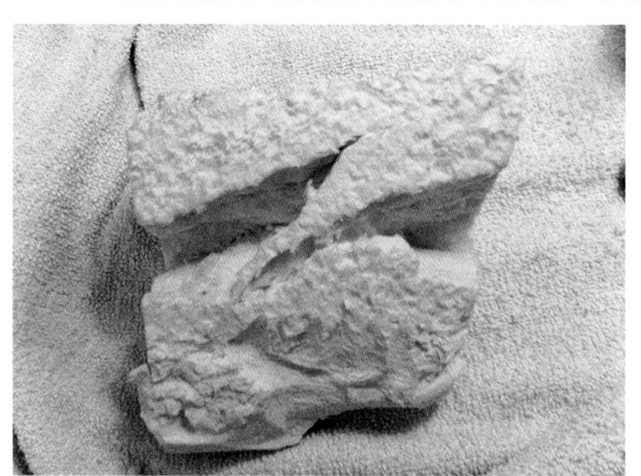

High exothermic heat can also cause blowholes and discoloration in closed-cell foam.

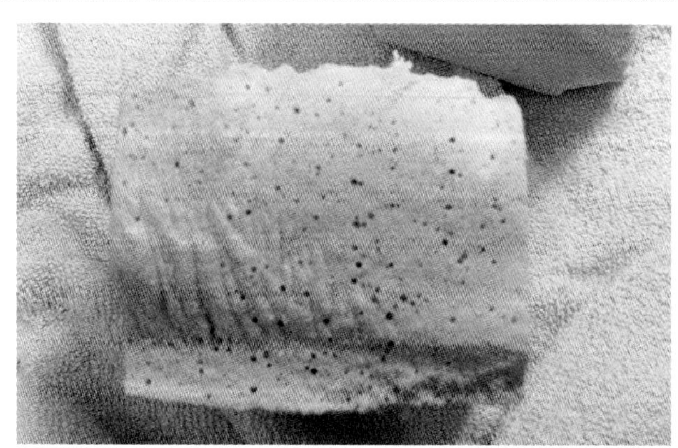

Cracks, fissures, and voids in closed-cell foam indicate either a poor mix or excessive lift thickness.

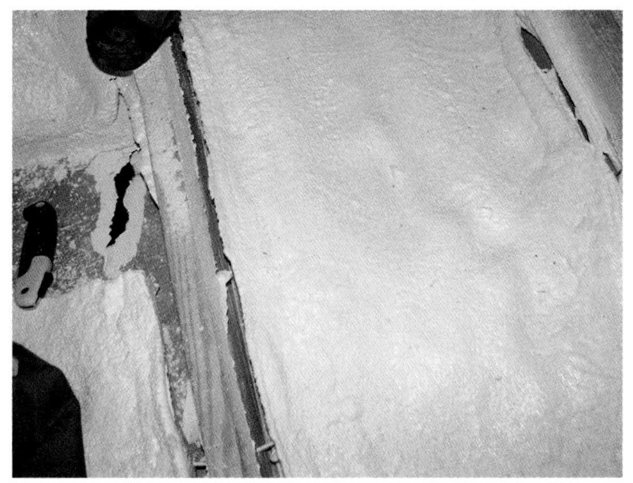

Closed-cell foam was sprayed too thickly into this stud bay and has shrunk away from the framing as a result of exothermic heat build-up. The foam should be removed and replaced.

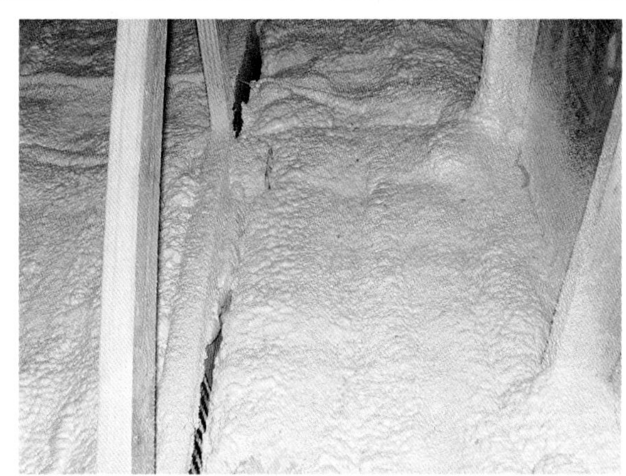

This foam has pulled away from the truss chord due to excessive exothermic heat. Closed-cell foam should be installed in lifts that measure less than 2 inches thick, and with enough time between lifts to allow exothermic heat to dissipate.

typical ½-pound foam installation would have a ¾-inch to 1-inch tolerance between studwall cavities. As a result, trimming is usually necessary after the foam has been sprayed (Figure 33).

Job-site protection. SPF insulation can drift a few hundred yards on a windy day if the doors and windows have been left open, and it sticks tenaciously to any surface it lands on. Therefore, every job should have a comprehensive overspray plan that includes careful masking and the removal of any items in the

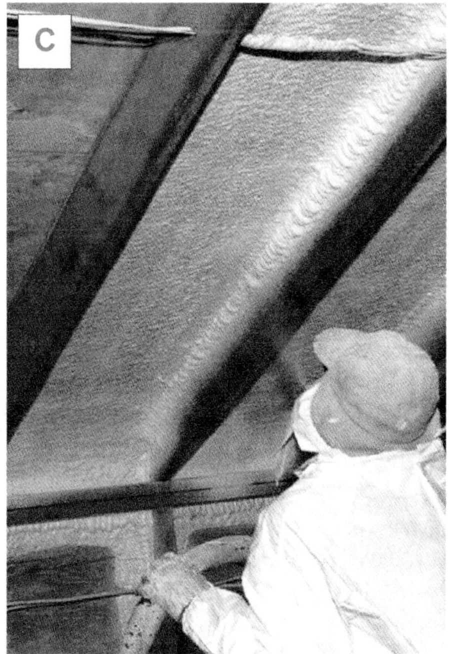

Figure 33. Open-cell foam can be installed in a single pass (A), but because of its high expansion rate it must typically be trimmed after installation, which produces considerable waste (B). Trimming usually isn't necessary with closed-cell foam, but to avoid excessive exothermic heat, it should be installed in lifts no more than 1½ inches thick (C).

immediate vicinity that might be damaged by overspray. And since the fumes and mist produced by an installation can be harmful, SPF contractors are responsible (per OSHA regs) for a written respirator plan for employees and for a safety plan that protects all nearby occupied areas and prevents nonworkers from entering the work area during spraying. (GCs are responsible for a safety plan as well.)

Fumes and mist usually dissipate within a few hours to a few days, depending on the amount of ventilation available. Since off-spec foam can create odors that linger much longer, any odors that last longer than a week may indicate a problem with the foam and should be investigated.

What to Look For

Ideally, every completed SPF installation should be inspected by a manufacturer's representative, an owner's representative, or a third-party inspection company. (For a list of inspectors accredited by the Spray Polyurethane Foam Alliance, go to www.sprayfoam.org.) With the cost of a third-party inspection on most residential projects ranging from $1,000 to $2,500, the most realistic option for a GC with an already stretched insulation budget is to request an inspection by the SPF manufacturer's or supplier's rep — especially if there are any concerns about the quality of the insulation sub's work.

When I inspect an SPF installation, my inspection report includes the name of the material supplier, the type and product number of the foam, the lot number, the specified thickness, photos, and a sketch of the sprayed areas. I measure and record foam depths at a minimum of 15 locations to verify that the contractor met thickness requirements and to evaluate his ability to uniformly install the foam. I also examine the foam quality and look for problems like poor adhesion; density irregularities; and voids, cracks, or gaps in the foam.

Cell structure and quality. Foam should have a consistent cell structure without significant color changes, cell deformation, or other anomalies. Dark or scorched areas in the middle of the foam indicate high exothermic heat, which can result in cracks and shrinkage.

Density. I've inspected enough foam to be able to tell whether it's approximately the right density simply by pressing it with my thumb. But when I'm in doubt, I take a sample and test it. For 2-pound foam, the density should be between 15 and 25 psi; for ½-pound foam it should be between 2 and 5 psi. Anything softer or harder is an indication of an off-ratio or poor mix.

Adhesion. Adhesion problems on closed-cell foam can usually be found by randomly pounding the foam. Delaminated foam will have a hollow sound and compress slightly.

When I find a suspicious area, I use a coring tool, a saw, or a knife to take a sample. If the sample is hard to remove and leaves little bits of foam on the substrate (the industry term is cohesive foam failure), there is no adhesion problem. Another acceptable result is when the sample comes away from the substrate with some force but is clean; this is called a mechanical bond. But if the sample is easily removed from the substrate, I know that the adhesion is poor and the affected area must be removed, since poorly adhered foam can lead to blisters, delamination, and shrinkage of the foam — all of which will affect the foam's insulating, air-sealing, and condensation-control qualities.

Repairs

Usually, cracking and other problems in a foam installation affect only small areas, and repairs can be made without a total tearout of the existing insulation. Unless the whole application is off-ratio, most repairs require the removal of 5 to 15 percent of the existing foam.

After the off-spec foam has been identified, it should be cut back at a 45-degree angle to where it exhibits good adhesion and good physical properties. After the substrate has been cleaned and — if necessary — reprimed, the area can be resprayed.

Mason Knowles, *formerly executive director of the Spray Polyurethane Foam Alliance, an industry trade group, is a building envelope and roofing consultant in Savannah, Ga.*

Chapter 4

FOUNDATIONS

Frost-Protected Shallow Foundations

by Bill Eich

Most building techniques that improve quality or save energy also increase construction costs. But the frost-protected shallow foundation (FPSF) is an exception: If you build in an area where frost heaves can cause trouble, frost-protected shallow foundations enable you to build a higher-quality, more energy-efficient building for less money than the traditional deep footing. Now that the technique is being accepted by the major model codes, it's time for builders to take a good look at FPSFs.

Frost-protected shallow foundations save energy while reducing building costs. Since heat loss is greater at building corners, the horizontal "wing insulation" is wider there.

How an FPSF Works

The frost-protected foundation concept is so simple it's surprising that it hasn't caught on sooner in the United States. Rather than install our footings below the frostline (which is 48 inches deep in much of the northern U.S.), we insulate the ground around the perimeter of our homes with enough foam insulation to permanently raise the frostline. We make the footings think they are in Florida, where they only have to be 16 inches deep.

The technique's success is based on a fundamental principle of physics: In conductive heat transfer, heat travels from warm to cold, and it will always follow the path of least resistance (Figure 1). The earth generates its own heat. In a deep frost footing, the soil around the foundation (along with snow cover) stores the heat and slows its movement from within the earth, keeping the deep subsoil warmer than freezing year-round. In an FPSF, well-placed foam insulation provides resistance that directs the heat flow under the shallow footings, where the soil, with its high heat-storage capacity, stays above the freezing point year-round.

A long history. FPSFs are different, but not new: They were first shown in the U.S. in Frank Lloyd Wright's Usonian house in 1936. In the mid-1950s, the Swedes and Norwegians began using the system extensively. Today, there are more than a million structures built in Scandinavia on shallow foundations.

Some U.S. builders have also demonstrated the value of the concept. My own company, for instance, has been building FPSFs with good success for many years in Iowa, where the frostline is 4 feet deep.

Code approval. FPSFs are finally gaining acceptance here in America. Provisions for FPSFs are included in the 2000 and 2003 IRC (Section 403.3) for buildings that will be heated to at least 64°F year round. In addition, the 2003 IRC and 2003 IBC reference the American Society of Civil Engineers Standard ASCE 32-01, "Design and Construction of Frost-Protected Shallow Foundations," which also covers semi-heated and unheated buildings. So these may be permitted under the IRC/IBC as well.

However, as with all construction methods, use of FPSFs is still governed by local building codes. For example, in areas with heavy termite infestation, codes may restrict the use of foam insulation on the exterior of the foundation or may require special termite-resistant insulation.

Resource available. Before you actually build one, you should study the *Revised Builder's Guide to Frost-Protected Shallow Foundations,* which you can download for free at www.toolbase.org (click on "Foundations" under "Design and Construction Guides"). The book contains important details that I won't cover here. But I will give you a general idea of how FPSFs are built, show some of the options they give you, and explain how they improve energy efficiency and reduce costs.

A. Uninsulated Foundation

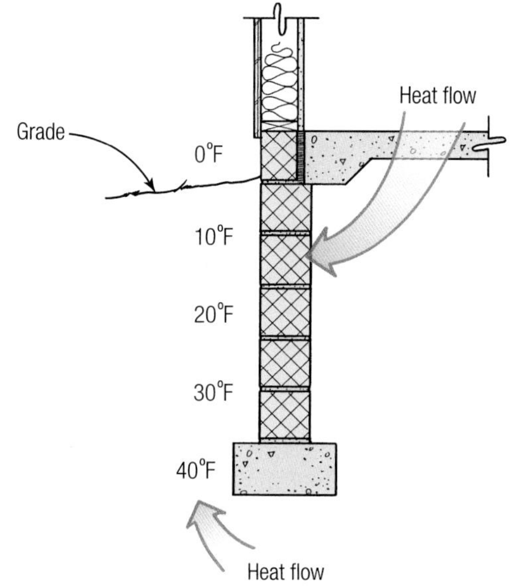

B. Interior Insulation

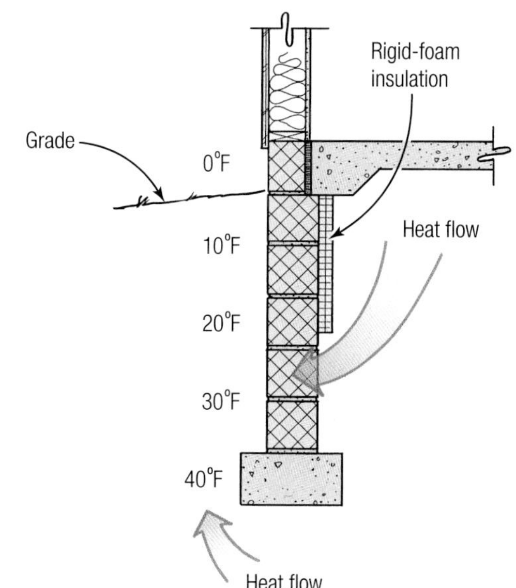

C. FPS Foundation (Heated)

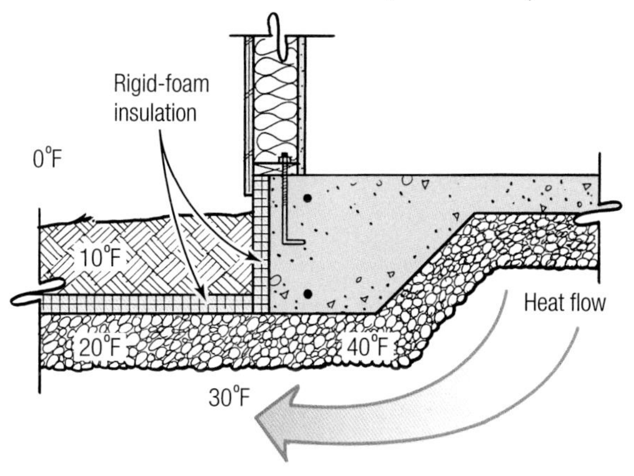

D. FPS Foundation (Unheated)

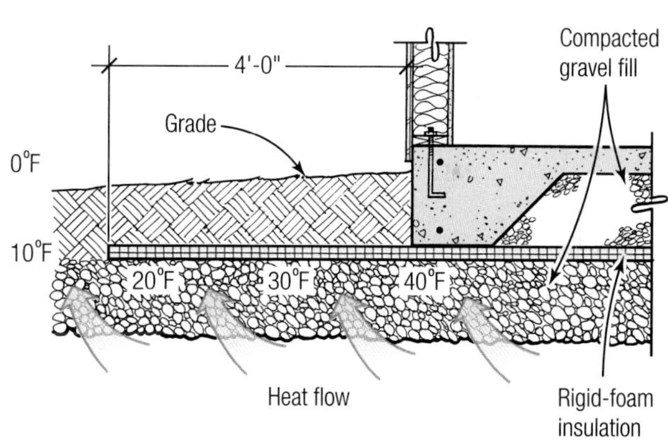

Figure 1. In an uninsulated foundation (A), the footing is warmed by the earth's heat, as well as by heat from inside the building. The deep soil above the footing provides the insulation and heat-storage capacity to keep the soil near the footing from freezing. With interior insulation (B), the footings still have to be below the frostline. But in a frost-protected foundation (C), foam insulation rather than soil depth keeps the soil at the footing from freezing. For unheated slabs-on-grade (D), the foam is placed under the entire slab to retain ground heat. The insulation must extend horizontally 4 feet beyond the footing.

Placing the Insulation

The placement of the insulation and the construction of the footing will vary depending on the situation. Heated buildings are insulated around the perimeter to direct interior building heat to a point below the footing. For unheated buildings, there is no interior heat to save; instead, the insulation is placed under the slab and footing to salvage ground heat. Walk-out basements and other special situations call for their own particular details. Let's take a look at some of the options.

Heated structures. For a heated building in our climate, the design guide calls for a 2-inch layer of foam placed vertically on the footing perimeter, and another 2-inch layer of foam placed as "wing insulation," extending horizontally 16 inches out from the footing's base (see photo, opposite page).

At the outside corners, where the floor area is exposed on two sides, the heat loss is greater. So more wing insulation is required there — in my climate, corners need 32 inches of wing insulation rather than 16 inches.

We sometimes use permanent wood foundations

instead of poured concrete. The cost is about the same, but in the winter, when poured concrete might freeze, it can be easier to place a wood foundation and put the shell up, then come back and pour the slab later. With the wood foundation, the foam is placed in the same position as with a shallow poured footing, but it's nailed to the wood (Figure 2).

Most of our buildings are framed with 2x6 walls. Typically, we offset the foundation by 2 inches all around, so the foundation insulation flushes out with the wall framing above. If that causes too much of a problem, we just taper the top edge of the foam, so water will drain off it.

Good drainage. Although the insulation can be relied on to prevent any water under the foundation from freezing, good drainage details provide further assurance — a belt-and-suspenders approach. All our buildings also have gutters and downspouts to direct roof runoff away from the building perimeter. And, as with any foundation, the finished grade should slope away from the building. On particularly wet sites or in areas with expansive soils, we also place drain tile around the perimeter of the house or leading from a subslab gravel bed to daylight, as appropriate.

Unheated Structures

Shallow foundations also work for unheated structures, like garages and sunrooms. The space inside these structures usually doesn't get quite as cold as the outdoors, but there isn't any source of heat inside that you're trying to save. So the purpose of the foam insulation is to salvage the heat from the ground below and also to salvage heat flowing from below the attached house. To achieve that, we put 2 or 3 inches of foam insulation under the entire garage floor, extending out 48 inches beyond the outside perimeter.

The *Builder's Guide* tells you how thick the insulation should be for your climate. The guide calls for a minimum 6-inch layer of compacted gravel as a base layer below the foam and allows for the insulation layer to be reduced for thicker layers of gravel. In general, the more compacted gravel you have below the foam, the less thick the insulation has to be, because the compacted gravel drains well and is not susceptible to heaving when it freezes. With 6 to 12 inches of gravel, we need only 2 inches of insulation in our area.

Most of the garage foundations my company builds rest on at least a foot of fill gravel. For an FPSF, we use the gravel to our advantage. When we place and level our fill, we bring it up to within about 14 inches of the point where the top of the finish slab will be. Then we place the 2-inch foam on top of the gravel and form the perimeter of our garage slab with 2x10s, driving our stakes right through the insulation (Figure 3). We fill the inside with 5 inches of compacted gravel. Then we spade out a thickened edge around the perimeter by hand, put two pieces of reinforcing steel in the trench, and pour a monolithic slab footing.

In this design, the footing and slab are bearing on top of the foam. Some builders worry that the foundation concrete may crush the foam. But it turns out that this is not a problem. For residential footings, the soil that the footing bears on is typically required to have a compressive strength of 2,000 lb./sq.ft. The foam that we use for frost-protected slabs has a density of 2 pounds per cubic foot and a compressive strength of around 3,500 lb./sq. ft., so it actually can bear more weight than the soil it rests on. If that margin of safety is not enough for you, there are foams available with even higher compressive strengths.

The IRC allows for either expanded polystyrene (EPS) or extruded polystyrene (XPS) foam in shallow foundations. The foam board must be in compliance with

Figure 2. Wooden concrete forms (top) are lined with foam insulation. After the monolithic slab and footing are poured, the forms will be stripped and horizontal "wing insulation" placed around the outside perimeter. In a permanent wood foundation (above) the foam board is nailed against it and wing insulation will be added later. The wood foundations let the author work in winter: He pours the slab after the shell is closed in.

ASTM Standard C578 and have adequate R-value and compressive strength for the specific application (Table 1). Be careful to get the right foam. Most expanded foam stocked by lumberyards is only ¾-lb. or 1-lb. density and lacks sufficient compressive strength.

Where FPSFs Shine

Frost-protected shallow foundations have particular advantages in a number of special situations:

Complex plans with angles are much easier to do with the FPSFs. Try to get a backhoe operator to dig an octagonal foundation and you'll see what I mean. With a shallow foundation on grade, you just scrape off a flat area, and you're ready to go.

Room additions on narrow lots are also much easier. Often you can hand-dig a shallow foundation, avoiding all the disruption of bringing heavy equipment on site.

Foundations over uneven, sloping terrain are easier. Houses with crawlspaces on sloping lots can be done "half and half": The footing on the uphill side is backfilled with enough earth to keep it from freezing, but on

Figure 3. Slabs and footings for unheated buildings, such as the attached garage shown here, are placed directly on top of the foam insulation, with a foot of gravel under the foam. Stakes for the footing forms are driven through the foam (above). A trench is hand-dug inside the perimeter to form the slab's thickened edge (right).

Table 1. Design Values for FPSF Insulation Materials[1]

Type of Polystyrene Foam	Type of Insulation	Minimum Density (pcf)	Nominal R-value (per inch)	Max. Effective R-value (per inch)		Allowable Bearing Capacity[2] (psf)	Minimum Thickness (inches)	
				Vertical	Horizontal		Vertical	Horizontal
Expanded (EPS)	II	1.35	4.0	3.2[3]	2.6[3]	-	2.0	3.0
Expanded (EPS)	IX	1.8	4.2	3.4[3]	2.8[3]	1,200	1.5	2.0
Extruded (XPS)	IV	1.6	5.0	4.5	4.0	1,200	1.0	1.5
Extruded (XPS)	V	3.0	5.0	4.5	4.0	4,800	1.0	1.0
Extruded (XPS)	VI	1.8	5.0	4.5	4.0	1,920	1.0	1.0
Extruded (XPS)	VII	2.2	5.0	4.5	4.0	2,880	1.0	1.0
Extruded (XPS)	X	1.35	5.0	4.5	4.0	-	1.5	2.0

1 Per ASTM C578, except for effective R-values (shaded column).
2 Bearing capacity developed for non-cyclic loading conditions at 10% deformation.
3 SEI/ASCE 32-01 adopted values and restrictions are referenced. Reprinted with permission, American Society of Civil Engineers, *Design and Constructicn of Frost-Protected Shallow Foundations*, 2001.

Reprinted with permission from the *Revised Builder's Guide to Frost-Protected Shallow Foundations*, by NAHB Research Foundation (2004).

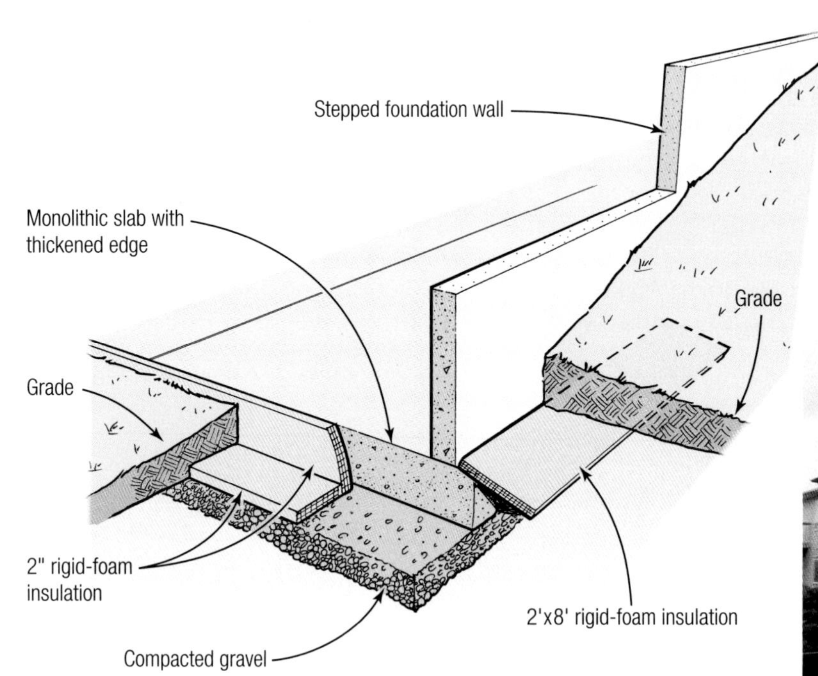

Figure 4. FPSFs simplify the construction of walk-out basements, like the one at left (and in the photo below), built by the author. He protects walk-out basement foundations with foam to avoid having to step down the excavation. A 2x8-foot length of foam board protects the footing of the main wall at the corner where the backfill is shallow.

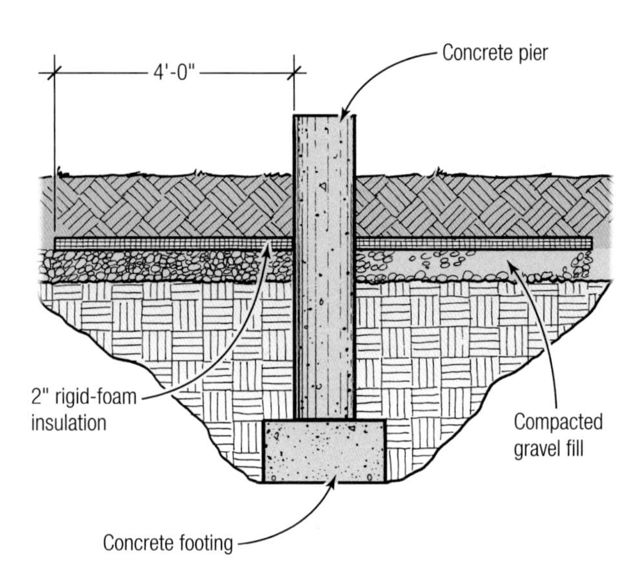

Figure 5. To prevent frost heaving of pier foundations, the author places 2-inch foam horizontally around the piers about a foot below grade.

the downhill side you can use insulation to keep the footing from freezing rather than stepping down the footing.

Walk-out basements are simpler. Where one wall of a basement is a walk-out, we don't have to excavate, form, and pour the traditional step-down footing. Instead, we use a frost-protected footing for that wall, usually with a monolithic slab (Figure 4).

Near the corners, the backfill above the footings of the full basement walls may not be deep enough to prevent freezing. So we place wing insulation above the footing as needed. In most cases, we just lay one 2x8-foot piece of 2-inch foam over the footing at the corner, then backfill.

You can winterize existing buildings that don't have a deep foundation. In one case we did this for a restaurant that had an unheated porch on two sides. Instead of putting a deep foundation under the porches, we insulated the perimeter of the porch foundations, and saved the customer almost $3,000. He turned around and spent that savings with us to extend his project beyond the original proposal.

Post-and-pier foundations for decks and porches can be frostproofed, too. In some soils, even a 48-inch-deep post footing will sometimes be heaved up by frost because of adfreezing: Tough clay soil will freeze to the surface of the foundation and lift the post. Although there is no provision for this situation in the design guide, we've found from experience that a 4-foot strip of foam around that post footing can keep the ground below from freezing and solve the problem (Figure 5).

Advantages of Shallow Foundations

Using the shallow foundation approach cuts my company's costs in many ways. We don't just save on the cost of concrete, we also spend less on excavation and backfill — there is just less fill to store on site or haul away.

Job-site convenience is also a factor. We don't have to work around the overdig from the foundations, or worry about storing the fill, hauling it off, and putting it back in — and there's no concern about trench safety. All of this means scheduling is also easier with shallow foundations: The whole job moves faster when you take a few steps out of the process.

Shallow foundations allow us to extend our concreting

season into December. We use the foam insulation to protect the ground prior to digging, and the foundation foam protects the footing before and after the pour.

We've also found that buildings on frost-protected shallow foundations provide better customer satisfaction. One big benefit is warm floors, even in homes with forced-air heating systems ducted through the attic and slab-on-grade construction.

With FPSFs, we can offer better value in the home: Because of the money saved on foundation and site work, the customer will be able to spend more on amenities like whirlpools or skylights. And compared with a crawlspace, slab-on-grade construction reduces sound transmission, resulting in a quieter home.

Another big advantage is energy savings. An insulated perimeter foundation significantly reduces heating bills. If you're considering radiant floor heat, the added insulation in an FPSF makes that option more cost-effective.

Bill Eich *is a builder and remodeler specializing in energy-efficient homes in Spirit Lake, Iowa.*

Super-Insulated Slab Foundations

by Alan Gibson

Twenty years ago, I built my first frost-protected shallow foundation here in Maine. It cost me less than $500 to install and has performed flawlessly ever since; I still live on it today. Admittedly, this type of foundation is eyed somewhat warily by those unfamiliar with its design principles. But, in fact, as foundations go, it's quick and cost-effective and provides an excellent base for the super-insulated homes we build.

Compared with a full foundation, a frost-protected slab can reduce construction costs in my market by about $20,000 for a house with 850 square feet on the first floor. Part of that economy comes from the fact that the base prep and formwork for a shallow foundation can be done by a crew of carpenters instead of a foundation contractor. That's one less sub to manage and pay. Other savings come from reductions in the amount of excavation and concrete needed. Also, there's no first-floor deck to frame.

A thick layer of foam on a bed of compacted gravel supports the building, prevents frost damage, and keeps the heat inside.

The Shallow Concept

A frost-protected shallow foundation (FPSF) relies on rigid foam insulation to protect the foundation from frost. (One-inch-thick extruded polystyrene foam — XPS — has an R-value of 4.5 and an insulating effect equal to 4 feet of soil.) On a typical FPSF, a layer of rigid insulation is placed vertically around the edge of the slab and extended horizontally for a given distance, depending on the severity of the climate. This "wing" insulation traps the heat of the earth under the foundation, ensuring that the soil there doesn't freeze.

Although FPSFs can be configured as crawlspace foundations, I've always favored the slab-on-grade approach, both for the economy of using the slab as the finish floor and for the thermal mass it provides in a passive solar design. Of course, this limits me to relatively flat sites. I've built FPSFs on slopes with a 3-foot change in elevation from one corner of the slab to another, but if the site is much steeper than that, the cost of elevating the low side with gravel fill becomes an issue. At that point, a frost wall or full basement probably makes better sense.

(Also keep in mind that not every locality approves FPSFs; regions with high termite infestations are less likely to allow buried foam. Check with your local building department for applicability.)

There's probably no single best way to design and detail an FPSF. A lot of information is available on the Web to guide the installation of these foundations. The NAHB document "Revised Builder's Guide to Frost Protected Shallow Foundations" is very useful (available free at www.toolbase.org). This document divides FPSFs into two categories, those for heated buildings

Sub-Slab Insulation: How Much Is Enough?

The question of how much R-value to place under a slab is not as simple as it may seem. Because concrete is a good thermal conductor, it makes sense to insulate beneath a slab to the same degree that you would insulate a wall or ceiling. But the difference between ground temperature and air temperature makes a big difference in how much heat is lost by conduction through a slab versus an exterior wall.

At a certain depth, the ground remains at a constant temperature. This varies by region; here in coastal Maine, it's about 50°F year round. Air temperature, however, can fluctuate greatly between the seasons. When determining above-grade insulation levels, the coldest winter temperature is the operational factor. Here, that temperature is around 0°F, while the sub-slab temperature will still be around 50°F. Thus, it takes less insulation to keep the slab's thermal resistance at the same level as a wall or roof assembly's.

So what is an appropriate quantity of insulation to install below a slab? We asked environmental building consultant Marc Rosenbaum, P.E., to do a heat loss analysis for an 8-inch layer of EPS foam board (R-4.5 per inch) beneath the slab and 4 inches of foam installed vertically on the foundation's edge. Rosenbaum used a software program called THERM to model our specific site conditions. (The software was developed by Lawrence Berkeley National Laboratory and is available free online at www. windows.lbl.gov/software/therm/therm.html).

Rosenbaum set up a case with a constant deep ground temperature of 50°F occurring 10 feet below the slab insulation. Soil conductivities can vary widely; he picked a soil conductivity that implied some dampness in the soil, making it relatively conductive. He set the outdoor temperature at 0°F and the indoor temperature at 70°F. The model allowed him to look at the entire slab surface and have THERM calculate its effective R-value.

In this case, the model indicated an equivalent above-grade insulation value of R-78. (Rosenbaum notes that values vary throughout the year because soil has lots of mass and its heat flow doesn't change as fast as the air temperature.) The outcome is analogous to saying that when it's 0°F outdoors, the slab will lose heat as if it were an above-grade surface insulated to R-78 — about twice the claimed R-value for the foam itself.

and those for unheated buildings, with different details for each.

Heated buildings. The theory behind FPSF design for heated buildings is that the indoor heat will move through the slab to the ground below and prevent it from freezing. In mild climates, only the slab's vertical edge has to be insulated. In colder regions, wing insulation of a given thickness and width is specified according to the specific regional air freezing index (AFI). You can find AFI data for 3,110 cities in the U.S. and Puerto Rico at the National Climatic Data Center (www.ncdc.noaa.gov). And IRC Table R403.3(2) categorizes the index for all 50 states by county.

Unheated buildings. Though garages, barns, and other outbuildings may not be heated, they can still be built on FPSFs. At a certain depth, which varies by geographic locale, the ground temperature remains at a constant temperature well above the freezing point all year round. By insulating the surface of the ground beneath the foundation, sufficient heat can be trapped to prevent freezing. That's the principle behind FPSF design for unheated buildings. Insulation is placed beneath the entire slab and out beyond its edges, again to a distance determined according to the regional AFI. Vertical perimeter insulation is unnecessary. In all but the most severe climates, 2- or 3-inch-thick sub-slab foam is all it takes to protect the foundation.

Super-insulated slabs. In coastal Maine, we have an AFI of less than 2,250. Here, according to the NAHB design guide, a slab foundation for a heated building requires neither horizontal rigid insulation underneath nor insulation extending beyond the slab's perimeter. But losing heat to the ground below is not consistent with the super-insulated approach our company uses. So even though the homes we build are heated, our shallow foundation design resembles that used for unheated buildings, except with much greater insulation levels. When insulating a slab, we aim for R-values as high as 30 or even greater (see "Sub-Slab Insulation: How Much Is Enough?," at left).

Which Foam Is Best?

Unlike a conventional foundation that bears directly on the ground, an FPSF foundation bears on a platform of foam. Our structural engineer specifies the appropriate foam density to support the weight of the building. Typically, for a two-story wood-framed house or barn, we've used foam with a density of 2.4 pounds per cubic foot and a compressive strength of 15 psi.

Depending on the energy goals of the project, we've placed between 2 inches and 6 inches of XPS or expanded polystyrene (EPS) under slabs, giving us sub-slab insulation values between R-10 and R-30. XPS is generally rated at R-5 per inch and EPS at R-4.5. The traditional view has been that XPS is best for burial because it absorbs less moisture over time. However, a more recent 15-year study indicates that EPS may actually absorb less water and retain a higher R-value over time than XPS.

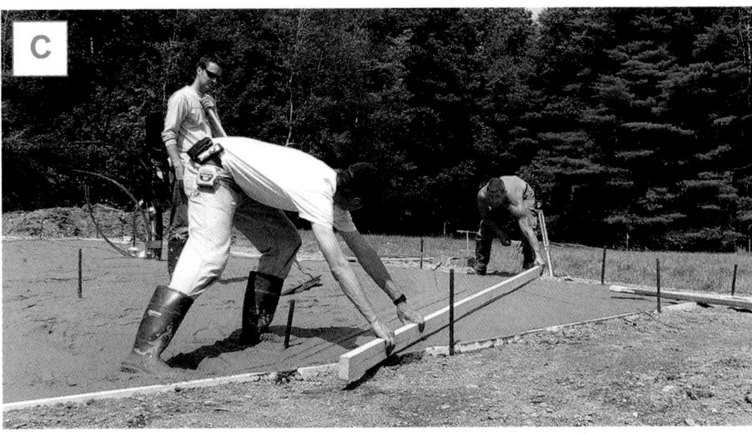

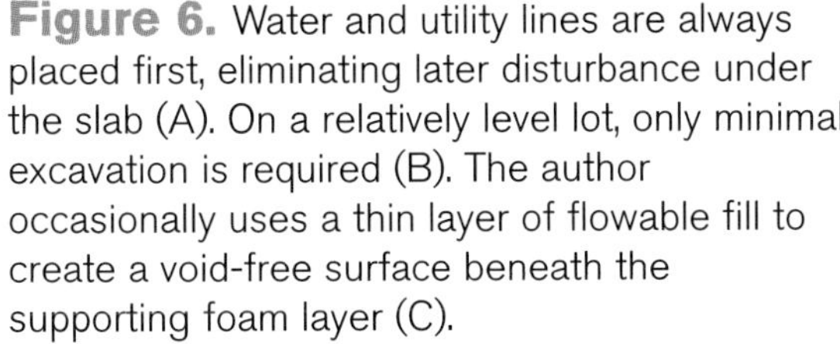

Figure 6. Water and utility lines are always placed first, eliminating later disturbance under the slab (A). On a relatively level lot, only minimal excavation is required (B). The author occasionally uses a thin layer of flowable fill to create a void-free surface beneath the supporting foam layer (C).

One important difference between the two types is that EPS is more environmentally friendly. Both foams are produced with blowing agents, but EPS is expanded using a relatively benign hydrocarbon such as pentane or butane, while XPS production uses HCFCs, which have implications for ozone depletion and global warming.

Available material thickness is another consideration. Although some sources imply that it's okay to place multiple layers of sub-slab foam, our structural engineer advises us to use a single layer to avoid the chance of sideways slippage between sheets or of voids occurring between them that could cause eventual settling. We can readily get 6-inch-thick EPS but have had no luck finding XPS in sheets thicker than 2 inches. For these reasons, we typically use 4-foot-by-16-foot sheets of 6-inch-thick Geofoam EPS (www.branchriver.com), which has a nominal R-value of 4.6 per inch, or R-27.6 overall. These sheets can be easily handled by two workers.

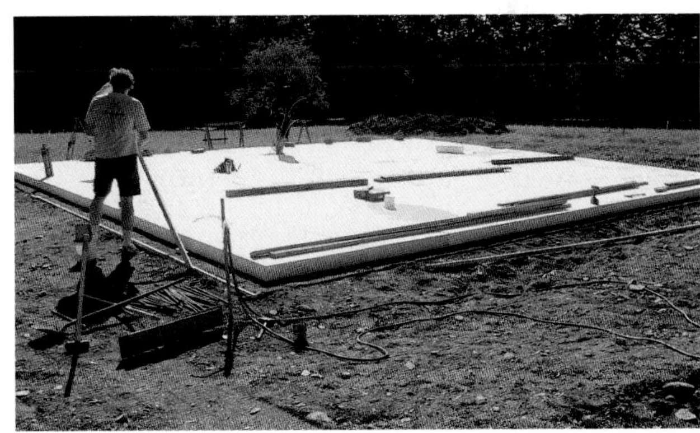

Figure 7. An insulating layer of rigid foam forms a structural base for a monolithic slab foundation. The foam covers the foundation's entire footprint, extending beyond it by about 24 inches on all sides.

Site Prep

We start by removing the topsoil from the building site and bringing in water, electric, and sewer lines as needed (Figure 6). Around these, we place good-quality bank-run gravel, compacted in 6-inch lifts, to a minimum depth of 12 inches. The gravel layer extends on all sides beyond the footprint of the building by at least 2 feet. To prevent voids underneath the foam, which might cause it to deflect, we take extra care to level the compacted gravel. Alternatively, we've used a 1½-inch layer of flowable fill — a thin, aerated concrete mix with sand aggregate — to true the surface. We form the area with leveled 2x3s, then screed the fill flat. This is a less forgiving method than moving gravel around, but

Super-Insulated Slab Foundation Details

Monolithic Slab

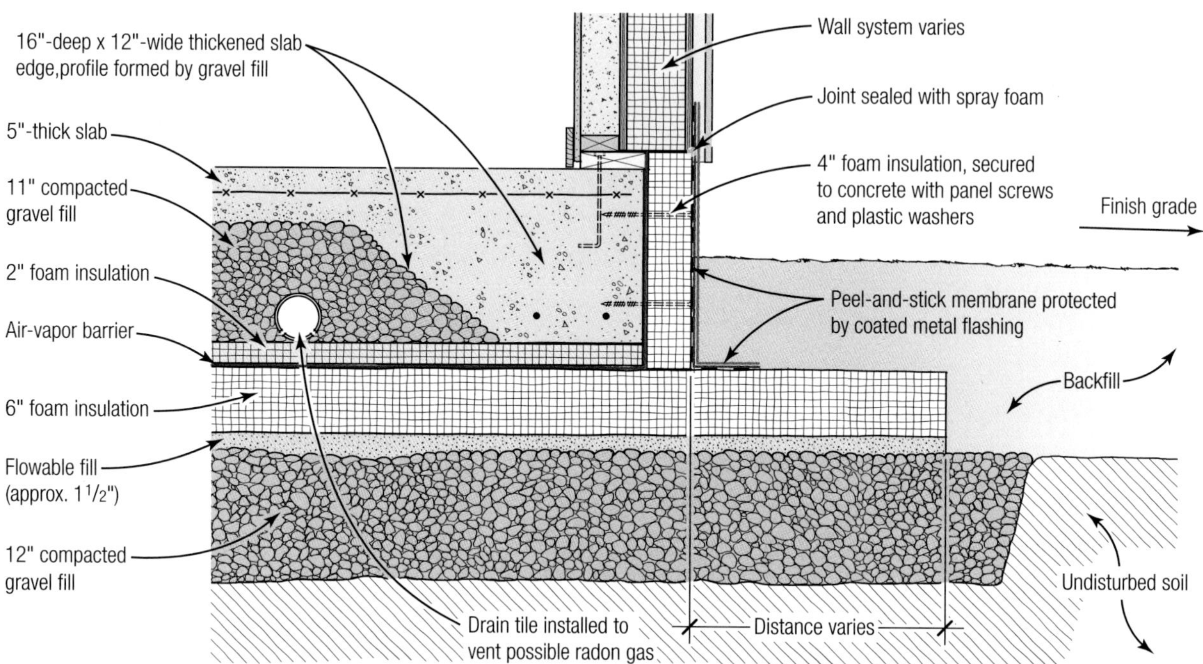
16"-deep x 12"-wide thickened slab edge,profile formed by gravel fill
5"-thick slab
11" compacted gravel fill
2" foam insulation
Air-vapor barrier
6" foam insulation
Flowable fill (approx. 1 1/2")
12" compacted gravel fill
Drain tile installed to vent possible radon gas
Distance varies
Wall system varies
Joint sealed with spray foam
4" foam insulation, secured to concrete with panel screws and plastic washers
Finish grade
Peel-and-stick membrane protected by coated metal flashing
Backfill
Undisturbed soil

Perimeter Grade Beam

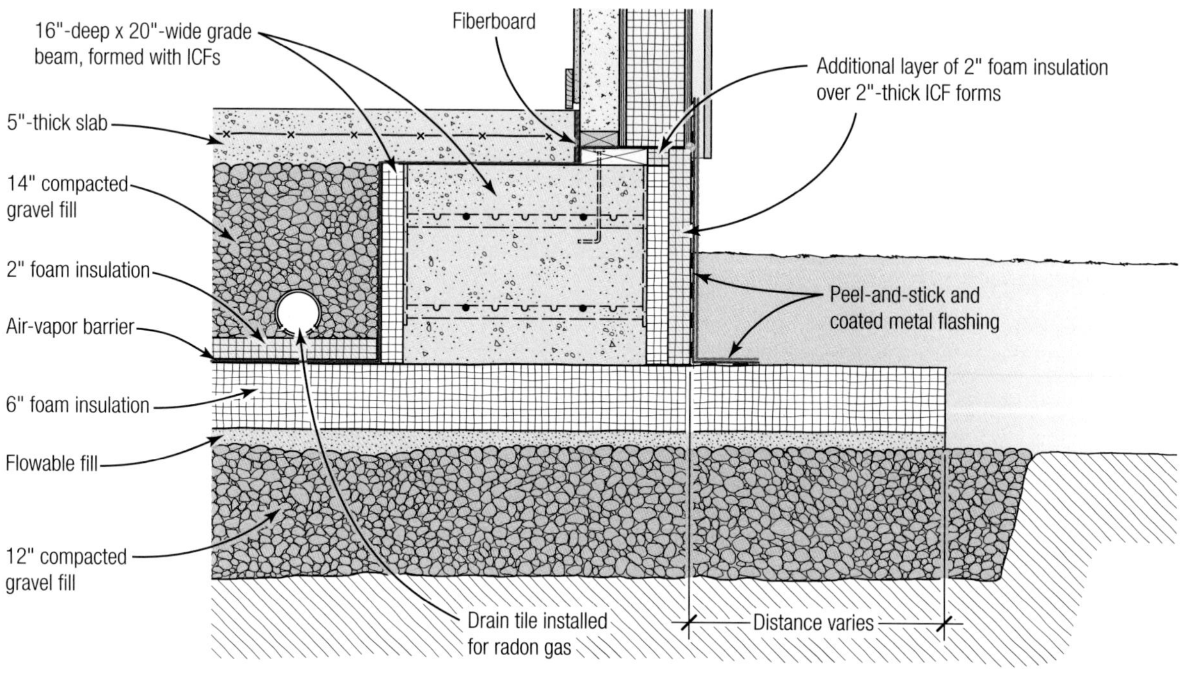
16"-deep x 20"-wide grade beam, formed with ICFs
5"-thick slab
14" compacted gravel fill
2" foam insulation
Air-vapor barrier
6" foam insulation
Flowable fill
12" compacted gravel fill
Fiberboard
Additional layer of 2" foam insulation over 2"-thick ICF forms
Peel-and-stick and coated metal flashing
Drain tile installed for radon gas
Distance varies

it produces excellent, void-free results.

Installing foam. We then lay the rigid foam over the leveled base (Figure 7), extending the sheets about 2 feet beyond the foundation footprint. The sheets are substantial enough to stay put until we're ready to place the concrete forms for either a monolithic slab or a perimeter grade-beam foundation.

Forming a Monolithic Slab

The more conventional of our foundation designs is the monolithic slab, which has an edge that's 16 inches thick and at least 12 inches wide at the bottom. Working on top of the foam base, we form the slab with stacked 2x6 framing lumber connected with 2x4 gussets (Figure 8). We line the inside face of the forms with 4 inches of foam. To make sure the foam will be secured to the concrete, we push long panel screws with plastic washers through from the back.

We stake and brace the forms at no more than 6 feet on-center. The closer, the better; wet concrete is heavy stuff and the last thing we want is a blowout. To prevent the forms from moving laterally at the bottom, we drive steel stakes along their edges down through the foam base into the compacted gravel.

Air-vapor barrier. On top of the foam, we place a continuous polyethylene vapor barrier, running it up the sides of the forms and bonding it to the foam with acoustical sealant. This prevents air and water vapor from rising through the seams between the foam panels. You can actually get quite a lot of air movement through the soil beneath a foundation. Air can find its way into the living space around utility and plumbing stubs, in some cases bringing radon gas with it.

We seal all the penetrations with tape, caulk, and additional pieces of poly. As an added precaution against radon, we also install a length of perforated PVC pipe on top of the foam, with an ell that brings it up through the slab. Then, if testing later reveals an unhealthy level of radon in the home, we'll vent the PVC through the roof to mitigate.

To make up the difference between the thickened edge and the 5-inch-thick slab, we place compacted bank gravel inside the forms (see illustration, facing page). Detailing the gravel to form the inner wall of the thickened edge is tricky; the slope has to be shallow enough to permit compacting, but if you make it too shallow, you have to make up the difference with a lot more concrete.

Forming a Perimeter Grade Beam With ICFs

I like monolithic slabs for their structural integrity and because they're easy to place — one pour and you're done. But forming and bracing the thickened edge can be time consuming. So recently we've gone to a two-phase process using insulated concrete forms (ICFs) to create a perimeter grade beam and then a separate pour for the slab (Figure 9 and illustration, facing page). While ICFs are typically used to form 8- to 10-inch-thick walls, our design requires a 12-inch-deep, 20-inch-wide grade-beam footing. We found an ICF manufacturer, Arxx Corp. (www.arxxbuild.com),

Figure 8. The author forms a monolithic, thickened-edge slab using 4-inch-thick foam board braced with framing lumber (left). After the air-vapor barrier is installed (below), the interior is filled with compacted gravel that's contoured to form the thickened edge. Long screws pushed through the vertical foam hold it to the hardened concrete.

Figure 9. In this alternative to the monolithic slab method, ICFs outline the foundation and are poured first (A). Forms are stabilized with framing lumber cleats, staked through the foam into the gravel base. Corners require extra bracing (B). Like the footings, column pads are set directly on the foam (C). A foam wrap helps prevent the vapor barrier from tearing over rough edges (D). On this job, an extra layer of 2-inch foam raises the nominal R-value by 10.

Figure 10. The ICF grade beam provides an immediate platform for framing (left). Once the building is enclosed, the slab can be poured without concern for temperature or foul weather (above).

Figure 11. Ice and water membrane covers the seams and helps prevent both insects and water from infiltrating the foam (A). Acoustical sealant ensures an airtight seam where the foam meets the frame (B). Galvalume cladding protects the foam against impact and UV degradation (C).

that offers form ties to accommodate thicker wall designs along with a variety of ICF sizes and configurations to suit our needs.

To keep the forms straight, we run lengths of framing lumber along the bottoms, secured through the foam base into the gravel layer beneath with steel stakes. Corners call for extra bracing. To support interior column point-loads, we form 3-foot-by-3-foot pads using 2x12 lumber. The pads get three rows of #4 rebar 3 inches up from the bottom and three more 3 inches down from the top.

As soon as the footing concrete hardens, we install the vapor barrier and radon vent. In some cases, we'll add another layer of 2-inch foam board over the vapor barrier, increasing the nominal R-value by 10. We fill the slab area to the top of the footings with compacted gravel, and we're ready to frame the building (Figure 10). Once we're closed in, the plumber roughs in the waste and supply lines, and we place the rebar or welded wire mesh to get ready for the concrete. Up to this point, the work has been done by my carpenters and our excavation sub, but we turn concrete placement and slab finishing over to a concrete sub.

Overall, the two-step grade-beam method actually takes less time and labor than the monolithic slab approach. While I can't make a completely accurate cost comparison, my sense is that the labor savings offset the added cost of the ICFs. The method offers another significant advantage, too: Pouring the slab inside a dried-in building minimizes the adverse effects of weather and temperature. Should a future job find us pouring the slab after winter sets in, it'll be relatively easy to heat the building above freezing until the slab is poured and has cured.

Before backfilling, we add 2 inches of foam to the outside edge of the foundation, over the ICF forms, which are only 2 inches thick. Here in Maine, carpenter ants find easy nesting in buried foam, so we do what we can to discourage them. We fold ice and water membrane into the corner between horizontal and vertical foam around the entire foundation (Figure 11). Later, after we frame and sheathe the walls, we cover the sill joint with another piece of membrane that overlaps the foundation strip. By code, a minimum 6 inches of vertical foundation edge must remain exposed between the wood line and the final grade. We cover it with Galvalume sheet metal, a neat and durable solution that's easy to repair if it becomes necessary.

We aim for a minimum of 8 inches of soil cover over the horizontal foam extending beyond the foundation. To encourage positive drainage away from the building, we've beveled the foam's surface with a hand saw with some success. As an alternative solution, we've poured a sloping cap of concrete over it, but the concrete can displace some of the topsoil necessary to support a healthy lawn or perimeter plantings. The right solution varies from one job to the next.

The advantages of an FPSF are considerable: lower cost, faster installation, less disturbance to the site, fewer subcontractors to schedule, and simpler detailing and finishing. Its ready applicability to super-insulated passive-solar design only adds to the list. But because it's an unfamiliar foundation, it's critical to resolve all structural questions and to address the clients' concerns about durability and aesthetics. We find that once these issues are covered, however, a frost-protected shallow foundation is a nearly ideal base.

Alan Gibson *co-owns G-O Logic, a design-build company in Belfast, Maine. His partner is architect Matthew O'Malia.*

Building an ICF Foundation

by Malcolm Meldahl

As a design-build contractor in an area with no shortage of upscale home buyers, I have quite a few clients who don't mind paying a little extra for a quality product. As a result, I often have a chance to try out new products and ideas. One thing I do with that freedom is try to steer my designs in the energy-efficient and "green" direction, while meeting the client's other objectives.

On a recent project, I used the Polysteel insulated concrete form (ICF) system to build the foundations for three connected buildings. I'm glad I gave this system a chance: The results were everything I had hoped for, and the few minor glitches we encountered will be easy to avoid next time around.

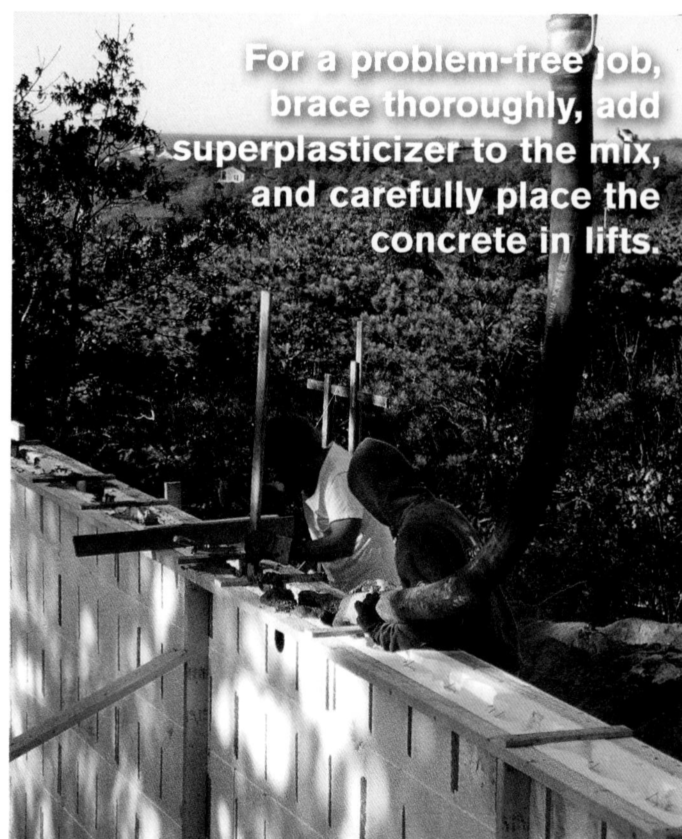
For a problem-free job, brace thoroughly, add superplasticizer to the mix, and carefully place the concrete in lifts.

Why ICFs?

The high insulation value of an ICF wall wasn't my primary reason for using the system. The main thing, frankly, was convenience: ICFs gave me more control over schedule and quality, and they gave me design flexibility.

In our area, you can wait a long time for a foundation contractor to fit you into his busy life. With an ICF system, my crew and I could form the footings and walls ourselves instead of having to work around a subcontractor's schedule.

Also, with the time pressure they face, poured-wall contractors don't always produce accurate work, and anyone who builds houses knows how much trouble it can be to adapt your wooden structures to a concrete foundation that is not quite true or level. By setting our own forms, my carpenters and I knew that if the basement didn't end up the way we wanted it, we'd have only ourselves to blame. It wouldn't take us any longer to place our own forms accurately than it would to level and square the deck on somebody else's concrete work.

Finally, ICFs made it easy to accomplish my stepped foundation design. I wanted to preserve a lot of the natural landscape on the site, and I wanted the building to conform to the contours of the existing terrain. The excavator I work with is willing to do things carefully, so instead of just hogging out a giant pit for the basement and worrying about the landscaping later, I planned to shape the foundation to the hillside. I ended up with a section of full 8-foot basement, a section of 4-foot crawlspace, and a section of 6-foot partial basement. Stacking 4-foot-by-16-inch ICF blocks let us easily match the walls with the stepped footings as we went up the grade.

Energy advantage. Although construction efficiency was my first consideration on this job, I don't mean to make light of the energy efficiency of ICFs. Above grade, ICF walls rate an R-20 or better, and they're impressively airtight as well. R-20 is heavy insulation for a basement, and the wall's performance when buffered by earth is probably quite a bit better than even that rating would indicate. I'm not sure how much the basement affected the whole building's heat-loss calculations, but I would say that this basement feels much more snug, warm, and dry than most basements I have built.

I would have gone to some trouble to insulate this foundation even if it had been a conventional basement. But when you stud out a basement and insulate the cavities, you're stealing living space; and you sometimes encounter moisture problems, too. If you put foam on the outside of a conventional concrete basement, you can have termite and ant problems, and aligning the siding becomes a concern (typically, you have to cantilever the sill out over the foam). Either way, there's labor involved. With ICFs, on the other hand, you're insulating at the same time you set up your forms.

Cost was not the main issue for my clients on this custom job, so I was expecting changes during construction. And I was right: We ended up moving some windows on the first and second floors. Needless to say, I was glad those above-grade walls were not cast in concrete.

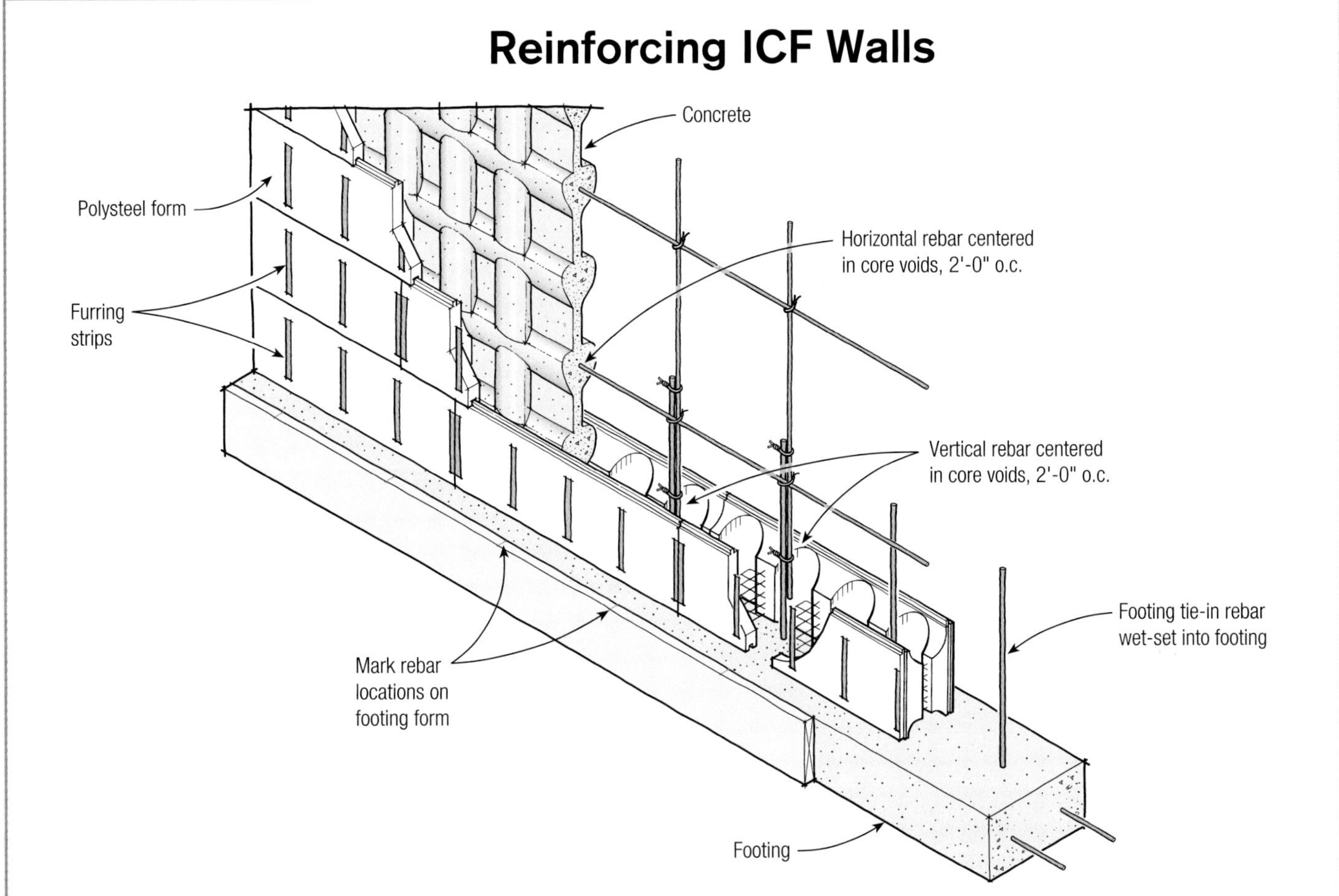

Figure 12. Rebar stubs must be accurately set into the footings to ensure that the vertical bars are centered within the core voids. The exterior of the completed wall has flat, parallel faces, but the waffle-shaped interior reduces the amount of concrete needed while still providing a high-strength product.

For a fixed design, however, such as a townhouse, I can certainly see some advantages to using ICFs for the whole house. The day may come when I take a chance on building a whole-ICF home.

Choosing a Manufacturer

This was my first ICF project, and I didn't know enough about the different ICF systems to favor one over another. Quite honestly, I picked Polysteel (American Polysteel, Inc., www.polysteel.com) because it had a distributor not too far away, and because they were the quickest to supply us with useful information. Polysteel's instruction booklet was clear and comprehensive enough that I didn't need to call the company for any help or advice during the project. They also sent us their video, which the crew and I watched together; that convinced us all that we'd be able to handle the job without any trouble.

Polysteel also has the advantage of being treated with borates to resist ant and termite infestation. That saved us from having to install termite shields between the foundation and the house frame, and it let us bury the foam and stucco over the above-grade portion, without any concern that bugs would cause hidden damage. If you chose a brand with no borate treatment in the foam, you need to think about insect protection issues.

I was very happy with the way the Polysteel forms worked. They were easy to assemble, and the steel fins on the outside face accepted screws readily, so it was easy to fasten bracing to the forms and to make splices when we needed to cut a form to length. Other forms might have other advantages, but all in all, I was satisfied with my choice.

Stacking the Forms

Polysteel forms are 4 feet long, and they come in 1-foot, 2-foot, and 16-inch heights. The top, bottom, and ends have a tongue-and-groove profile, so they stack precisely, and the forms lock together to a certain extent. Setting up the forms is simple: You pour your footing using conventional methods and snap lines for your foundation footprint the same way you would for conventional forms. The first course of forms is adhered to the footing with a thin, continuous bead of polyurethane foam. From there on up, setting the forms is something like building with toy Lego blocks: You just stack them up, using a little dab of foam at all abutting edges to "tack" things together. (We cemented all the blocks together with a continuous bead of foam because we had plenty on hand, and that worked fine — just don't use so much foam that it pushes things out of alignment as it expands.) When you come to a corner, you use a right-hand or left-hand corner form.

Layout. The footprints of my three connected buildings had a few jigs and jogs in them, but they weren't especially complicated, and there were only right angles — no odd bends or curves. So I didn't have to learn any of Polysteel's methods for making mitered corners (although their handbook provides detailed instructions for that, and it doesn't look too difficult). For the sake of efficiency, I based my plans as much as possible around the 4-foot and 2-foot modules. A few odd wall lengths required us to trim forms, and this was not a big problem, even though we had a minor incident during the pour when a splice started to give way. For the sake of simplicity, it's nice to avoid the odd dimensions if you can.

A more critical layout concern has to do with how you place your rebar. Every wall gets some amount of reinforcing steel, and the vertical bars within the wall are tied into short stubs that are wet-set into the footings. The rebar has to sit in the middle of the 1-foot-on-center core voids in the waffle forms, starting with a bar rising up the center of the corner cavity (Figure 12). So it's important to know how your foam forms will lay out and to mark the footing forms for the proper rebar locations (or else be ready to measure carefully as you place your rebar stubs into the footing).

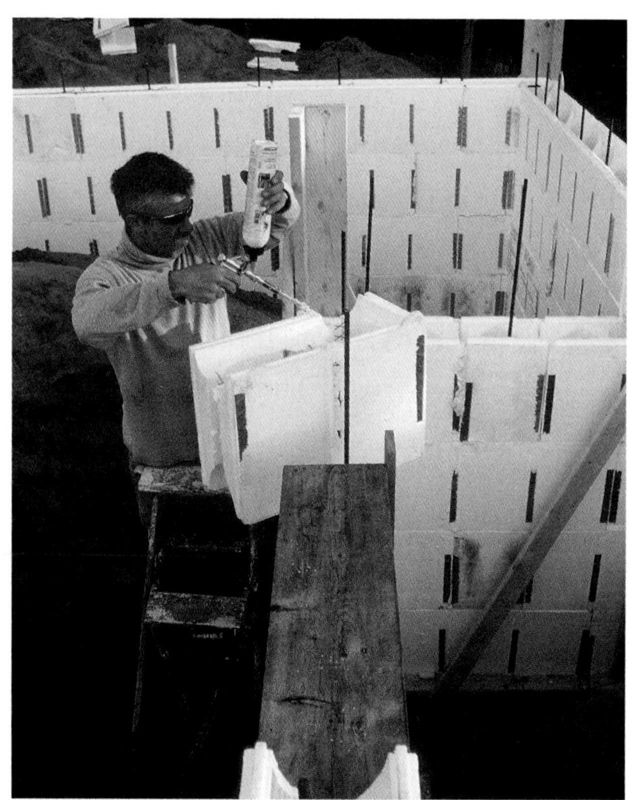

Figure 13. Walls are stacked one course at a time; corners are laid up using alternating left-hand and right-hand corner blocks. Polyurethane foam is used as "glue" between trimmed forms that lack the usual tongue-and-groove connection, but added exterior reinforcement is also needed in those areas.

Placing forms. You stack the blocks up one course at a time, always beginning in a corner (Figure 13). If your foundation is the right size, you can go all the way around the footprint without cutting any forms until you get back to where you started. But you'll usually have to cut at least one form at the end of the circuit, and you may need to cut one in every length of wall as you approach the corner. In any case, you alternate left and right corner forms as you go up the wall and stagger the end joints of the form blocks so they don't fall out above one another.

Cutting and splicing. Whenever you cut a form, you're trimming off the tongue-and-groove connection, and you need to replace it with a strong splice. Running a bead of polyurethane foam between the cut forms helps keep them in alignment, but the easiest way to provide the needed structural strength is to place a small piece of plywood to span over the joint and screw it to the nearest steel furring strips on the forms. In our experience, it's worth taking time with splices and even providing each splice with its own brace back against the soil. The only time we had trouble during our pour was when a splice started to give way.

Reinforcement. Polysteel's specs call for a minimum placement of #3 rebar at 2 feet on-center, horizontally and vertically. They also say to consult local building codes, but they provide a reinforcement engineering table that tells you how much rebar to place for walls of any height or thickness in various soil types.

On our job we placed the bar 2 feet on-center as specified, but I went up from #4 to #5 bar, just to be conservative. The added cost was insignificant, but according to the table, this change increased the strength of the wall considerably. We placed the bar as we stacked the forms (Figure 14). The vertical bars sit beside the stubs sticking out of the footings. Horizontal bars lie in metal chairs, or hammocks, that span the forms and keep the bars centered within the wall space. When you use the metal chairs, you don't need to tie the horizontal and vertical bars together with wire.

Window openings. There were two windows and a door in one of my basement spaces. Since Polysteel is designed for above-grade as well as basement walls, the company has given windows a lot of thought. They're not hard to detail: You just build a window buck of pressure-treated wood to the rough-opening dimensions and add bracing to hold them in place

Figure 14. Polysteel's instruction manual includes a reinforcement table that specifies the rebar size and placement for any soil condition, wall height, and wall thickness. Wire saddles placed across the forms keep the bars centered in the concrete core section (left). If saddles aren't used, the vertical and horizontal bars must be tied together with wire (right).

during the pour (Figure 15). The permanent attachment between buck and wall is provided by ½-inch lag screws, 4 inches long, which are driven through the wood into the form voids. When the concrete sets up around the lag screw threads, the whole assembly is firmly locked in place.

Bracing. Adequate bracing is a critical part of any concrete pour, and this is especially true of ICFs. Don't try to get by with fewer braces than the instruction manual specifies. We shot 2x4s into the footings on both sides of the wall at the bottom and then made a sort of ladder built of 2x4s to lie along the top edge of the forms (Figure 16). These upper and lower frames are connected with vertical 2x4 members spaced about 8 or 10 feet apart, and we braced them to stakes driven into the ground with additional 2x4s.

We also attached a working platform of 2x10s to the vertical braces at about half-wall height wherever access was at all difficult. It would be tempting to dispense with this working platform, but that would be a big mistake: It's very helpful to have good, comfortable access to the whole top of the wall as you pour so you can easily move the hose along and manipulate it.

The Pour

The waffle shape of the wall system conserves concrete: A Polysteel wall uses about 25 percent less concrete than a conventionally formed wall of the same nominal thickness. Polysteel's handbook provides a formula for estimating concrete quantities based on the number of form blocks you use, and it seemed accurate — we had enough concrete and little waste. The handbook recommends a 3,000-psi mix at a

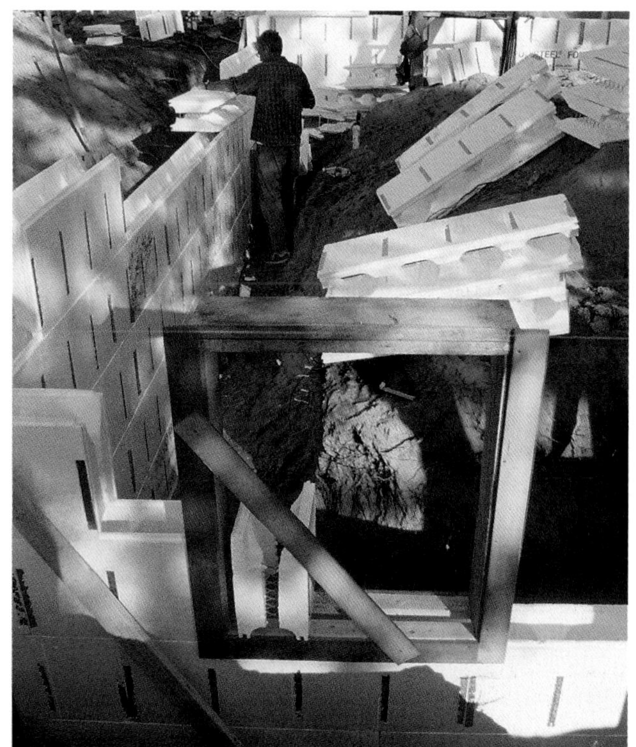

Figure 15. Window openings are created with simple site-built window bucks made from pressure-treated 2x10 stock. A slot between the two spaced 2x4s that serve as the bottom sill makes it possible to pour concrete into the forms below the window opening. Temporary wooden flanges help position the bucks (the inside flanges are not yet in place in this photo), while added exterior bracing keeps them plumb during the pour.

5-inch slump, with superplasticizer added at the job so the mix will flow easily into the forms and around the reinforcing.

To reduce stress on the forms, it's important to pour in 1-foot to 2-foot lifts, at a total rate of about 4 vertical feet per hour. The superplasticizer wears off quickly, and the concrete in each lift stiffens enough that the pressure will not build up too high as the pour progresses.

Pumps and hoses. The standard way to place concrete in foam forms is to pump it (Figure 17). A 4-inch hose won't fit between the forms and work around the

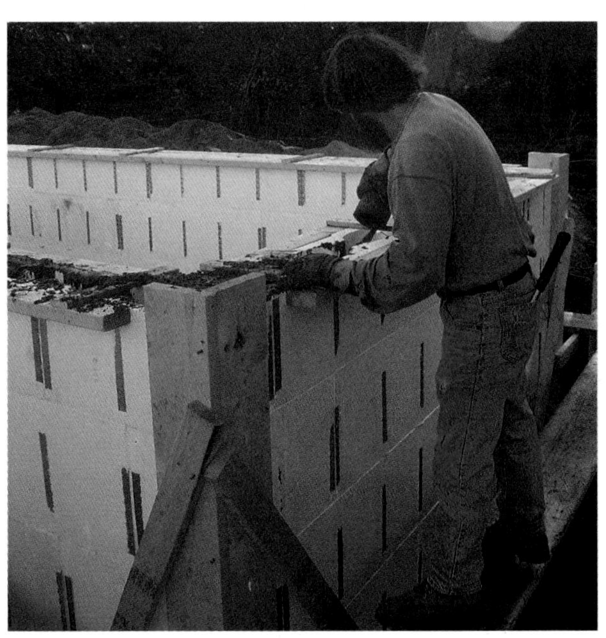

Figure 16. Vertical 2x4 braces spaced about 8 feet on-center tie into a 2x4 "ladder" laid over the top of the forms to stiffen them. Diagonal braces run from the vertical braces back to the ground (above), and a working platform tied into the bracing system provides easy access to the tops of the forms (right). It's important to use at least the minimum bracing specified in the manual.

Figure 17. A concrete pump delivers a 3,000-psi mix using small aggregate, and the mix is treated with a superplasticizer (right). The author's concrete sub did not use a 2- or 3-inch reducing adapter on the pump hose, which would have made the pour more manageable. Rapping the forms with a hammer and a block of wood during the pour helps consolidate the concrete and prevents the formation of voids and air pockets (below).

form ties and rebar, so Polysteel's instructions say to use a reducer to adapt the pump hose from 4 inches down to 2 or 3 inches. This lets the hose reach all the way to the bottom of the forms, allowing you to gently deliver the concrete into the bottom of the form on the first lift, rather than dropping it from a height of 6 or 8 feet.

We did not use a hose adapter on our job, and the effect was noticeable. At the beginning, we were dropping the concrete several feet, and at the bottom of the forms I later noticed some bulging — as much as 1/2 inch of convexity between vertical braces in a few places. Since there was no finish issue in our case, this wasn't a big concern, but I did think to myself that we were approaching the strength limit of the forms. Compared with conventional methods, using foam forms takes a bit of a delicate touch — the bracing and the placing methods really matter, because there is not a lot of tolerance for carelessness.

We actually did have a couple of minor blowouts — nothing catastrophic, but enough to cause some yelling and running around. One happened when the guy who was directing the pour mixed up his signals with the concrete pump operator. Instead of stopping the pump, the operator kept the concrete flowing, and very quickly we had a high mountain of concrete at one spot in the wall.

Under the increased pressure, a splice in a cut form about a third of the way up the wall bulged out and threatened to give way. Fortunately, we were able to contain the damage by jamming a piece of plywood over the tender spot and shoving in some new 2x4 braces against the side of the trench. We had a similar problem partway up a low section of wall where there was relatively little pressure involved (Figure 18). In that instance, we hastily shoveled some backfill back into the trench and tamped it down to offset the pressure of the concrete.

In hindsight, I think it would be wise to create some sort of augmented through-ties at any location where the form's strength is at all dubious. I would also make the plywood gussets stronger and thicker next time and brace them back more thoroughly. It's best not to allow wishful thinking into the work at all. Next time, I'll definitely use the adapter, even though it's tiring to have to continually slide the business end of the hose into the forms and lift it out again as you progress around the walls.

Curing. When you use ICFs, you're doing your concrete a huge favor. The insulation contains the warmth that the concrete creates as it sets, and it keeps the moisture from evaporating. The temperature stays more uniform across the entire concrete section, and the concrete cures moist. That decreases the internal stress that often forms within a mass of concrete as it dries and cools differentially from the outside in. As a result, the shrinkage cracks that form will tend to be fewer and smaller. Also, a moist cure adds significantly to the concrete's final strength — it's reasonable to estimate that concrete cured inside ICF forms would end

Figure 18. Inadequate bracing at a spliced form and a too-rapid pour in one area caused a section of form to bulge outward (far left). The affected area was located partway up a low section of wall, so the damage was contained by tamping backfill against the bulging form (left).

up at least 25% stronger than concrete that is wet-cured for seven days, and perhaps double the strength of concrete that is exposed to air a day or two after the pour.

Capping off. As you finish the pour, you place anchor bolts into the wet concrete just as you would for a conventional wall. In a few days, when the concrete is hard enough, you apply a pressure-treated sill in the usual way, although the sill itself is wider. The added thickness of the forms means that a nominal 6-inch wall is actually 9¼ inches across, which makes for a nice fit with a 2x10 sill. A nominal 8-inch Polysteel wall gets a 2x12 treated-wood sill cap.

The portion of the foam form on the exterior surface that's above grade, between the ground and the house, needs to be protected. We used a cementitious stucco called California Stucco, from Silpro (www.silpro.com). It comes dry in a sack, and you mix it with water on site. Polysteel's literature says you can apply the stucco directly to the foam if you rough up the foam with a wire brush first, and it's true — that's what we did, and the stucco does adhere. But in the future I think I would use expanded galvanized-metal lath, because the stucco we applied has developed some fine cracking. Another option would be to screw pressure-treated wood to the steel furring strips in the foam, or to apply some kind of fiber-cement sheet material.

Would I Do It Again?

When the forming and pouring were all done, and we stepped back to assess the results, my crew and I were impressed. I've got a crew of veteran tradesmen — each has been doing this kind of work for 25 or 30 years. And everybody, myself included, felt that this system was worth the effort and lived up to its promise.

I'm not sure at this point how the cost of this job would compare to the cost of bringing in a regular poured-wall subcontractor. There were a lot of wild cards in this particular project, including the unusual wall heights and my desire to protect the site.

But when I do figure up all the costs, I won't be surprised if I find that this way was actually cheaper as well as better. I avoided the separate cost of insulating, and I avoided having to bear the cost of a specialty contractor's markup and the cost of any delays caused by working around his schedule. The well-insulated basement space saves energy for the homeowner and is also more comfortable and livable than the usual basement.

In addition, by including a generous amount of steel reinforcement and by curing the concrete under ideal conditions, we've built what I am convinced is a very strong and durable wall.

I'll be using ICFs on my next basement, even though I'll be working at the opposite end of the market, building a small, bare-bones house with a tight budget. Even for a client of modest means, I think this system is worthwhile.

Malcolm Meldahl *is a design-build contractor in Truro, Mass.*

Insect Infestations in Buried Foam

by JLC Staff

When building contractor David Damroth first discovered termites in his coastal home, a local pest control expert advised him to remove a section of the exterior rigid foam insulation that covered the foundation so he could see the extent of the problem. What he found was a network of tunnels in the foam full of termites on their way into his house through unsoldered corners and overlaps in the copper termite shield. To stem the tide, Damroth removed a 6-inch band of foam all the way around his foundation. "I thought if I removed the foam and destroyed the mud tubes, my problems would be over," Damroth said. "Was I ever mistaken. Within a few hours the mud tubes had been rebuilt."

Termite and carpenter ant infestations have prompted builders, pest control operators, and code officials to rethink the use of foam board below grade.

Most readers wouldn't be surprised to hear this story from a builder or homeowner in the South, where termite infestations are a fact of life. But Damroth lives and works on the Massachusetts island of Martha's Vineyard, hundreds of miles north of what

Hidden Termite Entry Paths

Termite activity is hidden from view when a concrete foundation is insulated on the exterior with rigid foam (A) or when it is constructed of ICFs (B). The insects can enter through tiny openings, such as where pipes penetrate the wall, but they can also tunnel directly through the foam at any point. Termiticides applied to the ground will not affect the foam, which acts as a shield for the termites.

Homes without exterior insulation but with interior foundation insulation are not much better off (C). If shelter tubes along the exterior are spotted during regular inspections, termiticides applied to the ground may drive the termites further underground. By tunneling under the footing, the termites can enter through cracks and seams in the basement slab. Once inside, the

continued on next page

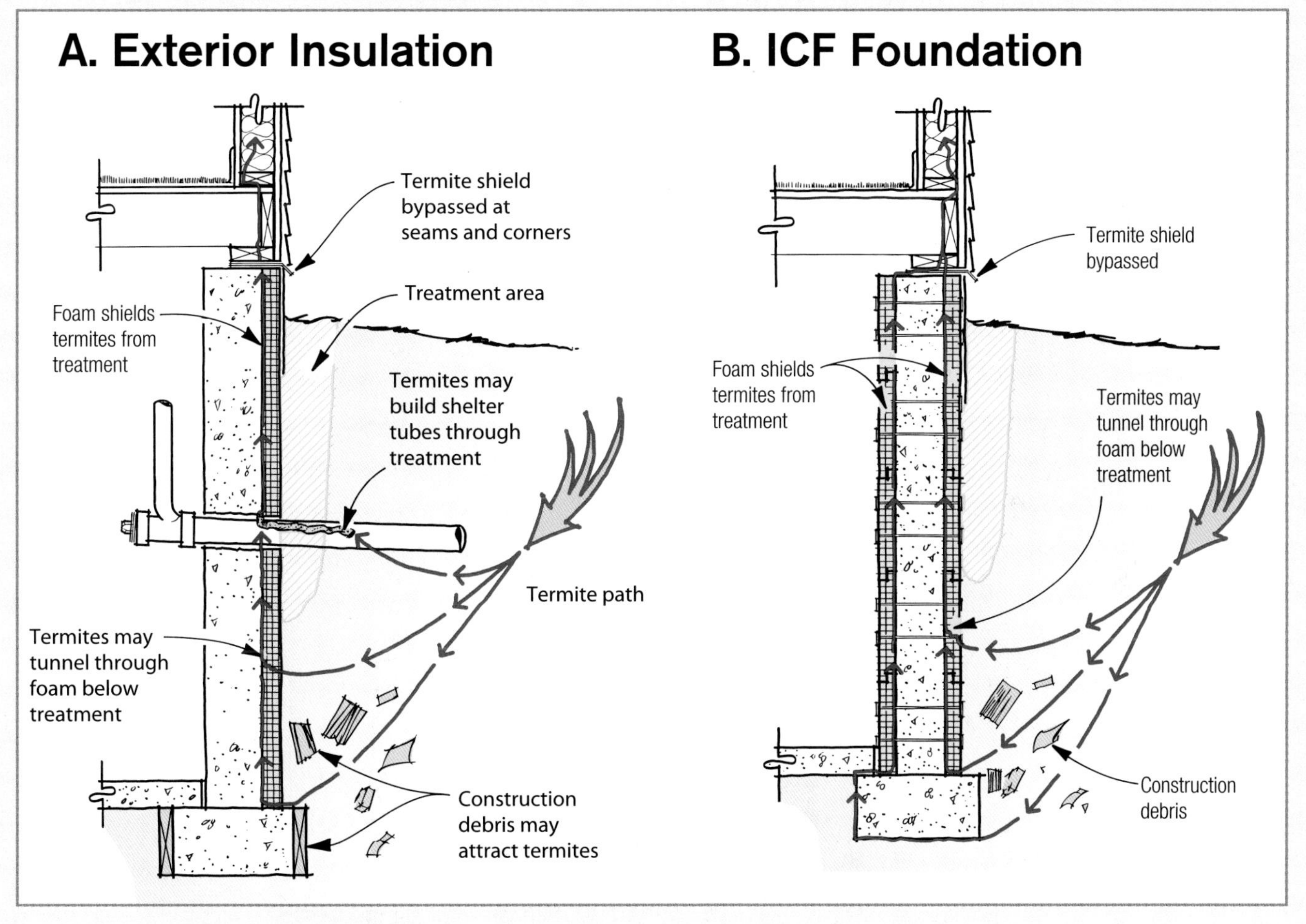
A. Exterior Insulation
Termite shield bypassed at seams and corners
Treatment area
Foam shields termites from treatment
Termites may build shelter tubes through treatment
Termite path
Termites may tunnel through foam below treatment
Construction debris may attract termites
B. ICF Foundation
Termite shield bypassed
Foam shields termites from treatment
Termites may tunnel through foam below treatment
Construction debris

has been traditionally considered termite country. In fact, according to the National Pest Control Association in Dunn Loring, Va., termites of one kind or another are found in every state except Alaska, and carpenter ants and other destructive insects can pose a similar threat well into Canada.

Obviously, wood-destroying insects don't stop at the Mason-Dixon line, but they don't always find entry into the house through the wood mudsill at the top of the foundation either. In Damroth's case, an initial do-it-yourself treatment of the exposed foundation with Dursban, an off-the-shelf termiticide, lasted for just two weeks. Then, while putting bikes away in the basement, Damroth noticed new mud tubes, this time on the basement floor. The termites had found their way under the footing and into the house through cracks in the basement slab and the foam beneath it (see "Case Study," page 108).

The Trouble With Foam

Wood structures have always been susceptible to damage from termites and other wood-destroying insects, but the presence of rigid foam appears to exacerbate the problem in two ways. First, once the insects tunnel through the foam, they are hidden behind it (see "Hidden Termite Entry Paths, " above). This gives the

continued from previous page

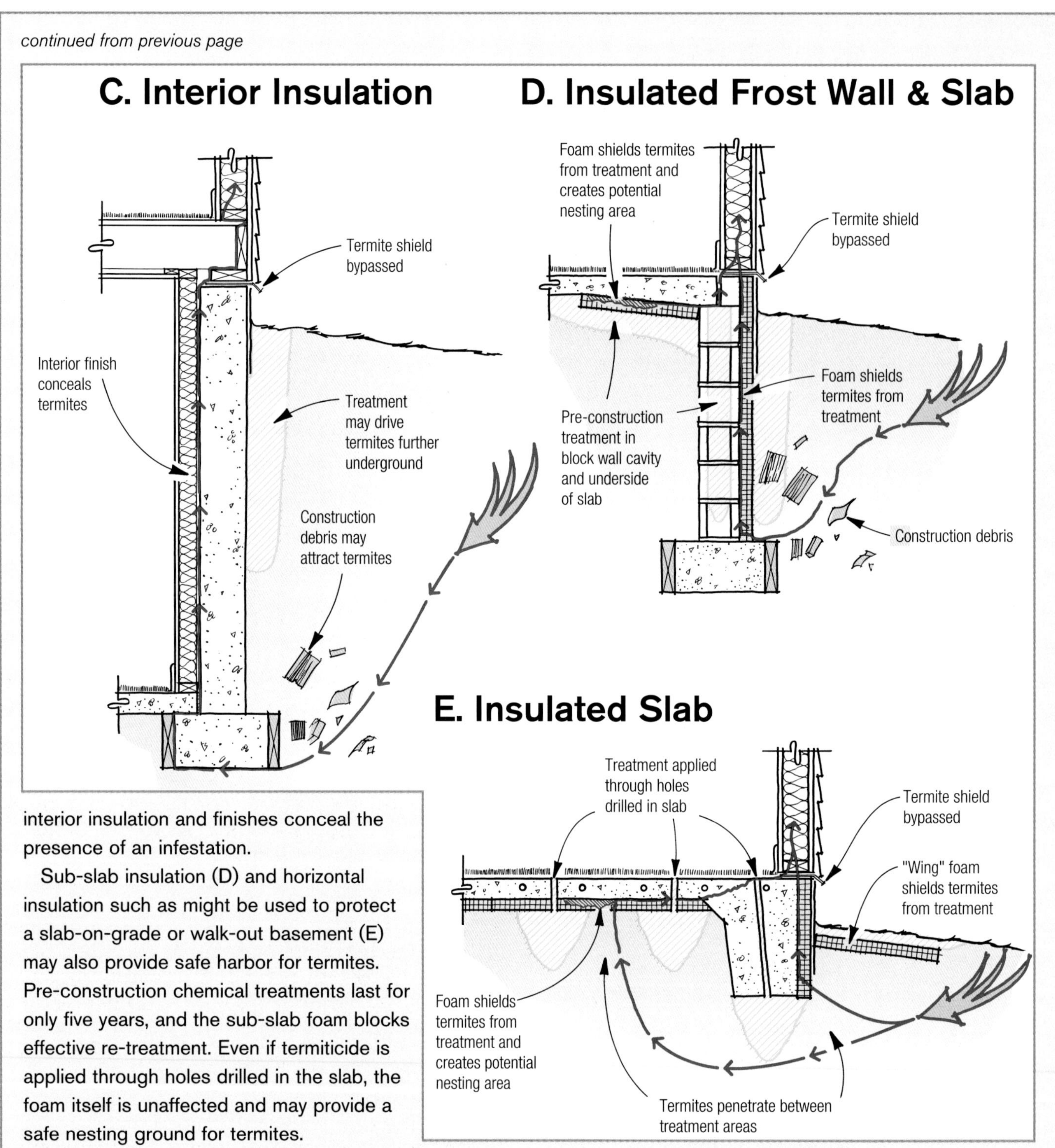
C. Interior Insulation
Termite shield bypassed
Interior finish conceals termites
Treatment may drive termites further underground
Construction debris may attract termites
D. Insulated Frost Wall & Slab
Foam shields termites from treatment and creates potential nesting area
Termite shield bypassed
Foam shields termites from treatment
Pre-construction treatment in block wall cavity and underside of slab
Construction debris
E. Insulated Slab
Treatment applied through holes drilled in slab
Termite shield bypassed
"Wing" foam shields termites from treatment
Foam shields termites from treatment and creates potential nesting area
Termites penetrate between treatment areas

interior insulation and finishes conceal the presence of an infestation.

Sub-slab insulation (D) and horizontal insulation such as might be used to protect a slab-on-grade or walk-out basement (E) may also provide safe harbor for termites. Pre-construction chemical treatments last for only five years, and the sub-slab foam blocks effective re-treatment. Even if termiticide is applied through holes drilled in the slab, the foam itself is unaffected and may provide a safe nesting ground for termites.

insects time to establish themselves before the infestation is discovered and may increase the extent of the damage to the wood structure.

With an exposed foundation, for example, a termite infestation can often be discovered early by looking for the telltale mud tubes that the insects use to protect themselves from light and air. If these tubes are hidden behind the foam, however, the first sign of trouble might not show itself until several years later, by which time the termites may have started satellite colonies in and behind the foam.

Second, regardless of when an infestation is discovered, the presence of foam insulation against the foundation can make complete chemical treatment impossible. Even if the soil surrounding basement walls or under slabs is treated, the foam, which itself remains unaffected, prevents the pesticide from reaching the concrete, effectively shielding insects that get behind or in it. According to Greg Baumann, director of field services at the National Pest Control Association

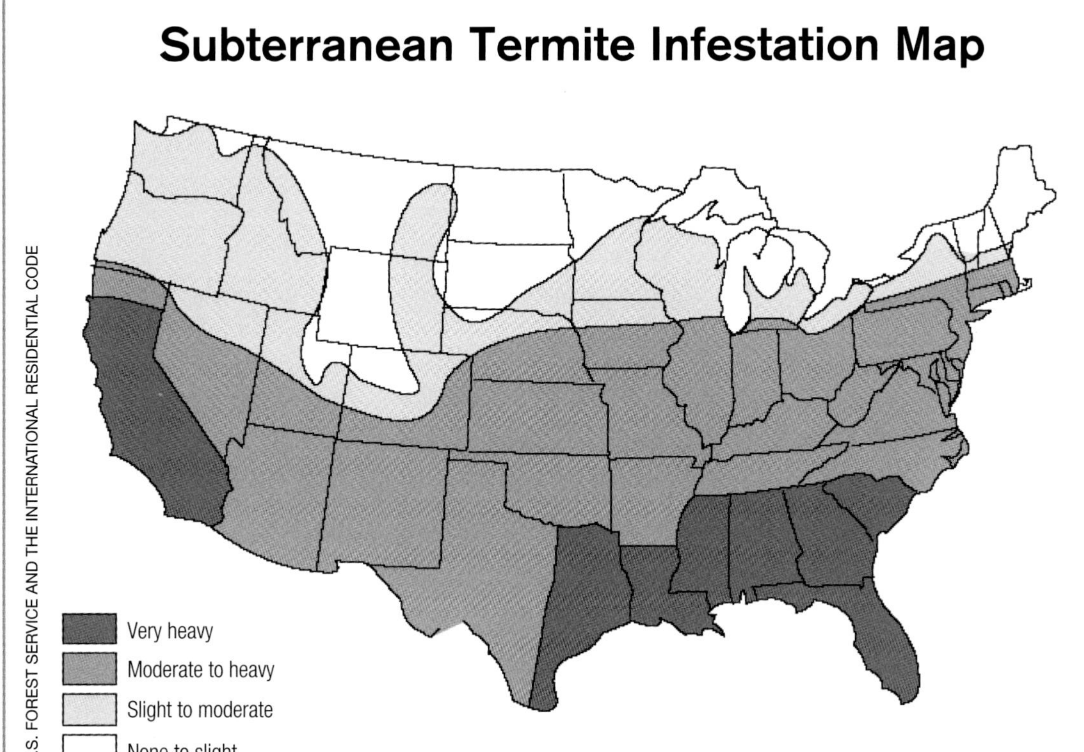

Figure 19. Building codes prohibit most uses of below-grade foam in areas of "very high" probability of infestation, including the Southeast and most of California. Some experts feel that this map, developed by the U.S. Forest Service in the 1960s, underestimates the current risk in some areas.

(NPCA), "There is simply no way to treat below-grade foam insulation once it is infested with insects. The only cure is to remove the foam. That could mean digging up foundations and jackhammering out slabs, but it's the only recommendation we have at this time." For this reason, some national pest control firms, such as Orkin, now refuse to guarantee the effectiveness of treatment in houses with below-grade foam, a big problem in southern states where insect inspections are often necessary to secure bank financing when a home is sold.

What's the Attraction?

Wood-destroying insects don't actually eat rigid foam, but because they tunnel through and nest in it, some experts have begun to wonder if foam holds some special attraction for the pests. For example, studies conducted recently in a lab at Colorado State University suggest that termites, like mosquitoes, might be attracted to low concentrations of carbon dioxide (CO_2). Since CO_2 is used as a blowing agent in some foams, the researchers concluded that the CO_2 may attract termites to foam.

However, while the study established that termites will move toward a CO_2 source, no actual foam was tested. A company spokesperson for Dow Chemical Corporation, which uses CO_2 to expand foam in some of its products, disagrees with the CO_2 theory, because "any residual CO_2 would be long gone by the time the product reaches the job site." Most pest control experts also discount the theory.

The question of whether foam acts as an attractant for wood-destroying insects is further complicated by the fact that many manmade chemicals can attract insects, and one or more of these may be present in foam, according to Harold Harlan, a staff entomologist at the NPCA. Common inks and dyes or one of the many residual chemicals in foam and other building products could be to blame.

On the other hand, Dr. Niel Ogg, assistant head of Clemson University's Department of Pesticide Regulation, is conducting studies of southern homes that have led him to believe that buried foam plays some role in termite infestations. "Statistically, new homes built without below-grade foam should show a low rate of termite infestation in the first five years — 5 to 15 percent. By comparison, we found 85 to 90 percent of houses in South Carolina and Florida with below-grade foam to be infested after five years. So it's not if but when," said Ogg.

One possible explanation is that nearly all homes in areas of high infestation probability, such as Florida and the Carolinas, where Ogg's studies are being done, are treated regularly with pesticides. These chemical treatments may be more effective on bare concrete foundations than on foundations protected with a layer of rigid foam.

The plastic foam industry maintains that its products aren't at fault. Betsy DeCampos, executive director of the Expanded Polysytrene Molders Association, which represents approximately 45 manufacturers of foam products, told JLC that "the data shows EPS

Case Study: Foundation Foam Conceals Termite Infestation

By David Damroth

During the course of a summer, I tackled the removal of 6 inches of foam insulation around the entire perimeter of my home. Within the first 3 feet I observed tunnels throughout the foam crawling with termites.

At the termite shield, the termites had built corridors along the top edge of the foam, apparently in an effort to find a point of entry in the house. Eventually, they found the corner of the building where the copper shields overlapped. The overlap was not soldered, because I assumed the pressure of the house and sill sealer would keep the joint tight. But my idea of tight was a termite's idea of a doorway, and they squeezed through the tiniest cracks. In one instance, the industrious little pests had built a tube that angled away from the foundation into midair, then went up and over the edge of the termite shield.

I thought that if I removed the foam and destroyed the mud tubes behind it, my troubles would be over. Was I ever mistaken. Within a few hours, the mud tubes had been rebuilt. Again I scraped the rebuilt tubes off, but they

David Damroth discovered the extent of a termite infestation in his home by removing a 6-inch band of insulation from the perimeter of the foundation (left). He found a dense network of termite shelter tubes behind the foam, as well as along the top of the foam (right), where the insects had traveled around the house looking for a point of entry.

products have no nutritive value to insects ... but we encourage our members to work on solutions to the insect problem within the limitations of building codes." Similarly, ABB Corporation, makers of BlueMaxx ICFs, tells its dealers in a termite position paper to "... point out that ICFs don't 'attract termites,' but that if [the homeowners live] in a heavy termite area, they are advised not to install the ICF below grade until we come out with the appropriately configured solution to the problem and/or the codes are reversed." (*Note*: ABB is now called Arxx Corp. and has renamed its product line the ARXX ICF system.)

When asked about ongoing research to find chemical solutions, DeCampos said that while most of the chemical research is being done by raw materials suppliers, "individual molders generally aren't going to have the financial resources to conduct their own research." Studies of that type may cost millions of dollars, can take years to complete, and must involve the EPA.

Dow Chemical, when asked about its in-house research, would say only that chemicals incorporated into foam "show promise" in the battle with insects.

Are Borates a Solution?

One manufacturer of expanded polystyrene (EPS) foam, AFM Inc., started incorporating borate in its Perform Guard line of foam building products in the early 1990s. Borate, a natural mineral compound, is known to be an effective deterrent for many destructive insects, including termites and carpenter ants.

However, little field research was available on the effectiveness of borates in buried foam. To establish reliable performance data and seek code acceptance for its borate-treated foam, AFM conducted extensive field trials using third-party researchers. The research reappeared. I had hoped to avoid using chemicals, but now it was clear I had no choice. I treated the area with a light application of Dursban. No new tubes appeared that day or for the next two weeks.

I had almost forgotten the entire problem until I went into my basement to put my daughter's bike away for the winter. As I descended the stairs, I saw new mud tubes, not just on the floor, but extending all the way up the wall to the rim joist. Those darned creatures had moved down under the footing and back up into my home. I removed the mud tubes, hoping to at least slow down the occupation, but within four hours, the tubes reappeared, rising like stalagmites into the air. I never imagined that termites would be quite that persistent.

My respect for the tenacity of these insects has grown dramatically. I've decided that the only way to protect the house in the long term is to preserve the ability to inspect the foundation. I don't want to excavate and remove the foam, because it holds in the heat and keeps the basement dry. Instead, I plan to leave the top 6 inches of the foundation exposed, capped with a custom piece of metal flashing to hold it in place. If I have to use chemicals again, however, this cap will have to be designed so I can apply termiticide behind the foam. And I'm still concerned about the potential for human exposure to the chemicals.

David Damroth is a building contractor in Martha's Vineyard, Mass.

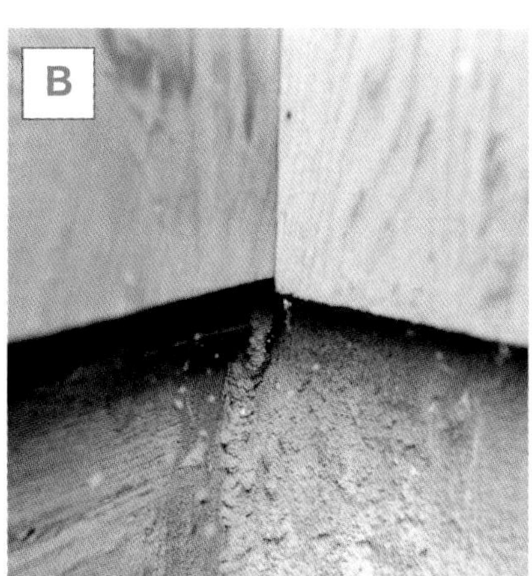

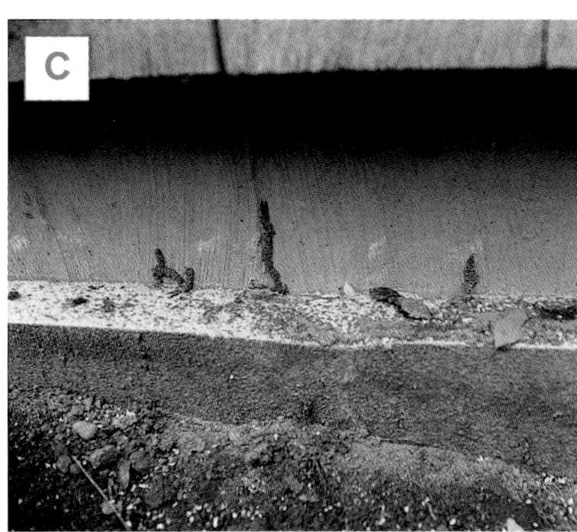

The termites were hidden from view by the foam, through which they carved numerous tunnels (A). They eventually entered the house between overlapped layers in the copper termite shield at the house corners; in some cases, they built shelter tubes around the termite shield (B). Damroth removed the tubes, but within hours, the termites had begun to build new tubes (C).

followed the stringent testing guidelines of the International Commercial Code (ICC) Evaluation Service. After five years of heavy termite exposure at three test sites in the deep South, the treated foam emerged with minimal damage. On average, the treated foam had 3 percent damage, compared with 24 percent damage in the untreated foam. Based on these tests, the ICC issued Evaluation Service Report ESR-1006 that recognizes Perform Guard as a termite-resistant insulation suitable for use in areas of heavy termite pressure.

AFM is quick to point out that the foam is treated to protect the insulation material, itself, not the building. President Mike Tobin told JLC, "Perform Guard is not a barrier system. Just like you wouldn't expect a pressure-treated sill plate to protect the whole house from termites," he said, "you can't expect PerformGuard to either."

Clemson's Niel Ogg also warned against relying on borate-treated foams below grade to deter termites. He explained that whether the foam is treated or not, once termites find it the basic problem remains unchanged: Any termites that find their way around the foam will be difficult to spot, and treatment of any infestation will be impossible with the presence of the foam. Echoing the opinion of most pest control experts, Ogg concluded, "The only sure fix if you have below-grade foam is to remove it."

What the Codes Say

The model codes have recently made efforts to address the problem of termites and other wood-destroying insects. Since 1999, the Southern Building Code Congress International (SBCCI) has banned the use of all below-grade foam products in states with a high-probability of termite infestation (Figure 19, page 107).

These restrictions were adopted by the 2003 and 2006 IRC building codes, which prohibit most uses of buried foam insulation in areas of "very high" termite infestation. With a few exceptions, described below, the code bars the use of rigid foam insulation below grade on the exterior of a foundation or underneath foundation walls or slabs. It also requires a 6-inch gap between above-grade foam, such as foam sheathing, and the finished grade.

The code does allow foam on the interior of basement walls. It also allows below-grade foam if the structure is made entirely of pressure-treated wood or non-combustible (metal or masonry) materials. A third, more general exception permits buried foam where builders use an "approved method of protecting the foam plastic and structure from subterranean termites." Exactly how to achieve that remains the topic of much debate (see "Termite-Resistant Foundations").

Alternative systems. An "approved" product or system is essentially anything accepted by your local code jurisdiction. In most cases, these decisions are guided by published supplements to the code or code evaluation reports issued by the ICC Evaluation Service. These reports certify that a new product or system has been adequately tested and deemed by the evaluation service to be in compliance with the code.

Approved insulation products include treated foam boards such as Perform Guard (www.performguard.com) or Dow Styrofoam Blueguard (www.building.dow.com). Approved systems for protecting the structure include alternative chemical treatments, such as baiting systems and physical termite barriers. Barrier systems can be costly and not widely used in the U.S., but they may be suitable for some projects. A unique barrier system called Termimesh (www.termimeshusa.com) blocks hidden termite entry points with a woven stainless-steel mesh. Some foundation waterproofing membranes have also been approved for termite control and may make sense for projects where a waterproofing membrane is being considered.

Interior foam. Most codes allow the use of foam on the inside of basement walls, because it is accessible for treatment. But interior foam will still shield termites from sight. Should an infestation occur, completely dismantling a basement family room to remove infested foam can be as destructive and expensive as digging up the foundation. Interior basement insulation with fiberglass batts is not a solution either. Whether the studs are wood or steel, the insulation will still hide termites traveling along the concrete wall, and getting rid of an infestation will still be difficult and expensive.

The soundest course is to leave out interior basement insulation and finishes to begin with. In the South, the energy loss is negligible; in a typical northern city, a completely uninsulated basement or slab might add between $600 and $1,000 to the annual heating costs. Given the cost of treating a termite infestation, this trade-off may be worth it.

Termite-Resistant Foundations

By Steven Smulski

Pest-control professionals are right not to guarantee treatments when faced with an insulated foundation, because it's impossible to inspect inside and behind the insulation.

A 1/32-inch gap is all termites need to sneak into a house. To eliminate these gaps, begin by choosing a foundation type and materials that present the fewest possible entryways.

Of all foundation types, slabs-on-grade are the most vulnerable. In the first design (A), for example, termites

A. Slab-on-Grade With Stem Wall

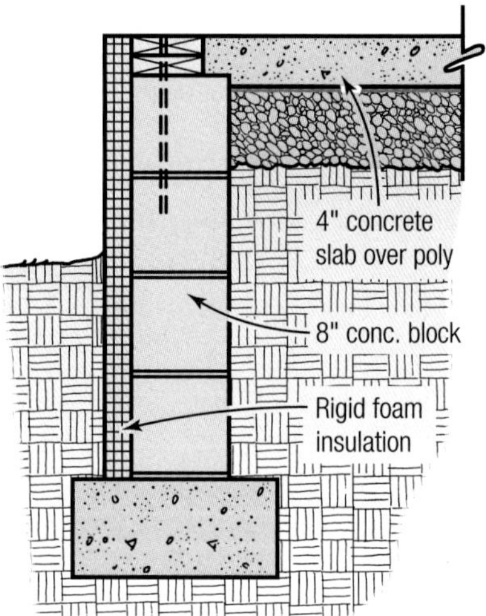

This slab-on-grade foundation is a poor choice in areas where termites are a problem. Termites can slip through the foundation/slab joint, inside the hollow concrete blocks, or between the insulation and foundation.

Good Building Practices

While the code offers clear guidance for builders in areas of "very heavy" infestation, in the rest of the U.S., the decision is often left to builders and homeowners with or without some guidance from local inspectors.

Since the map of termite risk adopted by the codes dates back to the early 1960s, it may not accurately can slip through the foundation/slab joint, inside the hollow concrete blocks, or between the insulation and foundation.

Monolithic slabs, where grade beam and slab are cast in one pour, lack joints and, therefore, present fewer entry routes than slabs supported on foundation walls. Likewise, a cast concrete stem wall, with its solid center and reinforcement to minimize cracking, is better than a hollow block wall. However, block walls can be made more termite-resistant by capping them with reinforced concrete or solid blocks, or by plugging the hollows in the top course with mortar.

Making *any* foundation termite-resistant requires treating the soil under the slab and surrounding the foundation with a termiticide. Treating the soil under the slab, of course, is best done before the slab is cast, and treating the surrounding soil should be done during finish grading.

Termites prefer wetter soils, so make sure water is directed away from the foundation by properly sloping finish grades and by using gutters and downspouts. Also, keep the below-slab drainage pad higher than the outside soil by elevating the slab surface at least 8 inches above the finish grade. Reinforce the slab to minimize cracking and design utilities so that the slab penetrations are minimized or eliminated. All penetrations and joints should be sealed with roofing-grade coal-tar pitch. Also, make sure that all wood (read "termite food"), such as stumps, grade stakes, formwork, and scraps, is removed and disposed of off site, and not buried during backfilling.

When detailing the insulation, you may have to sacrifice some energy efficiency in return for being able to properly inspect for termites. The details in B and C show two ways to leave the foundation exposed for inspection and also reduce the number of possible entries. The metal shields shown in these details should be thought of as only *one part* of a home's anti-termite defenses. They're seldom fabricated and installed as tightly and as carefully as is really necessary.

B. Monolithic Slab-on-Grade

Metal shield
8" min.
Treated fill
Treated soil

C. Basement or Crawl Space

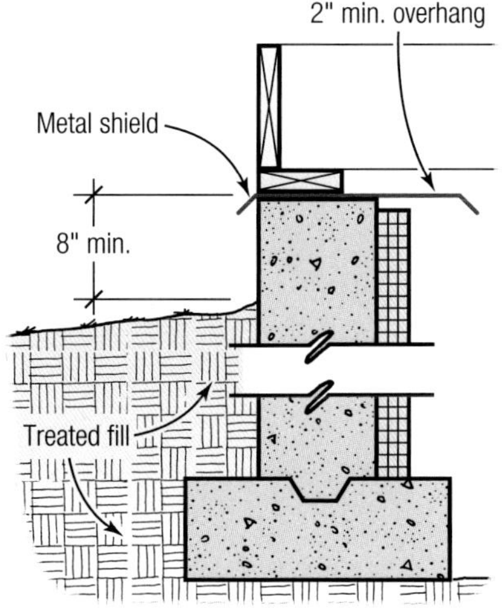

A monolithic slab (B) or a concrete basement wall (C) presents fewer entry routes than a slab resting on a stem wall. It's important to leave at least 8 inches of the foundation exposed above grade. Although some insulation value is lost, this allows an exterminator to inspect for the presence of termites.

Dr. Steven Smulski is a wood scientist and president of Wood Science Specialists in Shutesboro, Mass.

reflect current termite activity throughout the U.S. It is not known whether anecdotal reports of greater termite damage in some northern climates reflect greater termite activity, more homes in wooded areas, or just more homes in general. But your state's structural pest control authority, pest control operators, or code officials may provide a better guide to local conditions than the official code map of termite infestation.

In some areas, builders would be wise to follow the same precautions as outlined above for areas of "very heavy" infestation. In all areas, builders should use common-sense building practices that discourage termite attack. In areas of minimal risk, these good building practices may be enough to keep the critters at bay.

Key points are to keep the soil dry around the building perimeter and to keep termite attractors out of the backfill. These strategies are widely recommended for all buildings but too often ignored. As summarized by the National Pest Control Association, these include:

- Avoid water accumulation near your home's foundation.
- Divert water away with properly functioning downspouts, gutters and splash blocks.
- Reduce humidity in crawlspaces with proper ventilation.
- Remove old form boards, grade stakes, etc., left in place after the building was constructed. Never bury wood scraps or waste lumber in the yard.
- Remove old tree stumps and roots around and beneath the building.
- Most important, eliminate wood contact with the soil. Ideally maintain an 18-inch gap between the soil and wood portions of the building.
- Routinely inspect the foundation for signs of termite entry.

Foam at slab edge. Homes built with radiant slabs pose a special problem, because they often rely heavily on insulation at the edge of the slab. The warmth from the slab is inviting to ants and termites, which can make their way through cracks as small as 1⁄32 inch. Joints of this size and larger typically occur under wall plates at the edge of the slab, where termite traffic is hidden from view. The same techniques used to control radon — meticulous detailing of control joints and pipe penetrations — combined with chemical soil treatment before and after construction may be necessary to keep insects at bay. If foam must be used for perimeter insulation, placing it on the inside of the frost wall keeps the concrete or block accessible for chemical treatments outside.

Chapter 5

THE BUILDING SHELL

- Practical Details for Tight Construction
- Building a High-Performance Shell
- REMOTE Walls: Exterior Foam Details for Cold Climates
- Tight and Efficient Double Stud Walls

Practical Details for Tight Construction

by Paul Bourke

Over the years, I've developed a simple system to control random air leaks in the energy-efficient houses I build in Massachusetts. Of all the possible energy-saving upgrades, air sealing is the most cost-effective, since about 30 percent of the heat loss in a typical home is due to uncontrolled air leaks. Using the techniques described here, we build houses with consistently low infiltration rates — 0.6 square inches (or less) of leakage per 100 square feet of shell area, well under the Energy Crafted Homes standard of 2.0 square inches.

For a tight, energy-efficient house, plan your air-sealing strategy at the framing stage.

Creating a Tight Air Barrier

If you are committed to minimizing air leaks in the houses you build, you need to be sure that everyone on the job site, including the framing crew and the subcontractors, understands the basics of air sealing and understands your expectations for maintaining a tight air barrier.

In the colder parts of the U.S., builders typically install polyethylene under the drywall, calling it the "vapor barrier." But the most important function of polyethylene is as an *air barrier*. Moisture follows air leaks, moving through holes in a house, at much greater rates than it passes through solid surfaces as a vapor. Most of the problem-causing moisture that condenses in attics and building cavities is transported by interior air leaking through holes in the air barrier.

An air barrier should be continuous with the thermal insulation (see "Locating the Thermal Envelope," page 119). In most cases, the air barrier will be on the warm side of the thermal insulation, but it doesn't have to be. In some cases, it makes sense to establish the air barrier on the outside of the thermal insulation.

Assemble your materials. For a careful air-sealing job, you'll need to be sure you have a few important materials on hand: reinforced polyethylene (for example, Tu-Tuf, Good News Reused, or Tenoarm); Tremco

Figure 1. Installing 1 inch of rigid foam insulation under the basement slab keeps the slab warm enough to prevent moisture from condensing on it. The perimeter insulation between the slab and the colder concrete wall provides a thermal break. The cast-in-place pressure-treated window frames will receive low-E argon-filled windows.

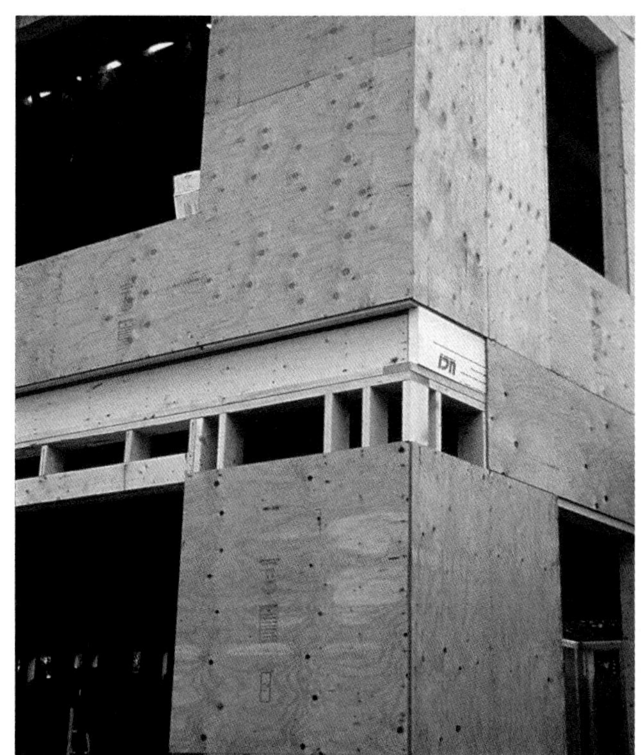

Figure 2. Recessing the band joist 2 inches provides room for exterior rigid foam insulation. To provide an air barrier, the foam is carefully caulked in place with Tremco acoustical sealant.

acoustical sealant (a multi-purpose air-sealing caulk that sticks to polyethylene); 3M Construction Seaming Tape (also called contractors' tape, it's used for polyethylene and housewrap); airtight electrical boxes (from LESSCO); and a good urethane foam gun (see "Sources of Supply," page 121).

Keeping the Basement Warm

We always install 6-mil polyethylene and at least 1 inch of rigid foam insulation under all of our basement slabs. Besides saving energy, the foam keeps the slab warm, greatly increasing comfort and helping to minimize condensation. After installing crushed stone to the depth of the footing, we lay down the poly and then the rigid foam. We also install a strip of 1-inch foam at the perimeter of the slab, between the slab and the foundation wall, as a thermal break (Figure 1). If the basement floor is getting radiant heat, we'll increase the thickness of the under-slab insulation to 2 inches.

Insulating basement walls. We no longer insulate our basement walls from the exterior, since exterior foam is vulnerable to insect damage, and above-grade foam is difficult to protect. Instead, we frame up 2x4 walls inside the basement, leaving a 2-inch gap between the back of the studs and the basement wall. This allows enough room for the installation of R-19 fiberglass batts, which we cover with flame-retardant poly from Poly-America. One advantage of interior insulation: With the 2x4 perimeter walls installed, all it takes is wiring and drywall for a customer to finish the basement.

Since most basement walls have few penetrations, they are relatively simple to air seal. But be careful of bulkhead doors, which are often leaky. The area between the door and the band joist, especially, needs to be sealed and insulated.

Preventing Drafty Floors

Most houses leak a lot of air through gaps at the perimeter of the floor system. To keep this area tight, four critical areas need to be addressed: under the mudsill; along the band joist; between the band joist and the subfloor; and between the subfloor and the wall plate.

Tight sills. Between the foundation wall and the mudsill, we use regular polyethylene foam sill seal, folded in half lengthwise. Doubled sill seal does a better job of air sealing than a single layer. Any gaps that are too big for the sill seal to handle are filled later, using our urethane foam gun.

Warm band joists. On many houses, the band joists are poorly insulated, so condensation forms on the cold interior surface of the lumber. Keeping the band joist warm with exterior foam insulation prevents condensation that can lead to rot.

Since we frame our walls with 2x6s, we can recess our band joists 2 inches. We attach 2-inch-thick rigid foam to the band joist with continuous beads of Tremco acoustical sealant (Figure 2). The rigid foam, once it is caulked in place, becomes the air barrier. Although Tremco sealant can be messy to apply (and is often referred to on job sites as "black death"), it's the best caulk to use for air sealing a wide variety of materials, including most types of plastic.

From inside the basement, we stuff a piece of R-19 kraft-faced fiberglass batt into each joist bay, behind the band joist. Finally, when we put the subfloor down, we put a continuous bead of construction adhesive along the band joist to prevent any air leaks at the perimeter of the subfloor.

Gasketed bottom plate. We install regular foam sill seal under the bottom plates of our exterior walls. To make the sill seal go twice as far, we usually cut it in half lengthwise. We roll out the foam and hammer-tack it to the subfloor just before we stand up our walls. Instead of foam sill seal, you can also use sticky-backed foam weatherstripping in this location.

Cantilevers. Cantilevered floors are particularly difficult to air seal, especially if wires or pipes create an air path through the floor and up the exterior wall. At the point where the cantilever begins, we install solid blocking between each cantilevered joist. The edges of the blocking, as well as any penetrations through the blocking, get carefully caulked. Because the plywood subfloor over a cantilever is the air barrier, be sure the subfloor is installed with construction adhesive. Finally, the bottom of the cantilevered joists need to be wrapped with housewrap.

Keeping Walls Tight

Most of our walls are framed with 2x6s, 16 inches on-center. If the studs are spaced wider than 16 inches, the dense-pack cellulose insulation pillows out, interfering with drywall installation. If the customer is willing to pay for an upgrade, we space the 2x6 studs at 24 inches on-center and then install horizontal interior 1x3 strapping at 16 inches on-center (Figure 3). The strapping restrains the cellulose and also provides a thermal break between the drywall and the studs.

Figure 3. When the budget allows, 2x6 studs are spaced 24 inches on-center, and 1x3 strapping is installed horizontally at 16 inches on-center. The air space provides a thermal break between the studs and the drywall. Red 3M tape is used to seal seams and tears in the poly air barrier.

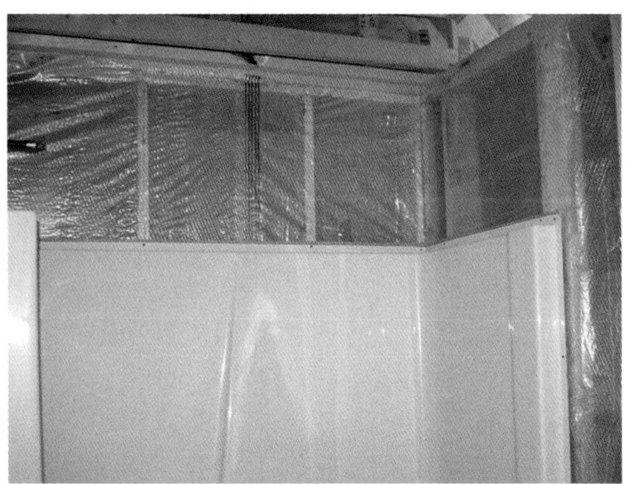

Figure 4. When a tub/shower unit is located on an exterior wall, the poly air barrier is installed before the tub goes in. To create a tight air barrier, the poly needs to be taped to the bottom plate of the wall.

When it comes to sheathing, we prefer to use plywood or OSB, unless the homeowner insists on foam. Foam sheathing causes several headaches: The walls need special bracing against racking; window and door openings need to be furred out; and siding can be attached only to the studs.

We always install Tyvek, which we consider the best available housewrap. We tape all seams with Tyvek tape, following the manufacturer's instructions.

Where an interior partition meets an exterior wall, we install a vertical 1x8, 1x10, or plywood piece as a drywall nailer. This nailer needs to be continuous (not a collection of scraps), and it needs to be wide enough to provide room to tape the poly air barrier in the corner.

Insulating Rafter Heels

In many houses, the insulation is thin at the rafter heels, where adequate space for insulation is lacking. This thin insulation can contribute to melting snow and ice dams. On the interior, thin insulation leaves the drywall cold at the corner, encouraging condensation and mildew.

One way to increase the R-value at the rafter heels is to install rigid foam insulation between the rafters. This is fussy work — first, installing ¾-inch strips of plywood against the top of the rafter faces to maintain a ventilation channel, then cutting each piece of foam for a snug fit.

If the roof is being framed with rafters, an easier solution is to install a band joist and raise the rafters (see "Attic Ventilation Details," page 166). Raising the rafters leaves plenty of room for insulation. If the roof is framed with trusses, use raised-heel trusses, which don't cost much more than regular trusses.

Windows and Doors

We build insulated door and window headers out of two 2x10s, a piece of ½-inch plywood, and 2 inches of rigid foam. The gap between a window and the rough opening should be sealed using a urethane foam gun or with backer rod and caulk, not fiberglass insulation. (Fiberglass insulation is not an air barrier.) We plan our rough openings for a ⅜-inch gap all around the window or door — just the right gap for a foam-gun nozzle. We use Pur-Fil low-expansion foam, which won't distort the frame and pinch the sash.

Attic hatches. Since an attic access hatch is just an exterior door located in a ceiling, it needs to be carefully insulated and weatherstripped. A piece of drywall dropped into the opening is obviously inadequate. In winter, hatches without weatherstripping are often ringed with ice and deteriorated attic insulation.

We build our attic hatches from plywood and glue 4 inches of rigid foam insulation on top. Around the perimeter of the plywood hatch, we screw steel connector strapping. Along the top of the stop, we install magnetic door gasketing, which sucks that hatch down and seals it. When these magnetically sealed hatches are tested with a blower door, they are virtually leak-free.

Think Ahead

We've learned to recognize several areas that can be tricky to seal: walls behind tubs, interior soffits, recessed can lights, attic ductwork, zero-clearance fireplaces, chimney chases, dryer vents, and electrical boxes. If you plan the air-sealing details at the framing stage, sealing these areas will be much easier.

Tubs and showers. If a tub is located on an exterior wall, we install the poly air barrier, taped to the bottom plate, before the tub goes in (Figure 4). Then the area behind the tub is sheathed with plywood, which protects the poly and prevents the cellulose insulation from pillowing out. After the tub is installed, the stud bays can easily be filled with blown-in cellulose from the top.

Interior soffits. If the house has a second-floor soffit, don't forget to install the poly air barrier before the soffit is framed. The poly should be large enough to allow it to be taped later to the rest of the poly air barrier.

Recessed cans. In many houses, recessed can lights act like little chimneys, constantly leaking interior air into the attic (Figure 5). If we have to install a recessed can light in an insulated ceiling, we make sure it is an airtight unit rated IC for insulation contact. We mount the can fixture on a piece of plywood that spans two joists; the plywood provides a surface for taping the poly air barrier.

Wherever possible, especially in bathrooms, we install recessed cans in soffits or dropped ceilings. Because the poly air barrier is installed at the bottom of the joists before the soffit is built, the air barrier remains intact above the electrical fixtures.

Attic ducts. Most of our houses have some ductwork in the attic. At each ceiling register, and wherever a duct penetrates the ceiling poly, we install a section of ¾-inch plywood spanning two joists. We usually provide the hvac sub with a stack of 24-inch-wide pieces of ¾-inch plywood for this purpose, and the sub installs the plywood (Figure 6). The gap between the plywood and the duct or the flange on the register boot is sealed with a liberal amount of silicone caulk.

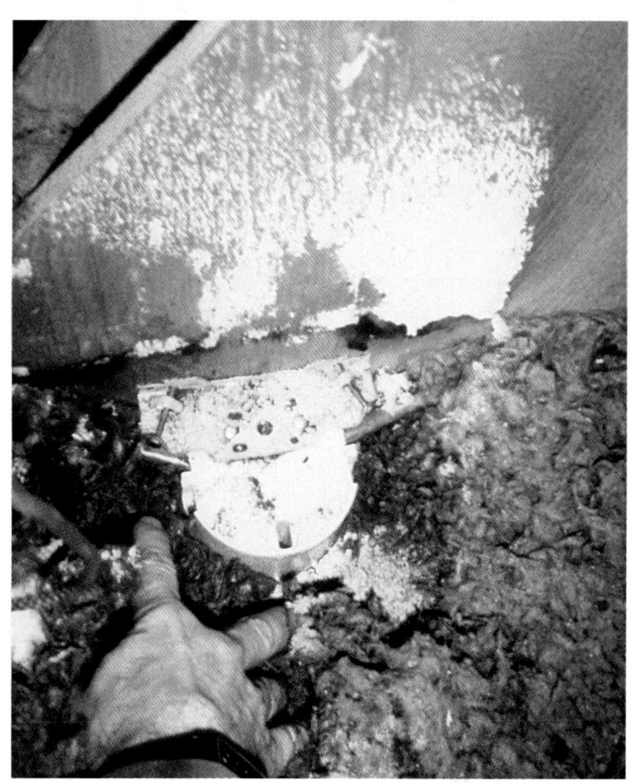

Figure 5. Poorly sealed ceiling-mounted light fixtures continuously leak interior air into the attic. When the warm, moist air hits a cold surface, the moisture condenses, leading to mildew or rot.

Figure 6. Here, a forced-air register is installed in a piece of ¾-inch plywood where it penetrates the attic air barrier. The register boot is caulked to the plywood.

The ceiling poly gets taped to the plywood.

All of the attic ducts are sealed with mastic or aluminum tape. After the hvac sub has installed the ducts, we always go into the attic to inspect the work to be sure all penetrations of the ceiling air barrier are well sealed. New subs usually take some training before they get it right.

Fireplaces. Zero-clearance fireplaces provide many opportunities for air leaks. Usually, we stop the air barrier one stud short of the fireplace to keep the poly away from high temperatures. We tape the poly to that stud and then install ½-inch cementitious backerboard between the stud and the fireplace. To maintain the air barrier, the backerboard is caulked in place with high-temperature silicone caulk, which we purchase at an auto supply store. The backerboard eventually gets covered with marble or brick.

Chimney chases. Most chimney chases allow interior air to rise to the attic through the 2-inch gap between the chimney and the ceiling joists. In many parts of the country, inspectors are being more stringent about enforcing the requirement for chimney firestops. That's good, because firestops improve energy efficiency.

For masonry chimneys, we make our firestops out of 8-inch-wide aluminum flashing, bent on a brake. Our mason cuts a ½-inch kerf into the masonry to insert the firestop, which doubles as an air barrier. Each chimney gets four pieces of flashing. We nail the flashing onto the framing, with a continuous bead of high-temperature silicone caulk under the flashing. We also install caulk at all of the flashing seams.

Metal chimneys require firestop kits provided by the chimney manufacturer. All of the gaps and cracks in these firestops need to be caulked with high-temperature silicone.

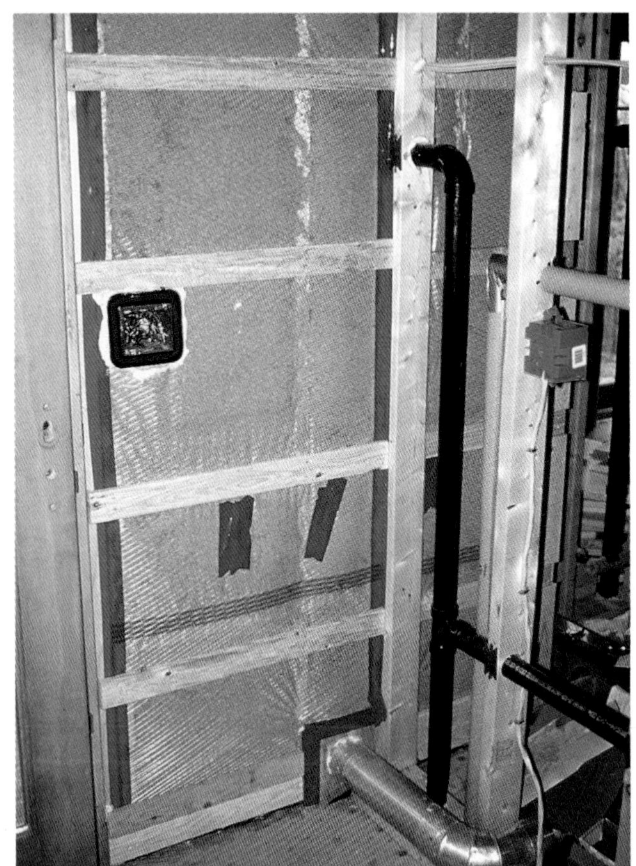

Figure 7. Where this dryer vent penetrates the exterior wall (at bottom of photo), a plywood block provides a surface for taping the poly air barrier. This house has horizontal wall strapping, so there was no need to recess the plywood block between the studs. Note that where the partition meets the exterior wall, the penetrations for the plumbing vent and electrical cable are sealed with urethane foam. The photo also shows an Enviroseal airtight electrical box.

Dryer vents. Where a dryer vent goes through an exterior wall, we usually install a plywood block between the studs, so that the vent duct has something to rest on (Figure 7). The plywood is attached to small 1x1 nailers and is mounted flush with the edge of the studs. We apply urethane foam between the dryer vent and the plywood and tape the poly air barrier to the plywood.

Electrical boxes. We use Enviroseal airtight electrical boxes. (Note: These are currently unavailable.) These boxes have a removable wide flange with a foam gasket designed to seal against the drywall. When we install the poly air barrier, we cut an X at each box and stretch the poly over the box. We tape the poly to the box, and then fit the flange on the box, locking the poly in place.

Enviroseal boxes are available only as one- or two-gang boxes. When we need three- or four-gang boxes, we buy airtight electrical boxes made by LESSCO.

Foam the gaps. After the framing is complete and the rough mechanicals are in — but before the insulation and poly — we inspect the house for gaps that need to be filled using the urethane foam gun. Places to check include between the foundation wall and the mudsill, where wires go through partitions that intersect exterior walls, and where wires and pipes penetrate the top plate into the attic.

Polyethylene Air Barrier

Some builders of energy-efficient homes advocate the Airtight Drywall Approach (ADA), creating their air barriers with gaskets installed under the drywall rather than with polyethylene. But since drywall contractors in our area are not familiar with ADA techniques, and since a poly barrier typically accompanies the installation of our preferred insulation, dense-pack cellulose, we don't use the ADA method.

Our insulation sub installs the reinforced poly air barrier according to our requirements. The poly gets stapled with ¾-inch staples using an electric staple

Locating the Thermal Envelope

The continuous barrier formed by the insulation and air barrier is called the thermal envelope. Where to locate the thermal envelope depends, to some extent, on builder preference. Should it follow a flat ceiling or the sloping rafters? Should it include the crawl space? In many cases, there is no single right answer to these questions. However, it is important to make a choice and stick with it, and then explain to your framing crew and subcontractors where the thermal envelope is located.

Air Sealing a Cape Knee Wall

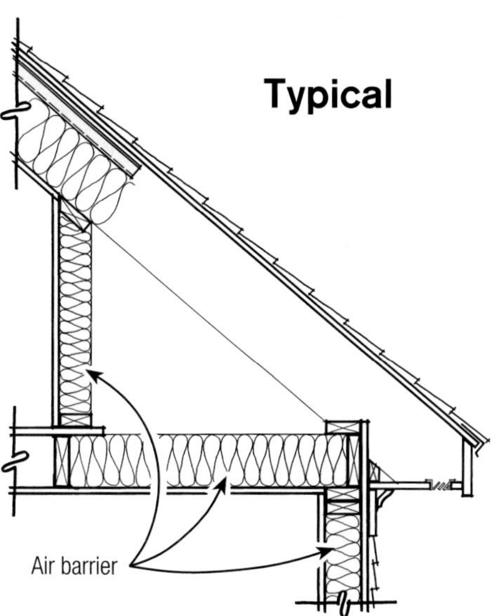

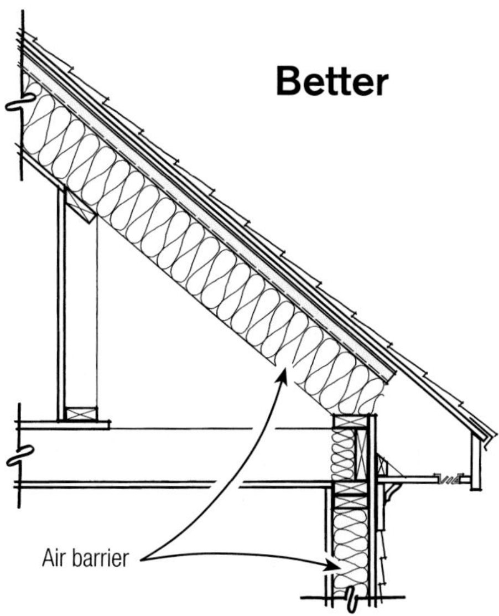

Creating a tight air barrier in a Cape kneewall is much easier if the rafter insulation is brought all the way down to the wall plates (above). The more typical approach of insulating the kneewalls and floor area (top) is more labor intensive to seal and more prone to air leaks.

In the past, many builders excluded basements and crawlspaces from the thermal envelope. However, building scientists now recommend sealing and insulating crawlspace walls.

In cold climates, the prescriptive requirements of the Model Energy Code mandate basement wall insulation. Including the basement inside the building's thermal envelope is usually simpler and no more expensive than building an uninsulated basement, because insulated basements do not require ceiling insulation, duct sealing, duct insulation, or pipe insulation.

In a typical Cape, the second-floor kneewalls are insulated, as well as a portion of the first-floor ceiling (see illustration). But when the thermal envelope is located at the kneewalls, air sealing becomes very difficult. Interior air can escape through the first floor ceiling into the cold area behind the kneewalls. Exterior air from the soffit vents, which should rise above the insulation in the rafter bays to ventilate the roof, often enters the living area through gaps in the kneewall. An access door in an insulated kneewall is awkward to build, because it needs to be carefully insulated and weatherstripped.

Air sealing is easier when the rafter insulation is extended down to the plates, bringing the triangular crawlspace behind the kneewalls within the building's thermal envelope. This also permits the area behind the kneewall to be used for storage without the need for an airtight access door.

—P.B.

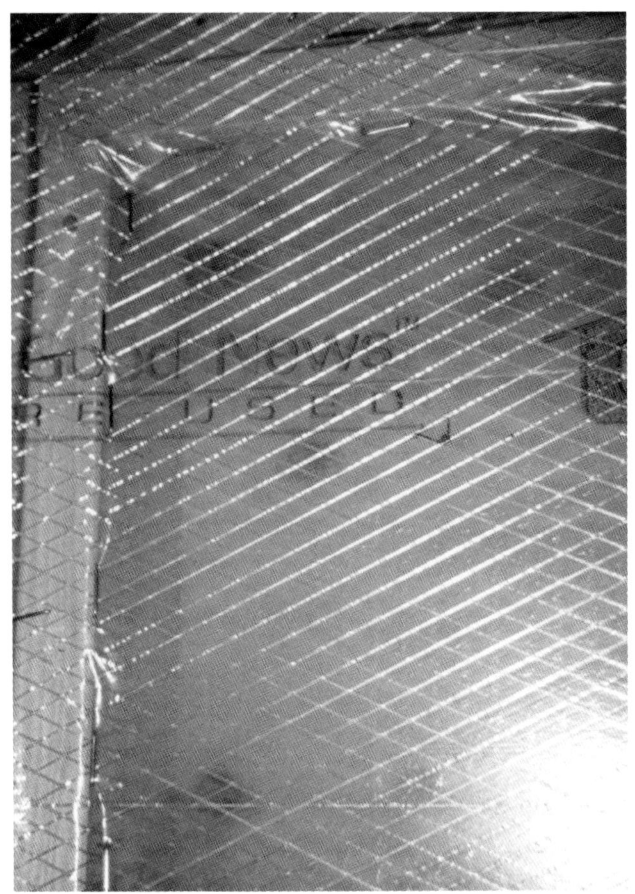

Figure 8. Most dense-pack cellulose systems require the installation of a reinforced polyethylene air barrier. Stapling the poly on the side rather than the edge of the studs helps keep the poly from bulging when the cellulose is blown in place.

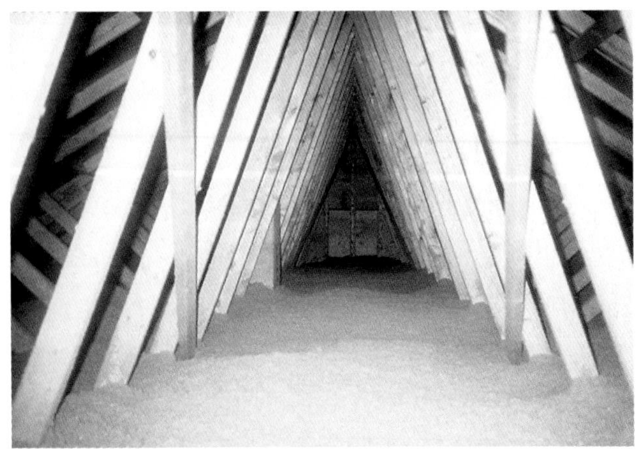

Figure 9. Cellulose insulation is inexpensive and effectively fills all of the spaces around the bottom chords of roof trusses. It should be installed at least 20 percent deeper than required to allow for settling.

gun. For walls that won't receive interior horizontal strapping, the staples are driven into the face (side) of the stud, about 1/4 or 1/2 inch back from the interior edge (Figure 8).

Although a vapor barrier with a 2 percent gap is still 98 percent effective, the same is not true for an air barrier. An air barrier needs to be continuous, since small gaps can lead to big problems. All seams and gaps in a poly air barrier must be taped or caulked. For a typical building, we'll use about 12 rolls of 3M red tape, which costs about $12 a roll. Where the air barrier is being sealed to a top plate or bottom plate, or at the rough opening for a window or door, the poly can be sealed with either 3M tape or Tremco acoustical sealant.

We have experimented with installing the poly air barrier on the entire second-floor ceiling before we put up the interior partitions. But since that makes it more difficult for our mechanical subs to access the attic, we don't do it anymore. Usually, our ceiling poly is installed room by room and is carefully taped to the top plates of the walls. At the exterior walls, the ceiling poly gets taped to the wall poly.

Ceiling strapping. We usually strap our ceilings with 1x3s. In most cases, we install the poly air barrier on the bottom of the joists, before the strapping goes up.

Time to Insulate

Any insulation material can work well, as long as it is installed carefully. But if you expect fiberglass batts to match the performance of a blown-in insulation like dense-pack cellulose, you need to install the batts meticulously, without voids. How many fiberglass installers actually take the time to split the batts at every pipe and wire in the walls, much less in the attic?

Our preferred insulation is dense-pack cellulose, installed at a density of 2 1/2 pounds per cubic foot. Dense-pack cellulose helps reduce air infiltration and fills in especially well around mechanicals, wires, plumbing, and odd-shaped or tight spaces.

Because blowing cellulose in an attic is relatively inexpensive, you can pile it deep (Figure 9). Before insulating an attic, we install sections of fiberglass batt insulation against the ventilation baffles to prevent the cellulose from blowing into the soffits. When using blown-in cellulose in a cathedral ceiling, we install extra-rigid ventilation baffles (Durovent from ADO Products), since the cellulose pressure can cause standard baffles to collapse.

Our insulation sub slits the poly air barrier at each stud bay to insert the 2-inch blowing hose. It is the sub's responsibility to patch each hole with 3M tape. When the insulation job is complete, I check that the slits have all been taped. I also check the insulation density by feel, especially near the top of the stud bays. Well-installed cellulose should feel as firm as a car seat, not soft like a down pillow. The poly air barrier should be taut.

Build Tight and Ventilate Right

A tight house, which can't depend on random air leaks for ventilation and combustion makeup air, needs mechanical ventilation and sealed-combustion appliances.

We ventilate many of our houses with Panasonic bathroom exhaust fans, which are quiet fans designed for continuous operation (see "Simple Exhaust Ventilation for Tight Houses," page 294). We follow the guidelines of ASHRAE 62-1989, which requires 15 cfm per person. Depending on the size of the house, this requirement is easily met with one or two Panasonic bathroom exhaust fans, each controlled by an Airetrak timer/fan-speed controller.

Multiple Benefits

The package of air-sealing details we provide adds between 2 and 2½ percent to the cost of our homes — about $4,000 to $5,000 in construction costs on a $200,000 house. However, these details also result in savings. The houses require smaller heating and air-conditioning units, as well as less radiation or ductwork. Because we use sealed-combustion appliances, there is no need for a chimney. In many cases, these savings pay for the cost of the air-sealing measures.

Besides lowering the customer's heating bills, an energy-efficient house is less drafty and, therefore, more comfortable than a conventional house. During the winter, the indoor air will not be as dry as the air in a leaky house, so residents will have fewer bouts of respiratory infections, asthma, and allergic rhinitis. With fewer air leaks, there is less chance that warm, moist indoor air will leak into cold walls or the attic, where moisture can condense. Because of this, a tight house will be especially durable.

So if you build energy-efficient houses, your customers will be healthier. And they'll be pleased to know that their durable, comfortable, energy-efficient house will have a higher than average resale value.

***Paul Bourke** is a builder based in Leverett, Mass. He is a former instructor in the Energy Crafted Homes program and a member of the New England Sustainable Energy Association.*

Sources of Supply

3M
Construction Products Dept.
3M Center
St. Paul, MN 55144-1000
www.3M.com
3M 8087 Construction Seaming Tape

ADO Products
P.O. Box 236
Rogers, MN 55374
www.adoproducts.com
Durovent heavy-duty polystyrene attic ventilation baffles

Energy Federation Inc.
40 Washington St., Suite 3000
Westborough, MA 01581
www.efi.org
Retailer of air-sealing, energy-saving, and ventilation products, including Tu-Tuf polyethylene, 3M Builders' Sealing Tape, Pur-Fil aerosol urethane foam, and Enviroseal and LESSCO airtight electrical boxes

LESSCO
W1330 Happy Hollow Rd.
Campbellsport, WI 53010
www.lessco-airtight.com
Airtight electrical boxes

ParPac
P.O. Box 153
South Bristol, ME 04568
www.parpac.com
Good News Reused reinforced polyethylene air barrier

Poly-America
2000 W. Marshall Dr.
Grand Prairie, TX 75051
www.poly-america.com
Flame-retardant polyethylene sheeting, which can be left exposed in a basement

Resource Conservation Technology
2633 N. Calvert St.
Baltimore, MD 21218
www.conservationtechnology.com
Distributor of Tenoarm, a reinforced polyethylene air barrier from Sweden

Sto-Cote Products
Box 310
Genoa City, WI 53128
Manufacturer of Tu-Tuf reinforced polyethylene air barrier

Tamarack Technologies
P.O. Box 490
W. Wareham, MA 02576
www.tamtech.com
Distributor of ventilation products, including the Airetrak timer/fan-speed controller

Todol Products
P.O. Box 398
Natick, MA 01760
www.todol.com
Distributor of Pur-Fil aerosol urethane foam and Pur-Fil foam guns

Tremco Sealants
3735 Green Rd.
Beachwood, OH 44122
www.tremcosealants.com
Tremco acoustical sealant

Building a High-Performance Shell

by David Joyce

We recently completed a new home using a number of strategies to improve the home's energy performance. The home was designed by architect Betsy Petit of Building Science Corp. for owners who wanted a sustainable home with monthly energy costs that would remain fairly constant from one season to the next. They also wanted a building that was ahead of its time, so that 30 years from now, should they decide to pass it on to their children or sell, they wouldn't be handing off a dinosaur.

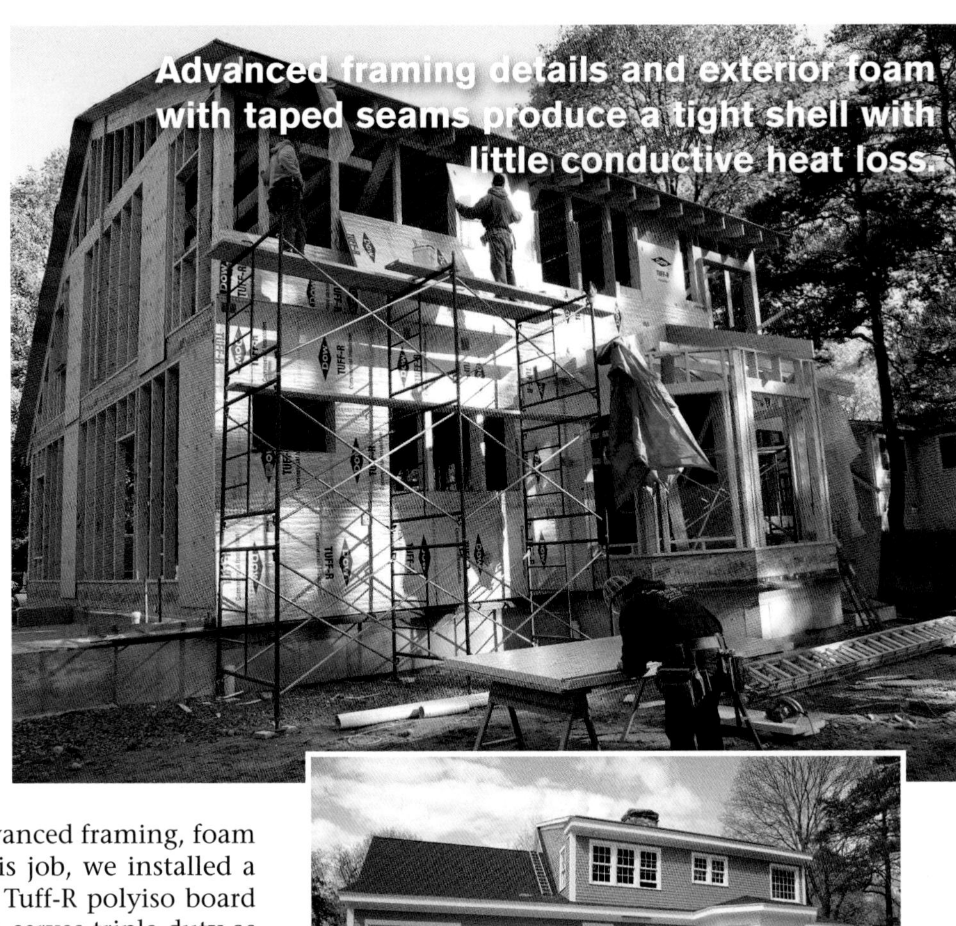
Advanced framing details and exterior foam with taped seams produce a tight shell with little conductive heat loss.

Among the performance-boosting strategies was the use of "advanced framing" — which eliminates redundant and structurally unnecessary lumber — and an exterior skin of insulating foam. Although not an essential ingredient of advanced framing, foam sheathing is a natural fit. On this job, we installed a double layer of 2-inch foil-faced Tuff-R polyiso board directly over the studs. The foam serves triple duty as a thermal break, a drainage plane for any water that gets past the siding, and an air barrier, with no need for supplemental housewrap. All seams and any tears in the foil facing are taped to provide an airtight, waterproof surface. To provide lateral strength to the frame, we installed vertical ½-inch plywood shear panels at specified intervals, covering the plywood with 1½-inch foam to match the thickness of the first foam layer.

Advanced Framing in the Field

The NAHB developed the advanced framing concept — originally known as "optimal value engineered," or OVE, framing — back in the 1970s, with the intention of making more efficient use of building materials. In this approach, all framing is strictly aligned from the first-floor deck up to the rafters on 24-inch centers. Walls have single top plates, corners are built with two studs instead of three or more, and structural headers are reduced to single members or insulated cores; in non-load-bearing walls, headers are eliminated (see "Framing, Insulation, and Air-Sealing Details," facing page).

Tying top plates together. Single-member top plates serve only to position and secure the studs, not to support or redistribute offset point loads. When butting plates together, it isn't necessary to land the joint on a stud. Instead, we use a Simpson TP49 metal splice plate or a piece of wood blocking. Blocking is cheaper and faster to install; where it just won't fit, as in corners, we use the metal plates. To prevent joint stress and separation, we install the metal plates after standing the walls. Before nailing them off, we throw a strap around a few studs on either side of the joint and pull it tight.

Because a single plate is more flexible than double top plates, it takes a little more time and a few more braces to straighten walls. When we brace the walls, we pull them slightly inward, about ¼ inch from plumb. Throughout construction, the top plates tend to get forced outward, mostly by rafter thrust before

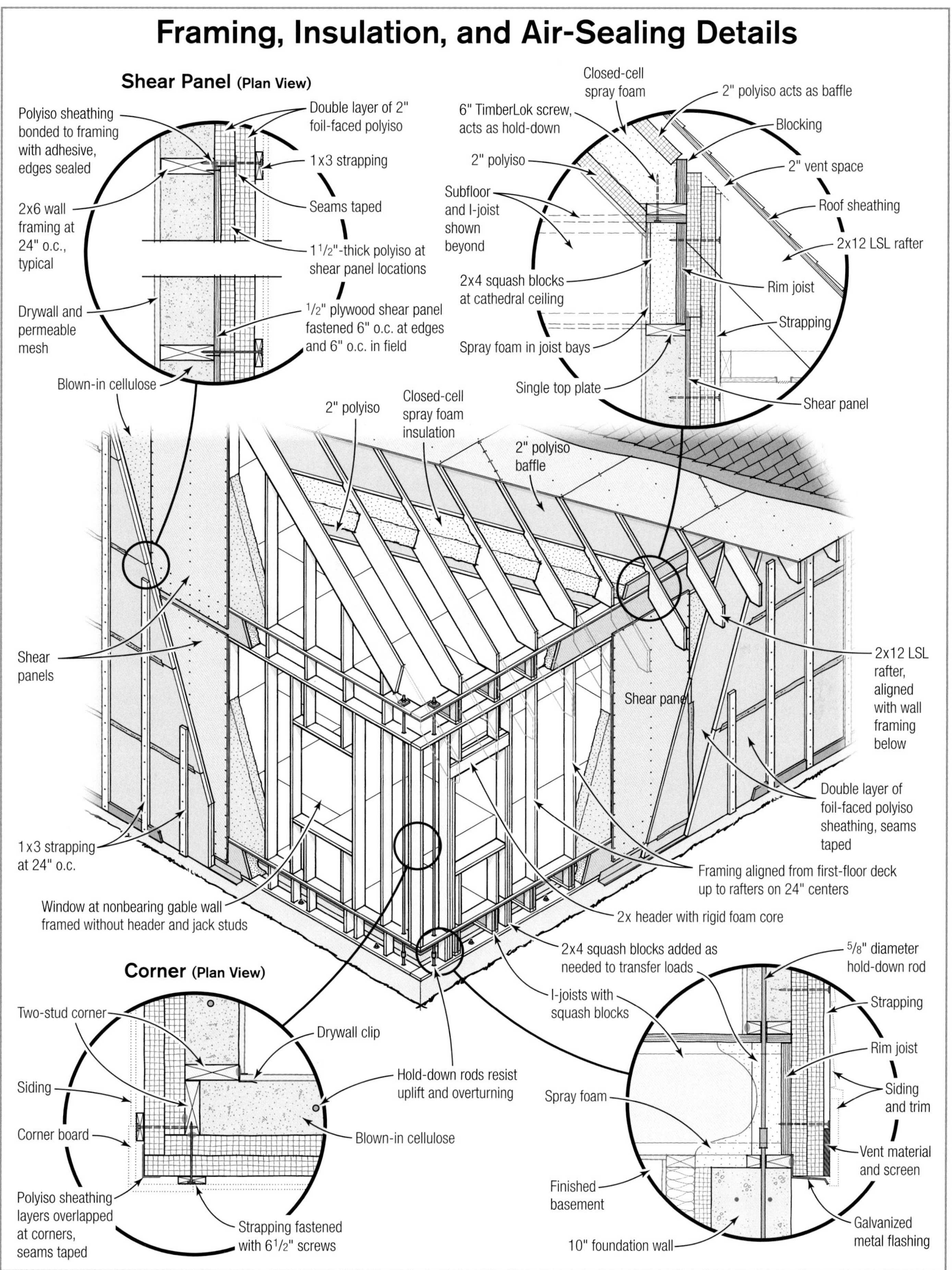
Framing, Insulation, and Air-Sealing Details
Shear Panel (Plan View)
Polyiso sheathing bonded to framing with adhesive, edges sealed
Double layer of 2" foil-faced polyiso
1x3 strapping
Seams taped
2x6 wall framing at 24" o.c., typical
1 1/2"-thick polyiso at shear panel locations
Drywall and permeable mesh
1/2" plywood shear panel fastened 6" o.c. at edges and 6" o.c. in field
Blown-in cellulose
Closed-cell spray foam
2" polyiso acts as baffle
6" TimberLok screw, acts as hold-down
Blocking
2" polyiso
2" vent space
Subfloor and I-joist shown beyond
Roof sheathing
2x12 LSL rafter
2x4 squash blocks at cathedral ceiling
Rim joist
Strapping
Spray foam in joist bays
Single top plate
Shear panel
2" polyiso
Closed-cell spray foam insulation
2" polyiso baffle
Shear panels
Shear panel
2x12 LSL rafter, aligned with wall framing below
Double layer of foil-faced polyiso sheathing, seams taped
1x3 strapping at 24" o.c.
Framing aligned from first-floor deck up to rafters on 24" centers
Window at nonbearing gable wall framed without header and jack studs
2x header with rigid foam core
2x4 squash blocks added as needed to transfer loads
5/8" diameter hold-down rod
Corner (Plan View)
I-joists with squash blocks
Strapping
Two-stud corner
Drywall clip
Rim joist
Hold-down rods resist uplift and overturning
Siding
Spray foam
Siding and trim
Blown-in cellulose
Corner board
Vent material and screen
Finished basement
Polyiso sheathing layers overlapped at corners, seams taped
Strapping fastened with 6 1/2" screws
Galvanized metal flashing
10" foundation wall

the collar ties are installed. Later, it's a lot easier to push a wall outward to plumb it than it is to haul it back in, so I like to start with that advantage.

Wall layout modifications. When laying out the front walls, we had to keep in mind how to support the second floor and roof. Although the general framing was consistently lined up from bottom to top, five rough openings didn't coincide with the 24-inch-on-center layout. The situation was further complicated by two doghouse dormers, each with doubled rafters on both sides, that landed off-layout. To transfer these loads, we had to add studs on both floors and squash blocks at the rim joists (Figure 10). Generally, we found that the simplest approach was to lay out the wall according to the plan and install the supplemental framing as needed later.

Figure 10. In an advanced frame, headers are minimized in favor of insulation cavities. All framing is vertically aligned and point loads are distributed directly through to the foundation. In this sloped ceiling section, squash blocks carry the rafters' load path over the second-floor rim joist (A). Where interior partitions intersect exterior walls, horizontal ladder blocking will secure the end stud, keeping the wall bay fully open and accessible for insulation (B). Structural headers are packed with foam board to create a thermal break (C). Openings in nonbearing walls are minimally framed, with single-member headers installed on the flat (D). The $^1/_2$-inch plywood lining the rough opening extends out to cap the edge of the 4-inch-thick foam sheathing.

When framing the gables, we adjusted the layout to accommodate the foam sheathing. The first layer of 4-by-8-foot foam sheathing is installed with its edges aligned on stud centers, but because it's also overlapped at the building corners, it falls off standard layout by its 2-inch thickness. To compensate, we centered the first stud in from the corner at 22 inches and established the 24-inch layout from that point. We used simple two-stud "L" configurations at corners, which allows for slightly better insulation.

Figure 11. For the 24-foot lengths required to frame the main roof, the author used LSL (laminated strand lumber) rafters and collar ties in place of old-growth dimensional lumber (top). The floors are framed with 14-inch I-joists on 2-foot centers. TimberLok structural screws replace metal ties for faster, code-approved rafter hold-downs (above).

Rough openings on nonbearing walls don't typically require structural headers or jack studs, so there we installed king studs only, with single 2x6 head and sill members installed on the flat. If sheathing the frame with plywood, you'd cut the headers and sills to the exact rough opening width. But in this case, we lined the openings with ½-inch plywood bucks that projected out 4 inches to cap the edges of the foam sheathing. To accommodate the bucks, we added an inch to the height and width of each rough opening.

Partition backers. Instead of standard partition backers, we used single studs at wall intersections and installed ladder blocking to attach them. Again, this eliminates an interruption in the insulation layer typically created in conventional framing.

Floor and roof framing. There was nothing unusual about the floors or the roof. We used wood I-joists aligned with the 24-inch on-center wall layout. At the gable ends, we substituted OSB rim-joist material for the I-joists and installed vertical 2x4 squash blocks directly below the studs. We took the blocks from the scrap pile and saved the cost of a few I-joists. On top of the plates, we nailed 2x4 cleats on the flat. Stopped by the squash blocks, they provided a 1½-inch attachment surface for the ceiling drywall while still leaving the end bays accessible for insulation — in this case, closed-cell spray foam at all rims.

Standard dimensional lumber in the 24-foot lengths we needed for the rafters has to come from old-growth trees, which we prefer not to use (Figure 11). And for the 4-pitch roof in the rear, solid lumber joists on 24-inch centers wouldn't have had the capacity we needed to handle the area's snow load plus the weight of the solar panels we'd be installing. So we used 2x12 laminated strand lumber, or LSL, which cuts just like solid dimensional lumber and doesn't require additional reinforcement at the plates. It's much harder than solid lumber, though — our standard pneumatic nails bent when we were nailing off the collar ties. We switched to the heaviest-gauge nail the guns would handle and still had to hammer the last ¾ inch home.

We saved a little time by eliminating conventional metal rafter ties. Instead, we drove 6-inch-long TimberLok (www.fastenmaster.com) screws up through the top plate into the rafters. Where they can't be driven directly up through the plate underside, they can be sent into the rafter from the front corner of the plate at a 22-degree angle. According to a technical bulletin on the company's Web site, these screws are code-approved replacements for straps or ties, which is nice because they're also faster and less obtrusive.

Shear Panels

Because foam sheathing doesn't provide racking resistance, we applied vertical 4-by-10-foot sheets of ½-inch CDX plywood at intervals specified by code.

Nailed every 6 inches around the edges and in the field, the plywood spans from the first- to the second-floor rim joists; on gable walls it's continued up to the second-floor ceiling rim (Figure 12). According to the IRC, intermittent shear panels must be installed at no more than 25 feet on-center, and a 40-foot-long wall must have a minimum of three shear panels over its run. Here in the Boston area, wind-speed provisions are moderate, so these are fairly basic standards. In high-wind and seismic zones, these specs are unlikely to be adequate.

We installed the shear panels after completing the framing, when everything was straightened, plumbed, and braced. It was a lot easier to make the necessary final adjustments to the frame without the panels providing resistance. There was a total of 16 panels, most of which required no cutting or fitting; it took two workers about three hours to install them all.

In addition to the shear panels, the plans called for continuous ⅝-inch hold-down rods from the foundation up through the uppermost top plates, at all corners and most shear-panel locations. These rods resist building uplift and overturning. They required accurate placement when pouring the foundation, which was a bit of a pain, but running the 10-foot links up through the walls was easy. To install and tension 16 rods required six man-hours.

Foam Sheathing

We started the first layer of sheathing on top of a galvanized metal flashing strip set an inch lower than the top of the foundation (Figure 13). To help with air-sealing and to keep out bugs, we set the strip in GreenSeries high-performance adhesive (www.osipro.com) applied to the pressure-treated sill and foundation. The flashing projects out 4½ inches, then bends down in a drip edge. It protects the bottom of the foam from insects, rodents, and flying sparks. We nailed a 10-inch-wide strip of insect screen over the flashing, to be folded up later over the sheathing.

We installed the first layer of 2-inch-thick 4-by-8-foot sheets vertically, with their long edges centered on the studs. To aid in air-sealing, we bedded all edges in a heavy bead of GreenSeries adhesive against the framing. The adhesive bonds and seals the sheathing to the framing; we used only a single screw and a 3-inch washer — the kind used to fasten rubber membrane roof underlayment — near the center of the sheet to hold it until the glue set. To match up with adjacent 2-inch-thick material, we applied a 1½-inch

Figure 12. Intermittent vertical 4-by-10-foot sheets of ½-inch CDX plywood applied directly to the frame brace it against wind racking (A). Hold-down rods — required with intermittent bracing — are installed at building corners and at regular intervals around the perimeter. They're anchored in the foundation and continue up the walls (B) through the topmost wall plate (C).

layer of foam board over the shear panels. We taped every seam in both layers of foam with Dow Weathermate tape, which sticks well in both wet and cold conditions. Around window openings, we taped the first layer of foam to the plywood bucks.

We installed the second layer of 2-inch foam horizontally, starting with a 2-foot-wide panel to ensure that few if any seams would align between layers. At building corners, we also made sure to overlap the edges. There's no adhesive between the layers; instead, we temporarily held the outer layer in place with FastenMaster HeadLok screws driven through plywood scraps. Ultimately, the vertical strapping for the siding would secure it.

The project included an attached two-car garage that isn't conditioned or insulated. Before framing it, we applied the foam sheathing to the common gable wall (Figure 14). Later, we tied the two structures together using 8-inch HeadLok screws through the foam. We used the same approach when framing the roofs over an ell and a walk-out bay window, first sheathing the main structure and then overlaying the rafters.

Strapping for siding. To provide an attachment point for the fiber-cement siding, we applied vertical

Figure 13. A galvanized metal flashing, air-sealed to the rim and foundation with adhesive, provides a starter strip for the foam sheathing and protects the bottom edge from burrowing bugs, rodents, and flying sparks (A). The attached insect screen was later folded up over the ends of the vertical vent strips behind the siding. Expanding foam seals random cutouts in the rim joist. The first layer of 2-inch foam is installed vertically and sealed and bonded to the frame with adhesive (B). The second layer installs horizontally (C), overlapping in an alternating weave at building corners. Note the air-sealing tape on the first layer where it intersects the projecting window bucks (D).

Figure 14. Before framing the unheated attached garage, the author applied foam sheathing to the common wall, establishing a thermal break between the two structures (above). Structural screws driven through the foam tie the isolated frames together. Here, the author anchors a walk-out bay rafter to the wall framing (right).

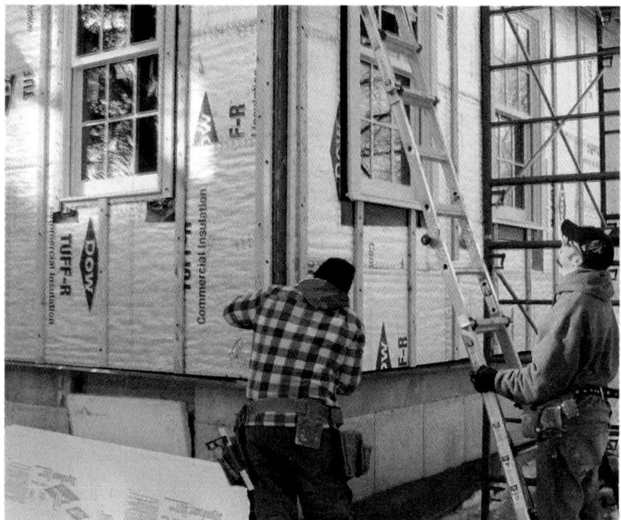

Figure 15. With the foam sheathing serving as a drainage plane, 1x3 vertical strapping creates a venting and drying space behind the siding. Additional strips around windows and doors provide separate backing for trim and siding.

1x3 strapping, screwed through the foam into the framing with 6½-inch HeadLok screws (Figure 15). The strapping creates a drainage cavity for any water that may penetrate the siding and allows drying air to circulate behind it. At the base, we cut strips of Cougar nylon-matrix ridge-vent material (www.benjaminobdyke.com) to fit between the strapping, to help pin the insect screen against the back of the siding. Around window openings, we installed strapping to back the exterior trim, and adjacent pieces to catch the siding. To provide attachment points for some of these screws, we had to add 2x4 blocking to the framing around the rough openings.

Windows and Doors

To terminate and seal the double layer of 2-inch foil-faced Tuff-R polyiso board around the rough window openings, we lined them with ½-inch plywood bucks that project 4 inches beyond the framing. The thickness of the sheathing ruled out installing the windows — Marvin Ultimate aluminum-clad low-E argon tri-pane double-hungs — using their vinyl nailing fins. Instead, we attached Simpson ST9 strap ties (www.strongtie.com) to the windows' side jambs, two per side, with ½-inch wood screws (Figure 16). After

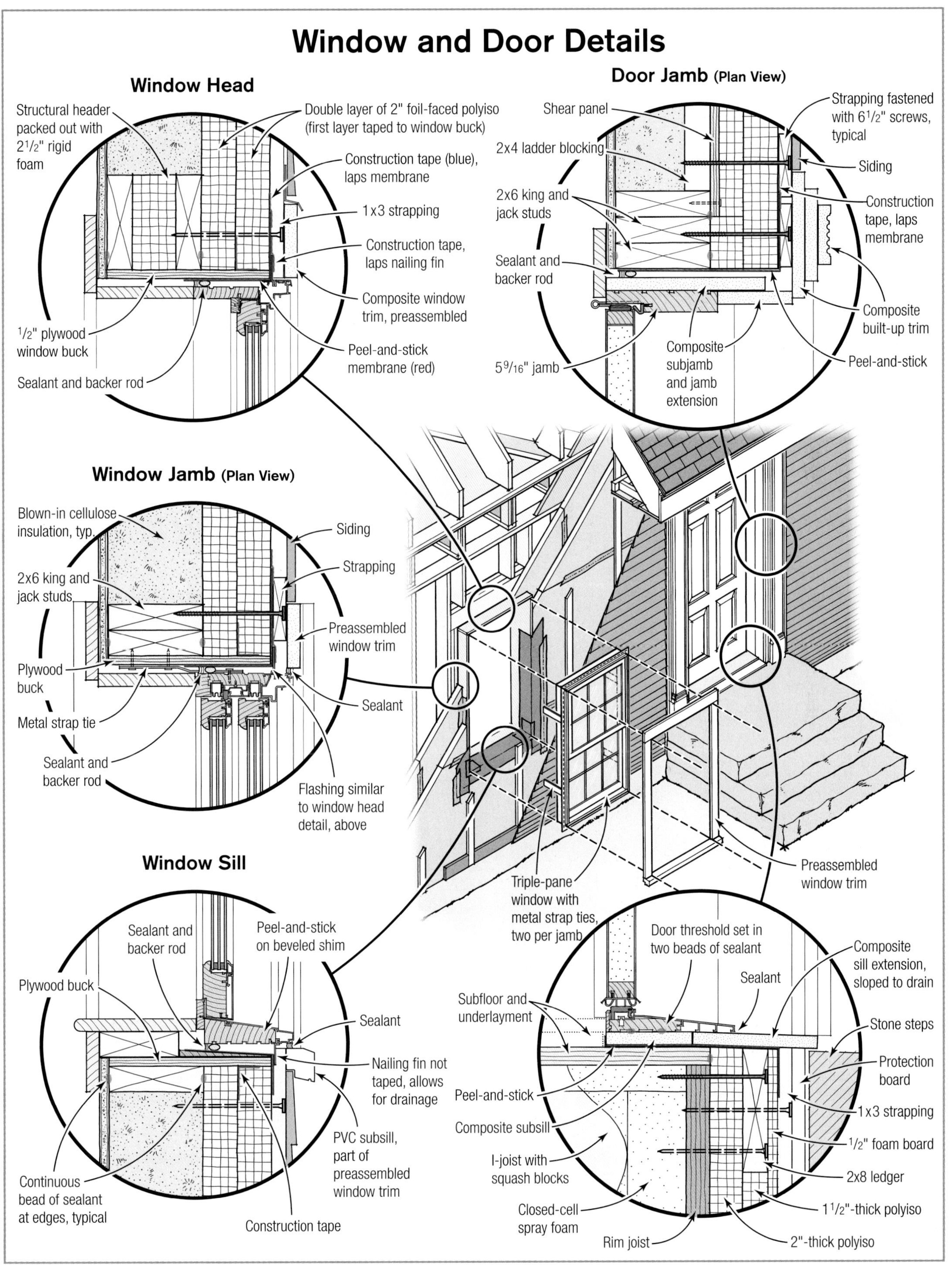

Window and Door Details
Window Head
Structural header packed out with 2 1/2" rigid foam
Double layer of 2" foil-faced polyiso (first layer taped to window buck)
Construction tape (blue), laps membrane
1x3 strapping
Construction tape, laps nailing fin
Composite window trim, preassembled
Peel-and-stick membrane (red)
1/2" plywood window buck
Sealant and backer rod
Door Jamb (Plan View)
Shear panel
Strapping fastened with 6 1/2" screws, typical
2x4 ladder blocking
Siding
2x6 king and jack studs
Construction tape, laps membrane
Sealant and backer rod
Composite built-up trim
5 9/16" jamb
Composite subjamb and jamb extension
Peel-and-stick
Window Jamb (Plan View)
Blown-in cellulose insulation, typ.
Siding
Strapping
2x6 king and jack studs
Preassembled window trim
Plywood buck
Sealant
Metal strap tie
Sealant and backer rod
Flashing similar to window head detail, above
Window Sill
Sealant and backer rod
Peel-and-stick on beveled shim
Plywood buck
Sealant
Nailing fin not taped, allows for drainage
PVC subsill, part of preassembled window trim
Continuous bead of sealant at edges, typical
Construction tape
Triple-pane window with metal strap ties, two per jamb
Preassembled window trim
Door threshold set in two beads of sealant
Composite sill extension, sloped to drain
Sealant
Subfloor and underlayment
Stone steps
Protection board
Peel-and-stick
1x3 strapping
Composite subsill
1/2" foam board
I-joist with squash blocks
2x8 ledger
Closed-cell spray foam
1 1/2"-thick polyiso
Rim joist
2"-thick polyiso

adjusting for an even gap around the jambs, we screwed the straps to the framing. The straps have enough flex that we'd be able to shim the jambs plumb later.

On the exterior, we added flat casings and subsill extensions, made and installed as preassembled units ("Window and Door Details," previous page). For all exterior trim, we used TUF Board (www.tufboard.net), a wood-PVC composite that doesn't expand and contract nearly as much as some of the solid cellular vinyl trim we've tried. We used a complementary Azek molding under the window sills. The window trim is simply butted around the outside of the windows, installed over vertical strapping that vents both the

Figure 16. Metal strap ties screwed to the jambs secure the windows to the framing (A). Exterior window casings were fastened over the 1x3 siding vent strapping (B). The author preassembled the window trim using composite lumber and PVC subsills (C). Water that bypasses the siding and trim is shed by the foam sheathing's foil face (D).

Figure 17. To provide an unobstructed swing, exterior doors were installed as if in a conventional 2x6 wall (left). Exterior extensions to the jambs and threshold rely on composite lumber and caulk (above).

trim and siding (there's more discussion of the venting ahead). With the windows sealed against the foil-faced sheathing, any water that gets past the trim and siding will drain back out at the bottom of the wall. The painters caulked the joints between the trim and the window jambs but kept the bottom edges caulk-free for drainage.

When installing the exterior doors, we aligned the outside edge of the 5⁹⁄₁₆-inch jambs with the framing rather than with the foam, creating a 4-inch inset. If we had used a deep extension jamb on the interior, it would have prevented the doors from fully opening. Instead, we ordered the doors without exterior trim, applied exterior extension jambs and trim, and extended the sill with TUF Board (Figure 17). Over the rim joist below the door openings, we installed a single layer of foam with a 2x8 ledger bolted above it for threshold support. We then covered the ledger with ½-inch foam board and installed a self-adhering flashing pan in the rough opening.

Back-Vented Siding

The prefinished WeatherBoard (www.certainteed.com) fiber-cement siding chosen for this project is installed over vertical 1x3 strapping, installed at 24-inch centers over the studs. This strapping creates a venting and drying space behind the siding. The foam sheathing's foil face sheds any water that may be driven past the siding.

We screwed the strapping through the 4-inch-thick sheathing using 6½-inch HeadLok screws (www.fastenmaster.com). At this length, the screws get a 2-inch bite into the studs. Passing as they do through 4 inches of foam board, you might expect them to eventually bend under the weight of the siding and allow it to sag. In fact, though, we used the exact same assembly on another job more than four years ago, and the siding shows no signs of movement — so it appears to work pretty well.

We started the strapping flush with the bottom edge of the sheathing. Lengths of 4½-inch-wide galvanized metal flashing, overlapping the mudsill and foundation, protect the bottom edge of the foam sheathing (Figure 13, page 127). We attached a continuous strip of nylon insect screen to the flashing and let it hang until the strapping was installed (Figure 18). We blocked between the strapping with strips of Cobra plastic-matrix ridge-vent material (www.gaf.com), then folded up the screen and tacked it to the strapping. The vent material holds the screen against the back of the siding, helping to keep bees and other bugs from nesting in the vent space. To prevent the flashing from drooping, we screwed it to the strapping ends.

Blocking for trim. At the two-stud outside corners, the 4-inch offset created by the foam board places the strapping conveniently behind the 1x8 corner boards without the need for any supplemental blocking. We preassembled the corner boards from the back using pocket screws and attached them to the strapping with stainless steel trim-head screws.

The strapping installed over the studs on both sides of the windows supports the window trim. But at inside corners and around windows and doors, we needed additional strapping to catch the ends of the siding. In these places, we installed 2x4 ladder blocking in the framing cavities and screwed the added

Figure 18. The sheathing is strapped on 2-foot centers, directly over the wall framing (above). The top of the venting channels is open to the soffit, ensuring positive airflow from the bottom up. Ridge-vent material blocks the gaps between strapping, forcing an insect barrier screen against the back of the siding (right).

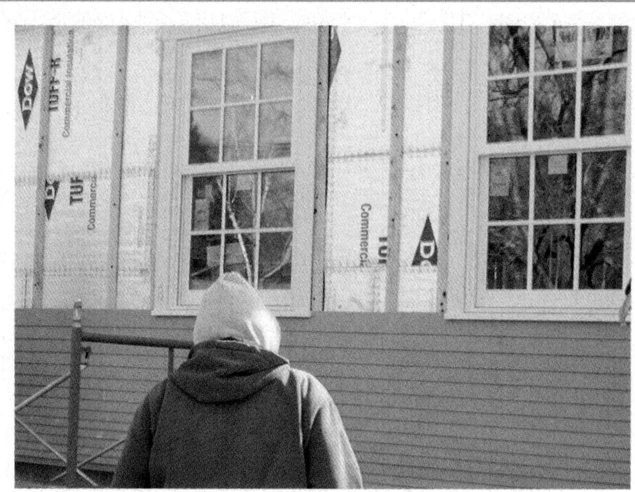

Figure 19. The fiber-cement siding was custom-ripped to allow narrower courses and tighter stacking at the base of the wall.

strapping to the blocks through the foam. Because the ladder blocking is installed on the flat in the wall bays, it would eventually be buried in blown-in cellulose insulation and wouldn't add greatly to the conductive heat loss.

Siding installation. The client wanted a particular look for the siding, one typical of older Cape-style homes: The courses start narrow at the base of the wall, with a 1⅞-inch exposure, and gradually widen over about 15 courses to the standard 4½-inch face (Figure 19). You can't effectively overlap 5½-inch-wide fiber-cement siding at those narrow exposures; it stacks up in a thick pile on the wall. So we played with some mockups and found we had to rip each course to maintain the 1¼-inch overlap prescribed by the manufacturer — a dusty and time-consuming process. The siding is blind-nailed in this overlap zone, which is pretty tight. We discovered that if we nailed a little too close to the top edge, the material tended to break out, something we haven't seen when installing Hardiplank.

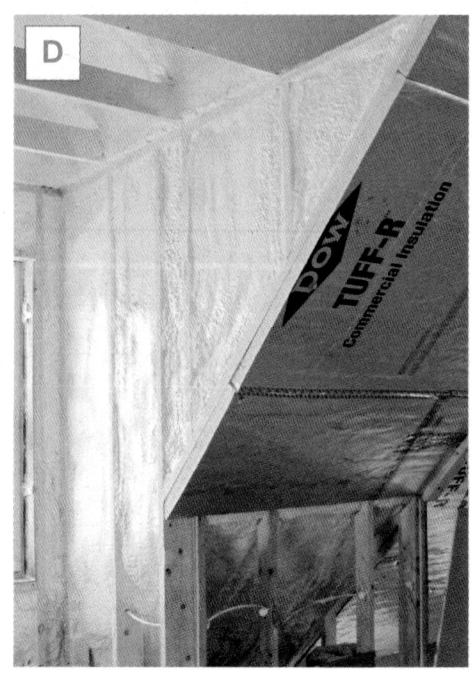

Figure 20. Foam-board vent baffles prevent wind-washing of the cellulose insulation in the attic ceiling areas (A). A 3-inch layer of spray foam effectively air-seals the vent baffles against the framing and insulates the rim joists to about R-18 (B). Sloped ceiling rafter bays were fully baffled with 2-inch foam board, then filled with closed-cell foam (C). Note the insulated rim joist and squash blocks below the single top plate. A layer of 2-inch R-13 foam board completes the sloped ceiling insulation, yielding a total approximate R-value of 70 (D).

In general, the thinner, less-expensive WeatherBoard required gentler handling than we were used to during installation, and I'm not inclined to choose it again.

We painted both the trim and the siding with two coats of acrylic latex. The vented installation will help ensure a long-lasting, low-maintenance finish.

Air-Sealing and Insulation

To insulate the walls, ceilings, and roof, we used a combination of foam board, spray-foam, and cellulose. Our general goal was to achieve R-values of 45 for the walls and 65 for the level and sloped ceiling areas. In the basement, which would be finished, we insulated the walls to R-25 and installed 2-inch R-10 XPS foam under the slab.

The asphalt-shingled roof is conventionally vented at the ridge, the Cobra vent balanced with aluminum strip vent in the soffits. For vent baffles at the eaves and in sloped ceiling areas, we used 2-inch R-13 foam board, spaced down from the underside of the roof sheathing with 2-inch foam spacers (Figure 20). We glued the spacers to the sheathing and tacked the board over them, running it to a point about 1 foot higher than the 16 inches of cellulose to be placed in the attic. The eaves baffles are air-sealed against the 2x12 rafters and top plate with a 3-inch layer of spray foam. Over the baffles in the sloped ceiling areas, we sprayed 7 inches of closed-cell foam with a nominal value of R-45; we then installed 2-inch foam board over the rafters. The combined values of the board and spray foam results in a total R-value of around 70.

We also used closed-cell foam to insulate and seal all rim joists, the sloped ceiling areas, and the two doghouse dormers (Figure 21). A 3-inch layer of foam at the rims has an R-value of about 18 and provides additional air-sealing at this typically leaky junction.

Basement walls. In the basement we installed 2-inch XPS foam on the foundation walls, overlapping it at the top with the closed-cell foam insulating the rims. We framed 2x4 walls in front of the foam and insulated them with fiberglass batts instead of cellulose. We did this because basement flooding is common in the area; if a flood overwhelms the subslab drainage and sump pump, the insulation will drain and dry to the interior without settling. In fact, in an effort to keep things dry, we installed the foundation with its top about 3 feet above finished grade, placing the slab a few inches above the average water table.

Even though the foam sheathing was taped at every seam in both layers and sealed to the framing with adhesive caulk, we still didn't consider it a fully effective air seal. Before blowing in the cellulose, we worked on sealing the framing from the interior, caulking every seam that might constitute an air leak in the shell

Figure 21. Complex framing areas are ideal spray-foam candidates (A). At roughly R-6 per inch, the 2x8 framing bays approach a nominal R-44. Two doghouse dormers were also insulated with closed-cell foam (B). The finished basement walls were insulated to R-25 with a combination of 2-inch XPS foam and R-15 fiberglass batts (C). Note the air-sealing tape over the seams. Spray foam on the rim joist laps onto the XPS on the foundation walls, creating an air seal along the top of the board (D).

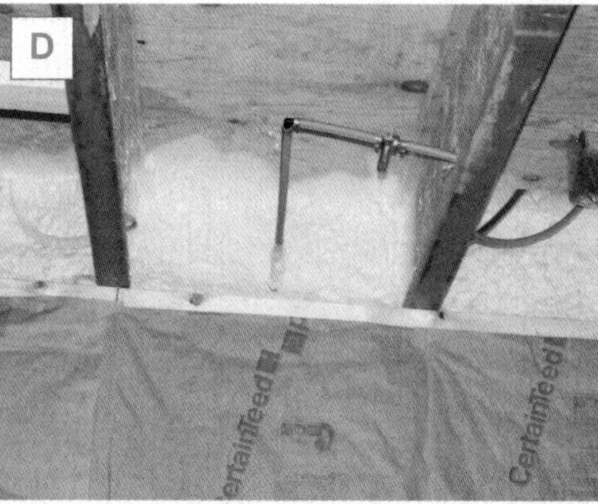

(Figure 22). This proved to be an extensive and expensive undertaking. We used acrylic latex caulk on every joint between double framing members in the exterior walls. We'd put a generous bead of subfloor adhesive under the bottom plates before standing the walls, but you can't visually check for voids or gaps, so we went ahead and caulked all seams between the bottom plate and subfloor. In the basement, we caulked where the 2-inch XPS foam on the foundation walls met the slab, and we sealed the seams with WeatherMate tape (www.building.dow.com). We spent about $800 on caulk and more than $8,000 in labor over two weeks, during which time someone from Building Science Corp. periodically came out and identified still more areas that could be caulked.

The air-sealing effort also included a labor-intensive treatment around all the windows and doors. We avoided using expanding foam around the jambs, not because it doesn't seal well, but because it too thoroughly fills the gap. If water were to get past the jamb, it could remain trapped and lead to rot. Instead, we inserted foam backer rod around the jambs, pressing it just beyond the interior edge, then capped it with caulk. This way, any water that gets in still has a chance to dry to the outside, where the underside of the sill is caulk-free and can drain. We caulked around the metal tie-straps, too, and along the edges of the self-adhering membrane protecting the rough openings.

Figure 22. Leaving little to chance, the crew caulked all seams between framing members and subfloor (A). Foam backer rod, sealed with caulk, was used in lieu of expanding foam around window and door jambs (B). Window sealing was time-consuming, with caulk outlining the metal installation straps and the interior edges of the self-adhering window flashing (C).

Figure 23. Dense-pack cellulose insulation was blown behind a permeable membrane stapled to the studs (left). Attic ceiling areas were drywalled first to support the insulation. Attics received a 16-inch layer of loose-fill cellulose with an R-value of 65 (above).

Insulation

The 2x6 wall bays were insulated with dense-pack cellulose, blown in behind a permeable plastic membrane. To support the cellulose in the attic spaces, we had to hang those ceilings first, using stiffer, ⅝-inch drywall to avoid a "quilting" effect over the 24-inch framing centers (Figure 23). After hanging the board, we checked from above for light leakage through seams and fixtures, and caulked them all tight. We also caulked the perimeter of the drywall to the top plates, from below.

Against the architect's recommendation, the homeowners insisted on recessed can lights. The fixtures weren't airtight, so we covered them from above with expanding foam. We hope the homeowners will use compact fluorescents to help prevent the cans from overheating and tripping the thermal breaker.

We performed a blower-door and smoke test before installing the cellulose. Even at this intermediate stage, the result — 1.37 air changes per hour at a pressure of 50 pascals (ACH50) — easily met the 1.5 ACH50 we'd targeted as our goal for the finished home. We identified a few leaks along the top plate where air found its way between the sheathing and the framing, and applied more caulking to seal these areas.

Figure 24. Drywall clips replace lumber backers in wall and ceiling corners.

In retrospect, I believe that rather than putting all that time and caulk into air-sealing, it would have been more economical to have had every wall bay "picture-framed" between the sheathing and the framing with closed-cell spray foam. Our insulation contractor estimates that this would have added $1,500 to the job cost, but it would have significantly reduced our labor.

Drywall

With two-stud corners and backerless wall intersections, we used drywall clips instead of nailers to support drywall corners (Figure 24). Both the hangers and I were surprised at how easy the clips were to use. Their purpose is threefold: First, they reduce lumber usage; second, without a nailer in the way, areas above the top plates and behind wall tees and corners are easier to insulate; and third, they help prevent drywall cracks in the corners, where wood movement can otherwise introduce stresses. Cracks aren't just unsightly; they also can contribute to air leakage through the wall assembly.

The blueboard and skim-coat plaster serve as the primary barrier to air movement through the walls and ceiling. When hanging the sheets, we ran a bead of acrylic caulk at all top and bottom plates; at wall ends; and around all openings, fixtures, and electrical boxes. At drywall clip corners, we simply caulked the vertical seams after installing the board — good insurance should the plaster crack in the corners despite the clips.

Mechanical Systems

This home is heated by forced hot air, with the ducts sized for air conditioning and installed entirely in conditioned space. The furnace is a natural gas-fired Evolution System Plus 95s (www.bryant.com) with up to 95 percent AFUE. Instead of installing a cooling-only unit, we used a heat pump that can supply both cooling and heating. It provides heat at temperatures of 35°F and above, relieving the furnace and saving

Figure 25. A 7-kW PV array on the shed-dormer roof is projected to supply more than 100 percent of the home's electrical consumption (far left). A digital electric meter displays a constant readout of power delivered to and from the grid (left).

some fuel. A Fantech VHR 1404 (www.fantech.net) heat-recovery ventilator provides whole-house ventilation with minimal heat loss. Both the furnace and the Rinnai RC98HP on-demand water heater (www.rinnai.us) are sealed combustion units.

Although the cooling load for the house was calculated at 1½ tons, a 2½-ton 18 SEER unit was the smallest available. It's possible this could lead to short-cycling of the system; that remains to be seen. Presumably, as tight-home construction becomes more common, smaller systems will, too.

Solar power. On the roof, a 7-kilowatt photovoltaic array of 230-watt OnEnergy panels (www.sharpusa.com) helps offset electrical usage, with excess power generation being fed back into the grid (Figure 25).

Home Performance

Effectively air-sealing a home is a tall order, but redundant taping and caulking of seams — along with careful attention to detail — clearly paid off in our preliminary test results. This was confirmed by the blower-door test we did after completing the interior: We achieved .72 ACH50 — nearly 50 percent lower (and better) than the outcome of our preliminary test. Our focus throughout the job on energy and resource conservation has already helped place the home well above the 100 mark required for a LEED Platinum designation.

More important, our efforts will pay back in the home's overall efficiency and performance. Whenever there's leeway in a construction budget, I push for higher levels of insulation. Done properly, it's one investment that can pay for itself fairly quickly and, over time, continue to reduce operating costs.

David Joyce *owns Synergy Companies Construction in Lancaster, Mass.*

REMOTE Walls: Exterior Foam Details for Cold Climates

by Thorsten Chlupp

As a custom home builder in Alaska, I've seen how poorly conventional wall assemblies perform in extremely cold weather. In Fairbanks, where I work, a "typical" wood-frame wall might consist of 2x6 framing with R-19 batt insulation, OSB sheathing, and housewrap on the outside, and a 6-mil poly vapor retarder on the inside.

There are two problems with this construction. The first is that the wall framing members act as heat conductors between the warm interior and the cold outside. There's nothing to slow the transfer of heat through the framing. But the bigger issue is air leakage. It's nearly impossible to do a perfect job sealing all the penetrations in the vapor retarder, and just as hard to make the housewrap airtight. On cold winter days, warm, moist indoor air is driven into the wall cavities, where it hits the inside of the cold sheathing, condenses, and freezes. When the weather warms up, the moisture is trapped between the vapor retarder and the relatively impermeable sheathing, where it degrades the insulation and causes mold and even rot.

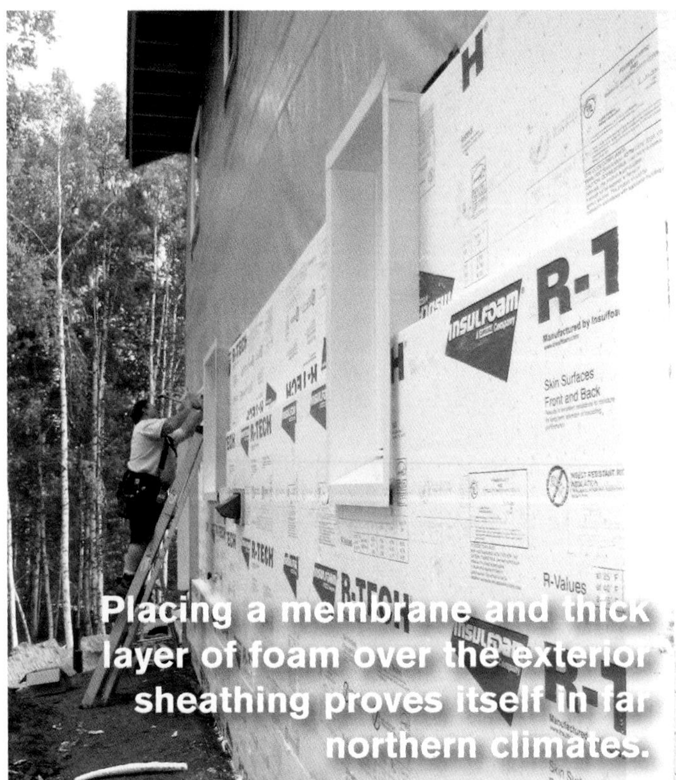

Placing a membrane and thick layer of foam over the exterior sheathing proves itself in far northern climates.

CCHRC Research

Moisture infiltration into wall cavities is a concern anywhere, but especially in climates like Alaska's, where extreme winter temperatures and a short drying season exacerbate the problem. To address the shortcomings of standard frame construction, my company has adopted an insulation and air-sealing method developed by builders and researchers working with the Cold Climate Housing Research Center (CCHRC, www.cchrc.org) here in Fairbanks. Nicknamed the REMOTE Wall System (for Residential Exterior Membrane Outside

REMOTE Wall Details

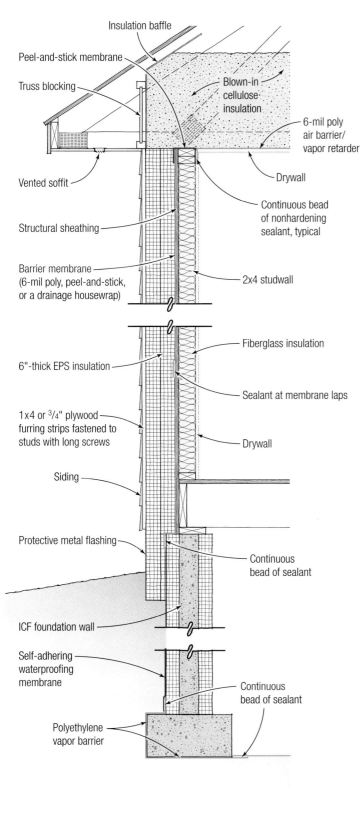

Insulation baffle
Peel-and-stick membrane
Truss blocking
Blown-in cellulose insulation
6-mil poly air barrier/ vapor retarder
Vented soffit
Drywall
Continuous bead of nonhardening sealant, typical
Structural sheathing
Barrier membrane (6-mil poly, peel-and-stick, or a drainage housewrap)
2x4 studwall
Fiberglass insulation
6"-thick EPS insulation
Sealant at membrane laps
1x4 or 3/4" plywood furring strips fastened to studs with long screws
Drywall
Siding
Protective metal flashing
Continuous bead of sealant
ICF foundation wall
Self-adhering waterproofing membrane
Continuous bead of sealant
Polyethylene vapor barrier

Window Installed Flush With Sheathing

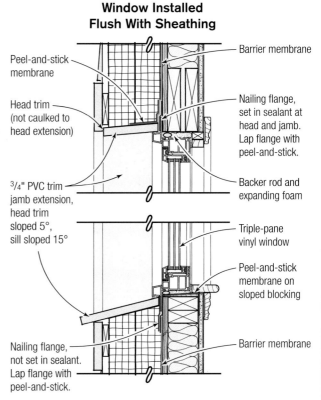

Peel-and-stick membrane
Barrier membrane
Head trim (not caulked to head extension)
Nailing flange, set in sealant at head and jamb. Lap flange with peel-and-stick.
3/4" PVC trim jamb extension, head trim sloped 5°, sill sloped 15°
Backer rod and expanding foam
Triple-pane vinyl window
Peel-and-stick membrane on sloped blocking
Nailing flange, not set in sealant. Lap flange with peel-and-stick.
Barrier membrane

Window Installed Flush With Outside Face of Wall

Peel-and-stick on sloped blocking
Barrier membrane
Sealant
Nailing flange, set in sealant at head and jamb
2x window buck
Backer rod and expanding foam
Triple-pane vinyl window
Peel-and-stick on sloped blocking
Nailing flange, no sealant
2x window buck
Peel-and-stick wraps window buck at sill and jamb
Barrier membrane

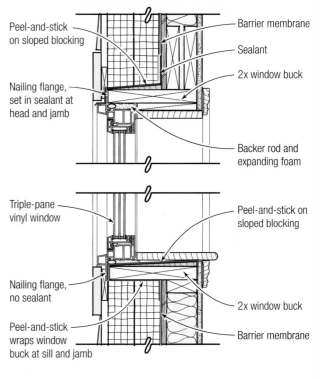

Foam Thickness & Dew Points

The illustrations below show the predicted temperatures within walls with insulated vapor-barrier sheathing in Boston, Mass. These predictions are based on a simple calculation described by Joseph Lstiburek of Building Science Corporation:

Interface temperature =
Indoor temp. – [(Indoor temp. – Outdoor temp.) X (Cavity R / Total R)]

You can use this equation to calculate the temperature at the inside face of the exterior foam insulation (the "interface temperature"). In walls where the interface temperature is above the dew point for the indoor air, there is little risk of condensation in the wall caused by interior moisture. If the inside surface of the foam falls below the dew point, there is a higher risk that water vapor will condense inside the wall and lead to moisture problems. In that case, increasing the thickness of the exterior foam will raise the interface temperature, reducing the chance of condensation.

For this calculation, the indoor conditions are assumed to be 70°F and 35 percent relative humidity — reasonable values if the rest of the house system is functioning well.

At this temperature and humidity, the dew point is 40°F, so the idea is to choose a foam sheathing R-value that will result in a calculated interface temperature above 40°F. (*Note*: the dew point is the temperature to which air must be cooled for moisture to condense out of the air.)

The outdoor design temperature is found by averaging the temperatures for the three coldest months for the year. For this example in Boston: 33°F (Dec.), 28°F (Jan.), and 30°F (Feb.), for an average of 30.3°F. (*Note*: These represent monthly average temperatures, not the much lower design temperature used to size heating equipment.)

After running the numbers, Case A is found to surpass the energy code, but risks condensation because the vapor-barrier temperature is below the dew point for the design indoor conditions. Case D does not risk condensation, but falls below the R-19 energy code minimum for wall insulation. All other cases satisfy moisture concerns as well as energy codes.

***Ted Cushman** reports on the building industry from Great Barrington, Mass.*

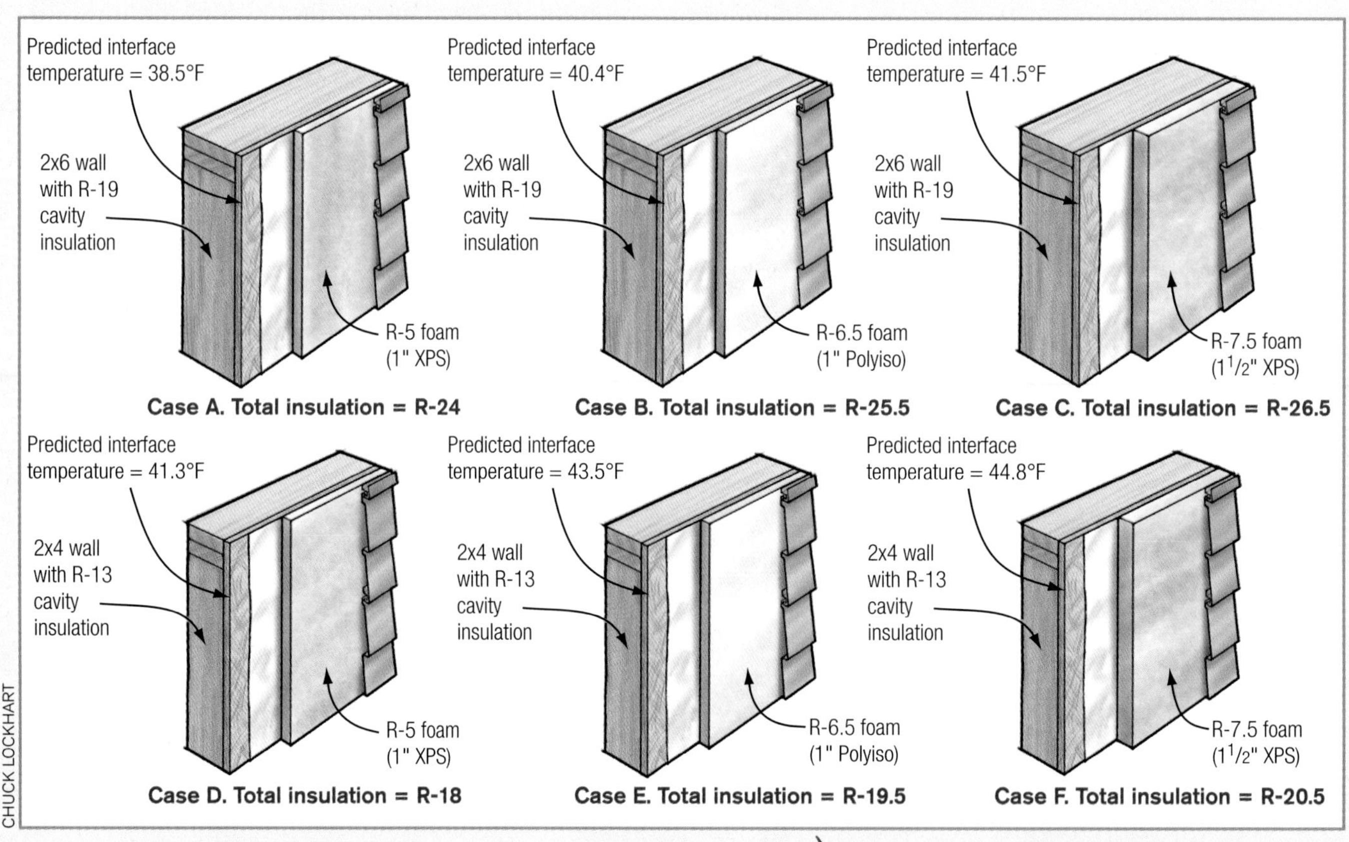

Case A. Total insulation = R-24

Case B. Total insulation = R-25.5

Case C. Total insulation = R-26.5

Case D. Total insulation = R-18

Case E. Total insulation = R-19.5

Case F. Total insulation = R-20.5

Insulation Technique), it involves installing a barrier membrane on top of the structural sheathing, followed by several inches of rigid foam insulation (see "REMOTE Wall Details," page 136). The membrane provides an air seal, while the thick insulation keeps the sheathing and framing above the dew point temperature and so prevents condensation from occurring in the wall.

The rigid foam can be supplemented by installing a lesser amount of fiberglass batt insulation in the frame wall. The goal is to increase the wall's total R-value from the inside, but without allowing the sheathing to cool to the dew point. (See "Foam Thickness and Dew Points," facing page.) It's a balancing act: You have to put enough insulation on the outside to keep the sheathing membrane warm, but not so much on the inside that you isolate the sheathing and framing members from indoor heat. This is critical, because besides providing an air barrier, the membrane — either by itself or in combination with the sheathing and exterior insulation — acts as a vapor retarder. So there's no doubt that in a REMOTE wall, interior moisture vapor will be stopped at the sheathing plane.

Concerns With Exterior Membranes

Mindful of the dangers of a "wrong-side vapor barrier," the CCHRC has been monitoring REMOTE wall projects around Alaska, in both dry northern areas and the humid coastal region. Using HOBO data loggers (available from www.onsetcomp.com) that record temperature and humidity over time, the research has confirmed a rule of thumb long used by builders wishing to place vapor retarders inside of walls: **It's generally safe to put approximately one-third of the total R-value to the inside of the vapor barrier.** This holds true even for an extremely cold climate like that of Fairbanks, which has 14,000 heating degree days. (Keep in mind this is just a rule of thumb; the ratio may change somewhat depending on project specifics.)

Data loggers on some REMOTE projects have indicated short periods when humidity levels in certain wall cavities rose. The good news is that the cavities also dry out again as soon as conditions are right, because there's no poly vapor retarder on the inside face of the studs. So if condensation does occur in the wall — say, in extreme cold weather — it can dry to the interior.

I've used the REMOTE method on 14 homes to date, with excellent results. I learned years ago that to create a durable, energy-efficient home in a cold climate, you have to meet four goals: adequate insulation, airtightness, moisture control, and good indoor air quality. The REMOTE wall method allows me to meet all of these.

Insulation

I generally use R-Tech IV EPS (expanded polystyrene) on the exterior. It's made by Insulfoam (www.insulfoam.com) and has an R-value of 4.8 per inch at 40°F. (The R-value actually increases as temperatures drop.) I typically install 6 inches — two layers of 3-inch foam. R-Tech has a polyethylene facing that helps it shed water, though the edges are unfaced. This has led to some concern that moisture might get into the foam board at joints and be unable to get out. But CCHRC tests in the rainy southeast of Alaska have shown that R-Tech performs well in REMOTE walls and that moisture entrapment is not a problem.

Some builders have used XPS (extruded polystyrene) foam, which has a slightly higher R-value, and it has also performed well on monitored projects.

Note that in cold Fairbanks, I can carry the EPS below grade with no fear of insect damage. Although some foams contain a borate additive intended to repel insects, the treatment may leach out over time in wet soils. In situations where insect damage poses a threat, holding the exposed foam above grade and using a termite shield is a safer option.

On the inside, I supplement the exterior foam with fiberglass batts.

Airtightness and Blower-Door Test

Covering the house with rigid foam board creates a potentially tight structure, but it's the barrier membrane applied to the sheathing that does most of the work (Figure 26).

The earliest REMOTE walls used peel-and-stick membranes; this produced an incredibly airtight, waterproof shell, but it was expensive. So most builders switched to less expensive materials — 6-mil poly or, in very wet zones, vapor-permeable drainage wraps such as Tyvek StuccoWrap or DrainWrap. Poly works fine in Fairbanks, which is fairly dry; in rainy southern Alaska, the Tyvek products are the usual substitute for peel-and-stick. The reason is that rainwater might travel through a nail hole and get trapped behind poly, whereas using a housewrap will allow for evaporation to the outside. (StuccoWrap or something similar is also used on REMOTE houses that receive an EIFS cladding, per the EIFS manufacturer's specifications.)

On the inside, the 6-mil poly continues across the ceiling below the attic. To avoid stack-effect exfiltration, we refuse to install recessed light fixtures in the ceiling poly and even avoid putting sealed electrical boxes there, pushing customers to put upper-floor lighting fixtures in the walls instead. On most of our jobs the plumbing stack is the only thing that penetrates the lid. Access to the attic is through a gable wall, preferably above an attached garage.

Performance test. Installing the barrier membrane and exterior foam doesn't in itself guarantee that the structure is airtight. The only way to do that is to do a blower-door test. This is a critically important step in achieving a tight shell, and you have to do it when you can still access the leaks. If you hold off doing the blower-door test until the insulation and drywall are installed, it'll be too late.

We wait until the electrical, plumbing, and mechanical subs have done their rough-ins, then hang the drywall over the ceiling air barrier. The blower door depressurizes the interior and shows us where the leaks are. There's no insulation in the stud bays at this point, so it's easy to seal wall leaks from the inside, using spray foam and acoustical sealant. The attic has not yet been insulated, so we can plug those leaks working from above. When the house is finished, an independent energy rater performs a second blower-door test as part of an energy audit.

Our goal is an airtightness of 0.6 air changes per hour at a pressure of 50 pascals (ACH50) — the same standard required for a Passive House. We've achieved this with the 6-mil poly barrier and have gotten down to 0.3 ACH50 with a peel-and-stick membrane. The best we've done with StuccoWrap is 0.8 ACH50.

Moisture and Air Quality

In buildings this tight, it would be a mistake to rely on natural infiltration for whole-house ventilation. Even exhaust-only fans (which require makeup air) would be a mistake. The home would have poor air quality and moisture and condensation problems. So I put a heat-recovery ventilator (HRV) in every house I build. The HRV provides a measured supply of fresh air and recovers much of the heat that would be lost with a simple fan system. HRVs also address the issue of indoor humidity by replacing stale humid air with drier outside air.

Installing the Membrane

Most of the houses I build have wood or vinyl siding; on those jobs we typically install a 6-mil poly barrier membrane, lapping the seams shingle style and sealing the laps with a non-hardening acoustical sealant.

Poly is slippery to walk on and will tear if you drag trusses across it, so when we get to the top of the wall we switch to a strip of 9-inch peel-and-stick flashing. The flashing adheres to the top plate and laps an equal distance onto the poly and the inside face of the plate (Figure 27).

Pencil marks will not show on this material, so we use a white marker to lay out truss locations. Once the trusses are set, we install the ceiling membrane, lapping its edges onto the peel-and-stick flashing and sealing the lap with acoustical sealant.

Installing Windows

Windows can be installed either at the face of the sheathing — in a recess — or out at the face of the wall. From a performance standpoint, a recess is better, because the window is somewhat protected from wind-washing and the interior glass is more easily warmed by the heat in the room. By contrast, windows installed at the face of the wall are in an interior recess, separating them from the warm air inside (especially if a curtain is drawn) and exposing the outer layer of glass to cold wind. I've observed that in

Figure 26. In a REMOTE wall, the sheathing is covered with a barrier membrane — either peel-and-stick (A), 6-mil polyethylene sheeting (B), or, in wet climates or beneath EIFS cladding, a wrinkled drainage material such as StuccoWrap (C). Installed before the roof is framed, the barrier membrane extends over the top plates and is later sealed to the poly air barrier on the ceiling of the house's top floor.

extremely cold weather — when it's 25°F below zero, for example — frost tends to form inside windows installed at the face of the wall, whereas frost rarely occurs on inset windows.

Recessed installation. I've installed windows both ways, but because of the frost problem I now do only recessed installations. A recessed installation is more complicated because the sides of the recess must be covered with exterior jamb extensions. On vinyl-sided homes, we make the extensions from 20-gauge metal coil stock (Figure 28). The bottom is sloped to shed water, and there are flanges on both edges — an inner flange that gets fastened to the sheathing and an outer flange that laps over the 1x4 strapping that we install on top of the EPS around the window.

We've also made extensions from wood and cellular PVC. These solid extension jambs are glued and screwed at the corners and fastened to the wall over a thick bead of sealant. We either toe-screw them to the framing or fasten them from the inside with metal clips.

Window bucks. Because it's less expensive, many of my past customers chose to have doors and windows installed at the outside face of the wall. We did this by extending the rough openings with bucks ripped from 2-by lumber. The buck fits inside the opening and extends from the inside face of the frame to the outside face of the furring that goes over the foam.

The window is installed in the buck and the fins

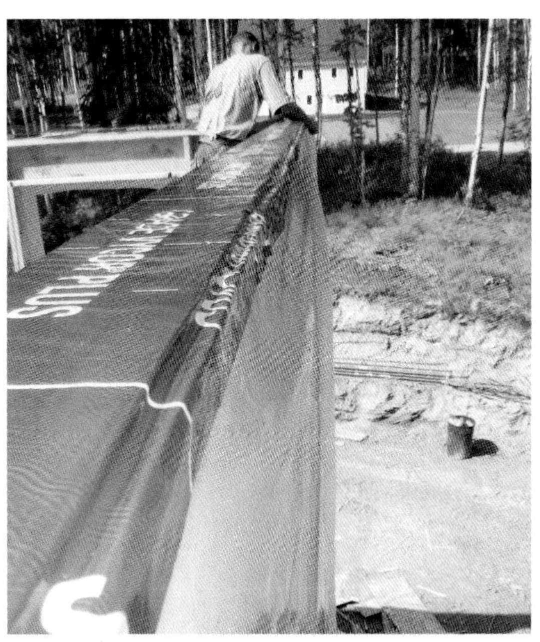

Figure 27. The author's crew applies a 9-inch-wide peel-and-stick flashing to the top plates, adhering it to the inside edge of the plates (top) and lapping it onto the 6-mil poly membrane on the sheathing (right).

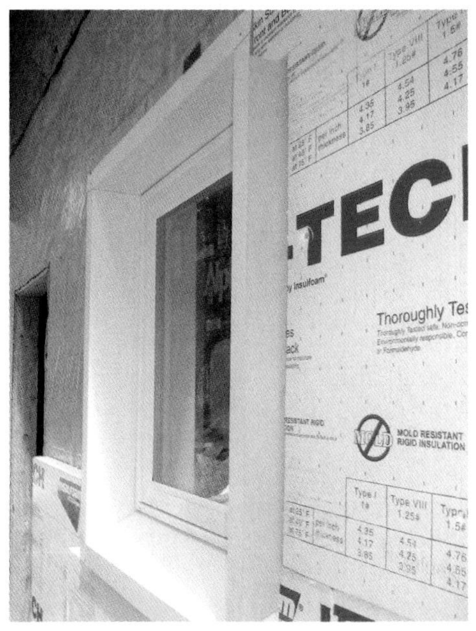

Figure 28. When installing recessed windows, the author uses sill and jamb extensions bent from coated sheet metal. The flanges at the outer edges (far left) are carefully placed to allow for the thickness of the foam, ¾-inch strapping, and the vinyl siding, which will tuck underneath. Note the lines of black acoustical caulk used to seal the jamb extensions to the poly membrane and the poly seams (left).

Figure 29. On past jobs, the author installed windows at the face of the wall by setting them in solid lumber bucks protected with peel-and-stick flashing (A). The bucks are attached to the inside of the rough opening and taped or flashed to the wall membrane (B). Bucks are sized so that when foam insulation and furring are installed, the siding will be in the proper plane (C).

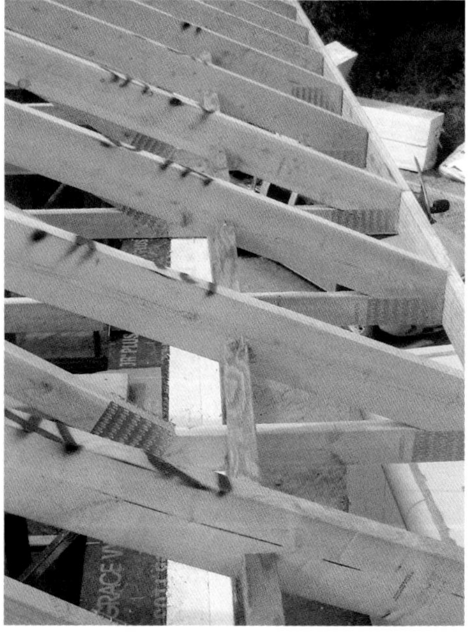

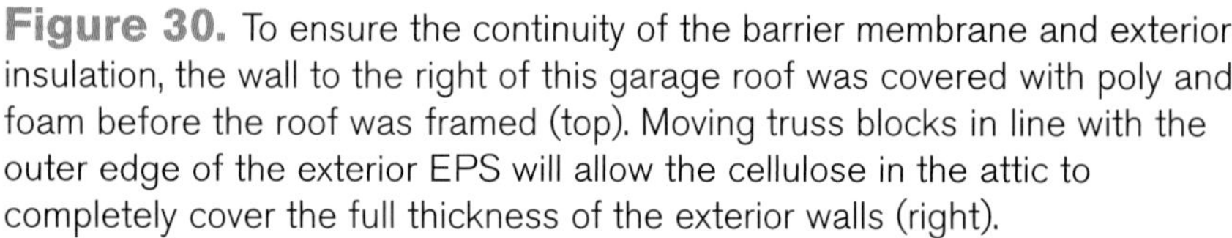

Figure 30. To ensure the continuity of the barrier membrane and exterior insulation, the wall to the right of this garage roof was covered with poly and foam before the roof was framed (top). Moving truss blocks in line with the outer edge of the exterior EPS will allow the cellulose in the attic to completely cover the full thickness of the exterior walls (right).

lapped with peel-and-stick flashings that extend back to the wall membrane (Figure 29). Though this method is less expensive than fabricating jamb extensions, it requires more care with the flashing. From the standpoint of moisture intrusion, I felt comfortable doing it around Fairbanks because we don't get a lot of rain, but in a wetter climate I would recommend recessing the windows. As I mentioned above, I no longer use this technique because of the icing problem my customers experienced. But for builders in a warmer climate, it could still be a reasonable approach.

Installing the Exterior Insulation

The EPS insulation can be lightly attached with framing staples or nails because the furring strips, which get screwed through into the studs, will securely hold it in place. We stagger seams and lap corners in successive layers so that air doesn't have a direct path

Figure 31. The EPS insulation is first tacked in place, then secured with long screws fastened through furring strips into the framing (A). Wide furring members are needed at corners (B) and around openings (C) to provide backing for trim.

through to the wall. The boards are butted to the sides of window bucks and jamb extensions, and gaps between sheets and around windows and doors are filled with minimally expanding spray foam.

Some areas have to be insulated and sealed before the framing is complete. For example, where the roof of an unheated attic butts to a sidewall, we'll insulate that wall before framing the roof (Figure 30).

We insulate attic gables at least as high as the top of the attic insulation. The area above does not have to be insulated, but it needs to be built out to the plane of the foam below, which we often do with scrap pieces of insulation.

If the inspector and engineer will allow it, we push the truss blocks along the eaves out to the face of the foam so that the blown-in attic insulation will cover the entire top of the wall, including the EPS. Otherwise, we carry the insulation boards up to the top of the attic insulation by fitting them around the rafter tails.

Furring

We provide nailing for siding by installing 1x4 furring or strips of ¾-inch plywood over the foam, fastening through to the studs with long screws (Figure 31). We space the screws about 12 inches on-center and make sure we penetrate at least 1½ inches into the framing. These long fasteners have to be mail-ordered; we use Wind-Lock W-SIP screws (www.wind-lock.com) and FastenMaster HeadLok and OlyLog screws (www.fastenmaster.com).

Screws are very heat-conductive and can cause condensation where they miss the studs. We always check from the inside for missed fasteners, reinstall them, and use spray foam to seal the holes.

Cost and Payback

Though the REMOTE method is more expensive than conventional construction — EPS costs more than fiberglass and there's extra labor involved — the added costs are offset by reduced energy use and a longer building life cycle. The CCHRC has estimated a three- to five-year payback period from energy savings, and there's no question that a building free of moisture problems will have a considerably longer life. But what's equally important is that good insulation, tight construction, and proper heat-recovery ventilation add up to a comfortable, healthy house to live in.

***Thorsten Chlupp** owns REINA, LLC, in Fairbanks, Alaska. Special thanks to Ilya Benesch of the CCHRC for providing technical advice.*

Tight and Efficient Double Stud Walls

by Dan Kolbert

I'm a building contractor in southern Maine with a focus on energy- and resource-efficient homes. Our approach is to do everything we can during the design phase to minimize the heating load (cooling isn't much of an issue in our region); then we figure out the best, most cost-effective way to meet the goals we've set.

The project I'll discuss in this article is a 2,500-square-foot house with an airtight double shell, high levels of insulation, triple-glazed windows, and a low-maintenance exterior. Roof-mounted evacuated-tube solar collectors (www.apricus-solar.com) supply hot water to a radiant system embedded in a well-insulated slab. The solar system is designed to provide most if not all of the heat and hot water in the fall and spring. In winter, an electric on-demand heater (www.seisco.com) will provide reliable heating, with solar offsetting its use. A propane-fueled fireplace, which can operate without electricity, will furnish emergency back-up heat, along with some ambience. Because of the high R-values in the slab, walls, and roof, there is no heating loop on the second or third floors of the simply configured home.

By keeping finishes and trim details simple (drywall returns at windows and doors, for example), we kept costs in line with those of standard custom homes while guaranteeing lower operating expenses over the building's life.

A double stud wall allows for plenty of cellulose insulation and reduces thermal bridging.

Energy Modeling

I was brought into the project by Kaplan-Thompson Architects. They had already settled on the essential elements of the shell using REM energy modeling software (www.archenergy.com); their goal was to achieve an airtightness rating of 0.6 air changes per hour at 50 pascals, the standard set for a Passive House (www.passivehouse.us). This high performance level allowed us to dramatically downsize the heating system, saving money up front on equipment and long-term on fuel. Energy modeling predicts that this house will use 15.9 million Btu per year, as opposed to the 72.9 million

Figure 32. Four-inch-thick foam board provides R-20 insulation under and around the edges of the radiant floor slab (left), which is tinted chocolate brown to serve as the finished floor. The inside 2x4 wall of the 11 1/4-inch-thick double framing will cover the exposed foam around the perimeter (above).

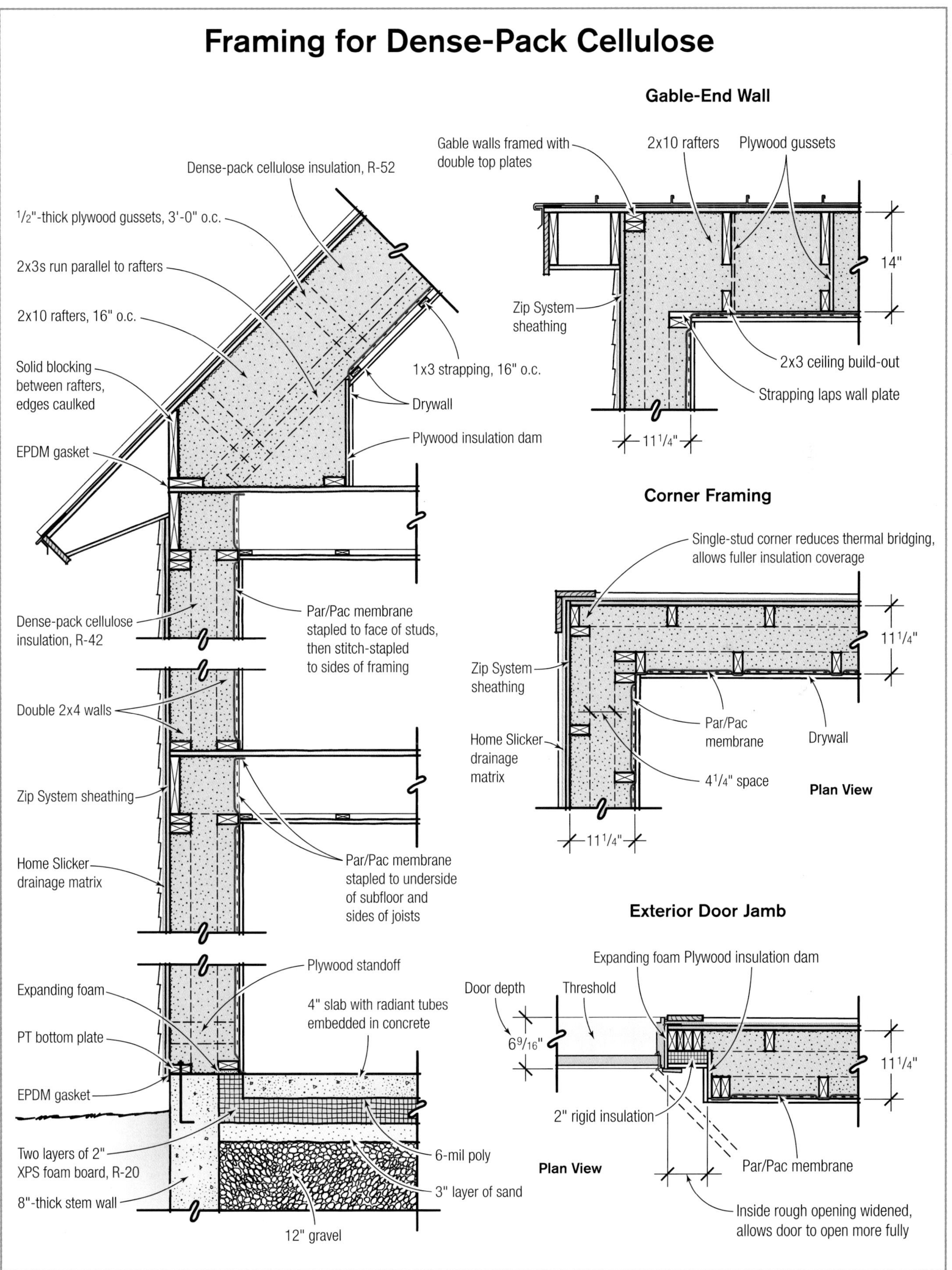

Framing for Dense-Pack Cellulose
Dense-pack cellulose insulation, R-52
1/2"-thick plywood gussets, 3'-0" o.c.
2x3s run parallel to rafters
2x10 rafters, 16" o.c.
Solid blocking between rafters, edges caulked
EPDM gasket
1x3 strapping, 16" o.c.
Drywall
Plywood insulation dam
Dense-pack cellulose insulation, R-42
Par/Pac membrane stapled to face of studs, then stitch-stapled to sides of framing
Double 2x4 walls
Zip System sheathing
Home Slicker drainage matrix
Par/Pac membrane stapled to underside of subfloor and sides of joists
Expanding foam
Plywood standoff
4" slab with radiant tubes embedded in concrete
PT bottom plate
EPDM gasket
Two layers of 2" XPS foam board, R-20
6-mil poly
8"-thick stem wall
3" layer of sand
12" gravel
Gable-End Wall
Gable walls framed with double top plates
2x10 rafters
Plywood gussets
14"
Zip System sheathing
2x3 ceiling build-out
Strapping laps wall plate
11 1/4"
Corner Framing
Single-stud corner reduces thermal bridging, allows fuller insulation coverage
11 1/4"
Zip System sheathing
Par/Pac membrane
Drywall
Home Slicker drainage matrix
4 1/4" space
Plan View
11 1/4"
Exterior Door Jamb
Expanding foam Plywood insulation dam
Door depth
Threshold
6 9/16"
11 1/4"
2" rigid insulation
Plan View
Par/Pac membrane
Inside rough opening widened, allows door to open more fully

Btu that a "standard" house of the same size would use — a 73 percent reduction.

Foundation

We poured a standard 8-inch-thick stem wall on footings set 48 inches deep, below the frost line (see "Framing for Dense-Pack Cellulose," page 145). After backfilling and compacting the gravel and sand subgrade, we installed two layers of 2-inch square-edge extruded polystyrene (XPS) foam board inside the stem wall and across the ground in preparation for placing the 4-inch slab. We staggered the seams to block air paths. With an R-value of 5 per inch, the XPS provides a total of R-20 under the concrete. The slab also serves as thermal mass, storing heat on sunny winter days and releasing it at night. (Since this gain is incidental, it didn't enter into the heat calculations.)

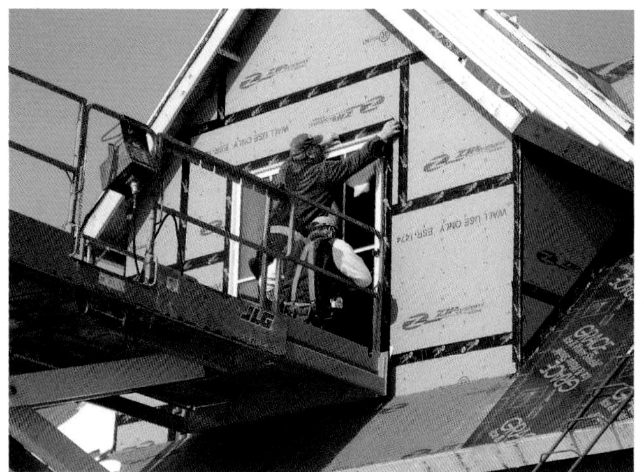

Figure 33. With the seams taped, Zip System sheathing provides a water-resistant air barrier under the siding.

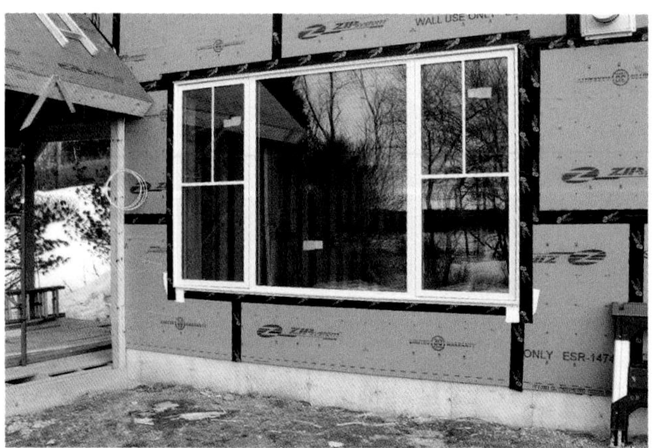

Figure 34. Triple-glazed windows cost up to 50 percent more than comparable double-glazed units but — according to computer modeling — will represent a 20 percent gain over double-pane glazing in the building's energy performance.

The 4-inch band of vertical perimeter insulation would ordinarily show in a conventionally framed wall (Figure 32). In this house, though, the double 2x4 walls are spaced 4¼ inches apart, giving an overall wall depth of 11¼ inches — enough to cover all but ¾ inch of the foam, which disappeared under the drywall and baseboard trim.

We had the concrete tinted a rich chocolate brown using ColorFlo iron oxide pigment (www.solomoncolors.com). The clients didn't care for the look of shiny polished concrete, so we simply cleaned the slab and sealed it with Seal-Once, a multisurface waterproofing compound (www.seal-once.com).

Framing for Thermal Efficiency

We framed the exterior walls first, completing and closing in the shell before building the interior walls. We used 2x4s at 16 inches on-center, with single studs at the corners, since we only had to catch the plywood sheathing and not the drywall. Similarly, the interior walls only have to catch the drywall. Thus, the heat loss seen in typical wood-heavy corners is minimized but not eliminated (our thermal scans showed the corners somewhat colder than the general wall area, presumably because there's still a greater concentration of studs there).

The joint between the sill plate and the foundation is the source of one of the biggest air leaks in a new home, even with conventional foam sill sealer installed. To address this area, we used a cellular EPDM structural gasket from Conservation Technology (www.conservationtechnology.com) that gets stapled to the underside of the plate before installation. It stays flexible down to –60°F, effectively fills irregularities, and keeps its flexibility for the lifetime of the building, according to the manufacturer.

We knew that the shell had to be as air-tight as we could make it. For that reason, I wanted to tape-seal all the seams in the sheathing and decided to try the relatively new Zip System sheathing (www.huberwood.com), an OSB panel with a moisture-resistant skin and proprietary seam tape. Although the panel-and-tape system has code acceptance as a "water-resistive barrier," relying on the proprietary seam tape made me somewhat nervous (Figure 33). I still didn't feel comfortable eliminating the roofing underlayment, so we prepared for the standing-seam metal roof with a full-coverage self-adhering underlayment membrane. But I am confident that the seam tape played a big role in the success of our blower-door test results.

We did note minor swelling at the edges of some sheets after wetting, along with some slight original variation in thickness from one panel to the next. The Home Slicker drainage material (www.benjaminobdyke.com) we installed behind the siding helped absorb the variations, but I'm hoping Huber will continue to improve the product.

Figure 35. Fixed awnings shade south-facing windows from high summer sun while allowing lower-angled solar gain during the winter months.

Figure 36. The bottom plates of the inside walls sit directly atop the slab's perimeter insulation, preventing a direct mechanical connection to the concrete. To hold the walls parallel to the exterior walls, the author used plywood standoffs and sealed beneath the plates with expanding foam (right). Single-stud corners reduce thermal bridging and allow fuller insulation coverage. Wall plates running parallel to the ceiling joists are nailed to 1x3 ceiling strapping, eliminating redundant framing (far right).

High-Tech Windows

We installed triple-glazed Thermotech fixed and casement units (www.thermotechwindows.com), which are fiberglass windows made in Canada (Figure 34). Compared with most double-glazed units, they're expensive. Depending on the manufacturer, you'll pay somewhere between 25 and 50 percent more for a triple-glazed unit than for double glazing. However, our energy modeling showed a 20 percent reduction in the heating load if they were used, suggesting a pretty aggressive payback over initial cost.

For budgetary reasons, we didn't use triple-glazed exterior doors — but the house has only three and they represent a tiny percentage of the building envelope.

Because the water view was too good to pass up, we put more glass than prescriptively recommended — typically no more than 10 percent of the aggregate glazing area — on the west-facing wall. The architect sized south-facing window overhangs to provide shade during the summer months. We framed them using local eastern white cedar and hackmatack and topped them in steel to match the main roof (Figure 35).

Double Wall Details

We framed the interior walls about ½ inch short so that we could tilt them up without hitting the ceiling joists. Since the bottom plates land over the 4-inch band of perimeter foam, we nailed the walls through the top plate into the floor joists above and used plywood standoffs bridging the exterior and interior walls to hold them in parallel alignment (Figure 36). To close the gap between the XPS and bottom plate, we injected expanding foam along the joint. The XPS has a compressive strength of 25 psi, and the thin bead of expanding foam should be adequate to distribute the load.

Figure 37. To allow the main entry door to open more fully in the thick exterior wall, the author widened the inside rough opening and applied rigid insulation to the inner face of the exterior wall studs, then sealed all seams with expanding foam.

On the second and third floors, we used solid shims between the subfloor and bottom plates, again foaming the gap against drafts. Where the interior wall framing ran parallel to the ceiling joists, we first strapped the ceiling with 1x3 furring on 16-inch centers, then nailed the plates to the strapping.

Entry door. The deep wall framing restricts the range of in-swinging doors to a roughly 95-degree arc. We accepted the restriction on the side doors, but to create a wider swing for the main entry, we enlarged the rough opening through the inside wall (Figure 37). We faced the exterior wall framing with 2-inch foam board and sealed all seams with expanding foam.

Deep Roof Build-Down

Our original roof framing detail called for standard 2x12s, cross-strapped with 2x3s set on edge on 16-inch centers. While this system would result in a nearly 14-inch-deep insulation cavity with minimal thermal bridging, I was concerned that the 2x3s might twist, creating nail pops and an irregular ceiling surface. (I

Figure 38. Ties made from Zip sheathing scraps connect 2x3 extensions to the 2x10 rafters to create a 14-inch-deep insulation cavity (A). Blocking between rafters is fully caulked around the edges to prevent air movement and moisture migration through the cellulose insulation (B). Gable walls are framed with double top plates in lieu of end rafters, breaking conductivity through framing members and creating an unobstructed insulation cavity (C).

avoid using 2x12s whenever possible anyway, under the assumption that they come from old-growth trees better left standing.) Instead, we used 2x10 rafters and created a deep insulation cavity by nailing 14-inch-wide ½-inch-thick plywood gussets to 2x3s about every 3 feet, then nailed these assemblies to the sides of the rafters to create a new lower ceiling plane (Figure 38). The reduced contact between framing members — along with the 2¼-inch gap between the members — further minimizes thermal bridging. We opted for an unvented roof and installed solid blocking at the eaves between rafters, caulking all the edges for airtightness.

Air-Sealing and Insulation

Even though correctly installed spray-foam insulation has built-in air-sealing properties, we chose cellulose for its lower installed cost — about one-third that of open-cell foam. Dense-pack cellulose can slow and even stop air movement, but leaks in the shell will definitely degrade its performance and allow moisture to enter framing cavities.

Before insulating, however, we routinely call for blower-door testing while the frame is still open and we can get to the leaky spots. It costs about $200 per test and is well worth the expense. We ran the first test after closing in the shell and making every effort to tighten it with caulk and tape. With the aid of a torpedo heater running inside the building, the infrared camera allowed us to find and caulk the few cold spots we found, mostly in the seams between built-up posts and headers on exterior walls (Figure 39). Our results at this stage were about 2.2 ACH at 50 pascals, a level of leakage around half that of many new homes. Not bad for an unfinished shell.

We also own a Bulldog 2K negative air machine (www.abatement.com) that we bought to help with dust control on renovation jobs. We've been using it to air out the house and have discovered that its 2,000-cfm fan makes a good substitute for a blower door. It doesn't allow us to measure the leakage, but it has shown us a couple of spots that required more caulking.

Figure 39. Blower-door testing at the weathertight stage is effective for early detection and treatment of air leaks in the envelope. The author achieved remarkable levels for this stage of construction.

Insulating With Cellulose

In new construction, dense-pack cellulose is commonly installed behind a membrane. In this case the membrane was Par/Pac (www.parpac.com), a stretchy, reinforced poly sheet that the installers first staple to the face of the studs, then "stitch" to the sides to keep the face from bulging beyond the wall plane (Figure 40). To prevent the cellulose from flowing over into interior ceilings, the installers run the wall membrane up into the joist bays and staple it to the joists and underside of the subfloor. The stapling schedule is

Figure 40. Triple-ply Par/Pac membrane is stretched around framing edges and rigorously stapled to prevent the cellulose insulation from bulging past the wall plane. Cellulose is blown through slits in the membrane to a density of 3.5 pounds per cubic foot. The slits are then resealed with tape.

intense, about one per inch. At doors and windows, we installed the drywall returns before blowing, to retain the insulation.

A good cellulose installation is a mix of art and science; installers develop a feel for when they're achieving the proper density, about 3.5 pounds per cubic foot. This job was complicated by the double walls and gusseted roof. Normally, bays are filled one at a time, but here there was nothing to keep the cellulose from flowing laterally. Fortunately, our installer, Ace Insulation, had already done several double-walled houses and had a handle on the slightly different technique for ensuring complete and proper density.

Figure 41. An energy recovery ventilator (ERV) provides whole-house ventilation while capturing heat held in humid indoor air and transferring it to the incoming fresh air.

Figure 42. Condensation on a very cold day during construction indicated gaps around this window that were not revealed during blower-door testing. The author stripped back the drywall returns and caulked around the jambs.

Ventilation

To ensure good indoor air quality and control moisture, a house as tight as this requires mechanical ventilation. My hvac contractor prefers ERVs (energy recovery ventilators) to HRVs (heat recovery ventilators) and installed an American Standard unit (Figure 41). Like an HRV, an ERV uses an air exchanger to transfer exhaust heat to the incoming air, but it also adjusts humidity levels by transferring moisture between air streams. While there have been concerns about a freezing risk to certain ERV cores in cold climates, my hvac contractor uses them exclusively and hasn't had any problems. Since unit specifications and performance vary, it's a good idea to check the manufacturer's recommendations.

We installed ducting to supply fresh air to the bedrooms and to draw moisture-laden return air from the bathrooms. While the ERV replaces conventional bathroom fans, we still installed a conventional range hood in the kitchen.

Second Test

Following insulation, we ran another blower-door test. The outcome — .88 air changes per hour at a pressure of 50 pascals (ACH50) — was among the best results our energy auditors had seen anywhere. We found slight drafting under the door pans and caulked them along the interior edges. We also found that pushing the doors tight against the weatherstripping affected our results, so we'll carefully adjust the strike plates when we install the final door hardware. Both doors and windows call for careful installation and air-sealing to ensure top performance.

In fact, after we set up temporary heat to dry the drywall, the dramatic temperature difference between indoors and outdoors revealed a cold spot on a large window unit that even the blower-door tests hadn't caught. Our rough opening was a little tight on the bottom and one side, preventing the cavity spray foam from making a tight seal. So, we stripped back the self-returning drywall and caulked the edges (Figure 42).

Looking Back

The extra time and material consumed in double-wall framing is somewhat offset by the relative ease and lower cost of framing with 2x4s rather than with 2x6s or some deeper system. I estimate that our framing package cost about 10 percent more on labor and about 5 percent more on materials compared with a conventionally framed house with 2x6 walls and standard 2x10 rafters. Blown with dense-pack cellulose insulation, double framing also produces a high R-value shell with extremely low thermal bridging, ensuring a short-term payback in lowered energy use. The final blower-door test, after drywall, came in at .77 ACH50 — not the .6 we had hoped for, but darn close.

__Dan Kolbert__ owns Dan Kolbert Building & Renovations in Portland, Maine.

Chapter 6
WINDOWS & SKYLIGHTS

PHILIP KANTOR

- Selecting High-Performance Windows
- Daylighting With Skylights

Selecting High-Performance Windows

by Steve Easley

There are over 100 million homes and approximately 20 billion square feet of clear glass residential windows in the U.S. Most of these homes are more than 30 years old, and as a result, the market is growing for replacement windows with energy efficient insulating glass units (IGUs). High-performance options are now readily available in all regions of the country. Heating and cooling energy savings of 10 to 20 percent or more can be achieved depending on climate region and the replacement window choice. Similar savings are achievable in new construction by upgrading to high-performance glazing. Almost all of these new products reduce ultraviolet (UV) radiation compared with clear glass, and fading damage due to UV can be cut by 50 percent or more.

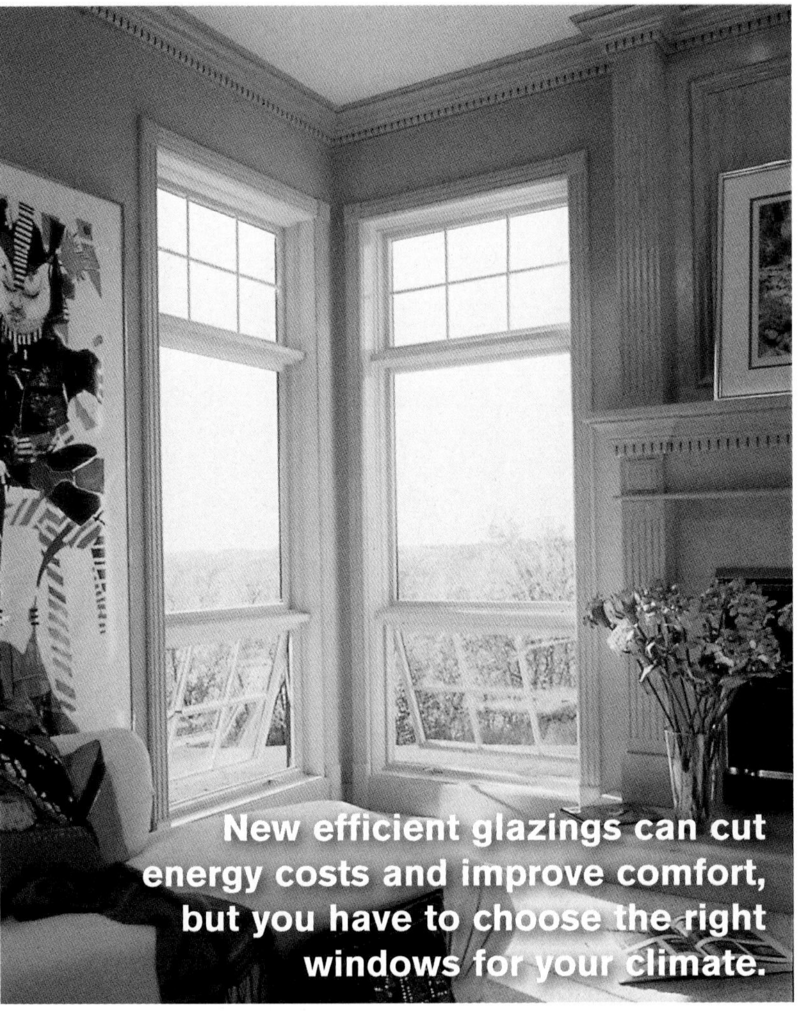

New efficient glazings can cut energy costs and improve comfort, but you have to choose the right windows for your climate.

A Profusion of Choices

Since there are hundreds of window manufacturers, each with many different product offerings, it's easy to get confused trying to sort through the trade names and marketing hype. Window options used to be limited to single-pane versus double-pane and wood frame versus aluminum frame. Today, there are three or four basic frame types, double- and triple-pane glass, and warm-edge insulating glass spacers. The low-E coatings used on most windows today can be formulated for low, medium, or high solar gain. The terminology alone is enough to make your head spin, and most of this technology is hidden inside the window so it can't readily be seen.

For example, all low-E coatings improve the insulating value of the glass and are clear to the human eye. Beyond the visible spectrum, low-E can be formulated to either allow solar heat gain into the building (great for passive solar in cold climates) or to significantly block solar gains (important for air-conditioning in all climates).

To make matters even more challenging, consumers have grown to expect high performance from their windows, even when they don't understand the technologies involved. I once received a call from a homeowner who had bought tinted windows. A few sunny days after the installation, she wanted the windows removed because she didn't feel they were doing anything to reduce heat gain, as the salesperson had so zealously promised. After a few questions, I discovered that she had a 10-foot-wide covered porch wrapping all the way around her house. She was right: Her windows never received direct sunlight, so there was no way a tinted window was going to affect her energy costs. She had been sold the wrong product.

Better Labeling

Thanks to the efforts of the National Fenestration Rating Council (the NFRC is a collaborative effort between manufacturers, the Department of Energy, utility companies, and others) most building codes now require windows to be labeled via the NFRC process.

This NFRC label gives you specific information about the *whole window performance,* not just the glass or components (Figure 1). For example, a piece of clear glass transmits about 90 percent of the visible light striking it, giving it a VT of 0.90. For the whole window, including sash and frame, however, the VT drops to about 0.60 or more, depending on the specific window.

U-factor measures how well a product prevents heat from escaping; the lower the U-factor, the greater a window's resistance to heat flow and the better its insulating value. The U-factor is the inverse of the more common R-value measurement. For example, a window with U-factor of 0.25 has an R-value of 4 (1/.25 = 4).

Solar heat gain coefficient (SHGC) measures how well a window blocks heat from incoming sunlight. The number, from 0 to 1, is the fraction of incident solar radiation admitted through a window. The lower a window's SHGC, the less solar heat it transmits into the house.

Visible transmittance (VT) measures how much light comes through a window and is also expressed as a number between 0 and 1. The higher the number, the more visible light gets through the window.

Air leakage (AL) is a measure of infiltration through cracks in the window assembly. The rating is expressed as the equivalent cubic feet of air passing through a square foot of window area. The lower the AL, the less air will pass through a window.

Condensation resistance (CR) measures the ability of a window to resist the formation of condensation on the interior surface during cold weather. CR is expressed as a number between 0 and 100. A higher rating indicates the product is better at resisting condensation formation.

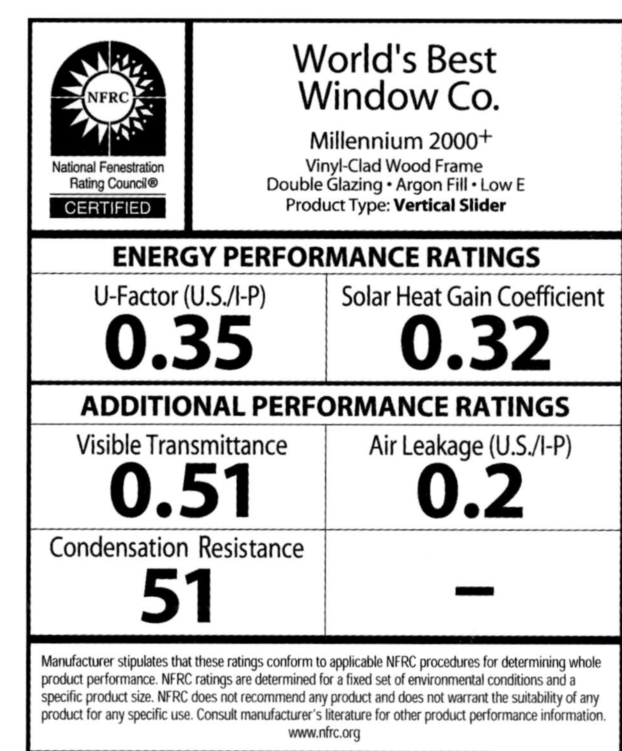

Figure 1. The NFRC label, found on most high-quality windows, makes it easy to assess a window's energy performance. Which U-factor and solar heat gain coefficient (SHGC) are optimal depend on the climate where the window will be installed. Optional ratings for air leakage (AL) and condensation resistance (CR) are included on the sample rating. AL indicates how many cubic feet of air leak through a square foot of window area, and generally ranges from 0.1 to 0.3. CR rates, on a scale of 1 to 100, indicates how well a window resists forming condensation on the inside of the glass. Higher numbers indicate better resistance to condensation.

Matching Windows to Climate

A companion to the NFRC label is the Energy Star label (Figure 2), which makes it easy to tell whether a given window is right for your climate. The Energy Star rating is based on minimum Department of Energy (DOE) performance specifications by region (Figure 3).

In the absence of an Energy Star label, follow the Energy Star guidelines in Figure 3. The program groups window requirements based on four climate regions.

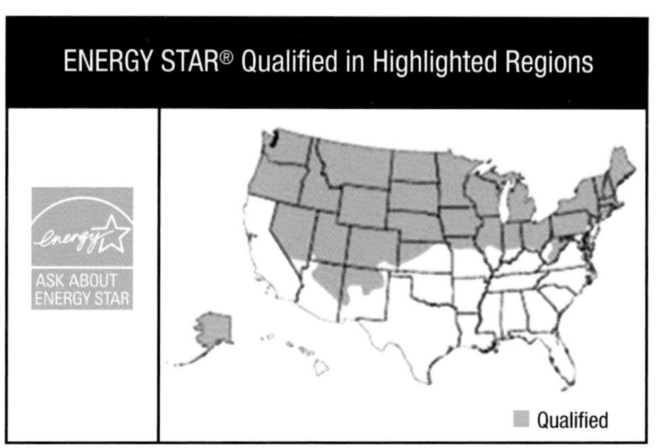

Figure 2. The Energy Star label uses color shading to show all the climate zones where a particular window or skylight will perform well. The Energy Star label appears on a window next to the NFRC label.

The Importance of Low-E

Of the many window technologies developed in recent years, none has had as great an effect on window energy performance as the low-E (low-emittance) coating. A low-E coating is a microscopically thin, transparent metal layer applied to one of the glass surfaces in the sealed space of the *insulating glass unit* (IGU). In an ordinary IGU (no coating) about two-thirds of the heat transfer across the gap is via thermal radiation. Low-E coatings will block most of this heat loss – the net effect is that double-pane glass with low-E insulates as well as uncoated triple- or quad-pane glass. This allows window manufacturers to offer high-performance windows using proven double-glazed window designs – particularly important for operable windows. All of the U-factors listed in the Energy Star criteria can be met using double glazing with low-E.

When the heat loss is reduced, the room-side glass surface temperature is warmer during cold weather. The infrared photograph in Figure 4 presents a visual representation of comfort with three different windows installed side by side on a cold winter night. The two window units on the left are double pane insulat-

Matching Windows to Climate

	Windows		Skylights	
Climate Zone	**Maximum U-Factor**	**Maximum SHGC**	**Maximum U-Factor**	**Maximum SHGC**
Northern	0.30*	Any	0.55	Any
North/Central	0.32	0.40	0.55	0.40
South/Central	0.35	0.30	0.57	0.30
Southern	0.60	0.27	0.70	0.30

* up to 0.31 if SHGC ≥ 0.35; up top 0.32 if SHGC ≥0.40

Source: Energy Star Requirements for Residential Windows Version 5.0

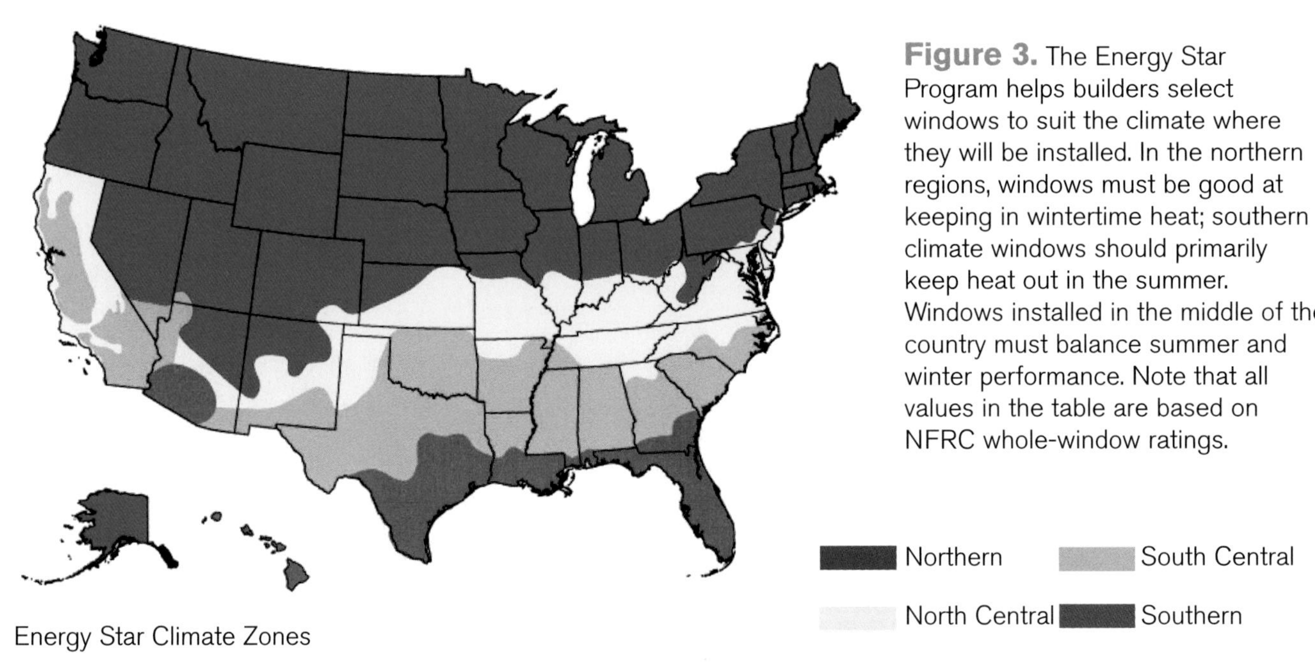

Energy Star Climate Zones

Figure 3. The Energy Star Program helps builders select windows to suit the climate where they will be installed. In the northern regions, windows must be good at keeping in wintertime heat; southern climate windows should primarily keep heat out in the summer. Windows installed in the middle of the country must balance summer and winter performance. Note that all values in the table are based on NFRC whole-window ratings.

Figure 4. The inside surface of the low-E windows (left and center panes) are much warmer than the clear double-pane (right). If this window had three bays of clear double-pane glass, the heating thermostat would have to be 2°F to 3°F warmer to deliver the same level of comfort you'd experience in the room with low-E glass.

ing glass with a low-E coating, while the unit on the right is ordinary double glass (no coating).

Low-E coatings increase comfort by making the inside surface of glass warmer, leading to less heat transfer from the person to the window on a cold day. Also, people are more comfortable when a room's escaping heat is reflected back at them by low-E coatings. A warmer surface on the inside of the glass also means less potential for condensation.

Spectrally Selective Low-E

Roughly half of the energy in sunlight is invisible to the human eye. Low-E coating manufacturers have learned how to design coatings that let most of the visible light pass through, with little tint or coloration, while either transmitting or blocking most of the solar heat. The different glass designs can be grouped into generic categories of *high, medium,* and *low solar-heat gain.*

Spectrally selective low-E coatings do a good job preventing winter heat loss and reducing summer heat gain while still allowing most of the visible light to enter the space (Figure 5).

Other Glass Technologies

Manufacturers have developed a number of technologies to improve window thermal performance in all climates. Some, like warm-edge spacers and gas fills, are widely used across the country. Others, such as tints and films, are only used for special applications.

Warm-edge IG spacer systems. The aluminum spacer bars traditionally used to separate the two panes in double glazing create a thermal short-circuit around the edge of the glass. Despite the warm center-of-glass temperatures achieved with low-E glass, the bottom edge of the glass was cold and had frequent condensation (Figure 6). Today more than 90 percent of the residential windows sold use some form of "warm-edge" system. The designs vary from low-conductance metals (e.g., stainless steel) to foam or plastic replacements of the aluminum spacer tube. The thermal performance improvement from warm-edge technology is reflected in the total window U-factor rating found on the NFRC label. In addition to thermal performance, however, it's important to pay attention to window durability. Be sure to compare manufacturers' warranty provisions – sometimes the best performer will lack long-term warranty support due to concerns about the durability of new materials and technologies.

Gas fills. Many manufacturers put low-conductance gases, such as argon or krypton, between the glazing layers to enhance the performance gains from low-E. Without low-E, the gas will have little effect. Even with the coating, the window U-factor will typically improve by less than 10 percent. Again, it's important to read the manufacturer's warranty to understand their provisions regarding gas retention.

Triple and quad pane glazing. Double-pane glass is optimized with a low-E coating and gas fill. To provide even better insulating values, some new window

How Spectrally Selective Low-E Works

Low-E Type (Double-pane glass)	**Visible Transmittance** (center-of- glass VT)	**Window Properties** (Typical)		
		U-Factor	**SHGC**	**VT**
None (clear glass)	81%	0.55	0.60	0.60
High Solar-gain	75%	0.33	0.52	0.56
Medium Solar-gain	70%	0.32	0.32	0.53
Low Solar-gain	66%	0.31	0.22	0.50

*Window U-Factor, SHGC, and VT are based on NFRC whole-window ratings, including sash and frame.

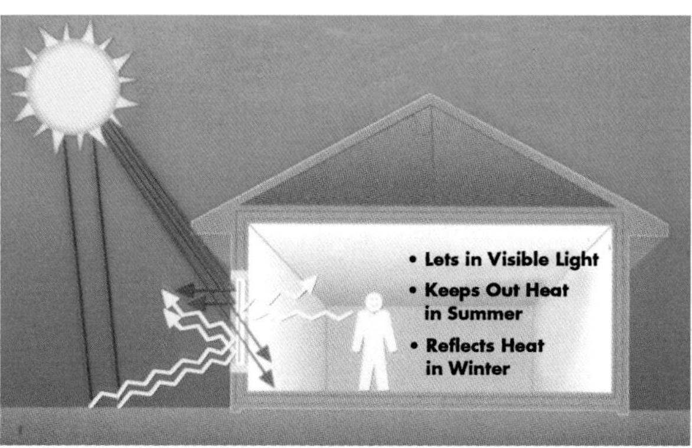
• Lets in Visible Light
• Keeps Out Heat in Summer
• Reflects Heat in Winter

Figure 5. Spectrally selective low-E coatings do a good job preventing winter heat loss and reducing summer heat gain while still allowing most of the visible light to enter the space, as indicated by high center-of-glass VT ratings. The chart compares the performance of standard clear glass to three types of low-E. Note the performance options available with advanced low-E. Going from high to low solar-gain cuts the SHGC by nearly two-thirds with only a modest loss of visible light.

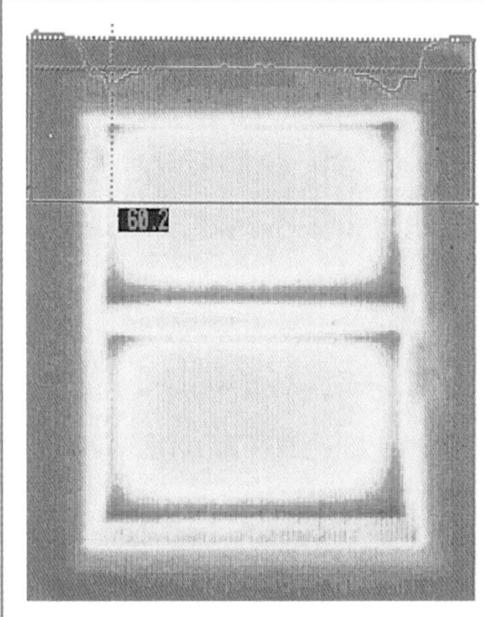

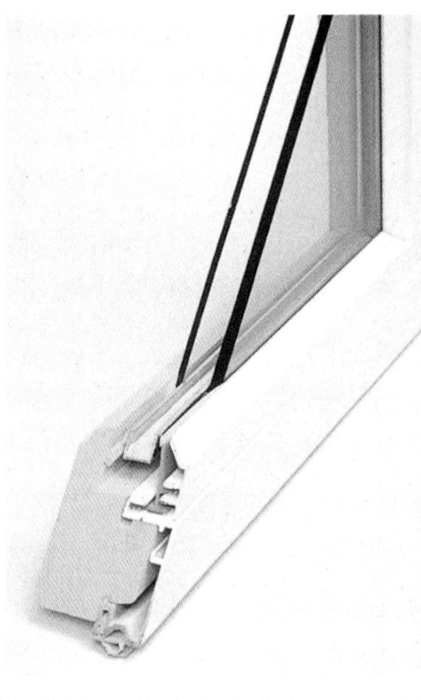

Figure 6. Conductive heat loss around the perimeter of insulated glass units (dark areas in the thermographic image, far left), caused by metal edge spacers, has led to recent innovations in "warm-edge" non-metal spacers, such as the PPG Intercept (left).

designs are incorporating triple and quad-pane systems with multiple low-E coatings (one coating in each air space). Concerns with weight and thickness have some manufacturers replacing the internal layer(s) with plastic or suspended films. Many remain skeptical of the durability of plastics encapsulated in the gap and exposed to sun and thermal cycles. Some newer window designs use thicker sash to accommodate all-glass triple or quad units. Refer to installation instructions to ensure that these products are compatible with your wall system.

Tinted glass. Tinted glass is sometimes used to reduce heat gain in hot climates. However, tinted glass gets hot in sunlight (from absorption) and suffers more loss of light transmission than spectrally selective low-E coatings. There are some spectral tinted glasses available today, usually light blue or green in color. However, residential windows usually avoid tints, given the market preference for clear glazings. Also, these tints don't improve the U-factor, so a low-E coating is still required to meet code and Energy Star standards.

Aftermarket applied films. Tint films are often retrofitted onto windows in rooms that overheat due to direct sunlight. While they can effectively address overheating, the films can be problematic because the low visible light transmission can excessively darken rooms. There can also be problems with film adhesion, and some window manufacturers will void their warranty if tint films have been applied. When buying new or replacement windows, look for products with a low SHGC, indicating that solar control is already built in to the window.

Reducing Fading With Low-E

The spectral selectivity of low-E coatings also allows them to block significant amounts of ultraviolet (UV) light. Research into the fading of fabrics, artwork, finishes, and home furnishings has shown that the radiant energy that affects fading includes portions of the visible light spectrum in addition to UV. The International Organization for Standardization (ISO) has proposed a damage-weighted scale called Tdw-ISO that accounts for the effects of both UV and visible light. The ratings for low-E glass (Figure 7) suggest that low-solar-gain low-E glass with a rating of 0.43 would reduce the rate of fading by over 40 percent compared with clear glass rated at 0.74.

It's not appropriate to claim that a glass type can "eliminate" fading altogether. If light passes through, there will always be a risk of fading. Also, the rate of fading will vary with the type of material and the exposure levels. Keeping a sensitive material out of

Reducing Fading With Low-E

Glass Type	Tdw-ISO
Clear	0.74
High-solar-gain low-E	0.66
Medium-solar-gain low-E	0.55
Low-solar-gain low-E	0.43

Figure 7. Although blocking UV light is important for preventing fading, some damage is also caused by portions of the visible light spectrum. To determine the actual fading potential of light passing through a glazing system, use the total damage weighted (Tdw) values. The lower the Tdw, the less fading will occur.

direct sunlight is always a good idea.

Comfort Is the Issue

A study commissioned by Pacific Gas and Electric several years ago discovered that the number one reason customers make energy-efficiency improvements to their homes is to increase their comfort. Windows have a huge impact on comfort. When it is 40˚F outside, the inside surface temperature of a single-pane window can be 20˚F colder than room temperature. Since our bodies radiate heat to colder surfaces, a room full of poorly insulating windows can make us feel uncomfortable (by radiant cooling) even if the home is well insulated. High-performance technologies can make windows feel warmer during cold weather by keeping the temperature of the interior glass surface higher (Figure 8).

Summer performance is important. Except in the Deep South, we tend to evaluate window products on their cold-weather performance. While winter performance is important, the right window can also have a big impact on comfort in summer as well as on air conditioning costs. Since more than 40 percent of existing homes and 80 percent of new homes have air conditioning, it makes sense to pay close attention to a window's solar heat-gain properties as well.

Surface temperature. Year round, and in all climates, windows can be a home's biggest source of thermal discomfort. The inside glass surface temperature is the dominant factor to consider regarding comfort (Table 1). We've already seen that a lower U-factor provides better insulation and warmer glass in the winter. This saves energy in two ways: less heat loss and a lower heat thermostat setting to provide comfort.

In warm weather, clear glass and high-solar-gain low-E will increase cooling loads and air-conditioner size. The combination of high solar gains along with the hot inside glass temperature,would require cooling thermostats set anywhere from 2°F to 4°F lower to provide the same comfort regimen as the medium or low solar-gain low-E.

In cold climates, solar gain can be used to offset heat losses, but this requires a system design approach. Windows should face south for best winter sun exposure, and overhangs should be designed to shade the glass in the spring and fall. If large amounts of south-facing glass are used, the building should be designed by an experienced solar designer, and it may need thermal mass to absorb solar gains and a circulation system to distribute the stored gains. Even with all this, many passive-solar buildings experience daily temperature swings that are beyond the comfort expectations of most homeowners.

Choosing the optimal glazing type for both winter and summer performance can be tricky. However, computer modeling indicates that the sweet spot for most

Figure 8. This infrared photo was taken on a cool (30°F) winter day. Notice how hot the high-solar-gain glass, at center, is relative to the other windows. Imagine the discomfort on a hot summer day.

Table 1. Glass Surface Temperature

		Interior Glass Surface Temperature	
Insulated Glass Type	**Low-E Coating**	**Winter night**	**Summer day**
Double Pane	None	44˚F	91˚F
	High solar gain	52˚F	98˚F
	Medium solar gain	56˚F	84˚F
	Low solar gain	56˚F	82˚F
Triple Pane	None	52˚F	94˚F
	High solar gain	61˚F	94˚F
	Medium solar gain	61˚F	87˚F

Note: Table assumes 0˚F and 15mph wind for winter conditions and 89˚F with bright sunshine for summer conditions. Note that low solar gain low-E glass is both warmer in winter and cooler in summer.

Annual Energy Costs Versus Type of Window

	Savings vs. Single Pane Glass					Savings vs. Double Pane Clear			
	Type II	Type III	Type IV	Type V	Type VI	Type III	Type IV	Type V	Type VI
Northern	20%	26%	25%	25%	28%	8%	7%	7%	10%
NorthCentral	19%	25%	25%	26%	27%	7%	8%	9%	11%
SouthCentral	17%	24%	27%	30%	30%	8%	12%	15%	15%
Southern	14%	19%	27%	30%	28%	6%	15%	19%	17%

Heating & Cooling Costs for a 2,000 ft² 2-Story Existing House

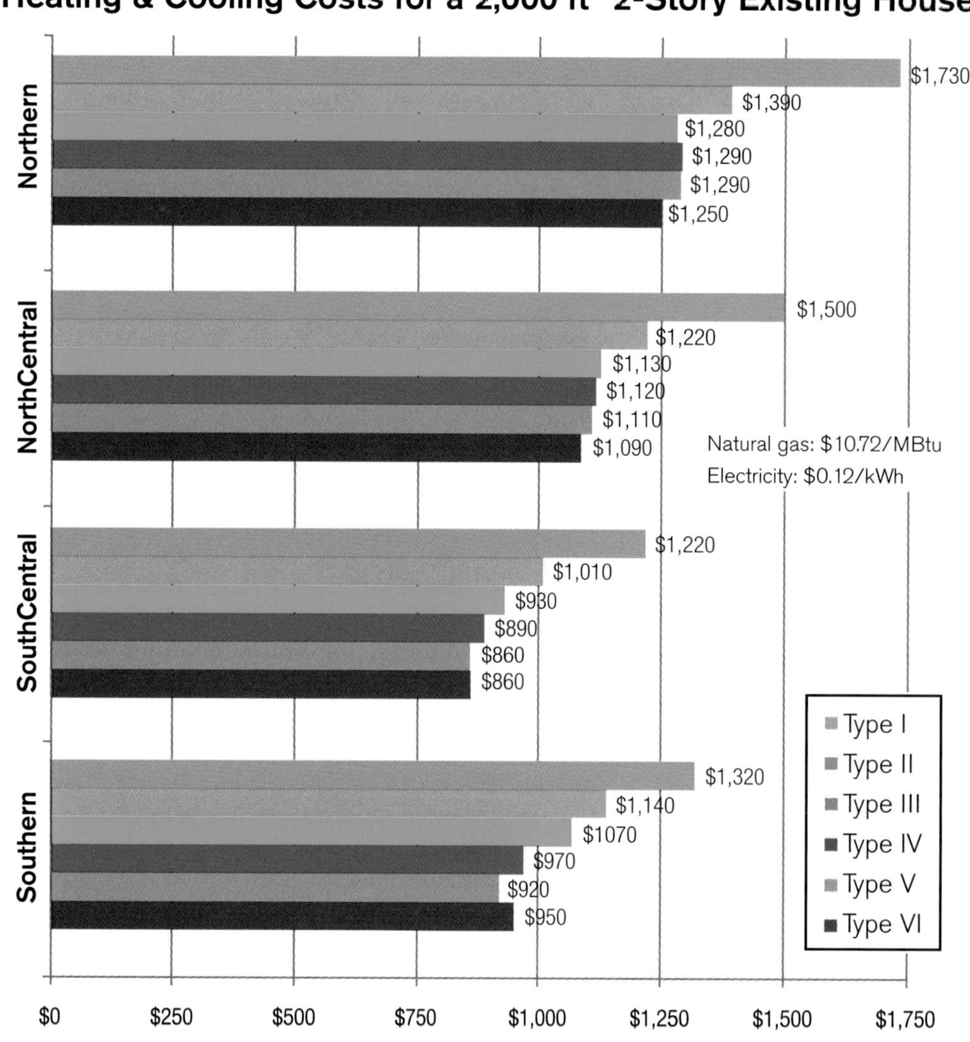

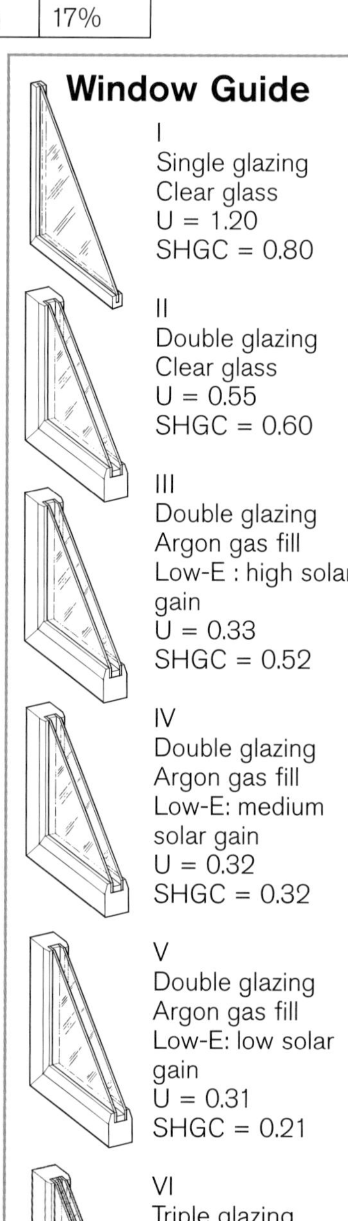

Window Guide
I
Single glazing
Clear glass
U = 1.20
SHGC = 0.80
II
Double glazing
Clear glass
U = 0.55
SHGC = 0.60
III
Double glazing
Argon gas fill
Low-E : high solar gain
U = 0.33
SHGC = 0.52
IV
Double glazing
Argon gas fill
Low-E: medium solar gain
U = 0.32
SHGC = 0.32
V
Double glazing
Argon gas fill
Low-E: low solar gain
U = 0.31
SHGC = 0.21
VI
Triple glazing
Argon gas fill
Low-E: medium solar gain
U = 0.25
SHGC = 0.29
All frames: wood, vinyl, or fiberglass
U = U-Factor
SHCG = Solar Heat Gain Coefficient

Note: Table courtesy of Jim Larsen, Cardinal Glass Industries. Energy savings were calculated using analysis performed by Lawrence Berkeley National Laboratory in support of the ENERGY STAR Window program (see www.windows.lbl.gov for detail). Building type was assumed to be an existing 2-story wood-frame house, 2,000 sq. ft. in size. National average fuel prices of natural gas and electricity for January 2011 came from the Energy Information Agency.

Figure 9. These graphs illustrate the total annual energy costs associated with seven common window types. In the northern region, for example, you reduce energy costs in an existing home by about $450 annually by switching from single glazing (Type I) to double glazing with low-E and argon (Types 3, 4, or 5). In the southern region, switching from single glazing to double glazing with low-solar-gain low-E with argon (Type V) would save about $400 a year. Similar savings would be realized in new construction.

homes in the U.S is argon-filled double glazing with medium-solar-gain low-E (SHGC from 0.25 to 0.35, U-factor of 0.28 to 0.32). This will provide warm inside glass temperatures on cold winter nights and limit unwanted heat gain in summer. In hot southern climates, it makes sense to use the lowest SHGC available.

Reasonable Cost

As we saw with the Energy Star program, national building codes have adopted window efficiency requirements that basically mandate low-E everywhere in the country. Given that the incremental cost of upgrading from clear double glass to a gas-filled low-E window is less than $1 per square foot of glass area, most studies show that the payback period for choosing low-E will be less than one year (Figure 9), and this does not even take into account the cost savings of a downsized furnace and air-conditioner. Nor does it take into account the improved comfort of occupants, one of the greatest benefits of the revolution in glazing technology.

Triple glazing may be cost-effective in extremely cold climates, but with a longer payback period that would need to be evaluated on a case-by-case basis.

In retrofits, while it may not be cost effective to replace old windows based on energy savings alone (depending on the new window and installation costs), once you have decided to replace the windows, upgrading from clear glass to low-E will provide a payback as quickly as in new construction.

***Steve Easley** is a construction consultant who specializes in helping contractors build and remodel homes for high performance and solving building science related problems. He also teaches best practice building techniques and can be reached at www.steve@steveeasley.com.*

Dealing With Condensation

Condensation on windows, which often causes disappointed customers and callbacks, can be reduced with new glazing technologies. With a simple chart (below), it's easy to predict under what conditions condensation will form on a given window. Low-E windows can prevent the formation of condensation until relative humidity levels reach 65 percent at an outdoor temperature of 20°F. Relative humidity levels above 65 percent are excessive and will likely cause other problems besides dripping windows. I always recommend that contractors carry a digital hygrometer to measure and record indoor relative humidity while they are in customers' homes. —S.E.

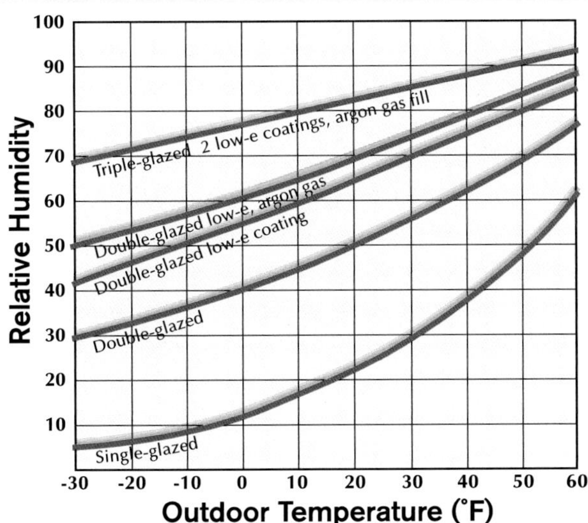

Given an outdoor temperature of 20°F, project up vertically to the desired glazing curve. A double-glazed clear window, for instance, corresponds to a relative humidity of 51 percent. Compare this with a double-glazed low-E argon product, which would allow almost 70 percent relative humidity before condensation would occur. This chart is for the glass only and not the frame.

For More Information

Efficient Windows Collaborative
www.efficientwindows.org

California Window Initiative, 604 Bancroft Way, Berkeley, CA 94710, 800/600-9050

Energy Star Windows Program
www.energystar.gov/windows

National Fenestration Rating Council (NFRC)
www.nfrc.org

Lawrence Berkeley Laboratory Building Technologies Program
www.windows.lbl.gov

Energy Efficient Building Association (EEBA)
www.eeba.org

American Architectural Manufacturers Association (AAMA)
www.aamanet.org

Daylighting With Skylights

by Doug Walter, AIA

Sunlight is nature's antidepressant. Have you ever noticed how the tables by the windows fill up first in a restaurant? Or how, in winter, people cross the street to walk in the sun? My personal belief is that no one should have to turn on a light during the day in any room. Skylights are often the most dramatic and effective way to make a difference in the daylighting of a new or existing home.

Why Skylights?

I think the reason that most people respond so positively to skylights is that they restore the natural canopy effect of being outside with a bright sky overhead. In effect, skylights are a way of bringing "pieces of sky" to important spaces in the home. They're an ideal way to highlight activity areas, such as kitchen islands, dining rooms, main stairways, hallways, or even a special piece of furniture. We use sun tubes to illuminate small utilitarian areas like closets, toilet rooms, and back stairs. The "punch" of daylight spilling into an area draws people to it, especially if it's deep within a wide floor plan where outside windows are impossible. The unexpectedness of daylight in such situations is a delight.

Table 2. Energy Star Standards for Residential Skylights

Climate Zone	Maximum U-Factor	Maximum SHGC
Northern	0.55	Any
North Central	0.55	0.40
South Central	0.57	0.30
Southern	0.70	0.30

Note: See Climate Zone map, Figure 3 page 154.

Energy efficiency. There's no reason to get all worked up about heat loss through a skylight or two. We use skylights that are typically 6 square feet, and always spec the highest efficiency flat-glass skylights possible, with a clad wood frame (Table 2). When used in a home that has 200 or 300 square feet of windows and doors, the energy loss is insignificant, and when compared to the energy saved by not having to turn on electric lights during the day, there's probably a net gain.

A much more important energy-related concern is

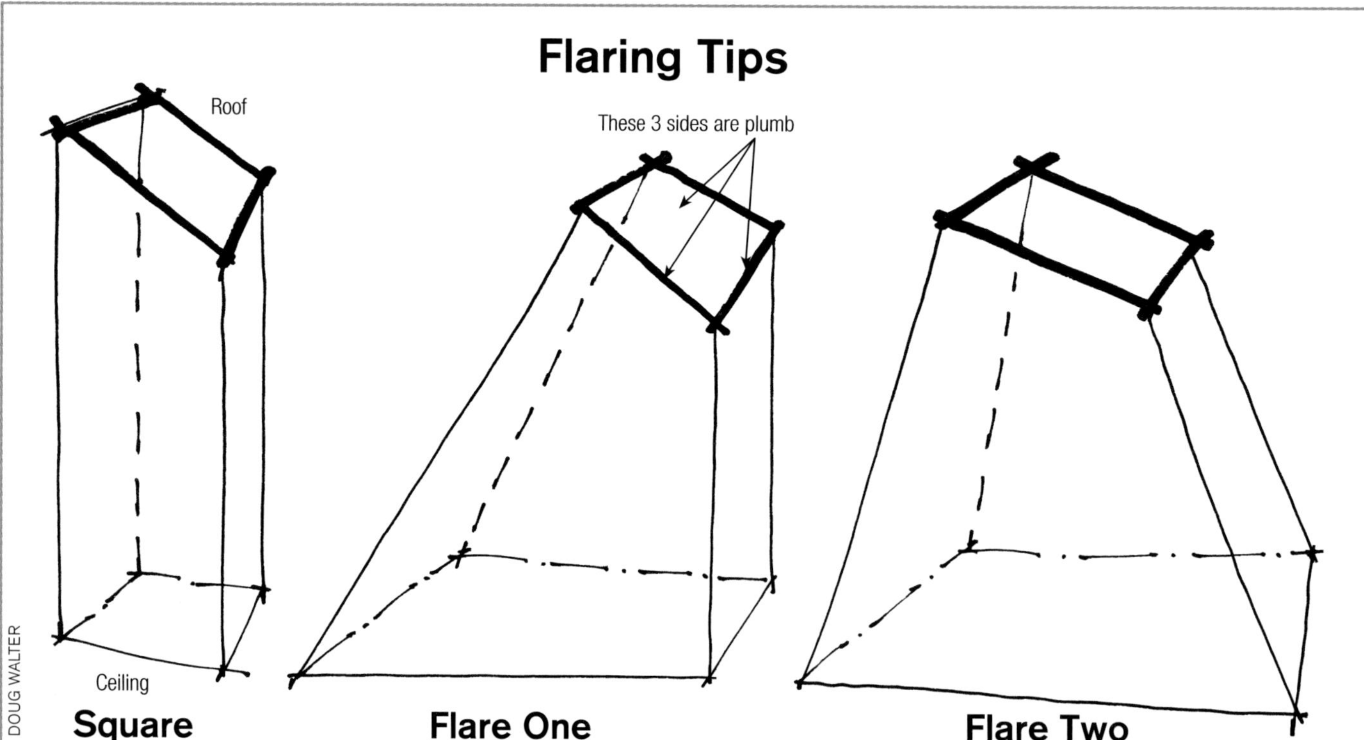

Figure 10. A perfectly plumb skylight shaft is simple to build, but yields a ceiling opening smaller than the skylight itself (left). Flaring one face of a shaft, usually the "uphill" face nearest the peak of the roof, allows light to penetrate more deeply, especially when the sun is low (center). A narrow space, such as a hallway, is a natural location for a shaft with two flared faces (right).

that of overheating during the warm months. In southwestern states, it can be a problem 12 months of the year. For that reason, it is our practice to use skylights minimally on west- and south-facing roofs, but more liberally on the east and north slopes of a roof.

Skylight Shafts

Many skylights require you to bring the daylight down through a 4- to 9-foot (or more) attic space. To complicate things even more, the best location for the skylight itself — away from hips and valleys on the back slope of the roof — won't necessarily be directly above where you want the light coming down through the ceiling. Balancing these needs can be a real challenge but offers some rewarding design opportunities. Also, make sure the shaft is properly insulated and sealed to prevent condensation problems in cold weather (see "Skylight Insulation Details, below).

Design with flare. If you plumb down from all four corners of a skylight in a sloped roof to a flat ceiling, you end up with an opening that is smaller than the skylight itself, resulting in a relatively small gain in daylight for the time and effort invested (Figure 10). In most cases, it's well worth flaring at least one of the four faces of the shaft. Our preference is to flare the top face — that is, the face nearest the roof peak — because this allows deeper penetration of the daylight, especially in the winter months when the sun angles

Skylight Insulation Details

By Terry Brennan and Chuck Silver

For insulating the skylight well, we prefer rigid foam insulation. This is one of those awkward areas where a sheet of foam board is easier to work with than fiberglass batts and sheets of poly. Cut the foam board to the sizes and angles you need, nail them in place, tape the seams, and seal the corners and any gaps with canned foam sealant. This provides the insulation, air barrier, and vapor barrier all in one shot. We install at least R-30—often using a combination of foam board and fiberglass insulation.

Be sure to seal and insulate between the rough opening framing and the skylight jamb–canned foam works best. If warm indoor air can get to the bottom side of the aluminum flashing when it is cold outside, there is a good chance that the dew point will be reached, and the skylight will appear to leak. Worse, it's a "leak" that no amount of roof cement slathered on the shingles and flashing will fix. So pay attention while installing the foam.

Carry the foam board insulation from the skylight frame all the way down the well to the ceiling level. It's too difficult to make an air barrier if you stop the foam up higher and try to insulate the rest of the well with the fiberglass ceiling insulation. The general idea is to wrap the chase in a tight layer of rigid insulation. This keeps the interior surfaces warm and the whole assembly free of air leaks and condensation.

Skylight Insulation Detail

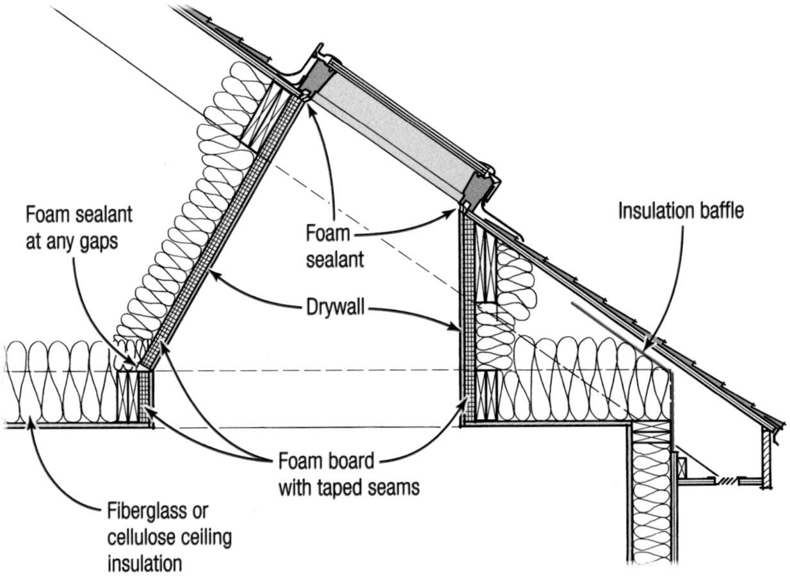

Installing rigid foam board is the most effective way to seal and insulate the skylight well. Be sure to seal around the jamb with foam sealant, or the underside of the flashing might reach dew point in cold weather. This can cause condensation to drip like a water leak.

***Terry Brennan** is principal of Camroden Associates, a building science consulting firm in Westmorland, N.Y. Chuck Silver is principal of Hudson River Design in Saugerties, N.Y.*

are low. Another option is to flare both the top and bottom faces of the shaft. That can be especially effective where the sides are confined within a hallway or other narrow space.

Ceiling coffers. We often use flared skylight shafts as giant ceiling coffers (Figure 11). That's a good way to lift the apparent height of a space to give it a more important feel.

Flaring more than two sides. It's also possible to flare three or all four faces of a shaft, although this involves some tricky geometry. Because each framing member must travel a different distance from the sloping sides of the skylight to the flat ceiling plane, the side faces of the three- or four-sided flare will describe parabolic planes — essentially, planes that have been twisted. The resulting shaft can be dramatic, but allow sufficient time for framing and fitting the drywall, which may have to be moistened to take the required curve.

Grouping and Placement

The deeper the shaft, the more we start to think about stacking or ganging multiple skylights (Figure 12). In bringing shafts down between roof trusses that are 2 feet on-center, this is your only option to give a room significant punch (Figure 13).

No matter what the length, a single 2-foot-wide shaft will probably look lost in a 12x15 foot room, so

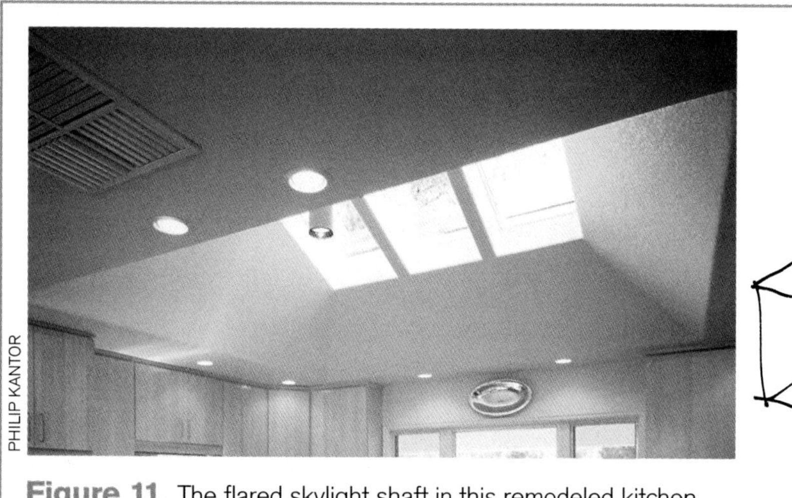

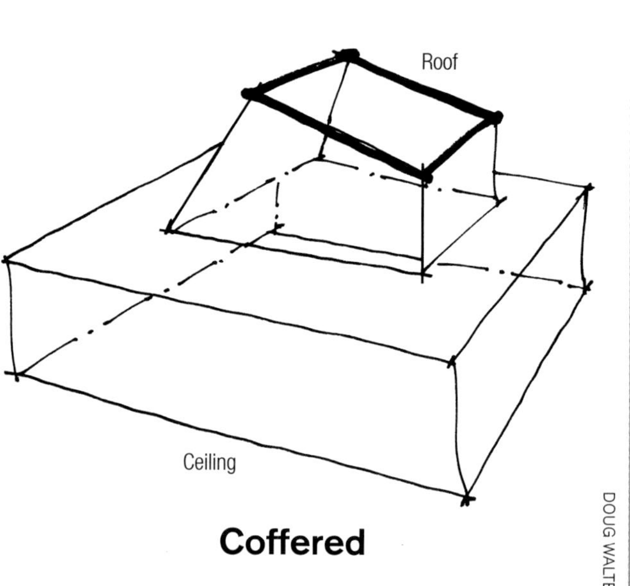

Figure 11. The flared skylight shaft in this remodeled kitchen acts as a giant ceiling coffer to admit daylight and define the space (above). Another option is to terminate a flared shaft within a square-sided coffer (right).

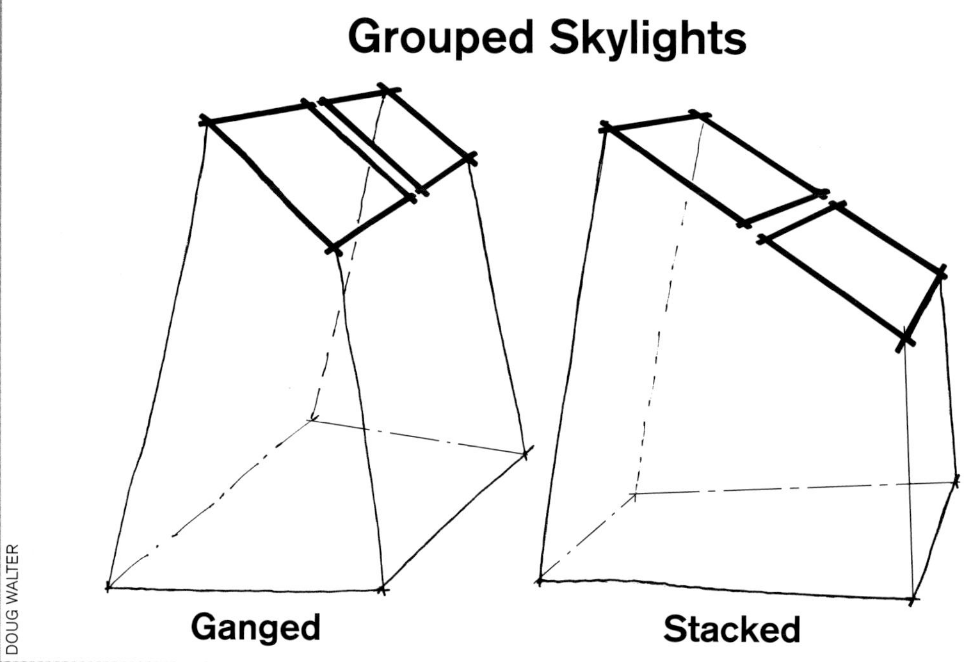

Figure 12. Ganging or stacking skylights are good ways to admit added light between existing roof trusses.

DON RILEY

Figure 13. Three 20-inch-wide shafts defined by roof trusses are interconnected by heating louvers, allowing excess summer heat to be exhausted by a thermostatically controlled exhaust fan.

we group two, three, or four together.

Deep and narrow shafts have the unexpected side benefit of softening the entering sunlight by bouncing it off the shaft interior. That can be especially useful for balancing the lighting in rooms that have only one outside wall, as these rooms tend to have a problem with glare. With all the light coming from one direction, it's as if you were in a cave with all the light entering through the mouth. If we are using skylights mainly to balance lighting in a room, we are likely to locate the shaft close to a wall, so the light can bounce off it.

Another imaginative possibility for an exceptionally deep shaft — especially one that punctures one floor plane on its way down to another — is to direct some of that light into the upper space by way of a window (Figure 14).

***Doug Walter**, AIA, is a residential architect based in Denver.*

PHILIP KANTOR

PHILIP KANTOR

Figure 14. Ganged skylights admit daylight to the kitchen through a wood-paneled shaft (top). An opening to the study loft above the kitchen allows the same skylights to illuminate that space as well (above).

Chapter 7

ATTIC & ROOF INSULATION

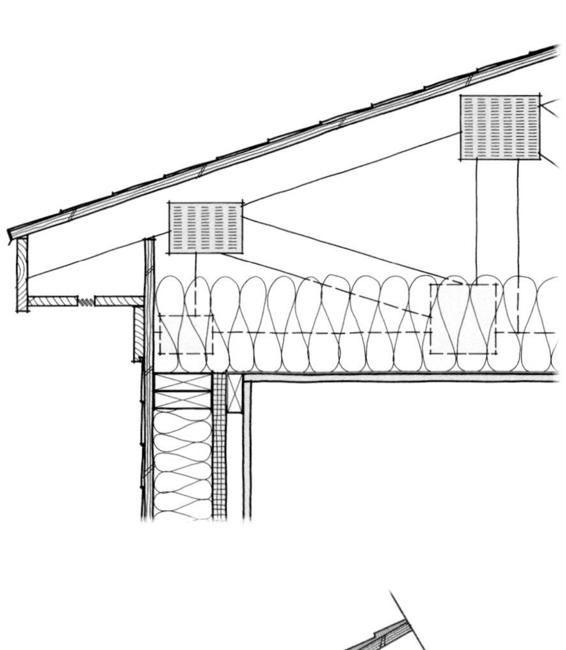

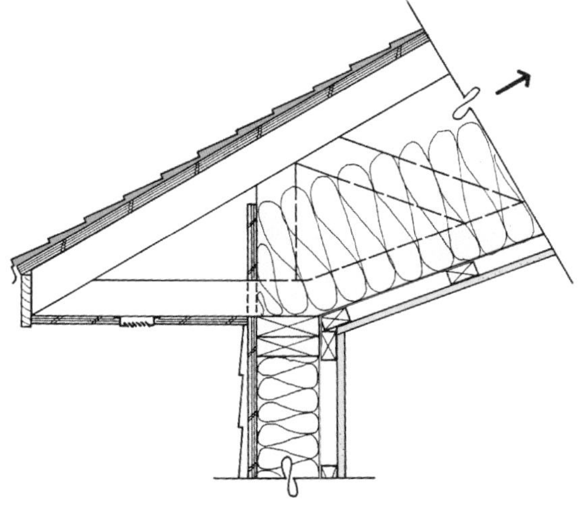

- Attic Ventilation Details
- Vented Cathedral Ceiling Details
- Insulating Unvented Attics With Spray Foam
- Insulated Cold Roof Retrofit
- Cool Roof Strategies for Hot Climates

Attic Ventilation Details

by Gordon Tully

A challenging place to design insulation and ventilation details is the intersection of roof and wall. The appearance of the exterior roof-wall intersection on the exterior is an important part of house design. What goes on inside is equally important and often influences the exterior appearance. In fact, solving the insulation details may lead you to better exterior eaves details.

Eaves at Unoccupied Attic Floors

In the typical one- or two-story house with an unoccupied attic, the eaves are at the same level as the attic floor (Figure 1). The rafters rest on the top plate of the wall and nestle alongside the attic or floor joists. If a roof truss is used, the lower and upper chords often intersect at the top of the wall. This joint is troublesome, because if not done properly it squeezes the insulation (just where you want it thick to prevent ice dams) and invites cold air from the roof ventilation system into the ceiling insulation.

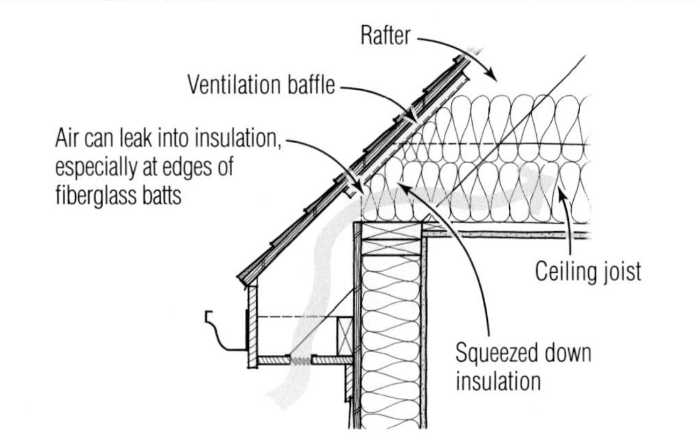

Figure 1. When the eaves are at attic floor level, the rafters squeeze the insulation just where you want it thick to prevent ice dams. This detail also allows cold air to blow through the ceiling insulation, causing heat loss and cold spots on the ceiling.

If you are using trusses, make sure you request shop drawings from the truss manufacturer. In my experience, no matter what you draw, the manufacturer will send through the design cheapest to build. But for a modest extra amount, they can easily create a "raised-heel" truss, either by blocking between the bottom and top chords or by adding another member underneath the top chord (Figure 2). Try for as much depth as you can at the eaves, ideally the full dimension of the attic insulation.

If you are using rafters, put a band joist around the attic floor and add a plate on top of the joists to receive the rafters (Figure 3). This will add the depth of the rafter to the depth of the joists and greatly improve the insulation at the eaves. However, don't overlook the structural requirements of the connection of the rafter ends to the eaves (see "Raised Rafter Plate Connections," facing page).

Eaves at Occupied Attics

When the attic is used for living space, as in a Cape Cod or a gambrel-roofed house, where do you run the insulation? When possible, run it between the rafters,

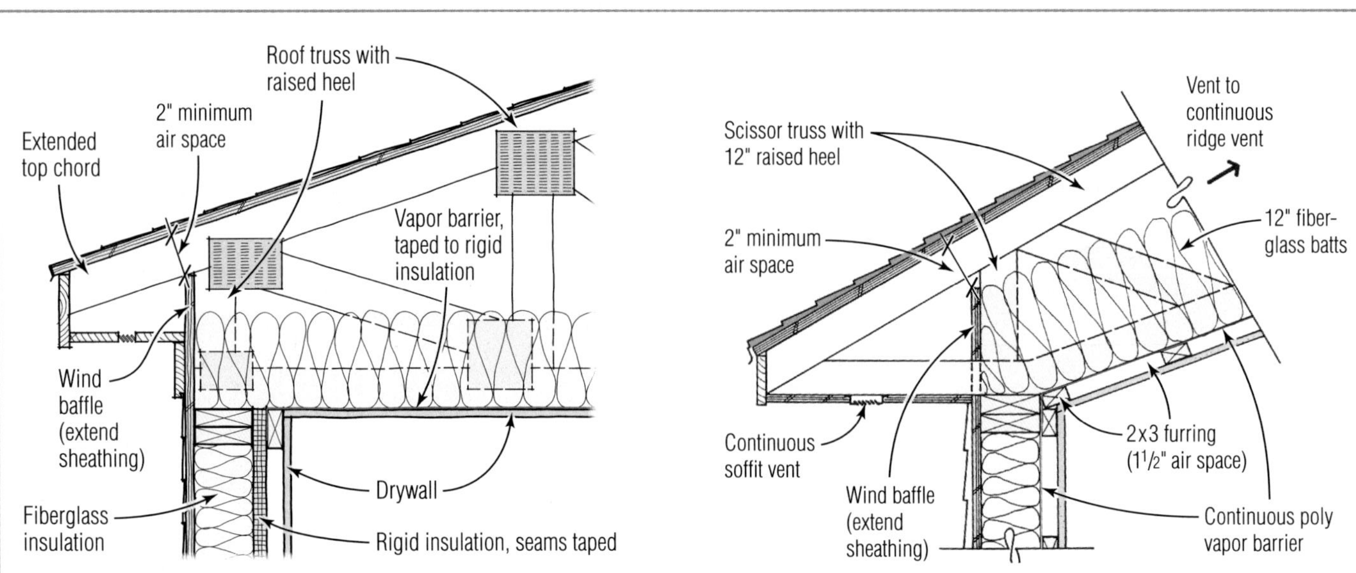

Figure 2. When using trusses, have the manufacturer add depth for insulation at the eaves, creating a "raised-heel" truss (left). For cathedral ceilings, use a raised-heel scissor truss (right).

because experience shows that insulated cathedral ceilings are much more airtight than insulated attic floors (Figure 4).

Insulating the cathedral ceiling creates the most continuous air barrier possible, preventing air leakage through the floor system into the building interior. While careful blocking of the floor joists can help, this is labor intensive and difficult to seal completely.

By insulating at roof level, you also avoid the nasty

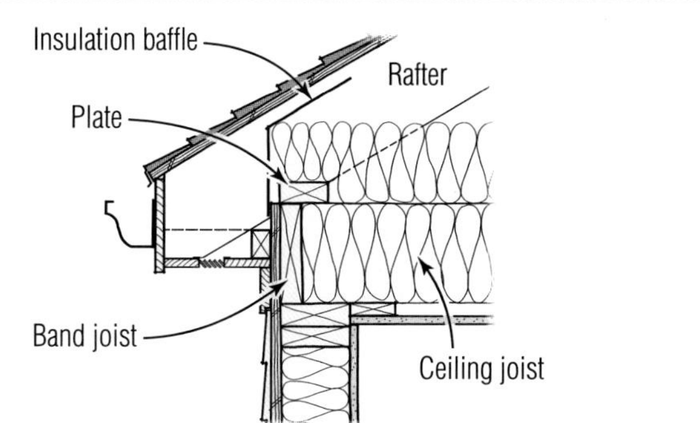

Figure 3. When using rafters, put a band joist around the attic floor and add a shoe on top of the joists to receive the rafters. This allows room for a full depth of insulation. However, structural reinforcement of the rafter-end connections is usually required (see "Raised Rafter Plate Connections," left).

Raised Rafter Plate Connections

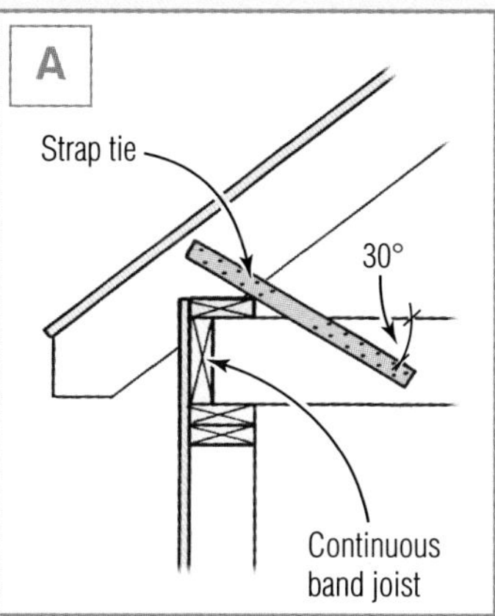

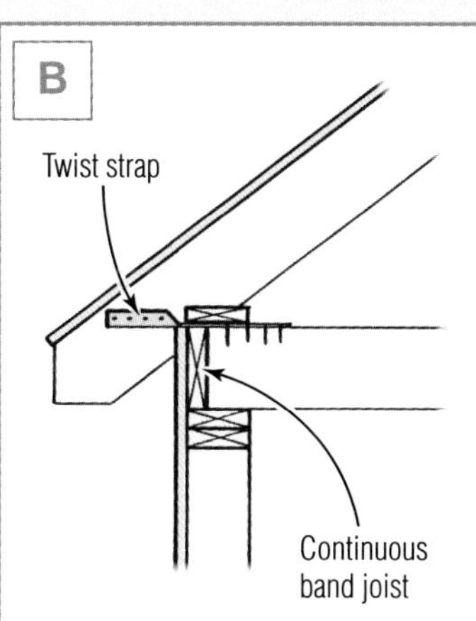

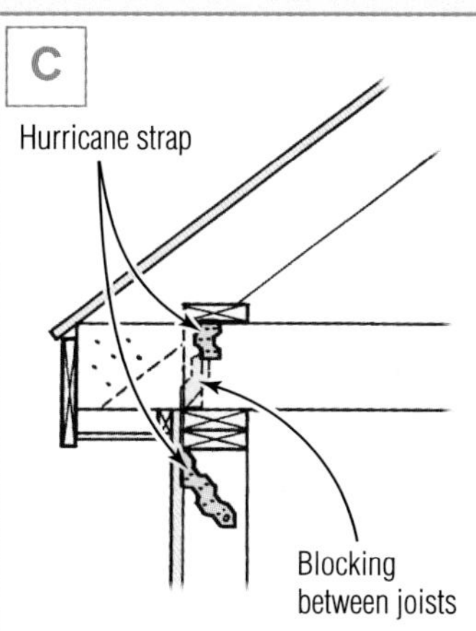

The raised rafter plate allows room for insulation above the wall plate, but the lateral thrust of the roof must be accounted for in the design. When using a raised rafter plate, Simpson strap ties (A) are the easiest way to resist roof thrust. When an attic floor is in the way, twist straps will work (B). Extending the attic joists beyond the walls (C) provides a strong rafter-joist connection, but may require additional hurricane ties to resist wind uplift.

Robert Randall, P.E., *a structural engineer based in New York.*

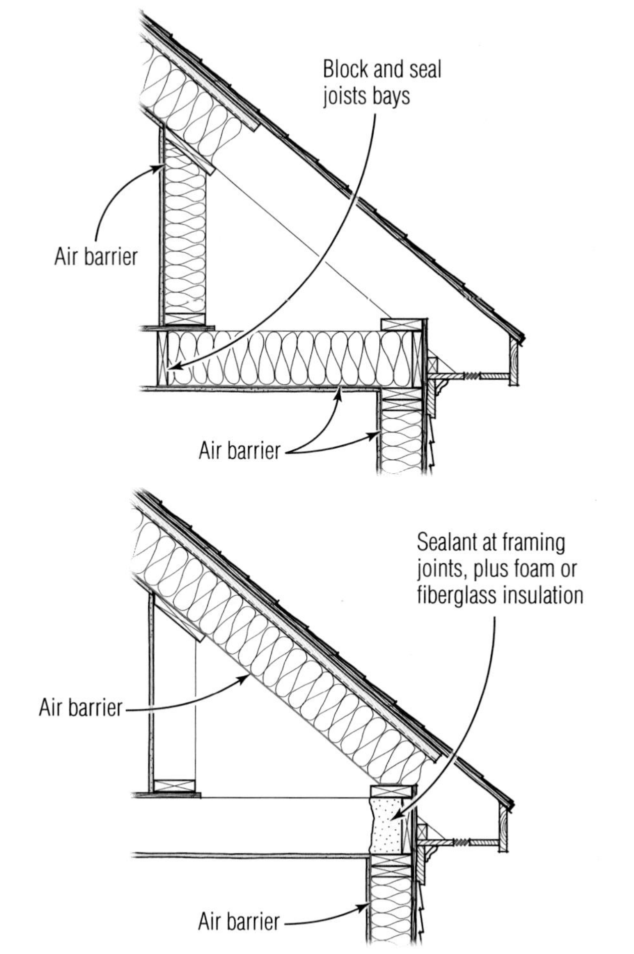

Figure 4. Avoid insulating knee walls, but where the detail is required, it is especially important to block and seal between the joists directly below the knee wall in order to maintain a continuous air barrier (top). Whenever possible, run the insulation between the rafters instead (bottom), making it easier to maintain a continuous air barrier and effective thermal boundary.

problems created when the homeowner insists on using the uninsulated space behind the knee wall for storage. Also, this gives you the option of leaving out the knee walls altogether or making them very short — often a nice detail for finished attics and Capes.

Notice that the rafters are thicker than needed for structure in order to accommodate a sufficient thickness of blown-in (my preference) or batt insulation. The floor deck runs right to the outside of the building, as in a normal second floor, and is well sealed and insulated to prevent cold spots and prevent air from entering the floor system.

To create the most continuous air barrier possible, and more important, to avoid drafty spaces between knee walls and roof, it is best to keep the insulation and air barrier running in the plane of the roof, not in the knee wall.

***Gordon Tully** is an architect in Norwalk, Conn.*

Vented Cathedral Ceiling Details

Few components in low-energy homes produce more diverse approaches — and more disagreement — than cathedral ceilings. The reason is simple: Trying to satisfy the insulation and ventilation requirements in such a tight space is a real challenge. Also, the air barrier on the interior should be near perfect to keep moist air out of the roof cavity.

It's often impossible to fit the required amount of insulation into the depth provided by 10- or even 12-inch rafters. A common solution for an R-40 ceiling is to use fiberglass batts between the rafters and then nail an inch of rigid insulation underneath the rafters. The seams of the foam board are taped so that it doubles as an air and vapor barrier. An alternative is to use deeper (but more expensive) engineered beams, such as I-joists or trusses, and to avoid the use of foam insulation. Other methods achieve a deeper cavity by building down from the rafters with gussets or 2x3s, providing a deep cavity for blown insulation.

Another problem is providing adequate roof ventilation. Most roofs are designed to have an eaves-to-ridge flow of air. These are called "cold roofs" because they keep the underside of the sheathing cold in winter. In a heating climate, the flow of cold air under the sheathing discourages moisture buildup within the roof and ice damming. In a cooling climate, ventilation relieves heat buildup.

With blown insulation, a continuous vent channel is stapled to the underside of the sheathing to maintain a free air space from eaves to ridge. When blowing cellulose into ceilings, make sure the vent channel is sturdy enough to resist crushing from blowing in the cellulose.

Vented versus unvented roofs. To complicate matters, not all builders and researchers agree that ventilation space above the insulation is necessary in heating climates. Cathedral ceilings that aren't ventilated are referred to as "hot roofs" and rely on a well-sealed air and vapor barrier to keep moisture out of the roof. Solid-foam roof systems, such as stress-skin panels, are a type of hot roof where the insulation acts as its own air barrier, and in the case of closed-cell foam, is also an effective vapor barrier. Most foams are undamaged by water as well (see "Insulating Unvented Attics With Spray Foam, page 171)

Shown here are vented cathedral ceiling details along with the pros and cons of each approach.

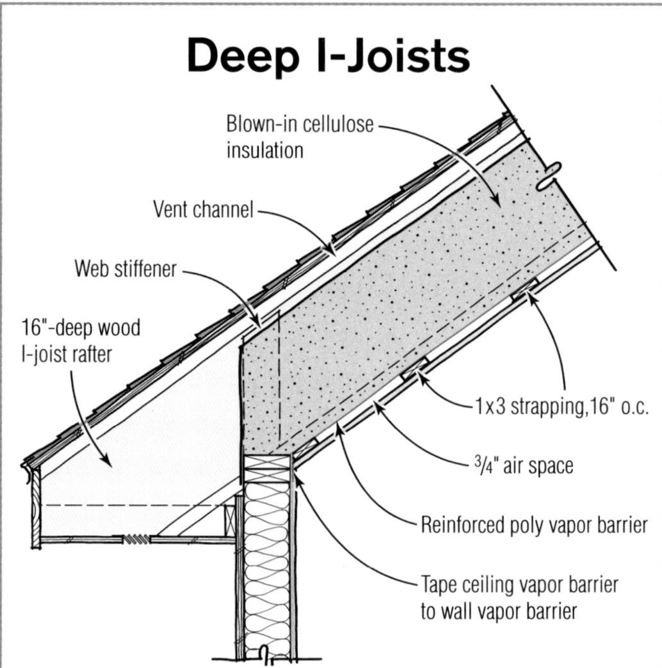

Deep I-Joists

Sixteen-inch-deep wood I-joists were larger than needed structurally, but they create a high-R cathedral ceiling when insulated with dense-blown cellulose. I-joists are straight and true, providing a nice flat ceiling. However, the high cost of the I-joists and the extra time needed to install them make this my least favored system. Attaching the joists at the plate and ridge is complicated, especially if there is a hip or valley, but eaves and rake details are the most tricky and time consuming. Attaching soffit and fascia to I-joists requires a lot of labor-intensive "packing out" compared with standard rafter tails.

– Paul Bourke, Bourke Builders, Leveret, Mass.

Plywood Gusset Build-Down

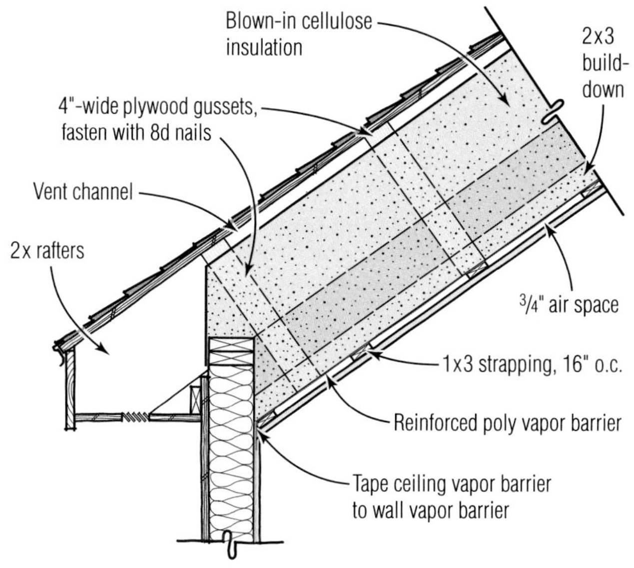

Building Down With Gussets

By hanging 2x3s below the rafters with plywood gussets, you can create a space as wide as needed for insulation without using larger rafters. The detail also creates a thermal break between the rafters and ceiling. On a big section of roof, the build-down goes quickly but slows down where the roofline is cut up by valleys or hips. To keep the ceiling flat without resorting to strings, the best approach is to cut the gussets a uniform length equal to the insulation depth and nail the gussets onto the build-down pieces first. Then the framers can just hold the pieces up so the gusset ends butt against the underside of the sheathing and nail the gussets into the sides of the rafters. We select reasonably straight 2x3s for the build-downs and compensate by eye for any excessive rafter crown. Most of the time this gives us a good result quickly. After installing a reinforced poly vapor barrier and strapping, we fill the cavity with dense-blown cellulose. — *P.B.*

Crisscross Build-Down

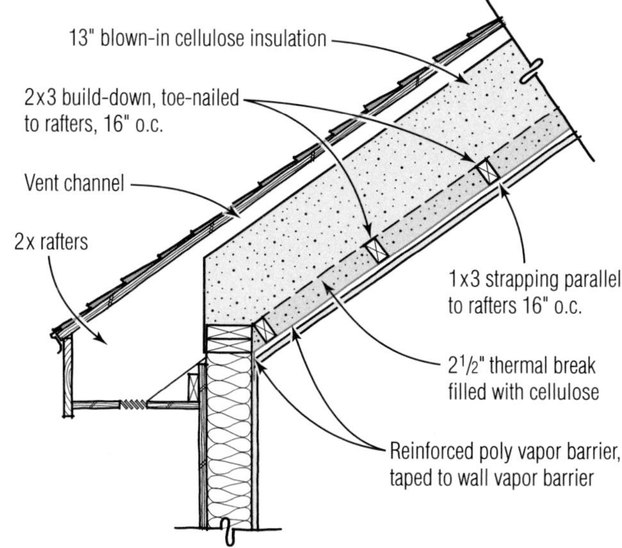

Crisscross Build-Down

This provides most of the benefits of building down the ceiling without the need to install gussets. The method is quick and simple as long as you plan ahead for the air/vapor barrier and strapping details. Under the 2x12 rafters, we use 3½-inch pneumatic nails to spike 2x3s on edge across the rafters (Figure 5). Next, we install a reinforced poly vapor barrier and strapping (parallel to the rafters) and blow 13 inches of dense cellulose. Besides creating a 13-inch-deep insulation cavity, the crisscross build-down also provides a 2½-inch thermal break below the rafters. — *P.B.*

Figure 5. The contractor spikes 2x3s on edge across the rafters (A), installs a reinforced vapor barrier and stapping (B), then blows the cavities with cellulose. The vent chutes must be strong enough to resist crushing while the cellulose is blown in (C).

Foil-Faced Foam

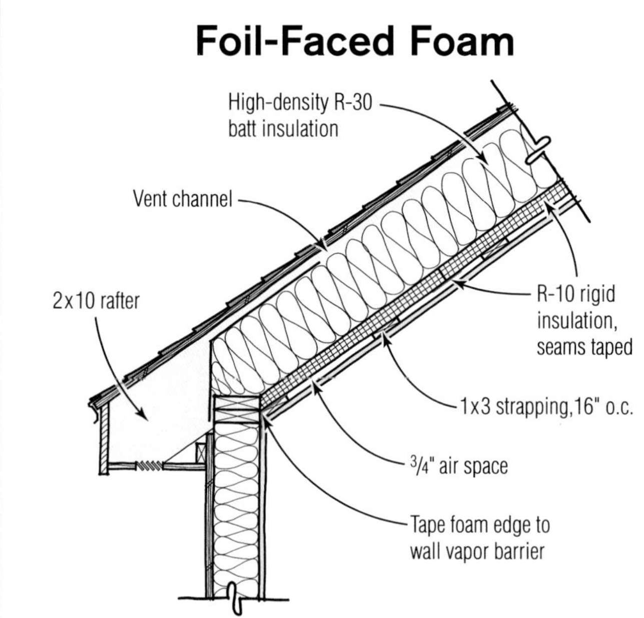

Foil-Faced Foam

If space is limited, leaving no room for build-downs, or on a small area of ceiling that we want to complete quickly, we apply foil-faced foam sheets to the bottom faces of the rafters for added R-value and a thermal break. Taping the seams where sheets meet creates a good air and vapor barrier. Using high-density batts, you can pack a touch over R-40 into 10¾ inches. I strap over the foam to provide a good screw base for the drywall, and the dead air space facing the foil adds a little R-value. While this system is simple and quick to install, with foam and fiberglass batts it costs more than blown cellulose in a built-down cavity. We can't use cellulose here, because the foam board can't resist the pressure the dense cellulose exerts. — *P.B.*

2x12 Rafter with BIBS

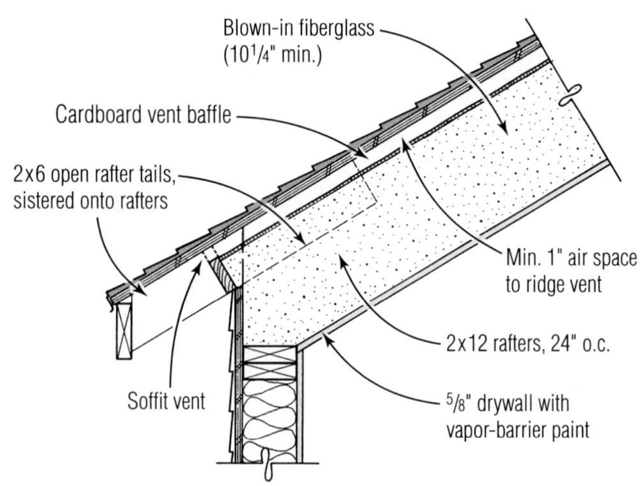

2x12 Rafters With BIBS

This method achieves R-38 to R-40 with standard framing and blown insulation, making it fast and efficient. It requires 2x12 rafters, typically larger than are required for structural reasons. The insulation is blown-in fiberglass (BIBS), which achieves a higher R-value than batt insulation and is not subject to settling. The only drawback is the higher costs of the oversized framing and BIBS system.
— *John Raabe, designer, Langley, Wash.*

Scissor Trusses

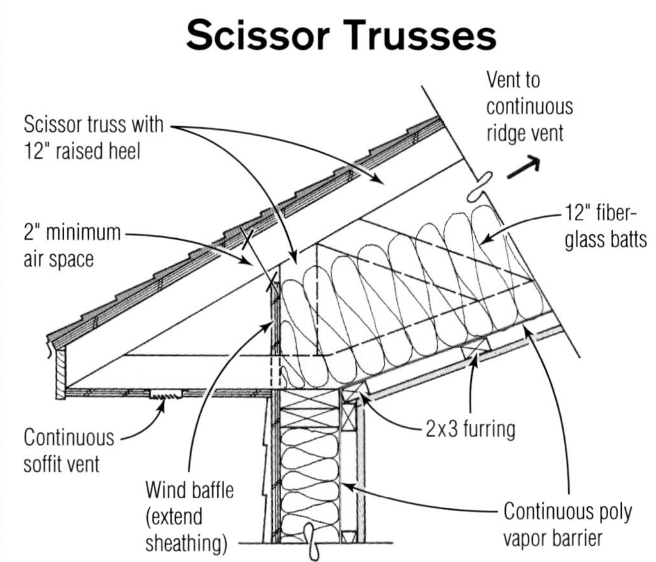

Scissor Trusses

Scissor trusses provide a fast, cost-effective way to frame cathedral ceilings with ample space for insulation and ventilation. Standard fiberglass batts can be used, but the batts must be carefully fitted to minimize short circuiting at truss chords. Make sure the trusses are designed with raised heels to allow full insulation at the eaves.
— *William Baldwin, Johnston, R.I.*

Insulating Unvented Attics With Spray Foam

by James Morshead

As a general contractor, I was taught that attic and cathedral ceiling assemblies should always be vented. Since then, however, studies have shown that properly designed and installed unvented attic assemblies outperform vented assemblies. They reduce energy loss and protect against rot and mold by preventing moisture from passing through the insulation and condensing on cold surfaces. Although many builders — and even some building inspectors — are unfamiliar with them, unvented assemblies are already part of the 2006 IRC and will soon be allowed by most building codes (see "IRC No-Vent Provision," page 173).

I work for a company in northern California that installs spray polyurethane foam or "SPF" insulation, and we are frequently asked to insulate unvented assemblies. Sometimes the building has a flat roof or a cathedral ceiling that would be difficult or impossible to ventilate (Figure 6). In other cases, the existing framing cavities are too shallow to accommodate a sufficient amount of insulation plus a vent space. And occasionally customers request unvented attics because they make the building more comfortable and energy efficient.

Why Install Roof Venting?

Traditionally, venting has been used to deal with problems that occur when heat or moisture escapes into the attic. In cold climates, the escaping heat can cause ice dams by melting the snow on the roof. Venting the space above the insulation helps keep the roof cool by carrying this heat away. If moisture enters the attic through the ceiling (usually as an air leak), the vents are supposed to allow it to exit before it condenses on something cold.

However, ventilating above fiber insulation comes with an energy penalty. Fiber insulation is designed to be enclosed in an airtight cavity. When air flows over and through fiber insulation, there is a substantial loss of thermal performance (Figure 7).

Also, most HVAC ducts and air handlers leak to some degree, so when these are installed in vented attics, conditioned air is lost to the exterior. And because vented attics are subject to extreme high and low temperatures, additional energy is lost through the thin insulation on the hvac equipment.

In cooling climates, venting the attic can bring humid outdoor air into contact with attic ductwork. If the ducts are not properly insulated, they can be cold

Figure 6. Spray foam is a good choice for roofs that are difficult to vent, like a turret with converging rafters (far left) or a flat roof with its rafters hung between flush beams (left).

enough to cause condensation.

Venting and shingle temperature. It's a common misconception that code-required venting significantly lowers the summer temperature of the roof surface. In fact, tests have shown that it lowers the surface temperature of asphalt shingles by at most about 5°F.

For many years, roofing manufacturers required that shingles be installed over vented substrates, but today, several companies — including Elk and CertainTeed — will guarantee shingles installed over properly constructed unvented roofs.

How Unvented Assemblies Work

A properly constructed unvented attic is immune to the moisture problems that occur in vented assemblies and is much more likely to be energy efficient.

In an unvented assembly, anything below the insulation — including an attic — is considered conditioned space. Turning the attic into conditioned space saves energy; if heat or air escapes from the hvac equipment, it remains within the conditioned space (Figure 8).

If enough energy is saved in this manner, the hvac system can actually be downsized, reducing installa-

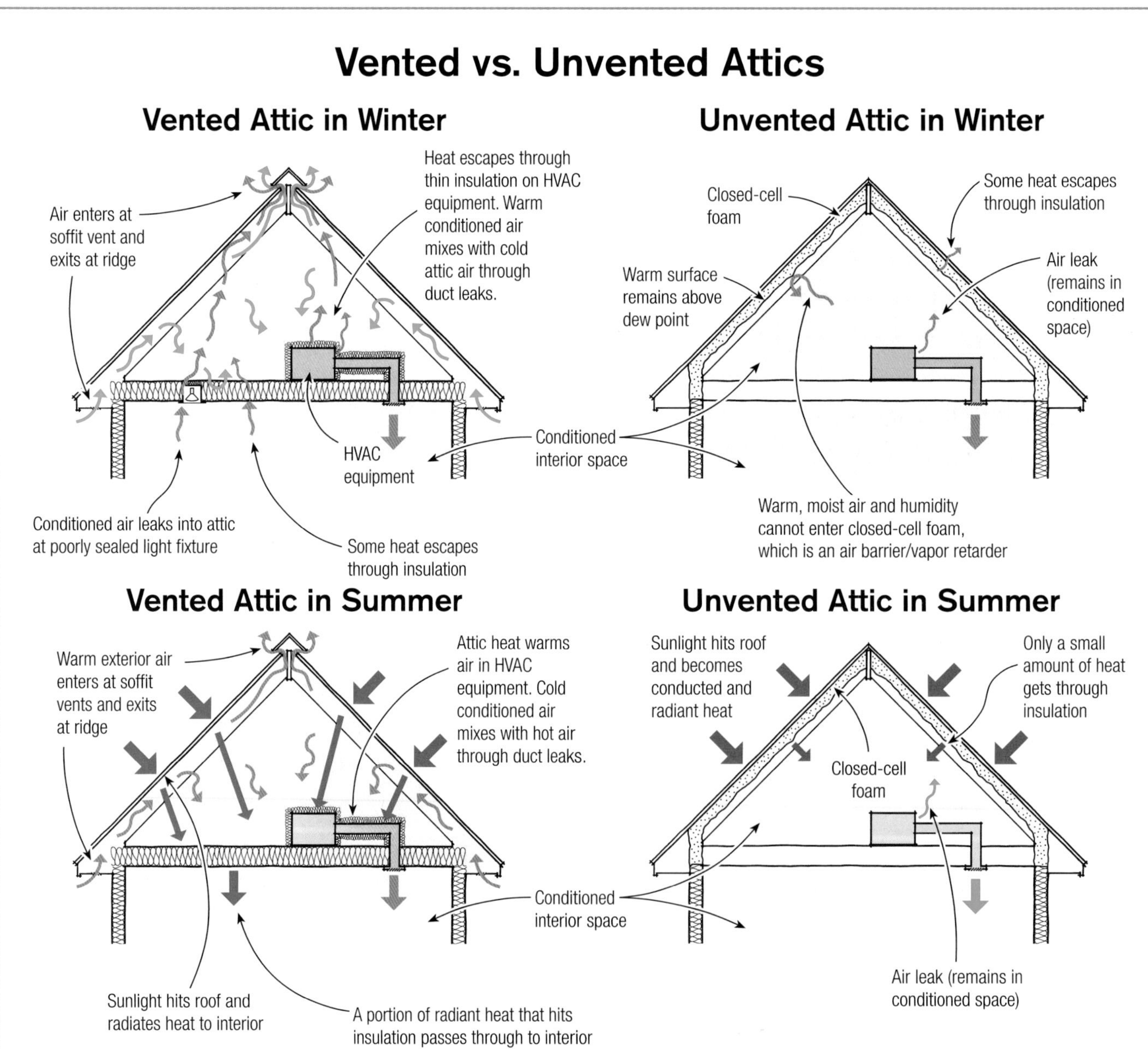

Figure 7. While attic ventilation can mitigate problems caused by ineffective insulation, air leaks in the ceiling, or inadequate vapor retarders, a better approach is to build the attic as an unvented assembly. The foam insulation used for unvented attics stops air movement and with it the transport of moisture. Any hvac equipment located in the attic is within the conditioned shell of the house, which also cuts energy losses.

tion and operating costs.

A number of insulation materials can be used in an unvented assembly, but the one with the greatest applicability across the country is spray polyurethane foam (SPF). It's an extremely effective insulation and air barrier all in one, and since it's spray-applied, it conforms to irregular shapes that otherwise might be difficult to insulate and seal (Figure 9).

Despite the multiple brands of SPF, there are only two main kinds: open-cell foam and closed-cell foam. Chemically, all brands are nearly identical — contrary to some advertising claims — and contain about the same proportion of agriculturally derived resin from corn, sugar beets, sugarcane, or soybeans. None of the spray foams contain formaldehyde or use toxic or ozone-depleting blowing agents.

The important differences between products have to do with density, R-value, and permeability.

Open-cell foam. The typical open-cell foam weighs 0.5 pound per cubic foot and has an insulation value of R-3.5 per inch of thickness. This type of foam is relatively permeable; at 5 inches thick it is rated at about 10 perms. Open-cell foam is an air barrier but not a vapor retarder.

When sprayed, open-cell foam expands to about 100 times its liquid volume, so it usually has to be trimmed flush to the framing. Fortunately, it's soft and easy to trim.

Closed-cell foam is denser and less permeable than open-cell material. The typical closed-cell foam weighs 2.0 pounds per cubic foot and provides R-6.6 per inch of thickness.

When sprayed, closed-cell foam expands from 30 to 50 times its liquid volume, making it easy to apply without completely filling the framing bay. If the bay must be filled completely, the applicator can overfill it and then trim off the excess.

Trimming closed-cell foam is not as easy as trimming the open-cell material, but it can be done.

Figure 8. The ducts visible in this unvented attic will be concealed after drywall is installed. But because they are in conditioned space, they won't be subject to the extremes of temperature typical of attics.

Advantages of Closed-Cell Foam

Both types of SPF are excellent insulation materials, but our company uses closed-cell material in unvented assemblies because we think it provides the best overall performance. With it, we can pack more R-value into a small space, which is helpful when the existing rafter bays are shallow; for example, we can get R-30 into a 4½-inch space.

In our climate zone, it's important to avoid excessive vapor diffusion, and we think the best way to do this

IRC No-Vent Provisions

All states with state building codes, and most municipalities across the U.S., have adopted some version of the IRC.

Until recently, the IRC required all attics and enclosed rafter spaces to be vented. But the latest version allows unvented attic assemblies if certain conditions are met.

According to Section R806.4 of the 2006 IRC, unvented assemblies are allowed if "no interior vapor retarders are installed on the ceiling side (attic floor) of the unvented attic assembly" and if "air-impermeable insulation is applied in direct contact with the underside/interior of the structural roof deck."

There is an exception that allows air-permeable insulation (fiberglass and cellulose) to be used in unvented assemblies in certain parts of the South (climate zones 2B and 3B).

It has long been possible to get an unvented assembly approved by the inspector as an "alternate construction method." But once states update their codes to the 2006 IRC, it will no longer be necessary to get special approval for unvented assemblies.

In the meantime, the fact that the 2006 IRC allows unvented assemblies should make it easier to get special approval in states that have adopted earlier versions of the code.

Do not build an unvented attic assembly without first talking to the local building inspector. Unvented assemblies are new in the IRC, and your state might be using an older version of the code. Also, the committee that wrote this section is still working on it, so more changes may be on the way.

is to use closed-cell foam. One of the great benefits of closed-cell foam is that if you install it to a thickness of at least 2 to 2½ inches, it will have a permeance of 1.0 perm or less.

This means that in addition to being an air barrier, closed-cell foam is a vapor retarder. It's actually a vapor retarder from both sides, so it ends the debate about which side of the insulation to put the vapor retarder on in climates where interiors are both heated and cooled.

Some companies that make both open-cell and closed-cell foam advise insulation contractors not to use the open-cell material in unvented assemblies — or to do it only in certain climates where vapor diffusion will not be a problem.

In conditions of extreme vapor drive — an indoor pool or spa, for instance — it may be necessary to further reduce the permeability of closed-cell foam by coating it with a spray-applied liquid vapor barrier.

Cathedral Ceilings

In a vented cathedral ceiling, the insulation is in contact with the back of the drywall, and there's an air gap (the venting space) above. But in an unvented

Figure 9. This barrel ceiling (left) would be difficult to insulate and seal with traditional materials. It's an ideal candidate for spray foam, which conforms to its irregular surfaces (right).

Figure 10. Open-cell foam, which expands to about 100 times its liquid volume, typically has to be trimmed flush to framing members — an easy task, since the foam is so soft. Because of its lower expansion rate and higher R-value per inch, closed-cell foam doesn't usually have to be trimmed. When it does, as in this shallow rafter bay (left), the author's crew uses a scraper — in this case a horse curry comb — to clean the framing in preparation for drywall (right).

assembly, the insulation must be against the bottom of the sheathing.

Sometimes, if the rafter bays are unusually shallow, we have to fill them all the way up with closed-cell foam (Figure 10). But because this type of foam has such a high R-value, in most cases we have to fill the cavities only part way.

Contractors often ask about the air space below the foam; most were taught that it's bad to leave an air space below insulation. This is true of fiber insulations because convection currents can form in gaps and degrade the insulation's thermal performance, particularly if there is an air space on both sides of the insulation. But this is not true of foam, which can't be infiltrated and is relatively unaffected by surrounding air currents.

Any space left below the foam is considered conditioned space (Figure 11).

Dealing With Can Lights

It's easier and more energy efficient to build a cathedral ceiling as an unvented assembly, but dealing with recessed light fixtures can be a real challenge.

There are two issues: how to insulate and seal the area above the fixture and how to provide enough space around it so it doesn't overheat. Even if the fixture is an IC unit, you can't embed it in foam.

Insulating above. If we're lucky, there will be room to spray a full thickness of foam above the fixture and still maintain the desired 2 to 3 inches of clearance between foam and fixture.

If there isn't enough space or access to spray above

Figure 11. Fiberglass and cellulose insulation are usually installed in contact with the back of the drywall; the concern is that leaving a space on both sides of fiberglass insulation allows convective air currents to degrade the insulation's thermal performance. Because closed-cell foam is unaffected by air movement, the space between it and the drywall is not a problem.

Figure 12. Code requires that a space be left between can lights — even IC-rated cans — and spray foam insulation. In shallow bays, the author's crew installs foil-faced rigid foam above fixtures and creates a seal by lapping the spray foam onto it (left). An alternate method, which may soon be required in California, is to isolate fixtures from the foam by installing them in metal boxes (right).

a fixture, we sometimes install a piece of nonperforated foil-faced rigid foam above it instead. Before spraying, we mask the fixture to keep it clean, then create an airtight seal by lapping the SPF onto the rigid foam (Figure 12). If the rigid foam butts to framing, we caulk that joint with polyurethane sealant.

Clearances. Few building codes contain specific requirements about clearances between foam and can lights, so it's a good idea to talk to the building inspector about the issue. SPF is such a good insulator that it can cause a fixture to overheat, tripping the temperature-limit switch and cutting power to the light. Excess heat could also damage the wire sheathing or even the foam itself.

In California, new code provisions are being developed that will require builders to take one of three measures with recessed lights: leave 3 inches of clearance around a fixture, box around it, or wrap it with 2 inches of mineral fiber. A 3-inch clearance is already required around hot appliance vents.

SPF is compatible with PVC and CPVC, so it's okay to spray it on Romex, PVC pipe, and CPVC sprinkler pipe.

Air Sealing

Any surface we spray will be sealed against the movement of air, but there are always some surfaces we can't spray. For example, the gaps between doubled-up framing members are too small to spray with foam, yet a significant amount of air can leak through at these spots. It's best to seal these joints during framing by installing compressible foam gaskets between the members. If that isn't done, you can caulk the joints after the foam is installed.

When the gaps are too wide for caulk, we fill them

Unvented Roof Details

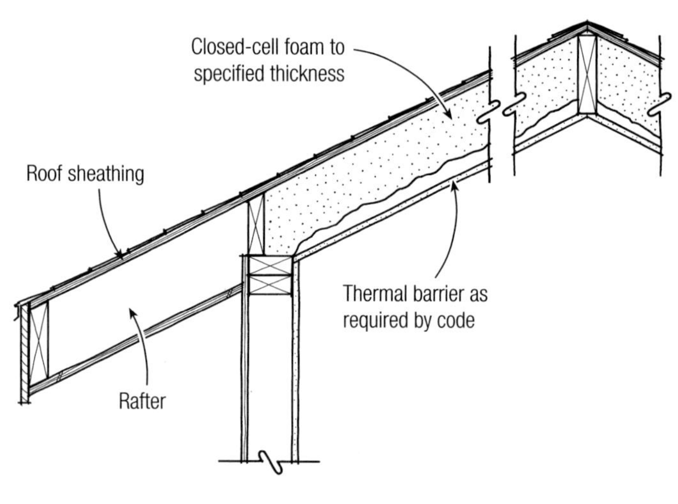

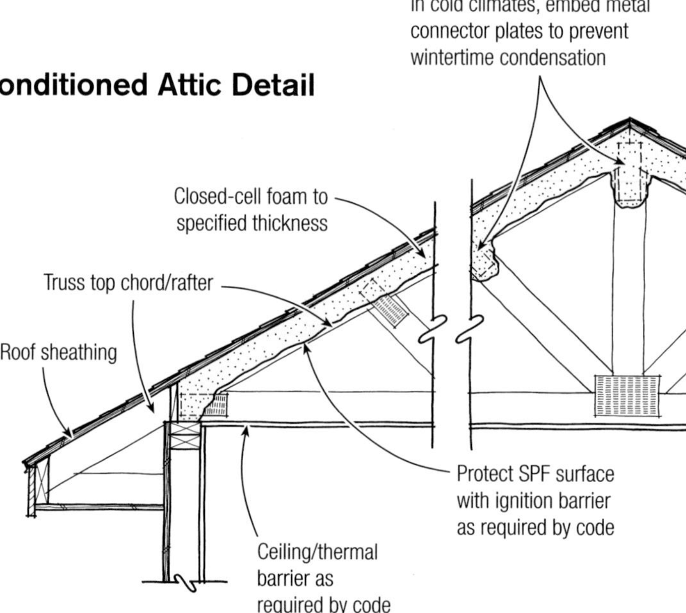

Figure 13. When insulating an unvented roof assembly, the author prefers closed-cell to open-cell foam because it's both an air barrier and a vapor retarder. To finish an unvented cathedral ceiling insulated with closed-cell foam, most codes require a layer of 1/2-inch drywall or an equivalent thermal barrier (left). Depending on local code, the spray foam in an unvented, or "cathedralized," attic (below) may not require drywall covering unless the area is accessible for servicing equipment. In some cases, the foam may have to be sprayed with an intumescent coating.

with foam from a can. The canned foam should be the low-expansion type; it contains more closed cells than the high-expansion material. We stay away from the latex foams because they're very permeable.

Fire Resistance

When the unvented assembly is a cathedral ceiling, the foam will be covered with drywall, which is a code-approved thermal barrier. In an attic, though, the rafter bays are not normally covered by drywall, so the issue of fire-resistance comes into play (Figure 13).

This can be a gray area in the code, so be sure to check with your building department before building an unvented attic space. Most codes state that if the attic is accessible for the service of utilities, the foam must be covered with an ignition barrier. Certain water-based intumescent coatings qualify as ignition barriers.

If the attic area is not accessible or is not "accessed for the service of utilities," it may be possible to leave the SPF exposed. Many contractors are confused about how to treat this enclosed attic space. Providing access through a ceiling hatch is okay but not necessary; venting to the room below is prohibited by the fire code.

Other Issues

Unlike fiber insulation, which can be blown through a hose or stuffed into hard-to-reach areas, SPF can't be installed without sufficient access. The applicator must be able to get close enough to the sheathing to spray from 16 to 24 inches away — and do it from pretty much straight on.

Cost. In our area, the installed cost of an average-size closed-cell foam insulation project is between $1.10 and $1.40 per board foot of material.

For R-30, that comes to about $5 per square foot of roof area. That's more than other insulation materials would cost, but not much more if you factor in all of SPF's advantages — future energy savings, increased comfort and moisture control, the greater design flexibility that comes with being able to fit the necessary R-value into small framing cavities, and the possibility that the mechanical system can be downsized.

James Morshead *is senior project manager and technical director for American Services Co. in Dublin, Calif.*

Insulated Cold Roof Retrofit

by Dan Perkins

As a metal-roofing contractor in northern Michigan (over 8,500 degree days), I am frequently asked to fix "roof leaks" that have less to do with roofing than with insulation and moisture problems. For example, warm, moist air from inside a house may escape into the attic and condense on the underside of the roof sheathing; when the homeowners see water stains on the ceiling of the room below, they assume there's a roof leak.

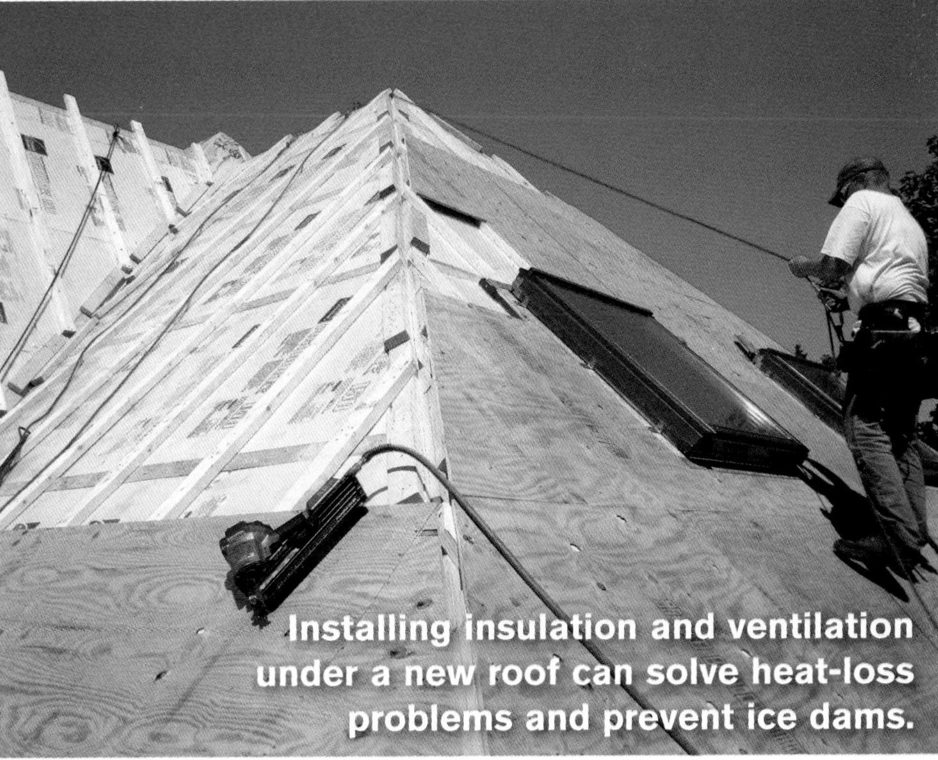

Installing insulation and ventilation under a new roof can solve heat-loss problems and prevent ice dams.

But by far the most common problem in our area is ice damming, which occurs when heat from the attic melts the snow on the roof. The snowmelt runs down the roof beneath the accumulated snow, refreezes when it hits the cold air at the eaves, and blocks the flow — causing an ice buildup and, often, a leak.

Ice dams happen for a number of reasons, but mostly they involve insufficient insulation or poor roof venting. We see ice dams all the time on the older Capes in this area, which have second-story sloped ceilings underneath 2x4 or 2x6 rafters. Typically, the rafter bays are stuffed full of batt insulation, but this

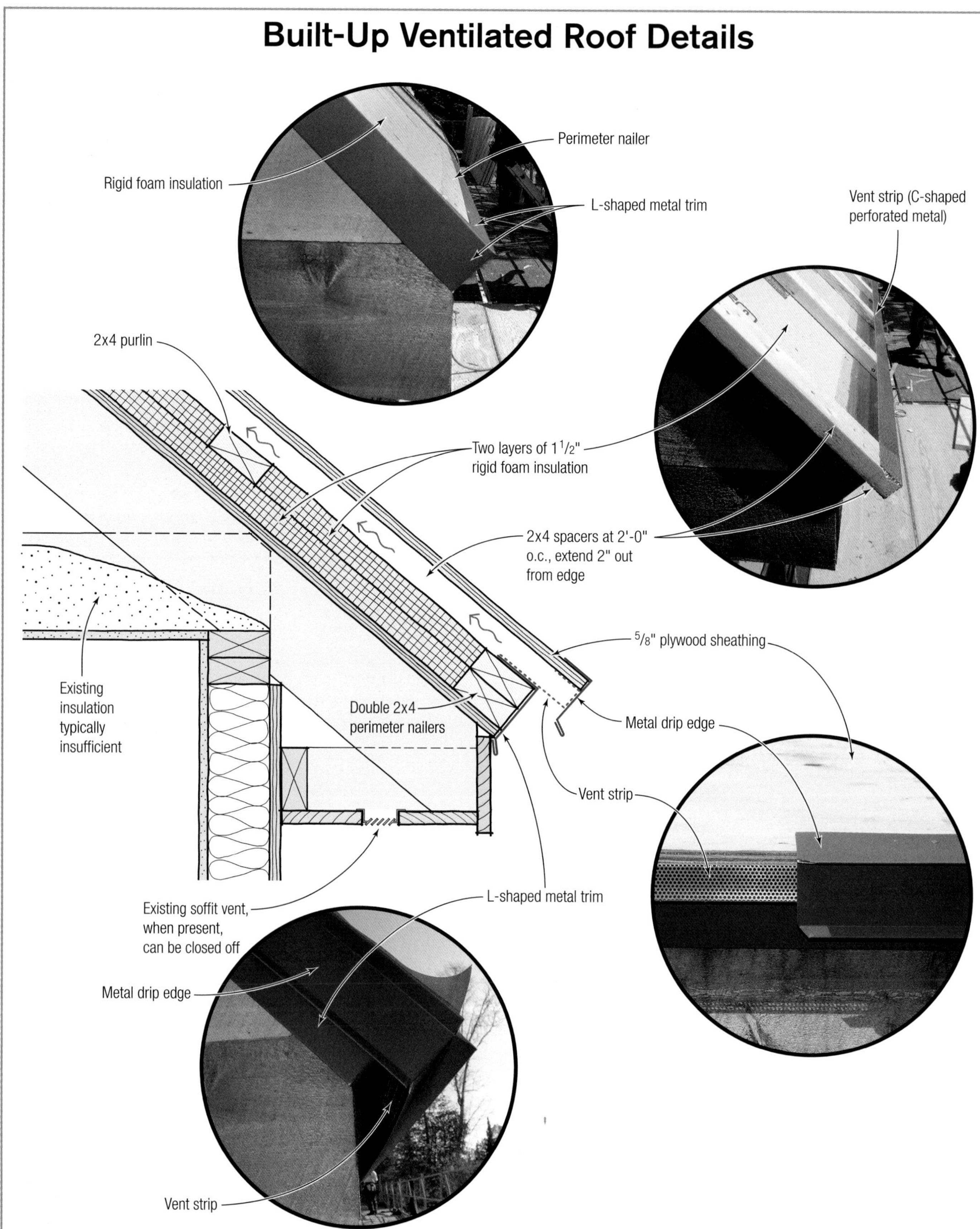

Figure 14. The original insulation in an older knee-wall Cape is often insufficient, which can lead to ice dams in cold climates. Adding rigid insulation and an air space over the existing sheathing creates a thermal break and increases the overall R-value of the roof, slowing the loss of indoor heat and preventing ice buildup.

means the roof is only insulated to R-11 or R-19 — not R-38, like it should be. And with no vent channel to allow outside air to keep the inside surface of the roof cold, the snow on the roof quickly begins to melt.

Another common problem is that the attic insulation is thin or compressed where narrow rafters land on exterior walls. This creates another spot where interior heat can easily bleed through to the roof, melting the snow at the eaves. The wider rafters on newer homes don't necessarily guarantee good ventilation in sloped ceilings. Even if the bays are deep enough, skylights, hips, and dormers can block the flow of air.

While it's possible to fix these problems from inside, we've found it's often cheaper and easier to deal with them from the exterior while reroofing the house. Our company installs about 30 roofs per year; for two-thirds of them, we create an insulated, ventilated cold roof on top of the existing sheathing.

Our system contains one or more layers of rigid insulation, wood or metal edge trims, perforated metal vents at eaves and ridge, and a new layer of sheathing held off the insulation by 2x4s (Figure 14). The 1½-inch air channel created by the 2x4s provides sufficient ventilation above the insulation to maintain a cold roof surface and prevent ice damming. The insulation creates a thermal break and increases the R-value of the roof assembly.

In cases where the roof or attic was not well insulated or ventilated to begin with, we always add enough rigid foam to turn the area below into conditioned space. We can then close off or remove the existing roof vents, secure in the knowledge that the underside of the existing roof sheathing will never drop below the dew point.

Initial Work

On a typical job, we remove the existing roof, then cover the sheathing with a synthetic roof underlayment like Titanium UDL-30 (www.interwrap.com) or RoofTopGuard II (www.rooftopguard.com). The underlayment isn't strictly necessary, but we install it to protect the house while we're doing the work. On jobs where we are certain that we can complete the buildup and dry in the roof in one day, we'll skip this layer of underlayment.

Plumbing stacks. In our region, snow can accumulate on a metal roof and creep like a glacier, which can damage plumbing stacks that are close to the eaves. To avoid this, we reroute the stacks so they penetrate closer to the ridge.

Insulation

Next, we install a 2x4 nailing plate around the perimeter of the roof — a single 2x4 thickness for 1½ inches of insulation and two 2x4s for 3 inches of insulation. After that, we cover the area inside the nailers with 4x8 sheets of 1½-inch extruded polystyrene (XPS) rigid foam, securing them to the existing roof sheathing with cap nails.

When there are two layers of insulation, we alternate the 4x8 sheets with 2x4s on the flat all the way up to the ridge (Figure 15). This second layer of rigid foam is fastened to the first layer with cap nails, and the horizontal 2x4 "purlins" are secured with long Torx-head screws (www.grkfasteners.com).

The purlins provide nailing for the 2x4s that will create the vent space. Although they do interrupt the double insulation layer, we prefer to use them because it's faster and easier to nail the spacers to purlins than to fasten them to rafters with 8- to 10-inch-long screws.

If the roof is getting only a single layer of foam, we may skip the 2x4 purlins and fasten the spacers by screwing all the way through to the rafters. At about R-5 per inch for XPS — more if we use polyisocyanurate — a 3-inch layer of rigid insulation adds R-15 to the building.

Edge trim. We cover the edge of the perimeter nailer with an L-shaped metal trim, which we prefabricate in our shop on a heavy stationary brake. We use 24-gauge

Figure 15. After installing a double 2x4 nailer around the perimeter of the roof, the crew fills in the field with a layer of 1½-inch rigid foam (left). A second layer is installed over the first, with 2x4 purlins between each row to provide nailing for the spacers to follow (right).

Galvalume steel with a Kynar paint coating, to match the new roof.

The insulation trim looks best when it's installed over a single 2x4 nailer; with a double nailer, it can look too wide, depending on the other fascia details. In that case, we may use a piece of flat wood trim instead of the metal.

Vent Space

The ventilation strip along the eaves is formed from perforated metal — 20-gauge Galvalume with ⅛-inch holes drilled on a 3⁄32-inch stagger that we buy from Direct Metals (www.directmetals.com) or McNichols Co. (www.mcnichols.com). We bend it into a C-channel that will accept flat 2x4s — the ends of the ventilation spacers that run up the roof slope.

To ensure a straight edge, we nail the vent strip to a snapped line. The perforated metal projects 2 inches beyond the edge of the roof. When its top and edge are covered with roofing material, this leaves a 2-inch vent space along the bottom.

We install the 2x4 spacers 2 feet on-center, tucking the bottom ends into the vent strip and running them up the slope to the ridge on top of the insulation and edge nailers (Figure 16). We run the spacers long at the top, then snap a line at the ridge and cut them to

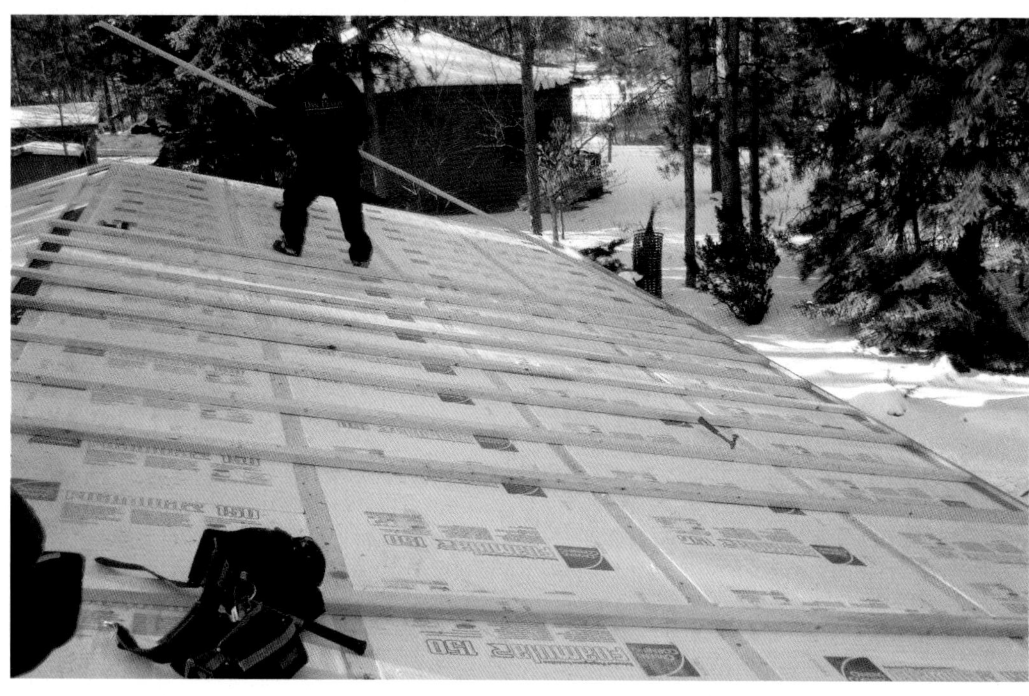

Figure 16. Crew members slide long 2x4 spacers into the C-shaped perforated metal vent fastened to the bottom edge of the roof. They run the spacers long, then cut them in place at the ridge.

Figure 17. The roof sheathing is fastened to the 2x4 spacers, creating a 1 ½-inch vent channel above the rigid foam insulation (left). The sheathing stops short of the peak to allow airflow through the ridge vent (right).

length in place. If the roof has sagged, we can straighten it by shimming under the spacers.

Sheathing. We nail the spacers to the purlins or — on roofs with a single layer of rigid foam — secure them with screws to the rafters or decking below. We then sheathe the new roof surface with 5/8-inch CDX plywood, stopping it short of the ridge so that the roof can vent to a ridge cap (Figure 17).

When the sheathing is complete we install a custom-bent metal drip edge — an L-shaped piece with a hem on the exposed edge. The vertical leg is 3 inches long, which covers the sheathing and the outer edge of the vent strip and leaves a reveal that helps conceal the bottom of the perforated vent.

At this point we're ready to put down underlayment and then roof. We always install standing-seam metal (Figure 18), but there's no reason composition shingles or some other roofing couldn't be installed over this buildup.

Dan Perkins *owns Dan Perkins Construction in Ishpeming, Mich.*

Figure 18. A standing-seam metal roof completes the job. The vent strip is inconspicuous.

Cool Roof Strategies for Hot Climates

by Danny Parker

Reduce cooling costs and increase comfort with reflective roofing, radiant barriers, or better insulation.

Even in hot, sunny climates, it's common to see dark shingle roofs. Because dark shingles absorb much of the solar radiation that falls on the roof, they carry a significant energy penalty. In sunny climates, heat gain through the roof makes up a major share of a house's cooling load.

People use different strategies to limit heat gain through the roof. Extra ceiling insulation, extra ventilation, under-roof radiant barriers, and sealed attics with insulated roof decks can all help in certain circumstances. But research shows that the single most effective way to cut the cooling loads from a hot-climate roof is to make the roof reflective. There's a reason all those quaint little cottages in Bermuda have white roofs — they work.

Reflective roofs work because they stop the heat before it enters the roof or building. The sun's rays hit the roof surface at the speed of light, and at the speed of light they bounce back into space. White or light-colored materials work best, but some new dark pigments reflect enough invisible infrared radiation to reject a lot of solar energy. And whether you're applying tile, metal, membranes, or even asphalt shingles, choosing a more reflective version seldom adds cost.

Let's look first at reflective roofs, then consider some of the other options for cutting heat gain through the roof.

1 Standard dark shingles (base case)
2 Terra Cotta S-tile roof
3 Light-colored shingles
4 Standard dark shingles with sealed attic and R-19 roof deck insulation
5 White "barrel" S-tile roof
6 White flat tile roof
7 White metal roof

Peak Attic Temperatures

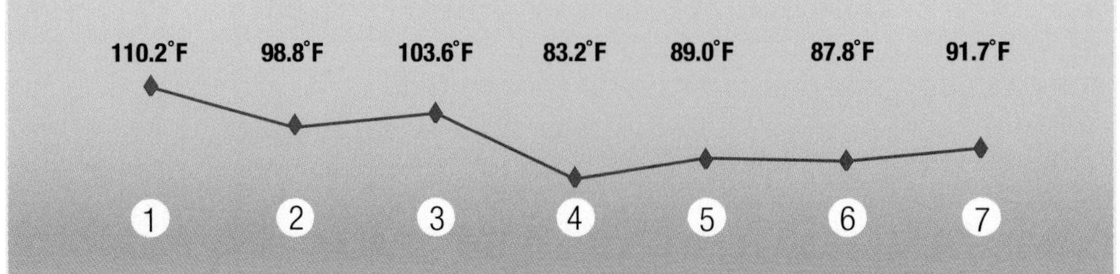

Percent Reduction in Peak Cooling Load

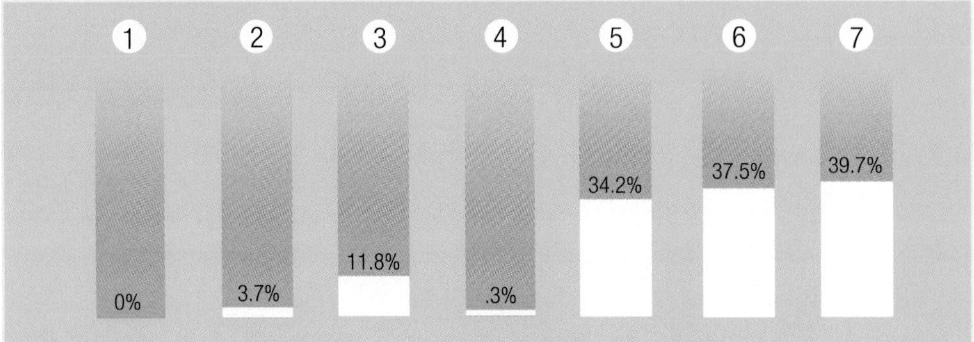

Percent Reduction in Total Cooling Energy

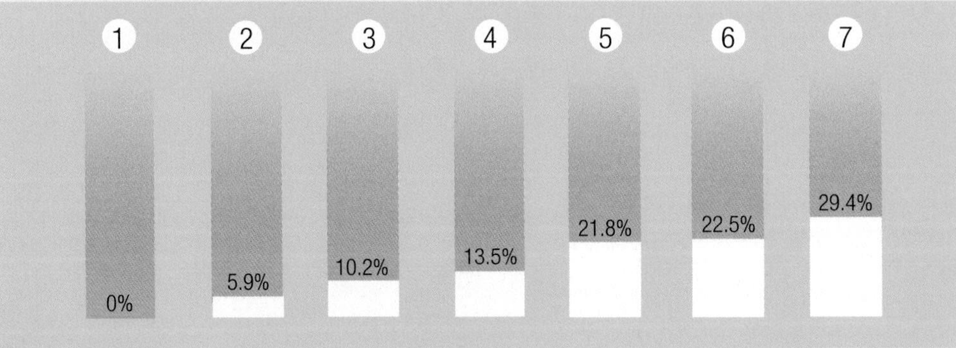

STEVEN SPENCER, FSEC

Figure 19. Florida Solar Energy Center researchers compared the air-conditioning power use of seven identically built houses with different roof coverings. Reflective roofing dramatically reduced total power use (bottom chart) and had an even greater effect on peak A/C power demand (middle chart). Insulating the roof deck and sealing the attic, without using a reflective roof, cut total energy use somewhat but did not reduce peak cooling loads noticeably.

Reflective Roofing

It's well established that reflective roofing materials can lighten the load on home air conditioners. When researchers at the Florida Solar Energy Center (FSEC), where I am a principal scientist, whitened the roofs of nine occupied homes in the summer of 1994, air-conditioning savings averaged 19 percent. We got even better information by comparing seven otherwise identical new homes with various roof types in a study sponsored by Florida Power & Light (FPL) during the summer of 2000 (Figure 19). All these homes had R-19 ceiling insulation, but each had a different roof covering. Clearly, reflective roofing made a huge difference.

One house of the seven had an insulated roof deck to keep the ductwork within the sealed, conditioned attic. That modification did save energy on average, but not as much as the reflective roofs — and it had little effect on peak loads.

Cool colors. Until recently, to have high solar reflectance, a roof had to be white — not something every customer wants. But we now have tile and metal roofing systems made with "spectrally selective" paints, which absorb some colors of light in the visible range but reflect rays in the infrared and ultraviolet spectra that account for much of the sun's heat. These colors give designers more choices, while still saving considerable energy (Figure 20).

BASF Corporation's ULTRA-Cool metal-roof coatings (www.basf.com), which use spectrally selective pigments from Ferro Corporation (www. ferro.com), have a 38 percent solar reflectance in colors that achieve only 25 percent reflectance when made with standard pigments. And at least two companies, Classic Products (www.classicroof.com) and MCA Tile (www.mca-tile.com) now supply metal or clay tile in a range of colors with solar reflectance around 30 percent. Classic's "Musket Brown," for instance, reflects 31 percent, while the same color in traditional paint would reflect only 8 percent. It even outperforms a standard white shingle with a reflectance of about 25 percent.

Bare metal roofs. Unfinished galvanized or "tin" roofs are still fairly common in the hot Southeast. Galvanized steel is highly reflective when new, but its reflectivity soon drops as the zinc oxidizes; and the material also has low infrared emittance. The high absorptance and low emittance can combine to keep the roof blazing hot.

When FSEC researchers put a white coating on the ten-year-old galvanized steel roof of a retail strip mall, the roof's reflectance went from 30 percent to 77 percent. The average air-conditioning reduction in seven monitored shops was more than 24 percent (Figure 21).

If you want unfinished metal roofing, Galvalume (an alloy of aluminum and zinc) is a much better cool-roof choice than galvanized steel, especially in mixed heating and cooling climates. Galvalume maintains its reflectance as it ages, and its low emissivity means it holds heat well in winter even though it reflects well in summer.

Tile Roofing

It's conventional wisdom that tile roofs are cooler than shingle roofs. To a small extent, that's true: S-tiles permit cooling airflow between the tile and the roof deck, and their thermal mass stores energy during the day and re-radiates it at night, instead of passing it all through to the attic.

But the color of the tile matters. For instance, we painted some dark gray tiles bright white at midsummer in central Florida in 1996, and we measured an 18 percent drop in space-cooling energy.

Shape appears to be far less important than color. In the seven-home side-by-side study for Florida Power & Light, one of the homes had flat white tile, and another had white S-tile. We didn't see much difference — both

Figure 20. Kynar roof coatings using spectrally selective pigments from Ferro Corporation allow Classic Roofs to produce aluminum and steel shingles in several dark colors that meet Energy Star standards with solar reflectances better than white asphalt shingles. Tests indicate that the colors will sharply reduce solar heat gain through the roof.

roofs did about 20 percent better than the dark asphalt shingle roof. An S-shaped red tile roof in the same study was only 3 percent better than dark asphalt shingles.

In general, light-colored metal roofs will outperform tile in a hot climate like Florida's. At night, they actually radiate attic heat upward into the night sky, cooling the attic to below the ambient air temperature. The thermal mass of tile will not let attic heat escape so readily.

Radiant Barrier Systems

When a house has a dark, sun-absorbing roof, radiant barriers in the attic can cut heat gain and save energy. But they don't necessarily work in every case, and they're not always the best solution.

The basic radiant barrier is a layer of aluminum foil placed with its shiny side facing a clear air space. Placed under the rafters, aluminum's low emissivity prevents heat from radiating off the shiny surface onto the insulation below (Figure 22). If the surface gets dirty, it won't work as well; that's why radiant barriers work best with the shiny side facing down so it won't collect dust.

There's now a range of material choices for attic radiant barriers, including radiant-barrier sheathing, spray-applied low-emissivity coatings, and a wide variety of foil products. Homes with complex attic geometry and poor access to the space are not great candidates for a foil application, but a radiant barrier sheathing is easy to apply to any new house, and a spray-applied low-e coating such as Lo/Mit from Solec, Inc. (www.solec.org) makes a practical retrofit.

Energy savings. Radiant barriers are effective. Our research indicates that under-roof foil barriers reduce heat flow through the ceiling by 30 to 50 percent and can bring annual cooling electricity savings of 7 to 10 percent in the Southeast climate.

Radiant barriers also have a strong effect on peak loads for the air conditioner. A nine-home retrofit study we conducted for Florida Power Corporation found that radiant barriers reduced air-conditioning power use by 9 percent and cut afternoon air-conditioning peak loads by 16 percent. In a six-ton system, that's a ton of cooling. Attic temperature peaks dropped by about 8°F. Perhaps most important, indoor temperatures fell by an average 2°F — a boost for homeowner comfort.

But that was in the South. In colder climates, radiant barriers could create a risk of wintertime condensation, because some foil products also act as vapor barriers. For cool-climate homes, it's wise to search out a product that has high permeability as well as low emissivity (manufacturers can supply data sheets with perm ratings, emissivity ratings, and other useful information).

And be aware that if you have a reflective roof to begin with, a radiant barrier is overkill — and may even

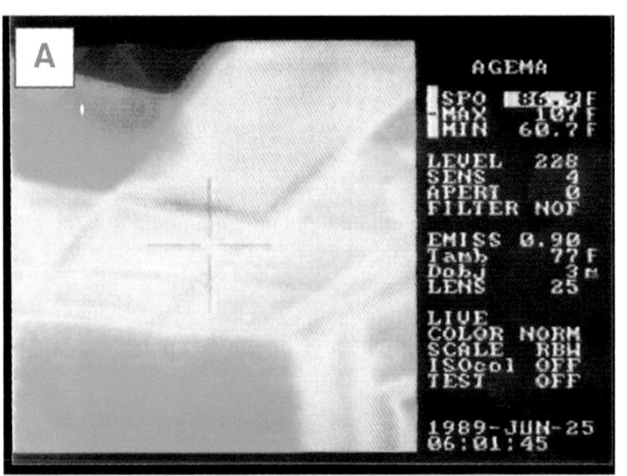

Figure 21. Unfinished galvanized steel roofs may look shiny when new, but they age quickly to become very nonreflective. The infrared thermal scan (A) shows the drop ceiling (B) at a radiant temperature of almost 90°F under the metal roof of a strip mall building, despite insulation below the roofing. When FSEC researchers applied a reflective coating (C), the building's air-conditioning power use dropped 16 percent, and tenants reported improved comfort. One tenant even called to thank the landlord for fixing the air conditioner. (He hadn't.)

be counterproductive. Since the underside of a reflective roof does not get hot, a radiant barrier under the roof adds little benefit. On the other hand, by reflecting heat inward, the radiant barrier will impede the ability of the attic to radiate excess heat to the night sky.

Another word of caution: We installed our test radiant barriers in midsummer, so we could immediately measure the benefit. But the attics we worked in were dangerously hot — one of our people actually had to stop and get medical attention. It's much safer to install attic radiant barriers in the cool season, or at least during the early morning before the attic is baking hot.

Boosting Attic Ventilation

If the attic is too hot, is more ventilation a good idea? Maybe, but maybe not. Increasing the roof's passive air vents can reduce the cooling load, but it is usually one of the least effective options. The incoming ventilation air is hottest just when you need the cooling.

In retrofit work, we have seen increased ventilation bring a 5 percent reduction in building cooling loads. But in humid or coastal locations, it can also create problems: At night, the vents bring in moist outside air that may condense on duct systems.

Since passive vents work inconsistently, some people recommend powered ventilation fans. But the electric power used to operate the fan usually outweighs the air-conditioning savings. And there's another drawback: Power attic ventilation can depressurize the house and cause gas water heaters to backdraft. It may also draw conditioned air out of the house into the attic, creating a further energy penalty.

We've conducted tests of photovoltaic solar-powered attic fans in Florida. They run whenever the sun is shining, and we found savings of about 6 percent on electric bills. But at around $600 for the solar panels plus the fan, the savings don't really justify the cost in simple financial terms.

Added Insulation

Added insulation is another option for cutting heat gain through the roof. It certainly works: One of our studies for a Florida utility showed that boosting ceiling insulation from R-19 to R-30 cut space cooling by about 9 percent in summer.

But your savings may vary. Duct systems in many homes run through the hot attic and may be insulated to only R-4 or R-6. So the air conditioner is sending 55°F air into the duct in a space that can reach 130°F on a hot day. That's a temperature difference of 75°F, across just an R-6 insulated duct wall — much greater than the 20°F difference you might see from indoors to outdoors across an R-11 or R-19 building wall. And duct surface area is much greater than you might think — often as much as 25 percent of the house floor area. During the hottest hours, as much as 30

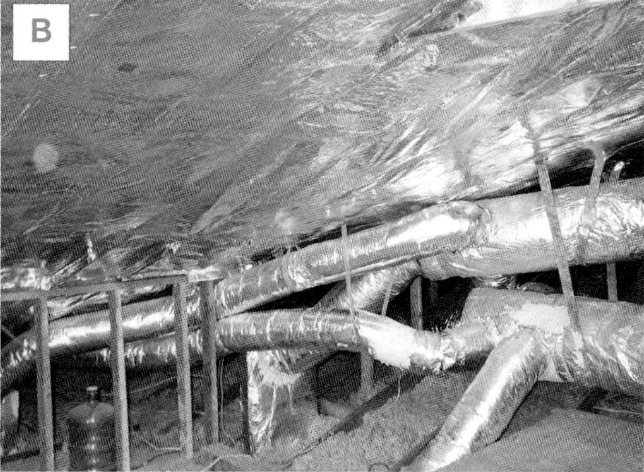

Figure 22. Radiant barrier foil under the rafters stops heat from radiating into the attic, because the foil will not emit heat radiation even when it's hot (A, before foil, and B, after). Lo/Mit low-emissivity silicone coating spray-applied to the roof underside (C) is a cost-effective alternative method.

Options for Stopping Rooftop Heat Gain

Field research at the Florida Solar Energy Center (FSEC) has found several effective ways to limit rooftop heat gain in sunny conditions. Using a highly reflective roofing material (top) is the simplest and most effective: It stops the sun's energy before any heat is absorbed, so that even the roof sheathing and framing stay cool.

If the existing roof is dark colored or the customer prefers a darker roof, heat can still be blocked by adding a radiant barrier foil just below the roof deck, with the shiny side facing down (middle). Savings from this method are roughly comparable to the saving achieved with reflective roofing; however, some conductive heating of the attic space will still take place, and the roof deck and shingles will experience some increased heat stress. To reduce this heat stress and maximize energy savings, it's best to combine radiant barriers with effective ventilation below the roof deck. Ventilating the space between the radiant barrier and roof deck will increase energy savings about 5 to 10 percent, or even more with higher performance ventilation.

A third option is to increase the insulation between the attic and the living space below and to run the hvac ductwork within the conditioned space rather than in the unconditioned attic. This method has a smaller effect on cooling loads than the reflective or radiant barrier roof systems but is effective at reducing heating loads as well as cooling loads, making it the most cost-effective option in mixed heating and cooling climates.

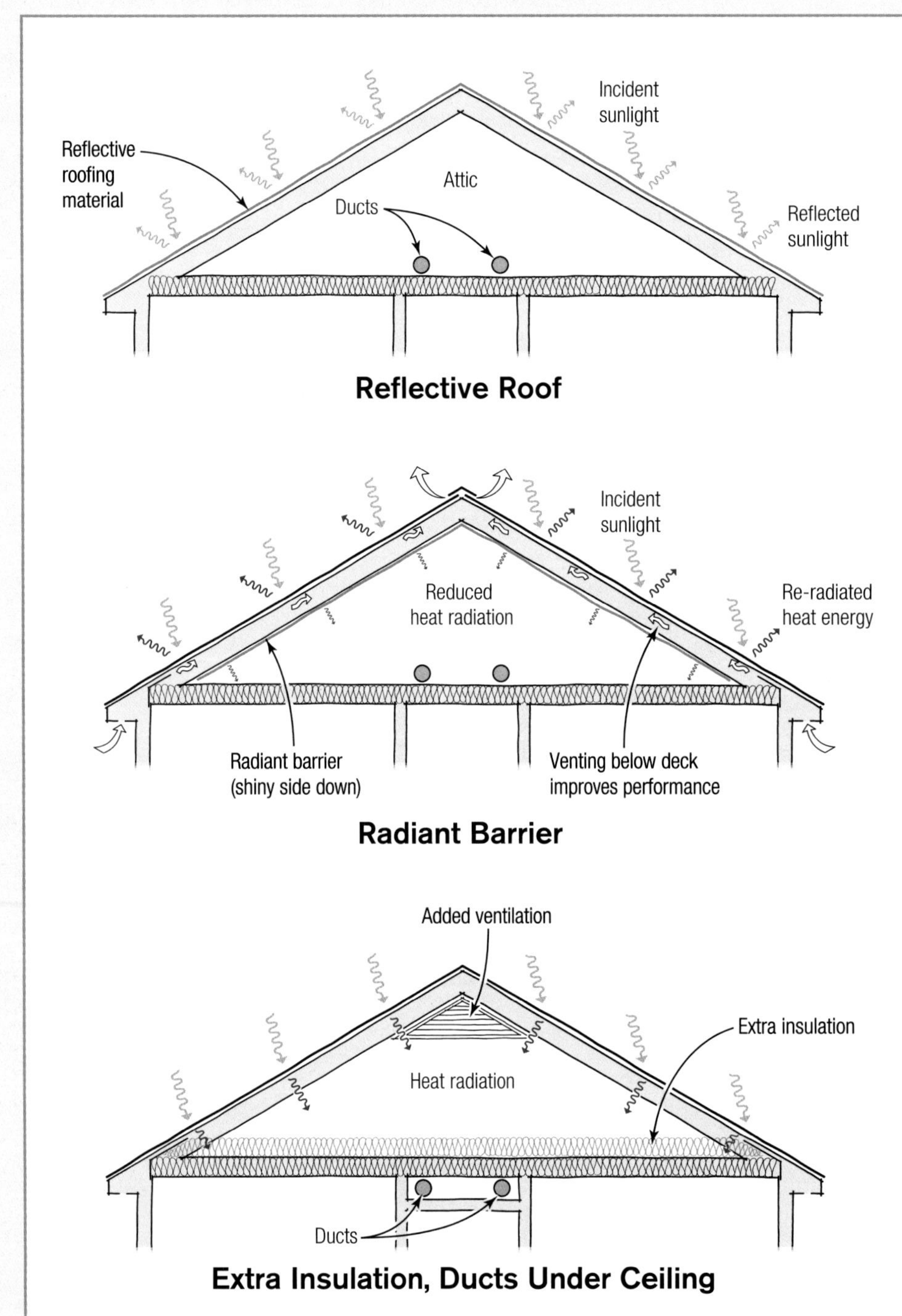

percent of the cooling system's capacity can be lost to heat gains in the duct system. Besides the wasted energy, this means it takes longer to cool down the house when the air conditioner kicks in.

Unlike a reflective roof or attic radiant barrier, ceiling insulation does little to address duct system losses. So if your design relies on ceiling insulation to limit roof-related cooling loads, try to locate the duct system within the thermal envelope, below the insulated ceiling. Even running the ducts through the crawlspace, though they might be exposed to outdoor air temperatures, will add less to the load than running them through the solar-heated attic.

Insulated Roof Deck With Sealed Attic

Sealing the attic and insulating the roof deck is another way to get the duct system into a more friendly environment. Some code officials may not like this roof design, and researchers don't recommend it in colder climates, but it does save energy. It also creates semiconditioned storage space in the attic, reduces interior moisture loads in hot climates, and avoids the risk of condensation on air handlers and ducts.

In our seven-home side-by-side comparison, the house with a sealed and insulated attic used 9 percent less energy than the base case house, even though both had dark shingles. Some of us were expecting greater savings, but several factors limit the benefit of this method.

The big advantage is that the ductwork is inside the thermal envelope. However, while a ventilated attic can flush some heat out through the vents, an insulated roof deck fights its whole battle at the roof surface. Also, the air conditioner has to treat the additional air volume of the attic space.

Beyond that, an insulated roof deck contributes more heat to the house than an insulated attic floor does. Heat transfer is proportional to the temperature difference and also to the area of the surface. In a ventilated attic on a hot day, the top surface of the ceiling insulation may hit 130°F — a 55°F difference with the 75°F interior. But the deck of an insulated roof in the direct sun may reach 170°F while the attic reaches 85°F, for a difference of 85°F across the insulation. That wider temperature gap drives faster heat gain. And that faster gain is multiplied by a greater area, since the roof area is anywhere from 5 to 40 percent greater than the ceiling area, depending on the pitch of the roof (not to mention the gable ends).

So with an insulated roof deck and a sealed attic, it is very worthwhile to block that solar gain right off the bat: Use a lighter tile, white shingles, or a more reflective metal. In our study, the sealed system with dark shingles did about 9 percent better than a ventilated attic with dark shingles. With a reflective roof, the sealed attic would likely post savings of 25 or 30 percent. Even matched with white shingles (with a reflectance of 25percent), we estimate that the insulated roof would have scored about a 13 percent savings compared with the dark shingles and vented attic. Also, it's worth noting that we carefully sealed the ductwork in all the test houses to avoid confusing the results. If the ducts are leaky, the benefit of a sealed attic is much greater, because those leaks can't communicate with the outdoors.

Smart Choices

Good roof details can save energy anywhere in the country. But climate and other building details do affect the choices. Here's how to approach the decision:

Northern climate options. If you build in the North, reflective roofing materials or radiant barriers bring only modest savings. Adding insulation in the attic is a much more cost-effective upgrade. Insulation cuts both heating and cooling costs, and the heating savings in northern winters add up to much more money.

For the full benefit, it's important to run ductwork within the insulated envelope. In both winter and summer, ducts in the attic will bypass the ceiling insulation and reduce its effectiveness.

Not that cooling doesn't matter up north, however. In summer, attics get hot everywhere. So even in the North, reflective roofing or radiant barriers may be worth installing simply to improve summer comfort and to reduce peak loads on the air conditioner. But if you want a reflective roof in the North, look for a material like Galvalume that is both reflective and low-E. This conserves attic heat during the winter as well as providing a summer cooling benefit.

Southern choices. Down south, reflective roofs are a no-brainer — they're money in your pocket. Air conditioning is the big energy cost, and reflective roofs can cut it by a third in the hottest months. Increasing the attic insulation can't hurt, but reflective roofs are more cost effective, particularly if the ductwork runs through the attic.

If you're stuck with a dark roof, attic radiant barriers can achieve savings comparable to a reflective roof's performance. But if you use radiant barriers under an asphalt shingle roof, you're wise to also choose white shingles, just so the shingles themselves won't get quite so hot.

Good ductwork location (inside the thermal envelope) is beneficial on its own, as is using reflective roofing or radiant-barriers. Using the two strategies together, however, is best since they complement each other. For example, if you have a dark roof and a hot attic, bringing the ductwork below the insulated ceiling will help quite a lot. If the ducts are in the attic, switching from a dark roof to a reflective roof can help. But combining the two tactics — applying reflective roofing and bringing the ducts inside — provides the greatest total benefit. In a hot climate like Florida's, your summer cooling loads could drop by as much as 40 percent.

Danny Parker *is a senior research scientist with the Florida Solar Energy Center.*

Chapter 8

FORCED-AIR HEATING & COOLING

- Installing Efficient Forced-Air Heat
- Fine-Tuning Forced-Air Heating & Cooling
- Air Conditioning for Humid Climates

Installing Efficient Forced-Air Heat

by Gary Bailey

Whether you're installing a heating system in a new home, replacing a worn-out furnace, or just need to add a few duct runs for an addition, it's important to take the time to select the right equipment and install it properly. If your clients can't sit in the new family room without shivering, or can't afford to keep the home at a comfortable temperature during the heating season, they're not going to be happy with your work.

Scope Out the Job

Before you can recommend a specific furnace, you have to know what will and won't work with the job conditions at hand. When I survey a job, I'm trying to find out three things:

1. Which fuel to use — natural gas, LP, or oil — and how to vent the flue gas
2. How much heat the house is losing so I can size the new furnace
3. Whether the ductwork is adequate

Once I have my answers, selecting the right furnace is straightforward. The only decisions left are what features the customers want and how much they are willing to invest in their heating system.

Fuel Choices

What's the best fuel — oil, natural gas, or LP? The answer depends on which is most commonly installed in your area and its local cost. In our area and in most parts of the U.S. served by natural gas, it is available at the relatively low cost of about $1/Therm (2010 data). For an apples-to-apples comparison of different fuels, always compare their costs in dollars/Therm (1 Therm = 1000 Btu).

Add the convenience of never having to schedule a fuel delivery, and natural gas is a smart choice where available. In rural areas, however, it's usually a toss-up between oil and LP gas. Oil is generally cheaper ($1.90/Therm for oil vs. $2.38/Therm for LP in 2010), but oil doesn't burn as cleanly as gas so the furnace will require more maintenance. Also very few oil furnaces can offer the efficiency or features of the best gas units. In my opinion, the drawbacks of burning oil outweigh the lower fuel costs. Unless I can install an oil furnace without having to repair the chimney or replace the oil tank, I often suggest that rural customers switch to a high-efficiency LP gas furnace.

Venting Options

Proper venting of flue gases is critical. An improperly vented warm-air furnace often results in frequent call-

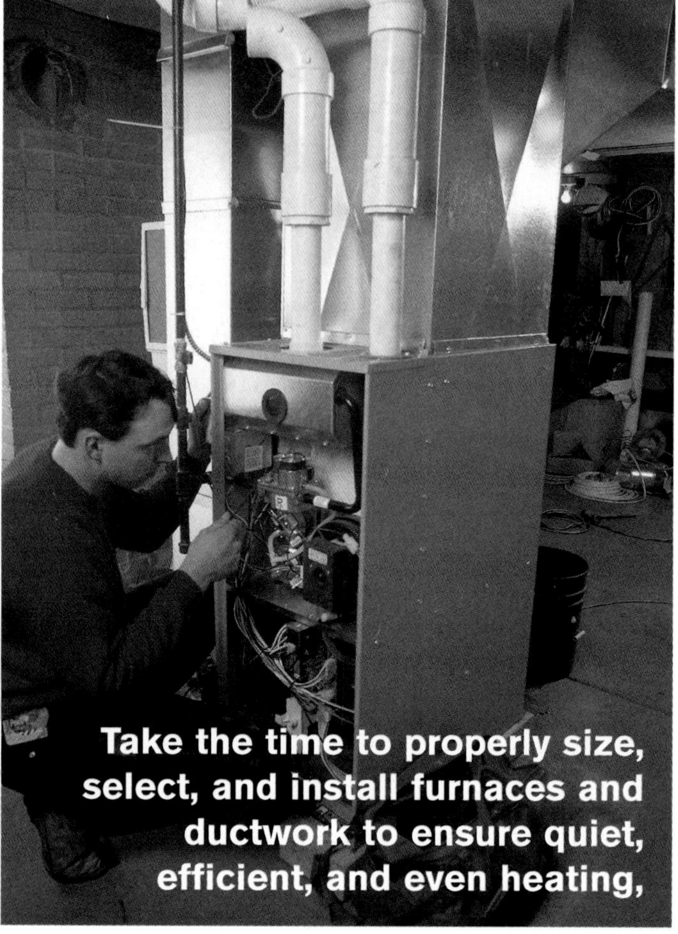
Take the time to properly size, select, and install furnaces and ductwork to ensure quiet, efficient, and even heating,

backs and nuisance no-heat calls. In the worst case, it will do irreparable damage to your client's home or produce life-threatening carbon monoxide gas.

Oil venting. Oil furnaces require either stainless steel "all-fuel" chimneys or well-built masonry chimneys with masonry or stainless steel liners. (Aluminum liners will quickly corrode.) Some inspectors allow sidewall power-vent kits to be installed on oil equipment, but don't be tempted. These units can cause overdraft, producing excess soot and reducing efficiency. The few hundred dollars you save by not building a chimney will be burned up in higher fuel costs and endless maintenance.

Mid-efficiency gas venting. Builders often confuse mid-efficiency (80 percent AFUE, or Annual Fuel Utilization Efficiency) furnaces with true "condensing" (above 90 percent AFUE) furnaces because they look mechanically similar. Beware: Although some mid-efficiency furnaces on the market are approved for sidewall venting, many are not and, therefore, require a properly sized and lined masonry chimney or a B-rated metal chimney system. The combustion products from a gas furnace are as acidic as the mix-

Figure 1. This standard-efficiency furnace (left) vents into an unprotected chimney on an outside wall. The poor draft has resulted in excessive flue gas condensation, which has corroded the galvanized flue pipe. Instead of repairing a damaged chimney, it is often less expensive to install a PVC-vented high-efficiency furnace (right).

ture used to clean mortar off brick and will quickly destroy an unlined masonry chimney by reacting with the portland cement in blocks and mortar. I've seen chimneys actually collapse only a few years after installing a mid-efficiency unit. Masonry chimneys on cold outside walls are the worst offenders, because the flue gases will cool and condense very quickly (see Figure 1).

You can't tell if a chimney is lined by looking just at the top. The only way to know for sure is to look in through the thimble with a flashlight and mirror. If the chimney lining is questionable, a flexible, one-piece aluminum liner, such as the Flexi-Liner (Flex-L International, Columbus, Ohio), can be installed. Or select a furnace that is approved for side venting and closely follow the manufacturer's instructions.

High-efficiency gas venting. If the chimney is beyond repair or if your customer wants the greatest savings possible on heating bills, a condensing gas furnace is your best option. These vent through a PVC pipe directly out the sidewall or up (one story) through the roof. These furnaces must be vented exactly as the manufacturer requires, which often limits the length and position of the vent pipe.

Many condensing gas furnaces are available as "sealed combustion" units, which bring combustion air to the firebox in one pipe and send exhaust back out another. There are many advantages to sealed combustion — no backdrafting of other nearby appliances and cleaner, drier air for combustion, which means longer component life. There are also pitfalls, the most common being "recirculation lock-out," where the unit sucks moisture-laden exhaust back through the inlet. The best defense is to follow the manufacturer's installation instructions exactly, use the approved two-pipe termination method, and keep pipe lengths as short as possible.

Sizing the Furnace

Many customers who are tired of being cold will want a furnace that is the same size or larger than the one I'm taking out. I have to educate them that with warm-air furnaces, oversizing is the cause of a host of problems. Instead of providing steady, even heat, an oversized furnace will quickly come up to temperature internally and shut down. This "short cycling" will make rooms close to the furnace too hot and rooms at the end of the line too cold, because the blower never operates long enough to fully mix and circulate the air in the house. People can feel temperature differences as small as a couple of degrees, but if the furnace is oversized, it's not uncommon to experience swings of 10°F or more.

Equipment life. Short-cycling also wears out furnace components, including the blower motor and the heat exchanger, three to four times faster than if the furnace were running normally. I've seen high-quality furnaces that should have lasted for 20 years or more fail completely in three or four years as a result (Figure 2).

Condensation and soot. Burning fossil fuel produces moisture, and like a car that only gets driven around the block, an oversized furnace will never dry itself out or warm up enough to keep a clean flue. Like a car tailpipe, the result is extra soot, scale, and rust — all enemies of metal parts.

Noise. Heating technicians will often boost the

blower speed in an attempt to move the heat off the oversized furnace as quickly as possible. While this may protect the furnace from damage due to overheating, it can also cause a sound reminiscent of a jet plane taking off every time the furnace comes on.

Figuring Heat Loss

When my grandfather started in this business, he ballparked furnace sizes based on the volume of the house or some other basic rules of thumb. Today, furnaces are more sophisticated, and the only right way to size one is with a heating load calculation, which tells you the rate at which the house is losing heat. You don't have to be a mathematician to produce a usable load calculation; basically, you are figuring out the area of any surface exposed to cold, then plugging in numbers from a chart.

Future additions. If an addition is part of the current project, you'll need to calculate it right along with the existing house and size the new furnace accordingly. Sometimes, however, people want to know if the furnace I'm proposing will be big enough to handle an addition "in the future." I'm reluctant to size a furnace for something that may never happen, especially when doing so will cost the homeowner extra heating dollars year after year. The better solution is to wait until the addition is actually planned and address the heating at that time with a separate system or zone.

Basic Heat Load Calculation

To size a furnace, you have to know the house's rate of heat loss in the worst case scenario, which would be on the coldest winter night with a brisk wind – called the heating "design temperature." The difference between the interior temperature and the design temperature is called the Delta T, often written as ΔT (Δ is the Greek letter Delta, which is often used to mean *change*).

In our area of New York State, we use the design numbers of 70˚F indoor temperature and -10˚F outdoor temperature, producing a ΔT of 80˚F. Figure 3 is a chart giving heat loss for common building assemblies at ΔTs ranging from 40˚F to 100˚F. Use the values from the column that best represents your area. If you're not sure what design temperatures apply to your area, any good hvac contractor should be able to tell you. These numbers have been adjusted for average air infiltration.

To calculate heat loss for assemblies not listed, use the formula

$$\frac{\Delta T \times SF}{\text{R-Value}}$$

where SF is the total square footage of the assembly, ΔT is the commonly used number for your area, and the R-value is the sum of all the R-values in your assembly.

You might want to add 15 percent to the total heat loss figure for average air infiltration, 30 percent if the house is known to be very drafty, or nothing for a new tight house. A small mistake probably won't affect your totals, but use common sense and adjust the figures accordingly.

Figure 2. Because it was oversized, this 90,000 Btu furnace had to be replaced. The four 7-inch-diameter ducts carried only half the hot air the furnace was capable of producing, causing the heat exchanger to overheat and crack.

Figure 4 is the worksheet our company uses to perform heat load calculations (we also use it for cooling loads). In the top portion, we sketch the walls of the house, including doors, windows, and other relevant information. Each square of the graph paper represents a 5-foot square. For complex houses, we'll use more than one sheet, dividing the house up as necessary. The sample house is a simple single-story ranch with an uninsulated concrete foundation.

Here's how to use the worksheet:

1. Gross wall area: Unless the entire house above grade is the same construction, you must calculate each wall type separately. First measure the outside perimeter of the house. Our sample house has an uninsulated concrete foundation, with 16 inches exposed above grade and insulated 2x4 exterior walls. For each type of exposed wall, multiply the total length of the wall by its height. Include the rim joist area in the stud wall.

Masonry Wall:
140 ft. x 1.34 ft. (16 in.) = 188 sq. ft. wall (gross)

Frame Wall w/ Rim Joist :
140 ft. x 9 ft. = 1260 sq. ft. wall (gross)

2. Windows and doors: Measure all the windows and doors and round to even feet. A standard entry door is 3 ft. x7 ft., or 21 sq. ft., for example. List each by type of glazing — single pane, single pane with

Heat Loss of Building Assemblies (Btu/hr)

Assembly Windows	Approx. R-value of assembly	ΔT 40°F	60°F	80°F	100°F
		Values are per square foot			
Single pane	NA	55	85	110	140
Single pane w/ storm	NA	38	60	75	94
Thermal pane	NA	33	50	65	82
Doors					
Wood, no storm	NA	125	188	250	313
Wood, w/storm	NA	75	113	150	188
Steel insulated	NA	50	75	100	125
Garage, weatherstripped	NA	75	113	150	188
Walls					
Above-grade masonry - uninsulated	R-2	18	27	36	45
Above-grade masonry w/2" EPS	R-12	4	6	8	10
Uninsulated wood, 0" insulation	R-3	11	17	22	28
Insulated wood, 1 1/2-2" insulation	R-5	6	9	12	15
Insulated wood, 3-4" insulation	R-13	3	4	6	8
Insulated wood, 5-6" insulation	R-19	2	3	4	5
Ceiling					
Open, no insulation	R-1.5	23	34	45	56
1 1/2 - 2" insulation, plaster or drywall	R-5	6	9	12	15
3-4" insulation, plaster or drywall	R-12	3	4	6	8
5-6" insulation, plaster or drywall	R-20	2	3	4	5
8-9" insulation, plaster or drywall	R-30	2	2	3	4
11-12" insulation, plaster or drywall	R-38	1	2	2	3
Floors		Values are per linear foot			
Radiant slab edge, no insulation		125/LF	188/LF	250/LF	313/LF
Slab edge, no insulation		75/LF	113/LF	150/LF	190/LF
Slab edge, 1" EPS insulation		45/LF	68/LF	90/LF	113/LF
Radiant slab edge, 1" EPS insulation		75/LF	113/LF	150/LF	190/LF
		Values are per square foot			
Basement slab, below grade	NA	1	2	2	3
Wood floor, uninsulated, 0"	NA	11	17	22	28
Insulated wood floor, 1 1/2-2" insulation	R-5	6	9	12	15
Insulated wood floor, 3-4" insulation	R-12	3	4	6	8
Insulated wood floor, 5-6" insulation	R-20	2	3	4	5
Insulated wood floor, 8-9" insulation	R-30	2	2	3	4
Insulated wood floor, 11-12" insulation	R-38	1	2	2	3

For building assemblies not listed here, calculate the heat loss in Btu/hr with the formula: $\frac{\Delta T \times SF}{\text{R-Value}}$
Add 10-30% to the total building heat loss for air infiltration.

Figure 3. Use this chart to find the heat loss in Btu/hr of various building assemblies. Use the ΔT (design temperature) that applies to your region. The design temperature is the difference between the coldest night of the year and a 70°F indoor temperature.

storms, and double pane (see Worksheet, below). We don't consider the improvement provided by low-E or other films or coatings. As a fudge factor, we instruct our estimators to use only two values for windows in existing construction: 110 Btu/sq.ft. for single pane, 75 Btu/sq.ft. if the window has a good storm or is double-pane.

Window/Door Heat Loss Worksheet

Quantity	Glazing/ Door Type	Size (ft.)	Total sq.ft.	Heat loss per sq.ft.	Heat loss total (round up to nearest 100)
2	Insulated steel entry door	3x7	42	100 Btu	4,200 Btu
1	Single-pane window	10x5	50	110 Btu	5,500 Btu
6	Double-pane window	3x4	72	75 Btu	5,400 Btu
0	New double-pane window, tight installation	----	----	65 Btu	----
Total Btu loss for all windows/doors					15,100 Btu

We use the 65 Btu/sq.ft. value only in new construction where we can verify how the window was installed. Experience has taught us that new windows are often poorly sealed and insulated around the perimeter.

3. ***Net wall heat loss:*** Subtract the window/door area from the gross wall area above grade (wall heat loss values are from the table in Figure 3):

1,260 sq.ft. wall area – 164 sq.ft. window/door area = 1,096 net wall

Area x 6 Btu/sq.ft. = 6600 Btu/hr (rounded up)

Calculate exposed basement wall:

140 ft. x 1.34 ft. (16 in.) = 188 sq.ft. X 36 Btu/sq.ft. = 6800 Btu/hr (rounded up).

Note that if there were basement windows, they would be calculated the same as windows in the above grade framed walls.

4. ***Cold ceiling:*** Calculate the exposed ceiling area:

30 ft. x 40 ft. = 1200 sq.ft. x 3 Btu/sq.ft. = 3600 Btu/hr.

If there are areas of the house insulated differently, they must be measured and calculated separately. If there is no batt or fill insulation above the ceiling or you can't confirm the amount, assume the plaster and wood has at least minor R-value. Rarely will you find a totally uninsulated ceiling except in an unfinished structure like a garage or warehouse.

5. ***Cold floors:*** You either pretend the house is on stilts with the main floor exposed to cold or you calculate the basement slab and walls, but not both. In this case, we are including the basement in the calculation, so the first floor is neutral to heat loss, and we figure the concrete basement slab instead. Surprisingly, the result will be very close either way, once you correct the total for basement area loss (step 7, below). Rounded up, the area is the same as that of the ceiling:

30 ft. x 40 ft. = 1200 sq.ft. x 2 Btu/sq.ft. = 2400 Btu/hr.

Other examples of cold floors might be the floors of living spaces above garages, enclosed porches, cantilevered areas on raised ranches, or upstairs rooms above open porches.

6. ***Add up the losses:*** You're almost done. Once you've calculated the losses through windows/doors, walls, ceilings, and floors, add up the result, rounding up as necessary.

7. ***Basement factor:*** Add an additional 20 percent of the total net loss to account for basement area heat loss and air infiltration at the sill. This is a factor we calculated based on information from more than 1,000 jobs. It works well to account for heat loss through below-grade basement walls, and it saves us from having to do a full analysis on each basement surface for every house. We use this factor only for uninsulated, unfinished basements; if the basement is insulated or finished, calculate it the long way.

Windows/doors	15,100
Basement wall (above grade)	6,800
Frame walls	6,600
Ceiling	3,600
Floor (basement)	2,400
Total net loss	**34,500 Btu/hr**

34,500 Btu/hr x .20 = 7000 Btu/hr(rounded up)

8. ***Output required:*** Add the total net loss to the basement factor (if any). The result is the output needed from the furnace. The furnace output is often listed on the rating label.

34,500 + 7000 = 41,500 Btu/Hr output required

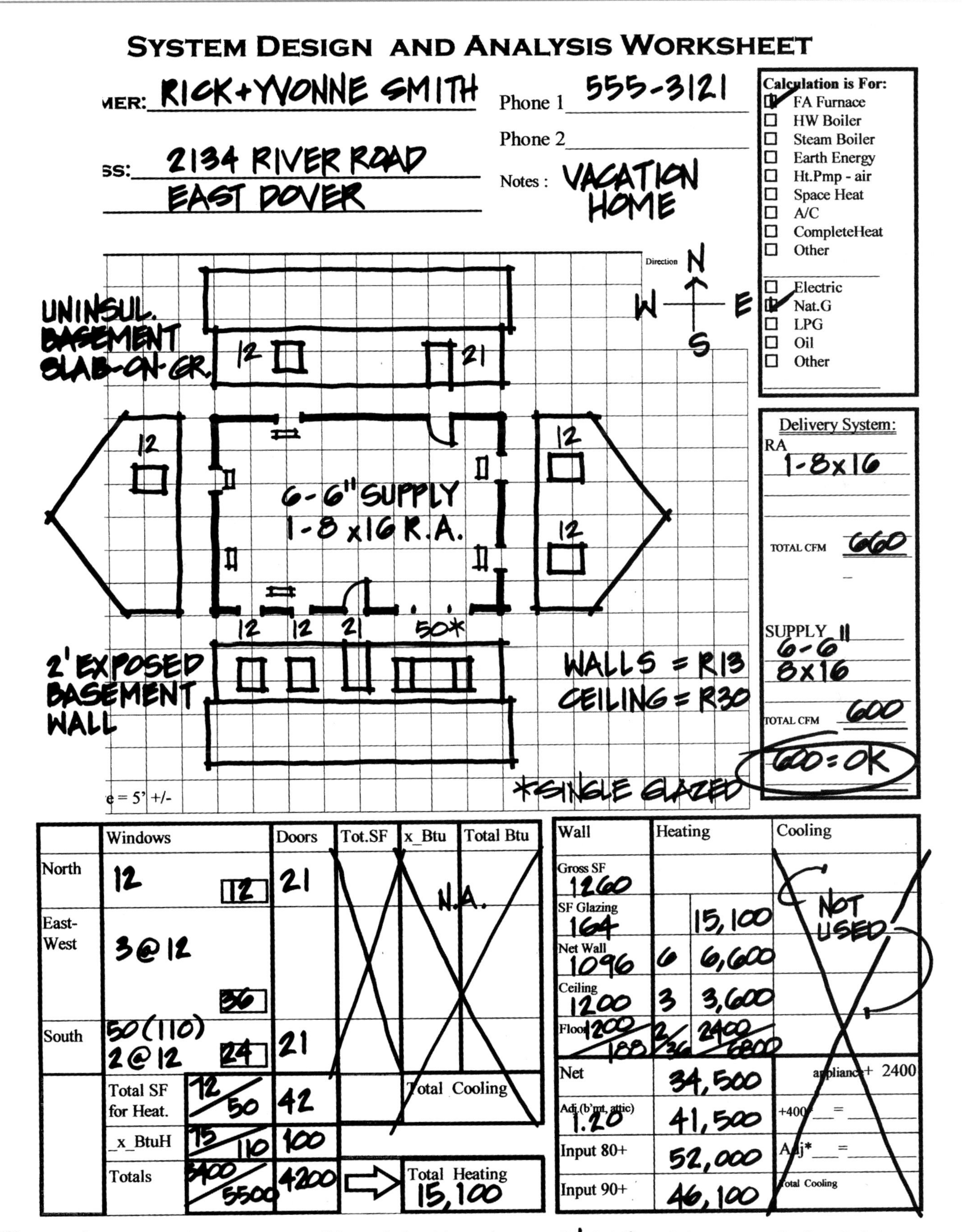

Figure 4. The author's company uses this worksheet to perform building heat loss calculations. In the sample calculations shown here, the heat loss for building assemblies is based on a design ΔT of 80°F.

9. Furnace input required: Furnaces are generally sold by the input rating of the burner, not by the output. Input required is dependent on efficiency. To calculate the required input, divide the output by the AFUE rating on the furnace label or literature. To keep things simple, we typically use 80 percent for a mid-efficiency furnace and 90 percent for high-efficiency units. (For ultra-high efficiency units — 95 percent AFUE, for example, I would use the actual rating.)

41,500/.80 = 52,000 Btu/hr Input at 80% AFUE (rounded up)

41,500/.90 = 46,200 Btu/hr Input at 90% AFUE (rounded up)

Since furnaces are not sold in oddball sizes, in this example, a furnace with input of 60,000 Btu/hr would be required for a mid-efficiency unit, but one with input of 50,000 Btu/hr would do the job at high efficiency. It's not uncommon for us to see an oversized 80,000- to 100,000-Btu furnace installed in a house like this one.

Moving Hot Air

Like the furnace, the ductwork must be properly sized. Otherwise, a bottleneck in the duct system will have

Typical High-Efficiency Furnace

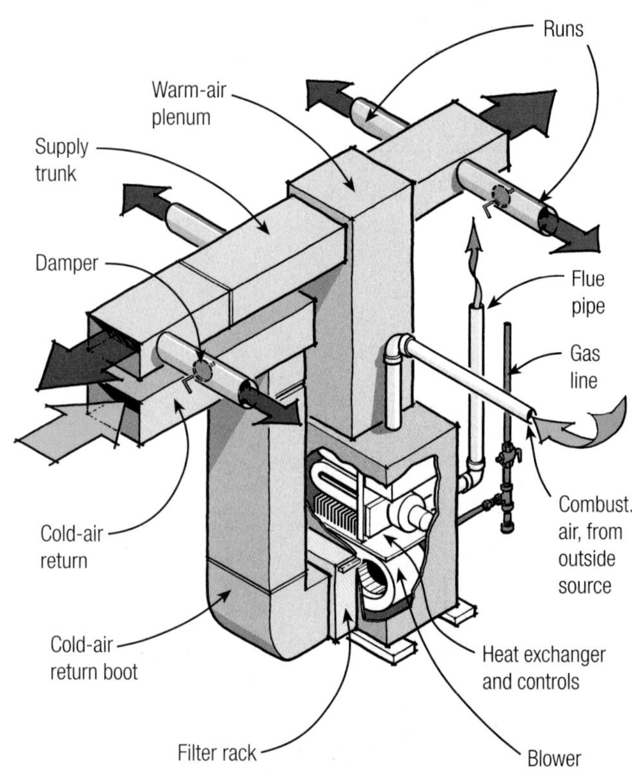

Notes for Chart

The CFM and Btu capacities in this chart are based on a maximum distance of 60 feet from the furnace to the supply register. To use this chart, first select a furnace whose output matches the heat loss for the building. Size individual room ducts based on a room-by-room heat-loss calculation. Size each trunk line to carry the total CFM of all the branch ducts that it supplies. Step down the trunk line to maintain air velocity, making sure that each new trunk section has the capacity to carry all the branch lines connecting to the trunk downstream from that point.

Sizing Ducts for Forced-Air Heat

Round Pipe (in.)	Square Duct (in.)	CFM	Heating Btu
4		32	2,400
5		60	4,400
6	3 1/4 x 10	100	7,400
	3 1/4 x 12	120	8,900
7	3 1/4 x 14	145	10,700
	8 x 6	180	13,300
8		210	15,600
	8 x 8	270	20,000
9		290	21,500
	8 x 10	370	27,400
10		390	28,900
	8 x 12	460	34,000
11		500	37,000
	8 x 14	560	41,500
12		620	45,900
	8 x 16	660	48,900
13		770	57,000
	8 x 18	800	59,300
	8 x 20	900	66,700
14		930	68,900
	8 x 22	1,000	74,100
	8 x 24	1,100	81,500
15		1,140	84,400
	8 x 26	1,200	88,900
16	8 x 28	1,300	96,300
	8 x 30	1,400	103,700
17	10 x 24	1,500	111,100
	10 x 26	1,700	125,900
18		1,800	133,300
	10 x 28	1,900	140,700
	10 x 30	2,000	148,100

Figure 5. Use this chart to assess existing ductwork or plan for additional runs. The total Btu capacity of the ductwork (both supply and return) must match the Btu output of the furnace.

the same effect as a furnace that is too big — short cycling and uneven heat distribution. If you're dealing with new work, my best advice is to have the whole system professionally designed by someone willing to guarantee performance. But if you're putting on a small addition or adding a couple of extra heat runs, that responsibility will probably be yours.

Overall system capacity. Fortunately, checking existing ductwork is not much more complicated than figuring heat loss: A tape measure, an airflow chart like the one in Figure 5, and some basic knowledge are all you need.

The bigger the ducts, the more air and heat they can carry into the building. In the sample heat-load calculation, the house is losing 42,000 Btu per hour. A 6-inch round duct, common in forced air systems, can deliver approximately 100 cfm (cubic feet per minute) of air, which in turn can carry about 7,000 Btu. So it will take 600 cfm of air to deliver the entire 42,000 Btu (6 x 7,000). The plenum, trunk lines, cold air returns, and the sum of all individual heat runs must be able to deliver that much air at a minimum. The chart in Figure 5 shows that the trunk lines would have to be at least 8x16 inches (660 cfm), with at least six 6-inch heat runs (6x100 = 600 cfm).

Cold air returns. Watch out for choked-off cold-air-returns, which are common in older homes: The total return capacity should be the same or greater than the supply air. Ideally, each room should have its own return; at a minimum, there should be one return for each major section of the house. The shorter the path from a supply register to a return, the less drafty the house will feel.

Unlike supply runs, which must be in ductwork, it's perfectly acceptable to "pan" joist bays and stud cavities — enclose them with well-sealed sheet metal or drywall — to carry return air back to the furnace. Always measure the actual size of the cavities used to make sure there is enough total volume.

Not enough or undersized runs. Instead of the typical 6- or 7-inch-diameter runs, some older systems were designed to work at much higher pressures and faster air speeds than modern furnaces and used runs as small as 4 inches. Again referring to the chart, dropping duct diameter from 6 to 5 inches reduces air flow from 100 cfm to 60 cfm at the same static pressure. If the sum of all runs doesn't equal the total required airflow, you'll have to increase duct size or add more ductwork.

Bad System Design

Think of the duct system as a big drinking straw with holes punched in the sides and your finger on the end. When you blow in the straw, the pressure from your finger makes the air go out the side holes in a controlled way. This delicate balance can, however, be easily upset. If your clients are complaining that some rooms are colder than others and everything else measures up, be on the lookout for the following trouble spots:

Runs bunched on one end of a long trunk or taken directly off the end have the same effect as taking your finger off the end of the straw: All of the air rushes out the end, so very little enters the smaller branch runs.

Figure 6. Trunk lines commonly step down to maintain air velocity. The capacity of the trunk at each step-down point must equal the capacity of all the branch runs that come after it.

Trunks that are not "stepped down" properly slow the air velocity and result in poor delivery. To keep air speed constant along their entire length, supply trunks often have to be reduced in size as they travel away from the furnace (Figure 6). Each section of trunk must be big enough to support all the branch runs farther down the line. It does little good to carefully step an 8x20-inch trunk down to 8x8 inches if all the runs are jammed at one end.

Missing branch run dampers make it difficult to balance a system. A damper is nothing more than a flapper that can be adjusted to direct air into or away from a branch run. If the dampers are missing, be sure to add them whenever possible. Don't count on adjustable registers in the rooms to do the same job: The dampers need to be close to where each branch run leaves the trunk.

Choosing a Furnace

Once you've sized up the job, you can start exploring equipment options. I like to present a good-better-best scenario to clients (Figure 7), then let them decide what features and costs work best for them.

What's the efficiency? Manufacturers often use misleading terminology when describing their products — for example, calling an 80 percent efficient furnace "high efficiency." This can lead to confusion or even legal problems for builders and homeowners. By current industry standards, furnaces from about 80 to 83 percent AFUE are called "mid-efficiency," and those above 90 AFUE are referred to as "high-efficiency."

Single- versus dual-stage. A single-stage furnace has only one burner setting — high. By comparison, two-

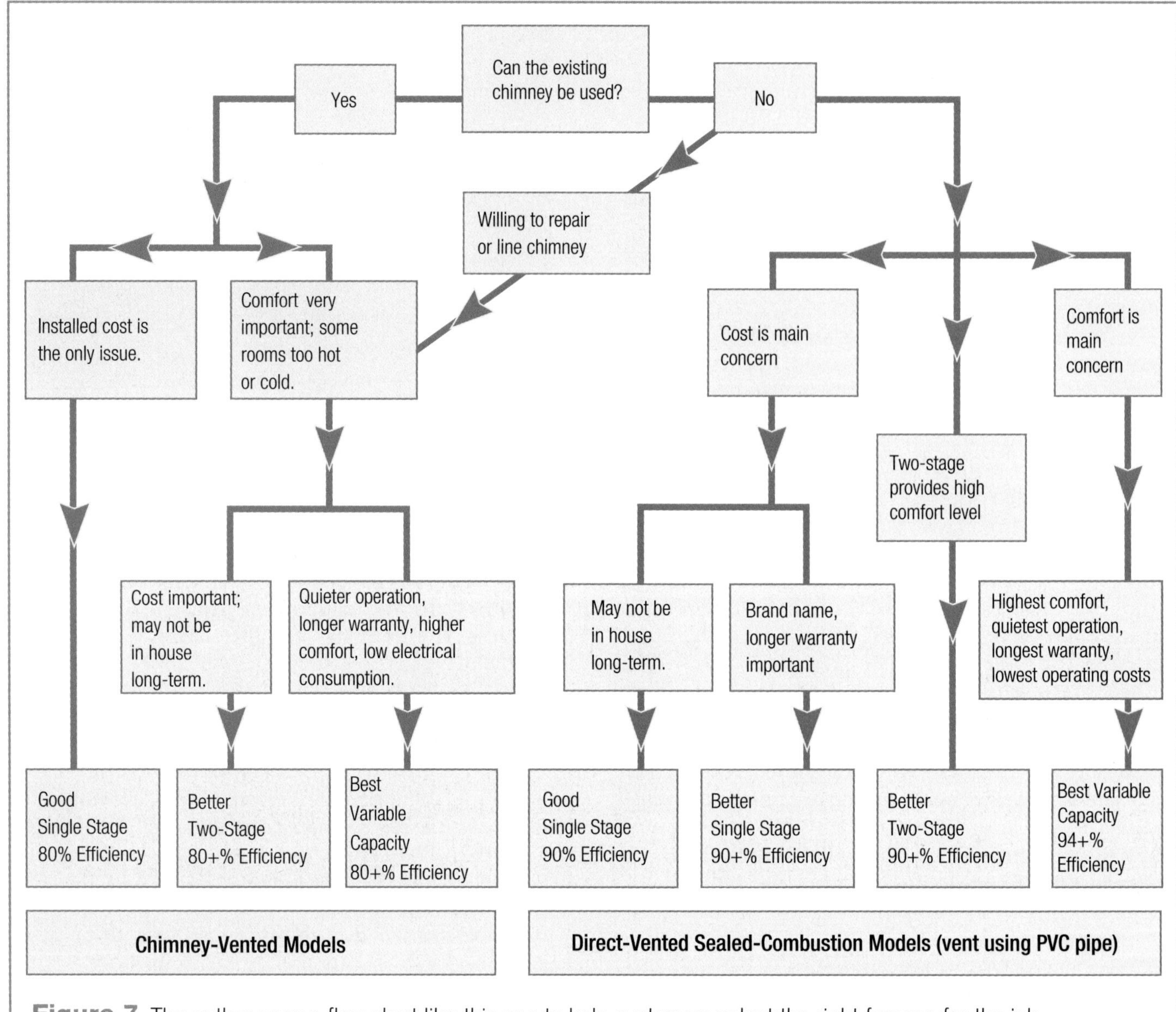

Figure 7. The author uses a flow chart like this one to help customers select the right furnace for the job.

stage units have two settings and multi-speed blowers. They operate most of the time on a lower burner and fan setting, idling along until they need the extra power of full capacity. Two-stage furnaces are quieter during low-stage operation, and provide more even heat and greater comfort because they run longer on a lower setting. Two-stage units may also provide a small efficiency boost, although this is still debated by industry groups, and the answer seems to depend largely on which efficiency test is used. Nonetheless, many customers report lower heating bills with mid-efficiency two-stage furnaces than with single-stage units in comparable houses. This makes sense, because we size furnaces for the worst-case scenario, which only occurs 10 percent of the time in our area of central New York. Two-stage furnaces are also ideal for zoned forced-air applications, where often only half the heating capacity is required at any one time.

Variable speed. Some manufacturers have added variable-speed blower motors and even infinite capacity burners to their top-of-the-line models. Instead of distinct high-low operation, these furnaces can be wired to "ramp up" slowly in response to heating requirements. The result is quiet, even heat that can rival the comfort of hot water heating systems. Variable-speed blowers (also called ICM or ECM) are more expensive to purchase, but operate at a fraction of the cost of conventional blowers, saving as much as $150 annually in electrical costs. Many top-of-the-line models also have auxiliary terminals for hooking up electronic air cleaners, humidifiers, and multi-stage air conditioning without having to add separate controls.

***Gary Bailey** owns and operates a third-generation heating and cooling company in Elmira, N.Y.*

Fine-Tuning Forced-Air Heating & Cooling

by Jeri Donadee

Hydronic, or hot water, heating is seeing a surge in popularity at present, mainly because of the increasing use of radiant floor heating, which is known for providing even, comfortable heat. Yet contrary to popular belief, not every home needs hydronic heat to achieve this level of comfort.

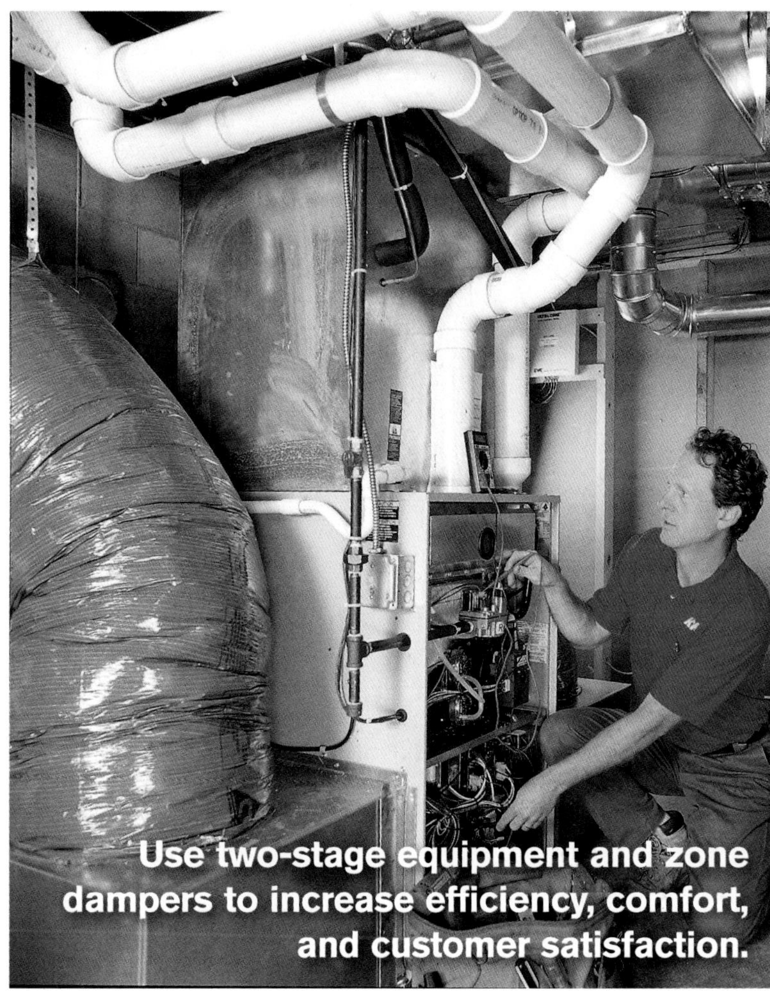
Use two-stage equipment and zone dampers to increase efficiency, comfort, and customer satisfaction.

Apples to Oranges

Hydronic heat is sometimes touted as more comfortable than forced-air heat. But since the typical hydronic system is significantly more expensive than the typical hot-air system — especially if cooling is included — this is an apples-to-oranges comparison. Customers willing to invest in a quality hot-air system, rather than a bare-bones package at the lowest price, will find that forced hot air can be as comfortable as hydronic heating.

The least expensive forced-air system usually includes a single-stage furnace with a single-speed blower motor. The entire house is ducted as a single zone and, therefore, has just one thermostat. If the system is sized by a contractor who uses a rule-of-thumb formula to estimate heat loss and heat gain, the homeowner can end up paying high energy bills for a noisy, inefficient system that provides uneven temperatures from room to room.

A quality forced-air system would probably include a two-stage furnace with a variable-speed blower motor. The house would be separated into several zones with separate thermostats, and the air would be distributed through well-sealed, insulated ducts. In many cases, such an upgraded hot-air system will still cost less than a hydronic system.

Ask the Right Questions

One of the most important steps to designing a quality heating and cooling system is to take the time for a long talk with the homeowner. Don't assume that you know what the customer wants and is willing to pay for. Most homeowners are not aware of all the available options. Here are some of the questions you need to ask:

What is your budget for this work? This is a tough one to get answered. Often the answer is, "Gee, I really have no idea." However, someone building a 2,500-square-foot home with an $8,000 budget is not looking at the same system as a person with a $13,000 budget.

What type of system do you have now, and what do you like and dislike about it? The answer to this question will tell you what the customers expect from their new system. Different customers have different priorities when it comes to efficiency, comfort, noise, and ease of operation.

Does anyone in the home have allergies? If the answer is yes, the customer may want to consider a high-performance air filter. There are three basic types of high-performance air filters used today: Pleated media filters ($350 to $425), electronic air cleaners ($775 to $900), and HEPA filtration systems ($1275 to $1600). A fourth type, electrostatic filters, have fallen out of favor due to restrictive air-flow.

What type of fuel is available at your site, and what fuel do you prefer? If a client has a phobia about gas or an aversion to oil or heat pumps, you should know about it before you design their system.

Finally, you need to explain to the homeowner what your standard design temperatures are — for example, 70°F inside on a 0°F day, and 75°F inside on a 95°F day. Make sure you're in agreement on these parameters up front, and if they have other ideas, incorporate them into your design, as long as their ideas are reasonable.

Choosing the Right Sub

Heating contractors vary in their attention to detail. Ask your prospective heating sub how load calculations and duct design are performed; the answers will help you evaluate the sub's expertise.

Load calculations. Does your heating contractor calculate accurate room-by-room heating and cooling loads? In order to perform these calculations, your sub needs to know the insulation values of the floor, walls, and ceiling; the fresh air infiltration rate; the R-value of the windows; and the orientation and measurements of any skylights (see "Installing Efficient Forced-Air Heat," page 190). Many heating contractors still use rule-of-thumb square foot formulas for calculating heating and cooling loads. But since glass-to-wall ratios can differ significantly from one floor plan to the next, "square-footing it" is a dangerous practice.

Duct design. Not all heating subs pay close attention to duct design. The standard duct design manual is Manual D — Residential Duct Systems from the Air Conditioning Contractors of America (www.acca.org).

One common duct design error is inadequate return ductwork. A system with multiple return grilles is preferable to a system with a single, central return grille. Another basic error is supply ductwork that is not matched to the output of the furnace. In extreme cases, undersized ductwork is unable to remove the furnace's heat fast enough, causing the heat exchanger to overheat and crack.

Supply air vents should be placed where they can deliver air along the exterior perimeter walls, where the greatest heat loss and gain occurs. Avoid low sidewall supplies, which can cause drafts and result in dissatisfied customers.

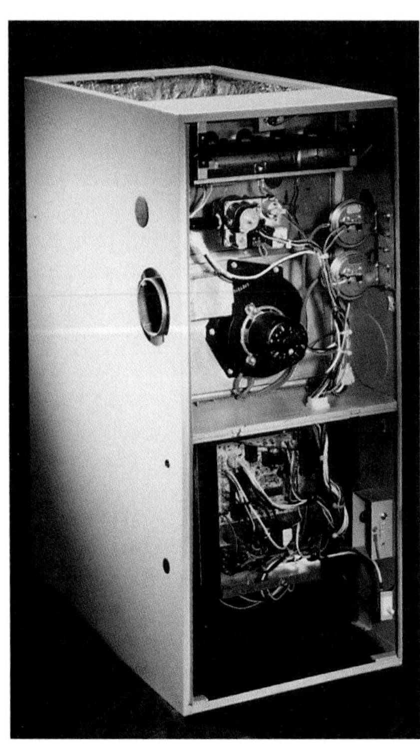

Figure 8. Two-stage gas furnaces, like this model from Goettl Air Conditioning, have two levels of Btu output and airflow. Since low-stage operation is adequate to meet the heating demand most of the time, such units are quieter and more efficient than single-stage furnaces.

Two-Stage Equipment

The calculated loads will show the Btus per hour (Btu/hr) required at peak load conditions (the coldest outdoor temperatures in winter and the hottest outdoor temperatures in summer). In most areas, peak conditions are reached only for a few hours in a typical season, so most of the time, a correctly selected unit is oversized for moderate conditions. That's why it's important to offer the customer a two-stage system.

Two-stage models are available in mid-efficiency and high-efficiency gas furnaces, as well as air-source and geothermal heat pumps (Figure 8). These units offer "Btu staging" — for example, a two-stage gas furnace might have a 65,000 Btu/hr input on low, and a 100,000 Btu/hr input on high. Several manufacturers offer variable-capacity units, which are even more precise at delivering heat that matches the load requirements at varying outdoor temperatures.

If you burn oil, you probably will be limited to choosing a single-stage furnace. While gas burners can be equipped with a two-position gas valve, an oil burner is equipped with a unique nozzle that is optimized for a single firing rate. Two-stage oil pumps are usually not available for residential furnaces.

In heating mode, two-stage units operate at low speed for 80 percent of the time. Two-stage units quietly deliver consistent indoor comfort through longer run cycles at lower speed than conventional single-speed systems. A typical furnace allows the air temperature in a space to fluctuate up to 4°F, while a two-stage system reduces the temperature fluctuation to less than 2°F, while improving air circulation at the same time.

This has several benefits to the owner. First, two-stage units offer improved comfort, because of consistent temperatures throughout the zone. Second, two-stage units are extremely quiet, because their two-speed fans are usually operating at low speed. Last and most important, operating costs are lower, because the Btu per hour output is matched more closely to the actual load and because the unit fires for longer cycles, reducing the start-up and shut-down cycles experienced with a single-speed system.

Variable-speed blower motors. A furnace with a variable-speed blower motor provides improved comfort and efficiency. A variable-speed motor, which is available for either a gas or oil furnace, slowly ramps up on the initial call for heat, so that the air-speed increase more closely follows the increase of heat available at the heat exchanger. Conversely, on the shut-down cycle, the fan will slowly ramp down, extracting the maximum Btus from the heat exchanger surface. In contrast, the blower in a standard furnace usually has a timed on/off control, which can cause an objectionable "cold blow" on start-up and shut-down.

A variable-speed blower can also be set up to operate at very low "fan-only" speeds. The fan-only feature, which is controlled by a manual on/off switch at the thermostat, is especially important for systems with high-performance air filters, because the only time the air filter will work is when the air is moving through it.

Fan-only operation may also be useful for a room that is not on a dedicated zone and is located far away from the thermostat. Constantly introducing new air into the room will bring the temperature more into line with the temperature in the rest of the home. The cost of running an efficient variable-speed blower on fan-only for a year is less than $40, while a standard motor running for the same year would cost more than $200 to operate.

Two-speed condenser. For the cooling side of the system, consider upgrading to a two-speed condenser. Homes with skylights and large window areas will often have very high heat gains on sunny days, dictating the size of the cooling unit. But on warm, humid days without a bright sun, the house will not have as much heat gain, and a single-speed condenser will not run long enough to remove the high humidity.

A two-stage condenser (which usually includes both a two-stage compressor and a two-speed condenser fan motor) coupled with a variable-speed blower fan can remove up to 30 times more moisture than a standard fixed-speed system, because it will not be short-cycling as often.

Smart controls. Some manufacturers offer communicating thermostats that use microprocessor technology coupled with temperature/humidity sensors to control the system. Examples include the Carrier Infinity and Honeywell IAQ lines, which have controls that look like an electronic thermostat but are capable of displaying the outdoor temperature and indoor relative humidity. These will precisely operate the system based on desired indoor temperature and humidity set points. In addition these devices can operate programmed set-backs, control ventilation functions, and provide maintenance reminders.

When this type of control is coupled with matching heat-pump components, it will regulate the variable-speed fan motor to maintain consistent air discharge temperatures.

Such systems can provide a minimum air temperature delivery of 100°F, up to a maximum of over 120°F — about 20°F warmer than previous-generation equipment. Most users report higher comfort levels with these warmer air delivery temperatures.

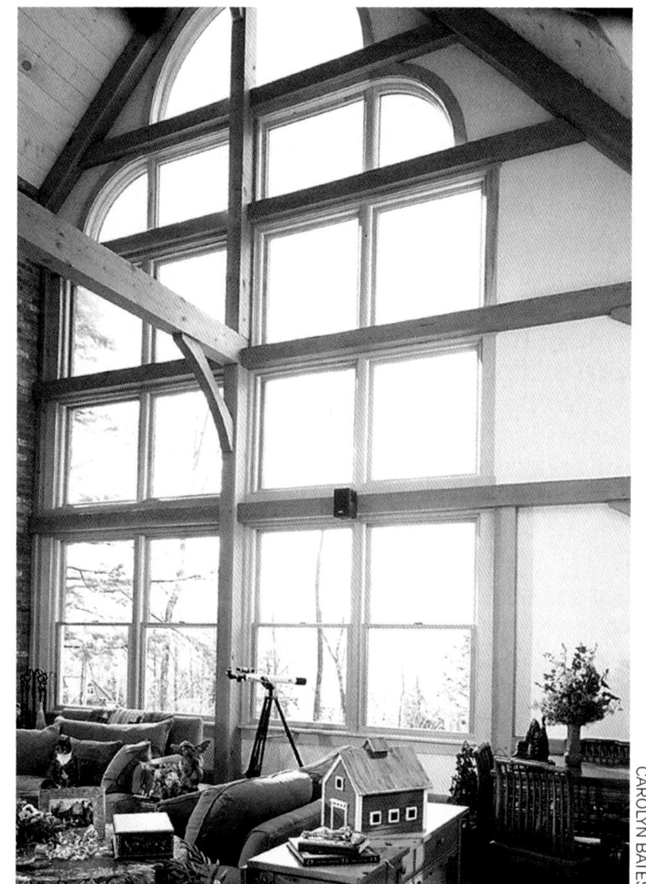
CAROLYN BATES

Figure 9. A room with an unusually large area of glass tends to have high heat loss at night and high heat gain on sunny days. Such a room is a good candidate for a separate zone.

Several Zones

Many contractors do not recommend or install zoning equipment, due to the mistaken belief that zoning is complicated. But if the homeowner's lifestyle requires different temperature levels in different areas, zoning probably makes sense, especially in larger homes.

Another reason to zone is to provide good temperature control in any area of the house that has much greater heat loss (or gain) than other areas of the house. Typical examples are areas with many windows or rooms that are oriented toward a different direction than most of the other rooms in the house (Figure 9). During your initial meeting with the owner, look for such areas — for example, a sunroom or a finished area above a garage.

How do you decide whether an area needs its own furnace or just a zone off the main unit? Assuming you have sufficient capacity, it is usually less expensive to install (and always less expensive to operate) a zone off of the main system than to install a separate dedicated unit. In some cases, though, the location of the zone or the building's total heating and cooling loads may dictate a separate unit.

When designing a zoned system, the first step is to know the Btu and airflow demands of the zone. Once the actual air requirements are verified, the ductwork should be designed and installed at a slightly larger size

(10 to 15 percent larger) than standard ductwork. Oversizing each zone's ducts helps to dissipate any extra airflow when only one zone calls for heating or cooling.

Zoning is accomplished by installing motorized zone dampers (Figure 10). Since the premise for zoning is to reduce the air going to the area where the temperature is satisfied and deliver air to the area that needs the heating/cooling, each zone will need dampers. Manufacturers of zone dampers include Carrier, Honeywell, and EWC Controls (see "Sources of Supply," page 206).

If there is room for a dedicated trunk line to serve the zone, it is usually easier and cheaper to install a zone damper in the trunk line. In that case, the individual branch lines that are tapped off the dedicated trunks will not require zone dampers. When there is no room for a dedicated trunk line, the area can be zoned by installing a series of dampers in the branch lines serving the area, and then controlling the dampers together with a multi-damper enabler. Usually, the enabler is purchased from the zone damper supplier.

A multi-zone system requires individual thermostats to regulate the temperatures of each zone. The low-voltage thermostat wire is fed to a main zone panel. Wires are then run to the equipment and each zone damper. High and low temperature sensors are usually placed in the supply-air plenum to serve as unit safeties in the unlikely event of a zone damper failure.

Supply ductwork is the only part of the system with dampers. When one zone calls and gets supply air, the returns are still being drawn from the entire home. Therefore, it's important to locate adequate returns in each zone. Two-story homes should have a combination of high and low return grilles.

Extra air. When only one zone in a multi-zone system calls for heat, there needs to be some way to dissipate the extra cfm output of the furnace. Some brands of zone control ignore this problem and let the high airflow howl through the small duct. Other brands will allow for the other zone(s) to open slightly and allow for the air to "leak" into areas that do not actually require conditioning. A third option is to install a bypass damper that allows the excess air to be recirculated back to the return. How the "extra" air is handled is a matter of contractor preference. The surplus air issue is much less of a problem with a communicating thermostat system on a two-stage gas furnace or a two-stage heat pump, especially one with a variable-speed fan — one more reason for installing two-stage equipment.

Doing Ductwork Right

In unconditioned spaces like crawlspaces and attics, insulated duct for both supply and returns is required. For ducts in conditioned spaces, insulation is highly recommended, but not required. During the cooling season, uninsulated metal ducts can become cold enough to sweat.

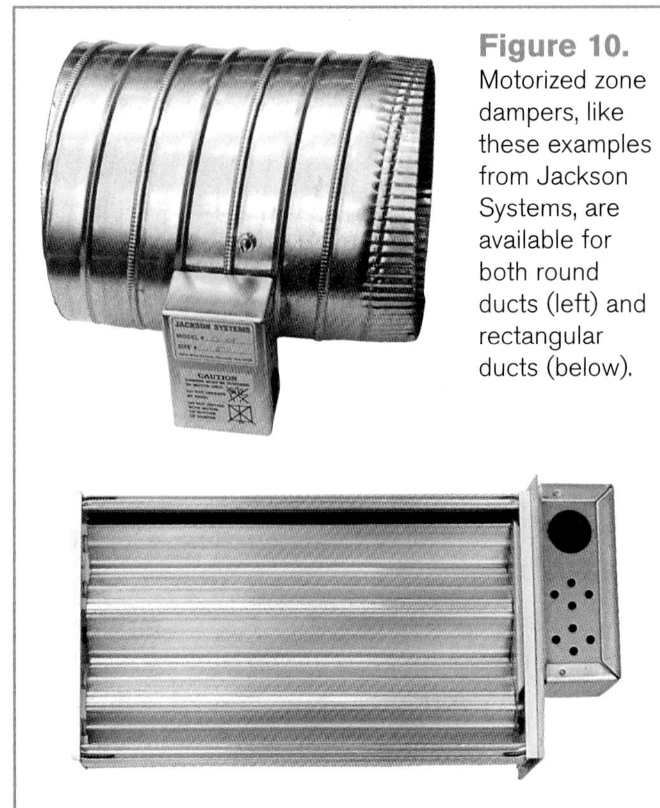

Figure 10. Motorized zone dampers, like these examples from Jackson Systems, are available for both round ducts (left) and rectangular ducts (below).

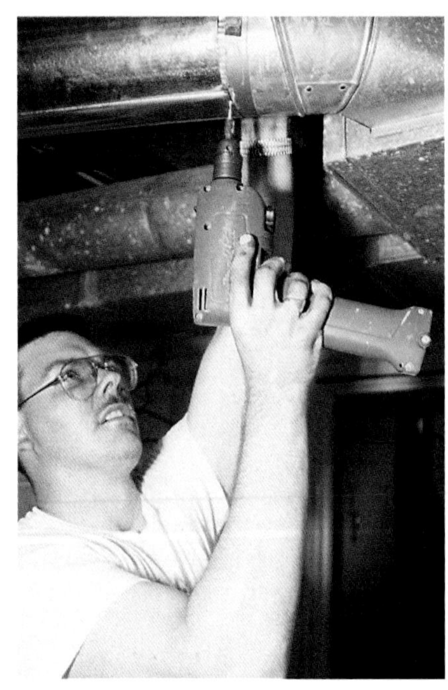

Figure 11. Sheet-metal duct joints must be screwed together before mastic is applied.

Minimizing leaks. Many studies have shown that the typical forced-air system has leaky ductwork. Leaky ductwork wastes energy dollars and can lead to pressure imbalances in a house.

Joints in sheet-metal duct should be screwed together and sealed with mastic (Figure 11). Using mastic is always good practice, although some contractors omit

continued on page 205

Duct Tape Update

by Martin Holladay

By now, most people know that regular hardware store duct tape is good for almost anything but ducts. Duct tape has been used to make makeshift tow-chains to pull vehicles from ditches and for various emergency repairs on Apollo space missions. When used on ducts, though, generic cloth duct tape fails when the heat dries out the adhesive.

Perhaps you're wondering, then, "Why isn't there any industry standard for duct tape?" It turns out that there is one — at least for duct tape used on flex duct and fiberglass duct.

Underwriters Laboratories reports on its website (www.ul.com) that UL first published a standard for duct tape in October 1995. The standard, UL 181B, is called "Standard for Safety for Closure Systems for Use with Flexible Air Ducts and Air Connectors," and covers duct tape for use on flex duct. Another standard, UL 181A, "Standard for Safety for Closure Systems for Use with Rigid Air Ducts and Air Connectors," covers duct tape for use with rigid fiberglass duct (duct board). There are two types of UL 181A tape: heat-activated tape and pressure-sensitive tape. In general, heat-activated tapes, which are sealed with a tool called a heat seal iron, perform better than pressure-sensitive tapes.

According to the UL website, "The Standard requires that duct tape pass a series of tests, including evaluations of tensile strength; peel adhesion strength; shear adhesion strength under a variety of weights, temperatures and humidity levels; long-term high-temperature effects; and surface burning characteristics. UL also evaluates the tape for its ability to inhibit fungi from growing."

If you want a duct tape that actually works on ducts, look for the UL 181 designation, which should be printed every 6 inches on the tape. These UL 181 duct tapes are backed with aluminum foil, so they don't look like old-fashioned gray duct tape.

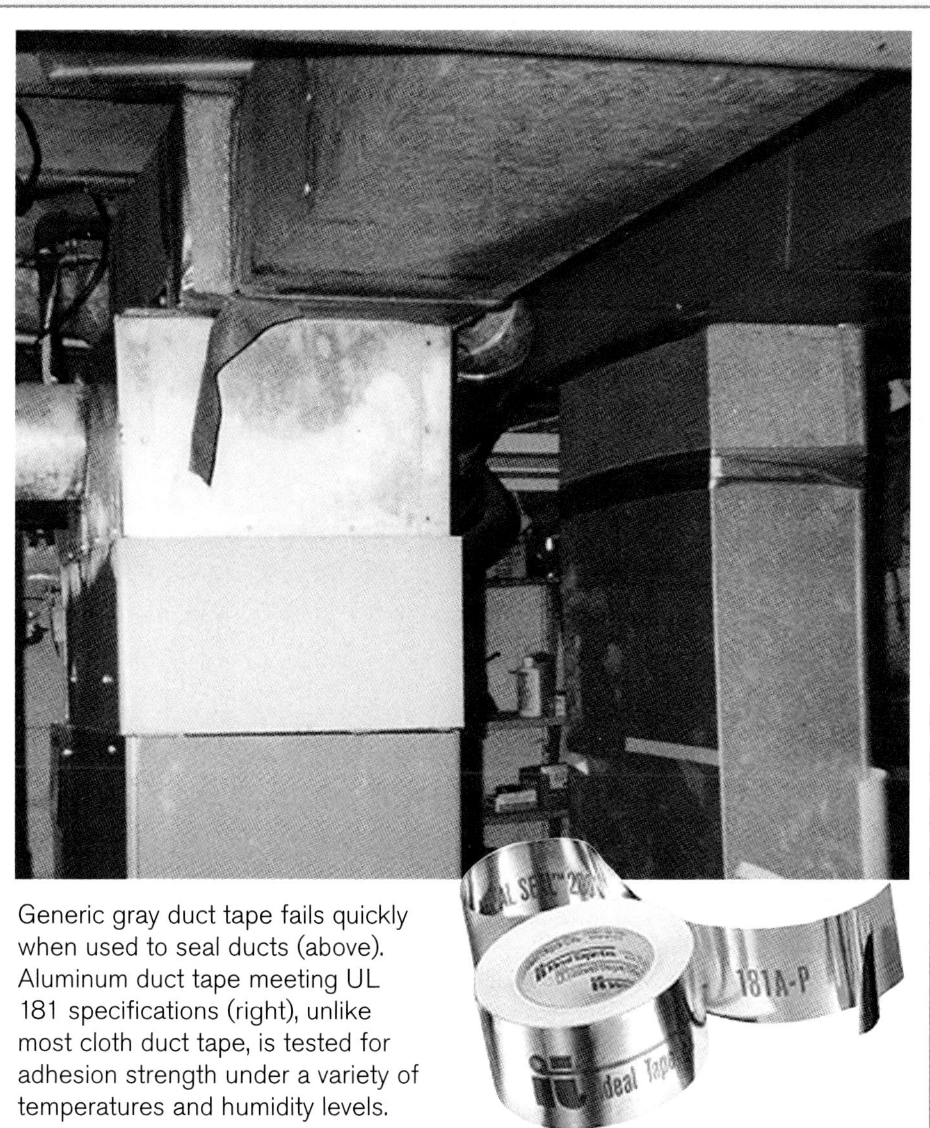

Generic gray duct tape fails quickly when used to seal ducts (above). Aluminum duct tape meeting UL 181 specifications (right), unlike most cloth duct tape, is tested for adhesion strength under a variety of temperatures and humidity levels.

For sealing sheet-metal duct, rather than flex duct or fiberglass duct, use mastic, not tape. No standard exists for duct tape used on sheet-metal duct.

***Martin Holladay** is senior editor of www.GreenBuilding Advisor.com and was formerly the editor of Energy Design Update.*

Making Mastic Stick

by Bruce Sullivan

Recent research shows that ducts can be responsible for 20 to 60 percent of the total air leakage in houses.

Some contractors use standard duct tape to seal ducts, but cloth tape becomes brittle and loses its adhesion within a couple of years. So more residential contractors are turning to the treatment used in many commercial buildings — duct mastic. Applied properly, it can all but eliminate air leakage from ducts.

Where to Use Mastic

Air handler: Fill all openings for wiring, plumbing, and refrigerant lines. Seal all seams in the air handler and plenums. Tape around access panels, so they can be opened for service.

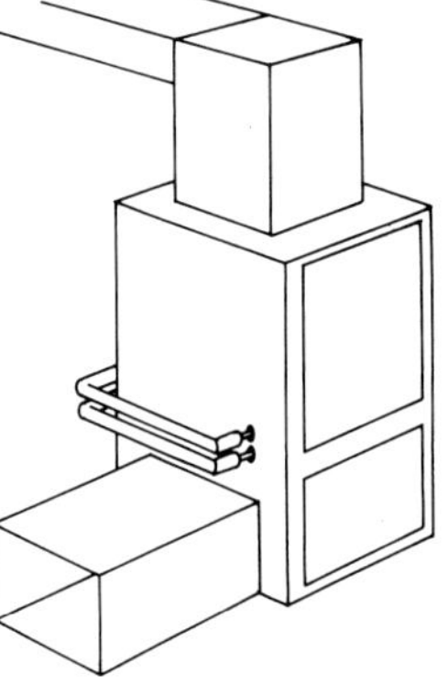

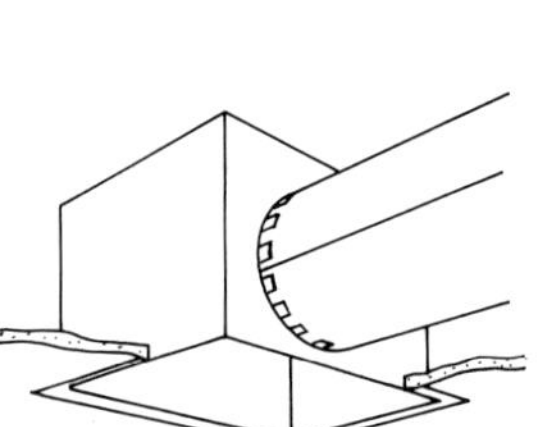

Transitions: Use mesh tape to strengthen the joint where ducts of different shapes meet. Seal all seams, even manufactured ones.

Register boot: Few manufactured seams leak, but for insurance it's worth hitting the ones you can easily. The transition between the duct and boot may require mesh tape. Folded corners don't need sealant.

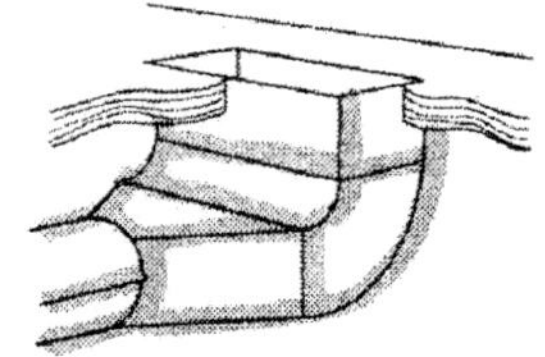

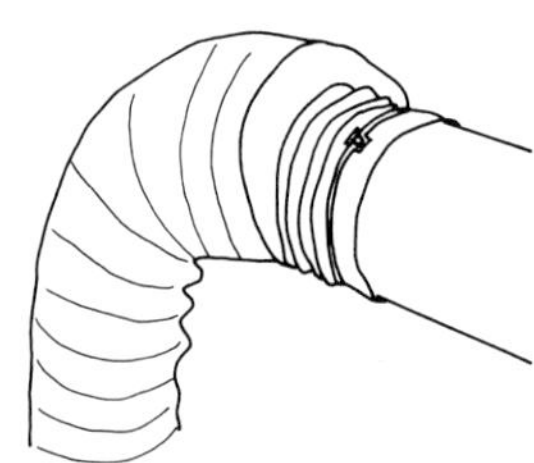

Flex duct connections: Plastic strap holds the inner liner firmly to the duct or fitting. Mastic should cover the end of the liner. Then tape the outer liner to the metal fitting.

Building cavities: Seal all joints and openings in cavities used for air movement. Seal sheet metal to framing.

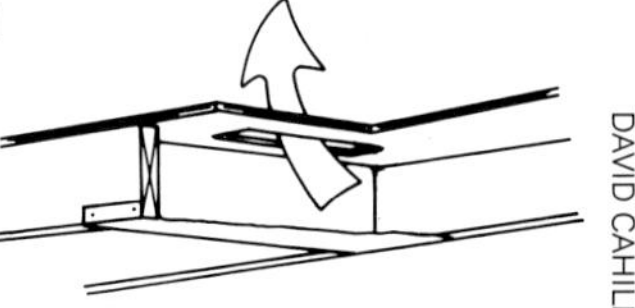

DAVID CAHILL

Duct mastic doesn't hold ducts or their seams together. That's a job for screws, rivets, and straps. Mastic does, however, serve as a high quality flexible sealant. Because it never fully hardens, mastic stretches as the duct expands and contracts. It withstands wetness. Some mastics contain tiny strands of fiberglass to increase strength.

Mastic products vary in consistency from that of mashed potatoes to yogurt. It comes in cartridges (like caulk), tubs, and buckets. You can apply it with a caulk gun, brush, or trowel, or with your gloved hand. In the past, most mastics used a petroleum solvent base, but manufacturers now offer many water-based products. These are safer to handle and easier to clean up.

Finding the Good Stuff

The lack of uniform standards makes it hard to judge the sealing qualities of a mastic without trying it. You'll have to try several and choose one that works best for you. A good duct mastic has these characteristics:

High solids content. Solids content (usually listed on the product literature) should be at least 50 percent. Some have as much as 70 percent. As with paint, higher solids means less shrinkage as the material cures.

Excellent adhesion. Duct mastic is used mainly for metal ductwork, but since you'll probably occasionally seal plenums, you'll want a product that sticks well to wood, drywall, plastic, concrete, and just about any other material you might find in a house. Since these surfaces are seldom clean, a mastic should adhere well to dirty or oily surfaces.

Water resistance. Condensation may collect on ducts during cooling, so the mastic must hold even when exposed to water.

Low toxicity. Check the product's Material Safety Data Sheet for warnings. If you like to spread the material with your hands, wear gloves. Water-based mastics are generally less irritating than petroleum-based ones.

Surface burning characteristics. Duct mastics should meet standards for flame spread and smoke development (ASTM E-84 and UL 723). The National Fire Protection Association Standard 90A requires mastics to have a flame-spread rating no higher than 25 and a maximum "smoke developed" rating of 50.

Viscosity. Some installers like thicker mastic that they can apply with a trowel or gloved hand; this lets you reach and feel places that are hard to see. Others like it thinner so they can brush it on. Viscosity is measured in units called centipois (cps) — the higher the number, the thicker the mastic. For mastic, the mashed-potato-like high end is around 100,000 cps; the 60,000- to 70,000-cps range will be more like yogurt, requiring a brush.

Storage. Mastics have a shelf life of a year or less, so don't overbuy. Mastic should not be allowed to freeze, so store it in a conditioned space and don't leave it in your truck on freezing days.

Color. If the ducts will be visible, you may want to select a pleasing color.

Application

To seal ducts effectively with mastic, you must install it properly.

Clean the surface. Wipe off loose dirt and oil with a dry rag. You want the mastic to stick to the duct, not the dirt.

Secure the joint. Mastic will stand normal duct expansion and shrinkage, but not the movement of unsecured joints. Secure connections and plenums with screws, rivets, or other mechanical fasteners. For flex duct, use plastic straps and tightening tools to secure the ducts to metal collars before sealing.

Gaps between 1/4 inch and 1/2 inch wide need reinforcement; use fiberglass mesh tape. Buy the special mesh tape made for ducts, because it differs in two crucial ways from the drywall product: It is treated to reduce smoke development, and it is generally 3 to 4 inches wide. You can usually buy it wherever you buy the mastic itself. You may need to repair holes larger than 1/2 inch with a rigid material, such as metal.

Apply the mastic. Gaps and openings up to 1/4 inch wide can be sealed with mastic alone. Spread the material at least one inch beyond the opening or on either side of the seam. Apply a thick coat, filling all crevices.

Bruce Sullivan, *a writer and editor specializing in energy topics for builders, is the principal of Iris Communications.*

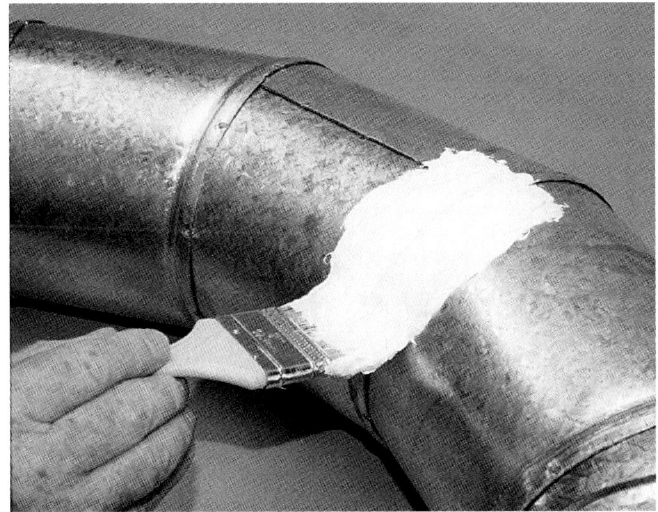

Figure 12. Joints in sheet-metal duct should be sealed with mastic, which can be applied with a paint brush (left). When mastic is used on duct board, the joint should first be bridged with fiberglass tape or scrim (right).

continued from page 202

mastic on ducts in conditioned spaces (see "Making Mastic Stick," page 204). Four water-based duct mastics are Glenkote 181, Hardcast Versa-Grip 181, RCD, and Uni-Mastic 181 Duct Sealer. Duct mastic has the consistency of mud and is spread with gloved hands or a paint brush (Figure 12). Wide gaps in ductwork can be bridged with fiberglass tape before applying mastic.

Joints in rigid fiberglass duct (duct board) should be sealed with a UL-181 heat-activated tape, like Ideal Tape #490 (Figure 13). Heat-activated tape works better and lasts longer than the aluminum pressure-sensitive tape (See "Duct Tape Update," page 203).

Keep flex duct short and fat. Insulated flexible duct is usually much faster to install than rigid duct. However, flex duct must be sized correctly and installed properly. Flex duct should be supported every 4 to 6 feet. Flex duct has high friction losses because of the coiled interior spring liner, so sharp bends should be avoided. The diameter of flex duct must be adequately sized for the airflow required, especially for runs longer than 12 feet.

Avoid pressurized rooms. If a room has a supply grille but no return grille, the room can become pressurized. To avoid this problem, such rooms need a low-resistance path for the return air. Verify that the door is undercut by 1½ to 2 inches or that transfer grilles are installed in a partition between the room and the hallway.

Costs

How much will the suggested upgrades cost? The cost of upgrading a 100,000 Btu/hr gas furnace from a single-stage unit to a two-stage unit with a variable speed fan is between $750 and $900. A very basic 3-ton air-source heat pump with a 13 SEER efficiency rating can be upgraded to a two-stage compressor, variable-speed indoor unit with a 16 SEER rating for an added cost of about $2,300.

Customers who choose the upgrades will reap returns on their investment, not only in increased comfort, but also in energy savings from the improved efficiency of the equipment.

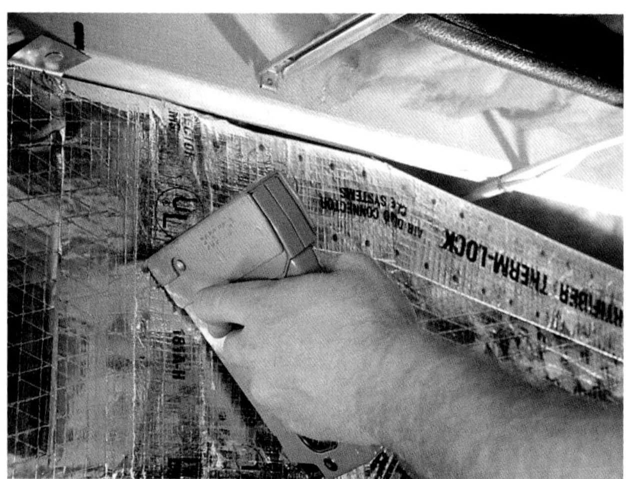

Figure 13. The female end of a duct board joint is pulled taut and stapled through to the male end (top). The joint is completed by applying heat-activated tape, which is warmed with an Amcraft duct board iron (above).

Jeri Donadee *is vice president of H.B. McClure, a heating and cooling contractor in Harrisburg, Pa.*

Sources of Supply

Amcraft
www.amcraftinc.com
Amcraft 7150 heat seal iron for sealing heat-activated duct tape

Carrier
www.carrier.com
Zone dampers

EWC Controls
www.ewccontrols.com
Zone dampers

Hardcast Carlisle
www.hardcast.com
Versa-Grip 181 duct mastic

Honeywell
www.yourhome.honeywell.com
Controls and zone dampers

Ideal Tape, a Division of American Biltrite Inc.
www.abitape.com
UL 181 heat-activated duct tape

McGill AirSeal
www.mcgillairseal.com
Uni-Mastic 181 Duct Sealer mastic

RCD
www.rcdmastics.com
Duct mastic

ITW TACC
www.itwtacc.com
Glenkote duct mastic

Air Conditioning for Humid Climates

by Dwayne Akers

No matter where you work, air conditioning for comfort has always been challenging: Comfort is a subjective quality, and the expectations vary from one person to the next. But in hot, humid areas like the southern coastal states, heating and cooling design can pose particularly tough problems. As a custom heating and air conditioning contractor in North Carolina, I know how hard it can be to keep a home comfortable during humid weather. In this part of the world, both the outdoor temperatures and the atmospheric humidity levels can vary through a wide range, and not necessarily together. Controlling both temperature and humidity with the same comfort system, 365 days a year, calls for a lot of technical savvy.

I work mainly in the custom home market, and my customers have high expectations. Even so, I have to compete against typical fly-by-night contractors who are willing to cut all kinds of corners to undercut my prices. Rarely, if ever, do they take the time to properly estimate even the total cooling load for a new system; you'll surely never see them correctly evaluate the split between dehumidification requirements ("latent cooling load") and simple cooling requirements ("sensible cooling load"). And they don't have the knowledge, skill, or training to design and install a system that properly deals with both kinds of loads and does it efficiently.

Yet that's the key to comfort in my climate. Temperature is the only factor a thermometer shows you, but humidity is often the more important factor in the comfort equation, and on many days humidity is the bigger energy load for an air conditioning system. Handle humidity well, and you're on your way to licking the problem. Fail to handle it, and the problem will lick you.

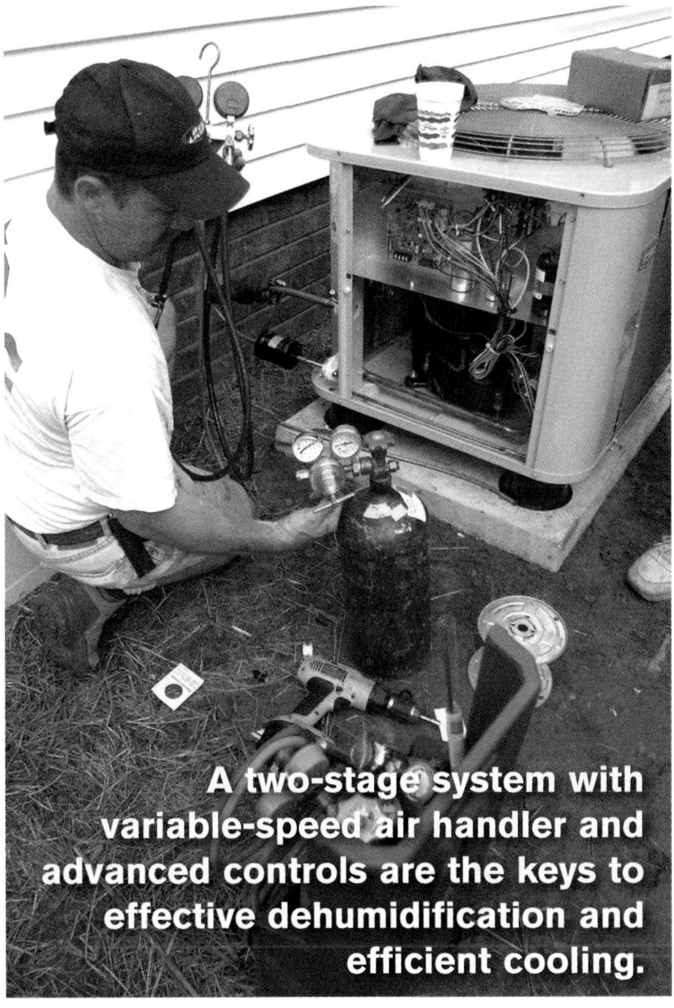

A two-stage system with variable-speed air handler and advanced controls are the keys to effective dehumidification and efficient cooling.

"Temperature is the only factor a thermometer shows you, but humidity is often the more important factor for occupant comfort."

Sensible Versus Latent Heat

Any discussion of air conditioning needs to recognize the two kinds of heat load that affect our indoor comfort level: sensible heat and latent heat. Sensible heat is simply heat that can be sensed by the body and that is easily measured with a thermometer. Latent heat is heat that is added to or subtracted from a substance without changing its temperature. You can boil a gallon of water into room air or pull a gallon of water out of the air with a dehumidifier and not change the room air temperature. But evaporating water into the air nevertheless adds the water's "latent heat of evaporation" to the total heat in the air, and pulling that water back out removes that same amount of latent heat.

Warm air will hold more water vapor than cool air will. That's why we speak of "relative humidity" (RH), not just "humidity." At 100 percent relative humidity, air is saturated and can't hold any more moisture. At 50 percent RH, the air contains only half the amount of moisture it could hold.

Cool air cannot hold as much moisture as hot air. So cooling the air temperature without removing moisture at the same time increases the air's relative humidity. Take a roomful of air at 95°F and 50 percent

RH, for example. If we cool that air down to 75°F but don't remove any moisture, it will end up at 95 percent RH. That air is very near its dew point, the temperature at which the water vapor in the air will begin to condense into liquid water. So you'll see moisture condensing on any cold surface (such as a pitcher of ice water).

Humidity and comfort. When it comes to human comfort, there is a direct relationship between temperature and humidity levels. Scientific studies back up the personal experience of most people: When the air is dry, occupants feel comfortable at a slightly warmer temperature than when the atmosphere is moist. So properly addressing the latent cooling loads allows comfort to be achieved at higher thermostat set points.

During humid conditions, the air conditioner or heat pump has to remove the latent heat load from the space, not just cool the air. That's why you expect to see condensate draining from the air handler or evaporator coil whenever the comfort system is operating.

For every pound of condensed vapor that drains away, 970 Btus of heat are removed from the space. In fact, the dehumidification part of air conditioning accounts for a big part of the system's workload. Evaporation takes a lot of energy, and adds a lot of heat, compared with a simple temperature increase.

Reversing the process, that is, condensing water vapor into liquid water to remove it from the air, takes the equivalent amount of work. For example, to cool the air in a room by 20 degrees, from 95°F to 75°F, we have to remove 5 Btus of sensible heat per pound of air (a pound of air is equivalent to about 12.3 cu. ft.). But pulling enough moisture out of that air to get it back down to its original 50 percent RH requires the removal of an additional 8 Btus of latent heat per pound of air. So on a hot, humid day in a house with a properly sized 5-ton cooling system, 3 tons of that capacity might be working to dehumidify the air, while only 2 tons are working to actually cool it.

The balance between the latent load and the sensible load varies from place to place and from season to season (Figure 14). In Arizona, you may be able to design a system based on peak outdoor temperatures, with no worries about humidity. But in my climate, a system needs to be sized to dehumidify as well as to cool — or better yet, to switch between dehumidification and sensible cooling as needed.

Efficiency Versus Dehumidification

Since the early 1990s, manufacturers have redesigned

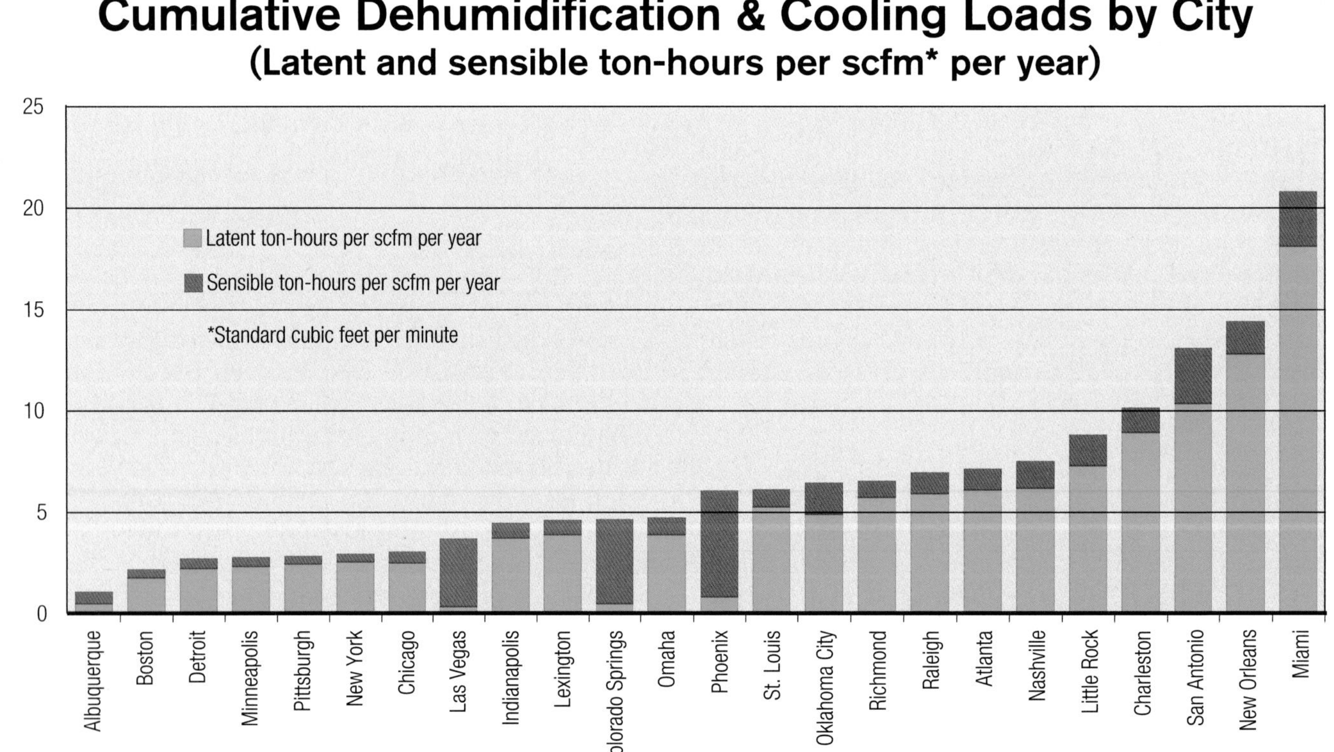

Figure 14. From region to region and season to season, air conditioning systems are asked to handle wide variations in load conditions. This chart compares the balance between sensible and latent loads in a sampling of locations within the United States, on an annual basis. Systems have to meet local needs: Dehumidification requirements are a negligible part of the load in some areas, but are the dominant factor in other locations.

heating and cooling equipment in order to meet tougher energy-efficiency standards. Seasonal Energy Efficiency Ratio (SEER) ratings have increased as a result of these changes. A system manufactured in the early '90s typically had SEER ratings around 8. As of 2006, the minimum rating allowed by law is 13, and for Energy Star rated systems it is 14. Indeed, some manufacturers have exceeded that requirement, earning ratings upward of 18-SEER on their top-performing units.

To achieve these gains, engineers have modified the condensing units (the outdoor coils and compressors, which transfer heat to the outside air when the house is being cooled). Condensers have been redesigned to decrease the head pressure, which reduces the power needed to operate the system. This is accomplished by increasing the condenser coil size, which increases the heat transfer area. Thinner refrigerant tubing that is "rifled" increases refrigerant surface contact and speeds heat transfer. This causes a lower refrigerant saturation temperature, allows for additional "sub-cooling" of the refrigerant, and increases the refrigerant's ability to do work.

The indoor evaporator coil, which cools air in the house, has also been modified. Evaporator coils in high-efficiency units operate at higher saturation temperatures than do the older SEER-8 system coils, resulting in a warmer coil surface contacting the airstream. But a warmer coil reduces the latent capacity of the system, since the coil cannot condense moisture out of the airstream as quickly. This means that longer cycle times are needed to remove the latent load. Air needs to flow over the coil for more minutes per hour to allow time for the moisture to condense on the coil and drain away.

This becomes a critical problem whenever the system has more than the required capacity: Oversized systems will cool the air and satisfy the thermostat before the latent load can be reduced, resulting in high humidity levels in the building. Homeowners end up setting the thermostat to a colder temperature to get the same comfort level that could be obtained at a higher indoor temperature if humidity were lower. And a house that is continuously cool but remains damp is at risk for mold and mildew, causing unpleasant odors, allergic symptoms, and respiratory discomfort for the occupants.

"Oversized systems will cool the air and satisfy the thermostat before the latent load can be reduced, resulting in high humidity levels in the building."

If the system is oversized for peak load conditions, it will fail to dehumidify properly even on the very hottest days. But even systems that are properly sized for the peak load conditions may not dehumidify well on days when temperatures are more moderate but atmospheric humidity remains high. If the system can't adapt to the seasonally changing balance between cooling and dehumidification needs, the thermostat will be satisfied long before the air is sufficiently dry: You'll see a lot of short-cycling, with rapid cooling but poor moisture control. That's the particular problem we face in North Carolina for many months of the year.

Practical New-Tech Solutions

Faced with the combined challenges of efficiency and load balancing, several companies have developed new systems that adjust throughout the day to changing conditions. This new generation of air conditioners is designed to solve the humidity problem while maintaining high operating efficiencies.

Every contractor has his own favorite brand of equipment. I don't have time to baby-sit the systems after installation, so I want to install a product I'm familiar with and whose performance I can predict and rely on. I have developed a preference for Bryant's solution. I know how the Bryant systems perform, how they last, and what they do. Those are the systems I install on a daily basis, and the ones I'm going to discuss for the rest of this article.

These systems have four main elements:

- a two-stage compressor with its own control board in the
- condenser unit
- a variable-speed air handling unit
- electronically controlled zone dampers
- a high-tech circuit-board control module

The control unit manages every aspect of the system: Indoor and outdoor sensors continually monitor air temperature and humidity, and the microprocessors adjust the compressor, fan, and dampers as needed to maintain the desired conditions that are programmed into the control center. When the house needs moderate cooling and a lot of moisture removal, the system can provide that; when there's a need for rapid cooling without extra dehumidification, the system can accomplish that as well.

Two-Speed Condensing Units

It's standard practice to size cooling and heating equipment using the ACCA Manual J method, or with a computer program that implements the Manual J technique. Using climate data appropriate to the geographic location and a description of the building to be cooled, Manual J totals up room by room the maximum heat gains and heat losses the building will experience. The system is then sized so its maximum capacity matches the load predicted during the peak 5 percent of the total cooling hours.

But during the remaining 95 percent of the cooling season, the system's full capacity isn't needed. So manufacturers have developed systems that ramp down to lower speeds to match low-load conditions. Two-speed condensing units for air conditioners and heat pumps are now available in a range of sizes suited to meet most of the load conditions likely to be encountered. Some units, like the Bryant 698B Evolution model (Figure 15), use a single compressor that can run at either high or low speed, while others couple two compressors together in the same refrigerant circuit, using one at a time for low-load conditions and both together to handle maximum-load conditions.

On low speed, a two-speed system operates at 50 percent of rated capacity, but with longer run times than if it were operating at maximum capacity. Given the seasonal and weather conditions typical in my climate, a two-speed system operates on low speed nearly 80 percent of the time.

This has many benefits. The longer run times allow better humidity control and improve comfort by eliminating frequent sharp temperature swings. Operating for more minutes per hour also promotes a continual mixing of the air in the home, which results in more even, consistent temperatures throughout the home's living space. Long, slow running of the compressor also lowers the system's energy consumption and reduces start-and-stop stress on the motors and bearings.

Variable-speed air handlers. Inside the building, most of my systems use the Bryant FV4 air handler (Figure 16), which is designed to partner with the outdoor units I install. Like some other advanced air handlers, the FV4's fan is driven by an electronically commutated motor (ECM), which can precisely adjust the fan speed. Airflows can be custom tailored for each job, and with the sophisticated control system Bryant supplies, motor speeds can change continuously to suit the needs of the moment. ECM motors operate quietly and are highly efficient, typically using 60 to 75 percent less energy than older low-tech models use. The new motors add to the system's installed price, but lower operating costs pay that back in just a few years.

ECM motors can correct for slight resistance in the duct system and for dirty air filters by adjusting the motor speed to maintain optimum operation. The motor's instruments can estimate the static pressure of the duct system on shut down by monitoring the number of revolutions it takes for the motor to come to a complete stop. The program in the motor determines the static pressure of the duct system, then adjusts the motor speed on the next start-up cycle.

During operation, ECM motors can change speed 60 times per second, at the peak of each electrical hertz cycle. They can adjust to lower the airflow and increase latent capacities or to increase the airflow and increase sensible capacities: At slower speeds, the air has longer "dwell time" on the coil and more humidity will condense; at faster speeds, the moving air will give up less moisture but more total heat to the coil. The motors can also be instructed to run continuously at low speed between cooling and heating cycles to

Figure 15. Bryant's top-of-the-line Evolution heat pump has a two-speed compressor controlled by a dedicated circuit board. The compressor experiences fewer on/off cycles than one-speed models, operating at low speed for most of its service hours, and achieves 15-SEER cooling performance with effective dehumidification. Other manufacturers have comparable systems that adjust to low-load or part-load situations.

promote air mixing and to maximize the effect of air cleaners and filters in the duct system. This broad flexibility in fan settings gives the hvac contractor the ability to customize each home's conditions to satisfy different comfort preferences.

Taking advantage of the motor's capabilities, the Bryant system can be set to precondition the cooling coil at initial startup, and to give the fan a two- or three-minute soft "ramp up" to full speed at the start of the cycle and a soft "ramp down" at the end. That way, the system provides a slow, quiet inflow of air at a comfortable temperature, instead of coming on each time with a sudden blast of unconditioned air that has been sitting in the ducts.

Zone dampers. I do a lot of zoning with my systems. Zoning is something of an art, and ten different contractors could tell you ten different ways to do it. Sometimes different parts of the house need their own independent systems, each with its own condenser, air handler, and controls. But in typical cases, I prefer to install a single air handler and duct system and to divide up the zones using controllable dampers in my ductwork (Figure 17). For the house shown in these pictures, I used zone dampers to create two zones, one for upstairs and one for downstairs. The dampers are controlled by the same electronic module that controls the condenser and the air handler. The system can provide different humidity levels and temperatures in each zone; and it can dehumidify, cool, or heat one zone at a time if need be.

Advanced Controls

A device called the "user interface" (Figure 18) is the brain center of the zone system: It continually senses temperatures in the home, checks the outdoor temperatures, and tells the control boards in the air handler and the condenser unit what to do. It will also talk to the zone dampers, opening and closing them as needed to condition each of the home's various zones.

The Bryant board I use can handle any combination of residential heating and cooling. It can control heat pumps, gas furnaces coupled with central air conditioning, or gas furnaces with piggyback heat pumps. It can run variable-speed systems or two-speed systems and is capable of independently managing as many as eight zones.

The Bryant controller will work with any brand of equipment, from any manufacturer. I use it with virtually every system I install. I am qualified to sell other brands of control unit, but this is the most flexible and capable zone-control product I have ever used.

The thermostat for this device has a seven-day independent control program. You can program it for four different periods per day, per zone. When I install a system, I program the boards on the equipment, I talk to the homeowners about what conditions they want in the home, and I program the user interface for the customer. Once everything is set up, no one has to touch it again.

This component is one of the keys to the Bryant

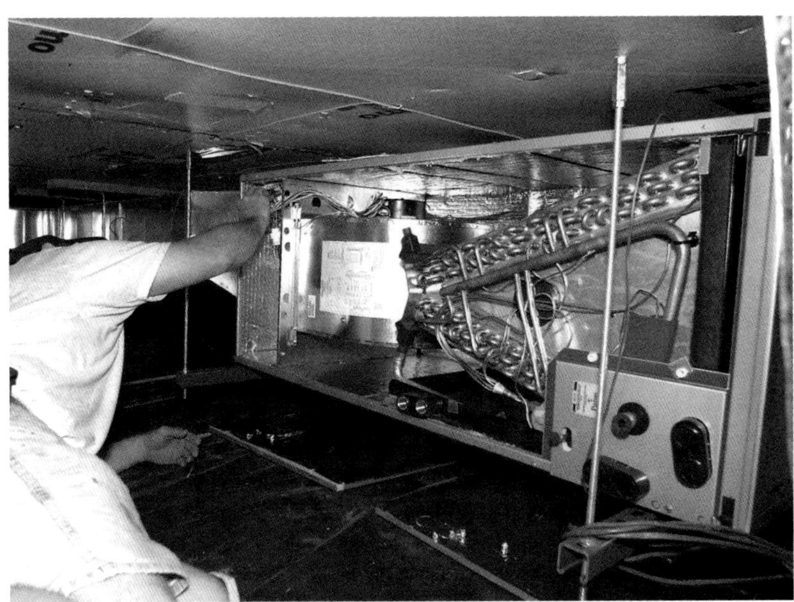

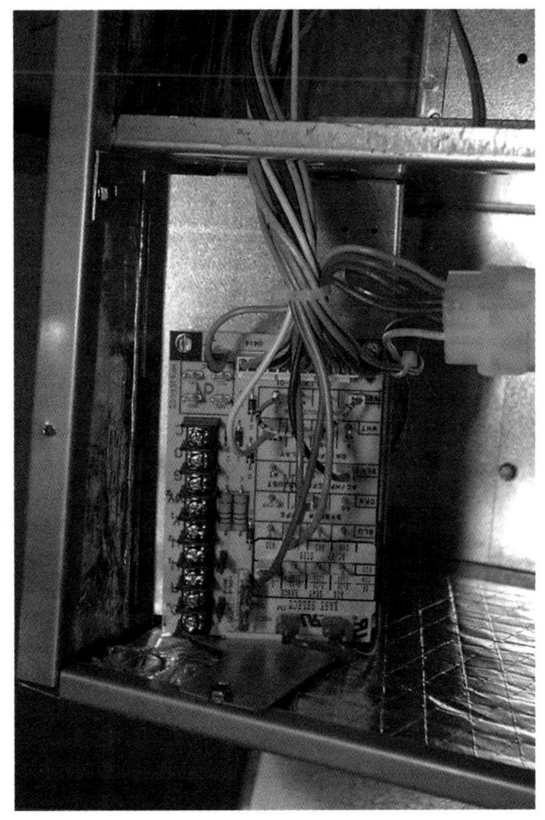

Figure 16. Inside the house, the author installs a variable-speed air handler that is matched to the outdoor condenser. Controlled by advanced electronic circuitry, the air handler's motor can continually adjust to changing loads, ramp up and down gradually as needed, and even sense and adjust to changes in static pressure in the duct system.

system's effective humidity control. A typical thermostat senses room temperature and initiates a call for cooling when the temperature rises. But the Bryant Thermidistat, matched with an air handler equipped with a variable-speed blower, offers an option for those times when it is cool in the home but the humidity is high, causing that "sticky" feeling.

This control can be set to maintain humidity levels in the cooling mode as low as 50 percent RH. If the humidity level rises in the home, the control initiates a call for cooling. During the dehumidification mode, the indoor blower speed is reduced approximately 40 percent. This allows the evaporator coil to become much colder than normal; meanwhile, lower airflow velocity allows the air to maintain contact with the coil longer, allowing the cold coil to wring the humidity from the air. This drastically increases the latent capacity of the comfort system without overcooling the structure.

A Case Study

To monitor how the system works, I installed data-logging devices in one home where conditions were particularly severe. This house was built on totally saturated soil, downhill from a pond. To provide accessibility, the floors had been set level with the

Figure 17. The author likes to zone heat pump or air conditioner setups using zone dampers within the ductwork, controlled by the same master circuit board that manages other aspects of the system. If one zone requires more or less cooling or dehumidification, the master controller can address that zone's needs independently of other zones.

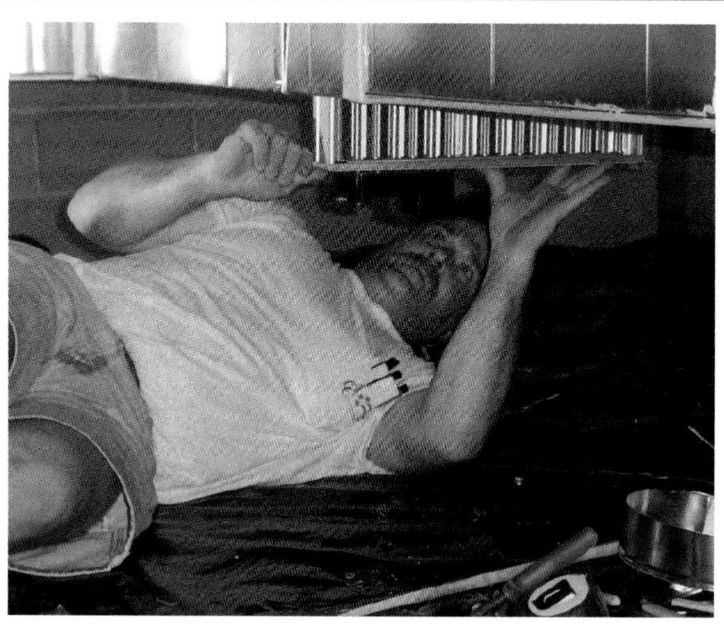

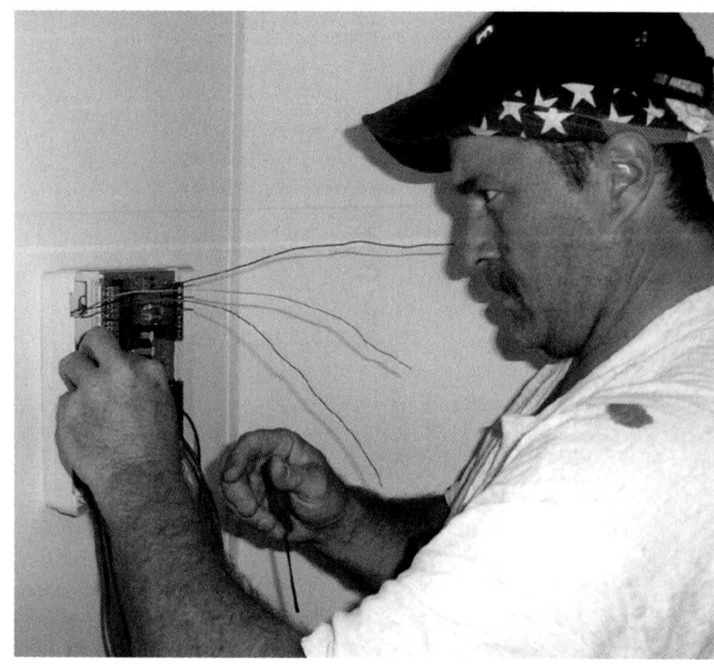

Figure 18. The "user interface" circuit board is the brain of the comfort system. It continually adjusts the air handler, outdoor heat pump, and zone dampers based on sensor input and its programmed settings. The board shown (right), a Bryant Evolution control, is capable of managing a wide variety of mechanical systems and can serve as many as eight independent zones.

outdoor grade. During construction, the excavation had to be continuously pumped in order to stay dry enough for the foundation stemwalls to be built and for concrete to be placed for a crawlspace slab.

Unfortunately, no vapor barrier was installed under the crawlspace slab for this house, and the concrete constantly wicks moisture into the house from the saturated soil beneath it. My system was designed according to Manual J standards, with no allowance made for this extreme and unusual moisture source. But the data I collected show that the system I installed, which is much like the one I've described in this story, has been able to maintain the exact design conditions I set it up for: 75°F temperature and 50 percent RH, with variation of no more than one degree or 5 percent RH.

While the new system provided excellent comfort for the occupants, the data I collected indicated that the system's efficiency was lowered by the excessive humidity levels in the house. The electrical bills for running the system were somewhat higher than I would have expected if the house had not had this type of moisture problem. In houses that have mainly atmospheric humidity to contend with, my systems are typically very economical to operate.

Workmanship Crucial to Performance

Installation is the critical part of any comfort system. You can go out and buy the best system on the market, but if it's not properly installed, it won't do the job. I can't cover every aspect of workmanship in one short article, but let's take a look at a few important details.

In Figure 19, I'm brazing a joint in a refrigerant line as I attach a refrigerant dryer to the line. The dryer's purpose is to clear oxidation and moisture out of the refrigerant. These systems use a lubricant that is particularly vulnerable to moisture; if the line isn't kept dry, there's likely to be corrosion and excessive wear.

The refrigerant dryer is a mandated standard item that has to be installed on every new system. Any time the line is opened for repair or modification, the dryer should also be replaced. What's not standard, however, is the solder I'm using to braze the tubing joints. I like to use a 15 percent silver formula, because it is the most compatible formula with the copper in the lines. Less expensive phosphorus-based formulas are more commonly used, but they don't provide the strength and durability of the 15 percent silver joints. It's not critical in this particular case, but when we place copper lines underground, as I do for some of my geothermal installations, it's very important.

When I braze a joint, I clamp a set of tubing cutters onto the line to hold the plastic insulation back from the area where I'm applying heat. That keeps the insulation from melting. I've also wrapped the valve in a wet rag, to keep it cool while I apply my torch to the joint and melt the brazing compound. When the joint has cooled, I'll take the cutter and the rag off and put the insulation back in place.

Figure 20 shows us flowing nitrogen through our refrigerant loops to clear out any oxygen or water vapor before we load the system with refrigerant. Not all contractors do this, but it's a good idea — it eliminates the moisture and oxidation that can cause corrosion, the same contaminants that the refrigerant dryer is supposed to help protect against.

Ductwork

Proper duct installation is key. We use only metal ductwork— no fiberglass duct board or flexible duct. We also seal every duct joint with mastic (Figure 21). When ducts are leaky, the losses don't occur just when the system is running. Air never stops moving — you

Figure 19. Careful installation work is key to any system's success. Here, the author makes a brazed joint in a copper refrigerant line as he installs a refrigerant dryer that will protect the system against moisture and corrosion.

have leaks when the system is on and leaks when it's off. It's a continuous loss, not a momentary one. Air and moisture getting into the duct system cost money, stress the system, and contribute to all kinds of problems. Careful duct-sealing is well worth the trouble.

Figure 20. Before filling the system with refrigerant, the author purges the loops with nitrogen to eliminate moisture and oxygen that could corrode refrigerant lines and mechanical components.

Figure 21. Thorough sealing of all duct joints is a critical quality-control step. Leaks in the ductwork allow moisture into the airstream, which will decrease system efficiency and may lead to condensation and mold growth inside the ducts. Applying sealant mastic with brushes or gloved hands is the preferred method for achieving airtight ductwork.

Duct sizing and layout are also critical to system performance. Here are a few key points:

- Ducts should be well supported.
- Runs should be kept as straight as possible.
- Sweeping curves are better than sharp bends.
- Ducts should be insulated to R-6 or more.

All of these quality details help the system perform effectively and reliably. But providing first-rate comfort along with high efficiency is about more than workmanship — it starts with good design. If your hvac contractor makes a careful, room-by-room estimate of the sensible and latent loads for the particular house, and if he chooses equipment of the right capacity that can adjust to a changing balance between those loads, you're well on your way to meeting the homeowner's needs.

***Dwayne Akers** owns and operates Akers Custom Comfort, Inc., a residential and commercial hvac installation and service contractor in Stokesdale, N.C.*

Chapter 9

HYDRONIC HEATING SYSTEMS

- Installing an Efficient Oil-Fired Boiler
- Hydro-Air Heating Options
- Retrofitting High-Tech Heating and Ventilation

Installing an Efficient Oil-Fired Boiler

by Cary White

My small plumbing and heating company recently replaced a client's inefficient 25-year-old combination wood-and-oil boiler with an efficient new Buderus oil boiler. Oil was the obvious choice of fuel. The homeowners no longer wanted to deal with firewood, and natural gas isn't available in the area of Vermont where they live. And propane — though available — is prohibitively expensive.

After choosing oil, we still had one important choice to make: Did it make sense to go all the way and put in an ultra-high-efficiency condensing boiler, or should we opt for a slightly less efficient noncondensing version?

A noncondensing boiler was the best choice on this job despite its slightly lower efficiency versus a condensing unit.

Condensing vs. Noncondensing Boilers

Going for maximum efficiency offered one substantial carrot: a $1,500 federal tax credit available at the time the unit was installed in 2010. The credit applied only to systems with an AFUE rating of 90 percent or more. (The AFUE — or annual fuel utilization efficiency — of a given fuel-burning appliance represents the average amount of useful heat delivered relative to the amount of fuel used over the course of a heating season. A boiler with a 90 percent AFUE, for example, delivers 90 percent of the value of the fuel as heat, while venting the remaining 10 percent to the outdoors.) Although the tax credits aren't specifically reserved for condensing appliances, only condensing appliances have so far been able to meet the AFUE threshold. An average modern oil boiler, by comparison, will typically have an AFUE of around 85 percent.

Tapping latent heat. What makes condensing appliances so efficient? Combustion gases from any source contain a certain amount of water vapor. As the gas cools, that vapor eventually condenses, changing back to liquid form. And when the vapor condenses, the gas gives off a certain amount of latent heat, which is ordinarily lost to the atmosphere.

A condensing boiler, however, is designed to make use of that latent heat by sending the flue gases through a secondary heat exchanger before they're vented to the outdoors. Here, the hot flue gases are used to preheat water returning to the boiler. As the gases give up their heat to the return water, the water vapor they contain condenses inside the heat exchanger, surrendering a substantial amount of useful additional heat.

The downside of efficiency. A complicating factor in all this is that the condensate has to be disposed of somehow, usually by routing it to an existing sewer or septic system. Ideally, this can be done with a simple gravity line, but many applications will require a condensate pump. Either way, it's important to protect the condensate line from freezing. The condensate is also fairly acidic, with a pH in the 3 to 4 range, which is roughly comparable to that of orange juice. To ensure that the condensate won't corrode metallic fittings downstream, some local codes require passing it through a neutralizer containing granular calcium carbonate or a similar material to raise its pH before discharge.

Unlike a conventional boiler, a condensing boiler requires direct venting, typically through a sidewall. But we've found that direct-vented condensing boilers can have lockout issues in windy locations. Soot staining — caused by dirty fuel or lack of maintenance —

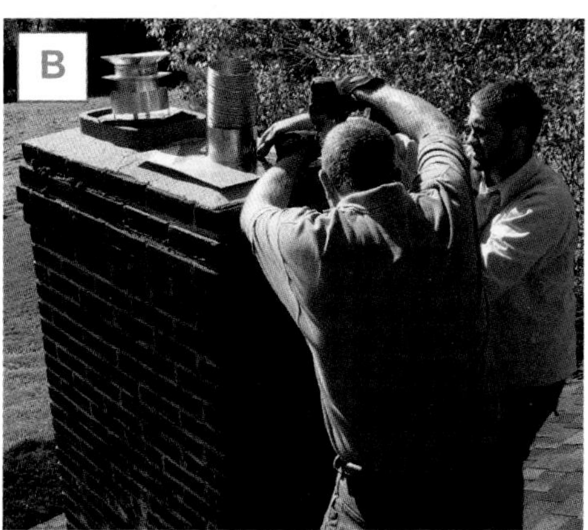

Figure 1. The Buderus G125BE noncondensing boiler can be vented either horizontally or vertically but needs a maximum 5-inch-diameter chimney liner when vented into an oversized masonry chimney flue (A). At the top, the liner's cap is set in sealant and screwed in place with masonry screws (B). At the base, the author packs the cavity between the new liner and old flue with mineral wool insulation and seals the opening with refractory cement (C).

can also be a problem, particularly in homes with natural wood siding, which can be very difficult to clean. Finally, flue gases produced by an oil burner contain less water vapor — and, therefore, less latent heat — than flue gases from a gas burner, so efficiency gains are smaller.

Making the right choice. We install and service both condensing and noncondensing versions of Buderus' new high-efficiency/low-emissions oil boiler — the condensing GB125BE and the noncondensing G125BE. The installed cost of the condensing boiler, with its 93.4 percent AFUE rating, would be about $11,300 on this job (or $9,800 after the $1,500 tax credit), compared with $9,500 for the noncondensing boiler, which has an AFUE of 89 percent. Although the difference in installed cost was fairly small, so was the 4.4 percentage-point difference between the efficiencies of the two boilers.

Given the home's existing fin tube radiators (condensing boilers work best with low-temperature heat sources, such as radiant floors) and windy location (which would have made sidewall venting problematic), we concluded that the noncondensing boiler was the way to go.

Sizing and Installing the Flue Liner and Boiler

My clients' 2,100-square-foot home was typical of those built in this area in the 1980s, with 2x4 walls, clear insulated glass windows, and moderate levels of insulation in the walls and attic. In new construction, I'd normally use ACCA (Air Conditioning Contractors of America) Manual J to calculate heat loss and size the boiler. But for this home, the largest 116,000-Btu version of the G125BE boiler closely matched the size of the existing Tarm wood/oil boiler. Since I knew the owners might add on to the house in the future, downsizing didn't make sense.

Flue requirements. The noncondensing Buderus boiler can be vented directly to a lined masonry chimney with a correctly sized flue. But because the existing chimney flue was oversized, we installed a 5-inch-diameter stainless steel chimney liner to guarantee a good draft and avoid potential corrosion problems from any flue gases condensing inside the chimney (Figure 1). Installing the liner accounted for about $1,300 of the project's overall cost. To help ensure proper draft, the exhaust flue is fitted with a barometric damper.

Higher efficiency, lower emissions. Even though the Buderus is a new boiler in the U.S., we're comfortable recommending it because of its 10-year track record in Europe, where fuel costs are high and emissions standards are stringent. It's equipped with a low-NOx (nitrogen oxide) burner designed to operate at a lower temperature than conventional burners, and features a ceramic burner tube in the combustion chamber (Figure 2). As it heats up during combustion, the burner tube recirculates flue gases through the burner until the vaporized fuel is completely consumed, leading to improved fuel efficiency and a decrease in smog-producing NOx emissions.

After the initial burn, the 800°F flue gases exiting the burner tube and combustion chamber make two additional passes through the center of the boiler. By the time the gases exit the rear of the boiler, baffle plates have slowed them down and cooled them to around 300°F. The smooth-wall design of the heat exchanger makes this boiler very easy to clean.

Modulating control. In most conventional boilers, a simple aquastat turns on the boiler when there's a call for heat or hot water. That causes the burner to fire until the boiler's internal temperature reaches 180°F, regardless of the season or weather. But the Buderus boiler has a remote sensor integrated with an electronic controller that takes outdoor temperatures into account when regulating the temperature of the boiler water (Figure 3).

In moderate conditions, when the boiler doesn't need to heat 6 or 7 gallons of water all the way up to 180°F to maintain the house at a comfortable temperature, the boiler may stop firing at only 130°F or 140°F. The Logamatic controller, as Buderus calls it, also manages the system's new indirect domestic hot-water tank. If my clients ever decide to upgrade, the controller can integrate solar panels or radiant heating into the system, too.

Fuel and Combustion Air

Buderus has incorporated some features that also help address the declining fuel-oil quality issues we've been noticing over the past year or so. In particular, refineries seem to be leaving more impurities in #2 heating oil, which can lead to clogged nozzles and filters and lower efficiency. I've heard that some of this has to do with the growth of a variety of bacteria that can live in fuel tanks. Whether that's true or not I can't say — I'm an hvac guy, not a microbiologist — but it makes sense, because I've noticed that fuel problems seem to be most common in systems with outdoor storage tanks warmed by the sun.

Bubbles and heavies. In addition to the standard tank prefilter, which catches most of the heavy particles in the fuel, the boiler comes equipped with a Tigerloop deaerator (www.westwoodproducts.com).

Figure 2. A perforated ceramic tube inside the cast-iron combustion chamber allows gases to recirculate past the burner before exiting the flue, resulting in more complete combustion — and boosting the boiler's efficiency rating.

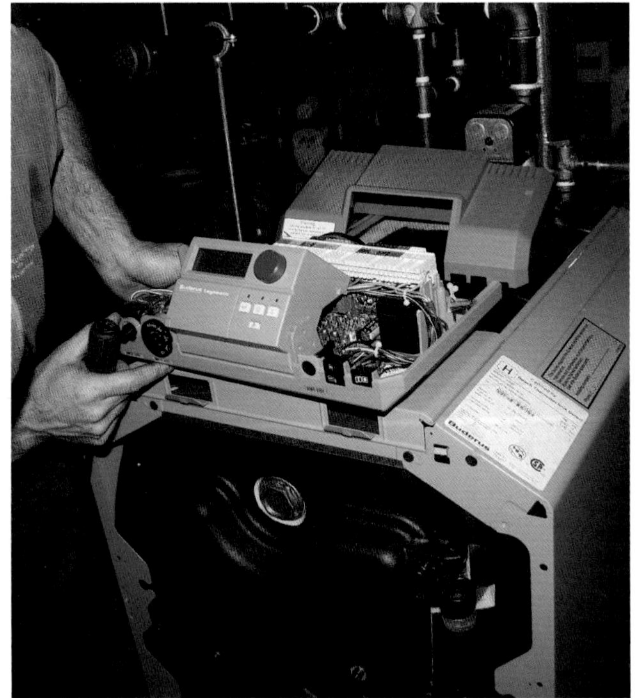

Figure 3. The boiler is controlled by a Logamatic 2107 microprocessor connected to an outdoor air temperature sensor, which modulates the boiler's firing temperature based on demand and weather conditions.

The deaerator has a secondary 10-micron filter that removes tiny air and gas bubbles that can interfere with combustion (Figure 4). There's also a fuel-line preheater, basically a low-wattage resistance element that briefly turns on when there's an initial call for heat, warming oil in the nozzle line. The burner operates more efficiently because it's using warm, clean oil instead of cold or dirty oil.

Bringing in outside air. Although Buderus recommends an outside air source for the G125BE, it's not strictly required. Given the age and construction of the home we were working in, it would not have been unreasonable to draw combustion air from inside the living space and count on air leaks in the building envelope to provide makeup air. But doing so would have been short-sighted: If the homeowner (or a future owner) were to significantly tighten things up at a later date, t he boiler could find itself starved for air.

With that scenario in mind, we installed a combustion air system using a screened intake air hood from Field Controls (www.fieldcontrols.com) and 4-inch-diameter 30-gauge galvanized steel pipe. The pipe connects to a termination collar on the back of the boiler (Figure 5). Buderus has specific clearance guidelines for the wall termination, but the basic rule of thumb is not to place it facing the prevailing wind (though with vertical rather than sidewall venting,

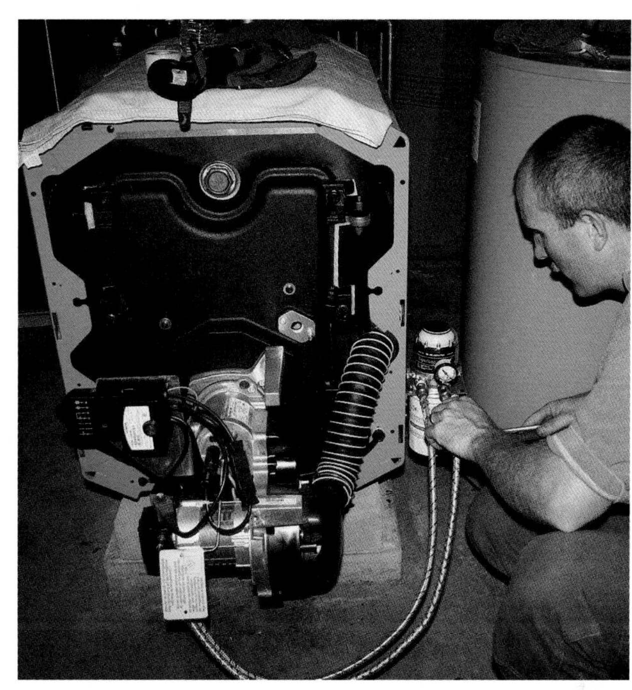

Figure 4. To provide warm, clean fuel for the burner, the boiler is equipped with a fuel line preheater and a 10-micron filter and deaerator, which removes air and gas bubbles in the fuel oil that can interfere with combustion.

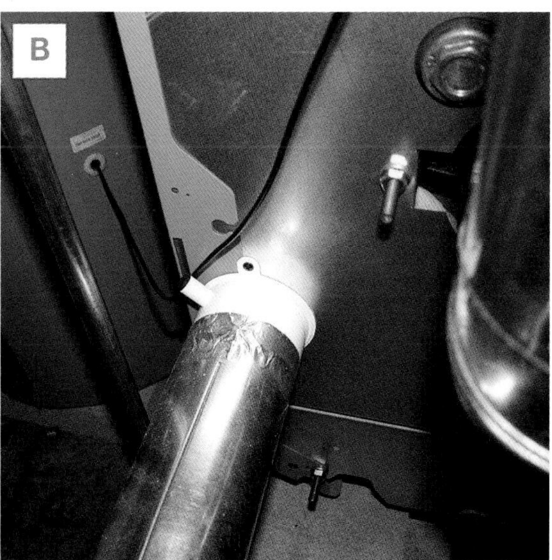

Figure 5. Outside combustion air flows through flexible metal duct (A) and 4-inch-diameter rigid duct to the rear of the boiler (B). The screened air-inlet fitting on the outside wall is protected by a metal cap (C).

Figure 6. As part of the system upgrade, the author installed new circulator pumps and expansion tanks (left) and an indirect-fired domestic hot-water storage tank (above).

this isn't as critical).

Cold air can cause some burners to operate at less than maximum efficiency, so many boilers require tempered combustion air. But because of the design of the low-NOx burner, this makeup air system doesn't require the vacuum relief valve we usually install to provide it. Valves are typically located as close to the wall termination as possible but inside the conditioned space, and they open partway in very cold conditions, allowing warm inside air to mix with cold outside air. If the wall termination gets blocked for any reason, the valve allows the boiler to draw combustion air completely from inside the basement. Since this system doesn't have that valve, we made it a point to remind the homeowner to keep the intake air hood clear of drifting snow.

Evaluating Performance

Because the Buderus boiler hasn't been in operation for a complete heating season yet, it's hard to predict how my clients' energy bills will compare with the ones they had under their old system. The old boiler had a tankless coil for domestic hot water — which is an energy hog during the warm months — so we replaced it with a new indirect-fired DHW tank (Figure 6). While we were at it, we also replaced the circulator pump, zone valves, and expansion tanks.

Based just on the difference in AFUE ratings, fuel consumption should be about 15 percent less annually — but AFUE ratings don't reflect the additional energy savings achieved by the Logamatic control and outdoor reset. I expect the actual annual fuel savings to be much closer to 30 percent.

Cary White is a plumbing and heating contractor with PerfectTemp in Jeffersonville, Vt.

Hydro-Air Heating Options

by Rick Groff

Choosing a heating system for a home is usually a process of balancing cost, comfort, and convenience. As an hvac contractor in Pennsylvania, I've seen a recent trend toward a unique type of hot water heating system called hydro-air. Hydro-air systems transfer heat from water to air, but they use a fan-coil heat exchanger instead of the familiar fin-tube or cast-iron baseboards. The warmed air is then distributed through traditional ductwork.

Hydro-air technology has been used for years in commercial and industrial applications with either hot water or steam as the heat source. Its popularity in the residential market is rising because it offers excellent comfort and versatility. When selling a client on the idea of a hydro-air system, I sometimes need to overcome their preconceived notion of a monster boiler lurking in the basement, feeding hot water to standing radiators. Improvements in boilers and heat exchangers have drastically enhanced operational efficiency, reliability, and control. Huge strides have also been made in how the heated water is used once it leaves the boiler, including sophisticated microprocessor controls, flexible radiant tubing, manifolds, mixing valves, indirect-fired water heaters, and a seemingly endless variety of water-to-air heat exchanger options.

A system we installed recently provides a good example of the flexibility offered by today's hot water systems. My involvement began when a general contractor asked me to recommend a mechanical system for a custom home he was going to build in Berks County, Pa. The client wanted all aspects of the house — frame, windows, insulation, and hvac system — to be state of the art. The 5,000-square-foot two-story residence, which would be built with 6-inch steel studs filled with Icynene insulation and clad with a brick veneer, was to be sited in an unsheltered setting with a design temperature of 0°F.

The client wanted radiant floor heat, but was only willing to pay for it in selected rooms. We designed a system that used a single boiler to provide heat to a radiant slab on the first floor and a forced hot air system on the second. The boiler also heated water for an indirect-fired domestic hot water heater (Figure 7). The heating load required 15 Btu per square foot to maintain a 70°F interior temperature when the outside temperature was 0°F. This isn't an abnormally low heating requirement, but it's pretty efficient, even for a well-insulated building with a low infiltration rate.

Where Radiant Slabs Fall Short

Even when cost isn't an issue, I usually recommend against using radiant heat in bedrooms, especially those on the second floor. That's because bedroom

For climates that require both heating and cooling, hybrid systems offer great comfort and flexibility.

floors are likely to be covered with plush carpeting and thick padding, whose high R-value resists heat transfer from a radiant loop. In addition, bedrooms are often filled with furniture — beds, dressers, nightstands, and so on — that limits the efficiency of floor heat.

What's more, many people enjoy a somewhat cooler bedroom. Since your head is always the warmest part of your body, you feel more comfortable if your head is surrounded by cooler air than the rest of your body. Large beds with thick covers that drop to the floor can trap a significant amount of the heat emitted from a radiant floor. Since this heat can't escape to warm the air, it may cause the bed to be warmer than is comfortable.

For these reasons, I rarely install radiant heating in bedrooms. I often install baseboard heat with separate thermostats in these areas. But many customers dislike the appearance of baseboard; plus, baseboard units may hinder future changes in room layouts.

That's where the hydro-air option comes in. This technique uses the same ductwork as the cooling system, but the heat comes from the boiler. A separately zoned circuit is piped from the boiler to a fan-coil unit in the air handler, which transfers heat from the boiler water to the cooler house air. Typically, water leaves the boiler at 180°F and returns from the coil to the boiler at about 160°.

Hydro-air systems can be used for entire homes as well. Zoning can be achieved by installing multiple systems, as we did here, or by using one system with dampered ductwork. Hydro-air also works great as a retrofit for an expired heat pump, and it generally supplies greater comfort at lower operating cost during heating months.

Sizing the Water Coil

Hot water coils come in varying sizes and must be selected to meet specific heating requirements. To size coils, you need to know the exact heat loss of the area being heated, the temperature of the water coming out of the boiler, and the airflow of the system in cubic feet per minute (cfm). It's also important to calculate how much heat the ductwork loses during severe weather conditions, as well as the flow rate of the water or glycol through the coil.

Some air handlers come with built-in hot water coils. These work well as long as they have the proper capacity, but they should also fit in with the overall design of the system. Built-in coils are usually small and have high friction factors. They work fine when trunk lines are large and duct runs are of moderate length, but they can restrict airflow when runs are long and trunk lines are small. We prefer to use separate components, because it allows us to select air coils that meet the specific requirements of the job. For example, if the duct system is long and stretched out, we use a less-restrictive coil with more square inches of surface area and fewer rows of fins (Figure 8).

For this job, we used a Rheem air handler mounted with a Rheem 69,000 Btu (at 1,450 cfm) hot-water coil. A Burnham PV-205-WNI LP-gas-fired boiler supplies heat to the coil and to a Burnham Alliance indirect-fired domestic water heater.

Sizing the Circulator

I usually figure on 4 gallons per minute (gpm), a standard circulator pump, and ¾-inch copper tubing with a 100-foot total *equivalent piping length.* ("Equivalent piping length" is the length of straight pipe plus added length to account for the pressure losses caused by bends and other fittings. If you use smaller tubing or make long pipe runs with a large number of bends, you may need a more powerful circulator.) The amount of *head* (the vertical distance to the air handler) and the type of fluid in the system can also affect circulator requirements. When in doubt, consult a chart or call the pump manufacturer. We generally use

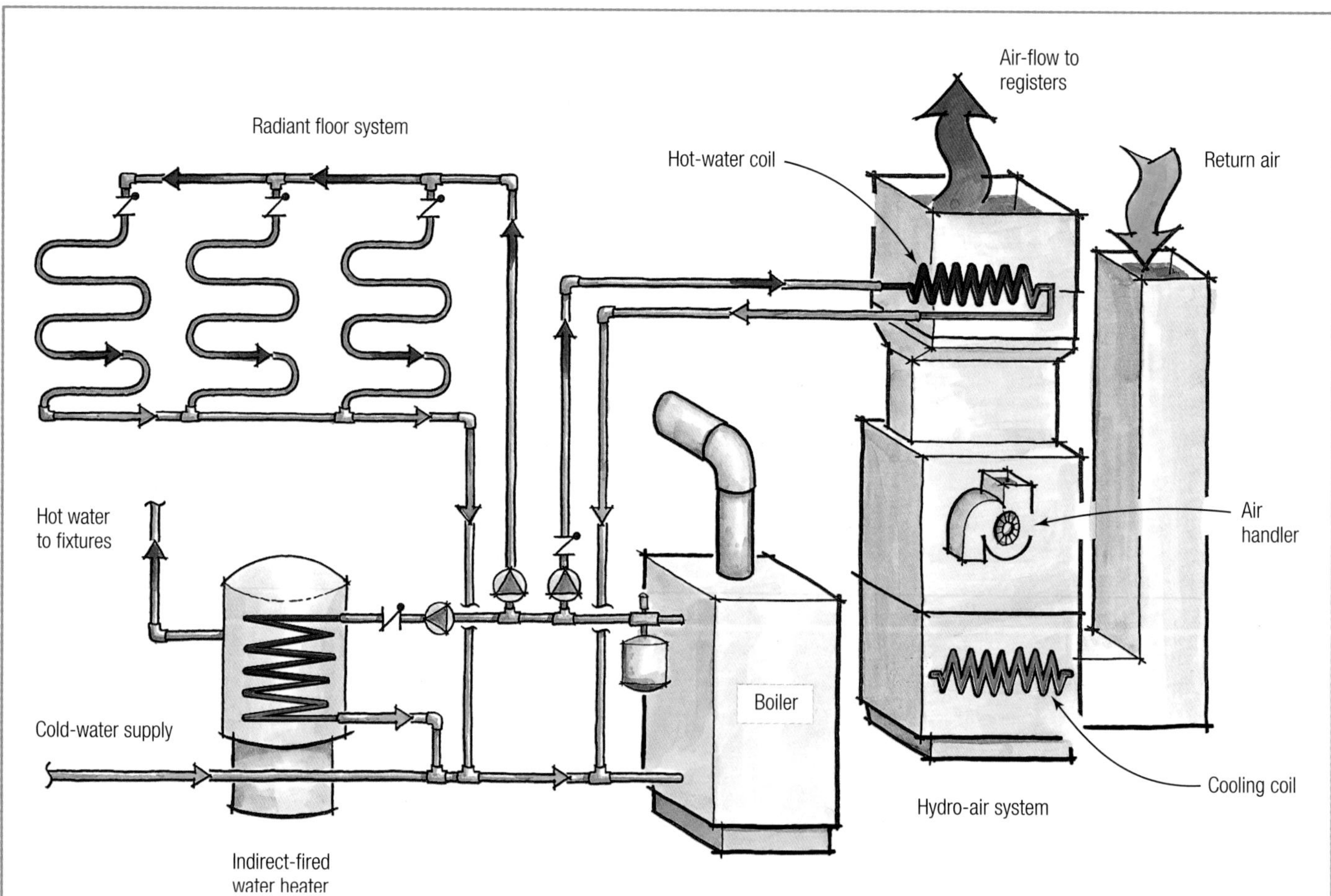

Figure 7. A hydro-air system provides the most versatility for custom homes in climates where both heating and cooling are needed. Using a boiler allows for radiant floor heat in some zones, while the heating coil, mounted to the top of the air handler, is able to share the air-conditioning ductwork. The boiler also provides domestic hot water.

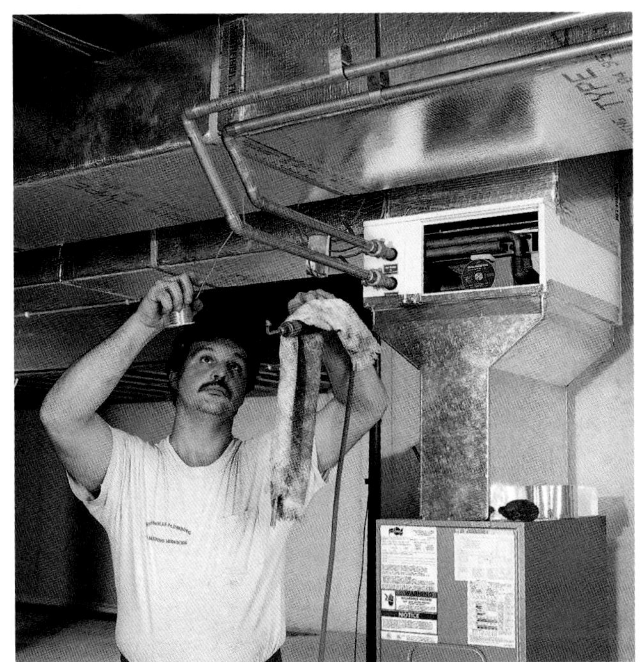

Figure 8. An hvac mechanic solders the hot water supply and return lines at the heating coil. The author prefers separate heating coils to built-in units, because they allow for more accurate sizing.

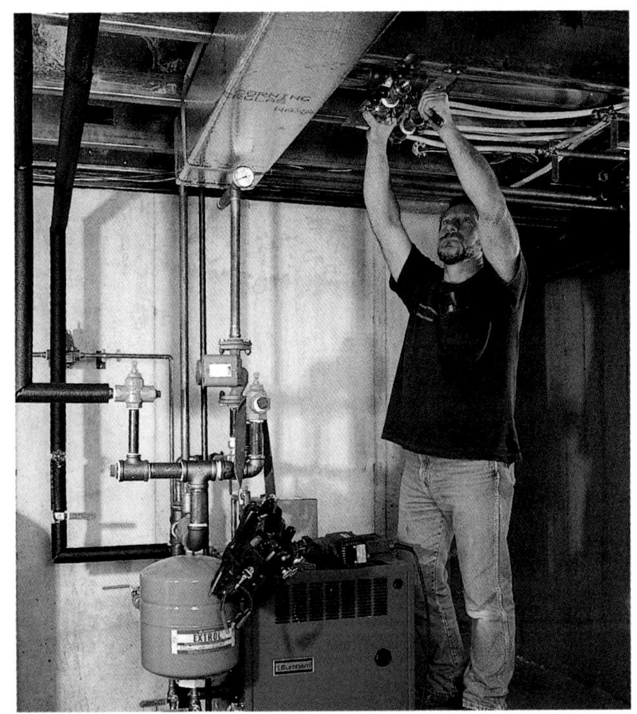

Figure 9. A mechanic connects floor manifolds to the PEX tubing that supplies heat to the slab on the first floor.

circulators made by Bell and Gosset, Jaco, or Grundfos. I prefer copper tubing because it makes for a professional-looking installation, but there's no reason not to use the new high-temperature PEX tubing.

Locating the Air Handler

Most contractors installing a hydro-air system would put the air handler for the second floor in the attic, because it's cheaper to install the air handler close to the area it supplies. Duct runs are shorter, and it takes less labor to put diffusers in the ceiling than it does to run ducts up or down stud bays. It's hard to argue with this reasoning if the bid is being awarded on price alone.

If a hydro-air system is installed in the attic, however, the liquid in it might freeze. To prevent this, contractors put a 50 percent glycol (a nontoxic antifreeze) solution in the water. Treating the entire boiler system makes for service headaches, so we only treat the portion that's susceptible to freezing. One way to do this is to use a liquid-to-liquid heat exchanger to transfer heat from the boiler water to the glycol solution, which is then pumped to the hot water coil in the air handler. Water for the radiant part of the system is unaffected, because it comes straight out of the boiler (Figure 9). Another option is to use a boiler that has a tankless coil. Typically, this coil is used to heat domestic hot water, but it can also be used to heat the glycol, provided there is enough capacity at the expected flow rate. Glycol is more viscous than water, so it's important to size piping with higher friction factors in mind. We haven't had problems using glycol, but then we always allow a lot of latitude on our piping jobs.

On the Berks County project, we decided to place the hydro-air system in the basement. The longer duct runs took more man-hours to install, but over time, energy consumption is lower when ducts run through 55°F basement air and conditioned wall cavities. Around here, the attic temperature in a well-insulated house might be anywhere from 0°F to 120°F, creating substantial heating and cooling duct losses when the system is installed in the attic. In addition, the building has better thermal integrity if there aren't any penetrations in the ceiling, which is exactly where diffusers are placed in the typical attic installation.

It also takes fewer labor hours to maintain equipment that's accessible, and air handlers that are jammed in closets or up in the attic are hard to get at. Invariably, the closet with the tiny access panel to the attic is jammed with off-season clothing. The service person might be thin enough to fit through it, but what about replacement parts?

An added bonus of placing equipment in the basement is that homeowners are less likely to hear it running, especially when they're trying to sleep in second-floor bedrooms. And there's no possibility that a leak in a glycol line or condensate drain will damage the ceiling.

Richard Groff *is one of the owners of Neffsville Plumbing and Heating Services in Lancaster, Pa. Photos by John Herr.*

Retrofitting High-Tech Heating and Ventilation

by Matt Golden and Adam Winter

As home performance contractors, we provide energy audits and a range of related services, such as air sealing, insulation, and hvac work. When we inspect existing homes, we usually find heating appliances that vary in age and efficiency and were never designed to work as a system. Recently we replaced the equipment in just such a home in San Francisco; we installed a new energy-efficient system that provides heat, hot water, and heat-recovery ventilation.

The 1,600-square-foot main floor of the house had been remodeled several years before, and at that time the furnace and ductwork were replaced. Despite the new equipment, the owners still had high utility bills, uneven heat distribution, and poor indoor air quality. When they decided to convert an unused ground-level basement into 800 square feet of additional living space, they contacted us to address the shortcomings of the heating system.

Our inspection uncovered a number of problems. For starters, the 100,000-Btu forced-air gas furnace was greatly oversized, even for the newly enlarged living area. The ductwork was also improperly sized and poorly sealed against air leakage. Domestic hot water came from an old, inefficient gas water heater.

Powered by solar collectors and a condensing gas boiler, this hydro-air system provides space heating, hot water, and fresh air from an integrated HRV.

Design Goals

After explaining the shortcomings of the existing equipment to the clients, we talked with them about their goals. They hoped to reduce the energy they consumed while increasing the home's comfort. With three young children, they were particularly concerned about indoor air quality.

We recommended replacing the existing equipment with a combined hydronic system, in which the same heat source — usually a boiler — provides both domestic hot water and space heating. The home would continue to have forced-air heating, but instead of the one zone there would be three; this would allow the family to selectively heat different areas. To improve indoor air quality, we would install mechanical ventilation and a whole-house air cleaner. The equipment would go in the garage, on the other side of the wall from the new living space.

The homeowners planned to install a photovoltaic system as well, so they asked about solar water heating. We explained that solar thermal collectors could supply a portion of their needs but the home would need a boiler as a backup heat source.

The system we designed relies on roof-mounted solar collectors and a small gas-fired boiler to heat the water in an insulated storage tank (Figure 10). Domestic hot water is drawn directly from the tank; space heating is provided by circulating hot water from the tank through a liquid-to-air heat exchanger inside a hydronic air handler.

Why Combined Hydronic?

We recommend combined hydronic systems for a couple of reasons: Replacing two combustion appliances with a single efficient boiler usually results in fuel savings, and hydronic systems work well with zoned forced-air heat. Because the stored hot water serves as a buffer against peak demand, the boiler can be smaller than it might otherwise be.

The boiler fires only when the water in the tank falls

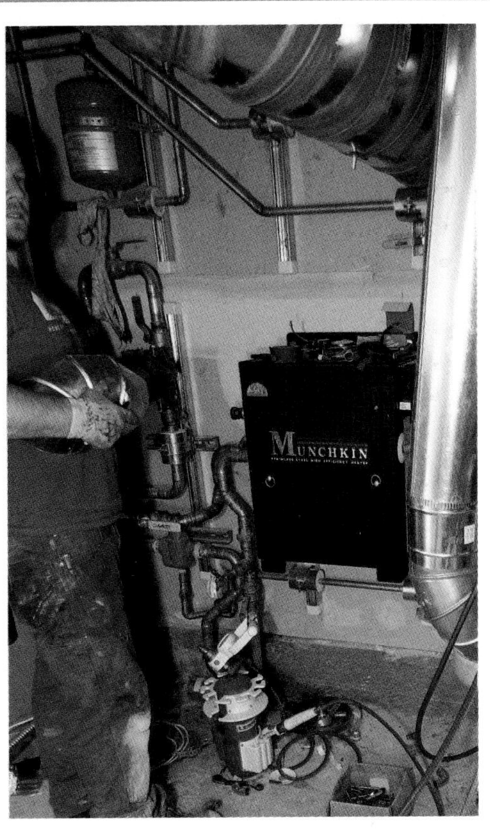

Figure 10. The solar thermal collectors (above) are expected to produce 40 percent of the yearly demand for heat and hot water. The Munchkin boiler (right) will fire whenever the collectors are unable to keep the water in the storage tank at or above 120 degrees.

below a certain low-end set point, and it continues to run until a higher set point is reached. This increases the system's efficiency by allowing the boiler to fire infrequently and for longer periods of time. By contrast, a forced-air furnace must fire every time a zone calls for heat. Using a traditional forced-air furnace to heat a single zone in a multizone system causes it to operate below optimal efficiency and reduces airflow over the heat exchanger — sometimes to the point where the heat exchanger overheats and is damaged.

Distribution System

To ensure proper airflow, our designer used Air Conditioning Contractors of America (ACCA) Manual D to size the ducts and Manual T to size the diffusers. Heat is supplied through a pair of 6x12 trunk lines, a rectangular profile that fits neatly inside a small soffit. The trunk lines run through conditioned space between the first and second floors, feeding branch ducts to individual floor and ceiling registers. To prevent leakage and heat loss, we sealed all the ducts with water-based duct mastic and wrapped the ductwork in the garage with foil-faced insulation.

Modulating Boiler

Our designer used ACCA Manual J to calculate the size of the boiler. We selected an 80,000-Btu Munchkin boiler (Heat Transfer Products, www. htproducts.com) with a rated efficiency of 95 percent. The Munchkin is a modulating condensing gas boiler. A condensing boiler is designed so that the water vapor in the combustion gas condenses and releases its latent heat before it reaches the flue. A modulating boiler varies its firing rate based on the temperature of the return water, a highly efficient mode of operation well-suited to zoned systems. When there is only a small demand for heat — if, say, only one zone is calling — the boiler fires at a lower rate. The model we selected can operate at full efficiency between 19,000 and 80,000 Btu.

Like other condensing gas appliances, the Munchkin has sealed combustion and uses PVC plumbing pipe for the air intake and flue (Figure 11). Combustion produces an acidic condensate that must be neutralized before discharge, which is done by running it through a cartridge filled with chips of marble.

Solar Thermal System

The solar thermal portion of the system is expected to produce 40 percent of the combined heat and hot water demand over the year — approximately 70 percent in the summer and 15 percent in the winter. When the collectors are not producing the required heat — when the sun isn't out or there's a high demand for hot water — then the condensing boiler becomes the backup heat source.

The system heats water indirectly by circulating a freeze-resistant fluid, food-grade propylene glycol, through a pair of roof-mounted solar collectors and a heat exchanger coil in the bottom of the storage tank. A set-point control (Tekmar Control Systems, www.

tekmarcontrols.com) monitors sensors in both locations. When the collectors are 15°F hotter than the tank, a circulator is activated, circulating the glycol until the temperatures in the collector and tank equalize (Figure 12).

The solar thermal array can heat the water to as high as 180°F in the summer and to almost as high on sunny winter days. To protect sensitive components like valves, gaskets, and air vents, the pump shuts down when the fluid in the collectors is below 55°F or above 180°F.

Stored Heat

The storage tank holds 119 gallons of water and contains two heat exchanger coils, which are located to allow for thermal stratification. The coil for the boiler is placed so that it heats the upper half of the tank, or about 60 gallons — enough to supply the combined demand of domestic hot water and space heating. The coil from the solar thermal collectors is at the bottom so that it can heat the entire tank, giving the solar collectors priority over the boiler. Since solar heat is more or less free, it makes sense to collect and

Figure 11. Aluminum cladding protects the insulation on the two pipes that carry fluid to the solar collectors (far left). Slightly lower and to the right are the PVC flue and air intake for the condensing boiler. The hood by the door is the HRV's air intake. Further down the wall (left) are the HRV exhaust hood and, to the left of the exhaust, a small outflow pipe for the boiler condensate.

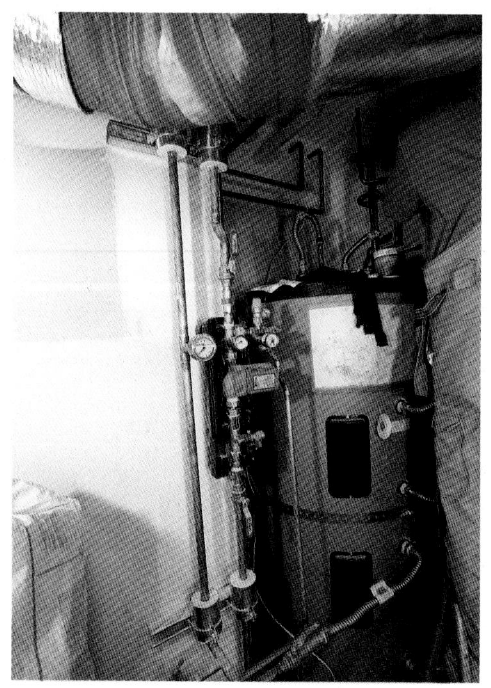

Figure 12. A circulator pumps heat-transfer fluid between the storage tank (far left) and the solar collectors in response to a set-point control (the white box with the screen, left). The control is programmed to activate the pump when the fluid in the collectors is 15°F hotter than the water in the tank. The gray box beneath the set-point control houses the zone controller, which activates the zone dampers and air handler when a thermostat calls for heat.

store as much of it as possible when the sun is out.

The boiler fires when the water in the upper half of the tank falls below 120°F and cuts off when the temperature reaches 130°F. To prevent scalding, the domestic hot-water supply passes through a tempering valve that reduces the temperature to 120°F.

Air Handler

To avoid having to integrate separate ventilation and air handler components — and to save space — we used a Lifebreath Clean Air Furnace (Airia Brands, www.lifebreath.com), a hydronic air handler with a built-in heat recovery ventilator, or HRV (Figure 13). To further improve indoor air quality, we installed an Aprilaire whole-house media cleaner (www.aprilaire.com) between the return air plenum and air handler.

The air handler is an updraft model; it has a pump and heat exchanger at the top, an HRV in the middle, and a blower and control wiring below. When a thermostat calls for heat, it sends a signal to a zone controller, which opens the appropriate zone dampers and activates the pump and blower. The blower is

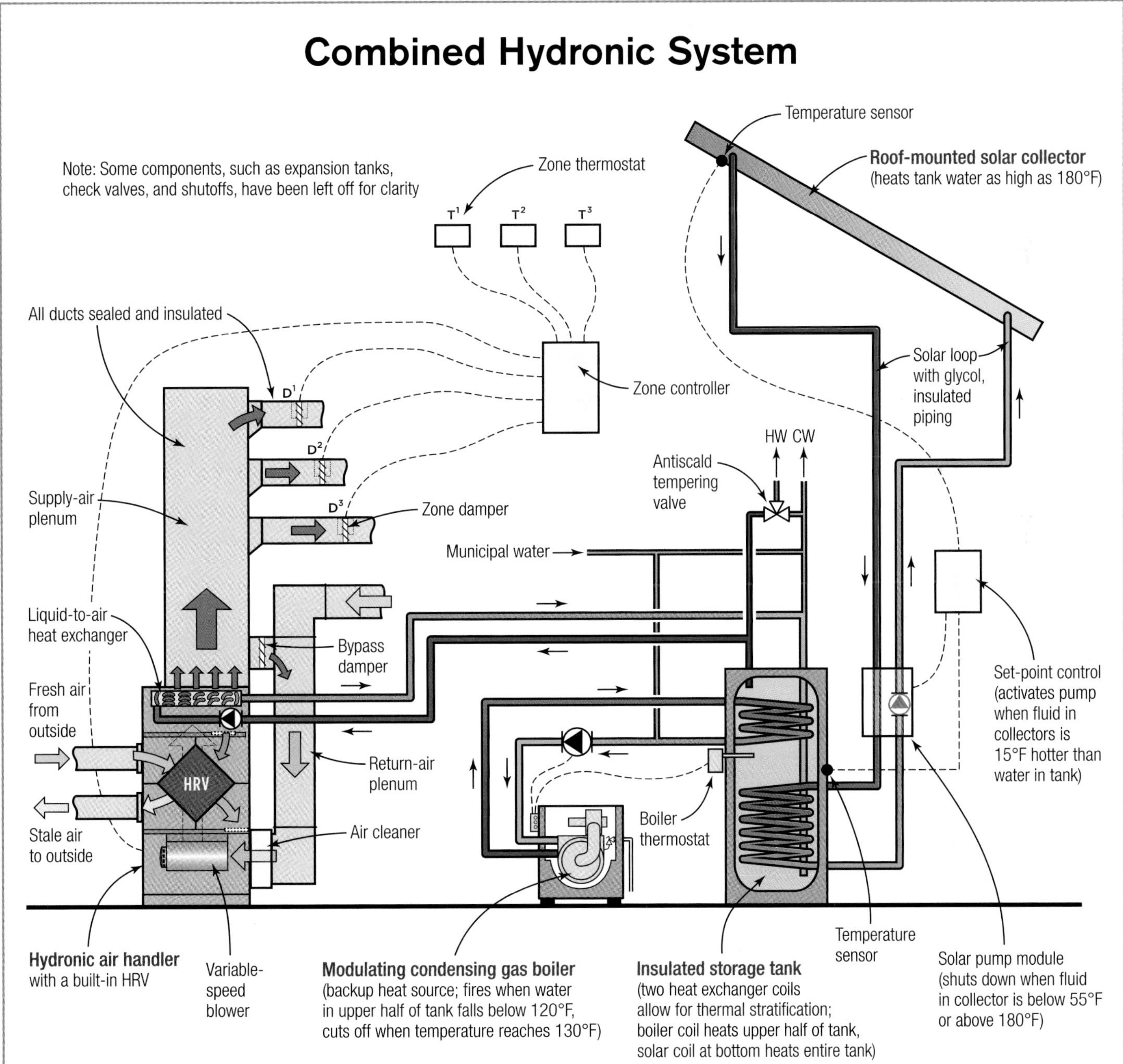

Solar thermal collectors and a backup gas boiler heat the water in the storage tank, which provides both domestic hot water and — by heat exchange in a fan-coil unit — forced-air space heating. An HRV built into the air handler brings fresh air into the house while extracting heat from the exhaust air.

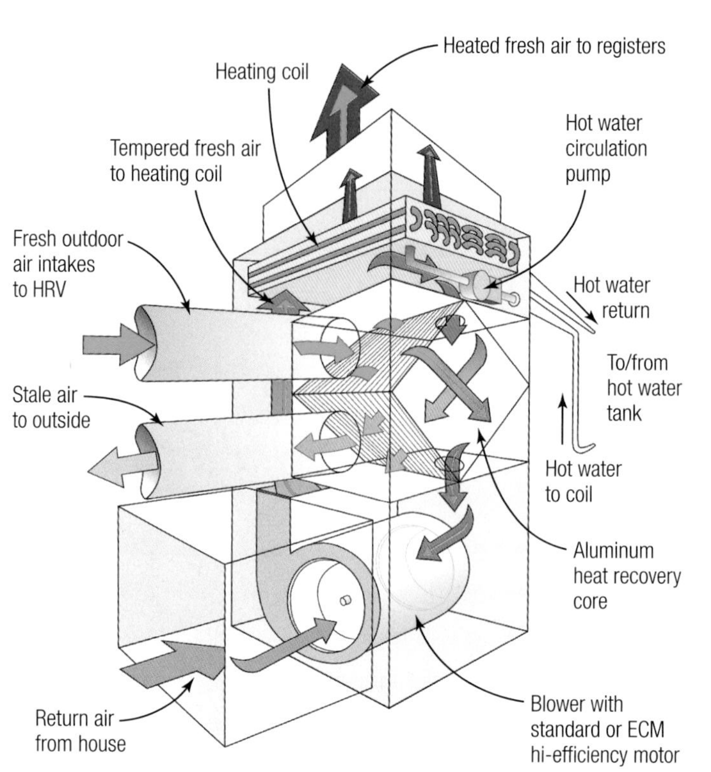

Figure 13. The air handler — a Lifebreath Clean Air Furnace — has a blower below, an HRV in the middle, and a pump and water-to-air heat exchanger coil above. Whenever a thermostat calls for heat, the blower is activated and the pump circulates hot water between the storage tank and the heat exchanger coil. The blower is powered by a high-efficiency motor that modulates between higher speeds in heating mode and low speed when only the HRV is operating.

powered by an efficient electronically commutated motor (ECM) that operates at high speed when the heat is on and at low speed when only the HRV is running. At low speed, the ECM uses 80 watts.

The HRV draws in fresh outside air while exhausting stale interior air. The two streams pass through opposite sides of an aluminum heat-exchanger core, which captures about 70 percent of the heat contained in the exhaust and transfers it to the incoming air. In heating mode, the HRV runs in tandem with the air handler and continuously adds outdoor air to the supply mix. Fresh air can also be introduced when the heat is off; when set to ventilation-only mode, the HRV runs for 20 minutes each hour. Ventilation can be controlled separately by a programmed seasonal setting or manually by the homeowner.

Bypass damper. The air handler is designed to produce a constant flow of air in heating mode. Closing off one or two of the zones increases the static pressure in the ductwork and causes the ECM blower motor to work less efficiently. To solve this problem, we installed an automatic bypass damper, which relieves excess pressure by allowing some of the air in the supply plenum to bleed back into the return.

The Results

The homeowners have reported that they are far more comfortable with the new heating system in place. We haven't yet got data on energy consumption. However, based on our experience with similar systems, we expect their energy use to be significantly lower than before, even with the newly enlarged living space.

Matt Golden and Adam Winter *are the cofounders of Recurve, a San Francisco–based provider of home performance services.*

Chapter 10

RADIANT HEATING

- Radiant Slab Heating
- Hardwood Flooring Over Radiant Heat
- Simple Radiant Floor Retrofit

Radiant Slab Heating

by John Siegenthaler

Radiant floor systems provide a very comfortable way to heat. The entire floor radiates heat, so occupants never feel far from the heat source. Moreover, floors wetted by foot or vehicle traffic dry quickly. And there are no floor registers, exposed pipes, or radiators to interfere with furniture placement and room layouts. For these reasons, homeowners and architects have become interested in these systems, and contractors are being asked to install them. Although there are several ways to install hydronic radiant floor (HRF) heating, the most economical HRF systems are installed in concrete floor slabs.

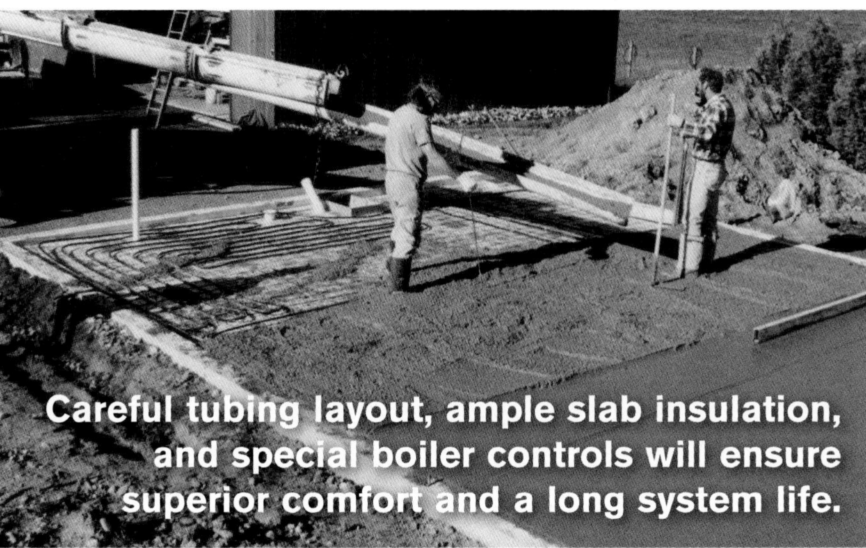

Careful tubing layout, ample slab insulation, and special boiler controls will ensure superior comfort and a long system life.

HRF Characteristics

There are several characteristics of HRF heating you should consider before installing this system. First, slab-on-grade HRF systems are slow to respond to changes in thermostat settings. If the homeowner leaves for an extended time during the winter and sets back the thermostat, an HRF system can take several hours to warm up a space when the owner returns. This is because the heat source must warm the thermal mass of the floor slab as it also warms the air and other materials in the room. This is not a problem when an occupant's schedule is known, since setback controls can be programmed to begin warming the space several hours before the owner comes home.

Likewise, space heated by a slab-on-grade HRF system can take several hours to cool down following a thermostat setback or power outage. This is a desirable characteristic because it allows the radiant slab to be tied into an intermittent heat source, such as a wood furnace, or an off-peak electrical or active solar system.

A second consideration affects the choice of floor coverings. HRF systems can be covered with a variety of finish floor materials, including certain types of hardwood, carpet, or tile. Each of these materials adds a different amount of thermal resistance to upward heat flow (Table 1). The average water temperature in the floor circuits must be increased as finish materials with higher thermal resistances are used over the slab. This is usually not a problem when a boiler is the heat source. But if you are relying on a hydronic heat pump, an active solar system, or another low-temperature heat source, the efficiency of the heat source will drop as the circuit temperature rises (see "Connecting to a Heat Source," page 247).

Also, if different areas of a slab are covered with different materials, each having a significantly different thermal resistance, you should make each of these areas a separate zone with its own distribution temperature. This will require additional mixing valves and higher associated costs (more on this later.) If you have more than two distribution water temperatures, it might be best to look at another type of distribution system.

Table 1. Heat Resistance of Common Floor Coverings

Floor Covering	Floor System R-Value	Avg. Water Temperature in Tubing
nylon carpet over 1/4-inch bonded urethane pad	2.5	135°F
3/8-inch floating hardwood over 1/8-inch foam pad	1.87	122°F
ceramic tile	1.00	105°F
1/8-inch vinyl	0.99	105°F
bare concrete	0.78	101°F

Note: This table shows the thermal resistances of some common radiant floor systems, including covering, slab and tubing, and estimates of the average water temperature needed to maintain a room air temperature of 68°F. The table assumes a 4-inch insulated slab with nominal 3/4-inch tubing spaced 12 inches on-center, and a slab heat output of 20 Btu/sq. ft. per hour.

Despite misconceptions to the contrary, wood floors can be installed over radiant slabs. Unfortunately, conventional wood flooring products that are either nailed or glued to an underlayment over the slab are often not guaranteed if used over a radiant floor heating system. The temperature fluctuations will reportedly cause problems with shrinkage or cupping. I recommend using a floating hardwood floor. These floors are typically made with three plies of laminated wood, so the material is dimensionally stable. And since the floors are not rigidly attached to a slab, they can expand and contract with temperature changes.

Most manufacturers of floating hardwood flooring will guarantee the use of their products over radiant slabs, provided the surface temperature of the slab is limited to about 85°F. However, this limits the upward heat flow to about 16 Btu per square foot per hour — sufficient to maintain a 68°F room temperature only in a very well insulated house. (See "Hardwood Flooring Over Radiant Heat," page 247.)

Planning and Layout

Before beginning an HRF installation, make a scaled drawing of the tubing circuit layout over the floor plan of the building. This is essential for specifying the right circuit length in each zone, ordering the proper length coils, and eliminating a time-consuming trial-and-error tubing placement at the job site.

An easy way of doing this is to overlay a copy of the ¼-inch scale floor plan with a sheet of vellum having a ⅛-inch grid. This grid corresponds to the 6x6-inch pattern formed by the welded-wire reinforcement. Circuit layouts done in this manner are easy to duplicate in the field since the installer can easily relate the plan to the welded wire grid.

Some tubing manufacturers even provide templates to expedite the drawing of serpentine patterns. HRF manufacturers recognize that design assistance is vital to proper installation of this technology. Most manufacturers offer some form of design assistance through manufacturer's representatives or direct from the factory. Some will take your floor plans and prepare a suitable design and cost estimate for a nominal charge. Others use design software to check special cases. Most manufacturers also publish design assistance tables in their catalogs.

Circuit Layout

All HRF circuits begin at a supply manifold and end at a return manifold. These two manifolds are usually located, one over the other, within an accessible wall cavity. I always try to choose a central manifold location. This minimizes the need to use long lengths of tubing between the manifold and individual rooms. The manifolds must be accessible through a removable or hinged wall panel exposed to finished space. If this is not acceptable to the client, try locating the manifolds in a closet.

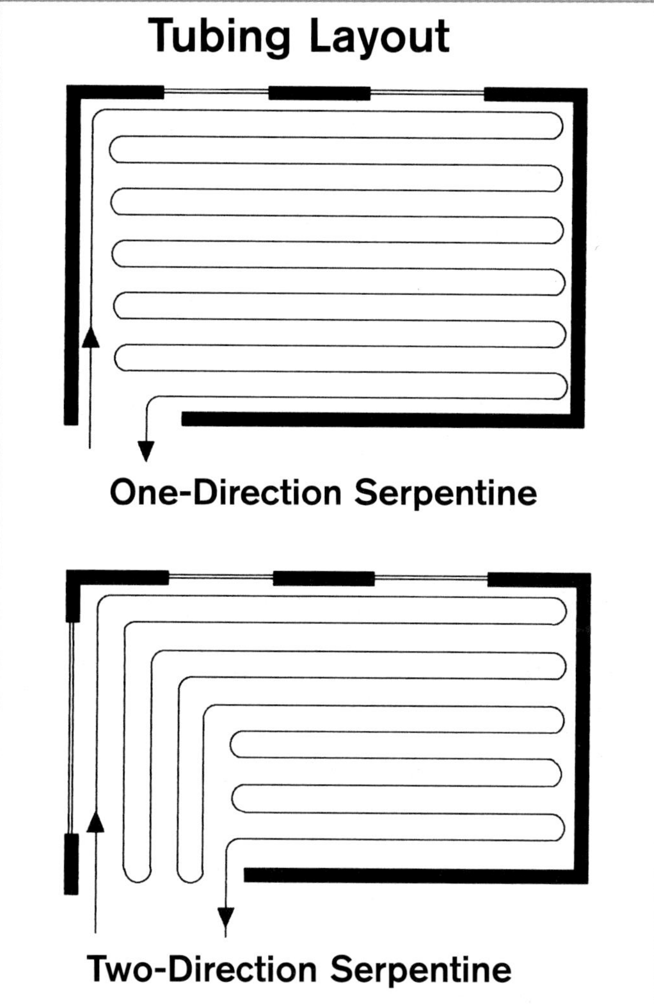

Figure 1. The author uses a one- or two-direction serpentine circuit layout pattern. In each case, the tubing circuits first run adjacent to the exposed walls, and then work their way toward the interior. This allows for a slightly higher heat output near the coldest areas of the room.

Circuits using nominal ¾-inch tubing should be limited to about 400 feet in length. Shorter circuits will have a smaller temperature drop from supply to return, which yields a higher average heat output per square foot. Longer circuits increase pump pressure requirements and yield lower average heat output per square foot due to the greater temperature drop from supply to return.

Also keep in mind that each floor circuit can be treated as an independent zone by controlling the circuit's flow rate either manually or automatically at the manifold. If you want to control each of several rooms independently, use a separate circuit for each room.

There are a number of possible circuit layout patterns for the HRF tubing. The simplest of these, and the one I use most often, is a "one-direction serpentine" (Figure 1). In this pattern, the straight portions of the circuit run along the length of the room. This speeds up installation since it minimizes the number of return bends.

Note that the tubing circuits first run adjacent to the exposed walls and then work their way toward the interior. This allows for a slightly higher heat output near the coldest areas of the room. Similarly, if the space has two exposed walls with large areas of glass, use a "two-directional serpentine" to keep the higher heating output near the exposed surfaces.

As a general rule, the tubing runs should be spaced 12 inches on-center. Occasionally, I might space the runs near the center of a slab 18 inches on-center. However, keeping the runs 12 inches apart ensures a

Connecting to a Heat Source

Because of the low water temperature requirements of an HRF system, it is critical to make a proper connection with a high-temperature heat source, such as a gas or oil-fired boiler. Failing to do this properly will result in possible damage to the boiler from internal condensation.

Condensation occurs when water vapor in the exhaust is cooled below its dew-point temperature. In a gas-fired boiler the dew-point temperature is typically around 130°F. Since return water in an HRF circuit is often below 100°F, continuous condensation within the boiler is almost guaranteed if the distribution is directly connected to the boiler. If the boiler is specifically designed as a condensing boiler, this effect is desirable and significantly adds to the efficiency of the boiler. However, standard boilers are not designed for prolonged operation in a condensing mode, and the acidic condensation can quickly corrode galvanized exhaust stacks and promote corrosion on the outside of the boiler.

Radiant Floor Boiler Hookup

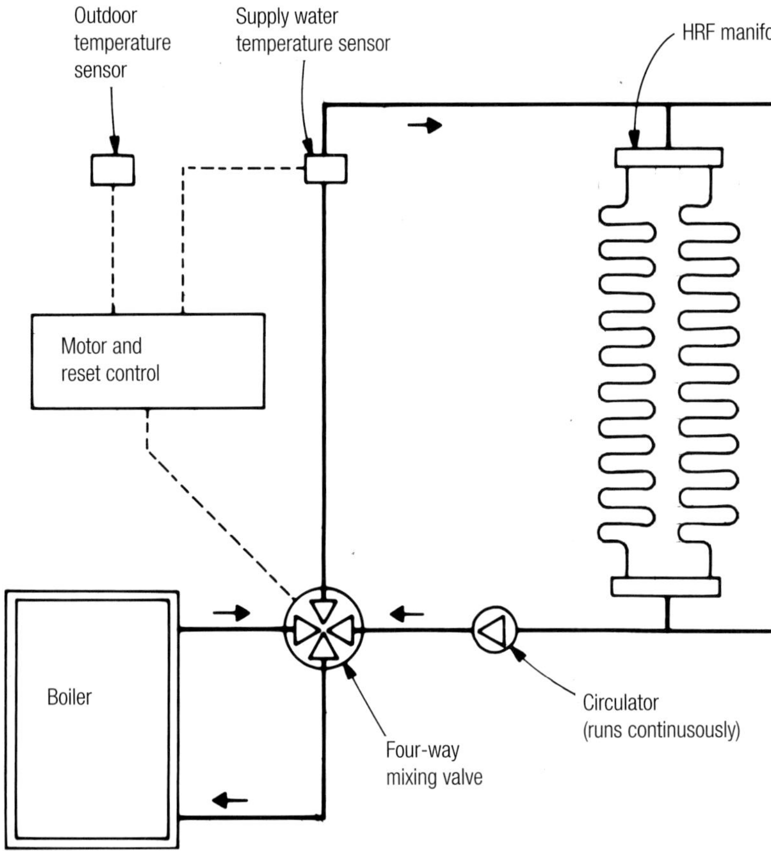

The author installs a four-way mixing valve to lower the water temperature in the tubing, while allowing the boiler to operate above the dew-point temperature. Sensors in the control measure outside temperature and the water temperature in the supply line and adjust the water mix accordingly.

To prevent condensation in standard boilers, install a four-way mixing valve between the boiler and the manifolds (illustration, left). This valve mixes cooler water with the hot supply water to bring it to the right temperature for the floor circuits. This allows the boiler to operate above the dew-point temperature, while also limiting the water temperature in the tubing.

The circulator runs continuously. Although the mixing valve can be operated manually, an electronic valve control can be installed. Sensors in the control measure outside temperature and the water temperature in the supply line and adjust the water mix accordingly. Several manufacturers offer complete systems of valves and controllers.

— John Siegenthaler

quicker response rate.

Try to avoid running tubing under partitions if there is any chance the partitions will be fastened to the floor slab with mechanical fasteners. If I can't avoid placing the tubing under the partition, I try to avoid using mechanical fasteners. On a recent job for a Sunday school that had several smaller rooms over a common floor slab, I specified that the partitions should be attached to the floor slab with construction adhesive. This allowed the circuits to pass under the partitions wherever necessary, greatly simplifying the tubing layout.

Ordering the Tubing

Once you have a sketch of the circuits, number each circuit and measure their lengths. Measuring off the plans can be a bit tedious, but it allows you to order the proper coil lengths and minimize waste. I use a small gear-driven measuring wheel to speed this work. I add an extra 10 feet to the measured length of each circuit to account for the risers to the manifold and for small measurement errors.

To minimize waste, I usually order long, continuous coils and cut the lengths I need for each circuit. Some manufacturers, however, only offer tubing in incremental lengths. Unless your circuits are equal to or just slightly shorter than the coil, you end up with a lot of expensive waste. You should never lay out circuits that require a buried joint.

There have been problems reported, mainly in Europe, with boiler corrosion from oxygen diffusing into the tubing. Although I haven't experienced this, I always use PEX or PEX-AL-PEX tubing, which is made with an oxygen diffusion barrier, just in case — it's cheap insurance.

Installing the Slab

All underslab plumbing and electrical conduit should be in place before beginning tubing installation. All underslab utility trenches must be filled and properly compacted. The final grade under the slab should be accurately leveled, allowing for the thickness of the slab and the underslab insulation. This is especially critical near the edges of the slab, where thicker insulation is used (Figure 2). Any loose rocks should be raked off to provide a smooth, stable surface.

Begin by placing a vapor barrier over the subgrade. Polyethylene sheeting is often used as this vapor barrier. Its purpose is to minimize water vapor migration from the soil into the slab during warm weather. Such migration, if unchecked, can discolor wood flooring placed over the slab. In areas with high radon potential, a special radon/moisture barrier may also need to be installed.

Underslab insulation is then installed over the vapor barrier. Although several options are available, extruded polystyrene foam is a commonly used material with a proven track record in such applications. It is available in several thicknesses and compressive stress ratings. It does not absorb moisture or outgas compounds that may be harmful to the environment. Designers should verify that local codes allow placement of foam insulation below concrete slabs, especially in areas where termites are present.

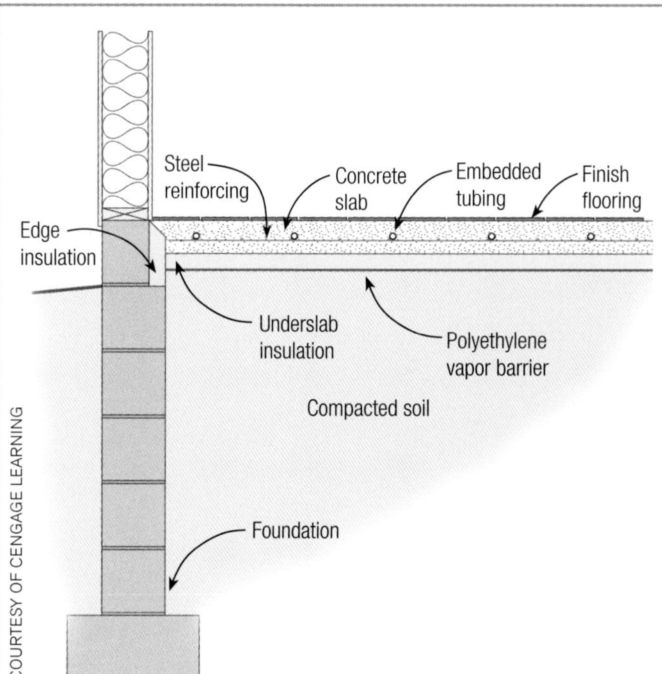

Figure 2. The exposed edges of a radiant slab should be insulated with a minimum of 2-inch extruded polystyrene. The recommended thickness of underslab insulation varies with climate. The tapered edge of the perimeter insulation allows concrete to be placed close to the foundation wall, where it will be covered with framing or finish materials.

Figure 3. Extruded polystyrene insulation around the slab edge has a beveled top to allow the slab to extend to the foundation wall.

The insulation should be neatly placed with all tongue-and-groove joints interlocked. If the site is windy, place sheets of welded wire fabric and/or wooden planks over the foam sheets as they are placed to avoid wind uplift.

The recommended R-value of underslab insulation varies with geographic location. In the absence of specific codes that require higher values, the Radiant Professionals Alliance recommends that the minimum R-value for underslab insulation be based on the following equation:

To calculate the minimum *R*-Value for underslab insulation use the formula:

$(R_{min}) = 0.125 \times (T_i - T_o)$ where

R_{min} = minimum *R*-value of underslab insulation (°F hr. ft.^{2}/Btu)

T_i = inside air temperature to be maintained at design load conditions (°F)

T_o = outside air temperature at design load conditions (°F)

Example:

If the outside design temperature is – 5°F and the indoor temperature is 70°F, the *R*-value of the underslab insulation should be:

$$0.125 \times (70 - (-5°F)) = 0.125 \times 75 = 9.4$$

Underslab insulation should *not* be installed under floor areas that support high structural loads from columns or bearing walls. Such columns and bearing walls, if present, are generally several feet away from the building perimeter, and thus omitting a relatively small area of underslab insulation will have minimal effect. However, the black polyethylene vapor barrier should remain intact across these areas.

Figure 3 shows 2-inch extruded polystyrene insulation around the slab edge. The insulation has a tapered upper edge, which allows concrete to be placed close to the foundation wall. With this detail, the edge of the slab will eventually be covered with framing and/or finish materials.

Most concrete slab-on-grade floors are reinforced with welded wire fabric (WWF) or steel rebar. When welded wire fabric is used, it should be placed over the insulation, with adjacent sheets lapped a minimum of 6 inches at all edges and wire-tied together.

The next step is to use the tubing layout drawing to locate the manifold stations within the building. These are the locations where tubing penetrates up through the slab surface and eventually connects to a manifold station.

Manifold stations are often housed within wall cavities that will eventually be built around them. It is crucial to carefully measure and place the manifold station at the precise location where such walls will eventually be built. A temporary manifold station support is constructed by driving two 3-foot stakes through the insulation and into the soil. A small plywood panel can then be fastened to these stakes and the manifold mounted to it, as shown in Figure 4. After the slab is poured and the manifold station is supported within the wall cavity, the stakes can be sawn off flush with the slab surface. *Be sure the manifold station faces a direction where it can be accessed when the surrounding wall is completed.*

After the manifold stations are placed, use the tubing layout drawing to mark portions of each tube circuit on the foam insulation using spray paint. Corners, return bends, and offsets should be marked as shown in Figure 5. This greatly speeds installation and reduces the chance of mistakes as the tubing is placed. Be sure to also mark flow direction arrows to help ensure that the ends of each circuit are connected to the proper manifold.

The tubing circuits can now be placed one at a time. Look up the length of the circuit being created on the tubing layout drawing. Select a coil of tubing long

Figure 4. This temporary support for a manifold station must be accurately located to ensure that the manifold lies within a partition, or on the finish surface of an eventual wall.

enough to create the circuit *without splicing*. Most tubing sold for radiant panel applications comes with sequential length numbers printed every 3 feet along the tube. By subtracting the smaller number at one end of the coil from the larger number at the other, the length can be quickly determined.

To prevent twisting, the tubing must be unrolled from the coil. *Never pull tubing off the side of a coil.* Most installers make use of an uncoiler, such as the one shown in Figure 6. This device allows the coil to freely spin as tubing is pulled from it. The uncoiler should be placed several feet away from where the tubing is being laid down. Several feet of tubing should be pulled off the coil to allow ample slack.

Connect the free end of the tubing coil to the supply manifold. Pull several feet of tubing off the coil and proceed along the supply side of the circuit, fastening the tubing along the way. Bends in PEX or PEX-AL-PEX tubing in sizes up to ¾ inch can be made by hand, taking care not to kink the tubing in the process. Bends in larger diameter tubing or especially tight bends may require a tube bender. Be sure to verify the minimum bend radius allowed with the tubing manufacturer. PEX and PEX-AL-PEX tubing always bends easier when warm.

Tubing is usually fastened to the welded wire fabric or

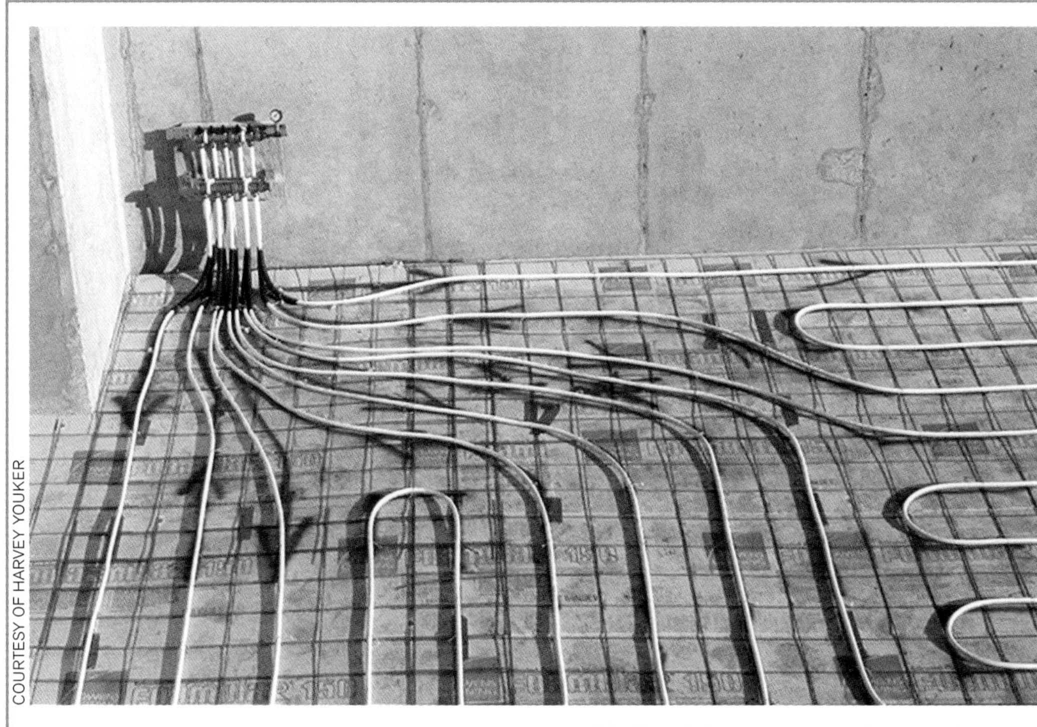

COURTESY OF HARVEY YOUKER

Figure 5. Spray paint is used to mark portions of each tubing circuit as well as the flow direction on the underslab insulation.

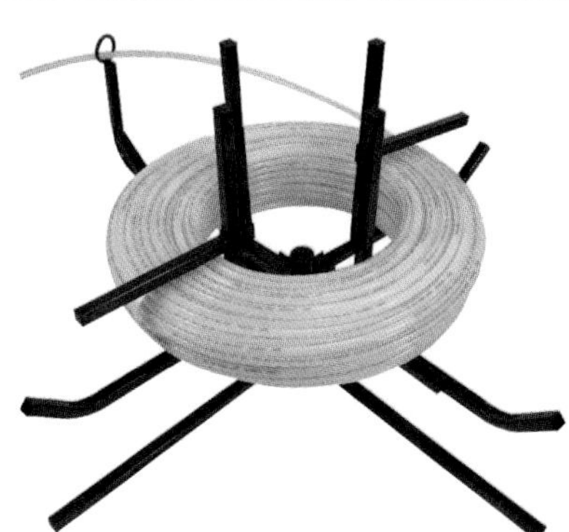

CREDIT: COURTESY OF UPONOR

Figure 6. The uncoiler, seen at right and inset, allows tubing to be pulled off the coil without twisting. Maintain ample slack in tubing to allow efficient placement. [Photo above]

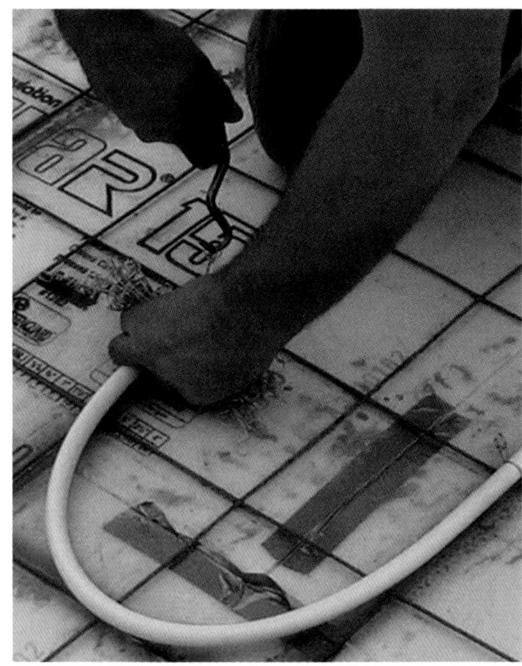

Figure 7. A worker secures PEX-AL-PEX tubing to welded wire reinforcing using wire ties and a "J-hook" twisting tool (top). The completed wire tie has the loop pressed to the side (above).

steel reinforcing using wire twist ties, nylon pull ties, or some type of plastic clip (Figure 7). The manufacturer may require that a specific type of fastener be used to retain the warranty on the tubing. Typical spacing for ties or clips is 24 to 30 inches on straight runs and at two or three locations on each return bend.

As tubing is placed, watch for any sharp ends on steel reinforcing. Either bend the reinforcing out of the way or slightly offset the tubing to avoid chafing its surface.

Some tubing suppliers require the installation of bend supports where the tubing bends from horizontal to vertical under the manifold stations. Some installation instructions also call for the tubing to be sleeved for protection where it penetrates through the slab surface, as shown in Figure 4. Verify the recommended details with the tubing manufacturer.

Control Joints

Most concrete slabs require control joints. The purpose of control joints is to intentionally weaken the slab at specific locations so shrinkage cracking occurs along the control joint rather than randomly across the slab. Control joints are usually made using a special saw the day after the slab is poured. The depth of the cut is often specified to be 20 percent of the slab's thickness.

Figure 8 shows how tubing should be detailed where it passes beneath a sawn control joint. The tubing is covered with a thin plastic sleeve that is centered on the eventual location of the control joint. This sleeve prevents the concrete from bonding directly to the tubing at this location. This minimizes stress on the tubing during any subsequent minor movement of the slab. Sleeving material is available from most tubing manufacturers for this purpose.

The thin-wall sleeving can be slit with a utility knife and wrapped around the tubing after the circuit has been fastened in place. Many installers mark the location of control joints using spray paint before fasten-

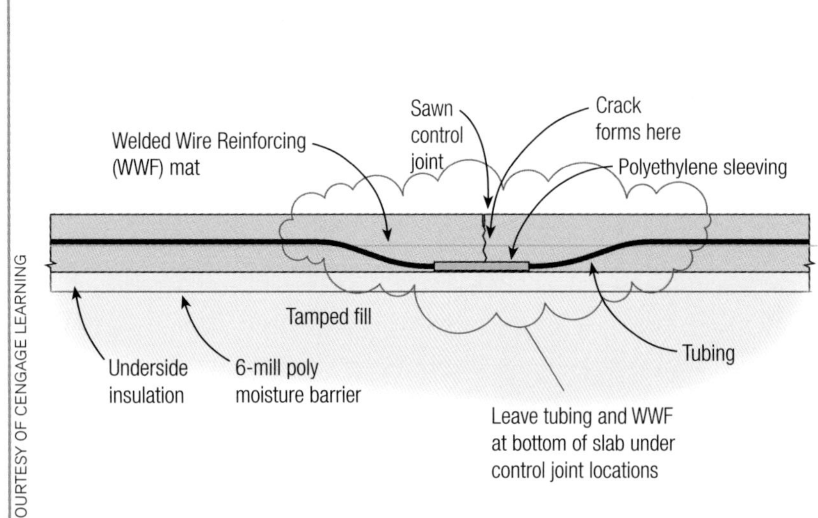

Figure 8. Where tubing passes beneath a sawn control joint, it is covered with a thin plastic sleeve centered on the control joint. This sleeve prevents the concrete from bonding directly to the tubing here, minimizing stress on the tubing from minor movement of the slab.

ing the tubing in place (Figure 9).

The tubing and welded wire fabric should not be lifted where it passes beneath control joints. This ensures a wide berth between the tubing and the bottom of the saw cut.

Another important installation detail is to hold tubing at least 8 inches away from any toilet drainage piping (Figure 10). This minimizes heating of the wax ring that is eventually installed on the closet flange.

Pressure Testing

Although leaks due to "defective tubing" are extremely unlikely, it is possible that careless equipment handling on the job site could damage the tubing before it is embedded in concrete. To ensure that no leaks are literally cast into concrete, all circuits should be pressure-tested prior to concrete placement.

Pressure testing is best done using compressed air, which is not subject to freezing during cold weather construction. A typical pressure-testing specification requires that all tubing circuits be pressurized to and maintained at 60.0 to 75.0 psi for at least 24 hours. Once the assembly has reached its test pressure, apply a soapy water solution to all manifold connections to check for any air leaks.

If the pressure drops significantly within a few hours, it is very likely the leak is at one of the manifold connections. Retighten and recheck with soap solution until the system is airtight. If the system will be left unattended for some time, the air pressure should be reduced to about 30.0 psi for safety. The tubing circuits should remain under pressure while the slab is poured. If a tube were accidentally punctured during the pour, the compressed air would give an immediate indication of the leak. The leak could then be repaired using a coupler specifically designed for that purpose.

Photo Documentation

After all circuits have been placed, several photographs of the tubing installation should be taken. Photos should be taken around each manifold station, as well as in any areas where tubing placement is tight or routed around objects such as a foundation pad. The use of digital cameras allows such photos to be quickly gathered and stored on disk or CD-ROM. A copy of the photos should be given to the building owner for future reference.

Placement of Concrete

There is no standard procedure for placement of concrete slabs. From the standpoint of the tubing, the placement procedure used should minimize heavy traffic over the tubing and ensure that the tubing ends up at approximately mid-depth in the slab (other than where it passes beneath control joints).

Wheelbarrow traffic over tubing that is under pressure is generally not a problem; however, care should

Figure 9. The location of the control joint is marked by the line painted on the underslab insulation. Short sections of thin-wall polyethylene sleeving protect the tubing where it passes under a sawn control joint.

Figure 10. Hold tubing at least 8 inches away from water closet flanges to prevent softening of wax ring.

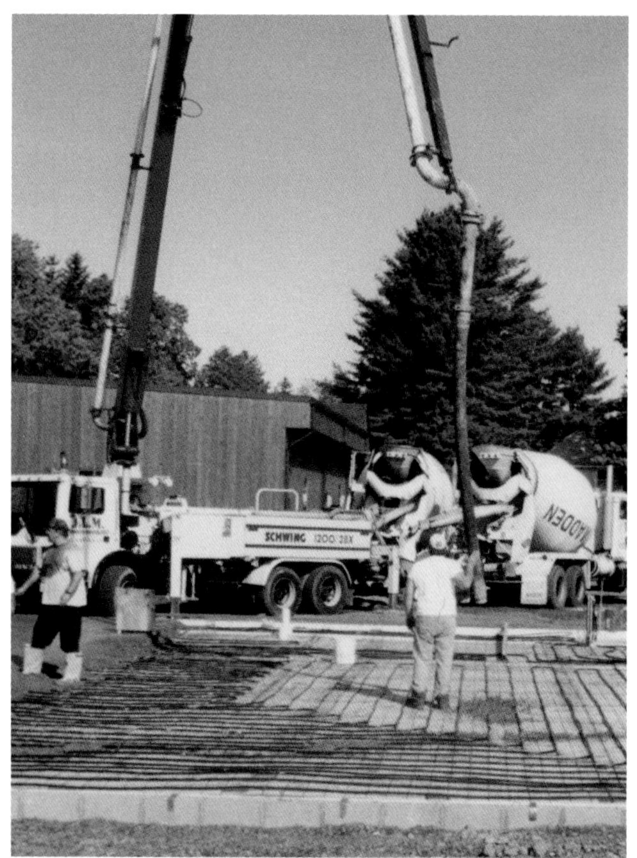

Figure 11. An aerial boom and pump help efficiently place concrete for large slabs-on-grade with radiant heating.

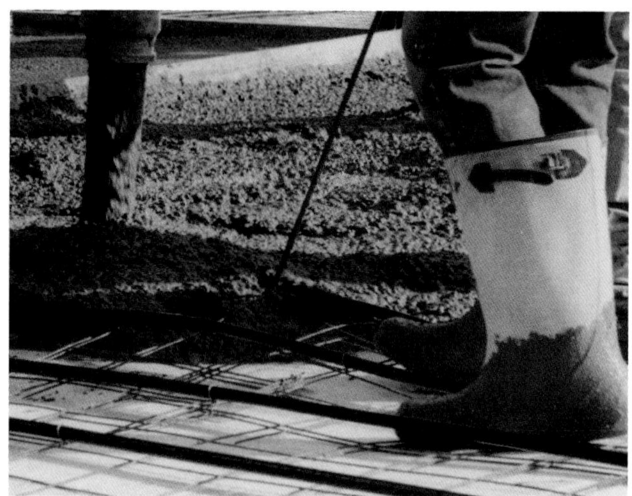

Figure 12. A mason uses a lifting hook to pull welded wire reinforcing and attached tubing to approximately mid-slab height. Note that hook is lifting reinforcing wire rather than directly lifting tubing.

be taken not to pinch the tubing under the nose bar of the wheelbarrow as it is dumped. So-called "power buggies" are too heavy to be driven over the tubing and insulation. Likewise, concrete trucks should never be driven over these materials. On small slabs, the concrete can often be placed directly from the chute of the delivery truck. For larger slabs, the use of a concrete pump truck equipped with an aerial boom is an ideal way to efficiently place the concrete with minimal heavy traffic over the tubing (Figure 11).

As the concrete is placed, lift the welded wire reinforcing and attached tubing to approximately mid-depth in the slab (other than at control joints). Ideally, one or more workers should be assigned solely to this task. The mesh is pulled up using a lift hook (Figure 12). After the coarse (stone) aggregate in the concrete flows under the mesh, it tends to support it quite well. After the concrete is placed, it is finished in the usual manner. Special care should be taken not to nick the tubing with trowels where it penetrates the slab under the manifold stations. Careless operation of tools, such as power trowels, can sever tubing circuits and lead to costly repairs.

The installation procedures just described call for good coordination of trades at the job site. It is important for the concrete placement crew to understand details, such as proper tubing depth and control joint detailing, before beginning concrete placement.

Thin-Slab Radiant Floors

There are many buildings where radiant floor heating is desirable, but where slab-on-grade construction is not possible. One of the most common is a wood-framed floor deck in a residential or light commercial building. One alternative is to install a radiant thin-slab over the subfloor. Thin-slab systems use the same type of PEX or PEX-AL-PEX tubing as slab-on-grade systems. The tubing is fastened directly to the wood subfloor and then covered with Gyp-Crete or a special concrete mix.

As with slab-on-grade systems, the thin slab provides an effective "thermal wick" that allows heat to diffuse laterally outward away from the tubing. It also provides moderate thermal mass to stabilize heat delivery. Because the slab is thinner than a typical slab-on-grade floor, lateral heat diffusion is slightly less efficient, requiring a slightly higher average water temperature (see "Thin-Slab Heating Over Wood Subfloors," opposite page).

This section was adapted from Modern Hydronic Heating: for Residential and Commercial Buildings, *3rd Ed., by John Siegenthaler (Cengage Learning, www.cengage.com). All photos and illustrations courtesy of Cengage Learning.*

John Siegenthaler*, P. E., is owner of Appropriate Designs (www.hydronicpros.com) in Holland Patent, N.Y., and has over 25 years of experience designing modern hydronic heating systems.*

Thin-Slab Heating Over Wood Subfloors

The usual method of installing a thin slab for hydronic floor heating uses a self-leveling, gypsum-based underlayment, such as Gyp-Crete. The underlayment is typically poured near the end of the job, after all the walls are up and the house has been closed in. These systems must be installed by a certified installer with a factory-trained crew. To save costs, we have also used a special concrete mix instead of Gyp-Crete, cutting the thin slab costs from $5 to $9 per square foot to $3 to $5 per foot, depending on local costs and the size of the job (based on 2011 prices). Smaller jobs are more costly on a square-foot basis.

The idea of using concrete for the thin slab came from a heating subcontractor, Harvey Youker of UnderSun Construction in Dolgeville, N.Y. We first tried this system, dubbed the "Youker" system, on the small, 900-square-foot building described here and have since used it successfully on several projects. It is well suited to renewable heat sources, such as geothermal and solar thermal, but adds a significant dead load to the floor (about 18 psf), It also requires that deflection in the floor system not exceed L/600. If in doubt, have the project reviewed by a structural design professional before proceeding.

Floor Prep and Tubing Layout

With the subfloor in place, we began by marking the locations of all exterior walls and interior partitions on the deck using chalk lines. We also marked the locations of the tubing circuits on the floor deck with a chalk line and lumber crayon, following an accurately drawn layout plan (Figure 13).

Manifold station. When drawing the layout plan for two or more tubing circuits, I first locate the manifold station where each circuit begins and ends. I always pick a central location, as shown in Figure 14. The manifold must allow all outgoing and returning tubing to come together in close proximity without the tubes crossing over each other. Also, the manifold should be easy to get to so the flow in each circuit can be balanced. To keep

continued on next page

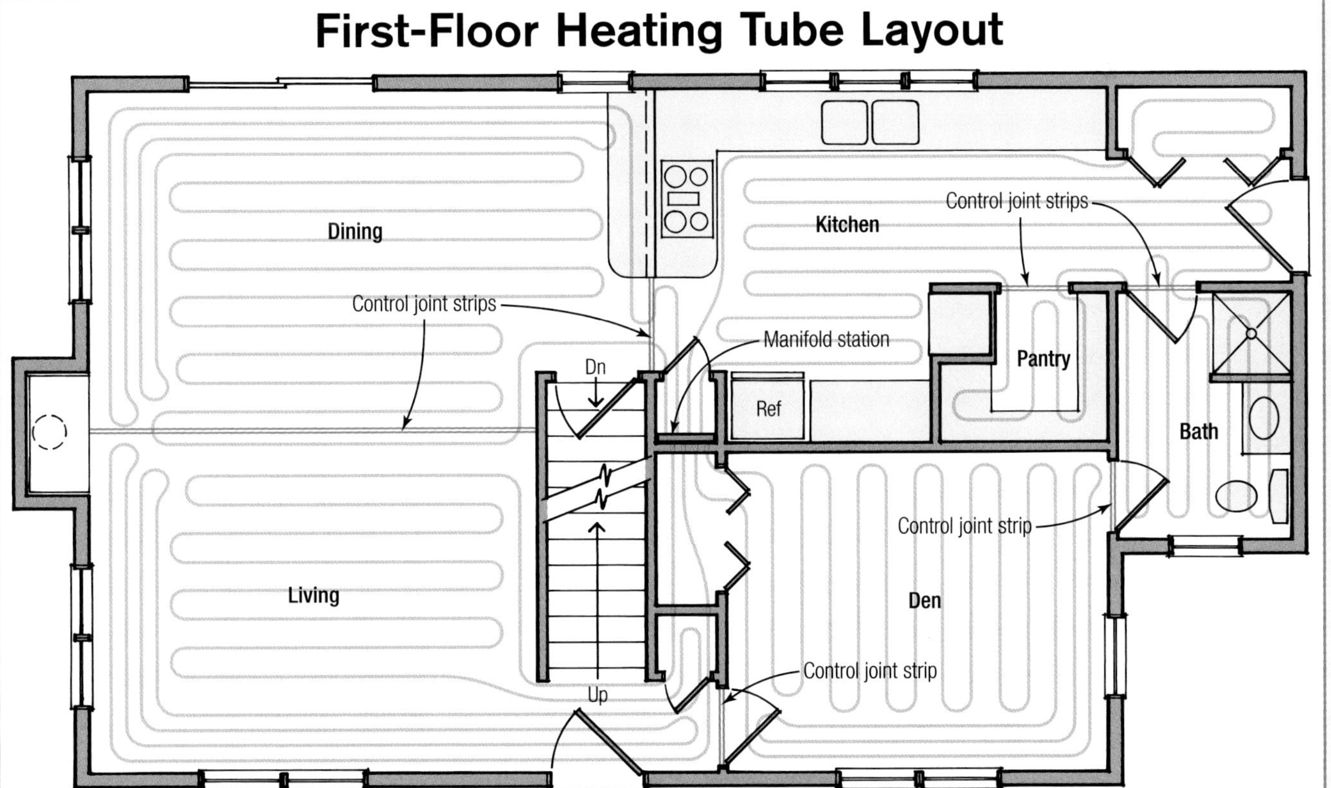

Figure 13. The author begins a tubing layout by picking a central location for the manifold station. In each circuit, the hottest water flows near the outside walls of each room, where the greatest heat loss occurs. Note the placement of control joints in the slab at each doorway and in the center of any expanse over 15 feet.

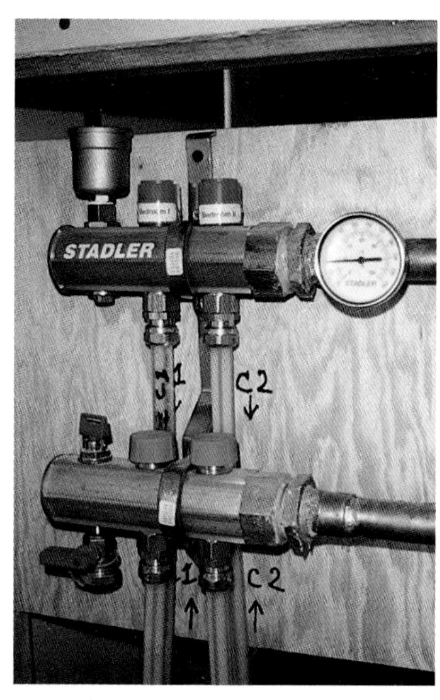

Figure 14. The four tubing circuits begin and end at a manifold station located in a wall inside a closet (left). Metal bend supports, supplied by the tubing manufacturer, protect the tubing from kinking as well as from the concrete finisher's trowels (right).

continued from previous page

must allow all outgoing and returning tubing to come together in close proximity without the tubes crossing over each other. Also, the manifold should be easy to get to so the flow in each circuit can be balanced. To keep the manifold accessible but still hidden, I like to install an access panel to the manifold station on an inside wall of a central closet.

Slip sheet. We then covered the entire deck with a transparent 6-mil polyethylene "slip sheet." This sheet mainly acts as a bond breaker between the wooden subfloor and the thin slab, and reduces the possibilities that shrinkage of the floor deck will cause random cracks in the slab. The poly sheet also protects the subfloor from rain before the building or addition is closed in.

Subplates and floor blocking. Next, we fastened down 2x6 and 2x4 subplates to the floor deck at all wall and partition locations. The slab will be poured flush with these plates, and they provide nailing for the walls. We also installed 2-by blocking where the toilet flange and other mechanicals that won't be routed through the partitions will be located (Figure 15). Later, this blocking can be removed to run piping or ductwork through the subfloor. We cut a slight taper on the edges of these blocks and install them with the narrow side facing down; square-cut edges make the blocks tough to get out.

Tubing. After this prep work was done, we were ready to run all the floor tubing over the premarked paths. Any fastener must be approved by the tubing manufacturer, otherwise the tubing's warranty may be voided. Typically, you can use hand-nailed plastic clips, gun-driven plastic staples, or metal staples. We used metal staples driven by a specially set-up Bostitch pneumatic stapler. This gun has a special nose attachment that controls the depth-of-drive to prevent compressing the tubing.

Figure 15. Prep for pouring the slab includes installing subplates for all the interior and exterior walls, and blocking for the toilet flange and other mechanicals.

After all piping is in place, the system should be pressure-tested the same as with any floor heating installation.

Control joints. Be sure to provide control joints within the slab. These joints allow the slab to crack along

Figure 16. To prevent random cracking of the slab, control joints were created by nailing PVC drywall corner bead to the plywood subfloor (left). Control joints across doorways (right) and in the center of large rooms ensure that the slab cracks only in these locations.

Figure 17. The crew unloaded concrete from the truck using a chute and wheelbarrows. They used a scrap of plywood under the nose of the wheelbarrow as it was dumped to prevent pinching the tubing.

predetermined lines as the concrete cures and the wood deck shrinks. We used 1x1-inch PVC drywall corner bead to make the control joints (Figure 16). We stapled the corner bead to the subfloor, placing them across all doorways and in the center portion of large rooms to break the slab area up into smaller segments (no more than 15 feet in any one direction).

To further guard against random cracking, we coated the edges of the 2-by subplates with one coat of form-release oil. This prevents the concrete from adhering to the side of the plates, thereby reducing tensile stresses within the concrete as it cures and shrinks. The form oil can be applied with either a brush or a small paint roller.

The Concrete

The Youker system relies on a thin concrete slab instead of the more typical gypsum-based underlayments. Concrete not only costs less and is more readily available, but once cured, it is not adversely effected by water. Gypsum-based underlayments can soften with continued exposure to water. Although normally this is not a problem, a leaking pipe or large spill at some point in the building's life might lead to major problems with the flooring. Also, the thermal conductivity of concrete (with a limestone aggregate) is about twice that of gypsum-based underlayments. This allows better lateral heat flow away from the tubing within the floor slab, producing less noticeable variations in the surface temperature.

Mix design. The mix design we used is shown in the table on the next page. Before adding the superplasticizer, this mix will have a slump of 2 to 3 inches. Once added, the superplasticizer increases the slump to 7 or 8 inches. This high slump, in combination with the small "pea stone" aggregate, allows the mix to easily flow around the tubing and makes for excellent thermal bonding. The water-reducing agent controls shrinkage of the concrete as it cures. The fibermesh provides tensile reinforcement to further resist shrinkage cracking.

Pouring the Slab

continued on next page

Youker Mix Design

Type 1 portland cement	517 lb.
Concrete sand	1,630 lb.
#1A (1/4" maximum) peastone	1,485 lb.
Air-entrainment agent	4.14 oz.
Hycol (water-reducing agent)	15.5 oz.
Fiber mesh	1.5 lb.
Superplasticizer (WRDA-19)	51.7 oz.
Water about	20 gal.

Note: These mix proportions make one cubic yard of 3,000-psi concrete floor topping (strength rated at 28 days). The high-slump concrete recipe creates an easy-to-pour mix that flows well around the tubing, providing excellent thermal conduction between the tubing and the concrete.

continued from previous page

used a scrap of plywood under the nose of the wheelbarrow as it was dumped to prevent pinching the tubing. In many places, the 2-by subplates served as screeds; in larger rooms where these plates could not be reached, temporary 2x4s were screwed down to the deck to serve as screed guides.

We found that a single worker on the wheelbarrow could keep up with two workers placing the concrete. For the 900-square-foot slab, this three-person crew placed, screeded, and floated 4 1/2 yards of concrete in about 45 minutes. We were able to continue framing the next day. Cracks over the control joints appeared a few days after the pour.

Added Dead Load

The concrete we used had a dry density of about 144 pounds per cubic foot. At a thickness of 1 1/2 inches, this added about 18 pounds per square foot to the dead loading on the floor. By contrast, a 1 1/2-inch-thick gypsum-based underlayment adds about 14.4 pounds per square foot.

In either case, it is critical that the floor framing is designed to handle the extra loading. In many cases, deeper or closer-spaced joists will be required. In our project, we used wood I-joists designed for the extra loading. It's important to inform the supplier of extra loading requirements when ordering the joists.

On all projects, I prefer to size the floor framing to limit deflection to no more than 1/480 of the clear span under full live loading. This results in a very solid deck. The extra cost associated with beefing up the floor deck will, of course, add to the square-foot cost of any thin-slab system.

Insulation. Any type of thin-slab floor-heating system also requires insulation under the subflooring to limit downward heat flow. I specify R-11 insulation when the space beneath the floor is fully heated, and R-19 over partially heated basements. The cost of installing this insulation should also be factored into the square-foot cost of the system if it would not otherwise be present.

Incorporate into Design

While this system can be modified for use in retrofit work, we found the key to using it on our project was to incorporate it into the design of the building as early as possible. This allowed us to optimize the floor framing for higher loading, and to adjust the procedure so we didn't have to worry about the heights of windows, doors, cabinets, and stair risers to compensate for an extra 1 1/2-inch-thick slab.

— John Siegenthaler

Case Study: Installing a Radiant Wall

In recent years, hydronic radiant floor heating has become increasingly popular. Radiant floors have limitations, however. A heavy carpet and pad, or full-thickness wood flooring, can act as an insulator and restrict heat output. The same is true where much of the floor is covered with furniture, cabinets, or other objects.

Boosting the water temperature in the tubing is generally not a good way to remedy this situation, because the exposed floor areas may get uncomfortably warm. Also, temperatures above 85°F increase stress on wood floors, possibly leading to excessive shrinkage and gaps.

Advantages of Radiant Walls

When radiant system designers take floor coverings into account, they may find that some rooms require more heat than the floor alone can provide. Why not use a drywall surface — a wall or even a ceiling — as a supplemental heat source? One scenario would be to use the floor to provide all the heat during partial load conditions, with the heated wall operating as necessary during very cold weather, or to speed up room temperature recovery following a setback period. Such a system could be controlled with a standard two stage thermostat. Another scenario would be to use the wall as the sole radiant panel for the room.

Undersun Construction and I had the opportunity to design and build a radiant wall using a 4-foot-high by 31-foot-long kneewall. The technique would also work well in a room with a chair rail 36 to 40 inches above the floor, which could provide a natural break between the thicker heated wall below and a standard-thickness wall above, eliminating the need to shim out the upper portion of the wall. This would also deliver the radiant heat into the lower, occupied portion of the room, where it would provide the most comfort. (It's also less likely that occupants will drive nails into the lower portion of the wall to hang pictures.) A chair rail could also provide a clean transition line in a retrofit situation.

A heated wall actually has certain advantages over a heated floor. For one thing, drywall isn't subject to the 85°F surface temperature limit often imposed on floors, so it's possible to get more heat from a wall than from a floor of the same size. This, and the fact that 1/2-inch drywall has relatively low thermal mass, make a radiant wall useful in areas that require fast recovery time. A heated wall would be well-suited for passive solar buildings, for example, which often have large, quickly changing heat gains and losses.

Just as with floors, the output of a radiant wall will be affected by objects placed against it. Before you commit to a wall heating system, find out if the owner is planning to line the wall with bookcases, an entertainment center, upholstered furniture, and so forth. Some coverage is probably acceptable as long as it's accounted for in the design.

Components

The system that we installed used common materials. For hydronic tubing, we used 1/2-inch AlumPex (Weil-McLain; www.weil-mclain.com). Unlike standard PEX tubing, which is all plastic, this PEX-AL-PEX tubing has a thin layer of aluminum sandwiched between inner and outer layers of cross-linked polyethylene. We chose it because its rate of thermal expansion and contraction is much lower than that of standard PEX, reducing the possibility of "ticking" sounds as the system warms up and cools down.

The tubing snaps into 6x24-inch aluminum heat transfer plates, also from Weil-McClain, which have a semicircular groove down their centerline that wraps around the tubing. (These are the same plates used in radiant floor applications.) The high conductivity of the aluminum conducts heat away from the tubing and spreads it out across the surface to be heated.

The plates mounted over strips of 3/4-inch Thermax foil-faced polyisocyanurate board, spaced to accommodate the tubing. The rigid foam adds about R-5.2 to the wall insulation, helping direct heat into the room (the foam is rated for service at temperatures up to 250°F). Although the aluminum facing is only about 0.001 inch thick, it helps conduct heat away from the tubing and disperse it across the wall surface. And because the foam has a very low thermal mass, it allows the wall to heat up quickly when warm water starts circulating through the tubing.

Under the foam board, we used standard 7/16-inch OSB, with 4 inches of fiberglass insulation behind that. The system described here can be used on either exterior or interior partition walls. In an exterior wall, the total R-value of the insulation behind the aluminum plates should be at least 50 percent greater than the R-value ordinarily specified for a standard unheated wall in a given climate.

In an interior partition, you can probably leave the fiberglass back-side insulation out altogether. In floor heating applications, we usually use a ratio of 10:1, downward to upward R-value as a guideline. The greater this ratio, the more heat is directed into the room. Even without back-side insulation added to the wall system,

continued on next page

continued from previous page

Inside a Radiant Wall

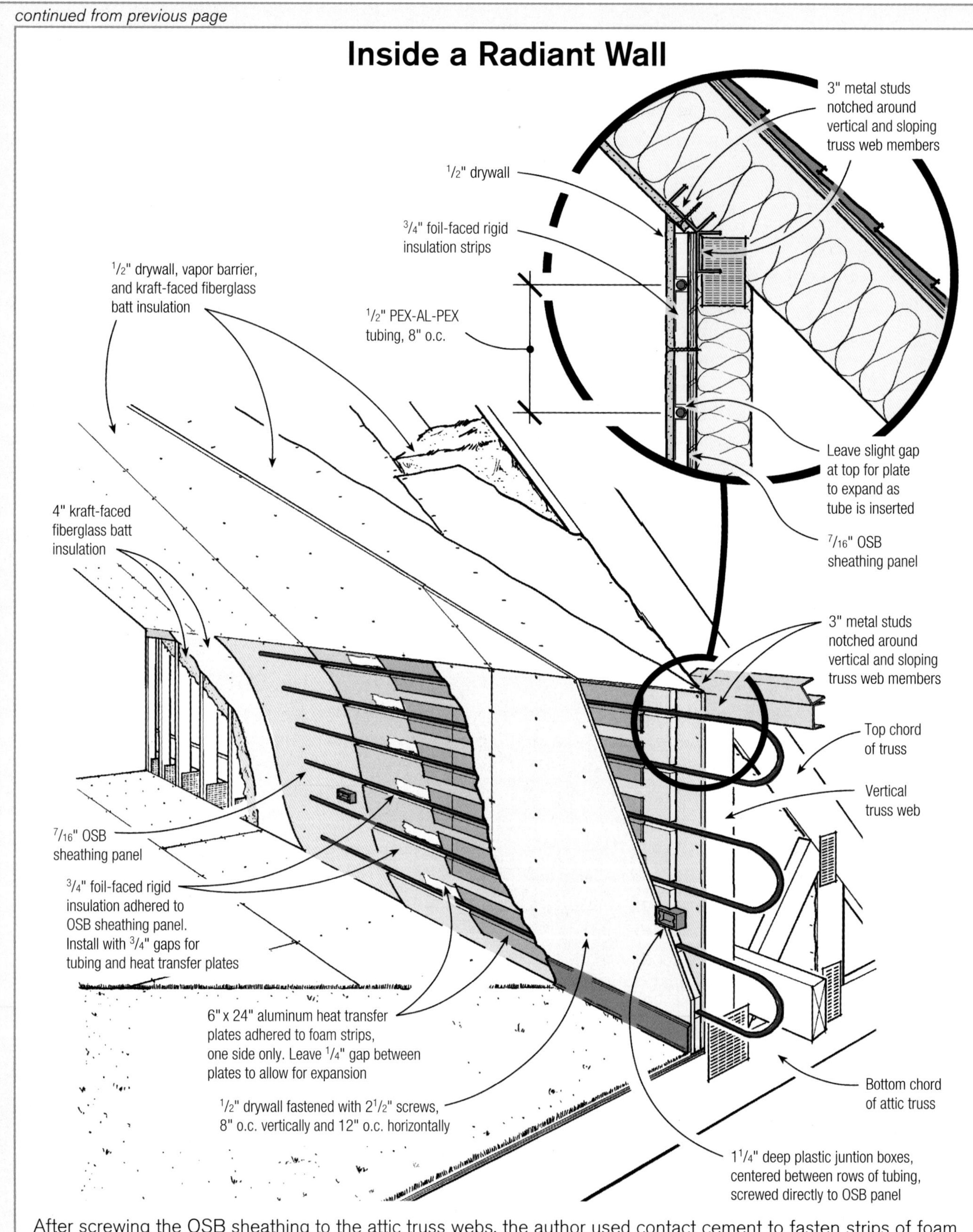

After screwing the OSB sheathing to the attic truss webs, the author used contact cement to fasten strips of foam insulation to the OSB. U-shaped aluminum heat-transfer plates were then cemented to the foam boards, but only along one side to allow the plates to expand as they heat up. Chalk lines snapped on the drywall ensured that no screws penetrated the PEX tubing.

the foam strips and OSB together constitute about R-5.5. Since the 1/2-inch drywall has an R-value of about 0.5, the back-side to room-side R-value ratio is 11:1. Keep in mind that back-side losses on interior walls are also usually heat gains to other rooms. Make sure there are no holes or notches in the top plate of the partition where the warm air can escape.

I've calculated that the radiant wall described here will deliver about 1.4 Btu/hr./sq.ft. for every degree the wall surface temperature exceeds the room air temperature. For example, if the mean wall surface temperature is 95°F and the room temperature is 68°F, the heat output should be about (95-68) x 1.4 = 37 Btu/hr/sq. ft.

Although many components in this wall are capable of operating at relatively high temperatures, the surface of the drywall should not be allowed to exceed 120°F. At higher temperatures, the drywall joints might discolor or hairline cracks might appear. Based on theoretical models of the wall's performance, I suggest limiting water supply temperatures to about 140°F.

Installation Is Straightforward

The first step was to provide a nailer between the trusses where the vertical and sloped webs meet. To avoid the tedious process of installing solid wood blocking, we used 2x3 metal studs turned on edge, notching the flanges at every truss web with metal snips (see illustration, facing page).

After insulating the stud cavities with high density fiberglass batts, we sheathed the knee wall with 7/16-inch OSB to provide a smooth, strong substrate for the rest of the system. We then ripped 7 1/4-inch by 8-foot strips from 4x8 sheets of 3/4-inch foil-faced polyisocyanurate board. We snapped horizontal chalk lines every 8 inches up the wall, starting 3 5/8 inches above the floor. These lines marked the top edge of each foam strip (Figure 18).

We bonded the foam strips to the OSB with contact cement, using a paint roller to apply the adhesive to both surfaces (Figure 19). (Again, we verified that the adhesive would not lose strength or pose outgassing problems at elevated temperatures.) We used a couple of 3/4-inch wood spacer blocks to maintain a consistent gap between the strips as we pressed them into place.

Tubing and final finish. Next we installed the aluminum heat transfer plates, again with contact adhesive. We used a 3-inch paint roller to apply the cement to only one side of the plate and the matching face of the foam board. Bonding only one side of the plate would allow the plate to expand and contract with changes in temperature. We also

continued on next page

Figure 18. To create the radiant wall surface, the attic truss knee walls (top) were first sheathed with OSB . Strips of foil-faced foam were then adhered to the OSB, with 3/4-inch gaps left to accept the aluminum heat-transfer plates and PEX tubing (above).

Figure 19. A paint roller is used to apply contact adhesive to foil-faced foam before mounting aluminum heat-transfer plates. Adhesive is used only on one edge of each strip to allow for thermal movement.

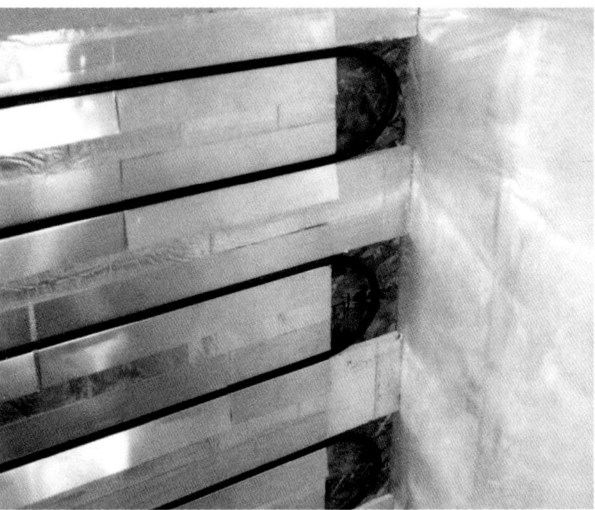

Figure 20. Return bends in the 1/2-inch PEX-AL-PEX tubing were easily formed by hand (left). With all the tubing in place, the drywall is installed, with lines snapped on the foam board to guide the screws (right).

continued from previous page

left a 1/4-inch gap between adjacent plates to allow for expansion and held the plates back about 4 inches from the junction boxes to avoid heating the receptacles.

Installing the tubing was a matter of snapping the straight runs of tubing into the grooved aluminum plates, then making return bends by hand at the ends of the wall (Figure 20). In laying out the tube, we made sure that supply and return ends of the circuit fell at the same end of the wall, to minimize tubing "leaders" that are not part of the heated wall.

The final step was to install the 1/2-inch drywall. We snapped guide lines half way between the rows of tubing and drove the screws to the line as usual. Using the OSB as a backer sheet, we placed 2 1/2-inch screws every 8 inches vertically and every 12 inches horizontally. The generous screw pattern ensures that the drywall is sucked in tight against the aluminum plates for good heat transfer. We taped and painted the wall as usual.

Figure 21. The author used this half-wall around a stairwell as a radiant wall on a later project. Delivering the heat into the lower, occupied portion of the room provides the greatest comfort.

How It All Works

An oil-fired boiler is the heat source for the wall (as well as the other hydronic systems in the building). A variable speed injection mixing system is used to control the wall's supply water temperature. The mixing system can be configured for either a fixed water temperature or a water temperature that increases as outdoor temperature drops. To date, I've operated the wall at a fixed supply temperature of 125°F.

The wall has been through several heating seasons, with positive results. From a startup temperature of 60°F, heat output is evident in about 10 minutes. The wall appears to reach steady operating conditions about 30 minutes after a cold start. The system operates silently, without any expansion sounds following cold starts. Part of the credit goes to the PEX-AL-PEX tubing, which has an expansion rate very close to that of the aluminum plates. We were also careful to leave an expansion space between the return bends and the end walls of the room; this prevents binding and the subsequent expansion "ticks" often heard in hydronic systems.

We have used the same basic design on several projects with success (Figure 21). It work well with low-temperature heat sources such as condensing boilers, geothermal heat pumps, and solar thermal systems.

John Siegenthaler, *with assistance from Harvey Youker of UnderSun Construction*

Hardwood Flooring Over Radiant Heat

by Doug Mossbrook

I've been installing radiant floors around New York state for a number of years. From the very beginning, I heard horror stories about hardwood floors shrinking, heaving, cracking, and swelling — all blamed on radiant heating. I wondered how all these problems could be caused by exposing the wood to such low, even temperatures.

From the outset, I wanted to make radiant floor heat a viable option for anyone who wanted it, and I knew that many clients would choose hardwood as their finish floor surface. I was determined to solve the hardwood flooring dilemma.

By following up on reports of wood flooring failures, I came to realize that many of the problems blamed on radiant heating would actually have occurred anyway — usually because of excessive job-site or household moisture. Where the radiant heating was a factor, in many cases simple modifications in the design and installation of the system could have prevented the problem.

Consequently, my program for success with hardwood flooring has two main points: careful control of job-site moisture levels and good hvac design. Following that advice, I've found that with the possible exception of wide plank floors, almost any type of hardwood floor — be it solid or laminated, nail-down, glue-down, or floating — can work with radiant floor heat, though some choices may perform better than others (see "Wood Flooring Choices for Radiant Heat," page 252).

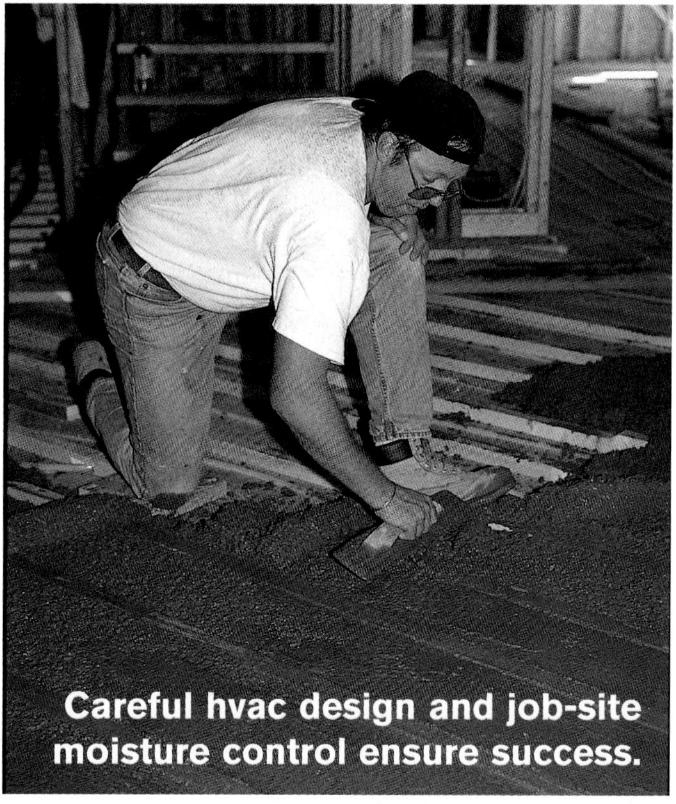
Careful hvac design and job-site moisture control ensure success.

Good Hvac Design Is Key

A perfect hardwood installation will fail if the radiant floor is not properly designed. Two enemies of hardwood are excessive floor temperatures and heat that is not evenly distributed, so I design the system accordingly. Here are four guidelines to keep in mind when you talk to your radiant system designer about protecting the hardwood floors.

1. Use the lowest possible fluid design temperature (the temperature of the water or glycol solution in the heating tubes).
2. Modify the tubing or insulation design instead of boosting the fluid temperature.
3. Use responsive controls to keep the heat as constant as possible.
4. Use supplemental heating when necessary.

Low Water Temperature

Radiant floors are designed to work at lower supply temperatures than hydronic baseboards or panel radiators. This is because floors warmer than about 85°F are uncomfortable underfoot. This is also the maximum temperature that a wood floor should be exposed to, according to the flooring industry. In fact, I've found that lower temperatures — around 80°F — are healthier for wood floors.

The fluid temperature required to produce that 80°F surface temperature will vary greatly, depending on floor construction and finishes and the type of radiant system used (see "Options For Warm Wood Floors," page 250). A bare concrete radiant slab, for example, offers little thermal resistance; 100°F water in tubes spaced 12 inches on-center may do the job. But lay down 2x4 sleepers, a plywood subfloor, and hardwood strip flooring, and now you've added an insulation layer that the heat output of the tubing has to overcome (Table 2).

The temptation is to increase the supply temperature to compensate for the added insulation. When hardwood floors are involved, fluid temperatures typically range from 105°F to 125°F for Gyp-Crete type floors and could be as high as 145°F for staple-up under-floor applications. It's hard to make generalizations about design because of the many variables, but if I'm having difficulty reaching a comfortable surface temperature, I'll add more insulation under the tubing, space the tubes closer together, increase the diameter of the tubing, or suggest a flooring with a lower R-value — anything except boosting the fluid temperatures.

Tube Spacing

Pipes spaced too far apart will create hot and cold streaks — a bad thing for a wood floor, which should expand and contract uniformly (Figure 22). A tubing design that works great in a warehouse with a bare concrete floor is probably not suitable for a living room. Many radiant floor designs are based on tubing layouts 12 inches or more on-center. For hardwood flooring, though, the spacing should be less, ideally 6 to 8 inches. The closer the spacing, the more even the heat will be, and the happier the wood flooring will be.

In some cases it may be necessary to decrease the diameter of the tubing as the spacing grows closer. Be careful not to exceed the maximum allowable length of each loop, which, depending on the pump size, could be as little as 100 feet for some types of 3⁄8-inch tubing. Closer tubing spacing means more individual loops. More loops mean more manifolds, which in turn means more advance planning.

High-Tech Controls

Controls for radiant floors have come a long way since the first systems were put in. The simplest control is the basic indoor wall thermostat. Setback thermostats, which are standard nowadays in conventional hvac systems, are of little value with radiant floor heat because of the slow response time of the floor. I encourage clients to find a temperature they're happy with and leave the thermostat alone.

With wood floors over radiant slabs, I encourage the use of more advanced controls and components that help to gradually modulate the heat output of the floor in response to outdoor temperature. I often install an outdoor reset control, which varies the temperature of the water in the floor depending on the temperature outside.

In great rooms with walls of windows, thermal gain can be a problem as the sun beats on the floor during the day, while at night the glass siphons the heat back out. Since wood floors don't like sudden changes in temperature, to minimize these solar swings, we may install sensors in the slab or thin-slab that signal the heating system to shut down a zone until the sun stops "loading" the floor. Another option we might consider is one of the new "modulating" boilers, which regulate fluid temperature by adjusting the gas flow to the burner based on different heating demands.

I also encourage the extra expense of injection pumps, which provide more responsive control of fluid temperature than the more conventional four-way mixing valves. When used in combination with the outdoor reset control, injection pumps help keep the fluid at the lowest possible temperature to satisfy the heating load for the room. This minimizes problems with the wood floor.

Supplemental Radiators

A properly designed radiant floor will produce around 20 to 25 Btu/hr/sq.ft. If that's not enough heat to satisfy the room, the common mistake is to increase the floor temperature — again putting the hardwood at risk. A better solution is to supplement the floor with radiant panels in the walls or ceiling, or add some conventional hot-water baseboard or a cabinet unit to the room.

Another common mistake is to ignore the area rugs that the owner may be planning to put down on the floor. An 18x20-foot great room may have a wool rug and pad in the middle that covers more than half of the floor area. This is basically a big insulating blanket that has to be factored into the design.

Moisture Control Is Critical

Because radiant floor heating is often the scapegoat for any wood floor failure, I take a proactive position when it comes to job-site moisture. Perfectly acclimated hardwood flooring laid over a perfectly cured slab will still fail if the basement or ground below is constantly wet. If we see something going on that could impact the final floor — for instance, a basement slab going down with no vapor barrier or a crawlspace with no ground cover — we step in and try to educate the builder as to why he needs to take the extra steps. Usually builders and homeowners are happy to oblige — they don't want problems with the hardwood floors any more than I do.

R-Value of Flooring Materials

Flooring Material	R-Value
1⁄2-inch plywood	0.62
3⁄4-inch plywood	0.94
Vinyl sheet flooring	0.21
Ceramic tile	0.22
3⁄8-inch hardwood flooring	0.54
3⁄4-inch hardwood flooring	0.93
1⁄2-inch acrylic plush carpet	1.71
7⁄8-inch nylon plush carpet	1.83
1⁄2-inch wool plush carpet	2.19
1⁄4-inch waffled rubber pad	0.78
3⁄8-inch urethane pad	1.61

Table 2. Finished flooring acts as an insulator on top of a radiant floor and must be accounted for in the design of the system. Ceramic tile provides little resistance to heat flow, so it works well with the low fluid temperatures used in radiant heating. A conventional hardwood floor with 3⁄4-inch subfloor has an R-value near 2. If the homeowners plan to add a rug on top, it becomes trickier for the designer to meet the heating needs of the room without overheating the hardwood flooring.

Another place I get involved is making sure there is enough time in the schedule. For example, a radiant Gyp-Crete floor can't be turned on for four to five days after it's poured to allow the Gyp-Crete to develop proper strength before being subjected to rapid heat. It might then take another two to three weeks with the heat on for the floor to reach its final moisture content so the hardwood can be installed. That's close to a month in the schedule that has to be accounted for. Since most of the homeowners we work with are prepared to spend more for a radiant heating system, it's not hard to convince them that rushing the job to save a few dollars on their construction loan is not in their best interest.

Checking for Moisture

The usual product literature that tells you to "let the flooring adjust to the room for 72 hours before installation" is in a word — baloney! It's important to keep track of moisture levels in the products being installed, but it is far more important that the house reach its "normal" moisture level before any finished flooring is even brought on site. A perfectly dry floor will swell as it soaks up job-site moisture — from a wet slab or subfloor or even the air inside the house.

Moisture levels should be monitored in both the substrate and the flooring before installation. The moisture content in the substrate should be no more than 11 to 12 percent, and the finish flooring should be about 4 percent less than the substrate. In no case should the finish flooring exceed 8 percent moisture content. Be sure to test all bundles.

Moisture meters. Anyone involved with wood flooring — or any kind of woodwork, for that matter —

How Tube Spacing Affects Floor Surface Temperature

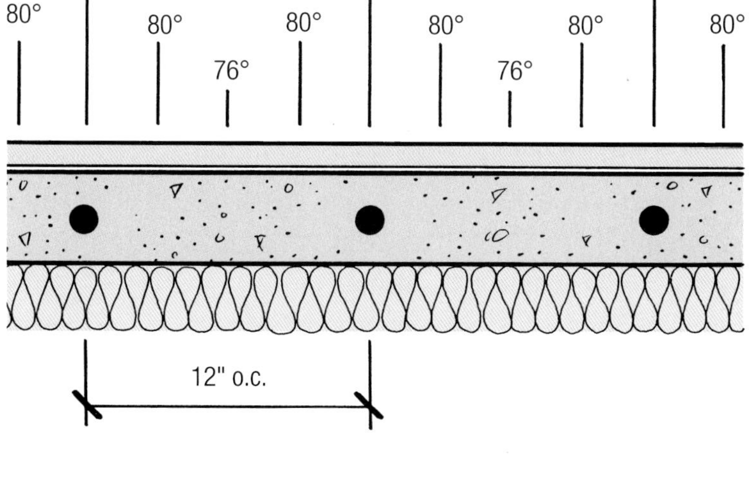

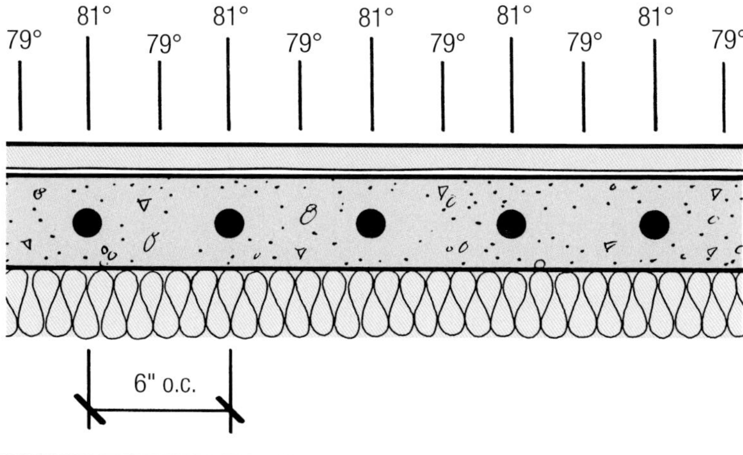

Figure 22. Each of the floors illustrated here has a 20 Btu/hr. output. Note that with 12-inch on-center tube spacing (left), the "striping" effect is much more pronounced. Six-inch spacing (below, left) produces the same heat with a lower surface temperature and a more even heat distribution — both of which are advantageous for hardwood flooring.

Options for Warm Wood Floors

The goal in designing a radiant system for hardwood floors is to provide continuous, even heat at as low a temperature as possible. There are several types of radiant floor systems, and some work better than others at meeting this goal.

Slab Systems

When I have my choice, I always prefer a system that uses thermal mass over a staple-up system. The mass helps even out temperature swings, which benefits the wood floor. I see no real differences in performance between full-thickness slabs (A) and thin slabs poured over wood framing. With thin slabs (B), I like Gyp-Crete because it's less likely to crack than a portland cement mix, though it's more expensive. Another thermal mass option we sometimes use is to substitute dry sand for the Gyp-Crete.

The maximum fluid temperature I use in a concrete or Gyp-Crete system is 140°F, to keep thermal swings and possible fracturing in the concrete or Gyp-Crete to a minimum. The only times the design temperature would need to approach 140°F is if plywood is used to provide a continuous nail base, or if sleepers are laid on top of a slab and the hardwood flooring is installed on the sleepers. In general, I prefer to set the sleepers close together for good nailing, pour the thin-slab mix in between, and lay the flooring directly over the slab and sleepers.

Staple-Up

In retrofit situations, when the wood floor is already in place, or when the designer, for whatever reason, doesn't want to pour a thin slab, my second choice is a staple-up system with a reflective insulating barrier below (C). This might be foil-faced rigid foam board or a reflective barrier with batt insulation underneath.

Some installers use aluminum plates to help spread the heat sideways and prevent the "striping" effect. I don't like the plates for a couple of reasons: They're expensive — about $3 apiece — and they're noisy when they're walked over and when they expand and contract. I've found that as long as I use the reflective barrier, stapling the tubes directly to the subfloor without plates works fine. I've never had a complaint about striping as long as the floor is designed with minimum water temperature in mind.

Another variation of this system, also designed to prevent striping, is the "suspended tube" approach — where the tubing hangs an inch or so below the subfloor,

A. Radiant Slab

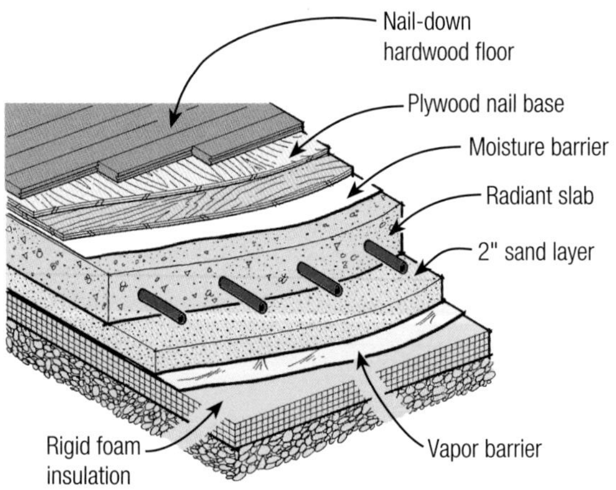

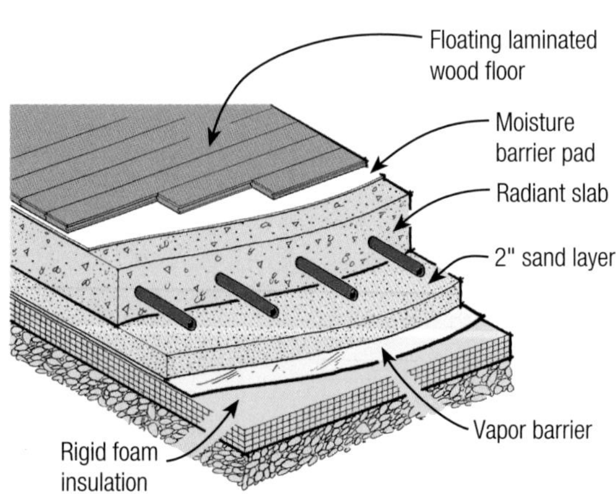

Whether you install nail-down strip flooring (left) or a floating laminated wood floor (right) over a radiant slab, be sure to include a moisture barrier on top of the concrete as well as below the slab. For nail-down flooring, lay a single sheet of 3/4-inch plywood or a double layer of 1/2-inch plywood as a nail base.

B. Radiant Thin Slab

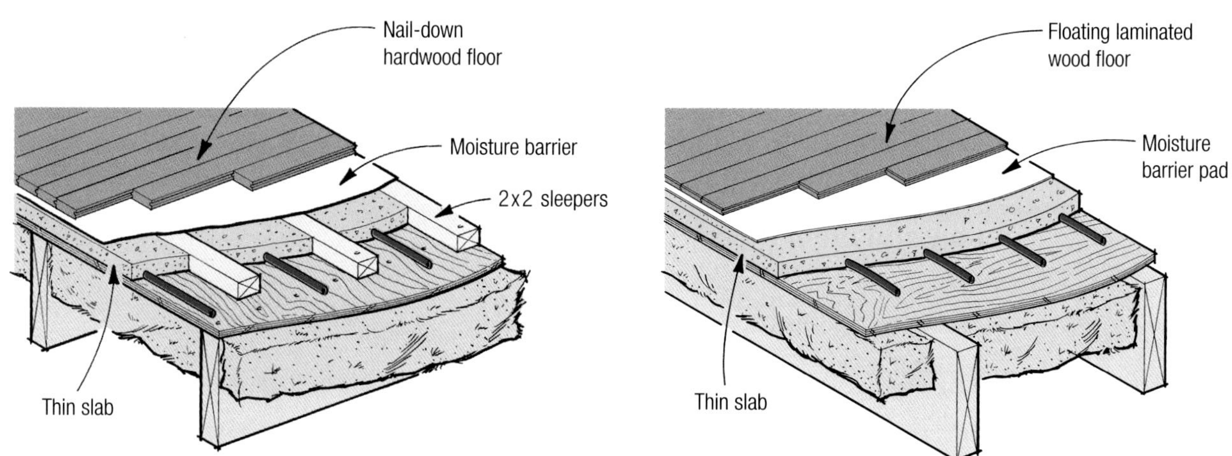

When installing nail-down strip flooring over a thin slab (left), the author recommends spacing the sleepers 8 inches on-center to provide good nailing. For wider sleeper spacings, you can use a plywood nail base, but the fluid temperature may need to be raised to overcome the plywood's thermal resistance. A floating wood floor system (right) installs directly over the thin slab.

with the reflective barrier below. In my experience, this makes it harder to install the tubing with little to gain for the trouble. Also, I've seen this technique misapplied, where the tubing was stapled to the sides of the joists — which does a good job of heating up the joist, but not the floor above. I prefer the direct contact of the tubing with the subfloor.

Staple-up systems require slightly higher fluid temperatures, with the maximum I'd use being around 160°F. Usually, it takes about 130°F to 140°F in the joist bays to produce an 80°F surface temperature. A critical factor in designing any staple-up system is to make sure that the insulation R-value under the tubing is at least four times as great as the R-value of the materials above the tubing. The goal is to direct the heat up.

— D.M.

C. Reflective Staple-Up System

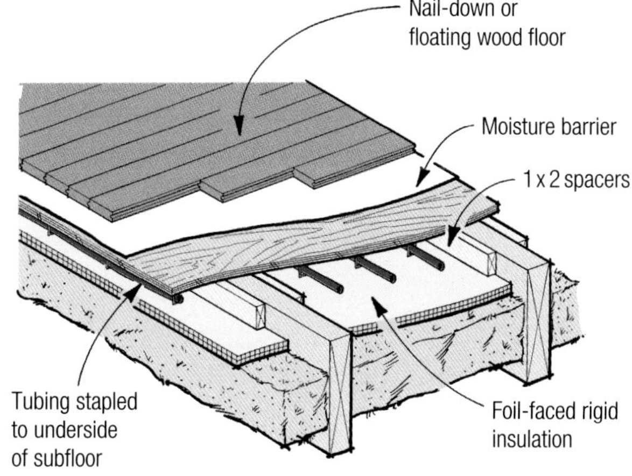

When installing underfloor radiant heating, the author staples the tubing directly to the subfloor, then adds an insulated reflective layer below — either foil-faced foam board, shown here, or a radiant blanket with batt insulation below.

Wood Floor Choices for Radiant Heat

Laminated wood flooring products are more dimensionally stable than solid wood floors, so they tend to perform better over radiant heat. Because solid wood behaves badly over a poorly designed radiant floor, always check with the flooring manufacturer for warranty details before committing to a product.

Avoid solid wide-plank flooring of any species; large gaps are guaranteed during the heating season. If the client insists, use a laminated product with a plank look.

When using conventional nail-down hardwood strip flooring, try to budget for a quartersawn product, which will move much less than a flatsawn flooring. Use strip flooring no wider than 3 inches; the narrower, the better.

Although the scientific data might lead to a different conclusion, expansion/contraction problems have been reported with solid sawn floors of very dense woods, like hard maple, possibly because the material is more difficult to acclimate.

Always follow manufacturer instructions exactly when installing over radiant heat. Pay attention to pads, moisture barriers, expansion clearances, and transitions.

Prefinished urethane flooring is a good choice because it is generally coated on all sides. Beware of wax finishes: They are harder to care for.

When applying a floor finish on site, use a sanding sealer first before applying the topcoats. This reduces the chance of side-bonding or "panelization" — the tendency for strip flooring to bond together at the edges, causing the flooring to open up wide cracks in only a few spots when the flooring shrinks.

Flooring made from quartersawn lumber (left in photo) will expand and contract much less than flatsawn lumber flooring (at right).

Prefinished flooring profiles with eased edges, or "micro-bevels," will show expansion and contraction less than square-edged products.

Be careful with glue-down flooring products. In some cases, the adhesive may not perform well because of the constant heat. Always check with the manufacturer.
— D. M.

should have a hand-held moisture meter. For around $300, you can get a meter that works on wood, concrete, and Gyp-Crete. Also, if you expect your moisture tests to stand up in court, in some states the meter must be capable of lab calibration. (A good source for moisture meters is the Professional Equipment catalog; www.professionalequipment.com).

Concrete slabs can start being checked for moisture content 30 days after placement, and Gyp-Crete after about a week. However, don't make the fatal mistake of just assuming a slab is okay because of its age — use a meter.

The polyfilm test. If you don't have a moisture meter, an easy way to check moisture in a slab is to duct tape 24-inch-square pieces of polyethylene at several points on the floor. After 24 hours, if any water is present or even if the concrete is darker under the plastic, then there is too much moisture in the slab. The test can be accelerated by placing a 60-watt light bulb 18 inches above the plastic. Keep performing the test until the moisture has dried up.

Acclimating the House

Once the radiant floor is ready to be turned on, we bring up the temperature to let it start drying the house. If the house also has central air-conditioning, we run that at the same time to further dehumidify and control the indoor temperature. If no a/c is available, large drying fans, available at rental yards, can be used.

Once the temperature and moisture levels stabilize, then the hardwood can be brought to the job site. If conditions are right where the flooring is stored and it is handled properly, there is no reason the hardwood can't be acclimated off site, which may shave a few days off the schedule.

Always Use a Moisture Barrier

The new urethane finishes common on today's hardwood floors put a moisture barrier on top of the wood. The last thing you want is for the unfinished back to absorb moisture from the subfloor — a common cause of cupping.

Hardwood always used to be installed over resin

Figure 23. For hardwood strip flooring over radiant heating, always use a moisture barrier like Moistop (above), a fiber-reinforced composite of poly and kraft paper popular with flooring contractors in the author's area. Under floating hardwood floors, a pad like Astro/Barrier (right) provides a foam cleavage layer and a poly moisture break.

paper or something similar. With a radiant floor, this "cleavage membrane" serves another function — to stop moisture from migrating from the subfloor or Gyp-Crete into the flooring. A moisture barrier won't help a chronically wet house, but it will buy a little time while a new house dries and will buffer seasonal moisture changes.

The one moisture barrier not to use under a radiant floor is black asphalt-impregnated felt — that is unless you enjoy the smell of asphalt every time the heat comes on. A sheet of poly would probably do the job, but the installers we work with prefer a moisture-retarding membrane such as Moistop (Fortifiber Corp.; www.fortifiber.com). This product is 12 mils thick, and consists of kraft paper and fiberglass reinforcing laminated between two sheets of black poly (Figure 23). Moistop has been used for years in the concrete industry, primarily as a sub-slab vapor retarder and also as a radon barrier. In the past few years, the product has found a niche in the flooring industry. At around 5¢ per square foot, it's cheap insurance.

If you're installing a floating laminated wood floor, use a product like Astro/Barrier (Innovative Energy, Inc.; www.insul.net), which is a high-density foam pad bonded to a poly sheet. It comes in 4-foot-wide rolls.

Finally, Educate

If you've read this far, it's probably clear to you that successful installation of a hardwood floor over radiant heat will involve coordination and cooperation — between the trades, the building designer, and the homeowner. I make it a point to have a preconstruction meeting with all the parties — the GC, the designer, the flooring contractor, and the owner — as early as possible to discuss the issues. At that point, I hope it's not too late to influence the decisions that have to be made — about the type of radiant floor, the hardwood products and finishes, the system controls, the need for supplemental heat sources, and so forth. I try to provide as much information as possible to make sure that all the parties are on the same page.

Many failures of hardwood flooring are not failures at all, but simply the owners' dissatisfaction with the tendency of wood to expand and contract. Even if the builder has done a great job of moisture-proofing the house, the hvac system is perfect, and the flooring is installed exactly as recommended, there will still be some seasonal movement in any wood floor. Let your clients know what to expect and how their choices will impact the end result. If the homeowner expects hairline cracks to show up in February, then it's no longer a "failure" when it happens.

__Doug Mossbrook__ is president of Eagle Mountain HVAC in Canandaigua, N.Y., specializing in radiant heating applications. Thanks to Joe Jackson of Bristol Mountain Hardwoods for providing background information for the article.

Simple Radiant Floor Retrofit

by Joel Boucher

Our company has had success installing radiant floor heat using a variety of methods. I'm always open to trying new and better installation techniques and was immediately interested when Stadler-Viega (now called Viega; www.viega.net) introduced its Climate Panel several years ago. These radiant panels are designed to be installed on top of the existing subfloor. They are made of ½-inch CDX plywood attached to an aluminum back that's about the thickness of aluminum flashing (0.012 inch). The panels come in two sizes, 7x48 inches and 10x48 inches. Each panel has a groove down the center of the plywood panel to accept a single run of tubing, so the tubing ends up being either 7 inches or 10 inches on-center, depending on the width of the panel. The Climate Panels use ¼-inch (I.D.) tubing, which is smaller than the typical ⅜- or ½-inch tubing used in most radiant floors.

These grooved plywood panels make it quick and easy to install radiant tubing on top of a wood subfloor.

In addition to the straight-run panels, Viega sells panels with U-shaped return bends for use at the end of a run. It calls these panels "U-turn strips."

Cost. The square-foot cost of a Climate Panel job is much more than a staple-up job, and generally more than a concrete pour. But in a remodeling situation where floor height is critical, a concrete or Gyp-Crete pour is usually impossible, so Climate Panel is an attractive option.

Heat output. The heat output of a Climate Panel floor is similar to that of other radiant floors. The limiting factor is usually the need to keep floor surface temperatures below 85˚F. Floor surfaces above 85˚F can be uncomfortable except in foyers or bathrooms, and most finish flooring manufacturers will not guarantee their products if the surface temperature is higher. A surface temperature of 85°F will produce about 35 Btu per square foot per hour. Most of my Climate Panel installations have had a maximum heat output of between 16 and 18 Btu, although higher outputs are possible. Our jobs generally have a maximum water temperature of 120˚F to 125˚F, although I have gone as high as 140˚F. Since all of our installations include weather-responsive controls, the maximum water temperature only occurs on the coldest days.

First Job with Climate Panel

The first installation we did with Climate Panels was in a family room addition on top of an existing deck. It wasn't possible to add 1½ inches to the floor height to accommodate a concrete pour, so staple-up would normally have been our next choice. With a staple-up system you must "drive" the heat through each layer of subfloor. Since the subfloor included the existing pressure-treated decking, a staple-up system would not have been very responsive in this case.

The radiant subfloor panels worked great. We installed the Climate Panels directly on top of the pressure-treated decking, which raised the subfloor height only ½ inch. We were able to use a lower water temperature than would have been necessary with a staple-up system, and we still delivered more Btu per square foot. When the thermostat called for heat, we

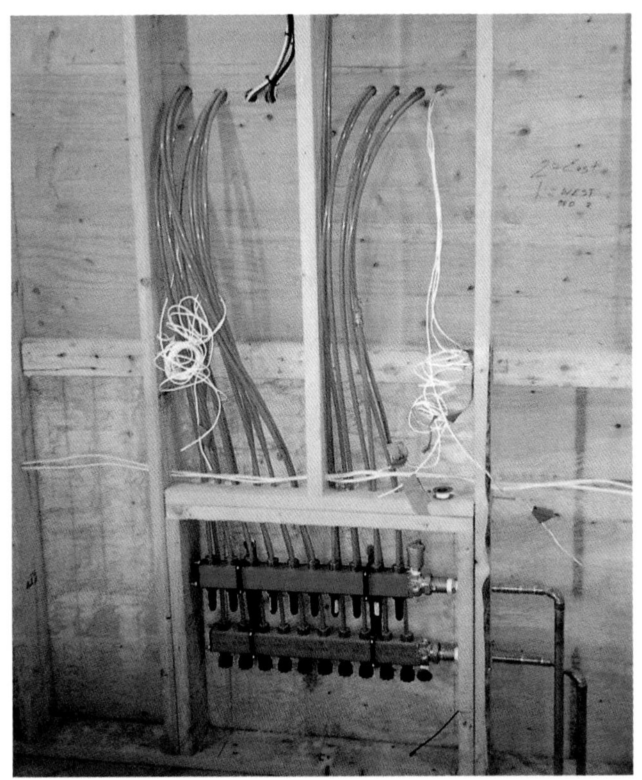

Figure 24. Because the Climate Panel system uses small-diameter tubing (1/4 inch I.D.), loops have to be kept relatively short, usually resulting in the need for more manifolds.

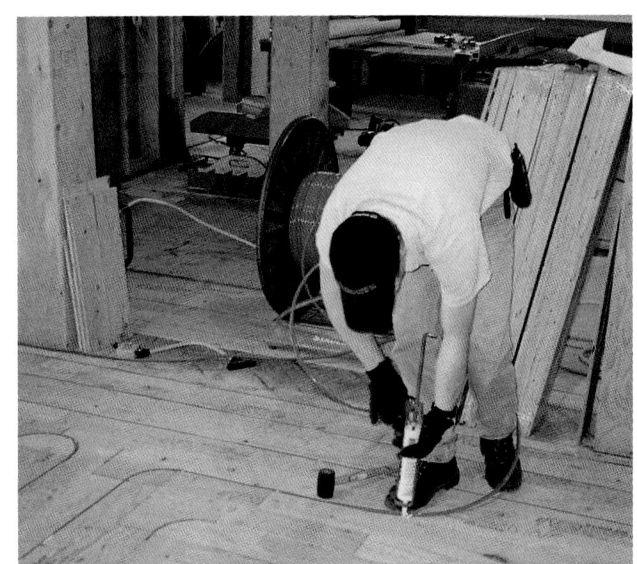

Figure 25. A continuous bead of silicone caulk is installed in each groove just before the tubing is installed.

didn't have to wait as long for the heat to arrive in the room, because it didn't have to push its way up through the decking.

Designing a radiant subfloor. For any radiant heating system, the first step is an accurate tubing layout and overall system design. The home shown on the facing page took considerable time to lay out, because the house was essentially half an octagon, and none of the rooms was square. For this project, we chose to use the narrower 7-inch panels, resulting in a tubing layout that was 7 inches on-center. (In high heat-loss areas, you can rip down the panels to pack the tubing closer together. This home had favorable heat-loss numbers, so this wasn't necessary.) To simplify installation, we didn't try to follow the angles of the house. Instead, we broke the areas with odd angles into rectangular sections. Next, we determined where to start and stop each loop of tubing. This is important to calculate, as each individual loop of tubing should not exceed 300 feet in length, including the run to and from the supply and return manifolds in the basement. Rather than push our luck with runs as long as 300 feet, we like to keep the loops to a maximum of 250 feet. Because of the need for short loops, we usually have to install multiple manifolds (Figure 24). Doing this simplifies zoning as well, as you can easily make each manifold a separate zone.

If hardwood flooring is expected, we design the tubing to run at 90 degrees to the intended direction of the flooring. We want to avoid having the edge of a board running parallel to the tubing, which would make the flooring impossible to nail.

Installation

Once the design work is done, we begin installing the panels. We start by laying out the straight panel sections on the floor, running them down to the return-bend panels. The panels simply butt up against each other, without a gap.

As we lay out the panels, we install just one screw per panel. Most of the screws will be installed later, after the tubing is snapped in the panels. With only one screw per panel, you can wiggle the panels slightly to line up the tubing track when you install the tubing. We generally lay all the panels in the room before installing any tubing.

Installing the tubing. It is important to make sure there is no debris in the panel grooves before installing the tubing. We use a shop vacuum to remove any loose debris — compressed air just blows debris into the adjacent panels, and you find yourself chasing the same wood chips all around the room. You need to run a 1/8-inch to 3/16-inch bead of silicone into the tubing track just before you lay in the tube (Figure 25). Be sure to use pure silicone that can handle temperatures of at least 180°F. The silicone holds the tube in place, so it won't make any noise as it expands and contracts, and slightly improves heat transfer from the tubing to the aluminum plate.

Don't get too far ahead with the silicone, or it will

set up before you can get the tubing in place. The tubing is installed by "walking" it into place (Figure 26). The tubing should not stick up above the panels. Carefully check this before the silicone sets up. We keep a rubber dead-blow hammer handy for extra persuasion. Be careful when using a hammer. If the tubing seems reluctant to go down, double check to make sure that debris hasn't inadvertently gotten into the tubing track.

Figure 26. Once the panels are loosely attached to the floor, the tubing is "walked" into the grooves. If necessary, the tubing can be persuaded into place with a rubber-coated dead-blow hammer.

Screwing down the panels. We use an auto-feed screw gun to finish fastening down the panels, using an average of ten screws per panel. You can use a nail gun for this instead, but then you have to bend over and crawl around. A "pogo stick" screw gun will be easier on your back. We have never had a complaint about a squeak or creak.

Once the panels are all screwed down, we install sections of regular ½-inch plywood to fill in the areas not covered by Climate Panels, such as door thresholds and areas under kitchen cabinets. It is best to keep any tubing runs well away from any areas where finish carpenters may be installing newel posts or special trim.

After the tubing is installed, we pressure-test the system for 24 hours with compressed air at 100 psi.

Insulation. At a bare minimum, 6 inches of fiberglass insulation should be installed in the joist bays underneath the floor. I prefer to see 12-inch batts. If there is a ventilated crawlspace rather than a full basement below, I would cover the fiberglass insulation with an additional layer of rigid foam.

Repairing damaged tubing. We try to install the finish flooring as soon as possible, to avoid accidental damage to the tubing. If installation of the flooring is delayed, you can cover high-traffic areas with plywood for temporary protection. Should a tube be damaged, it can be repaired. If the finish flooring is already down, we first remove the flooring in the area of the leak. We then cut the tubing at the point where it's been damaged and pull up about a foot of the tubing out of the track, on either side of the cut. Then we cut two slots with a Sawzall, each about ½x4 inches,

Figure 27. Hardwood strip flooring can be nailed directly to the Climate Panel. Leaving out the customary felt paper makes it easy to avoid the tubing when nailing.

Figure 28. For tiled areas, cement backerboard is installed on top of the Climate Panels.

right through the subfloor, and poke the ends of the tubing down through the slots. We then splice in a repair piece from below, using two couplings, leaving the patched section under the subfloor.

Finish flooring. Although Climate Panels are mostly used for remodeling jobs, they sometimes make sense for new homes. When a job involves a lot of hardwood flooring, we will often choose Climate Panel because it is by far the easiest system to use under hardwood flooring. The flooring is simply nailed directly on top of the panels (Figure 27). With Climate Panels, unlike a staple-up job, the brightly colored tubing is plainly visible on top of the floor, making it easy for the flooring installer to avoid nailing the tubing.

Some installers put a pad and carpeting directly over Climate Panels. Although such an installation is permitted by the manufacturer, it can leave the tubing vulnerable to damage. It is safer to install carpeting over 1/4-inch underlayment. Vinyl flooring will always require underlayment, and ceramic tile is usually installed over 1/2-inch cement backerboard (Figure 28). The backerboard serves two purposes: It raises the level of the tile floor even with the adjacent hardwood, and it provides a continuous, level surface for installation of the tile. Backerboard is also a good conductor, and spreads the heat out evenly.

Joel Boucher*, vice president of Boucher Energy Systems of Mendon, Mass., designs and installs radiant heat systems.*

Manufacturers of Radiant Subfloor Panels

Warmboard, Inc.
www.warmboard.com

Viega North America
www.viega.net

Uponor (formerly Wirsbo)
www.uponor-usa.com

Chapter 11

DOMESTIC HOT WATER

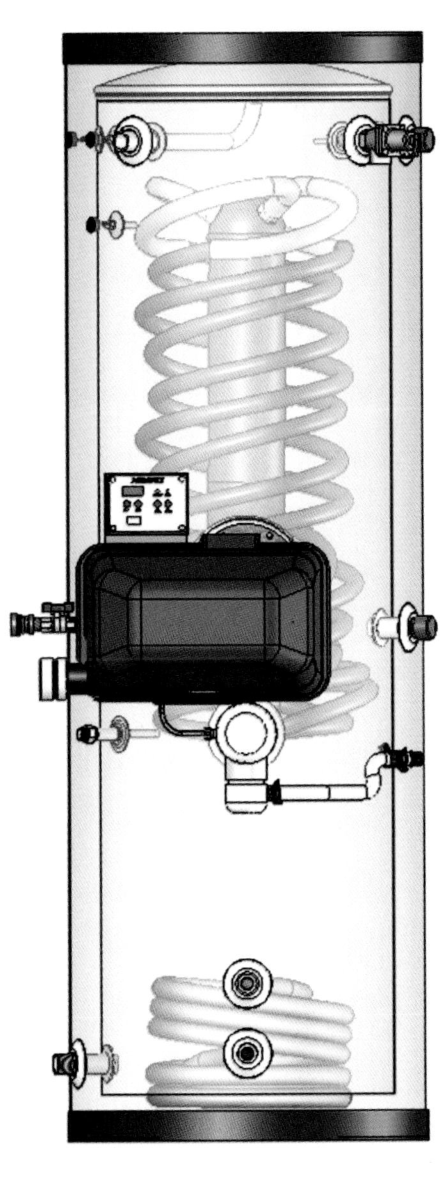

- Condensing Storage Water Heaters
- Indirect-Fired Water Heaters
- Installing On-Demand Water Heaters

Condensing Storage Water Heaters

by Jim Lunt

In my 30-plus years as a plumbing contractor, I've replaced countless water heaters. Our company, which works in the San Francisco Bay area, installs three basic kinds: conventional gas models, tankless models, and — increasingly — condensing storage heaters. Customers who want to save energy nearly always ask for a tankless water heater. That's no surprise — tankless heaters have been getting a lot of media coverage and are the only efficient heaters most people have heard of.

In most cases, however, we recommend condensing storage heaters to our replacement customers, because they are arguably more efficient than tankless models and — when used to replace an existing heater — frequently less expensive to install.

For homeowners, switching from a conventional heater to a condensing model is not a big change. If they consume the same amount of hot water as before, they'll have lower gas bills and run out of hot water less often. Switching to a tankless heater, by contrast, requires some lifestyle adjustments: The homeowners will have to wait for the heater to produce hot water, and they won't be able to get it at very low flow rates (see "Is a Tankless Heater Right for the Job?," page 275).

In this section, I'll discuss condensing storage heaters and how they're installed. Since natural gas is the primary fuel in our region, I'll be describing gas-fired models, many of which can be field-converted for propane.

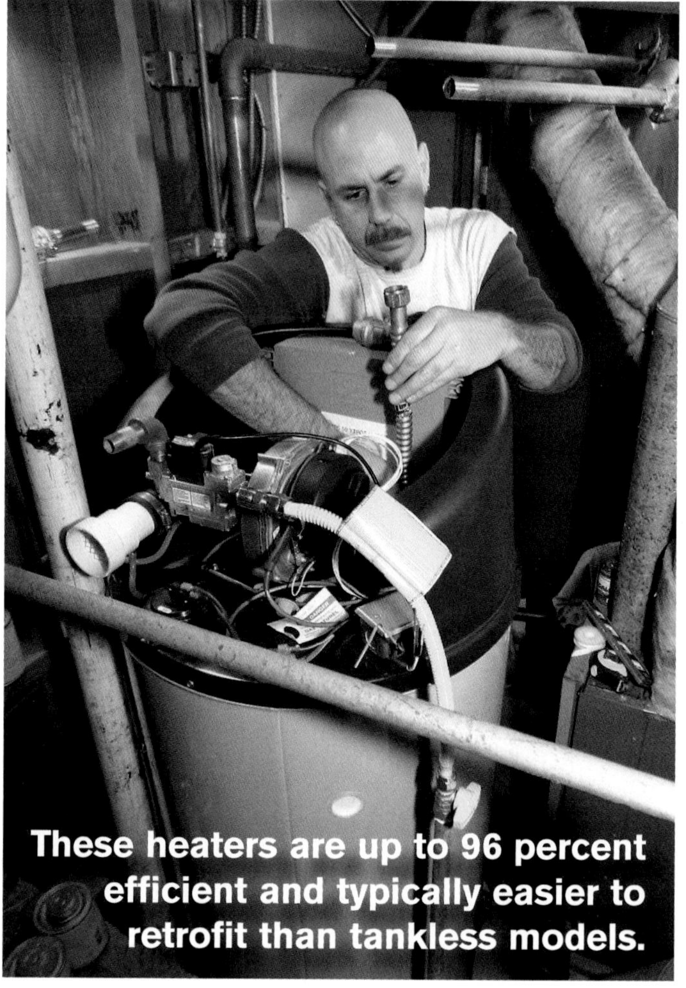

These heaters are up to 96 percent efficient and typically easier to retrofit than tankless models.

How They Work

In several respects, a condensing storage heater is like a conventional model. Both burn gas, have exhaust flues, and store hot water in an insulated tank. But a condensing heater is much more efficient because of how heat is transferred to the water.

In a conventional heater, the fuel is burned in an open chamber, and hot combustion gas rises through a flue in the center of the tank. A lot of this heat is transferred to the water in the storage tank, but a good portion exits through the vent pipe and is wasted.

In a condensing heater, a draft-inducing fan pushes air and fuel into a sealed combustion chamber inside the tank (Figure 1). As the fuel burns, combustion gas is exhausted through a secondary heat exchanger — a coiled steel tube submerged inside the tank. The combustion chamber and heat exchanger have large surface areas to maximize heat transfer to the water. So much heat is transferred that the combustion gases cool to the point where the water vapor in the exhaust stream condenses, releasing its latent heat, which is also transferred to the stored water. By the time the exhaust gas leaves the heater, it's cool enough to be safely vented through inexpensive plastic plumbing pipe. (Each manufacturer accepts different kinds of pipe; options include specified types of PVC, CPVC and ABS. All are far less expensive than stainless steel.)

The thermal efficiency (TE) of a condensing storage heater is quite high, typically between 90 and 96 percent. (For an explanation of thermal efficiency standards, see "Making Sense of Gas Water-Heater Ratings," page 262.) Standby losses are low because the storage tanks are covered with thick foam insulation — plus these units all have electronic ignition, so there is no standing pilot.

Heating Capacity

Most people think of storage heaters in terms of tank and burner size — as in a 40-gallon 40,000-Btu heater (see chart, facing page). The Btu rating is a measure of fuel input to the burner; output is measured in gallons of water heated per hour to a particular temperature rise. The condensing heaters we install have an input

Inside a Condensing Water Heater

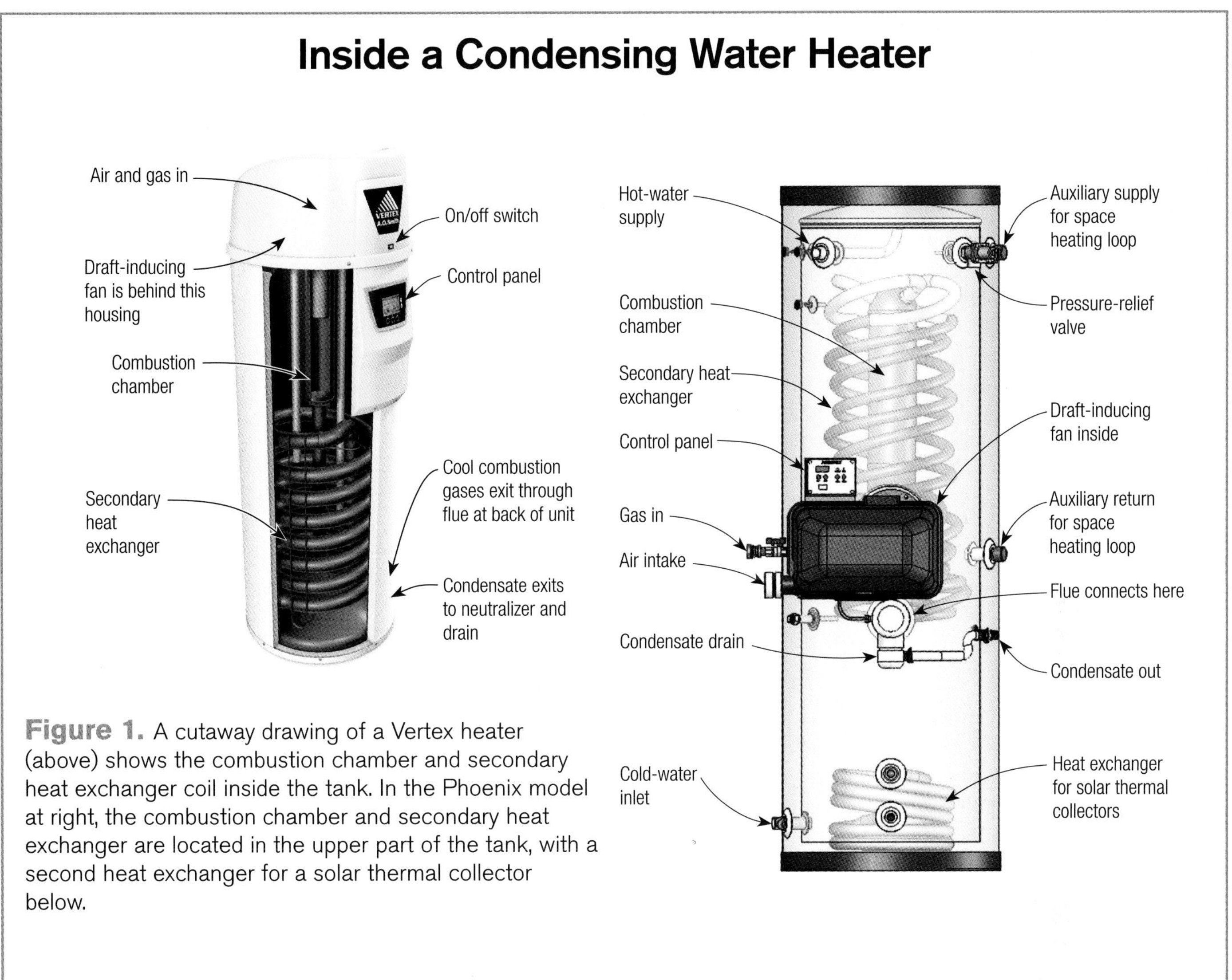

Figure 1. A cutaway drawing of a Vertex heater (above) shows the combustion chamber and secondary heat exchanger coil inside the tank. In the Phoenix model at right, the combustion chamber and secondary heat exchanger are located in the upper part of the tank, with a second heat exchanger for a solar thermal collector below.

Condensing Storage-Heater Specifications

Brand	Model No. (selected models)	Tank Size (gallons)	Maximum Input (Btu)	First-Hour Rating (gallons)	Recovery (gallons per hr. at 90°F rise)	Thermal Efficiency	Standby Loss (in Btu per hour)	Tank	Gas Supply
Phoenix Heat Transfer Products htproducts.com	PH100-55	55	100,000	169	128	95%	392	stainless-steel	3/4-inch
	PH130-80	80	130,000	227	167	95%	498	stainless-steel	3/4-inch
	PH199-119	119	199,000	335	256	96%	507	stainless-steel	3/4-inch
Polaris American Water Heaters americanwaterheater.com	PG10 34-100-2NV	34	100,000	153	129	96%	286	stainless-steel	1/2-inch
	PG10 50-130-2NV	50	130,000	201	166	95%	225	stainless-steel	1/2-inch
	PG10 50-199-3NV	50	199,000	292	257	96%	244	stainless-steel	3/4-inch
Premier Power-Vent State Water Heaters statewaterheaters.com	GP6 50 YTVIT	50	76,000	127	92	90%	364	glass-lined	1/2-inch
	GP6 50 YTPDT	50	100,000	164	129	96%	548	glass-lined	1/2-inch
Vertex A.O. Smith hotwater.com	GPHE-50	50	76,000	127	92	90%	364	glass-lined	1/2-inch
	GDHE-50	50	100,000	164	129	96%	548	glass-lined	1/2-inch

range from 76,000 Btu all the way to 199,000 Btu. (By comparison, the typical tankless model we install is rated at 199,000 Btu.)

Recovery. The recovery rate tells how fast the heater can replenish hot water as it is drawn from the tank. Recovery is measured in gallons per hour at a 90°F temperature rise; it's a function of the burner size (Btu input) and heat-transfer efficiency.

First-hour-rating. The number that we look at when sizing a storage heater is the first-hour-rating (FHR) — the amount of water it can provide in one hour at a 90°F temperature rise. FHR is a function of the size of the heater's tank and the recovery rate. The tank factors in because it's a reservoir of heated water, most of which is considered to be available for immediate use. The FHR is equal to the recovery rate plus 70 percent of the tank size.

Installation

Condensing heaters have the same footprint as conventional water heaters, so they work well for replacement jobs (Figure 2). The units cost more than tankless models, but because they're easier to install in existing construction, the higher equipment cost is often offset by lower labor figures. A typical tankless heater wholesales for about $950, and a 90-percent-efficient condensing storage model for about $1,700.

Many models can be connected to an existing ½-inch gas line (Figure 3), though some of the larger units require a ¾-inch line. All condensing heaters require a 120-volt electrical circuit to run the fan and electronics.

Flue. The existing flue can't be reused, but a new plastic flue is inexpensive and easy to install. The draft is fan-induced, so flue runs can be long — up to 128

Making Sense of Gas Water-Heater Ratings

In a perfect world, water heaters would be 100 percent efficient: Every Btu they consumed would be turned into hot water that was available for use. Of course, this never happens. Instead, heat is lost up the flue, and storage models contend with standby losses — which refers to the gas consumed by a pilot light (if there is one) and the heat lost through the jacket of the tank.

Apples and oranges. Under federal law, different efficiency standards apply to different kinds of heaters. Storage heaters with inputs at or under 75,000 Btu and tankless models at or under 199,000 Btu are considered to be residential models and fall within the scope of the National Appliance Energy Conservation Act (NAECA), which requires heaters to be rated on the basis of their energy factor (EF). Units with inputs greater than these are considered to be commercial units and fall under the Energy Policy Act (EPACT), which requires heaters to be rated on the basis of thermal efficiency (TE). It's illegal for manufacturers to put TE ratings on residential models or EF ratings on commercial ones. This presents a problem: EF and TE are so different that there is no way to use them to make an apples-to-apples comparison between residential and commercial models.

Energy factor. The EF test is intended to rate the efficiency of the heater over the course of a typical day. The test assumes that the homeowner uses 64.3 gallons of hot water at a temperature rise of 77°F and that the water is consumed in six equal draws. The EF is derived by calculating the amount of thermal energy added to the water and dividing it by the energy used to heat it. Also, if a fuel-burning water heater uses electricity (to power a controller or fan), the electrical consumption is measured, converted to a Btu equivalent, and added to the input amount. The test is performed over a 24-hour period, so standby loss is automatically accounted for. EF is used to compute the projected annual operating cost listed on the yellow Energy Guide label found on new residential water heaters. A typical conventional storage heater has an EF of about .59. For a typical noncondensing tankless model the EF would be around .82.

Thermal efficiency. TE refers to the ratio between the energy contained in delivered water and the energy consumed to heat it. It's derived by measuring the flow of water the heater can heat to a 70°F temperature rise with the burner at full fire, calculating the amount of energy that was added to the water, and dividing it by the energy used to heat it. The result is expressed as a percentage and does not account for standby loss. Condensing storage models are between 90 and 96 percent thermally efficient.

Standby loss. One of the descriptors for a commercial storage heater is standby loss, which for a gas model is expressed as the number of Btu lost per hour when the burner is not firing. Rarely listed on spec sheets, this number can be found in the Air-Conditioning, Heating, and Refrigeration Institute's Directory of Certified Product Performance (www.ahridirectory.org). When comparing two heaters with the same TE, the one with the lower standby loss will be more "efficient" overall.

***David Frane** is editor of Tools of the Trade and was formerly senior editor, The Journal of Light Construction.*

Figure 2. This 50-gallon condensing water heater (far left) will be installed in the space (left) previously occupied by a 40-gallon conventional storage model.

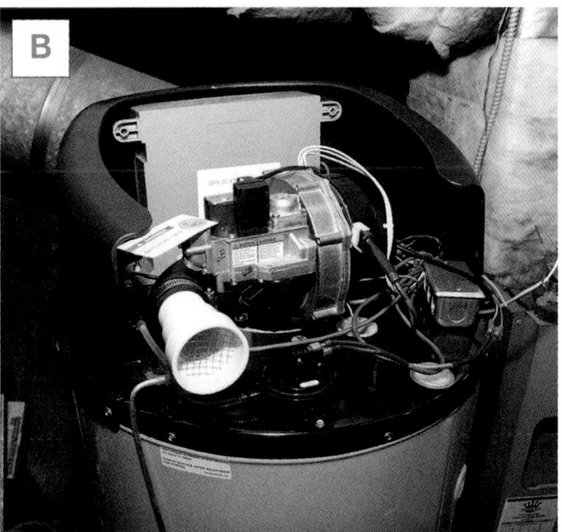

Figure 3. Condensing heaters can often connect to an existing 1/2-inch gas line. The plumber extends the line (A) to reach the inlet at the top of the heater. The air intake (B) — the PVC fitting with the screen inside — is connected to a draft-inducing fan. Combustion gas and condensate exit through a fitting near the bottom of the tank (C). The elbow connects to the flue and the condensate hose runs to a drain.

equivalent feet, depending on the heater and whether the vent is 2-, 3-, or 4-inch-diameter pipe. Makeup air can be drawn from the room or piped directly to the heater from the exterior. We try to terminate the flue at an inconspicuous location on the outside, because it may emit a visible plume of vapor and the fan may be audible there (Figure 4).

Condensate. The water that condenses in the heat exchanger and flue drains to a condensate trap and is fed through a plastic hose to the nearest plumbing drain. The condensate is acidic enough to erode concrete and metal, so it has to be neutralized before discharge; this is done by running it through a cartridge filled with crushed limestone or marble (Figure 5). The cartridge needs to be checked yearly and the stones topped off or replaced if they've dissolved.

Base Models

Condensing heaters have been used commercially for about 15 years; they're a proven technology. Because of the size of their burners, the heaters from the four manufacturers targeting the residential market are technically commercial units. Most of them have electronic controls and diagnostic sensors that can be accessed by a digital screen (Figure 6).

Vertex and Premier. The least expensive condensing

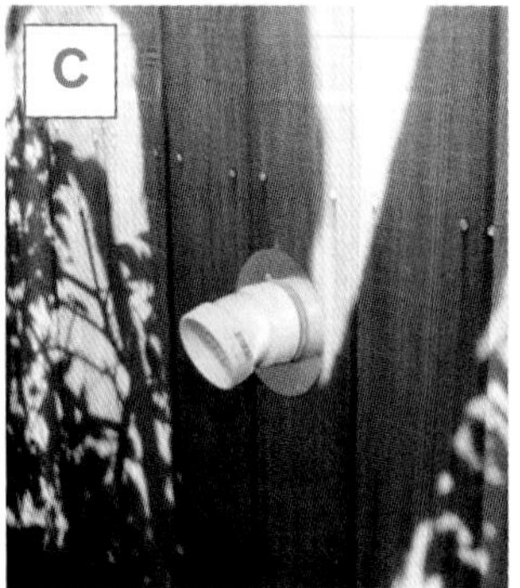

Figure 4. A plumber installs a section of flue pipe (A), taking care to slope it so that condensate drains back to the heater. With the particular heater shown here, the flue can be ABS or PVC; in this case, it's a combination of the two (B), because the plumbers ran out of ABS. The flue passes out through the wall and terminates at a screened fitting (C).

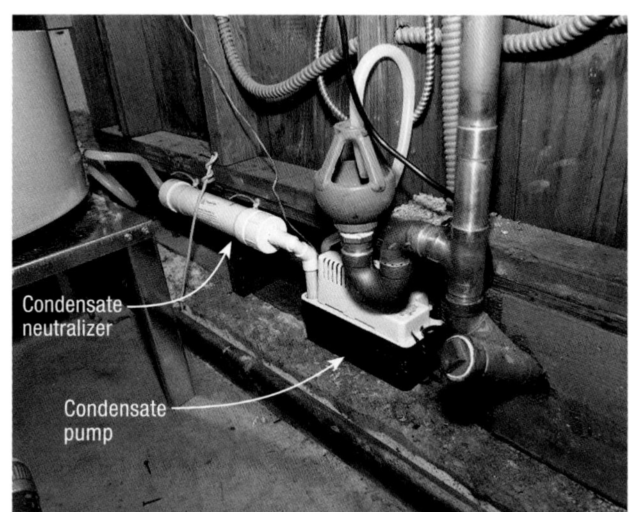

Figure 5. Condensate is acidic and should be neutralized, which is done by running it through a cartridge filled with marble chips or limestone. On this job (top), the condensate is pumped into an air-gap fitting on a drain line. Above, the condensate from a pair of heaters flows into a floor drain (both heaters have neutralizers, though only one is visible).

heater is A.O. Smith's Vertex. It's sold in two versions, both with 50-gallon tanks: a 76,000-Btu 90-percent-TE unit and a 100,000-Btu 96-percent-TE unit. Both have glass-lined tanks and taps that allow them to be used for combination space-heating and water-heating applications. The same heaters are also sold by State Water Heaters under the Premier brand.

We like these heaters for retrofits because they're easy to install. They can often use existing gas lines, so field-supplied materials are limited to piping and fittings near the heater, the neutralizer cartridge, and flue pipe. The heater itself is prewired; all we have to do is plug it into an adjacent outlet. As a replacement unit, the installed cost of one of these heaters is frequently less than the installed cost of a comparable tankless model.

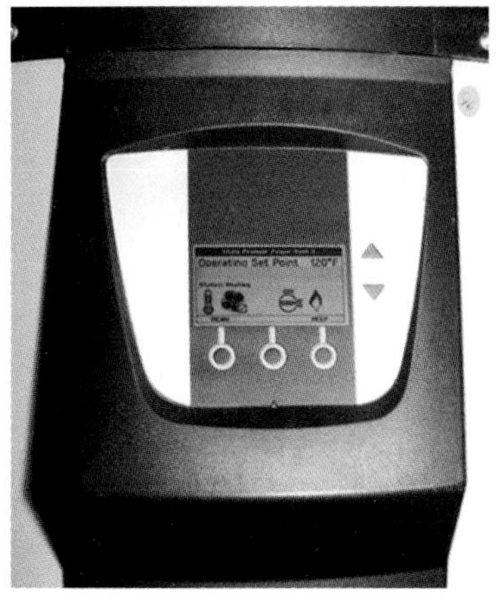

Figure 6. In this installation, the heater and condensate pump are plugged into a nearby electrical outlet (above). A digital readout (right) allows the homeowner to adjust the water temperature and the plumber to diagnose problems.

Premium Units

The next step up is to a Polaris, made by American Water Heaters, an A.O. Smith company, or a Phoenix, manufactured by Heat Transfer Products. These heaters have long-lasting stainless steel tanks and come in a variety of tank and burner sizes, with inputs up to 199,000 Btu. Both brands include taps that allow them to be used for combined space and water heating. Several of the Phoenix models also contain heat exchangers that can be connected to solar collectors for heating or preheating the water. Although we have installed both brands, we have more experience with the Phoenix, because it's readily available and better supported in our area.

Jim Lunt *co-owns The Lunt Marymor Co. in Emeryville, Calif., with Leigh Marymor.*

Indirect-Fired Water Heaters

by John Vastyan and Rich McNally

Indirect water heaters may be the most important technology enhancement to enter the residential hot water industry in the past 30 years. Two key needs have driven demand for these useful and practical heating units: fuel efficiency and an ever increasing desire for more hot water. Hot tubs, large baths, multi-head showers, and bigger homes with more bathrooms have increased America's appetite for hot water, and indirect water heaters can satisfy the need faster than any other technology.

For homes heated with a boiler, adding an indirect tank can provide efficient, reliable hot water.

Water Heating Choices

Before the advent of indirects, the options for heating domestic potable water included conventional direct-fired units or boiler-integrated "tankless coils."

Direct-fired water heaters (electric-, gas-, or oil-fired) are by far the most common technology, primarily because they have the lowest front-end cost. They have their disadvantages, however.

While electric water heaters are almost 100% efficient, operating costs can be high, given the high cost of electricity in most states compared with other fuels, as well as the growing demands of large, modern custom homes.

Fossil-fuel tank water heaters are typically inefficient, unless they're specifically designed for high efficiency, which means a substantially higher cost on the front end. Also, the difference in temperature between the combustion passages and the large tank of relatively cool water above or around them, depending on design, puts a lot of stress on metals and glass linings. That causes fatigue and shortens life span. This is especially true when they are harnessed for use as a heat source, because they really aren't designed for that much duty.

All tank-type water heaters collect mineral deposits from the water, called precipitates. The incoming water slows suddenly, heats up, and gives up its mineral particulates, which fall to the bottom, insulating the tank from the heat source over time, adding to thermal stress and decreasing efficiency.

Tankless coils. Although they're inexpensive, internal tankless coils, in either a gas or an oil boiler, are inefficient. As early as 1935, advertisements promised "free hot water" during the winter, but there was a cost penalty for having to fire the boiler all summer long to produce domestic hot water. Laboratory tests in the 1950s showed that tankless heaters with large-volume boilers were only about 18 percent efficient during the non-heating season.

Today's tankless units, like earlier models, rely on internal boiler convection and very high boiler temperatures. Because their gasketed attaching plates are made of metals dissimilar to the boiler's, over time they all leak at least a little, usually onto sensitive components. They're also notoriously troublesome because, as hard or otherwise untreated water passes through them, the super-heated coils collect mineral deposits that quickly diminish coil efficiency and then require costly acid bath cleanings.

Indirect-fired units, on the other hand, take advantage of the high efficiency and the inherent sturdiness of modern hydronic boilers by becoming an attached "zone." This arrangement directs the boiler's power to heating potable water in a well-insulated tank but without the stress on the tank common in direct-fired units.

As an indication of their efficiency and their ability to produce hot water, many indirect-fired water heaters provide two to four times the recovery rate of gas-fired water heaters. They also offer two to three times the peak flow of a tankless coil, and three to six times the peak output of comparably sized electric water heaters.

With indirects, the simpler tank designs and lower temperature difference between the heating medium and heated potable water also allow for the use of potentially longer-lasting tank materials, like plastics, cupronickel, and stainless steel, as well as high R-value insulations for optimal storage efficiency. Some indirect tanks have a glass or stone lining to protect the steel from corrosive electrolysis and natural oxidation. Most indirects do not require the use of a mixing valve, allowing better flow rates and fewer mechanical issues in the flow.

Sizing an Indirect-Fired Tank

The most common problem with indirect-fired units is undersizing. The indirect tank is typically the single largest zone attached to the heating plant and the most noticed if underpowered. It takes a tremendous amount of energy to heat water enough to raise its temperature 90 or 100 degrees at a flow rate sufficient to satisfy the modern family.

Proper sizing starts with the boiler. Most 30- to 40-gallon tanks with a 15- or 20-square foot EDR (equivalent direct radiation) coil can absorb a boiler output of 120,000 to 130,000 Btu, generally lots more than the average home's heat load. Thus, sizing the boiler to match the heating load rather than hot water needs can obviously adversely affect the indirect's performance.

What may not be quite as obvious is how critical it is to properly size the circulator pump and piping, and to use controls that give priority to domestic hot water when necessary. If the pipe and pump are too small and there's no priority control, there won't be enough hot water, no matter how big the boiler is.

Shopping for an Indirect Water Heater

Indirects, like many other popular products, are available in a wide variety of configurations and sizes from a number of European and domestic manufacturers, each claiming superiority in some way or other. There are similarities and vast differences among them.

Most use a heat exchanger coil submersed in the potable water that's to be heated. There are a diversity of coil profiles and materials. Among the best — and most expensive — is cupronickel, a copper alloy with good heat-transfer ability as well as good resistance to metal fatigue.

The coils are often finned to add surface area for more efficient heat transfer in a shorter length of tube. Some manufacturers claim that the fins lead to premature accumulation of precipitates, so they use a smooth-surfaced tube. To boost efficiency and output, these makers must use a longer tube, replicating the effective area for heat transfer.

Little standby loss. All of the leading manufacturers of indirect units insulate their tanks very well. Most claim losses of 2 degrees or less per hour during standby; some measure heat loss at less than ¼°F per hour. No water heater connected to a flue and chimney can make that claim.

Tank sizes among the many indirect manufacturers range from 20 to 120 gallons and more. Prices vary greatly, with a range at the 40-gallon size from $500 to $2,000, and from $1,000 to more than $4,000 for 120-gallon units. The wide variance in pricing is due to quality of craftsmanship, accommodation for faster heat recovery, ease of installation and maintenance, resistance to deterioration and mineral buildup, integration with boiler controls, efficiency, standby losses, and expected service life. These price ranges do not reflect differences in installation labor, which can be substantial. It's always good to seek an opinion from two or three installing professionals. Just be sure that they specialize in hydronic work.

It's worth mentioning that some of these suppliers are chiefly boiler manufacturers; the indirect-fired lines — whether they manufacture these as well or supply tanks made by others — are designed to complement their boiler systems.

Amtrol

Amtrol's BoilerMate uses a cold-water inlet that radially dispenses the water into the tank. According to the manufacturer, this reduces the mixing of stored hot water with the incoming cold water, allowing up to 87 percent of the tank's hot water storage volume to be used at temperature.

The heat exchanger is a finned copper material that permits high heat transfer. Amtrol claims that its vertical cylindrical coil creates a convective "chimney effect" that causes high flow rates around the coil, keeping it clear. The heat exchanger creates thermal layering that sends the hottest water to the top of the tank, where it's then drawn for domestic use.

Contact: Amtrol Inc.; www.amtrol.com.

Buderus

Buderus's Logalux tank capacities range from 30 to 130 gallons. The company states that its glass and steel tank coating provides safe protection against all forms of corrosion.

Thick magnesium anode rods draw corrosion away from the tank wall; an optional electric anode is

available. Among the best-insulated units available, Buderus tanks lose less than ¼°F per hour. Buderus offers both horizontal and vertical tanks (the vertical units provide the best recovery rates).

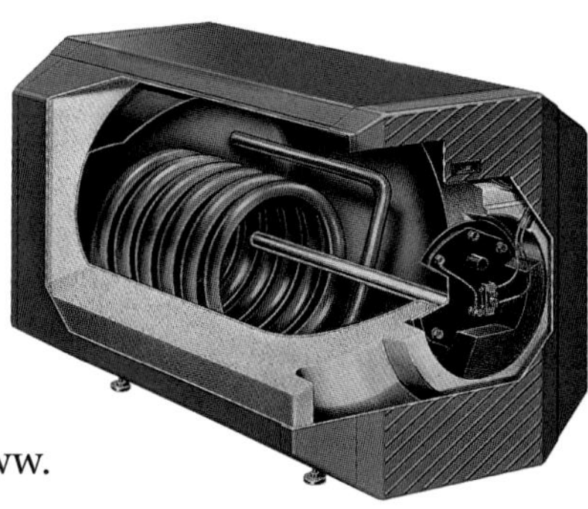

Contact: Buderus, www.buderus.net.

Burnham

Burnham Corporation's Alliance water heaters are well matched to its primary boiler line. The units are available in five sizes, from 27 to 119 gallons. A stainless-steel tank design ensures long service; and the smooth-surface, open-wound stainless coil offers excellent heat transfer to the domestic water in the tank. The tank's outer two shells sandwich an expanded polystyrene insulation. An inspection and cleanout opening is conveniently located. As with many indirects, these units can be installed in a modular or tandem arrangement to meet higher demands.

Contact: Burnham Corp., www.usboiler.burnham.com.

Ergomax

Ergomax indirect-fired units — more accurately termed "external tankless coils" or "heat exchangers" — are unique in that the tank is filled with boiler water and domestic water flows through multiple coils. Boiler water is kept in turbulent motion. Domestic hot water is not stored but produced instantaneously when needed, as it passes through several 50-foot copper coils surrounded by boiler water. According to the manufacturer, laboratory tests show that this design bumps heat-transfer efficiency to an astounding 99 percent.

The tank that's heated by the boiler is a closed loop. So, except for a very small amount of makeup water, no new minerals or oxygen ever enter it. This reduces the risk of scale buildup and, with no new oxygen in the water, avoids corrosion. The constant water turbulence prevents stratification and cold spots. Standby loss is less than ½°F per hour. There are six models to choose from, ranging from 26 to 119 gallons.

Contact: Group Thermo; www.ergomax.com.

Heat Transfer Products

Heat Transfer Products manufactures the SuperStor, made of high-grade 316L stainless steel with cupronickel coils. Two-inch-thick polyurethane foam insulation and good heat transfer within the unit keep heat loss to less than ½°F per hour. The Superstor Ultra is so efficient that it has a first-hour rating (the amount of water produced in an hour) of 154 gallons for the 30-gallon model, which is greater than that of many 80- to 100-gallon direct-fired water heaters. The Superstor is available in 14 models. Easy maintenance is an HTP hallmark.

The company's SSU-45 is a 45-gallon tank that contains a beefy 1¼-inch finned cupronickel coil, which provides low pressure drop at very high efficiency. Cold water entering the tank is directed at the coil to ensure a debris-free surface. Because the coil is so low in the tank, air stays out and good thermal layering is maintained.

Contact: Heat Transfer Products, www.htproducts.com.

Lochinvar

Lochinvar's Efficiency Mate heats domestic water when fluids pass through the internal heat exchanger, a double-wall highly conductive tube that surrounds the storage vessel. The Efficiency Mate features a heavy-gauge, glass-lined tank, a magnesium tank saver, factory-installed dielectric nipples, and a built-in thermostat. The unit's ample insulation reduces standby loss to less than ½°F per hour. It's available in four sizes: 40, 50, 65, and 80 gallons.

Contact: Lochinvar, www.lochinvar.com.

Peerless

Peerless units transfer boiler-generated heat through the use of cupronickel, fin-tube heat exchangers. According to Peerless, the coil is highly resistant to scaling deposits and is positioned so that entering water provides a "scrubbing action," eliminating the need for chemical cleanings. Domestic hot water is stored in a heavy-duty 316L stainless-steel tank. Two

inches of foam insulation keeps the water hot with a standby loss of less than ½°F per hour. These units come equipped with an adjustable, well-type Honeywell control and a T&P relief valve as standard equipment. Peerless indirects are available in nine models ranging from 30 to 119-gallon sizes.

Contact: Peerless, www.peerless-heater.com.

Thermo2000

Like the Ergomax units, the Thermo2000's Turbomax indirect-fired tanks work opposite the way many other units work. Rather than being stored in the tank, domestic water circulates through giant copper coils surrounded by boiler water. Domestic hot water is produced instantaneously as it passes through the coils. Inside each end of the Turbomax is an injector with perforated walls. The top injector creates multiple swirling jets that bathe the copper coils, spreading boiler water evenly throughout the tank to enhance heat transfer. Capacities range from 26 to 119 gallons.

The tank heated by the boiler is a closed loop, so, as with the Ergomax, the risk of scale buildup and corrosion is greatly reduced.

Contact: Thermo2000, www.thermo2000.com.

Triangle Tube

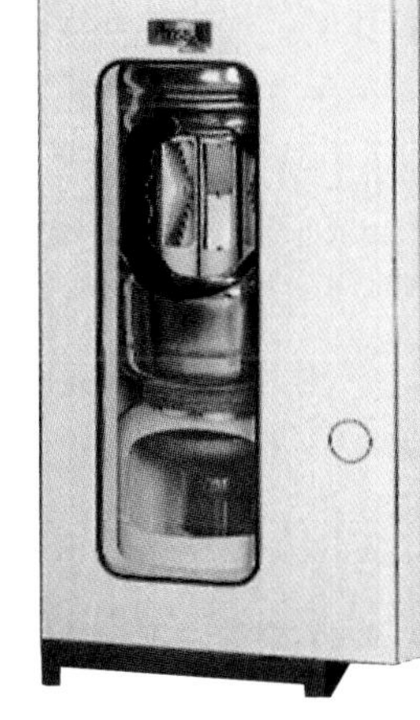

Triangle Tube's Smart Series indirect-fired water heater solves lime buildup challenges by imposing a tank-in-a-tank water barrier between the source of heat and the domestic water. A corrugated stainless-steel inner tank eliminates the need for coils and ensures excellent heat transfer and rapid recovery. The Smart Series is available in seven models, ranging from 28 to 119 gallons.

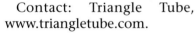

Contact: Triangle Tube, www.triangletube.com.

Vaughn

Vaughn states that its nonferrous, brass plumbing connections and seamless, ½-inch-thick "hydrastone" lining protect the steel tank from electrolysis and oxidation. According to the manufacturer, as water enters the tank, it's absorbed into the finely porous stone lining. Initially, aggressive water saturates the stone, reaching the inner wall of the tank. But doing that uses all of the oxygen in the water, changing it to an inert film, now trapped in place to blanket the entire inner tank.

Vaughn introduces the cold domestic water into the base of the tank to reduce stirring the water within the reservoir. A top-mounted, eight-bolt flange permits easy removal of the coil for inspection or future maintenance.

Contact: Vaughn, www.vaughncorp.com.

Viessmann

Viessmann offers a wide variety of exceptionally well-crafted vertical and horizontal stainless-steel- and glass-lined tanks. The high-alloy stainless-steel tanks are impeccably engineered. Across the product line, sizes range from 30 to 260 gallons. Fast, even heat transfer takes place with the 1¼-inch non-finned heat exchanger coil. The manufacturer's Vitocell U and B series and W-100 model can be used for domestic water heating applications that combine boiler and solar heat sources.

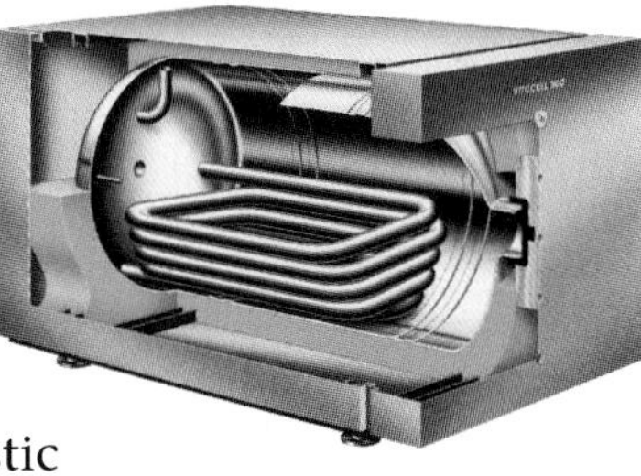

Contact: Viessmann, www.viessmann.com.

Weil-McLain

Weil-McLain's indirect-fired heater line offers seven sizes, ranging from 30 to 120 gallons, all with no coil to maintain. The tank-in-a-tank design combines a corrugated stainless-steel inner tank for domestic water and a carbon-steel outer tank for boiler water with a "self-cleaning" design that reduces calcification within the system. Weil-McLain also boasts the lowest pressure drop in the industry, with no high head pump required for residential applications. Two inches of rigid polyurethane insulation reduce standby loss to less than ½°F per hour.

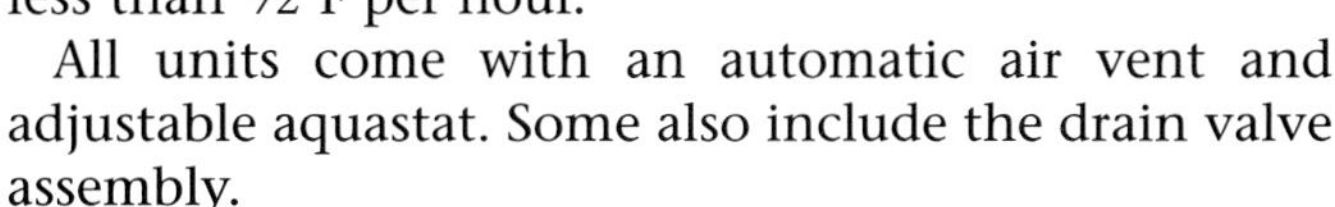

All units come with an automatic air vent and adjustable aquastat. Some also include the drain valve assembly.

Contact: Weil-McLain, www.weil-mclain.com.

***John Vastyan** is president of Common Ground, Uncommon Communications, based in Manheim, Pa. Chesapeake, Va.–based Rich McNally is eastern regional sales manager for Watts Radiant.*

Installing On-Demand Water Heaters

by David Grubb

In recent years, about half of my remodeling customers have chosen to replace their conventional water heaters with on-demand — or "tankless" — models. Long popular in Europe and Japan, on-demand water heaters first showed up here during the 1970s energy crisis. Their use never became widespread, however, because energy prices fell and early models had reliability problems that made plumbers suspicious of this technology. Today's fully electronic models are very reliable, and with energy prices on the rise, they are generating renewed interest.

Tankless water heaters free up floor space and save energy, but sizing and installation require a unique approach.

What Customers Want

The main reason my customers choose to go tankless is because it's a great way to pick up floor space in a remodel (Figure 7). They also want to reduce their energy consumption and are willing to spend more up-front to do so. Other reasons for installing on-demand heaters include the promise of never again running out of hot water and the security of knowing the equipment will last 20-plus years — much longer than conventional models.

The key question for contractors is whether on-demand heaters are better than conventional models (see "Is a Tankless Heater Right for the Job," page 275). I think they are, but it's important to understand the differences between the two types of heaters. Here I'll explain how tankless heaters work and how to install them on remodeling jobs.

Basic Operation

To appreciate the differences between conventional and tankless models, it helps to understand how each kind works.

Conventional water heater. A conventional residential water heater — let's assume it's gas — is built around a tank containing 40 to 75 gallons of water. When the water inside falls below the thermostat's set point, typically between 120°F and 140°F, the burner comes on and heats the water.

If the unit is properly sized, there should be enough stored hot water to provide a buffer against periods of heavy use. But if demand is too high, the store of hot water is depleted and the tap runs cold. The burner will eventually heat the incoming cold water, but it will take a while because the burner is quite small compared with the volume of water it has to heat.

Also, because hot water must be stored 24 hours a day, conventional heaters are prone to large standby losses (heat escaping from the tank).

On-demand water heater. On-demand heaters are smaller and more efficient than conventional units; they have no tanks and don't store any water. Instead, they are equipped with burners powerful enough to heat water almost instantaneously as it flows through the unit.

On-demand models are available for use with natural gas, propane, or electricity, but let's assume here we're talking about gas. When a hot-water tap is opened, cold water flows into the heater and passes through a control device that senses the amount of flow. If the flow rate is sufficient, the controls activate a burner that heats the water as it passes through a heat exchanger (Figure 8). The moment the flow stops or is interrupted, the burner turns off.

The burners in early tankless models had only two settings — on and off — so the temperature of the output water varied with flow. Most of today's models, by contrast, are modulating: If the flow increases, the burner puts out more heat. Water comes out at a consistent temperature that can be set on the machine or with a remote wall-mounted controller.

An Endless Supply of Hot Water?

Manufacturers market on-demand heaters with the claim that they're capable of providing an endless supply of hot water. This is true — but only if the heater is sized to meet peak demand, which is measured in gallons per minute (gpm).

For example, a heater might be just large enough to provide an endless supply of hot water to two show-

Figure 7. On this project, a conventional water heater occupied prime real estate near the back of the house (left). The author replaced it with a gas tankless model — installed in the crawlspace — and expanded the kitchen into what was formerly a utility porch (above).

ers. But if a third person were to turn on a shower at the same time, demand would exceed capacity and the temperature of the output water would immediately fall. There are several ways of dealing with this: stagger the showers, get a bigger heater, or buy a second heater and wire it to kick in whenever the first heater needs help.

Calculating peak demand. To calculate peak demand, add the flows of the appliances and fixtures that are likely to run at the same time. Here are some typical flow rates.

Low-flow faucet	0.5–1.5 gpm
Dishwasher	1.5 gpm
Showerhead	2.5 gpm
Clothes washer	4.0 gpm
Whirlpool tub	4.0 gpm

If the customer wants to shower and run the dishwasher simultaneously, the heater must be capable of producing at least 4.0 gpm — roughly the minimum required for whole-house water heating.

If two people want to shower while the dishwasher is running, the heater must produce 6.5 gpm at the desired temperature. The 2.5-gpm figure for showers assumes that the hot water coming from the water heater is reduced to 104°F at the shower's mixer valve. If the client likes it hotter, the shower will account for more than 2.5 gpm of output.

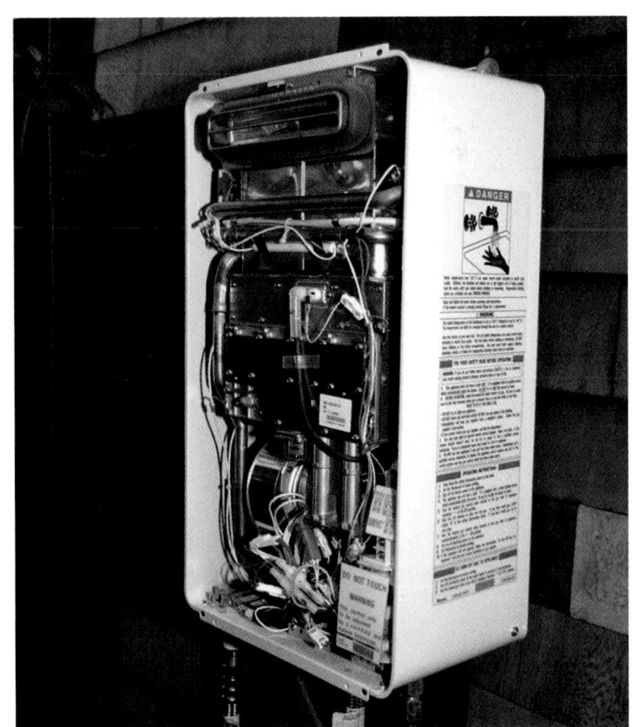

Figure 8. This on-demand gas heater (shown without its cover) has sophisticated controls to regulate the burner and combustion fan based on flow rate and incoming water temperature. It has more in common with a high-efficiency furnace than with a conventional water heater.

Temperature rise. The volume of water that an on-demand unit can heat is determined by the temperature of the incoming and outgoing water. A heater can produce more hot water when water comes in at 75°F (summer in Florida) than it can when water comes in at 45°F (winter in Wisconsin). Increasing the setpoint temperature of the outgoing water has the same effect on capacity as lowering the temperature of the incoming water.

Unless the customer wants to cut back on hot-water use in winter, you will need to install a unit powerful enough to produce the desired flow at that time of year. Heater specifications usually include test data showing how many gallons per minute a unit can heat for a given rise in temperature (Figure 9). Most — but not all — manufacturers list maximum output based on a temperature rise of 77°F.

Electric models. The average household uses more hot water than a single electric on-demand heater can heat. Most electric models produce less than 2.5 gpm; the largest I know of requires three 40-amp breakers and produces less than 4 gpm in cold weather.

Electric models are best suited to point-of-use applications (installing individual heaters in rooms where hot water is used). I wish I could install point-of-use electric heaters on my jobs, but where I work, the energy code makes it illegal to replace gas water heaters (even inefficient ones) with electric models. Conventional electric and tankless electric models can be extremely efficient, but because electricity is so much more expensive than gas in most areas, they are still more expensive to operate.

Running Hot and Cold

One problem with on-demand gas heaters is that "slugs" of cold water can get sandwiched between sections of hot water in the supply line. There are two ways this can happen.

Ignition lag. Before the burner can switch on, a control device must first measure the volume and temperature of the incoming flow. As a result, a certain amount of water passes through unheated. We have installed a number of Takagi heaters, and their manual says it takes three seconds for the burner to ignite. (The glitch is not confined to Takagi; all gas-fired models have similar lags.) Once on, the burner produces a steady flow of hot water, but if you turn the tap off and then back on again, more cold water passes through before the burner reignites.

Most homeowners don't even notice the slug of cold water, but some do. A remodeler I know installed a tankless heater for a client who liked to wash the counter with very hot water. She'd wet the sponge, turn off the water, and clean. When it was time to rinse, she'd turn on the water and rewet the sponge. Every time she did this, some cold water entered the hot-water line. Frustrated, she finally got the plumber to install a small conventional heater (10-gallon electric) between the on-demand unit and the sink. This approach worked but reduced the efficiency of the system.

Minimum flow. A second problem with gas on-demand models is that they won't switch on if the flow is too low. The cutoff is usually around .7 gpm (Figure 10); the exact level varies by model. Customers

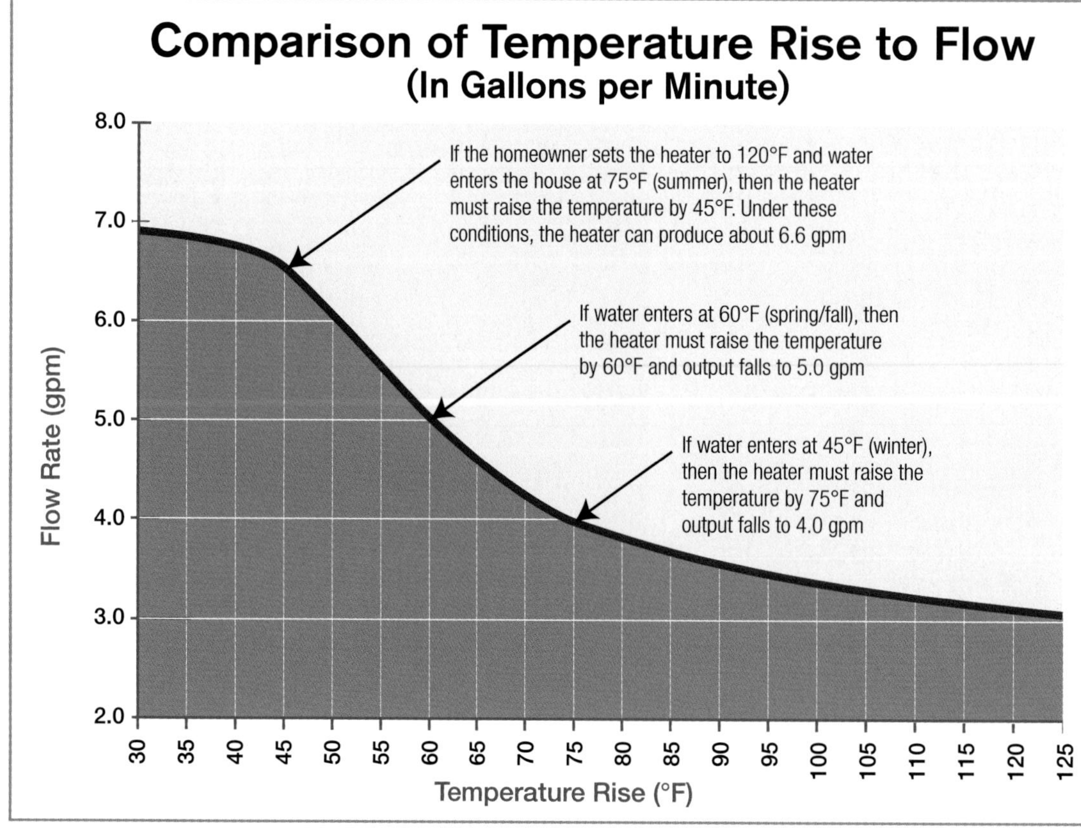
Comparison of Temperature Rise to Flow
(In Gallons per Minute)
If the homeowner sets the heater to 120°F and water enters the house at 75°F (summer), then the heater must raise the temperature by 45°F. Under these conditions, the heater can produce about 6.6 gpm
If water enters at 60°F (spring/fall), then the heater must raise the temperature by 60°F and output falls to 5.0 gpm
If water enters at 45°F (winter), then the heater must raise the temperature by 75°F and output falls to 4.0 gpm
Flow Rate (gpm)
8.0
7.0
6.0
5.0
4.0
3.0
2.0
30
35
40
45
50
55
60
65
70
75
80
85
90
95
100
105
110
115
120
125
Temperature Rise (°F)

Figure 9. The manufacturer's specs typically include a graph showing how much hot water the unit can deliver based on input temperature, output temperature, and flow rate. This graph is typical of 185,000-Btu gas models.

have complained that when they turn the water down to shave, it goes cold because the burner won't come back on. Also, if there is just enough flow to keep the heater going, flushing a toilet or opening a cold-water tap may cause the burner to shut off by temporarily reducing flow.

The default output temperature for most tankless models is around 120°F. Many people adjust this up, which increases the supply of warm water (by mixing it with cold). This works fine for most uses but makes it easier to accidentally switch off the burner during periods of low flow.

Installation Issues

An on-demand heater can be installed where the old water heater used to be, but the existing gas and water lines may be too small. Don't expect to use the old flue.

Electrical needs. The new unit will require 115-volt electricity to power an internal computer board, electronic ignition, and a venting fan for the flue (Figure 11). If the power goes out, the household will have no hot water. Although I haven't done it myself, I have heard of people installing battery backup units (the kind used for computers) to prevent the heater from suddenly turning off while someone is showering.

Bigger gas and water lines. One reason on-demand models heat so quickly is that they hold only about ⅓ gallon of water. (The other reason, of course, is that they put out an enormous amount of heat.) A conventional 40-gallon heater produces about 40,000 Btu, while an equivalent tankless model might put out 200,000 Btu — and thus requires a ¾-inch gas line. Most tankless heaters require ¾-inch water lines, but some need 1-inch lines. Undersizing either line can cause malfunctions.

Before installing an on-demand unit, check to see that the gas line into the home is big enough to power the heater and furnace at the same time. Having to replace gas and water lines adds cost, but if you're relocating the heater (as often happens in remodels), you'll be doing it anyway.

More expensive flue. Conventional water heaters use inexpensive B-vent flue. On-demand models typically require 4-inch Type III stainless-steel flue pipe

Figure 10. On-demand gas heaters will not switch on and deliver hot water if the flow rate is too low. The cutoff point is around .7 gpm, which is roughly the rate at which water is flowing through this faucet.

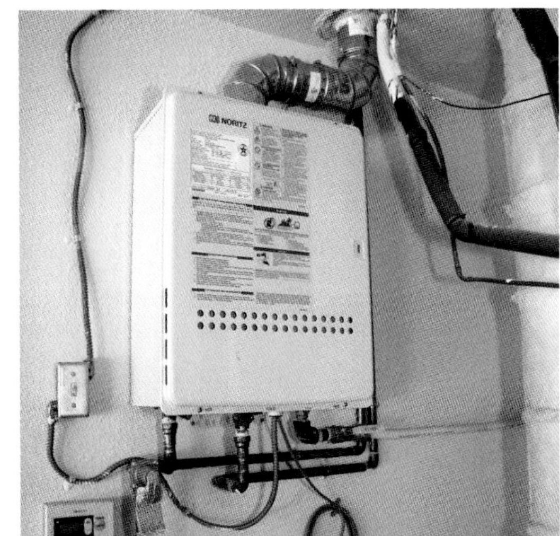

Figure 11. Like any gas water heater, this tankless unit (top) is connected to a gas line, water lines, a flue, and a temperature/pressure-relief valve. But it's also tied to a 115-volt power line and a wall-mounted temperature controller. With fan-induced draft, combustion gases must be vented through costly Type III stainless-steel flue (above). Flue joints must be gasketed or caulked with an approved high-temperature sealant.

— which costs about $16 per foot. Stainless steel is necessary because tankless models have a fan-induced draft, which can leave acidic combustion products in the flue when the burner turns off.

Locating the Heater

As a remodeler, the thing I like most about on-demand heaters is that they are small — typically 24 inches by 18 inches by 9 inches — and will fit in places conventional heaters won't. Since basements are not common in this area, water heaters have traditionally been housed in a closet or attached garage. Changing over to a tankless model allows us to put this space to better use (Figure 12).

It's possible to vent the heater through the roof, but venting through a sidewall minimizes the flue run and frees up additional space where the flue used to be. We frequently remove masonry chimneys that can't meet seismic code and, with no need for a vertical flue, pick up space on both floors of the house. If you consider what it costs to add square footage during a remodel, spending more for a tankless heater may be the least expensive way to go.

Combustion-air requirements. On-demand heaters burn gas quickly, so don't install them in enclosed spaces without providing an adequate supply of combustion air. The manual will tell you how much you need. One way to deal with this complication is to use a direct-vent model; combustion air is piped directly to these units from outdoors. We have installed a number of tankless heaters in crawlspaces, which is legal provided the access door is large enough to enter the area and service the unit (Figure 13).

Outdoor installation. The area where I work has a very mild climate — it never freezes. For this reason, it's common to install on-demand heaters outdoors on the side of the house. This frees up interior space and eliminates the cost of installing a flue. Units designed for outdoor use have an internal electric heating element that prevents freezing, allowing outside installations in climates cooler than ours. But if the power goes out, the heater can freeze and be seriously damaged.

Also be aware that the heating element protects only the heater — the water lines must be insulated and may require heat tape or a conditioned chase.

Clearances. As with any heating appliance, certain minimum clearances are required around the unit and between the flue and flammable materials. The rules are straightforward and can be found in the installation manual. Clearances apply indoors and out. For example, the flue outlet for a side-vented unit needs to be some minimum distance from doors, operable win-

Figure 12. The author gained floor space in this house by replacing a conventional water heater with an on-demand model installed outside. Designed for use in warm climates, outdoor units have an electric heating element that protects them from the occasional freeze.

Figure 13. The house was too close to the property line for the author to install this heater outside, so he put it in an accessible crawlspace (top), ran the flue into a joist bay, elbowed 90 degrees, and vented through a grille in the outside wall (inset).

dows, and intake vents.

Setback rules can be an issue, too. There have been instances where we were unable to install the heater on the side of the house because we were too close to the property line.

Cost to Install

When ballparking jobs, I carry a few hundred dollars in material for a conventional water heater and $1,000 or more for an on-demand model capable of providing water for an entire house. Depending on what you buy, you could easily spend $1,600 for the unit.

Installation labor and the cost for gas lines and flue are extra. If it's a remodel and we're changing the location of the heater, my plumber might charge $2,500 or more in material and labor to install a tankless model. This is about $1,000 more than it would cost to do the same installation with a new conventional heater.

In new construction, the cost would be less.

Efficiency and Cost to Operate

Every new water heater comes with an Energy Guide label that shows its estimated annual fuel cost. The estimate is based on a specified fuel price and a set of

Is a Tankless Heater Right for the Job?

When a customer asks us to replace a conventional water heater with an on-demand — or tankless — model, we often have to explain why a tankless unit may not be the right choice. In many cases, we'll steer the homeowner toward a condensing storage heater instead.

Prominent among the selling points of tankless heaters are that they're more efficient than conventional storage models and, within limits, able to produce an endless stream of hot water. However, the same can be said of condensing storage heaters. The unique advantage of tankless heaters is that they're small enough to fit where storage models will not.

Efficiency Claims

Much of a tankless heater's efficiency stems from the fact that it has no standby losses — no gas-consuming pilot light and no stored water losing heat through the walls of the tank. But its actual thermal efficiency (TE) is not all that high — typically around 82 percent. A number of companies have introduced condensing tankless heaters with TE ratings of up to 98 percent, but I won't recommend these to clients until they've been around for a while and have proved to be reliable.

The endless stream. The output of a tankless heater is rated in gallons per minute (gpm) of water at an assumed temperature rise of 77°F. However, advertised flow rates are frequently based on a 45°F temperature rise and may not be achievable — something we point out to customers.

Installation Details

Although tankless units may cost less than condensing storage heaters, installation costs can be a lot higher. This is particularly true in replacement jobs.

Gas line. Tankless heaters have very large burners, so existing 1/2-inch gas lines will have to be replaced with 3/4- or 1-inch line. This could entail the last few feet of line or everything all the way back to the meter.

Flues. Most tankless heaters require expensive Type III stainless steel vent pipe, which means existing flues cannot be reused in replacement jobs. In areas where the temperature doesn't drop below freezing, it's sometimes possible to eliminate the cost of the flue by installing the heater outside.

Operation

When a tankless heater's flow sensor detects a demand for hot water, it activates a vent fan and a burner that heats water as it passes through a heat exchanger. The burner will not be activated at flows less than about 0.5 gpm, and once activated, it takes 5 to 10 seconds for the flow to go from cold to hot. If the drain is open, that several seconds of flow results in wasted water. A recirculation pump can reduce the amount of waste, but most recirculation systems are not directly compatible with tankless heaters.

Cold-water sandwich. Cold water is introduced into the line every time the burner turns off — the so-called "cold-water sandwich." To eliminate this slug of cold water, some plumbers may install a tempering tank — a small electric storage heater — downstream from the tankless unit. In my opinion, this is a poor solution because it wastes energy and adds to the cost of the system.

Maintenance

There is a filter screen on the supply side that prevents rust and sediment from clogging the passages in the heat exchanger. The screen should be cleaned and the heat exchanger flushed and delimed annually.

Jim Lunt, *co-owns The Lunt Marymor Co. in Emeryville, Calif., with Leigh Marymor.*

assumptions about water temperature (intake and output), hot-water usage, and other variables. One assumption is that the homeowner uses 64 gallons of hot water per day.

Because there are so many assumptions involved, it's hard to gauge how closely the Energy Guide estimate will match your specific installation. But we do know that the cost to operate a water heater is likely to be much higher than the tag says. For example, whereas the label on a tankless model I installed last fall listed gas costs at 91 cents per therm, my most recent utility bill pegged them at $1.58 per therm (Figure 14). I consider this an argument in favor of on-demand models, because they use fuel more efficiently than conventional ones.

Water-heater efficiency is rated by energy factor, or EF. This number is calculated by dividing the energy delivered as hot water by the amount of energy consumed to produce the hot water. If no energy was lost and it all came out as hot water, the heater would have an EF of 1. Most conventional gas water heaters have an EF of around .59. On-demand gas heaters are typically rated between .81 and .85, making them on average about 40 percent more efficient than conventional models.

Payback period. If you know the EF and the local cost of natural gas (or propane), you can perform the same calculation used on the Energy Guide label and come up with an approximate yearly cost based on current fuel prices. And once you know the annual operating cost, you can determine the payback period for installing a more efficient water heater.

To find the cost savings achieved by switching from a conventional gas heater (EF .59) to an on-demand model (EF .82), use the following method.

Formula:
.41045 x cost per therm of gas x 365 / EF = yearly cost to operate with gas

Example 1, conventional model:
.41045 x $1.58 per therm x 365 /.59 = $401.20

Example 2, on-demand model:
.41045 x $1.58 per therm x 365 / .82 = $288.67

Yearly cost savings: $112.53

To calculate payback, I'd use the $1,000 difference my plumber quoted for installing a tankless model versus a conventional model in a new location in an existing home. Then I'd divide the added installation cost ($1,000) by the annual savings in operating costs achieved by going tankless, as follows:

$1,000 / ($401.20 – $288.67) = 8.9 years

The payback period will be shorter if energy prices continue to rise or if the homeowner uses more than 64 gallons per day. It will be significantly shorter if the homeowner is switching from a conventional electric model.

***David Grubb** is a remodeling contractor in Berkeley, Calif.*

Based on standard U.S. Government tests

ENERGYGUIDE

Water Heater – Natural Gas
Capacity (first hour rating):
218 gallons/hour

Rinnai Corporation
Model(s) V2532W/V2532WC
V2526W

Compare the Energy Use of this Water Heater with Others Before You Buy.

This Model Uses
182 Therms/year

Energy use (Therms/year) range of all similar models

Uses Least Energy 187 — Uses Most Energy 238

The Estimated Annual Energy Consumption of this model was not available at the time the range was published.

Therms/year is a measure of energy use. Your utility company uses it to compute your bill. Only models with maximum flow rates above 3.0 gpm are used in this scale.

Natural gas water heaters that use fewer therms/year cost less to operate. This model's estimated yearly operating cost is:

$166

Based on a 2004 U.S. Government national average cost of 91¢ per therm for natural gas. Your actual operating cost will vary depending on your local utility rates and your use of the product.

U245 677 3X02

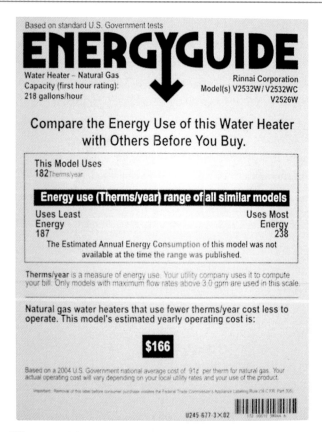

Figure 14. Every new water heater comes with an Energy Guide label that shows the estimated annual cost to operate it. But with current fuel prices rising so rapidly, the labels become out-of-date almost instantly.

Sources of Supply

Bosch Water Heaters
www.boschhotwater.com

Noritz America Corp.
www.noritz.com

Paloma Industries
www.palomatankless.com

Rinnai Corp.
www.rinnai.us

Takagi Industrial Co. USA
www.Takagi.com

Chapter 12

COMBUSTION AIR

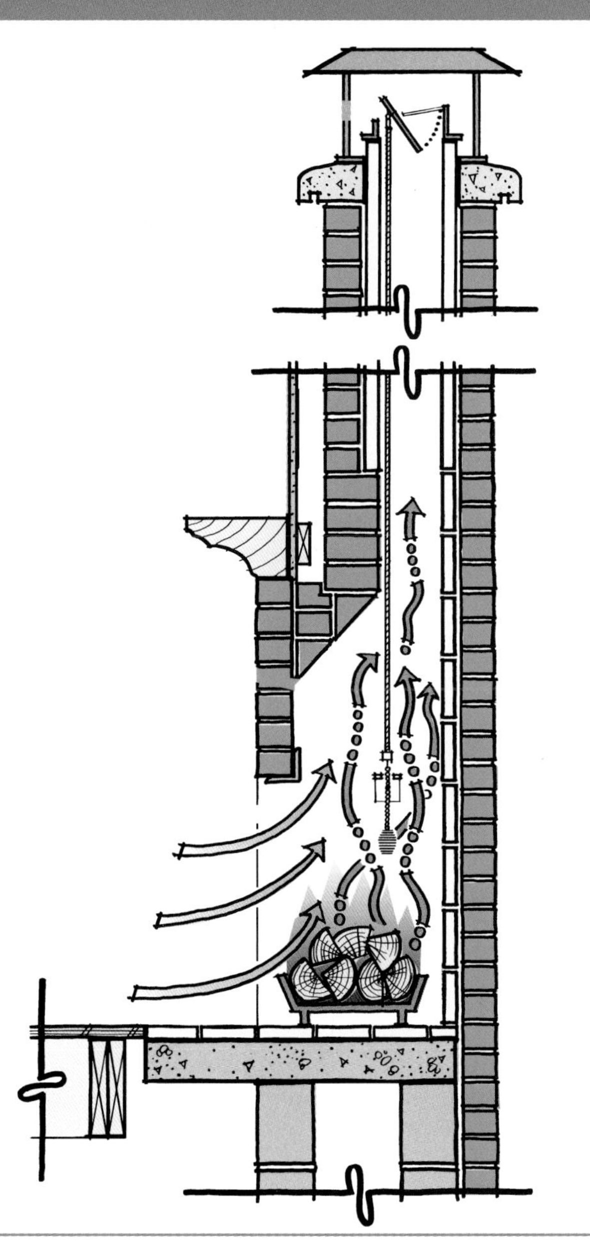

- Makeup Air for Combustion Equipment
- Successful Fireplaces in Tight Houses

Makeup Air for Combustion Equipment

by Carl Saunders

Try breathing through a soda straw. It takes effort, and you'll probably get dizzy quickly.

A fuel-burning boiler, furnace, or water heater can also end up gasping for air when installed in a very tight house or a confined space. The appliance won't get dizzy, but it can't burn its fuel properly — resulting in reduced efficiency and possibly exposing occupants to harmful gases, such as carbon monoxide.

A fuel-burning appliance needs a lot of air to burn properly. For example, a 100,000 Btu/h boiler or furnace needs 1,250 cubic feet of air per hour for proper combustion. With the exception of vent-free gas fireplaces and kitchen ranges, all gas- and oil-fired appliances are vented, using either fan-assisted venting or traditional atmospheric venting via a chimney.

Thanks to the natural buoyancy of hot flue gases — which rise rapidly up the vent pipe, just as a hot air balloon rises in the open air — vent pipes and chimneys suck flue gases out of appliances and suck in additional makeup air to replace outgoing flue gases. Here's the problem: You must replace the same amount of air that rises up the vent, and the makeup air must flow to the burner as easily as the flue gas was vented.

Causes of Poor Draft

If a vent pipe has poor draft, the burner may perform poorly. There are several possible causes of poor draft:

An undersized, restricted, or blocked vent. Try to locate the appliances as close to the chimney as you can. Long horizontal vent runs, called "lateral piping," decrease the capacity of the vent (Figure 1). The maximum length of lateral piping is listed in the vent capacity tables in the National Fuel Gas Code, as well as in the tables provided by vent pipe manufacturers.

A cold chimney. A cold chimney or vent will cool the flue gas and reduce its buoyancy. In some cases, this "cold stacking" is enough to allow the moisture in the flue gas to condense. Outside chimneys (chimneys exposed to the weather on three sides) are vulnerable to cold stacking, especially when a setback thermostat shuts down a heating appliance for several hours at night. To address the problems of cold stacking, the 1996 National Fuel Gas Code included new regulations covering the use of outside chimneys. In most cases, the new regulations require that an outside chimney have a metal liner with a surrounding air space, which allows a cold flue to come up to operating temperature as quickly as possible.

House depressurization. Under certain conditions, the indoor air pressure in a house may fall so low that it interferes with normal venting of flue gas (see "Warning: Building Depressurization May Be Hazardous to Your Health," facing page).

Wind downdrafts. Wind can interfere with normal chimney venting, especially if the chimney is lower than the roof ridge.

Lack of makeup air. If the house is extremely tight, the heating appliance may be unable to suck in enough makeup air to allow complete combustion.

Spillage and Carbon Monoxide

The most dangerous effect of poor or negative draft is spillage, which is the entry of flue gases into the home

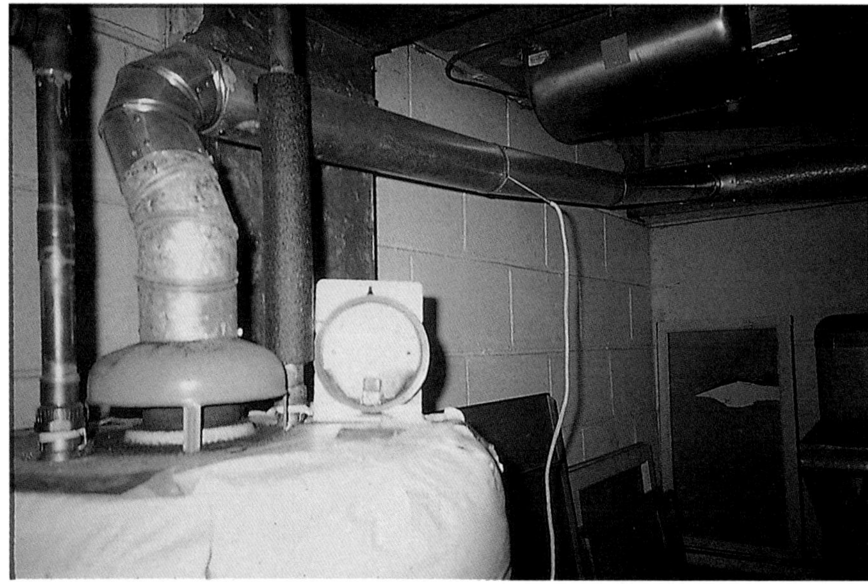

Figure 1. Avoid long horizontal runs of vent pipe, which can cool the flue gases and reduce the draft. This gas-fired water heater should have been located closer to the chimney.

Warning: Building Depressurization May Be Hazardous to Your Health

Although atmospherically vented appliances work well in many applications, some contractors and energy experts are so concerned about the dangers of spillage and the potential for carbon monoxide poisoning that they recommend that only sealed-combustion appliances should be used in today's tighter houses.

When a house is significantly depressurized, flue gas can spill into the living space (see photo). According to Ken Tohinaka, at Vermont Energy Investment Corp., the following appliances or conditions can contribute to house depressurization:

- ***Bath exhaust fans.*** Even small bath exhaust fans in the 50 to 75 cfm range can contribute to depressurization problems.
- ***Kitchen exhaust fans***. Downdraft exhaust fans are especially powerful, with ratings from 325 cfm to 1,200 cfm.
- ***A competing fuel-burning appliance.*** A strong draft from a wood-fired or gas-fired fireplace, or even an oil-fired boiler, can depressurize a house enough to cause spillage in another appliance, such as a gas-fired water heater.
- ***Powered attic ventilators.*** These fans, which turn on automatically whenever attic temperatures rise above a set point, can suck air out of the conditioned space below. This occurs even when the gable-end vents or soffit vents are sized according to code, because leakage paths between the attic and the occupied space are common.
- ***Unbalanced forced-air heating or air-conditioning systems.*** A house can be depressurized, for example, if a duct boot becomes disconnected from the main supply duct, allowing air from the duct to blow freely into the attic. The tighter the building envelope, the more likely it is that imbalances in the forced-air distribution system will change the house pressure.
- ***Other appliances that exhaust air to the exterior,*** such as clothes dryers or central vacuum cleaners.

A gas will tend to flow to a zone of lower pressure. If the house is so depressurized that the lower pressure in the house overwhelms the chimney draft, then the flue gas from a fuel-burning appliance will flow into the house instead of up the vent. Even when ducted exterior makeup air has been provided to the room with the fuel-burning appliance, strong exhaust fans can still depressurize the house enough to cause dangerous spillage. Since flue gas can contain carbon monoxide, spillage of flue gas can cause illness or death.

"When there is spillage, it's not a lack of combustion air that is the problem, it's house depressurization," says Don Fugler, senior researcher with Canada Mortgage and Housing Corporation in Ottawa. "Anyone considering installing a kitchen downdraft fan or an open masonry fireplace in a new house should avoid appliances with atmospheric venting."

Poor draft or house depressurization can lead to spillage of flue gas into the house. In this case, there is obvious evidence of spillage, since the backdrafting hot flue gas has melted the nearby pipe insulation.

"All of the designs for combustion makeup air are formulated on the assumption that there is no wind," says Gary Proskiw, a mechanical engineer in Winnipeg, Manitoba, specializing in residential energy issues. "If the wind is blowing, and if the combustion air inlet is on the leeward side of the house, then the air inlet could be exhausting air rather than providing makeup air."

Proskiw is also concerned about the long-term reliability of ducted makeup air systems. "The biggest problem with combustion makeup air systems is, will the homeowner defeat them by plugging the duct or disconnecting the makeup air fan? How many people will leave a 6-inch, 8-inch, or 10-inch hole open in the side of their house once winter sets in and they can feel the wind howling through their basement?"

Martin Holladay *is senior editor of www.GreenBuildingAdvisor.com and was formerly editor of Energy Design Update.*

(see "A Case of Backdrafting," page 282). Flue gases can contain dangerous levels of carbon monoxide, which is odorless and poisonous. Carbon monoxide detectors are now required in many locations. It is a good practice to install one, whether or not it is required by your local code.

Methods of Venting

A boiler, furnace, or water heater can be vented either by atmospheric venting (also called natural draft or natural aspiration) or fan-assisted venting. In atmospheric venting, flue gases flow to the chimney — and ultimately to the outdoors — under their own power. Until the 1980s, almost all residential fuel-burning appliances used atmospheric venting.

Fan-assisted venting, also called induced draft or forced draft, can use either a sidewall vent or a chimney. A boiler or furnace that has been designed with narrow flueways (to increase efficiency) often requires fan-assisted venting to help suck the flue gas out of the appliance.

Sealed combustion. Sealed-combustion appliances draw combustion air from the exterior directly to the burner (Figure 2). Because the fuel is burned in an environment that is entirely separated from the interior air of the living space, sealed-combustion appli-

Selecting the Right Vent

Appliance type			Vent pipe required
Category I appliances	Natural draft vent	Non-condensing	Lined masonry chimney or Type "B" or "BW" vent for gas or Type "L" all-fuel vent for oil
Category II appliances	Natural draft vent	Condensing	Type AL29-4C stainless steel
Category III appliances	Fan-assisted vent	Non-condensing	Type AL29-4C stainless steel or Type "B" vent (for vertical venting only)
Category IV appliances	Fan-assisted vent	Condensing	PVC or ABS vent pipe
Direct-vent appliances	Fan-assisted vent	Condensing	PVC or ABS vent pipe
Direct-vent appliances	Fan-assisted vent	Non-condensing	Type AL29-4C stainless steel

Figure 2. A galvanized pipe (foreground) provides combustion air directly from the exterior to the burner of this sealed-combustion boiler. A separate galvanized vent pipe conducts the flue gas through the sidewall.

Figure 3. An installer attaches the vent termination on the sidewall vent for a sealed-combustion boiler. The fresh air intake in the foreground will be terminated with a 90-degree elbow.

ances are unaffected by pressure differences inside the building envelope and are, therefore, the best choice for tight houses. Some sealed-combustion appliances draw air in by means of concentric pipes, with the smaller diameter vent pipe located within the larger diameter air supply pipe. Sealed-combustion appliances can discharge flue gas either to a side wall (Figure 3) or up through the roof. Most sealed-combustion appliances use fan-assisted venting, except for some direct-vent space heaters.

Condensing Versus Non-Condensing Appliances

Fuel-burning appliances are categorized as either condensing or non-condensing. Non-condensing appliances are limited to about 87 percent efficiency. Condensing appliances are more efficient, because they extract more heat from the flue gas by cooling the gas to the point where moisture is condensed out. This condensation provides a latent heat exchange, boosting the efficiency of the appliance into the mid-90 percent range.

Because of the corrosive nature of the condensate, however, condensing appliances have different venting requirements from non-condensing appliances. The condensate can contain acid (sulfuric, nitric, or hydrochloric) that can corrode masonry chimneys, as well as some types of stainless steel vent pipe.

The type of vent material that can be used depends upon whether the appliance is condensing or non-condensing, and whether the venting is natural draft or fan-assisted (see "Selecting the Right Vent," facing page).

Location of sidewall vents. When installing a sidewall vent, you must maintain certain minimum clearances from grade, as well as from openings, gas meters, and electric meters. These clearances differ, depending upon whether or not the appliance is a sealed-combustion appliance (Figure 4).

Code Requirements

In many parts of the country, the National Fuel Gas Code (NFPA 54) applies. Other applicable codes may include NFPA 31, Standard for the Installation of Oil-Burning Equipment;

Clearances for Wall Vents

Sealed-Combustion Appliance

Vent cap 12" min. from and below any door, window, or air inlet

Mount vent cap 12" min. from inside corners

Vent cap 12" min. horizontally from any electric meter, gas meter, or relief equipment

Vent cap at least 3' min. above any forced air inlet located within 10'

Locate vent cap 12" min. above grade

Vent cap must be installed with a vent termination clearance of 12" minimum from any air opening into a building

Power-Vented Appliance That Is Not Sealed-Combustion

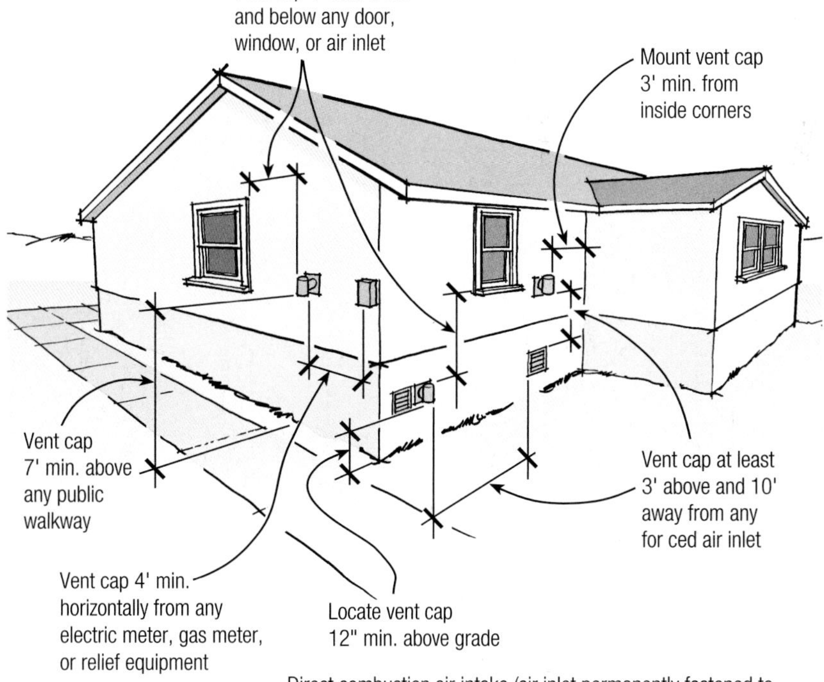

Figure 4. The required clearances between a sidewall vent and various other openings in a wall depend on whether or not the appliance is a sealed-combustion appliance. With a power-vented appliance that is not sealed-combustion, there is a risk that flue gas can be pulled back into the building through an open window if adequate clearances are not observed.

A Case of Backdrafting: Why Makeup Air Matters

Many years ago, we encountered a case of carbon monoxide poisoning that helped open our eyes to the importance of looking at the whole house as a system, not just at the appliance by itself. We also gained more appreciation for using test instruments to check system performance — both in testing the indoor air for carbon monoxide, and in testing the functioning of the appliance with combustion analyzers and draft test equipment.

The house was a one-story ranch with a full basement. Built in the late seventies, it was an early example of very tight construction — as we discovered. The husband in the family worked every weekday, and the wife stayed home with their two preschool children.

The wife had persistent health complaints — she felt headachy and tired all the time. The husband usually felt fine — except on weekends.

When we checked the appliances, located in a large, open basement, we found all the settings correct, but there was severe corrosion in the furnace and telltale damage around the draft hood of the water heater, indicating a lot of spillage. Theoretically, the huge open basement was an "unconfined space" with plenty of combustion air — but this was back before codes began to require makeup air vents in homes with tight construction. And this house was tight. A blower door test found only one tiny leak, at a can light in a bedroom closet.

It turned out that the wife followed a regular routine: She did all the family's laundry every Monday. The washer and dryer ran all day. This meant that the water heater ran all day, too — with its vent having to fight the suction of the dryer vent. Once defeated by the dryer, the water heater never reestablished a draft in the flue — it continued to run backwards all week.

At first, the water heater would burn cleanly. But the carbon dioxide it produced, being heavier than air, would settle to the bottom of the basement and gradually displace oxygen (see illustration). As the CO2 rose to cover the appliance air intakes, it began to starve them for oxygen, and they began to have incomplete combustion, producing carbon monoxide. The wife's symptoms were caused by CO poisoning — the husband was able to clear his system during his workdays outside the house and felt sick only on weekends.

The equipment had to be replaced. Beyond that, we had to build a tight enclosure for the equipment, a mechanical room in the basement — and we cut ducted air supply vents into the band joist, one low and one high. The family's health cleared up.

Today, the solution we applied is required by code in tight houses, although we don't always see the rules enforced.

We still run into that family from time to time, and it's a nice reward to think of the many years of good health they've enjoyed as a result of what we were able to do.

Bob Dwyer, *a technical trainer for Bacharach, Inc., and Mark Gronley, a quality control supervisor for Northwest Energy, a Montana utility.*

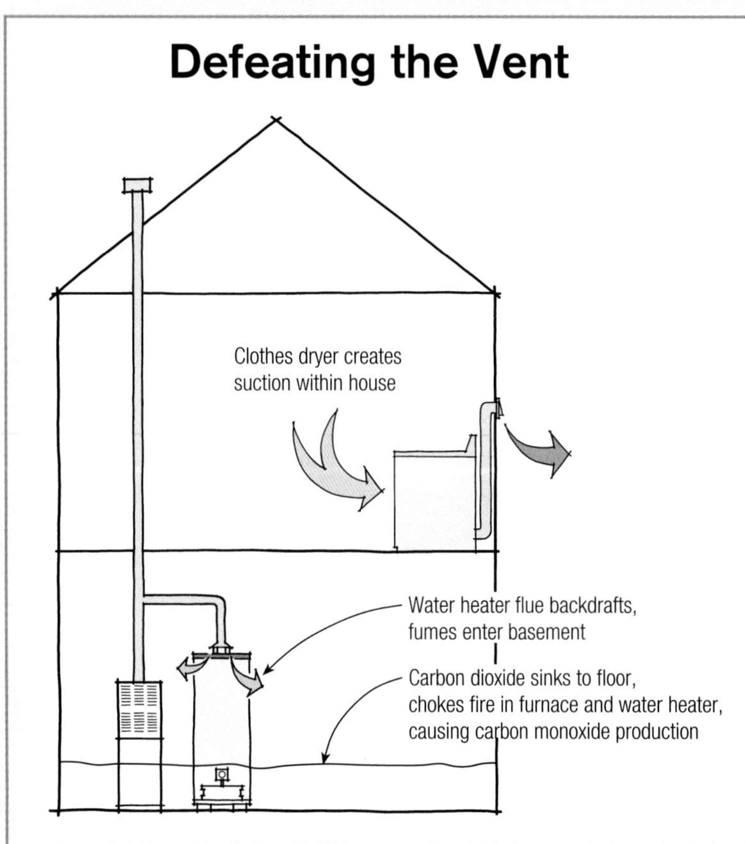
Defeating the Vent
Clothes dryer creates suction within house
Water heater flue backdrafts, fumes enter basement
Carbon dioxide sinks to floor, chokes fire in furnace and water heater, causing carbon monoxide production

NFPA 211, Standard for Chimneys, Fireplaces, Vents, and Solid Fuel-Burning Appliances; and Section 607 of the Uniform Mechanical Code. In addition, be sure to consult your local code and to adhere to the appliance manufacturer's instructions. If there is a conflict between your local code and the manufacturer's instructions, get the conflict resolved before installing any equipment.

The National Fuel Gas Code Handbook can be ordered from NFPA (www.nfpa.org).

Special Problems With Tight Houses

Thanks to the use of vapor barriers, housewrap, sill seal, weatherstripping, and caulk, we can now routinely build the kind of warm, draft-free homes our grandparents could only dream of. But if you build a very tight house without providing adequate ventilation, it can come back to haunt you.

Customers are increasingly concerned with indoor air quality. A while ago, a homeowner showed me his new superinsulated house, which included magnetic weatherstripping on the doors. Several months later, he called me for advice concerning the mildew and lingering odor problems in his house. He eventually decided to install a heat-recovery ventilator to improve the indoor air quality. A heat-recovery ventilator will improve ventilation levels, but it is not designed to provide makeup air for the heating appliances.

Makeup Air

All fuel-burning appliances require combustion air. Strictly speaking, combustion air has three components:

- ***stoichiometric air***, which is the air required for the chemical combustion process
- ***excess air***, which is the "little bit of extra air" that appliance manufacturers require to ensure that the amount of air available for combustion is adequate
- ***dilution air***, which is the air required to dilute the flue gases enough to allow their passage through the vent

The term *makeup air* is used to describe these three components of combustion air, along with cooling air, which is the air required to cool the room in which the appliance is located.

Appliances in an Unconfined Space

In an unconfined space, the makeup air for heating appliances is provided by the large volume of air present in the space where the appliances are located — usually, a basement or crawlspace.

According to the National Fuel Gas Code, a space is defined as unconfined if it has a volume greater than 50 cubic feet per 1,000 Btu/h of the combined input of the fuel-burning appliances. For example, if a house is equipped with a gas furnace with an input rating of 70,000 Btu/h, plus a gas water heater with an input rating of 40,000 Btu/h, the total input of the appliances would be 110,000 Btu/h. The space where these appliances are located would need to measure at least 5,500 cubic feet to be considered unconfined — equivalent to a space about 25x28 feet by 8 feet high.

Makeup air enters an unconfined space through uncontrolled infiltration from the exterior — for example, by finding its way between the top of the concrete foundation and the sill plate. With the advent of tight construction practices, however, some basements that meet the code definition of an unconfined space may not provide enough makeup air for fuel-burning appliances.

How Tight Is Too Tight?

How can a builder know when a house becomes too tight for uncontrolled infiltration to provide adequate makeup air to appliances in an unconfined space? Unfortunately, existing codes do not provide clear answers. NFPA 31 refers to the possibility that a building can have "insufficient air because of tight construction" (NFPA 31-1-9.3.2) without defining when that point is reached. The National Fuel Gas Code standards for makeup air assume that a building has at least ½ air change per hour.

If you are building houses with housewrap, sill seal, weatherstripped doors, and caulked windows, it is probably unwise to depend on uncontrolled infiltration to provide makeup air.

Appliances Installed in a Confined Space

Any space smaller than an "unconfined" space as defined in the National Fuel Gas Code is considered to be a confined space and must be provided with openings to admit makeup air. Usually, this requires the installation of a register or grille in the utility room wall (Figure 5), or the installation of one or more ducts leading to the exterior (Figure 6). The National Fuel Gas Code provides four options for providing these vent openings (see "Makeup Air Options," page 285):

- provide openings or grilles between the confined space and an adjacent unconfined space
- provide two ducts to a ventilated attic
- provide two ducts or openings to the exterior
- provide a single duct or opening to the exterior

This last option is a new addition to the 1996 code, and although the allowance of only one opening rather than two may appear to contradict the requirements of the previous three options, it is perfectly acceptable. This option was included to address the concern that two openings to the exterior might cause frozen pipes in colder climates.

Motorized louvers. If you are concerned that makeup

air from the exterior could cause pipes to freeze, you might consider installing motorized louvers on the air intake (Figure 7). Any motorized louvers used must be the type that lock out the burner circuit until the louvers are in the full-open position. Contact your heating contractor or supply house for more information on motorized louvers.

Figure 5. Combustion makeup air can be provided to a confined space through an opening in the utility room wall. Air enters the confined space from the adjacent basement area, which must meet the definition of an unconfined space.

Forced Combustion Air Systems

Another way to provide makeup air to appliances in a confined space is to install a forced combustion air system, also called a powered air intake system. This approach uses a fan to introduce ducted exterior air to a utility room (Figure 8). The fan is wired to be interlocked with the burner. An airflow switch in the intake air duct prevents operation of the fuel-burning appliance when the air duct is blocked, and a damper prevents off-cycle airflow.

The advantage of a forced combustion air system is the ability to use a small duct (usually, a single 3-inch round duct for a residential system) instead of the two larger ducts that would usually be required when exterior makeup air is provided passively.

Forced combustion air systems are sold by two different manufacturers, Tjernlund Products and Field Controls. These types of engineered systems are now accepted by the 2003 and later versions of the International Residential Code (IRC), as well as under NFPA 31 and 54.

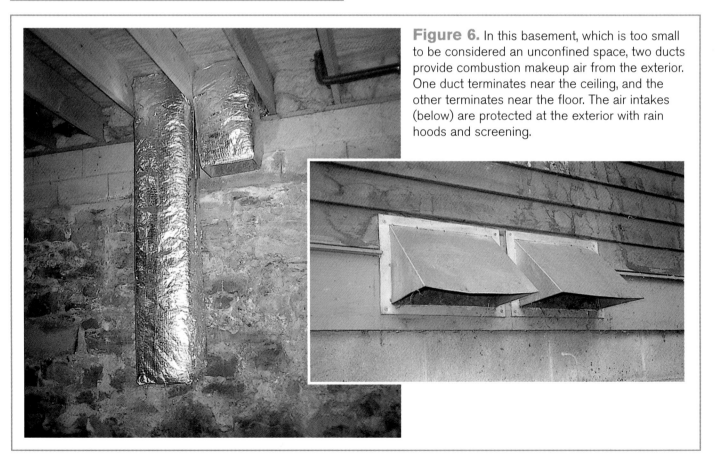

Figure 6. In this basement, which is too small to be considered an unconfined space, two ducts provide combustion makeup air from the exterior. One duct terminates near the ceiling, and the other terminates near the floor. The air intakes (below) are protected at the exterior with rain hoods and screening.

Makeup Air Options in a Confined Space

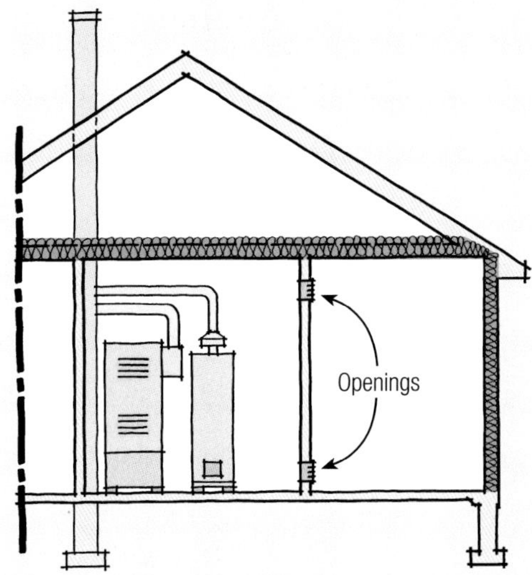

A. Makeup Air From Inside the Building

The space where the appliances are located must include two permanent openings communicating with an unconfined space, each of which must have a minimum free area of 1 square inch per 1,000 Btu/h of the total Btu/h input. One opening must be located within 12 inches of the ceiling, and one must be located within 12 inches of the floor. Neither opening can be smaller than 3 inches of free area.

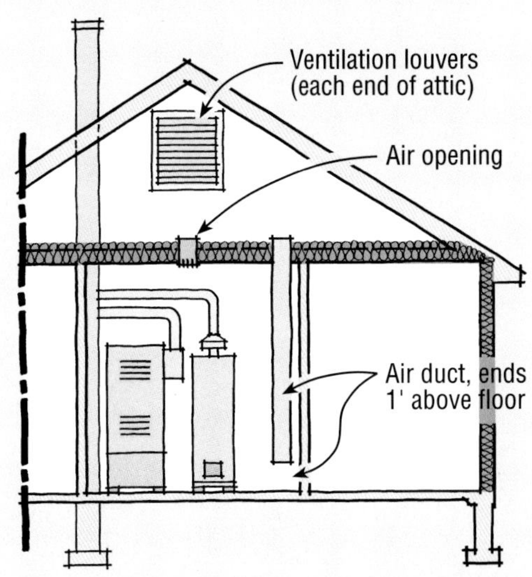

B. Makeup Air From a Ventilated Attic

The space where the appliances are located must include two permanent openings communicating with the attic, each with a free area of 1 square inch per 4,000 Btu/h of total Btu/h input. As with option A, one opening must be located within 12 inches of the ceiling, and one must be located within 12 inches of the floor, and neither opening can be smaller than 3 inches of free area.

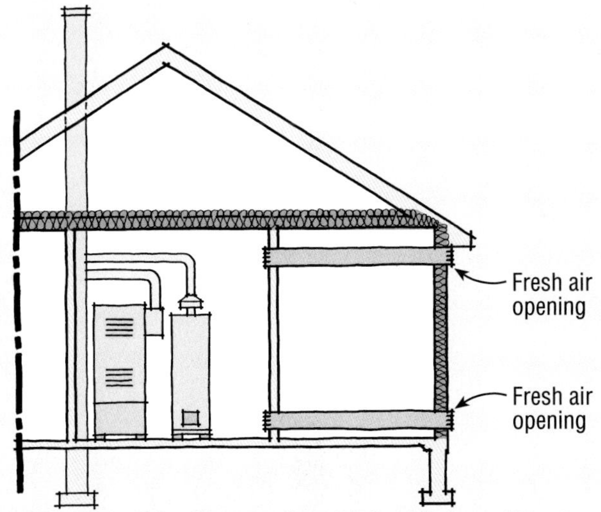

C. Makeup Air From Outside Using Ducts

The space where the appliances are located must include two permanent openings communicating with the outdoors, each with a free area of 1 square inch per 2,000 Btu/h of total Btu/h input. As with options A and B, one opening must be located within 12 inches of the ceiling, and one must be located within 12 inches of the floor, and neither opening can be smaller than 3 inches of free area.

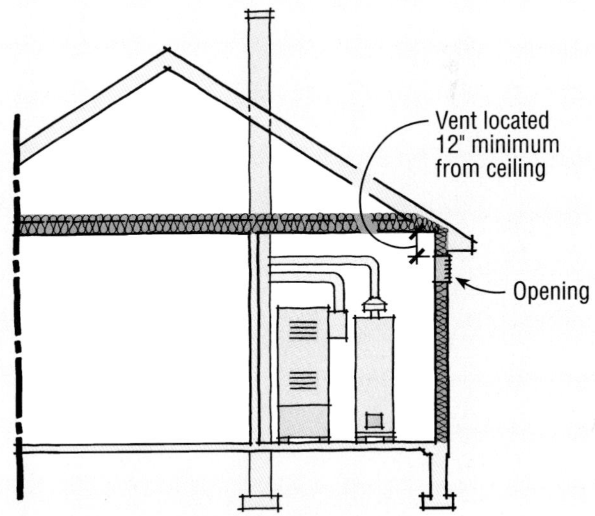

D. Makeup Air From Outside Using a Single Opening

The space where the appliances are located can include one permanent opening communicating with the outdoors. The opening must have a free area of 1 square inch per 3,000 Btu/h of the total Btu/h input, must measure no less than the total area of the vent connectors, and must be located within 12 inches of the ceiling.

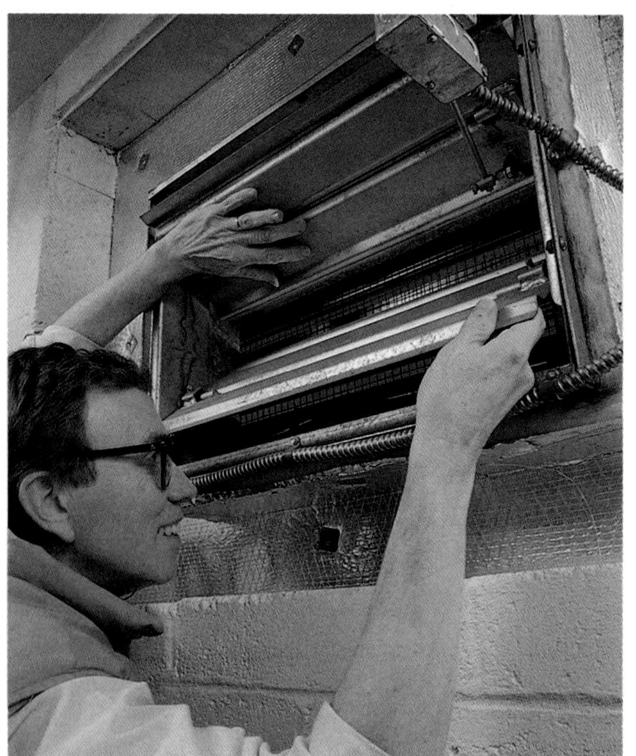

Figure 7. Motorized dampers are installed in very cold climates, where exterior makeup air might be cold enough to freeze plumbing pipes in a utility room or basement.

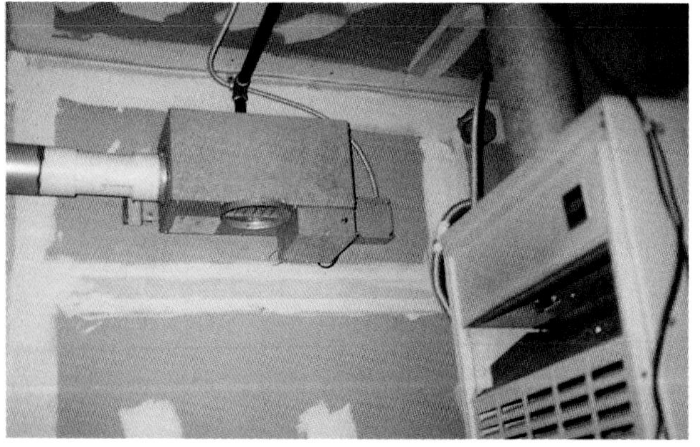

Figure 8. A forced combustion air system uses a fan to introduce makeup air into a utility room. This permits the use of a much smaller duct than when the makeup air enters by gravity.

Providing adequate makeup air for a fuel-burning appliance is essential not only for the proper operation of the equipment, but also for safety. Do the job right, and the building's appliances — not to mention its occupants and you, the builder — will be able to breathe easy.

***Carl Saunders** is director of training at Utica Boilers in Utica, N.Y.*

Manufacturers of Combustion Air Fans

Field Controls
www.fieldcontrols.com

Tjernlund Products Inc.
www.tjernlund.com

Successful Fireplaces in Tight Houses

by John Gulland

Builders are beginning to hear more complaints that traditional masonry fireplaces leak smoke and burn too much wood for too little heat output. The fact is, open site-built masonry fireplaces have always been filthy, smoky, and inefficient, but these drawbacks were less noticeable in drafty, uninsulated houses. Today's tighter homes, however, are less forgiving, and their occupants are less tolerant.

In addition, many modern fireplaces are used strictly as a design element, and many designers have no training in what makes one work. On top of that, many of the masons and other heating contractors who build fireplaces carry over outdated design traditions that are at the root of performance problems.

It doesn't have to be that way. Building scientists now understand why traditional fireplace designs perform poorly; and masons, manufacturers, and hearth installers have responded with new products and techniques that eliminate past problems.

In this article, I'll discuss the common causes of fireplace problems and propose solutions for masonry fireplaces and heaters, as well as for less expensive, efficient wood-burning metal fireplaces.

A central location, a tall chimney, and controlled combustion are the keys to a good burn.

Why Fireplaces Fail

When it comes to traditional open masonry fireplaces, masons have perpetuated outdated ideas about the smoke shelf, the mysteries of the smoke chamber, and the need for wide, but shallow-throat dampers.

Today, it is clear that all three of these features work against successful fireplace performance (Figure 9). The smoke shelf and shallow-throat damper both act as obstacles to straight exhaust flow. And the smoke chamber actually reduces the strength of a chimney's draft by slowing and cooling the fireplace exhaust. The performance of many brick fireplaces can be improved immediately by removing the throat damper and smoke shelf and installing a chain-operated damper at the top of the chimney. The results are a smooth, straight path for the exhaust and less smoking when a fire burns.

Cold Hearth Syndrome

But the biggest source of trouble is the location of the fireplace. Over the past 50 years of residential design, fireplaces have migrated from the center of the house to a position against the exterior walls, or even into chases that are completely outside the house. This causes cold hearth syndrome, which is the source of most fireplace failures.

The most dramatic effect of a cold hearth is a predictable blast of cold air when the fireplace doors are opened to build a fire. Smoke tends to fill the room when someone tries to light a kindling fire. This is a common, even chronic, characteristic of North American fireplaces.

The syndrome usually has its origin in the decision to place a fireplace outside an exterior wall in a frame or brick chase (Figure 10). The cold outside air sucks warmth from the fireplace and chimney structure, causing the temperature of the air in the flue to drop. When the flue temperature is lower than the house temperature, air begins to flow down the chimney and onto the hearth. This is called a "cold backdraft," and contrary to common belief, it does not happen because cold air is heavy and falls down the chimney. The air is not falling — it is being sucked down by the house.

Just as hot exhaust in a chimney produces a pressure difference called a "draft," so the relatively warm air in a house produces a pressure difference called "stack effect." The buoyant warm air rises, producing a slight low pressure zone downstairs and higher pressure upstairs. Since most fireplaces are installed on lower floors, they experience negative pressure due to stack effect when it is cold outside. As soon as the air in the chimney falls below room temperature, the house becomes a better chimney than the chimney itself, and a cold backdraft gets started. The backdraft tends to stabilize because as the chimney becomes full of cold air, it cannot produce any draft to resist the suction of the house.

Tall stack effect. A similar problem is caused by chimneys that fail to extend higher than all of the living space in a house. A chimney that is not tall enough competes with the living space above it to establish the dominant draft (Figure 11). If the upper part of a house envelope leaks enough air through windows, attic access hatches, and wall penetrations, the house will again act as a better chimney than the chimney itself. In these cases, the house is said to have a "taller effective stack" than the chimney. Air will tend to flow down through the chimney, then loop through the house to exit through the attic or upper-story wall leaks. To avoid these problems, chimney tops should always penetrate the highest section of the conditioned living space.

In all cases, the cold hearth syndrome has two necessary ingredients without which it will not occur: a misplaced chimney and a fireplace located low in the house. If we could move the fireplace and its chimney towards the center of a house, the syndrome would

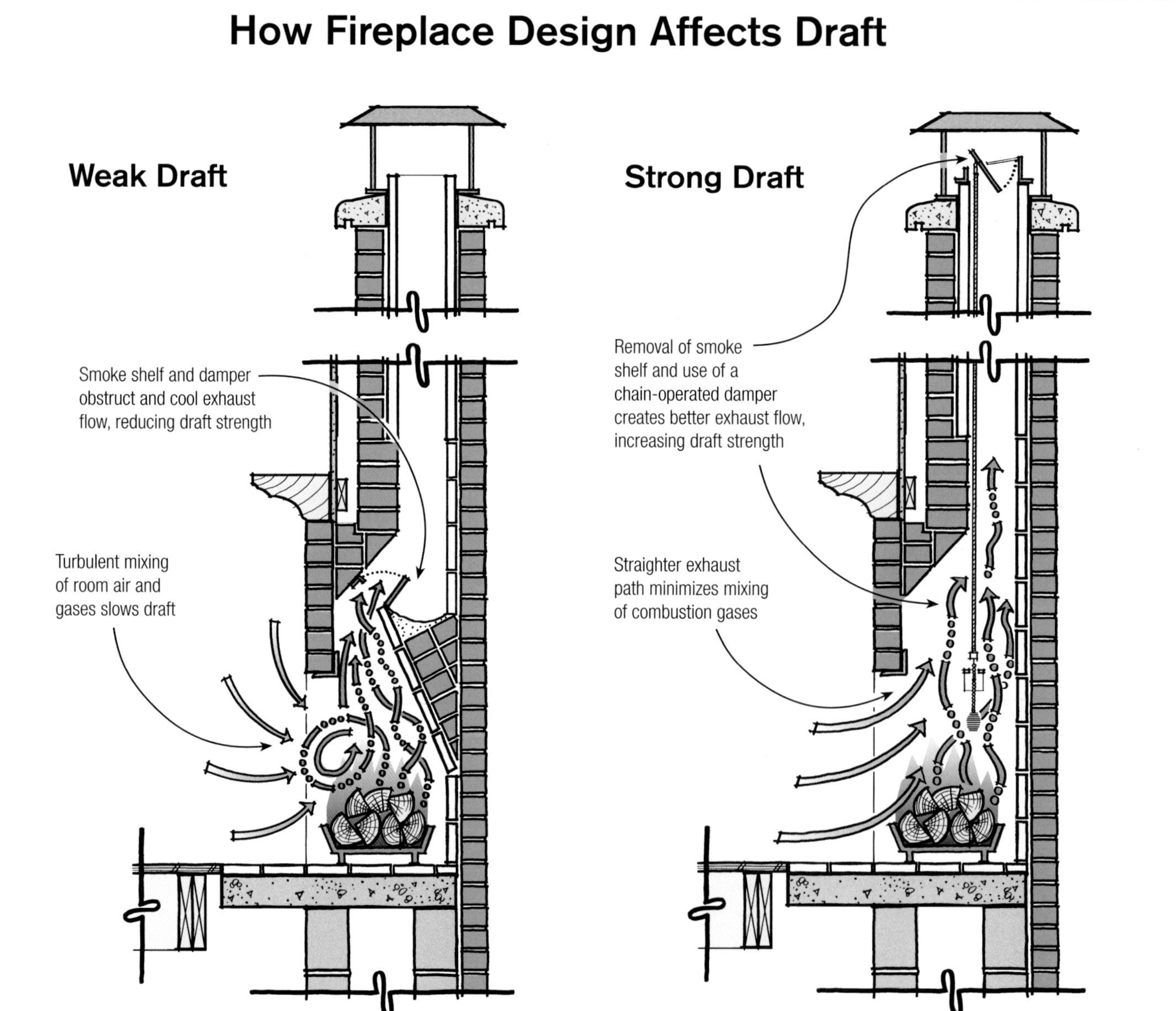
How Fireplace Design Affects Draft
Weak Draft
Smoke shelf and damper obstruct and cool exhaust flow, reducing draft strength
Turbulent mixing of room air and gases slows draft
Strong Draft
Removal of smoke shelf and use of a chain-operated damper creates better exhaust flow, increasing draft strength
Straighter exhaust path minimizes mixing of combustion gases

Figure 9. Traditional fireplaces leak smoke into living space and don't produce heat efficiently. The curving smoke chamber, the throat damper, and the smoke shelf all decrease the stability of the chimney draft.

vanish. Or we could move the fireplace to the highest floor of the house where the higher pressure caused by rising warmer air would ensure a good draft.

Unfortunately, moving a problem fireplace is not practical after it's been built, but you can still prevent cold hearth syndrome by keeping the chimney from falling below room temperature. One way to do this is to trick the fireplace into thinking it is inside. This requires building a sealed, insulated chase that thermally matches the house wall construction. The chase should be vented to the inside so that warm house air circulating in it will keep it at about house temperature.

A better solution is to design out cold hearth syndrome at the planning stage by bringing the fireplace and chimney in from the cold. Ideally the fireplace should be located centrally, in the heart of the home, so that the chimney will penetrate the roof closer to its highest point. This makes for a tall chimney with a large temperature differential between combustion exhaust and outside air — the two ingredients that make for the most reliable and stable draft. Straight venting systems also work better, so elbows and offsets in the chimney should be avoided.

Makeup Air

While improper design and location is a major cause of poor fireplace performance, tighter house construction and powerful exhaust fans must share some of the blame. By installing vapor barriers and using doors and windows that have sealing gaskets, builders commonly reduce air leakage by more than 75 percent compared with the standard construction of 20 years ago. And homes are now commonly equipped with high-volume exhaust fans, such as those in downdraft kitchen ranges, which can move air out of the house at a rate of 600 cubic feet per minute (cfm) or more. Because tightly sealed house walls will not allow this much air back into the house through leakage, these powerful fans create negative pressure that can cause a chimney to backdraft and fill a house with smoke (Figure 12).

One standard fix for smoky fireplaces has been to install a supply of outdoor air in the belief that air starvation is the root cause. While lack of combustion air may be a problem in some cases, supplying

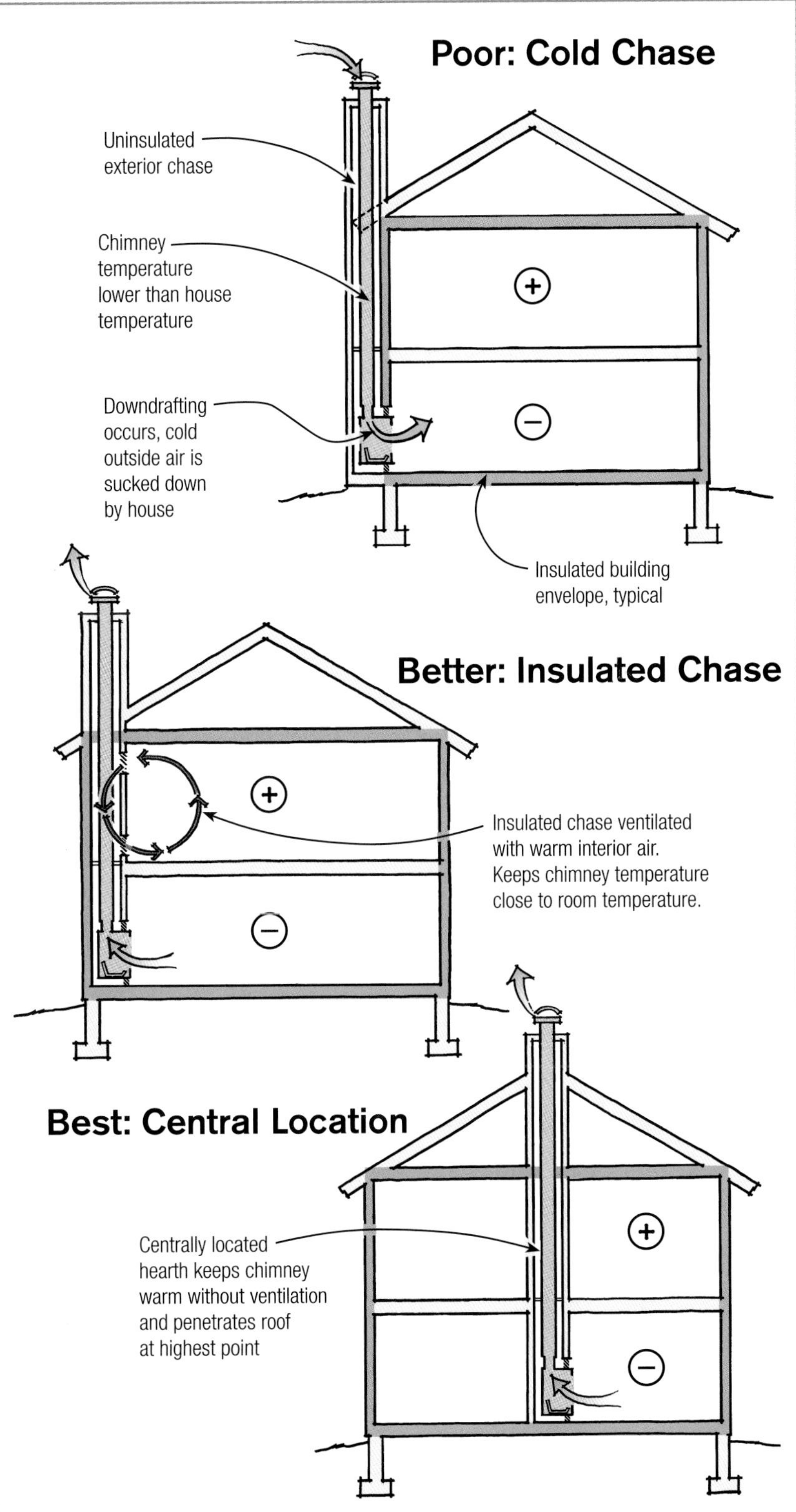

Figure 10. Chimneys built on an outside wall, whether exposed or boxed with an uninsulated chase, are prone to downdrafting (top). One solution is to insulate the walls of the chase and to vent the chase to the interior so warm air can circulate (middle). The best solution is to locate the chimney properly in the first place. The ideal location is in the center of the house (bottom) because the surrounding air will keep the chimney warm and the chimney will penetrate the roof at its highest point.

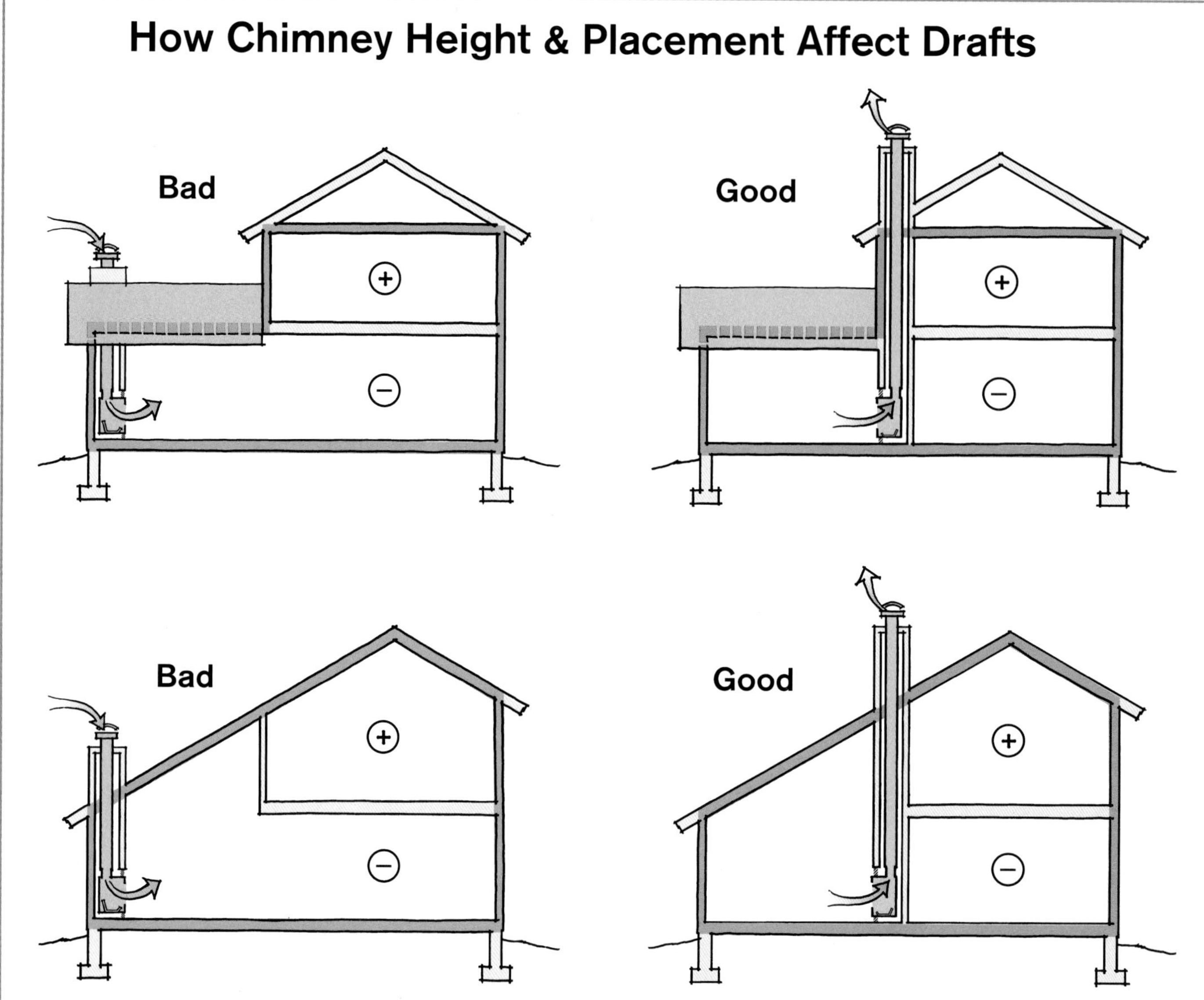

Figure 11. Chimneys built on outside walls are often too short to counter the house's stack effect and are prone to downdrafts. Again, moving the chimney closer to the center of the house ensures a tall chimney with a strong draft.

outdoor air to the fireplace through a duct is certainly not the cure. Two research studies, one conducted in Canada on a series of factory-built fireplaces and one done in the U.S. on a masonry fireplace, looked into the behavior of outdoor combustion air supplies. In both studies, the fireplaces were installed within chambers that could be depressurized continuously after a fire was lit. As the fires died down to charcoal, technicians monitored carbon monoxide readings in the chamber to see when exhaust began to spill from the fireplaces. Tests were done with and without combustion air supplied from outside the depressurized chamber. No consistent difference in spillage timing or amount could be found whether or not outdoor air was supplied.

The reason is simple: Air flows to zones of lower pressure. If a room is depressurized to the point where its low pressure overwhelms the chimney draft, smoke will flow into the room. Obviously, ducting makeup air to the fireplace doesn't work. In fact, building code authorities are currently removing mandatory outdoor air requirements for fireplaces that were added only a few years ago, just before research debunked the idea.

Where a notorious air-guzzling downdraft kitchen range causes excessive depressurization, many homeowners will simply not use their range exhaust when the fireplace is burning. But a better solution is to install a kitchen makeup air system that is interlocked to the range exhaust switch. This kind of makeup air system would force air into the house to compensate for the kitchen range exhaust flow. This would prevent depressurization, and solve the smoky fireplace problem.

Combustion Air vs. Makeup Air

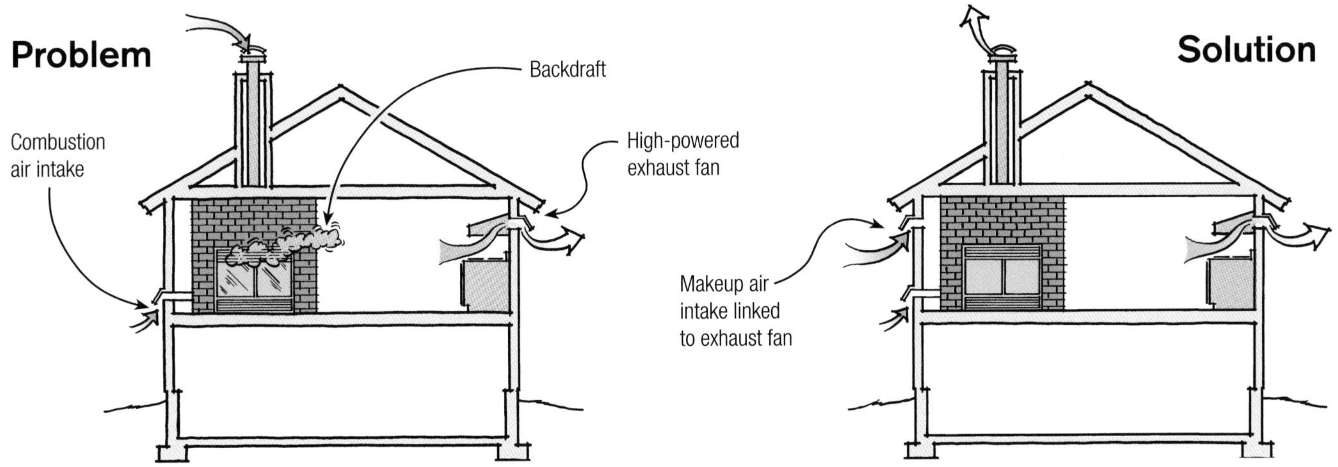

Problem

Backdraft

Combustion air intake

High-powered exhaust fan

Solution

Makeup air intake linked to exhaust fan

Figure 12. In tight houses, depressurization from cooktop vents, dryer vents, and other exhaust fans can cause fireplaces to backdraft and spill smoke into the room. Instead of ducting combustion air to the fireplace, which does nothing to change room pressure, add a makeup air system linked to the exhaust fans.

Controlled Combustion

The design of the fireplace itself plays a big role in the level of satisfaction it provides. The internal features that produce efficient, smokeless combustion tend to be the same as those that produce reliable chimney venting and trouble-free operation. To help guide fireplace design, here is a simple rule of thumb that neatly summarizes a lot of expensive research: The more air a fireplace demands for normal operation, the more fussy and spillage-susceptible it will be.

Open fireplaces are the worst because they consume huge amounts of air — much more than is needed for combustion — which cools the system, thereby reducing draft. If your clients insist on a traditional fireplace, make sure they also agree to equip it with tightly sealed doors. The more you control the combustion in the firebox, the higher the temperatures of the exhaust and the stronger the draft.

If your client doesn't want glass doors or much heat, direct them to a gas hearth. Do the same if the architect's plans call for a hearth in an outside chase situated at the low eaves of a cathedral roof. If the clients cannot be convinced to relocate the fireplace more centrally, you will both probably be happier with a direct-vent gas fireplace.

Several other alternatives to traditional masonry fireplaces are available. Metal stoves and fireplaces that meet Environmental Protection Agency (EPA) rules for low smoke emissions are the most resistant to leaking smoke into the house because they create a reliable draft (Figure 13). These appliances are equipped with internal baffles, firebox insulation, and strategically placed combustion air inlets, which produce a clean-burning fire, even at low heat output settings.

Figure 13. The Delta prefabricated metal fireplace is one example of an EPA-certified controlled-combustion fireplace (International Chimney Co., www.icc-rsf.com).

Figure 14. Masonry heaters, with their enormous thermal mass, are designed to burn very hot, then store and slowly release heat. Although more expensive than prefabricated metal fireplaces, they provide a reliable, high-performance wood-burning hearth.

Figure 15. Metal fireplaces don't have to look metallic. The masonry surround for this metal fireplace gives a traditional look along with predictable performance, at a savings over a site-built masonry fireplace.

Don't sacrifice performance for lower cost, however. Some cheap units are made out of lighter, thinner materials, and are often connected to lightweight air-cooled chimneys with flue diameters that are too small relative to the fireplace opening. All of these cost-saving elements hurt performance.

For customers who insist on a real brick or stone fireplace, a masonry heater is a good option (Figure 14). Masonry heaters use rapid combustion and heat stored in their massive structure to achieve high efficiency and excellent resistance to spillage.

Both types of appliances solve the smoky fireplace problem because they get hot and stay hot until the fire fades to a coal bed and goes out. Both types also produce net efficiencies of more than 60 percent, a welcome feature during a winter electrical power failure. In addition, high-quality prefabricated metal fireplaces are much less expensive than traditional masonry fireplaces — often less than half the cost, depending on the facade and the mantel design (Figure 15).

Trained Installers

In the last 20 years, building science research has clearly shown how fireplaces behave in houses. These insights are now being promoted through professional training programs. When planning a traditional masonry fireplace or metal heater, or even a wood stove, use suppliers, installers, or masons who understand the pitfalls of outdated ideas and impractical designs. Fireplace suppliers and installers who are certified by the National Fireplace Institute (www.nficertified.org) have a better handle on the issues that concern builders than those who are untrained. If a masonry fireplace is required, use only qualified heater masons who are certified under the Masonry Heater Association of North America professional training program (www.mha-net.org).

John Gulland *is a hearth consultant based in Ontario, Canada. He is author of "The Fireplace in the House as a System."*

Chapter 13

MECHANICAL VENTILATION

Simple Exhaust Ventilation for Tight Houses

by Andrew Shapiro

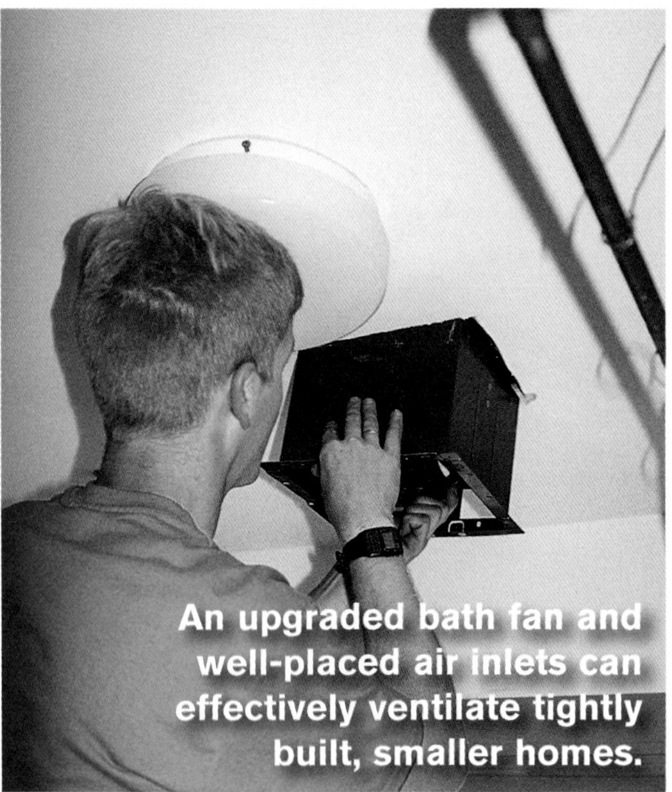

An upgraded bath fan and well-placed air inlets can effectively ventilate tightly built, smaller homes.

Indoor air quality has aroused increasing concern in recent years, with home buyers worried about everything from carpet fumes and formaldehyde to excess moisture and dust mites. These problems have been compounded by improved building practices that have created tighter homes. But a house doesn't have to be airtight, or even close to it, to have poor indoor air quality.

Of course, the best solution to indoor air problems would be to eliminate from the home all the products that emit air pollutants, but this is impractical and costly. And moisture from people, plants, pets, cooking, and bathing is a fact of indoor life. The most practical way to remedy problems from moisture and pollutants in a home is to install a simple ventilation system. Adding good ventilation is also an easy way to reduce callbacks from excess moisture on windows in cold climates.

Here, I focus on a system I've used that relies on a line of quiet, energy-efficient bath fans from Panasonic. However, many manufacturers now offer quiet and efficient bath exhaust fans. Look for those with Energy Star certification, indicating high efficiency and quiet operation.

Choosing a Fan

I typically use the Panasonic FV series of bathroom fans because they're affordable, extremely quiet, and energy efficient (Figure 1). This combination is critical for a ventilation system for a couple of reasons. First, most low-cost fans are so noisy you can't wait to turn them off, if you ever turn them on at all. If you expect a fan to be used, it must run quiet. The Panasonic fans run at under ½ sone for the 80-cfm models, and under 1 sone for the 110- to 150-cfm models. (One sone is about as quiet as a relatively new refrigerator.) Compare this with 2 to 4 sones for many cheap fans with similar capacities.

Figure 1. Panasonic was the first company to offer low-cost, low-sone, energy-efficient bath fans rated for continuous use, like the one shown above. Other manufactures now offer competing models.

Also, since the fan is going to run for long periods to exhaust a whole house, it must not consume too much electricity. The 80 cfm Panasonic fans use about 15 watts, compared with 100 or more watts for some cheap fans of similar capacity. A 100-watt fan used for 8 hours a day would cost about $29 a year to operate (at 10¢/kWh), while the 15-watt Panasonic fan would cost just over $4. Also, some of Panasonic's newer models offer variable speed for increased spot ventilation when needed.

Ventilation System Components

A fan by itself does not make a whole-house ventila-

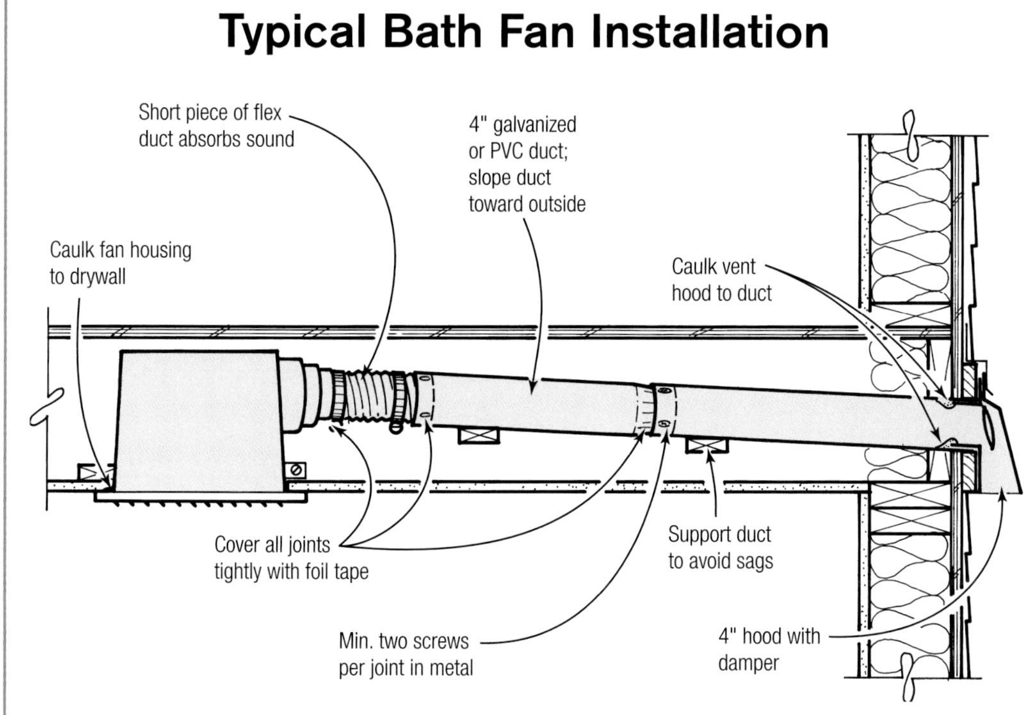
Typical Bath Fan Installation
Short piece of flex duct absorbs sound
4" galvanized or PVC duct; slope duct toward outside
Caulk fan housing to drywall
Caulk vent hood to duct
Cover all joints tightly with foil tape
Support duct to avoid sags
Min. two screws per joint in metal
4" hood with damper

Figure 2. For a quiet installation, separate the fan from the rigid duct with a short length of flex duct. Remember to support the rigid duct on blocking to prevent it from sagging. The illustration shows metal duct, which is required by some fire codes.

tion system. A complete system consists of a way to get stale air out, a way to get fresh air in, and a way to control the fans.

Out with the old. One FV-08 series fan, installed with less than 20 feet of smooth-wall duct and no more than two elbows, will deliver about 60 cfm. Just one of these is enough ventilation for a one-story, 1,700-square-foot house if the fan runs at least part of each hour that the house is occupied. Larger houses will require two or more fans (see "How Much to Ventilate," page 301).

Fresh air in. Whenever you have this much air exhausted from a house, you must provide a way for fresh makeup air to get in — and get in where you need it. Cracks around windows and doors, and other unavoidable air leaks, will also let in air, but this may not always provide enough fresh air in the occupied areas of the house.

I use through-the-wall inlets to do the job. I place one inlet in each bedroom, usually near the ceiling, where the colder outside air will mix with the warm house air before it contacts occupants. However, through-the-wall inlets can only be relied on in a very tight house. Otherwise the exhaust fan will pull makeup air from the nearest leak in the building shell, often not the installed inlet.

Controls. One key difference between a simple bath fan and a whole-house ventilation system is the length of time the fan runs. In most cases, the fan will run for 6 to 8 hours per day. Also, since most houses have more than one fan, the fans should be coordinated to run at different times to provide ventilation where and when it's needed. This requires reliable automatic timers.

Fans will need to run longer for people with "wet" lifestyles — lots of houseplants, cooking, Jacuzzis, and the like — and more during the first winter of occupancy in a new house when there is still a lot of moisture coming out of the building materials. This assumes that the occupants don't smoke and that there are no unusual sources of moisture or air pollution inside the house.

Sources of supply. Good mail-order sources for all the components of a whole-house system, including efficient exhaust fans, fresh air inlets, and automatic timers, are Energy Federation, Positive Energy, and Shelter Supply (see Sources of Supply, page 305).

Fan Installation

The Panasonic fans install in the bathroom ceiling just like any other bath fan (Figure 2). Be aware that the fan housing on some models is larger than that of typical bath fans. The one we typically use is 7⅞ inches deep, which fits in a 2x10 floor joist bay above the drywall. In a 2x8 floor system, however, you have to plan the installation so that the lower lip of the fan housing is flush with the bottom surface of the drywall. Panasonic provides a trim collar that can be secured with two thumbscrews from inside the fan housing. (A newer WhisperFit model fits in a 2x8 joist bay, but draws a little more power.)

Filters. Since the fan is going to be running frequently, it will collect a lot of lint and dirt. This can eventually clog fan blades and cooling holes in the motor, lowering air delivery and shortening the life of the fan. To protect the fan, use an ordinary cut-to-fit air conditioner filter. Cut a square that fits just inside the grille and push the grille springs through the filter before pushing the grille in place. Explain to the owners that this filter will need periodic cleaning or replacement. Also, if you run the fans during drywall finishing to help the mud dry faster, be sure the filter is in place during sanding and plan on replacing the filter before the owners move in.

Ductwork. If there is any "fine print" about Panasonic's FV series fans, it is that they cannot move air against a lot of back pressure, which is resistance to airflow caused by ductwork and other obstructions (see "Sizing Ventilation Fans," below). This means the ductwork needs to be full 4-inch-diameter rigid duct. A little flex duct — up to 2 feet or so — to connect to the fan and to the termination outside helps reduce noise and makes the installation easier without decreasing airflow too much.

For ductwork, I often use 4-inch thinwall PVC pipe — the nonperforated type used for foundation drains. This material is easy to work with and the joints can be sealed tight with PVC cement.

Sizing Ventilation Fans

Ventilation fans are sized to provide specific airflow rates in cubic feet per minute (cfm). The size of the fan needed for ventilation depends on the size of the house and the number of occupants. The older ASHRAE Standard, still widely used, recommends a minimum of 0.35 air changes per hour (ACH), but not less than 15 cfm per occupant during the time the house is occupied. You should calculate minimum whole-house fan size based on both house size and number of occupants, then use the higher number. (For the newer ASHRAE Standard, see "How Much to Ventilate," page 301.)

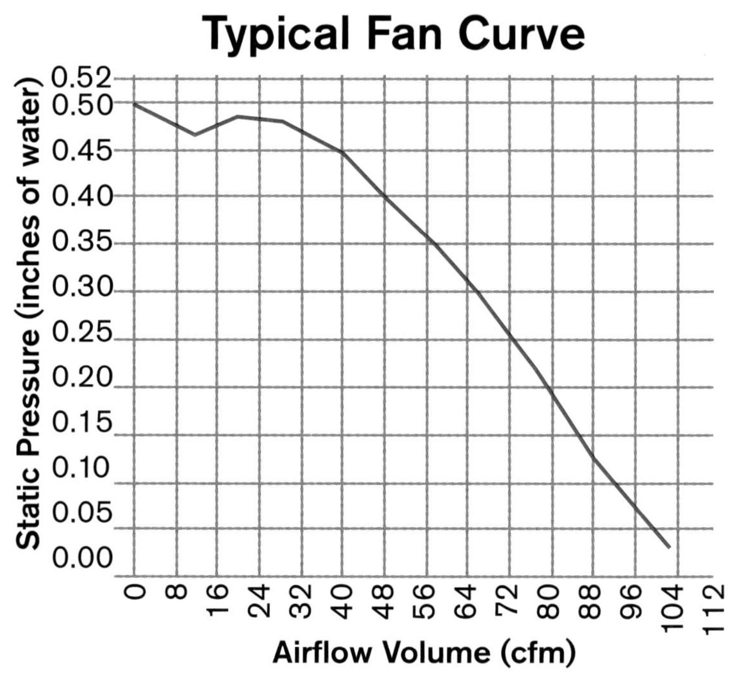

The fan curve shows how much air a fan will move as the static pressure increases with longer duct runs, elbows, grilles, and dampers. The 0.25" measure approximates the static pressure of a typical duct installation. So when choosing a fan, use the fan's airflow rating at 0.25", not 0.01".

Here's how to calculate 0.35 air changes per hour:

1. Multiply the exterior square footage of the house or apartment by the average ceiling height to calculate total volume. Then multiply by 0.85 to account for the wall and partition thicknesses.
2. Multiply the volume by 0.35.
3. Divide by 60 (minutes per hour) to get the required cfm.

So, for example, an 1,800-square-foot, three-bedroom house with 8-foot ceilings would need a ventilation rate of 71 cfm to ensure 0.35 ACH.

Now compare this with the other ASHRAE recommendation of 15 cfm per occupant. Since the number of occupants in a house or apartment changes over time, the assumption is made that there are two occupants in the master bedroom and one occupant in each of the other bedrooms. So a three-bedroom house requires 60 cfm of ventilation by this measure. Because the ACH measure — 71 cfm — is higher, that is the one to use. In this case, one Panasonic FV-08VQ2, which is rated at 75cfm at 0.25 static pressure, will meet the required ventilation needs.

Most fans' airflow ratings are listed at both 0.1 and 0.25 inches of water. When choosing a fan, make sure you use the cfm rating at 0.25 inches of water, which approximates the static pressure of a typical duct installation.

— A.S.

If you use galvanized ducts, put at least two screws per joint. Then use foil duct tape — the type with a peel-off paper back—not cloth duct tape. Conventional cloth duct tape will eventually deteriorate, releasing moist air into the attic or floor structure.

Flexible duct should be clamped first with metal hose clamps or straps, then taped to the rigid duct. Do it right from the start so you don't ever have to get in there again.

Keep the total duct run to no more than 20 feet, and use no more than three elbows or 2 feet of flex duct. In most cases, this will be plenty of duct to get to an outside wall. If you need more, reduce the number of elbows and eliminate as much of the flex duct as possible.

If at all feasible, avoid running duct inside 2x4 walls. However, running down and out may sometimes be the shortest route to the outside. If you run the duct in partition walls, use 4-inch oval duct. Don't reduce the duct size below 4 inches.

Vent termination. As a termination outside, I use a simple low-cost dryer vent with a flap-type backdraft damper. The dryer vent terminations with three louvers can freeze up in the winter, so I recommend the hood-type outlet instead.

Insulation. If the duct is in the attic, it should be under the attic insulation; otherwise, condensation will form on the ductwork and leak into the house. If this is not possible (as when the duct runs across the top of the ceiling joists), insulate the duct separately. If you are using blown-in attic insulation, you can put up "dams" using any available material, such as drywall, plywood, cardboard, or window screen. Fill the dammed-off area with insulation, mounding it over the ductwork to the proper insulation depth.

Support the duct with blocking to prevent any sags, and slope the rigid duct down toward the exterior as much as possible. With metal duct, face the long seams upward and "nest" the joints in the direction of flow, as a further hedge against water leakage from condensation problems.

Figure 3. A whole-house ventilation system needs effective controls. The author uses a Grasslin 24-hour automatic timer that can be set to run at 20-minute on/off cycles, with manual overrides.

Controls

An automatic timer gives occupants the most options for controlling the fans. I install one timer for each fan (up to two fans). If there are additional fans located away from normally occupied areas (a guest-room bathroom, for example), a switch for each of these is adequate.

Don't wire the fan into the light switch. Doing so makes it impossible to turn the fan on long enough for good ventilation without leaving the light on and wasting electricity.

I use the Grasslin KM2 24-hour in-wall timer (www.intermatic.com). The Grasslin timer (Figure 3) fits into a standard electrical box and can be programmed to turn on in 20-minute intervals. It can also be manually turned on and off. The timer needs a separate 2x4-inch electrical box, as the cover doesn't fit a ganged box.

Another good option is the Tamarack Airetrak timer (www.tamtech.com). This timer is a bit more expensive, but it allows the fan to cycle for part of every hour at full or reduced speed. You select the fraction of the hour, plus the speed of the fan. A single push-button allows you to bump up the fan to full speed for 20 minutes when the bathroom is being used.

Inlet Installation

Since the fans are exhausting air from the house, makeup air should be supplied through inlets. Although there are other air inlets on the market, I use Fresh-80s made by Therma-Stor (www.thermastor.com) (Figure 4). These are relatively inexpensive, easy to install, and have several good features, including an adjustable damper and an easy-to-get-to filter to keep out dust.

Install one air inlet in each bedroom and in any "extra" rooms such as home offices, dens, or other perimeter rooms that will be occupied. The goal is to move air from perimeter rooms toward the bathrooms. If the living room doesn't have any exterior doors, install an inlet in the living room as well. A typical small house will have three or four inlets.

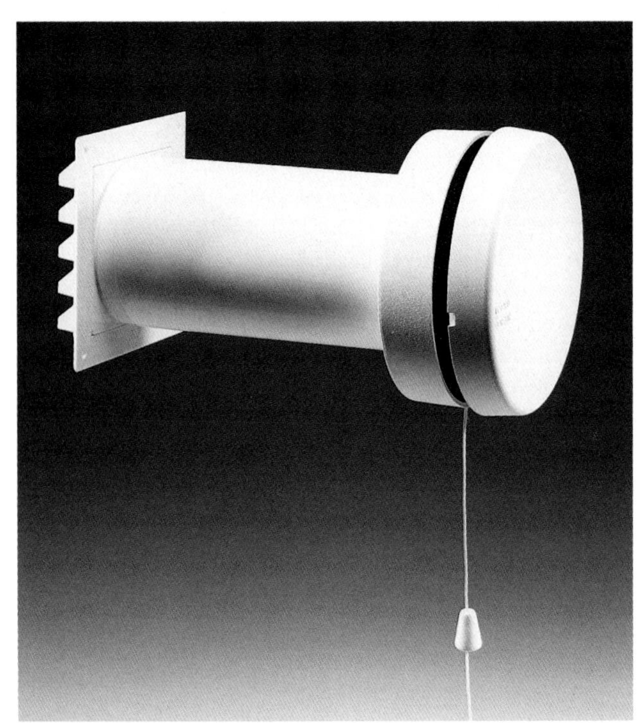

Figure 4. To provide makeup air to bedrooms and prime living spaces, the author uses through-the-wall Fresh-80 inlets. These are only effective, however, in a tight house.

Locate the inlet as near the ceiling as possible, and keep away from beds, couches, or other locations where cool, incoming air might be uncomfortable to occupants. Over a window is ideal, but this may mean drilling a big hole in a header, which isn't a great idea. If there isn't room over the header, locate the inlet anywhere in the exterior wall near the window. Keep the inlets near operable windows so that the vent's outside louver and screen can be cleaned (as often as once a year) by sticking a vacuum cleaner hose out the window.

These inlets install easily by drilling a 3¼-inch hole through the drywall, sheathing, and siding. The plastic duct that goes through the wall telescopes to fit various wall thicknesses. Caulk the duct to the drywall, to keep moist air from getting into the insulation, and to the siding or trim, to keep water out. For retrofit work, it's worth taking the time to align the hole so the outside grille, which is 4¼ inches square, fits on one clapboard. For new construction, install the inlet before the siding goes on so you can plan a 1-by block to go under the grille.

Be sure the inlets are away from garages, exhaust vents, and any other source of noxious fumes. Also be sure the doors in rooms with an air inlet and in the bathrooms are undercut a minimum of ¾ inch (1 inch is better) above finish floor height (including carpet) so that air can move through the room with the door closed.

Once the inlets are installed, adjust the inlet for maximum opening. With the filter, the outside screen, and the inside diffuser, these inlets don't let in very much air, and they don't do much at all if they are only partially open. The Fresh-80 has a string to open and close the inside diffuser. I usually open the diffuser, then wind up the string and stick it inside, so no one closes the inlet.

Backdrafting Cautions

An important caution about any exhaust-only ventilation system is the potential for backdrafting fireplaces, wood stoves, and natural-draft appliances, such as gas boilers and furnaces. While the negative pressure created by the Panasonic fans is quite low — much lower than that induced by a clothes dryer or most range hoods — there is still a chance for backdrafting when the bath fans, the dryer, and the range hood all run at once. The best way to avoid this is to use only sealed-combustion fuel burners and to supply combustion air to wood stoves and fireplaces.

Also, if the house is leaky, the fan will draw air from the nearest air leak. In this case, the inlets will not do their job, and the ventilation effect will be very localized. Dropped ceilings in the bathrooms can be a disaster — a leaky dropped ceiling can provide all the air the fan draws, leaving the rest of the house without any ventilation. In general, exhaust-only ventilation works well with houses with a natural leakage rate of about ¼ to ½ ACH (air changes per hour). This includes most reasonably tight new homes, built with vapor barriers and good seals around windows, band joists, and ceiling penetrations, such as vent stacks, chimney chases, and attic hatches. Older homes that are not built to these tightness standards should be air-sealed by a qualified weatherization contractor before retrofitting a ventilation system.

Andrew Shapiro *is an energy and sustainable design consultant and principal of Energy Balance, in Montpelier, Vt.*

Source of Supply

For fans, air inlets, and other ventilation components

Energy Federation
www.efi.org

Positive Energy Conservation Products
www.positive-energy.com

Shelter Supply, A Division of Dakota Supply Group
www.sheltersupply.com

Installing a Heat-Recovery Ventilator

by David Hansen

Poorly ventilated homes can have high levels of humidity, pollutants, and mold. Most homes depend on random cracks or exhaust-only systems for ventilation, but today's techniques for building tighter homes have made random cracks less common, and exhaust-only ventilation systems have a few disadvantages: They can contribute to backdrafting problems in combustion appliances, and they may draw their supply air from undesirable locations, like basements or crawlspaces.

An effective ventilation system requires careful attention to installation, duct sealing, and balancing.

The best way to improve indoor air quality is to provide a balanced ventilation system that includes a heat-recovery ventilator, or HRV. Such a ventilation system will create a gentle circulation of fresh air throughout the home, will lower the levels of indoor air pollutants, and will eliminate odors and window condensation.

How They Work

An HRV exhausts stale air from a house at a calculated rate, while simultaneously bringing in the same amount of fresh makeup air. The two airstreams pass each other in the heat-exchange core, allowing much of the heat energy in the stale air to be transferred to the fresh incoming air, without any mixing of the airstreams. In an air-conditioned home in a cooling climate, an HRV lowers the temperature of the incoming air by transferring some of its heat to the cooler exhaust air.

Core design. The heart of an HRV is its heat-exchanger core. Today's residential HRVs use one of three different core designs: a parallel-plate counterflow core, a parallel-plate crossflow core, or a rotary wheel core (Figure 5). Parallel-plate cores, whether

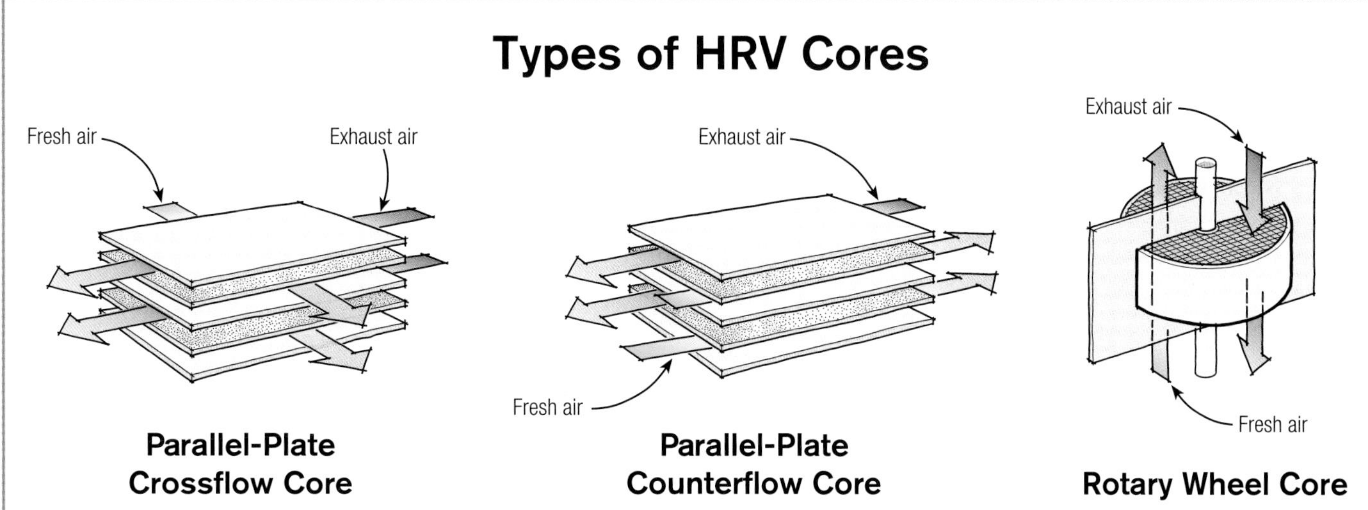

Figure 5. All three types of HRV cores are designed to encourage some of the heat from the exhaust air to be transferred to the incoming fresh air. There are two types of parallel-plate cores: In a crossflow core (left), the airstreams cross at right angles, while in a counterflow core (center), the airstreams travel in opposite directions. Parallel-plate cores can be made from either aluminum or plastic. A rotary wheel core (right) has enough thermal mass to absorb and release heat as the wheel turns through the two separated airstreams.

counterflow or crossflow, are made of aluminum, plastic, or in the case of an *energy-recovery ventilator*, a moisture-permeable membrane (see "Hot Climate Ventilation With ERVs," below).

Some manufacturers tout the theoretical superiority of counterflow cores over crossflow cores or aluminum components over polypropylene. In practice, however, HRV efficiency depends upon many design factors, not just core geometry or material type. The best resource for comparing HRV efficiencies is the Product Directory published by the Home Ventilating Institute (www.hvi.org). When choosing an HRV, small differences of efficiency may be less important than the level of service provided by a local ventilation contractor.

Frost formation. When the outdoor temperature drops below about 20°F, the incoming air is so cold that frost can build up in an HRV core. All HRVs have a defrost cycle to avoid frost problems. When an outdoor temperature sensor detects cold weather, a control module activates a defrost damper, which shuts for about six minutes every half hour. When the defrost damper is shut, the stale air recirculates through the HRV, thawing the core.

Hot Climate Ventilation With ERVs

An energy-recovery ventilator, or ERV, is a special type of HRV that tempers the extremes of humidity in the incoming fresh air. Like an HRV, an ERV transfers heat between the two streams of air passing through the ERV core. But an ERV also transfers some of the moisture from the more humid stream of air to the drier stream of air.

In winter, when outdoor air is usually dry, an ERV increases the humidity of the incoming air, while in summer, when outdoor air is usually more humid, an ERV can lower the humidity of the incoming air, as long as the house is air conditioned. (In a house without air conditioning, the humidity levels of the indoor and outdoor air are essentially the same, so an ERV can't help lower humidity.)

ERVs are recommended for air-conditioned homes in hot, humid climates. In cold climates, where winter indoor air can be humid enough to cause window condensation, one of the main goals of a ventilation system is to lower indoor humidity levels. For that purpose, an HRV makes more sense than an ERV. For the same reason, ERVs are not recommended for pool or spa rooms, where HRVs are more appropriate.

An ERV core, sometimes called an enthalpic core, can be either a fixed core or a rotary-wheel core and is usually made of treated paper or polyester fiber. Rotary ERV cores are often impregnated with a desiccant to improve moisture transfer.

– D.H.

Fully Ducted System

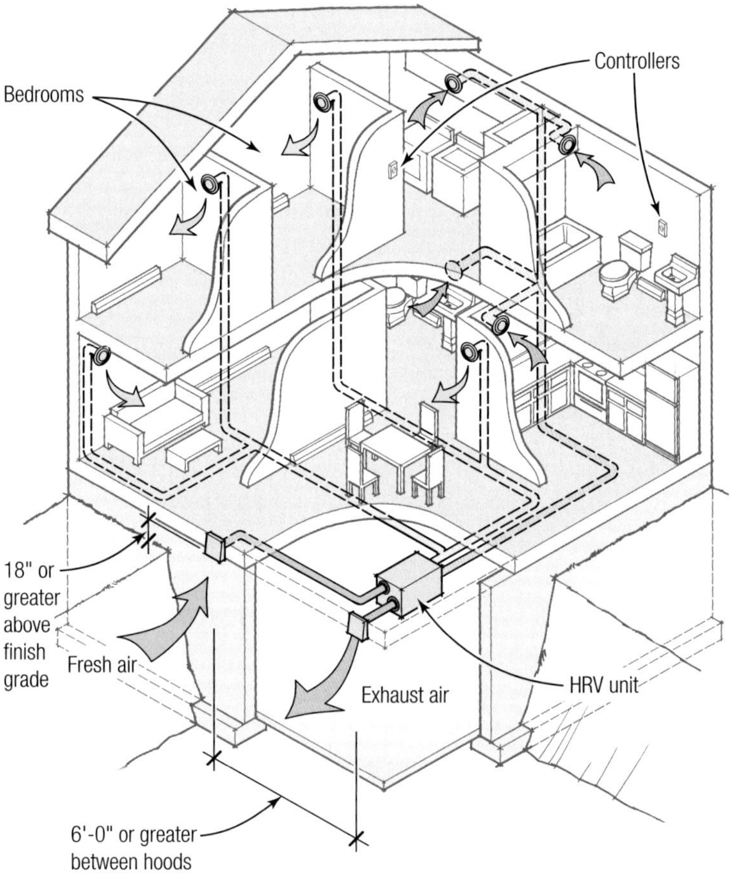

Figure 6. In fully ducted systems, habitable rooms are served by supply ducts, while rooms where pollution and humidity are generated get exhaust ducts. Kitchen range hoods should be vented directly to the outdoors, not through the HRV.

Energy performance. Because an HRV recovers some of the heat from exhaust air, it uses less energy than a ventilation system without heat recovery. Nevertheless, a home with an HRV uses more energy than a home without a ventilation system.

An HRV draws between 85 and 225 watts of electrical power. Most HRVs are only about 60 to 75 percent efficient at recovering the heat from exhausted air, although some models can achieve efficiencies of up to 90 percent. HRV operating costs, including the cost of the electrical power and the cost to temper the ventilation air, range from about $160 to $200 a year, depending on climate and electricity costs.

Ducting Options

An HRV system can be ducted one of several ways, depending on the existing heating system and the customer's budget. The three most common types of systems are simplified systems, modified systems, and fully ducted systems.

In a simplified system (installed in a home with forced-air heating or air conditioning), the HRV unit pulls stale air out of the main return duct of the forced-air system and introduces the fresh air downstream a few feet, in the furnace's return plenum. A simplified system does not provide point-source control of moisture or pollutants.

A modified system, which is an improvement over a simplified system, introduces fresh air into the forced-air duct system while exhausting stale air from the bathrooms.

A fully ducted system — the type described in this article — is typically installed in a home with hydronic heat and requires two duct systems dedicated to ventilation: one to exhaust stale air from areas that produce most of the moisture or pollutants, and another to supply fresh air to the living spaces (Figure 6).

Sizing an HRV

To size an HRV unit, first check whether any local

How Much to Ventilate

Continuous Ventilation Air Requirements (cfm)

Floor Area (sq. ft.)	Bedrooms 0-1	2-3	4-5	6-7	> 7
<1500	30	45	60	75	90
1501 – 3,000	45	60	75	90	105
3001 – 4500	60	75	90	105	120
4501 – 6000	75	90	105	120	135
6001 – 7500	90	105	120	135	150
>7500	105	120	135	150	165

Note: Table based on Table 4.1a in ASHRAE Standard 62.2-2007

The older ASHRAE ventilation rate of 0.35 air changes per hour (with a minimum of 15 cfm per person) of continuous ventilation is still followed by many installers. The newer ASHRAE Standard 62.2-2007 recommends a residential ventilation rate based more on occupancy levels. The new recommended rate is 1 cfm per 100 square feet of floor area, plus 7.5 cfm per person, assuming two people in the master bedroom and one in each additional bedroom.

For example, a 2,000 sq. ft. house with three bedrooms would require a minimum continuous ventilation rate of :

House square footage ÷ 100 + (bedrooms +1) x 7.5
2000 ÷ 100 + (3+1) x 7.5 = 50 cfm

ASHRAE also provides a table (above) to simplify the calculation. The formula, and table, assume a low natural infiltration rate of 2 cfm/100 sq. ft. of floor area. For older, more leaky buildings, the mechanical ventilation rate should be reduced to prevent energy-wasting overventilation. The ventilation rate should be adjusted higher if there is a higher occupancy rate than the formula assumes. Some installers also increase the ventilation rate for special conditions, such as higher than normal indoor humidity or other air quality problems that cannot be addressed more directly by eliminating the source of the problem.

The ASHRAE standard does not require mechanical ventilation in mild climates with less than 4,500 heating degree days (just open the windows), in buildings with no central air in a climate with less than 500 heating degree days, and in buildings that are heated or cooled for less than 876 hours per year.

— JLC staff

ventilation code applies. Some installers follow the older ASHRAE standard, which recommends 0.35 air changes per hour. To apply this standard, we start by calculating the volume of the house, using the following formula: square feet x ceiling height x .85. (This formula reduces the house's gross volume by 15 percent to account for interior walls and furniture.) To find the necessary ventilation airflow, we multiply the net volume by the design air-change rate (0.35 ACH) and divide by 60 (to convert air changes per hour to cubic feet per minute).

The newer ASHRAE Standard 62.2-2007, uses a formula based on the house size and number of occupants (see "How Much to Ventilate," page 301).

Either approach yields a ventilate rate in cubic feet per minute (cfm). With this information, we can select an appropriate HRV using the airflow fan curves supplied by the manufacturer for specific HRV models. The fan curve represents the amount of air a specific fan can move, depending on the resistance of the duct system.

Residential HRV systems move relatively small volumes of air. In most homes up to about 3,500 square feet, the total design airflow will be under 200 cfm, with each bedroom receiving 25 cfm or less. For the main ducts, 6-inch round duct, which has a maximum airflow capacity of 180 cfm, is usually sufficient. When moving such low volumes of air, it's important for duct to be as short, smooth, and airtight as possible. Every extra foot of duct and every elbow or transition add resistance (or static pressure) to the airflow. If plans are available, the ducts can be laid out on paper, although their final locations are best determined on site.

Laying Out the Ductwork

Ventilation ducts can be installed once the interior walls are framed. We try to be on site during the plumbing rough-in. Sometimes locating a pipe just a few inches to one side can make enough of a difference to allow a duct to fit into a tight joist bay. In a pinch, a wall can be shimmed out to make room for ducts to get past the plumbing or a chase can be located inside a closet, but by communicating with the plumber, we usually avoid such steps.

Locating the registers. Stale air is exhausted from bathrooms, the laundry, and the kitchen. (An HRV is not intended to handle grease or smoke, so a range hood should be separately exhausted to the exterior.) Fresh air is supplied to the bedrooms, living room, and other living areas. We try to locate bedroom registers away from the bed.

When we rough-in our duct drops, we always work from the top floor down. We locate both the fresh-air and the stale-air registers high on a wall or in the ceiling. After choosing tentative locations for the registers, we follow the intended duct routes down to the basement, to be sure there are no unworkable obstacles.

In most cases, all the fresh- and stale-air registers are wall-mounted 6x10 registers, and each gets its own separate duct down to the basement. To keep airflows as high as possible, we use 6-inch duct for stale-air pickups. For fresh-air supplies into bedrooms, 4-inch ducts are usually adequate.

We use mainly 30-gauge galvanized ductwork. In 2x4 partitions, we use 6-inch oval duct, which measures 3½ x 7½ inches and comes in 5-foot lengths. Oval duct has a smaller airflow capacity than round but is perfectly adequate for the individual wall stacks. Each register mounts in a 6x10-inch stackhead, a duct fitting that makes the transition from a rectangular register to oval duct.

Installing the Ducts

Stackheads are installed ½ inch proud of the studs, like electrical boxes (Figure 7). On most jobs, the top of the stackhead is installed about 4½ inches down from the top of the wall. If the room will receive crown molding, we install the stackhead lower.

Figure 7. Each wall-mounted fresh-air and stale-air register requires a rectangular duct fitting called a stackhead. Stackheads are installed ½ inch proud of the joists, like electrical boxes.

The crimped end of a stale-air duct always points toward the HRV unit, while the crimped end of a fresh-air duct points the opposite way, toward the stackhead (Figure 8). By consistently following this system, we can distinguish between stale-air and fresh-air ducts in the basement just by looking at which direction the crimped end is pointing.

We secure every galvanized duct connection with two or three ½-inch sheet-metal screws and aluminum duct tape (Figure 9). We've had good success with foil hvac tape (#1520 CW) from Venture Tape Co. (www.venturetape.com), which is easy to apply, because it has a paper release backing.

We extend all the stacks, both fresh and stale, down from the stackheads into the basement. Wherever an oval duct passes through the top plate of a wall, we use a piece of plumber's strapping to secure the duct to the plate. Because sweep ells for oval pipe take up too much room, we transition from oval to round duct as soon as possible, using straight transition fittings or transition elbows. Once the stacks are installed, we use aerosol foam to seal the gaps between the ducts and the bottom plates. This helps stop air leakage between floors and secures the stack to the framing (Figure 10).

PVC ducts. In houses where the installation of wall-mounted registers is difficult, we often install round ceiling-mounted diffusers, working from the attic.

Figure 8. Because this is a fresh-air duct, the crimped end of the duct points toward the stackhead. The photo shows two styles of 90-degree ells that can be used to make the transition from oval duct to round: The ell at the top of the photo is a longways ell, while the ell at the bottom is a shortways ell.

Figure 9. Ventilation systems remove relatively small volumes of air, so ducts should be as airtight as possible. All galvanized duct connections should be secured with sheet-metal screws and aluminum tape.

Figure 10. Where an oval duct penetrates a floor, aerosol foam helps secure the stack to the framing.

Since attic ducts, being cool in winter, are prone to condensation, we use 4- or 6-inch thin-wall PVC (sewer and drain pipe, type ASTM D 2729) for all attic ducts. (Because PVC is available in 10-foot lengths, it's also useful wherever a long section of straight duct is needed.) If condensation occurs, the glued joints of the PVC will prevent leaks. We always insulate any ducts that run through unheated space.

We like to use PVC pipe made by Flying W Plastics (www.flyingwplastics.com), because it is thinner than some other brands, making it easier to slide 6-inch galvanized duct into the pipe. To ease the transition, we chamfer the inside edge of the PVC pipe with a utility knife. The connection is then secured with screws and sealed with aluminum tape.

Wiring

Once we've roughed-in the stacks to the basement, we install the low-voltage control wiring, following the manufacturer's instructions. Usually, we run 4-conductor wire from the location of the HRV unit to each bathroom and laundry for an override timer, which permits the exhaust ventilation fan to be controlled from the bathroom. These override timers are located next to the room's light switch. We install a separate run of wire for the main control, which is usually located near the central thermostat on the first floor, about 5 feet from the floor.

Most residential HRV units come with a cord and a plug, so we coordinate with the electrician for the installation of a standard duplex receptacle near the HRV unit. When the stacks are installed and the wiring is complete, the first stage of our work is finished. We usually return later to complete the basement ducts and install the HRV unit.

Basement Ducts

In the basement, the various stale-air wall stacks are connected to a main round duct running to the HRV. A second main duct connects all of the fresh-air supply stacks. For most residential jobs, all basement ducts, galvanized or PVC, are 6-inch round ducts.

We determine the main duct run locations and then position a wye along this line with the leg of the wye pointing up into the joist bay of the stale-air stack nearest the unit. For galvanized ducts, we use #160 wyes, which come with three uncrimped ends, and crimp the ends as required. Because galvanized wyes aren't airtight, we seal all joints in a wye with silicone caulk, duct mastic, or aluminum tape before installation (Figure 11).

We then fasten the wye to a length of duct and use perforated nylon strapping to hang the duct from the floor joist. By adding adjustable elbows as necessary, we aim the branch of the wye toward the oval stack boot. The main duct runs should end near, but a little short of, the HRV unit. Once the ducts have been installed, we seal all connections not secured by aluminum tape, including the joints in adjustable elbows, with duct sealant or silicone caulk.

Installing the HRV Unit

The HRV unit is generally located inside the tempered space of the building, usually in the basement mechanical space close to the outside ports. Other possible locations include a closet, laundry room, workshop, top-floor kneewall area, or even a garage. We usually hang it from the ceiling joists.

We avoid the use of flex duct as much as possible, because its interior corrugations impede airflow. However, because insulated flex duct prevents prob-

Figure 11. Galvanized #160 wyes come with three uncrimped ends and are crimped as required on site. As purchased (at left, in photo), the wyes are not airtight, so the seams of each should be sealed with caulk before installation (at right).

Figure 12. An HRV system requires two exterior ports, an intake port and an exhaust port. These identical 6-inch ports are protected by vent hoods and are usually located at the rim joist.

lems with condensation drips, we use it to connect the HRV unit to the outside vent hoods. The flex duct needs to be sealed to both the HRV unit and the house vapor retarder. We also use short lengths of noninsulated vinyl flex duct to connect the HRV unit to the house ducts.

We keep our flex duct runs as short as possible, and we always seal any rips or tears in the outside cover of the flex duct. (If moist interior air comes in contact with the cold fresh air in the intake duct, condensation will saturate the duct insulation.) Where flex duct connects with the HRV unit, we seal the connection with silicone caulk and screw the duct to the collar on the HRV.

Outside vent hoods. Exterior vent hoods protect the intake and exhaust ports from weather and animals (Figure 12). A 6-inch exhaust duct needs a 6-inch or equivalent exterior hood, not a 4-inch dryer vent. The vent hood should include a cleanable rodent screen made from ¼-inch hardware cloth. We usually install Jenn-Air A406 wall caps (www.jennair.com).

The two outside vents are typically installed through the basement rim joist, level with one another. They should be located at least 6 feet apart to minimize the chance of the fresh-air intake pulling back any stale air. Sometimes a corner of the building can be used to better separate the fresh intake from the exhaust port. The fresh-air port should be as far as possible from any combustion flues, dryer exhaust vents, and places where cars may idle. An exhaust vent can be located under a deck or porch, but we avoid pulling fresh air from an enclosed space.

Since we usually install the vent hoods on trim blocks, we prefer to schedule this part of the work before the siding is on. We use a short (about 6- to 12-inch) section of 6-inch PVC pipe (including a bell end) to connect the insulated flex duct to the vent hood. We cut a series of 1-inch slots, about 1½ inches apart, in the male end of the pipe section, and then slip the flex duct over the PVC. The connection is sealed with aluminum tape and screws. We insert the bell end of the PVC through the hole in the building, flush with the outside face of the trim block. The Jenn-Air hood is then inserted into the PVC. We always seal the gap where the PVC duct penetrates the building with aerosol foam.

Registers. Once the drywall has been painted, we install the various controls and registers, and the controls are installed according to the manufacturer's instructions.

Both stale-air and fresh-air registers require a damper to allow airflow balancing. For wall-mounted registers, we use either a Lima 12V register (American Metal Products; www.americanmetalproducts.com) or a Hart

Sources of Supply

HRV and ERV Manufacturers

AirXchange, Inc.
www.airxchange.com

American Aldes Ventilation Corp.
www.americanaldes.com

Broan-Nutone
www.broan.com

Bryant Heating & Cooling Systems
www.bryant.com

Carrier Corp.
www.carrier.com

Honeywell Inc.
www.honeywell.com

Lennox International Inc.
www.lennoxinternational.com

Nu-Air Ventilation Systems
www.nu-airventilation.com

Nutech Energy Systems Inc.
www.lifebreath.com

RenewAire
www.renewaire.com

Research Products Corp.
www.aprilaire.com

Rheem Air Conditioning Division
www.rheem.com

Ruud
www.ruud.com

Stirling Technology Inc.
www.lychonia.com

Systemair.
www.systemair.com

Trent Metals Limited
www.summeraire.com

United Air Specialists, Inc.
www.uasinc.com

Venmar Ventilation Inc.
www.venmar-ventilation.com

A free directory of HRVs and other home ventilation products is available online from the Home Ventilating Institute (www.hvi.org).

& Cooley 661 (www.hartandcooley.com). We check the registers with a level before fastening them with screws through the ears of the stackhead. To provide better air distribution and hide the inside of the stackhead, we always adjust the register dampers to direct the airflow up toward the ceiling.

For round ceiling registers, we use molded plastic Scandinavian-style diffusers. These are secured to the inside of the round PVC duct with sheet-metal screws. Then we spin in the trim ring, making a friction fit, and adjust the damper rings to about three-fourths of the full opening size.

Balancing. Once the installation is complete, the system must be tested for airflow balance. Small airflows are hard to test, but most manufacturers provide a recommended balancing procedure, generally requiring the use of an airflow measuring station or unit-mounted pressure taps and a calibrated magnehelic gauge.

The final step of any job is an important one: homeowner instruction. We provide the homeowner with the operation manual and an on-site orientation, explaining:

- **Control operation:** Most HRVs can be set for intermittent operation, low-speed continuous operation, or high-speed continuous operation.
- **Humidistat function:** Most HRVs include a humidistat that automatically operates the fan at high speed when the indoor humidity rises above a user-adjustable level.
- **Filter cleaning schedule:** Every three months, HRV filters should be vacuumed, washed, or replaced.
- **Intake and exhaust ports:** It's important to keep the outside intake and exhaust ports free of leaves and mulch.

David Hansen *is the owner of Memphremagog Heat Exchangers, a ventilation contractor in Newport, Vt.*

Chapter 14

ENERGY RETROFITS

Effective Air Sealing in Existing Homes

by Bruce Torrey

As a contractor during the1980s energy crisis, I directed my energies toward building super-insulated homes. I experimented with my share of "cutting edge" strategies, with mixed results. It became quickly apparent that some of the experimentation — like site-built skylights — was less than successful. What was not so obvious at the time was that, in spite of beefing up the insulation levels in everything I built, I wasn't really getting the thermal performance I would have expected.

However, as more building diagnostic tools became available, I was able to see the flaws in my previous insulation strategies. I also saw a business opportunity: troubleshooting the all-too-common efficiency and comfort problems in buildings.

Over the last couple of decades, energy prices have continued to rise and energy codes have gotten stricter, but many of the same flawed insulation strategies are still being used in the field. Meanwhile, the consumer's demand for increased comfort often goes unanswered. Many of the calls we get involve existing homes that have new replacement windows and are already insulated. So what else is left to do?

Fortunately, advances in building science are helping the industry take a fresh look at how buildings really perform and what types of improvements are most practical and effective. The critical first step is to understand how a building loses heat. This may sound obvious, but there are still many misconceptions.

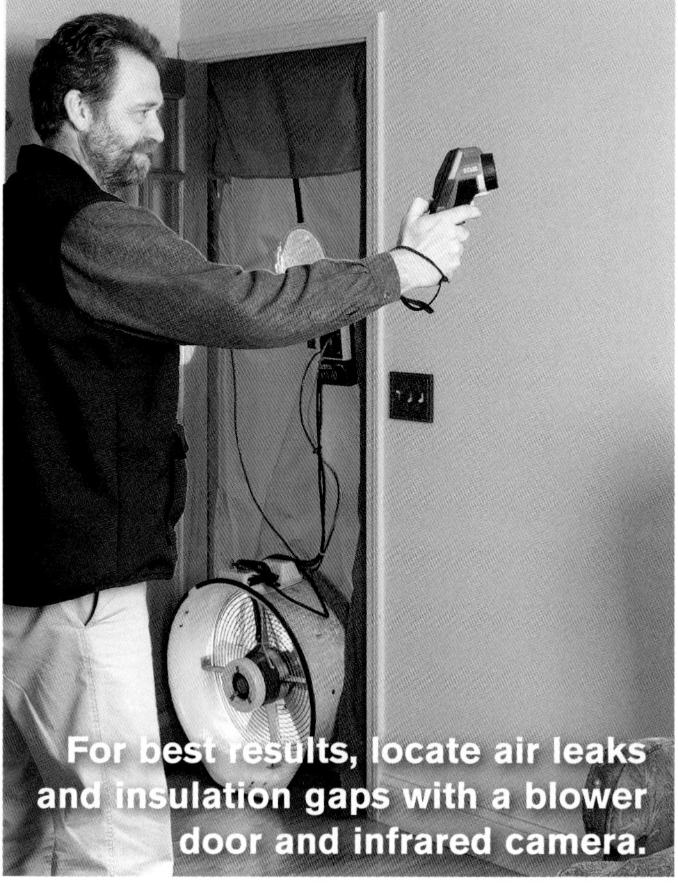

For best results, locate air leaks and insulation gaps with a blower door and infrared camera.

Flawed Assumptions

Probably the biggest misconception involves where a house loses most of its heat and what types of details can stop these "hidden" drafts. In most building configurations, fiberglass batt insulation — or even loose cellulose blown into an attic — doesn't do a good job of controlling air movement. Many studies have shown that air moves through fiberglass batts and degrades their R-value. And while cellulose can stop air movement when it's blown into closed cavities at densities above 3.5 pounds per cubic foot, loose-fill cellulose blown in an attic will not stop air leaks.

Most of the homes I visit have attic insulation, but they also have many air leaks from inside the house into the attic — at mechanical penetrations and plumbing chases, along partition-wall top plates, at framing intersections like soffits or other changes in ceiling height, around chimneys, and so on. In a typical home with a leaky attic, upward air pressure from the stack effect — the tendency of warm air to rise — can replace all of a home's heated inside air with cold outside air in just two or three hours.

Homes with knee walls or side attics have the further complication of horizontal heat loss and infiltration between heated floor cavities and the eaves (Figure 1). In many cases attic ventilation only makes this worse by connecting the interior to the outside and allowing wind to move far into the heated space.

New Tools, Better Results

These air leaks seldom get addressed during traditional home improvements because they're not visible from inside the conditioned space; they're concealed inside framed cavities, behind drywall or plaster. But with modern diagnostic tools, it's possible to find them and to complete an accurate, detailed heat-loss assessment of a home in just a few hours.

Using an infrared thermal camera in conjunction with a blower door, an energy auditor can identify leaks in the air envelope and locate insufficient or missing insulation in the thermal envelope.

On a typical job, I first set up the blower door and depressurize the house to 50 pascals relative to the outside. This approximates the range of pressures a building would be subject to on a very windy night and helps establish a consistent benchmark for comparing the leakiness of one building with another.

The blower-door fan draws outside air in through

Typical Thermal Bypass

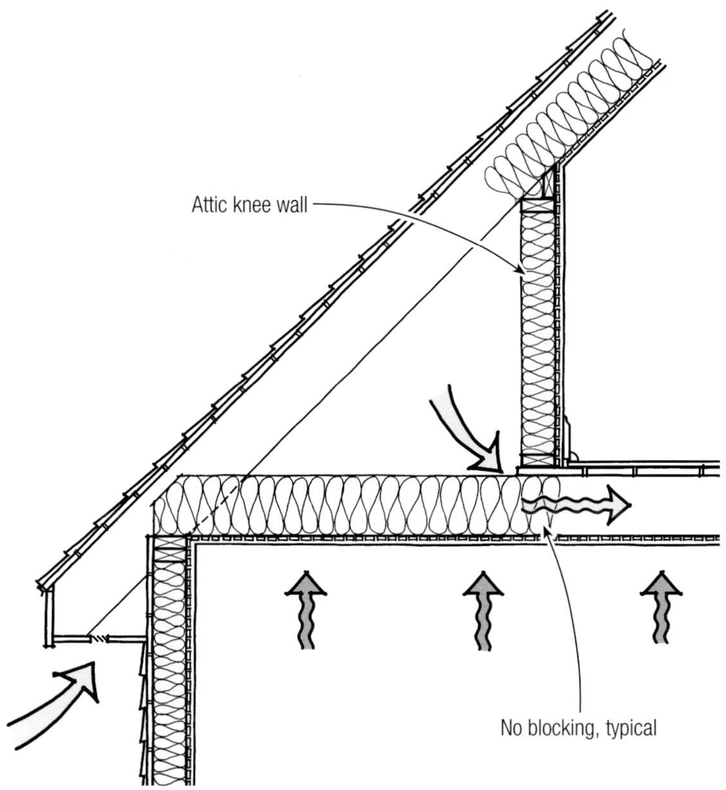

Attic knee wall

No blocking, typical

Figure 1. Even though they're often insulated, attic knee walls are a common area for thermal problems. Because there is typically no blocking below the knee-wall bottom plate, cold air from the attic, or outside air entering at the eaves, chills interior ceiling cavities, drawing heat away from the living space.

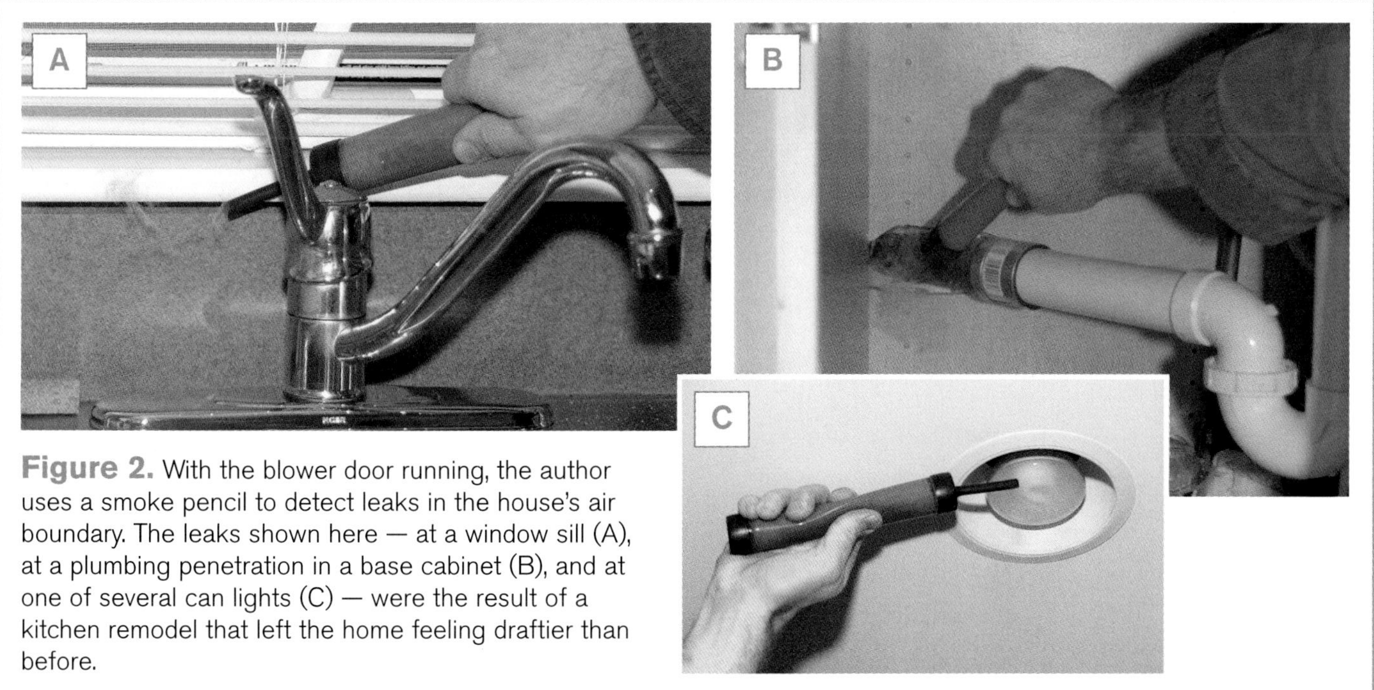

Figure 2. With the blower door running, the author uses a smoke pencil to detect leaks in the house's air boundary. The leaks shown here — at a window sill (A), at a plumbing penetration in a base cabinet (B), and at one of several can lights (C) — were the result of a kitchen remodel that left the home feeling draftier than before.

penetrations in the shell and exhausts it through a temporary entry door with a calibrated fan (see photo, facing page). The fan measures the cubic feet per minute of airflow required to maintain the 50-pascal pressure difference between inside and out. The draftier the shell, the higher the flow in cubic feet per minute. Simple math helps us convert the cfm reading to a whole-house air-exchange rate, stated in air changes per hour.

With the blower-door fan running, I make a visual inspection of the home, looking for any obvious leakage spots (Figure 2). A smoke pencil — a handheld

Figure 3. The darker spots in these thermographic images indicate the presence of cold in framing cavities behind the drywall surface — areas where cold air has infiltrated or heat has been lost through conduction. At top (A), the framing around a Palladian window lacks insulation, while the ceiling area above suffers from wind-washing at the eaves. An interior soffit (B) is cold because the batt insulation does not make good contact with the drywall; also, the gap around the ceiling register is drafty. The uninsulated wall around an interior fireplace (C) is chilled from cold attic air dropping down through the vertical chimney chase between the framing and the masonry.

device that emits a stream of chemical smoke — helps in tracing drafts.

After the blower has been running for a while, drawing in cold outside air, I take another tour through the house, this time using the infrared camera to scan for hidden air leaks and thermal bypass problems. The thermal image viewed through the camera reveals the radiant temperatures of the surface scanned. Since the R-values — and, therefore, the interior surface — of an insulated bay and the adjacent wood framing members are different, it's simple to identify the framing details as well as weak spots in the insulation (Figure 3). Thermal scans often reveal areas where the insulation has settled or is not dense enough, and wall and ceiling bays that were completely missed when the insulation was installed.

Because the blower door is drawing in cold air from the exterior or attic, the scan can identify and measure areas of air infiltration, recognizable by a plumelike thermal pattern (Figure 4).

The scans also show areas where the wall surface has become chilly, indicating that the cold air is moving through or beneath the insulation. These spots are common on ceilings near the eaves, due to the effects of wind-washing (outside air moving into the eaves and through the fibrous insulation), but they can also show up in interior locations where you might not expect to find them (Figure 5).

Sealing Strategies

Because framing details, air leakage paths, and insulation quality vary from home to home, there are no standard, one-size-fits-all solutions. Sealing air leaks into the attic is usually the most cost-effective improvement, but it can also be the most challenging. Fiberglass batts and loose-fill cellulose do not stop air leaks, so simply covering the leakage points with insulation doesn't work. Neither does sealing cracks in the attic floor above the insulation: Since the insulation is air permeable, you have to seal the leak below the insulation.

It's important to keep in mind that the drywall ceiling is discontinuous — it's interrupted by interior partitions and framed chases that enclose leaks. While those partitions and chases may appear airtight from inside the house, viewed from the attic, they are full of penetrations for electrical, mechanical, and plumbing runs (Figure 6). Even the long intersections between the edges of the top plates and the cut ends of the ceiling board provide air paths into the attic.

Figure 4. Wind-washing — air moving under and through the ceiling insulation at the eaves — degrades insulation performance, as is evident from the dark areas in the ceiling next to the exterior wall (A). Leaks in window framing (B) and around an exterior door (C) show up in a typical plumelike pattern.

Figure 5. The infrared scan revealed an unexpected cold area in this interior partition wall (A and B), which was traced to air leaking into the attic along the top plate, shown here being sealed (C).

Figure 6. Moving attic insulation uncovers a common cause of leaks: wire holes through partition-wall top plates (A). The double line of soot stains indicates upward air leakage between the drywall and a partition plate (B). Fiberglass stuffed into a plumbing wall (C) did not stop the air rising from below. Similarly, a double layer of fiberglass did not prevent air movement through an interior soffit into the attic (D).

The first step in the sealing process is to move the existing attic insulation to expose the air leaks. These include penetrations in the middle of a ceiling, like air supply registers and light fixtures, as well as the top plates of all partition walls.

Two-part foam. For sealing the leaks, most weatherization contractors use two-part polyurethane foam, which comes in cardboard containers in various sizes with an attached 30-foot hose and spray nozzle. The foam sticks well to dirty surfaces, and the high-pressure applicator makes it easy to spray in hard-to-reach places (Figure 7).

Small penetrations, like the gaps around light fixtures, fan boxes, and duct boots, can be sprayed directly. With larger bypasses — plumbing walls, unblocked balloon-framed cavities, the space under an attic knee wall — the opening can first be loosely stuffed with fiberglass, then sprayed. For extremely large openings, like drop soffits and large chases, it's best to fit a piece of plywood or rigid insulation board over the hole, then seal it in place with foam and screws (Figure 8).

Fire-code sealant. One place where you can't use foam — due to fire codes — is around chimneys and flues. Because of code-required clearance to combustibles, it's not uncommon to find leakage areas of 3 square feet or more around a masonry chimney. Here it's best to seal the gap with sheet metal sealed with an ASTM 136 high-temperature caulk.

Adding Insulation

Once penetrations have been sealed, the attic is ready for an additional layer of blown insulation, which fills gaps in the fiberglass batts and also covers the tops of the ceiling joists, reducing conductive heat loss.

Knee walls. Field and lab testing has confirmed that batt insulation works best when it's enclosed in an airtight space. This is rarely the case with attic knee walls, which are typically open on the attic side. So I often recommend adding a layer of rigid foam to the back of knee walls and taping the joints. This prevents air movement into the wall cavity from the attic side, and cuts conduction through the studs. Another method is to add a second layer of fiberglass horizontally across the backs of the knee-wall studs and secure it with a layer of housewrap — again, to reduce infiltration and conductive loss through the studs.

If for some reason an attic wall has not been insulated, I recommend securing housewrap across the studs and blowing loose-fill insulation into the cavities.

Some knee walls contain ductwork or pipes that make them impossible to insulate effectively. In these cases, it makes sense to move the thermal and air bar-

Figure 7. Because it sticks even to dirty surfaces, two-part urethane foam works well for sealing around attic penetrations (left). A worker seals beneath an attic ledger (above), after first chinking the gap underneath with fiberglass.

Figure 8. Rigid foam board is ideal for sealing large openings, like this oversized framing chase. After cutting the board to fit, the worker beds it in wet spray foam (left), then seals the edges (above).

rier to the outside roof slope by adding a code-approved rigid board to the underside of the rafters and blowing in cellulose. Where the budget can handle it and for spaces with limited access, an approved spray foam also works well.

Don't forget exterior walls. Although this article focuses on attics, it's worth noting that we often recommend additional blown-in insulation in the exterior walls below. I say "additional" because many of the homes I visit already have some type of wall insulation, but the scans frequently show that it's settled or insufficient. Be sure to have the insulation contractor blow in dense-pack cellulose at such spots; otherwise, cold air in the walls will find its way along floor and ceiling cavities and make the house cold and drafty.

Looking Ahead

With energy costs increasing, the demand for weatherization is also on the rise. If you're a remodeler, this might be a good time to consider providing your clients with a more comprehensive approach to thermal upgrades, in addition to the traditional home-improvement services.

After the first energy crisis, we learned that simply adding insulation is not enough — you have to address air leaks as well. Hopefully that lesson is not lost, and with a new generation of diagnostic tools on hand, there's no excuse not to get it right.

Bruce Torrey *is an infrared thermographer and building consultant. His company, Building Diagnostics, provides technical support and training to builders, architects, and insulation contractors.*

Retrofitting Exterior Insulation

by David Joyce

My company recently contracted to do an energy retrofit on an 80-year-old home in Arlington, Mass., a suburb of Boston. Energy efficiency is one of our specialties, so this wasn't our first energy retrofit, but it was one of the most comprehensive.

Because the owner wanted to replace the roofing, siding, and windows anyway, we had an opportunity to increase the R-value of the shell and eliminate thermal bridging by wrapping the entire exterior with rigid foam insulation (see "Is It Safe to Retrofit Exterior Insulation?", page 318)

The key to getting this type of installation right is deciding what role each layer of the installation will play. The house needs a drainage plane to make it watertight and an air barrier to keep it draft-free. The plans called for a layer of Tyvek housewrap over the existing board sheathing, followed by two layers of foam, a layer of vertical strapping, and cellular PVC clapboards nailed to the strapping, creating a rain-screen wall (see "Exterior Insulation Details," page 317). The outermost layer of foam would be the primary drainage plane, while the underlying foam and the Tyvek housewrap would serve as backups. The housewrap would also serve as the home's air barrier.

Adding rigid foam to the outside of the shell along with new windows dramatically increases comfort and performance.

Roof Down

We started with the roof, stripping it down to the sheathing, then installing two layers of 3-inch Dow Thermax foil-faced polyisocyanurate insulation, per the recommenda-

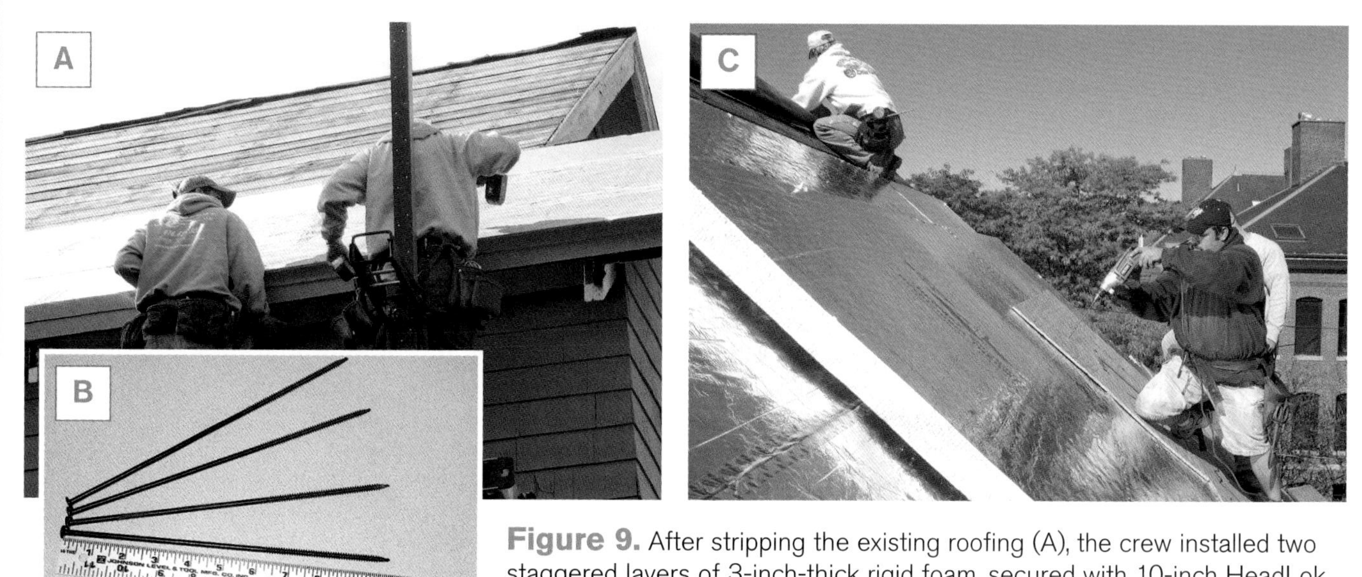

Figure 9. After stripping the existing roofing (A), the crew installed two staggered layers of 3-inch-thick rigid foam, secured with 10-inch HeadLok screws (B) driven through the sheathing into the rafters (C).

tion of Building Science Corp. in Somerville, Mass. We staggered the joints in both directions and taped the seams to prevent air movement through the edge gaps, then laid ⅝-inch plywood sheathing on top and attached it to the rafters with 10-inch FastenMaster HeadLok screws (www.fastenmaster.com) (Figure 9). We then installed the roofing right on top.

Next, we stripped the old shingle siding and installed the Tyvek. Because the housewrap was serving as both a drainage layer and an air barrier, we secured the bottom edge to the sheathing by embedding it in silicone caulking and taped all the seams with Dow Weathermate construction tape. We like this particular tape because it can be installed regardless of the weather. It sticks to wet surfaces and holds well even if it's left exposed for a long time.

Installation of the replacement windows followed. We used double-glazed Pella Impervia double-hung replacement units, sized so that we could keep the original interior trim intact (Figure 10). We flashed the rough openings with Grace Ice & Water Shield, then taped the housewrap to the peel-and-stick. As the windows were installed, we also attached 2-by blocking around the perimeters to provide backing for the deep exterior jamb extensions that we would be adding.

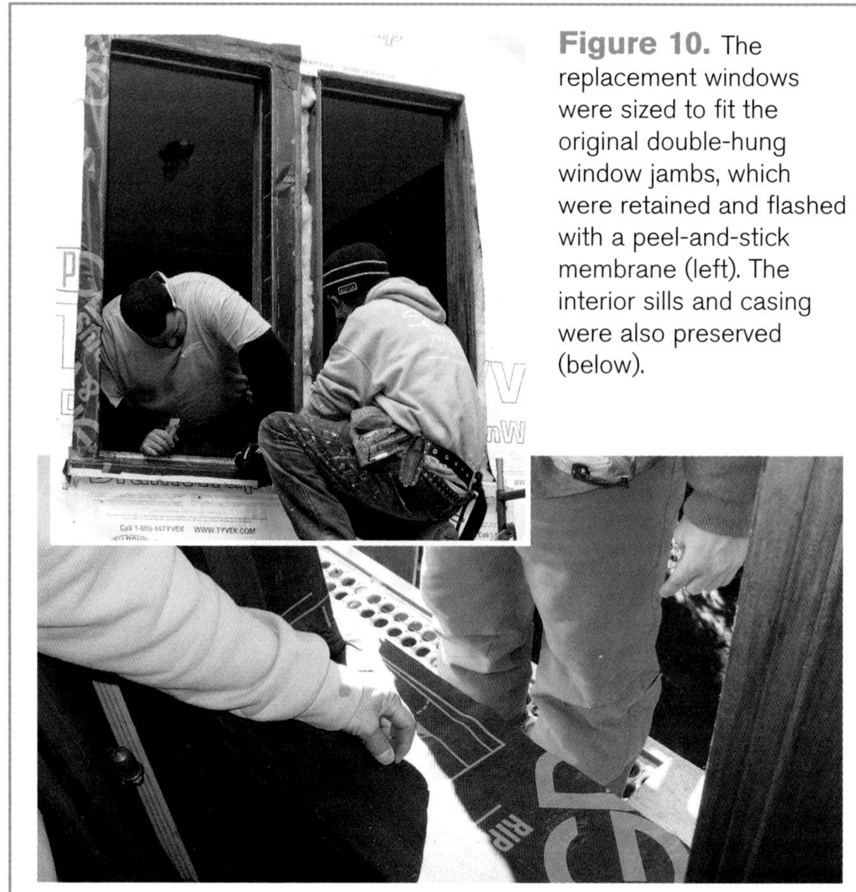

Figure 10. The replacement windows were sized to fit the original double-hung window jambs, which were retained and flashed with a peel-and-stick membrane (left). The interior sills and casing were also preserved (below).

Wrapping the Walls

Over the housewrap we placed two layers of 2-inch Dow Tuff-R, a foil-faced polyisocyanurate foam board. We started by fastening a 2x4 ledger across the bottom of the wall to provide support for the first layer of foam as well as nailing for the skirtboard. As we were installing the 2x4, we stapled insect screening to the wall; this would later be folded up and fastened to the strapping to keep bugs out of the air space (Figure 11).

We laid out the foam board with drainage in mind, making sure to stagger the field joints and weaving the edges on outside wall corners. That way, any water that gets past the first layer will hit solid foam rather than another seam. We also taped the seams on both layers.

Wall strapping. We held the foam board in place temporarily with long

Figure 11. One-by-three strapping screwed to the framing on 16-inch centers holds the double foam layer securely in place (above) and provides a drying and drainage channel behind the siding. Seams on both layers were taped to block air movement. Metal screen (seen hanging, right) keeps insects out of the drainage space.

Exterior Insulation Details

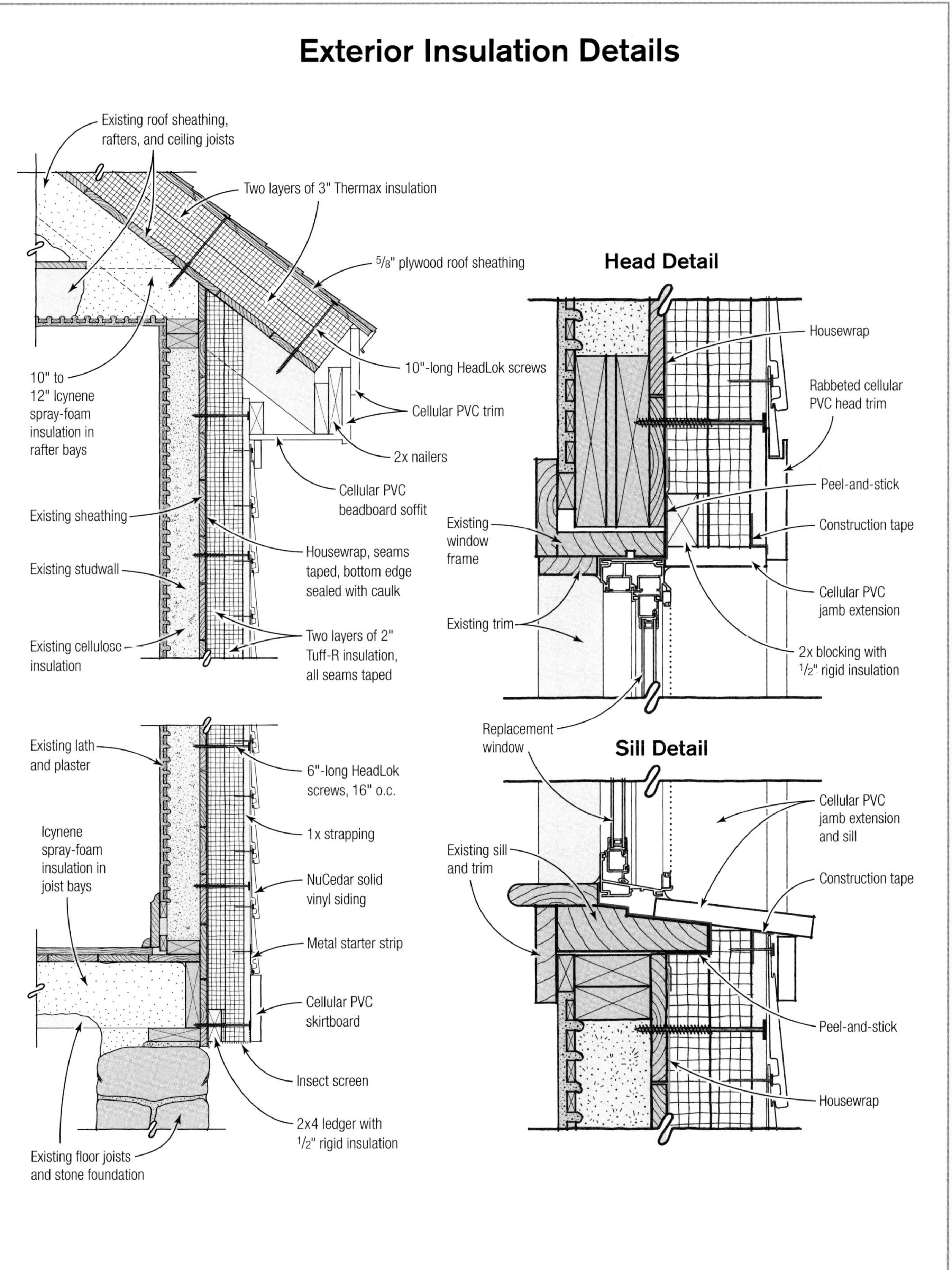

Exterior Insulation Details
Existing roof sheathing, rafters, and ceiling joists
Two layers of 3" Thermax insulation
5/8" plywood roof sheathing
10"-long HeadLok screws
Cellular PVC trim
2x nailers
Cellular PVC beadboard soffit
10" to 12" Icynene spray-foam insulation in rafter bays
Existing sheathing
Existing studwall
Housewrap, seams taped, bottom edge sealed with caulk
Existing cellulose insulation
Two layers of 2" Tuff-R insulation, all seams taped
Existing lath and plaster
6"-long HeadLok screws, 16" o.c.
1x strapping
Icynene spray-foam insulation in joist bays
NuCedar solid vinyl siding
Metal starter strip
Cellular PVC skirtboard
Insect screen
2x4 ledger with 1/2" rigid insulation
Existing floor joists and stone foundation
Head Detail
Housewrap
Rabbeted cellular PVC head trim
Peel-and-stick
Existing window frame
Construction tape
Cellular PVC jamb extension
Existing trim
2x blocking with 1/2" rigid insulation
Replacement window
Sill Detail
Cellular PVC jamb extension and sill
Existing sill and trim
Construction tape
Peel-and-stick
Housewrap

Is It Safe to Retrofit Exterior Insulation?

Q. *I built a lot of homes in upstate New York in the 1980s using 2x6 studs, fiberglass batts, and a poly vapor retarder. Given rising energy costs, some owners are now asking about energy upgrades to their walls. I'd like to suggest adding 1 or 2 inches of rigid foam on top of the existing sheathing, followed by new siding. Would the presence of polyethylene vapor retarders make this a risky retrofit strategy?*

A. Martin Holladay, senior editor of www.GreenBuildingAdvisor.com, responds: You may safely install exterior foam on most houses with a polyethylene vapor barrier, as long as the foam does not include aluminum-foil facing. In fact, exterior foam is a great idea, since it significantly improves the energy performance of walls.

As most builders now realize, polyethylene is a double-edged sword. Its ability to limit the outward migration of water vapor into a wall comes with a downside, since poly also prevents the useful inward drying of damp walls. In very cold climates—including your region, upstate New York—many builders still use interior poly. However, in warmer regions—Ohio and Connecticut, for instance—most walls perform better without any interior polyethylene.

The installation of exterior foam is not advised on any home that has suffered wet-wall problems like leaking windows, condensation in stud cavities, or mold. If you plan to install exterior foam during a siding replacement job, keep an eye out for any signs of moisture problems when stripping the old siding from the walls. Investigate any water stains on housewrap or sheathing to determine whether the existing flashing was adequate.

Dry and unstained sheathing may safely be covered with 1 or 2 inches of extruded polystyrene foam (XPS) or expanded polystyrene foam (EPS). One inch of XPS has a permeance of 0.4 to 1.6, while 1 inch of EPS has a permeance of 2 to 6; that means that walls sheathed with EPS have more ability to dry to the exterior than walls sheathed with XPS. Since aluminum foil is completely impermeable, the use of foil-faced foam is not recommended on walls with interior polyethylene.

Walls sheathed with exterior foam perform better when they include a rain-screen drainage gap beneath the siding — for example, vertical 1x3 strapping or a product like Cedar Breather.

screws, then followed with 1x3 vertical strapping screwed to the studs. To prevent noticeable waves and bumps in the clapboards, we took pains installing the strapping, making sure the surface of each piece was in the same plane as the pieces on either side. This is a good idea for any type of siding, but it was critical in this case because the PVC clapboards the owner had chosen — called NuCedar — have an interlocking edge that would make any irregularities in one course show up in the next course. The nailing surface needs to be almost perfectly flat — there's little tolerance for error.

We fastened the strapping to the underlying wall framing with 6-inch HeadLok screws, then pulled string or laid a straightedge over the faces. By tightening or loosening the screws, we could adjust the depth by ⅛ to ¼ inch to create a flat wall (Figure 12). Because it was an old house, we needed every bit of that adjustment in some areas.

Siding support. We've been asked several times whether, with 4 inches of foam between the strapping and the sheathing, we worry that the weight of the plastic siding will bend the screws and cause the courses to sag. Although the job isn't that old, we're confident that we won't have such problems. Another job we did had an identical rain-screen detail over 4 inches of foam — but in that case we installed fiber-cement siding, which is heavier than cellular PVC. Revisiting that job after four years, we saw no evidence of sagging.

Porch Ledger Over Foam

Installing the porch ledger was tricky, because we had to maintain the strength of the connection as well as the thermal break provided by the foam (Figure 13). We did this by cutting back the porch joists and removing the original ledger. We securely fastened a new 2-by ledger over the Tyvek into the framing, then covered it with ½-inch rigid foam. This created a total thickness of 2 inches, matching the first foam layer. We then installed the second layer of 2-inch foam, placed a second ledger on top of that, and again fastened through to solid framing. We flashed the ledger with Ice & Water Shield and aluminum.

Window Jambs

Anytime you add rigid foam to the outside of the shell, you end up having deep jamb extensions either inside or outside, depending on whether the windows are installed on the face of the sheathing or the face of the foam. We've done it both ways. On this job the windows were "innies," meaning we had to add exterior jamb extensions to cover 4 inches of exposed foam plus the ¾-inch strapping (Figure 14).

This is without a doubt the most vulnerable part of the installation; if there's ever a problem, it will be because of a leak around the windows. For that reason, I usually build and install the extension boxes myself, taking care to tape and seal every possible leakage point.

On this house I used cellular PVC boards supplied with the siding package, screwing the pieces together with stainless steel trim screws and applying silicone caulk in every joint. The sill has a 10-degree slope. I bedded the backs of the extension boxes in a generous bead of silicone on the window frame, then screwed them into the wood blocking around the perimeter. On the outside, I taped the sides of the extensions to the foil surface of the insulation board.

PVC Siding

The owner chose NuCedar siding to reduce maintenance costs; according to the manufacturer, it will never need to be painted. We found that it was scratch-resistant and easy to handle. Not only is it lighter than fiber cement, but it doesn't give off any

Figure 12. To keep the nailing surface as flat as possible for the PVC siding, the crew used straightedges and strings to line up the strapping. Final adjustments of up to ¼ inch were made by tightening or loosening the 3-inch Headlok screws.

Figure 13. Porch floor joists had to be cut off to allow the insulation board to pass behind (A and B). The new ledger was attached through the foam into solid framing with structurally rated screws (C).

noxious dust when it's cut.

The siding package we received included ½-inch clapboards; metal starter strips for the first course to lock into; flat plates for bonding adjoining clapboards; and premilled header, casing, and corner trim. When we did this job, NuCedar cost about 10 percent less than red cedar and about three times more than fiber cement.

We completed the job over the winter, in temperatures that varied from mild to bitter cold. The siding was flexible when temperatures rose above 50°F but became brittle at colder temperatures, which meant we had to handle the boards more carefully to keep them from cracking.

Accommodating Movement

With PVC siding you have to pay attention to movement, because any vinyl product expands and contracts a lot with changes in temperature. The siding we installed included a nailing flange at the top of each piece, fastened in place with roofing nails. To allow for movement, you have to leave a ⅟16-inch gap between the nail head and the flange, which required time-consuming hand nailing (Figure 15). (NuCedar has since come out with a clip system that is designed to work with a nail gun.)

Field seams are backed with a vinyl bonding plate that's glued to the back of the siding with PVC cement. The plate holds the siding in place but serves no waterproofing role. Because the plates are adhered with PVC glue, installing them in cold weather can be problematic; in fact, a few of the ones we installed on cold days later came loose.

Trim and Flashing

The NuCedar trim goes on after the siding and has a rabbeted edge that overlaps the clapboards. To allow for movement, the ends of the PVC clapboards have to land in the middle of the rabbet (Figure 16).

The package comes with sawtooth-shaped inserts that close the gap between the trim and siding. This method no doubt works fine on the flat walls of a new home, but with the retrofitted rain screen, we had to constantly adjust the strapping depth to get the inserts to fit tightly. These details added a lot of time to the job; the siding took about a third longer to install than wood clapboards.

The siding is also not as easy to replace as wood. You can't simply pull out a damaged piece and slip in a

Figure 14. In order to secure the deep exterior jambs needed to cover the double layer of foam, carpenters fastened 2-by blocking around the windows directly against the housewrap (A). The blocks were covered with ½-inch-thick foam, then buried beneath the second layer of 2-inch foam, effectively preventing thermal conduction (B). Stainless fasteners secure the PVC extensions, which were also taped to the foil-faced foam (C and D).

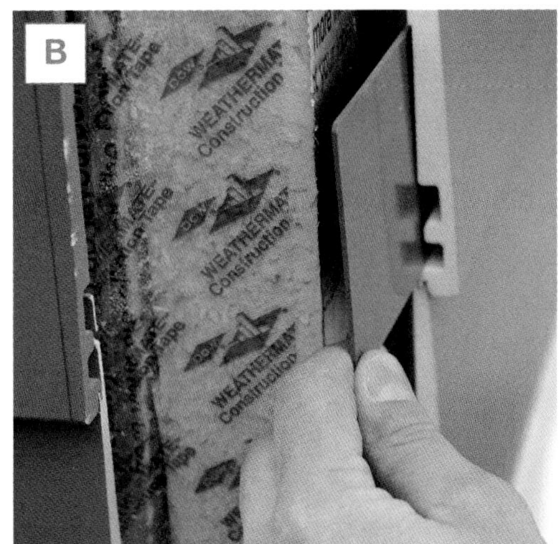

Figure 15. The cellular PVC siding had to be carefully hand-nailed through slots that allow for expansion (A). Backing plates provide glued reinforcement at butt joints (B and C).

Figure 16. Vertical trim pieces are rabbeted to allow the siding to move horizontally behind them (A). Sawtooth closure strips (B) plug the gaps where the clapboards run behind the trim (C).

Figure 17. Open-cell spray foam in the attic (A and B) boosted roof R-value to around 60. The benefits of the added insulation were apparent as the job progressed: Ice dams that used to form were gone (C and D).

new one. Each course is locked into the one above and below it, so you need to remove these pieces as well.

My overall impression of this siding? It's not ideal from an installer's point of view, and my top choices are still fiber cement and wood, both of which install quickly and are easier to replace. But with maintenance-free exteriors in demand, we can expect to see more of this product and others like it.

No More Ice Dams

On the inside, the owner added 10 to 12 inches of Icynene to the unfinished attic, bringing the total roof R-value to 60 or more. Added to the blown-in cellulose already in the wall cavities, the additional 4 inches of foam on the outside brought the wall R-value to around 39.

The benefits of the insulation retrofit were obvious to us as the job proceeded: Ice dams that used to form on the roof after every snow — a sign of heat leaking through the top of the building shell — were gone (Figure 17). New Fantech HRVs on the inside ensure good air quality for the two units in the building, and the occupants describe the house as warm, draft-free, and quiet.

***David Joyce** is owner of Synergy Companies Construction LLC in Lancaster, Mass.*

Case Study: New Life for an 80-Year-Old Home

by Terry Nordbye

We recently renovated a small, low-income rental unit in Point Reyes Station, Calif. Its owners, the local community land trust, wanted to replace the foundation, remodel the kitchen, and make some minor upgrades to the interior. They also mentioned that the utility bills were extremely high, so they wanted to add insulation.

The 80-year-old two-bedroom house didn't look too bad from the outside, but when I inspected the interior I found a variety of energy problems. The ceiling was insulated with R-13 fiberglass batts, and several batts installed between the floor joists hung down into the crawlspace. Some portions of the exterior walls had been insulated during an earlier remodel, but others contained no insulation at all.

There was also clearly a lot of air leakage. Fifty years of electrical and plumbing additions had left the house riddled with holes, and the siding was nailed directly to the studs with no sheathing or air barrier behind it. I told the owners that unless we air-sealed the building, adding insulation would do little to lower the heating bills.

Cost-effective strategies for air-sealing and insulation dramatically reduced air leakage and cut this home's energy bills in half.

Developing a Plan

The good news was that the house had a floor area of less than 850 square feet and 8-foot ceilings, so the amount of air-sealing needed was relatively small. We decided to try to make the house as tight as possible within the budget we had to work with, which wouldn't allow us to replace doors and windows. We also needed to preserve the interior finishes, so the stud bays would have to be accessed from the exterior.

The primary insulation in the walls and floor would be dense-pack cellulose, with blown loose-fill in the attic. A new layer of OSB sheathing would be followed by an inch of rigid foam and housewrap, with an exterior finish of fiber-cement siding applied over a vented air space (see "Insulation Details, page 329).

Cool and breezy. To measure our ability to eliminate leaks, we did blower-door tests at the beginning and end of the job. The initial test showed there to be 1,330 cfm of leakage at 50 pascals, or a very porous 11.9 air changes per hour (1,330 cfm x 60 minutes / 840 sq.ft. x 8 ft. = 11.9 ACH). When we saw those numbers, we weren't surprised that the previous tenants had complained about heating costs.

Preliminary Work

We began the project by replacing the foundation — a common repair in this area. After a house mover lifted the building onto cribbing, we removed the rotted pony walls and crumbling grade beams and poured reinforced concrete footings and stem walls capped by new pony walls (Figure 18).

Room to move. Although the building's footprint didn't change, the new foundation raised the structure by 2½ feet. Unlike the original crawlspace, which was only 1 to 2 feet high, the new one was tall enough for our crew and subs to do a good job replumbing, rewiring, and air-sealing from beneath the existing floor.

After the house mover lowered the building onto the new pony walls, we pulled off the old siding and carefully removed the doors and windows so they could be reinstalled later. We made various repairs to the framing, then turned our attention to the small front porch and a shed-roofed laundry room off the back of the house. Although the front porch was in good condition, the laundry room was so infested with termites we had to completely rebuild it. To conserve material and reduce thermal bridging, we framed it using the OVE (optimum value engineering) method (Figure 19).

Termite treatment. To prevent future infestations, we sprayed exposed framing with a glycol-borate preservative and termiticide called Borrada LP. According to its maker, the product had low toxicity to humans but kills insects up to 4 inches into the wood. We've since learned that Borrada LP has been discontinued, but similar termiticides are still available. One of the better known glycol-borate products is Bora-Care made by the Nisus Corporation (www.nisuscorp.com).

Air-Sealing

We began air-sealing by spraying canned polyurethane foam into the gaps surrounding pipes, wires, and electrical boxes where they penetrated framing and drywall (Figure 20). In the attic, we used two-component spray-foam kits from Touch 'n Seal at the eaves (www.touch-n-seal.com), applying a thick buildup where the rafters meet the top plate. The kits

Figure 18. After placing the house on a new foundation and pony walls (left), the crew removed the siding (above) so they could access the stud bays for air-sealing and then install sheathing.

Figure 19. The back laundry room was rebuilt with optimum value engineering (OVE) framing, a method that reduces thermal bridging and saves material. With OVE framing (left) there is 24-inch stud spacing, a single top plate, two-stud corners, right-size headers, and no jack studs. All of the framing in the house was sprayed (above) with Borrada LP, a low-toxicity glycol-borate preservative that kills termites 4 inches into the wood and prevents new infestations — a task made much easier by the additional crawl-space height provided by the new foundation.

come in several sizes; we used two of the largest, each of which yields about 600 board feet (50 cubic feet) of foam. In addition to sealing the penetrations, applying foam here increased R-value in an area where the low angle of the roof limited the amount of insulation that would fit.

We filled the holes in the backs of existing electrical boxes by plugging them with Arlington Industries' Duct Seal Compound (www.aifittings.com), a soft putty that does not harden over time.

After sealing every crack and penetration we could find, we sheathed the exterior walls and crawlspace ceiling with OSB, having already removed the original fiberglass batts from the framing cavities to make room for the dense-pack cellulose that would be blown in later. To further cut back on air leaks, we installed the wall sheathing over freshly applied beads of canned, one-component spray foam, which expanded to fill the gaps between sheets (Figure 21). There was no edge-blocking in the crawlspace ceiling, so we sealed the joints not backed by framing members with paper drywall tape embedded in a coating of

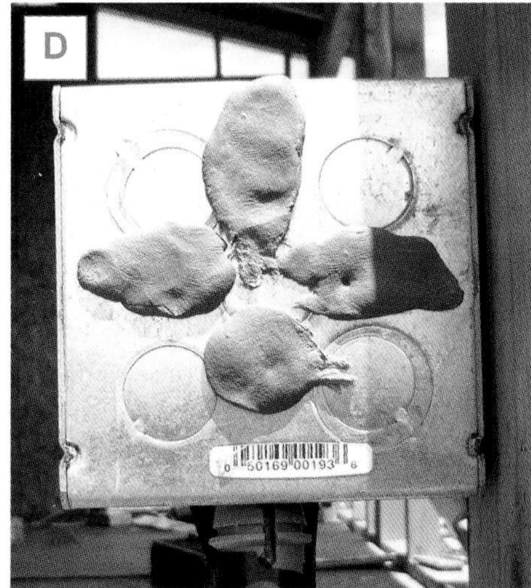

Figure 20. The author used one-component canned spray foam to seal plumbing and electrical penetrations through the walls (A), floor, and attic (B). To seal leaks at the eaves and provide added R-value in an area where insulation depth was limited, a thicker buildup of two-component foam was applied at the intersection of rafters and top plates (C). The holes through existing electrical boxes were plugged with a nonhardening putty (D) designed for sealing ducts.

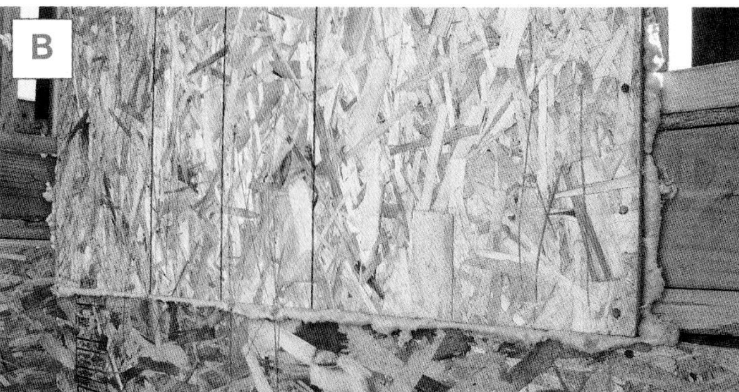

Figure 21. The carpenters installed the sheathing over beads of fresh spray foam (A), which expanded to fill any gaps (B). The seams in the OSB on the underside of the floor joists (C) were sealed with strips of paper drywall tape laid into a coating of duct mastic.

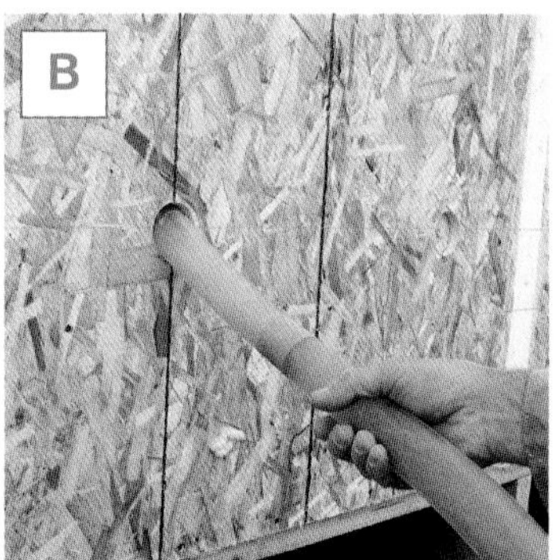

Figure 22. The insulation contractor used the dense-pack method to insulate the newly framed back porch, blowing cellulose through slits in mesh fabric that had been stapled across the studs (A). Where drywall was already up, he blew insulation through holes in the sheathing (B). The crew screwed temporary braces (C) across the existing drywall to keep it from popping off while cellulose was being packed into the wall.

DP 1010 duct mastic (www.designpoly.com). The gap at the perimeter of the ceiling was too large for mastic, so we sealed it with more spray foam.

Insulating With Cellulose and Rigid Foam

Dense-pack cellulose insulation is typically blown in from inside through holes cut in a mesh fabric that has been stapled to open framing. The fabric holds the insulation in the cavities, allowing it to be packed to a density of approximately 3.5 pounds per cubic foot. At this density, it has an R-value of about 3.4 per inch. Once the insulation is in, drywall is installed in the usual manner.

Inside out and outside in. Our insulation contractor used that conventional method on the walls and ceil-

Figure 23. The floor was insulated with dense-pack cellulose blown through holes in the joist blocking. To ensure the cavities were completely filled, the insulator connected a PVC pipe to the hose and began blowing from the far end of the bay (left), withdrawing the pipe as he went (above).

ing of the newly framed back porch (Figure 22). In areas where the drywall was already up he worked from outside, blowing cellulose through holes drilled in the sheathing. Early in the process, however, we found that the pressure exerted during installation could be enough to push the drywall off the studs. To prevent this from happening, we screwed temporary battens across the inside face of the wall. After the stud bays were filled, we patched the holes in the sheathing by inserting wood plugs and sealing them with duct mastic and mesh drywall tape.

Floor and attic. Instead of blowing insulation through the subfloor or the crawlspace ceiling, the insulation sub worked through holes bored in the blocking that served as a rim joist. To ensure that the cellulose reached the far end of the framing cavity, it was blown in through a long piece of PVC plumbing pipe attached to the end of the hose (Figure 23). The insulator started with the pipe all the way in and slowly withdrew it as the joist bay filled with insulation.

The attic was insulated to R-40 with blown-in cellulose. There was no need to install insulation baffles because the existing roof had no ridge or soffit vents. Ventilation was furnished by flat roof vents and a pair of gable vents.

An exterior thermal break. To provide a thermal break and an additional R-5 of insulation value, we covered the wall sheathing with one-inch XPS foam board, which was notched around the rafter tails (Figure 24). We cut the front porch free from the building and moved it temporarily away from the wall so the foam could be applied behind it without interruption. In framing the rear laundry room, we cut the rafters flush with the top plate so there would be no breaks through the foam. An overhang with short decorative rafter tails was later fastened to the wall from the outside (Figure 25).

Figure 24. A one-inch layer of rigid XPS foam covers the wall sheathing, providing added R-value and a thermal break. Flat roof vents and a pair of gable-end vents supply attic ventilation.

Rain-Screen Siding

To increase the durability of the wall assembly, we installed the exterior finish rain-screen style — that is, over a ventilated air space (Figure 26). This allows any moisture that gets behind the siding to drain to the bottom of the wall and promotes rapid drying of the back of the siding itself.

We began by ripping spacers from scraps of OSB, and nailing them over the foam around the perimeter of the door and window openings. Then we fastened the windows to the OSB spacers. Next, we covered the foam with housewrap, taking care to lap it over the window flanges and spacers. The remaining spacers went over the housewrap, aligning them with the studs, with window-screen material stretched across the open ends to keep insects from entering the air space. We completed the exterior by reattaching the front porch and nailing the casings, corner boards, and siding over the spacer strips.

Mechanicals

Before the remodel, the house had an electric water heater and in-wall electric resistance heaters. We kept the existing water heater but replaced the old electric wall heaters with new ones.

A house this tight should be equipped with mechanical ventilation. The budget on this project didn't allow for a fully ducted whole-house HRV, so we put a continuous-duty Panasonic FV-04VE1 in the main living area. This low-cost energy-recovery ventilator sells for about $350 and has a maximum capacity of 40 cfm. Except for the presence of a 4-inch outdoor air intake, it installs in the ceiling in much the same way as a bathroom fan (Figure 27).

Improved Performance

Near the end of the job, we performed a second blower-door test. It showed a more-than-tenfold reduction in air leakage — from the original 11.9 ACH

Figure 25. To maintain the continuity of the exterior rigid foam, the small front porch — shown here (left) with the siding applied — was cut free of the structure and then reattached after the foam had been slipped behind it. The back laundry room — a former porch — is fully insulated and lies within the building's thermal envelope (right).

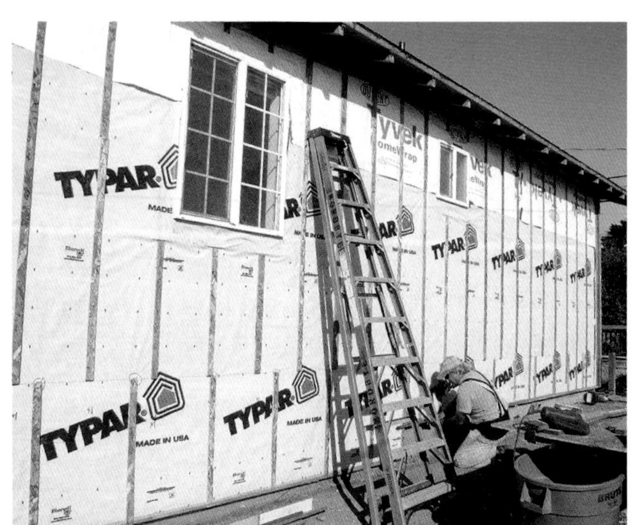

Figure 26. After reinstalling the existing windows, the crew covered the rigid foam with housewrap and vertical battens, which provide an air space and drainage plane behind the siding.

Figure 27. To improve indoor air quality in the now-tight house, the author installed a Panasonic energy-recovery ventilator in the ceiling of the living area. This small, inexpensive unit installs like a bath fan, except that there are two ducts to the exterior instead of one.

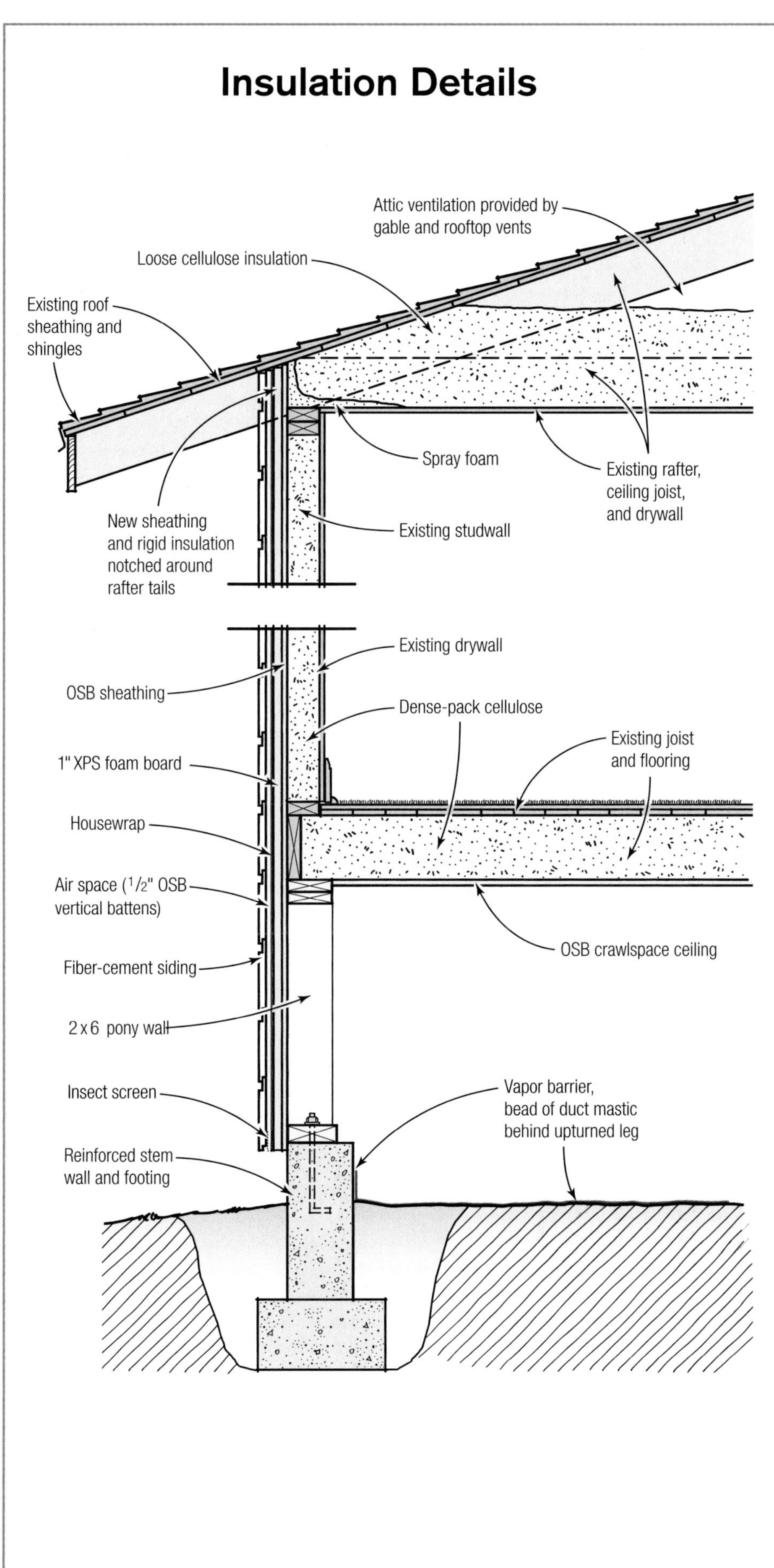

to just 0.9. We're confident that the leakage figure would have been even lower if we had been able to replace the existing doors and windows.

The owners have a few utility bills from the previous tenant and have been tracking electrical use after the renovation. Electrical use this past winter was half what it was during the same time period the year before — down from about 1,250 to 625 kilowatt-hours per month. We suspect that the bulk of current consumption goes to lighting and heating water, and hope to verify this through future monitoring. By my estimate, the air-sealing and extra insulation added about $15,000 to the overall $140,000 cost of the project.

Terry Nordbye is a building contractor in Point Reyes Station, Calif.

Chapter 15

BUILDING INNOVATIONS

High-Performance Shells With SIPs

by Gary Pugh

About 20 years ago, I watched a video about a house being built with structural insulated panels, or SIPs. It was the first time I'd seen the process: Instead of framing one stick at a time, the carpenters were installing entire sections of wall, which had arrived on site sheathed on both sides and insulated.

It impressed me as a faster and better way to build, so I tried SIPs on my very next house. That first one was difficult, because I had no one around to explain the technical details. But we stuck with it, and now my company builds only projects that include SIPs.

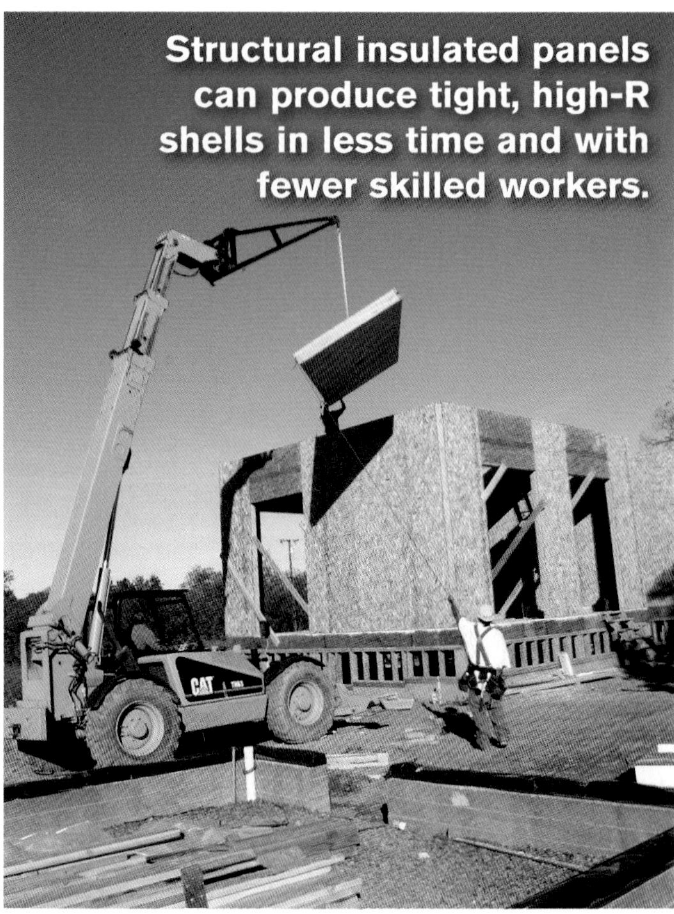

Structural insulated panels can produce tight, high-R shells in less time and with fewer skilled workers.
CAT

What Are SIPs?

SIPs are made by bonding a sheet material — OSB, plywood, steel, or fiber cement — onto both sides of an expanded polystyrene (EPS) or polyurethane foam core. By themselves, these materials are not strong enough to support loads, but once they're made into panels, they can be used for structural elements like walls, roofs, and floors. The most common panels consist of OSB over EPS (Figure 1).

Raw panels are produced in factories and then cut to size in fabrication plants or sometimes on site.

Size and thickness. OSB-faced panels come in sizes up to 8 feet by 24 feet. Foam cores are sized in thickness to match the width of standard framing lumber; that way, you can reinforce a panel or provide nailing by inserting a piece of framing stock. For example, a 6-inch panel is actually 6½ inches thick, made with a 5½-inch-thick piece of foam sandwiched between two sheets of ½-inch OSB.

Walls are typically made from 4- or 6-inch panels. Floors and roofs might be made from 6-, 8-, 10-, or even 12-inch panels.

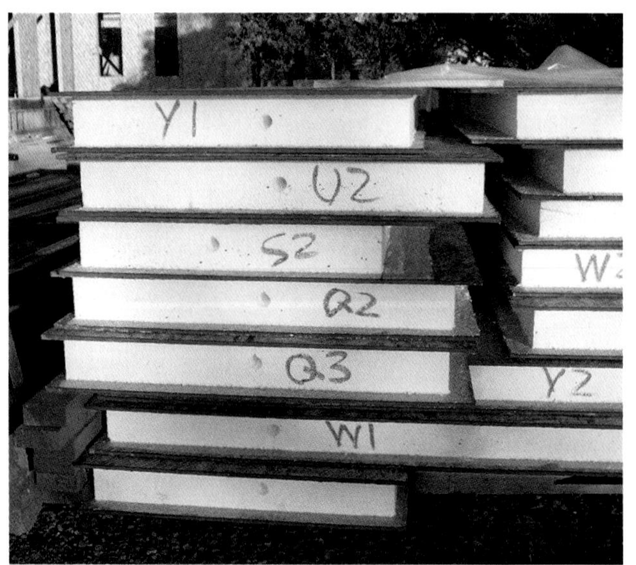

Figure 1. The most common type of structural insulated panel is produced by sandwiching EPS foam between two sheets of OSB. The face material can also be plywood, steel, or fiber cement, and the core can be polyurethane.

Why Use SIPs?

We use SIPs because it takes less time — fewer labor hours — and less skill to assemble precut panels than it does to stick-frame. The parts of the building made from panels are straight and true, and won't shrink or warp. Plus, they are exceptionally well insulated and sealed against air infiltration.

Our clients want their homes to be "green," and SIP buildings qualify because they're energy efficient and make good use of natural resources. The OSB skin is made from fast-growing trees that are plantation grown specifically for OSB.

Also, there's very little job-site waste with SIPs; the panels are cut by a fabricator, who can easily recycle cutoffs or use them when smaller panels are called for.

Insulation Value

The R-values associated with various building materials are misleading because they don't reflect how and where the material is installed. For example, 5½-inch fiberglass batts are rated R-19, but a wall insulated with these batts is not R-19, because there will be thermal breaks at every stud, plate, and header.

Whole-wall R-value. A more realistic way to look at insulation is to consider "whole-wall R-value," a method developed at Oak Ridge National Laboratory (ORNL) in Oak Ridge, Tenn., for estimating the R-value of various assemblies. The whole-wall R-value includes the insulation plus everything else that's in the wall.

According to ORNL, a 2x6 wall framed 24 inches on-center with plywood sheathing, drywall, and 5½-inch batts has a whole-wall R-value of 13.7. The same wall built with 6-inch OSB SIPs has a whole-wall R-value of 21.6. Why the difference? The foam in the SIPs has a higher R-value than the batts, and the SIP assembly contains fewer thermal breaks.

Ordering Panels

It's possible to buy raw panels and cut them to size on site, but it's better to pay a fabricator to do the cutting. Many fabricators have computer-controlled equipment that cuts panels far more accurately than we ever could.

Design. Like any building, a SIP structure starts out as a set of plans. Just about any stick-framed plan can be converted to SIPs (Figure 2), although it's easier when the initial design is done with panels in mind.

Either way, the first step in any SIP project is to produce a detailed set of shop drawings that show door and window openings, corners, edges, and wiring chases, as well as how the pieces will be joined on site.

Once the drawings are approved, delivery of the panels takes six to eight weeks. The process is a lot like ordering trusses, except in our case we produce the shop drawings in-house.

The fabricator could draw them, but we prefer to do it ourselves, because we gain more control over how the panels will go together.

Handling. SIPs arrive at the site on one or more semitrailers. Small panels are light — a 4x8 6-inch panel, for example, weighs about 115 pounds.

Larger panels are heavy, so we rent an all-terrain forklift to handle those.

Floor Structure

SIPs can be installed over any type of floor system. In our area of Northern California, most homes have wood-framed floors on stem-wall foundations with crawlspaces below.

Structurally, there's no reason we couldn't build the floor with SIPs. Doing so would be much faster than stick framing, and the insulation value would be very high.

But on most projects we still use conventional floor framing, as SIP floors aren't usually cost-effective in a mild climate like ours.

In colder areas, where insulating the floor is a major concern, building a floor with SIPs might make more sense.

Sound transmission. Even if they did cost less, we wouldn't use SIPs for upper floors.

The panels are good at preventing airborne noise from entering through the walls and roof, but walking on them creates a drumming effect that's annoying to the people below.

Setting Walls

Our panels arrive on the job cut to size with door and window openings, but without solid lumber nailers inserted.

The foam is recessed along the edges, so there's room to insert framing members. We install bottom plates to fasten panels to the floor, splines to join them edge-to-edge, and top plates to stiffen the top of the wall and provide nailing for the roof or floor above.

We install these lumber members over beads of sealant (provided by the panel manufacturer), then nail them in place through the face of the panel.

For an extra charge, some manufacturers will install the nailers for you.

Plates. With SIPs, wall plates are nailed, screwed, or bolted to the floor and then the panels are slipped over them.

If the wall lands on a stem wall or slab, the plate and

Figure 2. Panels can be used for any part of the building that isn't curved. The walls and roof of this traditional-style house are made from SIPs.

panel must be isolated from the concrete. To do this, we install a strip of pressure-treated plywood — sealed to the concrete with foam sill seal — and then install the plates over a bead of sealant.

Before installing the wall panel, we run sealant along the top and both edges of the wall plate, then stand the panel over it (Figure 3).

After bracing the panel plumb, we nail it to the plate through the OSB skin.

Hold-downs. In many regions, this nailed connection is all that's needed to hold panels to the floor or foundation. But we build in a seismically active area, so some of the panels are designated as shear walls and must be tied to the foundation with hold-downs.

The old way to do this was to connect threaded rods to the foundation and run them all the way up through the panels.

An easier method is to put double studs in the edge

Figure 3. Plates are installed first. Here, a 3x6 has been screwed to the deck over a continuous bead of sealant. In preparation for standing the walls, a carpenter runs sealant along the face and edges of the plate (A). The crew then stands the panel over the plate (B), braces it plumb, and nails it to the sides of the plate (C). When walls land on concrete, the plate is installed over a wider strip of pressure-treated plywood, which is also sealed to the concrete (D).

of the shear panel, cut a hole in the OSB, remove some of the foam, and install a conventional hold-down inside (Figure 4).

The hold-down is then bolted to the foundation and the double studs.

Another method is to run a strap up from the foundation and screw it to the outside of the panel at a double stud.

Joining Panels

We edge-join the panels with splines that fit into slots in adjoining edges and work like gussets. They're installed over beads of sealant and nailed in place through the skin of the panel.

We use three types of splines: solid pieces of lumber; surface splines, which are 4-inch rips of OSB; and block splines, which are basically a smaller SIP that fits inside the edges of adjoining panels (Figure 5). We prefer the foam block or surface splines because they don't produce thermal breaks.

We use solid lumber splines only where we need a doubled stud to carry a point load.

Solid nailers. Any vertical edge that is not joined to another edge with a spline must be filled with a piece of solid lumber. This provides nailing where there otherwise would be nothing to nail into.

Wall corners are made by butting the edge of one panel into the face of another and then screwing back through into the nailer (Figure 6). The exposed foam edge of the overlapping panel is filled with lumber to

Figure 4. The OSB and foam were cut from the corner of this SIP shear wall so that a hold-down could be installed. Later, the crew will foam in around it and replace the missing OSB.

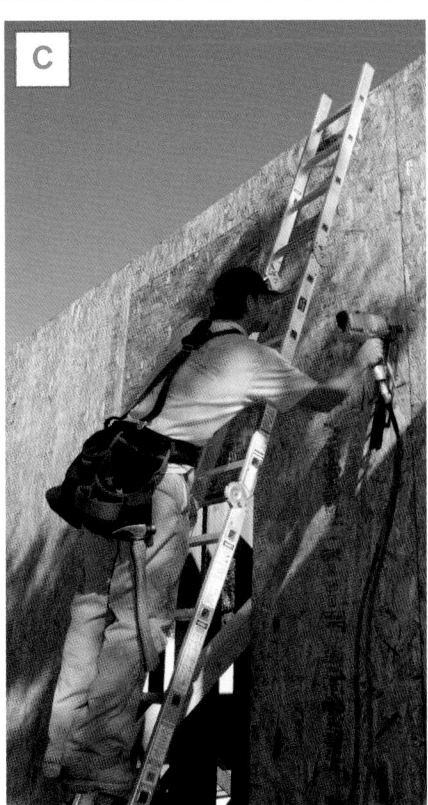

Figure 5. Panels are connected edge-to-edge with splines. Here, a carpenter prepares to install a block spline over continuous beads of sealant (A). The spline functions as a gusset and is held in place with nails driven first into the loose panel (B) and then into the adjoining panel (C).

Figure 6. At corners, the crew installs nailers flush to the edge of the panels, butts the panels together (far left), and uses screws to fasten through to the nailer beyond (left). These panels are 6½ inches thick, requiring 8-inch-long screws.

Foundation Detail

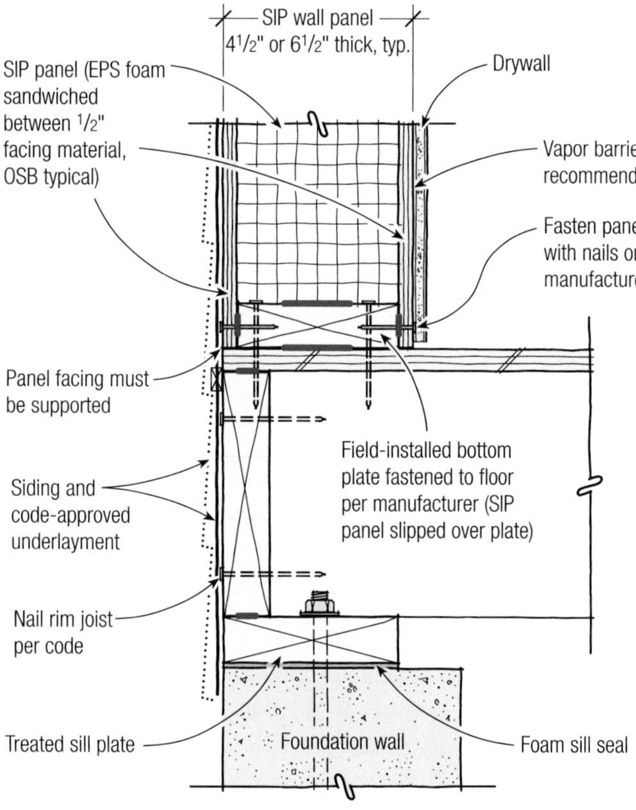

SIP wall panel 4½" or 6½" thick, typ.

SIP panel (EPS foam sandwiched between ½" facing material, OSB typical)

Drywall

Vapor barrier per manufacturer's recommendations or local codes

Fasten panel to bottom plate with nails on both sides, per manufacturer

Panel facing must be supported

Field-installed bottom plate fastened to floor per manufacturer (SIP panel slipped over plate)

Siding and code-approved underlayment

Nail rim joist per code

Treated sill plate

Foundation wall

Foam sill seal

Slab-on-Grade Detail

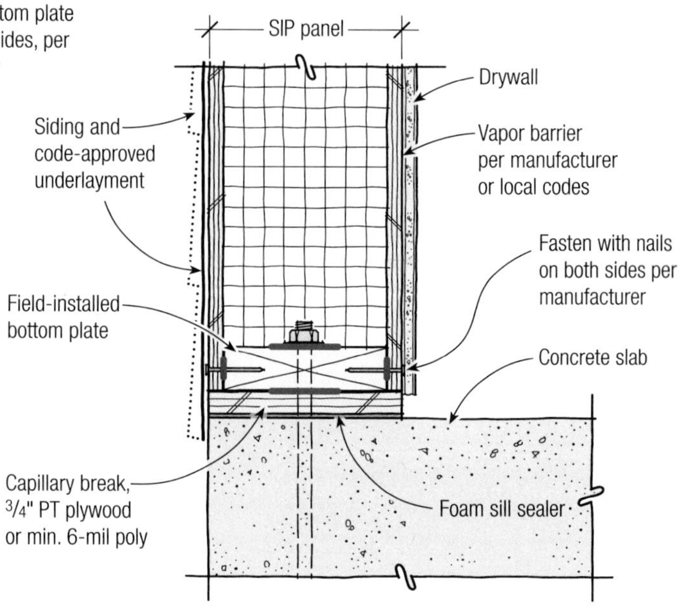

SIP panel

Drywall

Siding and code-approved underlayment

Vapor barrier per manufacturer or local codes

Fasten with nails on both sides per manufacturer

Field-installed bottom plate

Concrete slab

Capillary break, ¾" PT plywood or min. 6-mil poly

Foam sill sealer

Note: Areas with a continuous bead of sealant marked in RED

provide nailing for the wall finish.

Once the walls are up, we insert top plates. This stiffens the walls and provides solid nailing for the second floor or roof.

Sealing the Seams

There are a number of ways to seal the seams between panels. We run beads of panel mastic on mating surfaces, but you can also apply polyurethane foam from a can.

As an added measure, some panel manufacturers require you to surface-seal the interior joints by covering them with SIP tape, a type of peel-and-stick membrane. This is primarily a concern with SIP roofs in very cold, wet climates, because warm interior air will carry moisture through the gaps and can cause the outer layer of OSB to rot.

In some locales, the building code may require that you install a continuous vapor barrier inside the building. And to the extent that it reduces air leakage, a vapor barrier can be an improvement.

But the real issue with SIPs is not moisture diffusion through the panels — it's air leakage at the seams. In most climates, if you properly seal the seams you should not have problems, even without a vapor barrier.

Because SIP buildings are so tight, it is necessary to mechanically ventilate them to remove excess humidity and provide fresh air. The best way to do this is to install a heat-recovery ventilator (HRV).

The Roof

If the budget allows, a project might also have a SIP roof. A truss roof is cheaper and, if the roof is complicated, easier to install. But a SIP roof is tighter and better insulated.

With a SIP roof, beams are required, except where the panels span from wall to wall. There is typically a bearing ridge and beams at hips and valleys. Roof panels are joined edge-to-edge in the same manner as wall panels, then screwed to the beam or wall below.

Many of the photos in this article are from a house with a flat — or, more accurately, very low-slope — SIP roof surrounded by a short parapet (Figure 7). The panels are supported by interior beams and ledgers screwed to the inside faces of the walls. The ledgers are sloped to drain the rubber membrane roof toward

Spline Connection Details

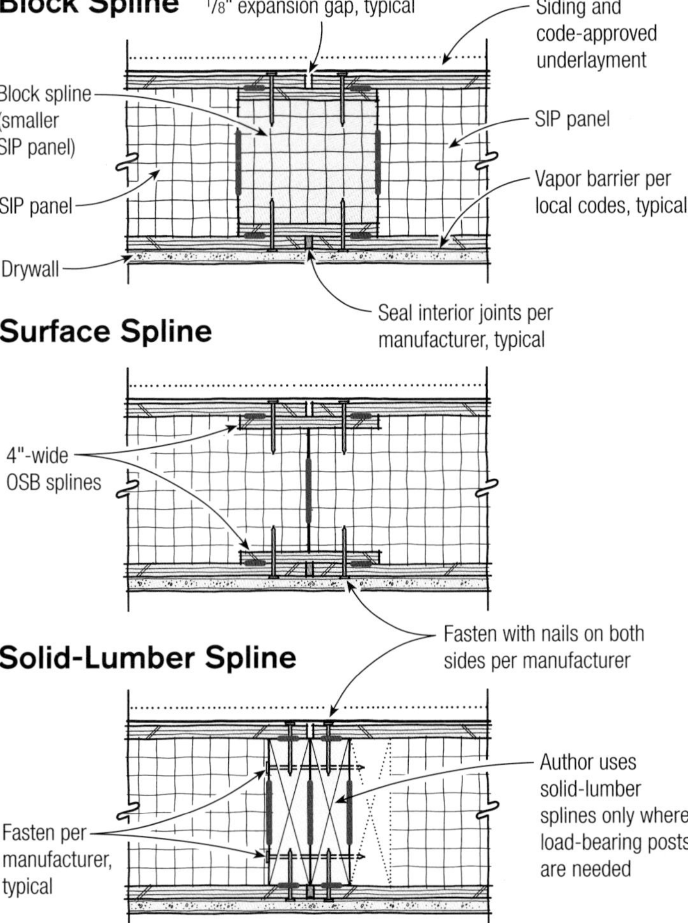

Corner Connection Detail

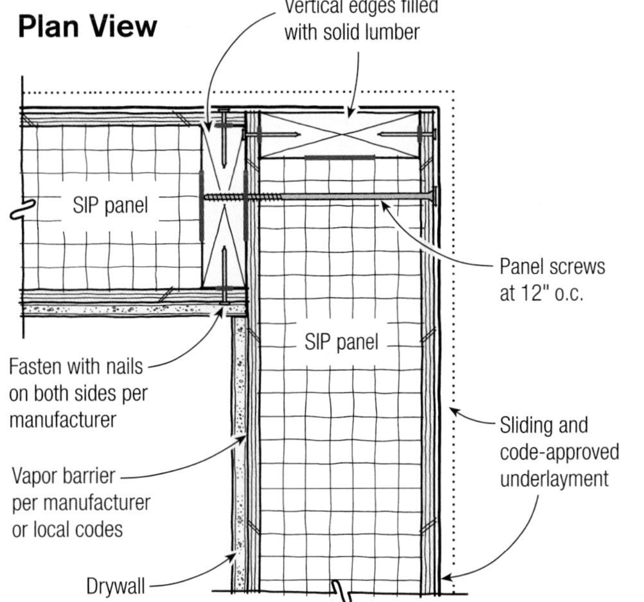

There are many different ways to join panels in the field; it's the responsibility of the fabricator — or an engineer — to specify the best approach for a particular job. Shown here are some common connection details the author often uses on his projects.

scuppers in the parapet. Inside the house, we dropped the ceilings to make them flat, leaving space for ductwork and wiring above (Figure 8).

Door and Window Openings

Door and window openings are often cut right through the panels. Headers are not usually necessary unless the opening is more than 5 feet wide or very close to the top. If the opening is large enough, you can save on material by piecing in around it. In such a case, the edges of the flanking panels should contain full-height studs plus jacks to support a panel or a header and panel above.

Cutting in the field. Occasionally the owner will want to add a window or make slight design changes after the panels are delivered. As long as the changes are minor, we can accommodate them by cutting the panels on site (Figure 9).

After cutting, we use a hot knife to neatly remove foam from the edge so there's room for a spline or nailer.

Because SIP buildings are engineered, we have to get changes okayed.

Effect on Subs

As with any alternative method, using SIPs affects the subtrades.

Drywallers and finish carpenters love SIPs because they are flat and straight, and they don't shrink or bow. Also, finding nailing is easy because the panels are continuously sheathed on both sides.

Roofing over SIPs is no different from roofing over any other sheathed roof.

Mechanical trades. Since partition walls in SIP houses are normally stick-framed, the hvac installer can easily run ducts in them. The only time there's a

Figure 7. Roof panels are lifted with an all-terrain forklift (A) and lowered onto glulam beams and sloped ledgers screwed to the wall panels (B). This carpenter fastens a panel by screwing through to the beam below (C). The parapets terminate with a double top plate (D), specified by the engineer.

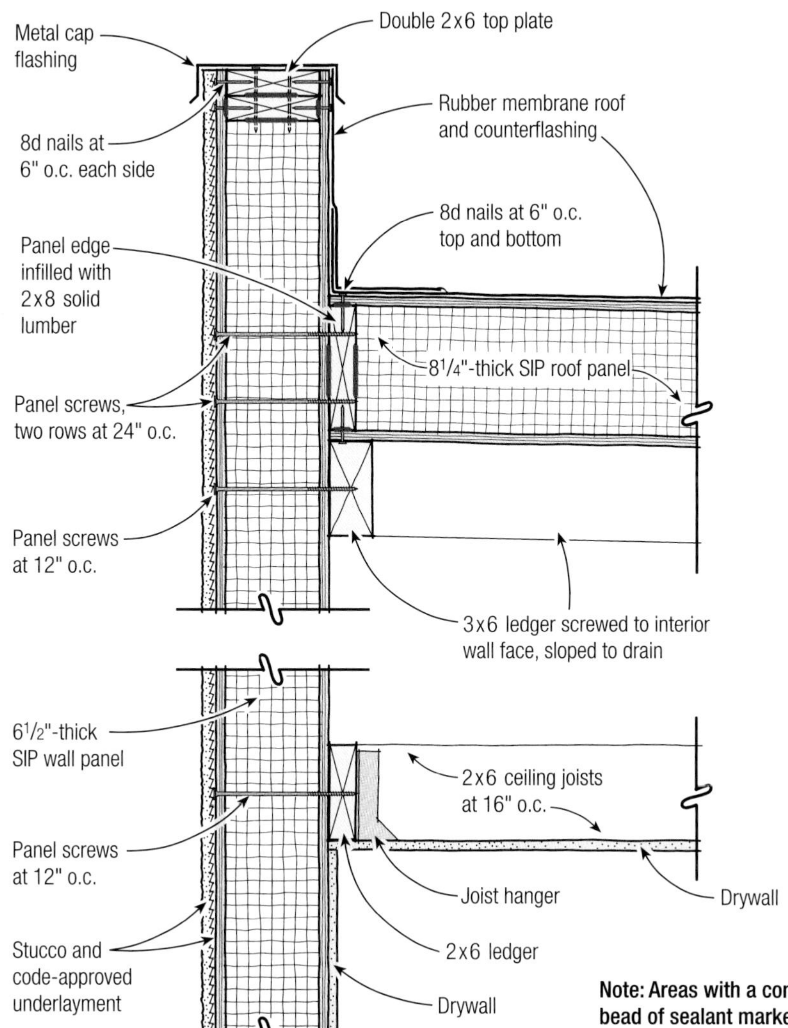

Figure 8. Many of the photos in this story are from a house with a flat SIP roof and parapet walls. The roof panels are supported by ledgers, which provide a slight slope toward drainage scuppers. Inside, the ceiling was dropped to provide space for ductwork and recessed lighting.

Figure 9. Mistakes and changes sometimes force the crew to alter panels in the field. Here, a carpenter trims a panel to size (left), then uses an electric hot knife (above) to neatly remove the foam so there will be room for a block spline.

Figure 10. To avoid putting pipes in the wall, the author had the plumber install the drain and supply lines for a sink just inside the panels at the sink-cabinet location (far left). If plumbing must go in an exterior wall, the author creates a chase by cutting out the panel and removing some of the foam (left). Once rough-in is complete, the author's crew uses spray foam to fill in around the pipes.

problem is when there's no attic and both the floor and roof are SIPs. Then we have to provide chases.

The plumber is in the same boat as the hvac contractor — most of the pipes go in partition walls. If the kitchen sink is on an outside wall, we either run plumbing through the toe space or bring it up through the bottom of the cabinet (Figure 10).

We typically build an interior chase for the vent pipe; when necessary, we leave an open space between two panels for pipes, then fill the space later with EPS and spray foam.

Electrical. The electrician faces the greatest challenge because it's hard to avoid putting switches and receptacles in exterior walls.

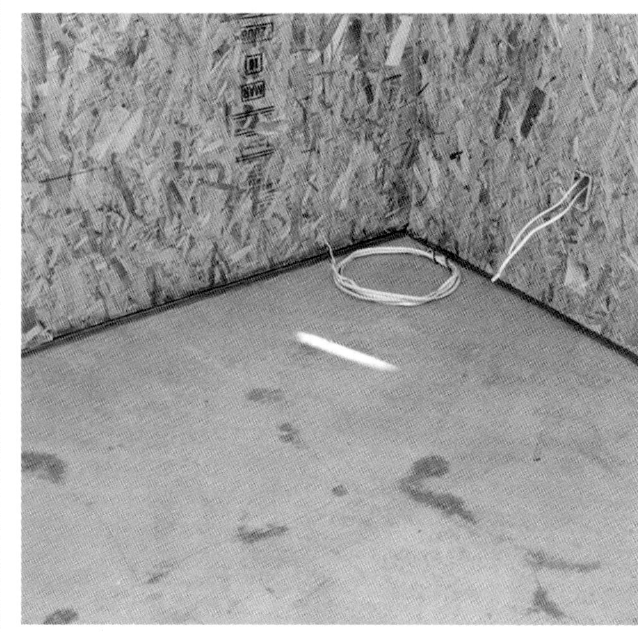

Figure 11. Wire chases are provided by panel manufacturers. The electrician accesses the chase by cutting a hole through the OSB and removing some of the foam. He can then fish wires through the chases and connect them to remodeling boxes in the panels.

We order panels with one vertical and two horizontal wire "chases" — 1¼-inch holes that run edge-to-edge through the foam (Figure 11).

The first horizontal chase is at outlet height and the second is at switch height. Since they're marked on the OSB, their location is obvious.

The electrician accesses the chase by cutting a hole through the face of the panel and digging out some of the foam. He is then free to fish wires vertically and horizontally and install remodeling boxes as needed.

When the wiring is done, we seal everything with spray foam.

With a little planning, you can run most of the wire through interior walls and minimize the amount that runs through panels.

Cost

Panels cost more than conventional framing material, but they require less labor.

In my business, building a house with SIPs costs somewhere between 1 percent less to 5 percent more than stick-framing the same plan.

Because a SIP house is tighter and better insulated, we can downsize the hvac system — but we have to install an HRV.

We don't have to hire an insulation contractor, and our dumping fees are lower because there is much less waste.

Gary Pugh *owns Alternative Building Concepts, a green building company in Santa Rosa, Calif.*

Building Complex Roofs With SIPs

by Mike Sloggatt

After 30 years of remodeling, I figured I had done just about everything there was to do — until I took on my first structural insulated panel (SIP) renovation. The project involved using SIPs to transform a modest cape into a country French–style home, with a roof featuring numerous irregular hips, turrets, steep pitches, and radius-top dormers.

Roofs with multiple hips and dormers can be assembled quickly using these energy-efficient panels.

Original estimates for stick framing the roof ran as much as $80,000 higher than the SIPs plan presented to the owners by project architect Bill Chaleff. Chaleff designs exclusively with SIPs and takes advantage of their structural characteristics — their ability to act as diaphragms, for example, or large flat beams. This means that roof loads are evenly distributed to the walls below, so that the complexities associated with stick-framing — structural ridges, hips, and valleys, and the point loads created beneath them — can be avoided. A SIPs roof goes together like a series of large planes (Figure 12). For this project, we used SIPs from Insulspan (www.insulspan.com).

Rebuilding the Walls

The cape — which was built in the 1930s — had already been remodeled three times. Because the first-floor deck wasn't level, we sized the wall panels ¾ inch short. This gave us room to shim the top of each one, so that the second-story subfloor would be level. Our benchmark was the ledger for the second-floor framing, which was attached to the first SIP wall section that we installed — the 14-foot balloon wall at the front of the house. From there we calculated the different top-plate heights, using various combinations of ⅜-inch through ¾-inch plywood, to ensure that the entire second floor came out level.

It took a three-man crew about three days to tack the first-floor wall panels into position. While this crew moved on to the roof, I brought in a few more crew members to secure the wall panels, which involved screwing the panels to the bottom plates on the deck and screwing the plywood splines at the joints. To prevent air infiltration where the panels butt, Insulspan SIPs have a small channel on the edge that must be filled with spray foam; we drilled holes along the joints at 8 inches on-center, then injected a two-part polyurethane — Dow's Froth-Pak 180 — into the channels.

Once all the first-floor wall panels were secured, a boom truck delivered the steel beams that would support the second floor. We framed the second-floor deck primarily with wood I-joists, though we used some SIPs wherever there was exterior exposure below.

The second-story floor joists are attached to the SIPs walls with top-mount joist hangers, hung from either a ledger fastened to the walls or from the blocking at the top of each panel. We attached the ledger with four 2-inch-long #10 screws and washers at 12 inches on-center, plus construction adhesive, as specified in the plans. The connection has to be strong enough to not only carry the floor loads, but also to enable the floor diaphragm to resist the lateral thrust from the roof.

Installing the Roof Panels

Stick framing can always be adjusted when sections of

a building don't align perfectly. SIPs are less forgiving, however, and the complexity of this roof allowed practically no room for error. If my layout was off by as much as ½ inch, the hips wouldn't come together, the dormers wouldn't fit, and the turrets would be a nightmare to install.

Layout. We had snapped lines on the first-floor deck to help us lay out the wall plates. We wouldn't be able to accurately locate the roof panels and turrets that spanned the two floors unless these lines were perfectly aligned with new lines on the second-floor deck. To do this, we projected points along the lower lines to the underside of the second-floor subfloor with a Stabila LaserBob, drove nails up through the plywood to locate these points on the second-floor deck, and then snapped new control lines to work from.

Assembling the panels. To assist in setting the roof panels, we had a 42-foot extending-boom, all-terrain forklift delivered and ready to go when the two tractor-trailer loads of SIPs arrived.

The roof panels arrived with bevel cuts at the ridges and plates. The foam cores were routed for blocking, which we ripped from 1¼-inch-thick OSB rim-board stock and installed with screws and adhesive. This was labor-intensive work; in hindsight, having it done at the factory would have saved time and materials.

Working off a set of sawhorses made from 24-foot-long LVLs, we assembled each roof plane on the ground. To keep the project as dry as possible (and to avoid having to staple paper on a steep 18/12-pitch roof), we installed Tri-Flex synthetic roofing underlayment before hoisting the sections (Figure 13).

Fitting the roof sections. Assembled SIPs are incredibly strong; Chaleff estimates that more than 90 percent of the load transfers across the joints, turning each panel assembly into a huge box beam. We didn't have to use any bracing when lifting the sections with the forklift. Locating the lifting point in the upper third of each one made it easier to drop the lower end onto the beveled top plates. We used tag lines to control the lift, and chain to prevent the lifting straps from slipping off the forks. The straps had a 5,000-pound rating; two of them provided plenty of capacity for lifting the panels.

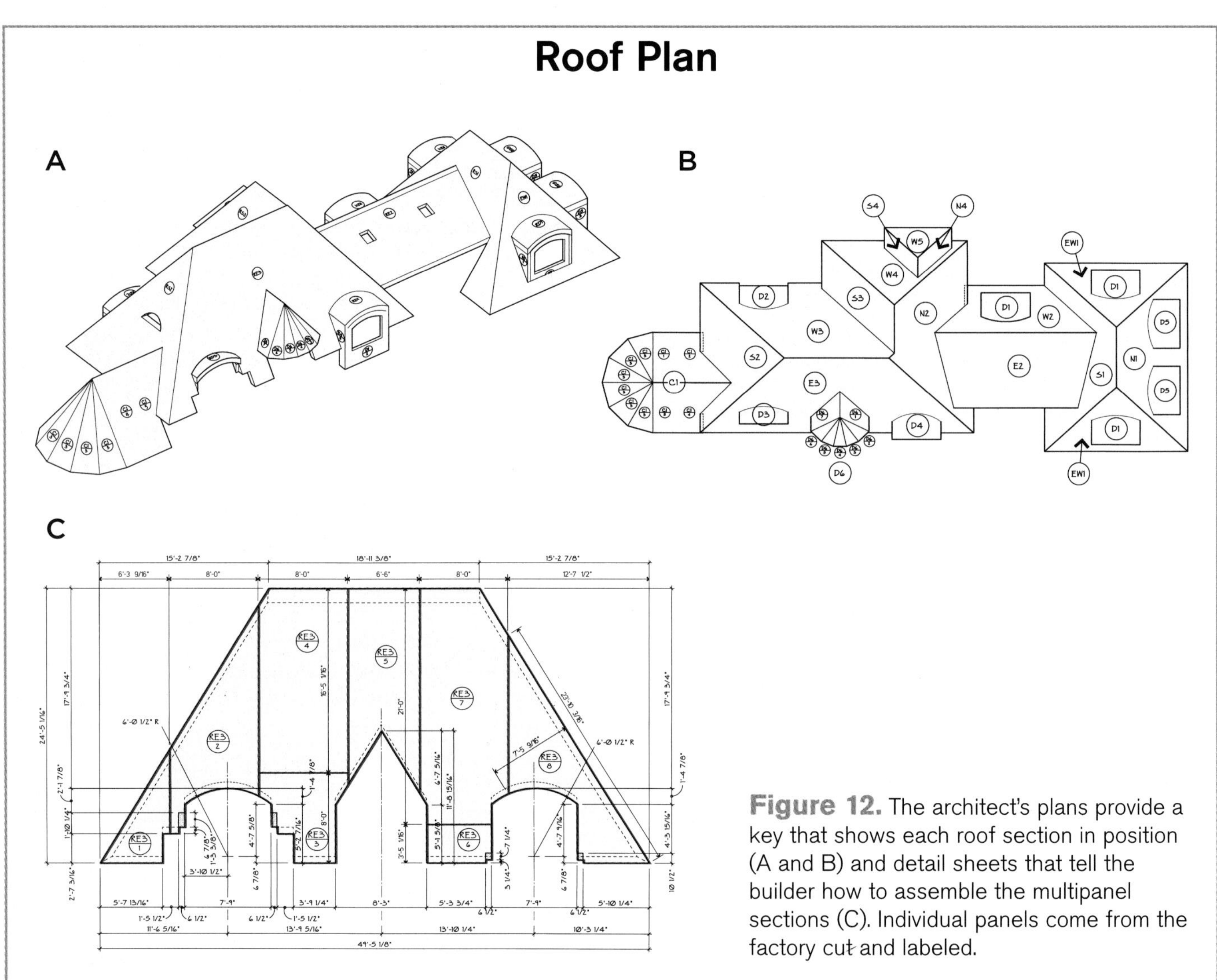

Figure 12. The architect's plans provide a key that shows each roof section in position (A and B) and detail sheets that tell the builder how to assemble the multipanel sections (C). Individual panels come from the factory cut and labeled.

The first roof section was the trickiest (Figure 14). We fastened it to the top wall plate with adhesive sealant and 10-inch-long structural screws 6 inches on-center — a connection strong enough that it requires no additional straps or hurricane clips.

After driving in the screws at the base, we braced the panel and also strapped it down to the deck to prevent wind from lifting it. We then rigged and set the opposing section, applying adhesive to the ridge blocking and fastening the ridge together with 3-inch-long #10 screws 6 inches on-center.

Once the main roof sections were fastened together,

Figure 13. Roof sections are assembled and prepped on the ground. Sealing the panel joints with asphalt cement helps prevent the OSB skins from absorbing moisture and swelling, while extra strips of underlayment laid over the patch keep the tar under control (A). Placing the panels on 30-inch-tall LVL sawhorses allows crew members to work underneath (B). After assembly, each section is rigged with lifting straps and hoisted into place with an all-terrain forklift (C).

Figure 14. To set the first roof section, the author projects the centerline of the ridge connection (marked on the deck) with a vertical laser line, then props the section into position with the forklift (left). After the roof pitch is verified with a digital level (right), the section is temporarily braced until the opposing roof section can be rigged and set into place.

Figure 15. With the main roof sections fastened together, the adjoining hips are installed (A). To save time, the author's crew preinstalled the connecting screws on the ground (B) before lifting the panels into position and preassembled small hip sections before placement (C).

Figure 16. When a panel has been trimmed in the field, foam must be removed with a hot iron to make room for new blocking.

it was easier to install the adjoining large and small hips (Figure 15).

Because the panels were so accurately cut, we had to modify only one roof section — by cutting 1 inch off the edge of a panel connecting two hip sections (Figure 16).

After the roof sections were assembled, we foamed all of the spline connections (like the walls), working from the inside. Then we applied an adhesive vapor-barrier sealing tape supplied by the manufacturer to all the seams and the underside of the ridge to prevent warm, moist air from migrating into these critical joints and condensing.

Turrets and Dormers

We preassembled the turrets on the ground before placing them with the forklift (Figure 17). Like the flat roof sections, all of the connections were made using adhesives and an assortment of 6- to 14-inch-long special SIP screws and washers.

The radius-roofed dormers came assembled from the factory; we simply lifted them off the back of the flatbed and dropped them into place.

Figure 17. Small and large turrets were assembled on the ground out of precut SIPs (A) and then hoisted into place with the forklift (B). The radius-roofed dormers — which were preassembled at the factory — were lifted straight from the delivery truck to the roof (C).

Even with all the extensive planning, we overlooked one thing: I was admiring a newly assembled SIP turret sitting in the driveway when I realized it wouldn't fit under the power line running across the front of the property. Rather than wait for the line to be lowered, we drove the turret around the property via the street, where the lines were higher. It was quite a sight for the neighbors to watch a roof drive by.

Roof assembly (not counting the time spent building the curved rafter tails) took about three weeks. I estimate that, for the same price, we could have framed a similar roof — but I would have needed more skilled carpenters (only two were available for this job), the project would have taken a little longer to finish, and we still would have had to insulate the roof.

***Mike Sloggatt** is a remodeling contractor in Levittown, N.Y.*

Case Study: My First ICF House

by Ralph Woodard

I had been building custom wood-frame houses on North Carolina's Outer Banks for more than 20 years when a local couple asked me to build a house for them using ICFs (insulated concrete forms). All I knew about this technique at that time came from reading magazine ads. A year later, I had successfully built a single-story 1,800-square-foot house using an ICF system and planned to build more.

This reinforced concrete system provided an energy-efficient shell with superior wind resistance for this coastal site.

Strong, Energy-Efficient Shell

Because they were building on the beach, the clients wanted to be sure the house would stand up to high winds. They discovered Polysteel at a home show in Pennsylvania and felt it addressed their concerns.

I figured it couldn't hurt to learn about a building system that's both strong and energy efficient. On the barrier islands where I build, we feel the effects of almost every hurricane and nor'easter that hits the East Coast. And because there's no natural gas service to the area, nearly all homeowners rely on electricity to heat and cool their homes. Insulated walls rated to withstand 200-mph winds and promising to cut electric bills in half might sell themselves.

I contacted the Polysteel distributor in nearby Virginia Beach, who invited me to come up and take a look at the product being installed on a job site. After this hands-on inspection, I took the manufacturer's user manual home and watched a couple of videos the company provides to builders. The instructions were detailed yet not that complicated. It was clear that anyone with a reasonable amount of construction experience could do it. The Polysteel distributor, Reid Pocock, who was also an engineer and contractor, helped me prepare a bid for the house, and I got the job.

Educating the Subs

Since getting my general contractor's license in 1980, I've used many of the same subcontractors. While some builders might find their subcontractors resisting a new way to build, I had worked with my subs long enough to know it wouldn't be a problem. I like a "can do" attitude, and that's what these guys give me. I didn't have one sub say he didn't want to work on the job — and when it was all done, each one of them said they'd be happy to do it again.

I realized that building with ICFs would affect my framers more than the other subs, so I took the framing crew to Virginia for another hands-on look at an ICF house in progress. I also gave them the instructional materials I got from Polysteel.

Stacking the Blocks

Because of flood regulations, most houses in this area must be elevated, and this house was no exception. It was designed with a 3-foot crawlspace under the entire house, which meant that our ICF walls were 12 feet tall. We poured a concrete footing 24 inches wide by 12 inches deep and stacked the ICFs directly on that.

Starting out level. The Polysteel literature recommends stacking the blocks the full height of the building, then shooting a level line around the top and sawing the top of the forms level. This seemed counterproductive to me, because if you start from a level footing, the blocks will stay level as you go. So we spent the time it took to get a perfectly level footing, using rebar grade stakes every 3 feet in the trench.

The Polysteel blocks are 48 inches long by 16 inches high by 9¼ inches wide, and have 6-inch-diameter vertical cores 12 inches on-center. (Polysteel also makes an 8-inch core block.) The foam is easy to cut with a handsaw, and we used a recip saw with a steel-cutting blade to cut through the expanded steel mesh and 1-inch steel furring strips that hold the forms together.

Rebar requirements. Before laying the first course, we had to install vertical rebar every 2 feet. We drilled ⅞-inch-diameter holes 6 inches deep into the footing and inserted 6-foot lengths of #6 Grade 60 rebar, securing them with Hilti epoxy. Our design also called for horizontal rebar every other course (Figure 18).

Figure 18. Vertical rebar, epoxied into place, extends from the footing (left) up through the Polysteel blocks. Horizontal rebar, laid in every other course, rests on the steel mesh that joins the sides of the blocks together and is tied to the vertical rebar (right).

Working from the corners. We began stacking at corners, just as you would a CMU or brick wall, and cut the forms as needed to fill in the middle of runs or at openings. We used batter boards and string lines to keep the walls straight. When we did this job, we had to miter the corner blocks. This is somewhat labor-intensive and also creates a potential spot for a blow-out. Polysteel now makes prefab corner blocks, which we used on later jobs.

To glue the blocks together, we used a low-expansion spray foam adhesive called Handi-Foam (Fomo Products Inc., www.fomo.com). It comes in aerosol cans with a spray attachment that mounts on top to dispense the foam.

We glued the first course directly to the footing, then shot 2x4s alongside it on both sides to prevent the bottom of the wall from moving. These 2x4 plates also came in handy later because they gave us a place to attach the bottoms of the vertical 2x4 braces (Figure 19). We used pressure-treated lumber for these bottom plates, because I knew the sand would cover them up during the job and they would be left in place.

As the forms went up, additional lengths of vertical rebar had to be wired on with a 24-inch overlap. The horizontal rebar also had to be tied to the vertical and to the galvanized mesh that it rested on. We used pre-cut wire ties and a pigtail to speed this job up.

There was one small gable on the house. It's possible to form rake angles with ICFs, but we opted to stack them level and frame the one gable.

Openings and Penetrations

Openings for doors and windows had to be cut out and framed with pressure-treated 2x10s. We also had to cut a 5-inch-wide slot in the bottom of each buck to get the concrete into the blocks below. A framework of 2x4s on the outside kept the bucks square. On the larger openings, we also installed vertical braces inside the bucks to keep the heads from sagging. The product distributor reviewed the plans to make sure the rebar in the lintels was adequate. For really large openings, like garage doors or where heavy loads come down, special rebar design may be required at lintels. On this house, the standard rebar design was adequate.

Once all the blocks were stacked, the plumbing, electrical, and hvac subcontractors came to create mechanical penetrations. It was a simple matter of drilling a hole through the foam and inserting a PVC sleeve through the blocks at every point where they needed access.

Installing Anchor Bolts

The wood-frame floor hangs from a ledger attached to the ICF wall with bolts. Installing all those bolts — ¾-inch J-bolts every 2 feet around the perimeter in most places — was easy though somewhat time consuming.

We first shot a level line around the inside for the top of the ledger. We then cut a 6-inch-square hole for every bolt location. To position the bolt before the pour, we cut a stack of 14-inch-square plywood pieces with a ¾-inch hole drilled in the center. We fastened the bolt to the plywood, then attached the plywood over the bolt holes with drywall screws into the steel furring strips.

After the pour, this left the bolts protruding from concrete pads that prevented the foam from being crushed when we installed the ledger (Figure 20).

We also installed bolts for attaching interior walls to the ICF walls, as well as anchor bolts 4 feet on-center to secure the double top plate we used.

Polysteel instructions called for ⅝-inch bolts, but the distributor was offering the larger bolts for the same price, so that's what we used.

Bracing the Forms

Even though we used the spray foam in the assembly process, a lot of wood bracing is still required to keep the lightweight blocks lined up and in place during assembly and the concrete pour. I figure we spent up to 120 man-hours on the bracing alone. With careful planning, we were able to reuse almost all the wood in the interior framing.

On a visit to the site, Pocock mentioned that I probably had more bracing than I needed, but for my first pour with ICFs, I wanted to be safe rather than sorry.

We installed vertical 2x4s approximately every 4 feet on both sides of the wall. We held them snug to the wall with tie wires that ran through the forms and around the 2x4s. We also nailed them to the bottom plate and capped them with a top plate as well. This top plate — one on each side of the wall — turned out to be very useful during the pour. Ordinarily, we would have had to set up scaffolding to work from, but these 2x4 plates provided an ample walking platform for the man working the hose. Some pump trucks have flexible hoses that can be pinched off to stop the flow of the concrete. The hose on our truck was stiff and never stopped flowing, so the guy on the top of the wall had to be able to keep moving continuously to prevent too much concrete from going in at any one point.

On this first job, framing the exterior walls took about two weeks longer than building with wood. On the next job with the same crew, I expect to come closer to matching a stick-built schedule.

Figure 19. Spray foam dispensed from a can (top) glues the blocks together as they are stacked. Two-by-four bracing holds everything in place for the pour (above). Note also the squares of plywood holding the anchor bolts for the ledger in place.

The Big Pour

Four weeks after breaking ground on the job, we pumped 30 cubic yards of concrete from a pump truck into the ICFs.

The concrete has to flow from the top of the wall all the way down to the foundation, through built-in steel mesh, and around rebar and bolts. You need a mix that flows well, but not one that is watery — too much water increases the likelihood of blowouts.

Pocock called in the concrete design to the ready-mix plant. He used a 3,500-psi mix with extra cement to improve flow. Generally, a 4.5 to 5.5 slump is good for ICF construction. According to Polysteel, most ready-mix companies are accustomed to ICF requirements.

The pour was labor-intensive. I had one guy manning the hose and another helping him, three carpenters prepared to deal with leaks and blowouts, and two guys walking around tapping the forms to help the concrete settle. The form makes a completely different sound when it's full, so this gave us our best indication that we were getting the concrete into the forms. At one point we tried using a vibrator, but it caused the concrete to liquefy and caused a blowout.

Otherwise, the pour went well, with only about 10 minor bulges that we had to fix. When the foam began to bulge, a carpenter would take a good size scrap of plywood and place it against the forms, then use a 2x4 brace, staked at the ground, to press it back into place — just as you would when plumbing a frame wall. The trick was to get the guy with the hose to move along quickly before more damage was done. We had some lengths of threaded rod on hand just in case we had a major blowout and had to pull both sides of a form back together; fortunately, we didn't need them.

It took less than five hours to fill the 12-foot walls of

Figure 20. After the pour, the ledger bolts that support the first-floor framing extend from 6-inch-square pads of concrete flush with the surface of the foam (left). These concrete pads prevent the foam from crushing when the ledger is attached. The author poured 24-inch-diameter concrete piers to support the first-floor beams (right).

the 50x36-foot house. After the concrete set, we cleaned up any small leaks and dribbles with a large sanding trowel provided by Polysteel. It was about 8 inches wide by 16 inches long and used the coarsest sandpaper I've ever seen. We also used it to flatten the walls anywhere there were bulges.

The original design for the house showed 12 concrete block pier supports under the floor framing. During the planning stage, I realized we could save time and money by using short, 24-inch-diameter cardboard tubes instead, and pouring these at the same time we filled the ICF walls. Once the floor ledger was bolted to the ICFs, floor framing proceeded in the usual manner, as shown in Figure 3.

Fine-tuning. When I build my next ICF house, I plan to do the concrete pour in two stages. I'll lay as many courses of block as it would take to get up to the floor level, fill them and the pier forms with concrete, then build the floor. This will allow my framers to work on the upper courses of block from step ladders and eliminate the need for scaffolding. The time saved stacking and bracing the blocks would more than cover the extra $500 for a second pump truck visit.

Roof Framing

Because my clients picked reinforced ICF construction for its strength and wind resistance, I needed to pay extra attention to the roof design. A roof built to code here is rated for winds up to 110 mph. I wanted to get the roof more in line with the 200-mph wind rating on the Polysteel walls. Before we began building, the homeowners agreed to change their gable-end roof to a stronger hip roof design, which we framed with 2x10s. We also used a heavier grade shingle for better wind resistance.

With most Polysteel houses, the builder adds a single top plate to the ICF wall and builds the roof. Because I'm building on the coast, I use Simpson H-10 hurricane clips on every rafter to meet state building code. Because the lower part of the clip would hang below a single top plate (and would normally be nailed to a wall stud), I doubled the top plate so that clips could be completely nailed into solid framing. The 10-inch anchor bolts were plenty long to pass through both plates.

Electrical, Mechanical & Drywall

The electrician had to recess all the wires and boxes into the surface of the foam blocks. I provided a hot knife for this job, and we played around with a spare block. It didn't take any time to get the knack of using it efficiently. Although most builders won't have to do this, our local building inspector required all wires to be run in PVC conduit. This cost about $1,000 extra for time and materials.

We designed the house so that no sinks or other plumbing fixtures came off exterior walls. This meant that except for running pipes through the Polysteel before the concrete pour, the plumber's work was no different than usual.

The hvac contractor didn't need to do things differently on site, but he spent several extra hours calculating the special pump requirements for the house. In our area, the hvac system is usually designed for heating efficiency. Because of the extra insulation value of the ICFs, he had to address cooling first. The heating load was 10,000 Btu/hr less than for typical new

Figure 21. Typically, the exterior surface of the foam blocks requires some flattening before installing siding. In this case, however, the finished structure was sided with panels of rough-textured wood shakes, which covered any slight inconsistencies in the foam's surface.

wood-frame construction, and cooling requirements were reduced by 3,000 Btu/hr.

While framing the interior of the house was no different from conventional stick construction, hanging gypsum board on the perimeter walls required a different technique. We glued the drywall to the steel furring strips, then secured it with screws into the strips.

Siding Installation

If any subcontractor was resistant to the idea of working with ICFs, it was probably the siding guy. We knew there would be more prep than usual to hang the siding, because the 1-inch width of the steel furring strips doesn't always give you secure attachment where you need it. The strips are also not continuous from course to course. To get around this, we used pieces of coil stock to bridge areas where we needed it. We screwed the coil stock to the strips with self-tapping, oval-head sheet metal screws. This process probably added about a day to the siding job.

The choice of siding also helped. We bid the job planning for vinyl siding and thought we'd have to spend considerable time flattening the wall. During construction, the owners decided to use Nailite Handsplit Shakes, which come in 3½-foot-long panels, two shingle courses high. The irregular texture and shape of the Nailite shingle pattern hid any irregularities in the foam substrate and made flattening the surface unnecessary (Figure 21).

Secret of ICF Success

It didn't take long for me to figure out how to build an ICF house. Most of the house could be built just like any other house I build. The instructions were easy to follow, and there were no unfamiliar materials, tools, or techniques. I could use ordinary exterior siding, conventional doors and windows, and hang drywall without a lot of special preparation. If I had a question, the Polysteel distributor, who had himself built a dozen ICF homes, was close by for consultation.

I had an advantage, too, because my subcontractors and I had a long history of working together. If I'd had to bid the job out to people I didn't know and who didn't know about working with ICFs, the price probably would have been 15 to 20 percent higher, and I might not have gotten the job.

Still living in a wood-frame world. I work in a resort area, where 90 percent of the homes are vacation and rental properties. With these houses, building cost is almost always the bottom line. My bid on this house was nearly 10 percent more than the same size wood-frame house would have been. Because my clients were motivated by their concern about hurricane damage, they accepted the extra cost. They will also keep their house long enough to recoup that cost through energy savings. But so far, my other clients are still opting for wood-frame construction.

Whenever prospective clients come into the office to discuss building a house on grade or a year-round house, I pull out the Polysteel block and do a little show-and-tell for them. I don't push it, but I like to get them thinking about the possibility of building a stronger, more energy-efficient home. Now that I've finished one house, I think in time I'll see more interest.

Ralph Woodard *is a custom home builder in Kitty Hawk, N.C.*

Custom Construction With Insulated Concrete Forms

by Victor Rasilla

Curved walls and arch-topped openings were no problem for this ICF veteran.

When we first worked with ICFs, we — like most contractors — used the foam forms only for foundations and simple structures. Eventually, though, we began to build entire houses with them.

The Alamo, Calif., custom home featured here was such a project. The plans called for curved walls with large arch-top openings. Given that combination — curved walls and arched windows — most builders would have chosen to stick-frame. But the house was also designed to be extremely energy efficient, with triple-glazed windows, radiant-barrier roof sheathing, a NiteBreeze ventilation system for cooling, and vacuum-tube solar collectors backed up by on-demand water heaters for hot water and hydronic heating. For all these elements to work, the walls would have to be airtight and well insulated — which made ICFs a good fit.

The house sits on a hill — two stories in front and one in back — with a crawlspace, garages, and mechanical rooms below and a single level of living space above. The upper floor is framed with I-joists attached to the ICF walls (see "ICF Wall Section," next page). The exterior finish is synthetic stucco applied directly to the ICFs.

The home's foundation — a poured-concrete grade beam on poured concrete piers — is typical for hillside residences in this area. Because the piers are designed to carry the weight of the house, the grade beams don't need to be as wide as conventional footings; on this house, most are 12 inches wide. We took great care to lay out and form an accurate foundation so we could install the ICFs flush to the outside face of the grade beams. In the few places where the grade beams were wider, we used the more standard method of installing the blocks to snapped lines.

Stacking the Blocks

Our company uses Logix blocks (www.logixicf.com). Like most brands of ICF, they're based on a 48-inch-long by 16-inch-high module and come in a variety of wall thicknesses. On this job we used 11½-inch blocks, which have a 6-inch cavity flanked by 2¾-inch EPS foam.

When setting blocks, we start from corners and work toward the center. Ideally, the length of every wall

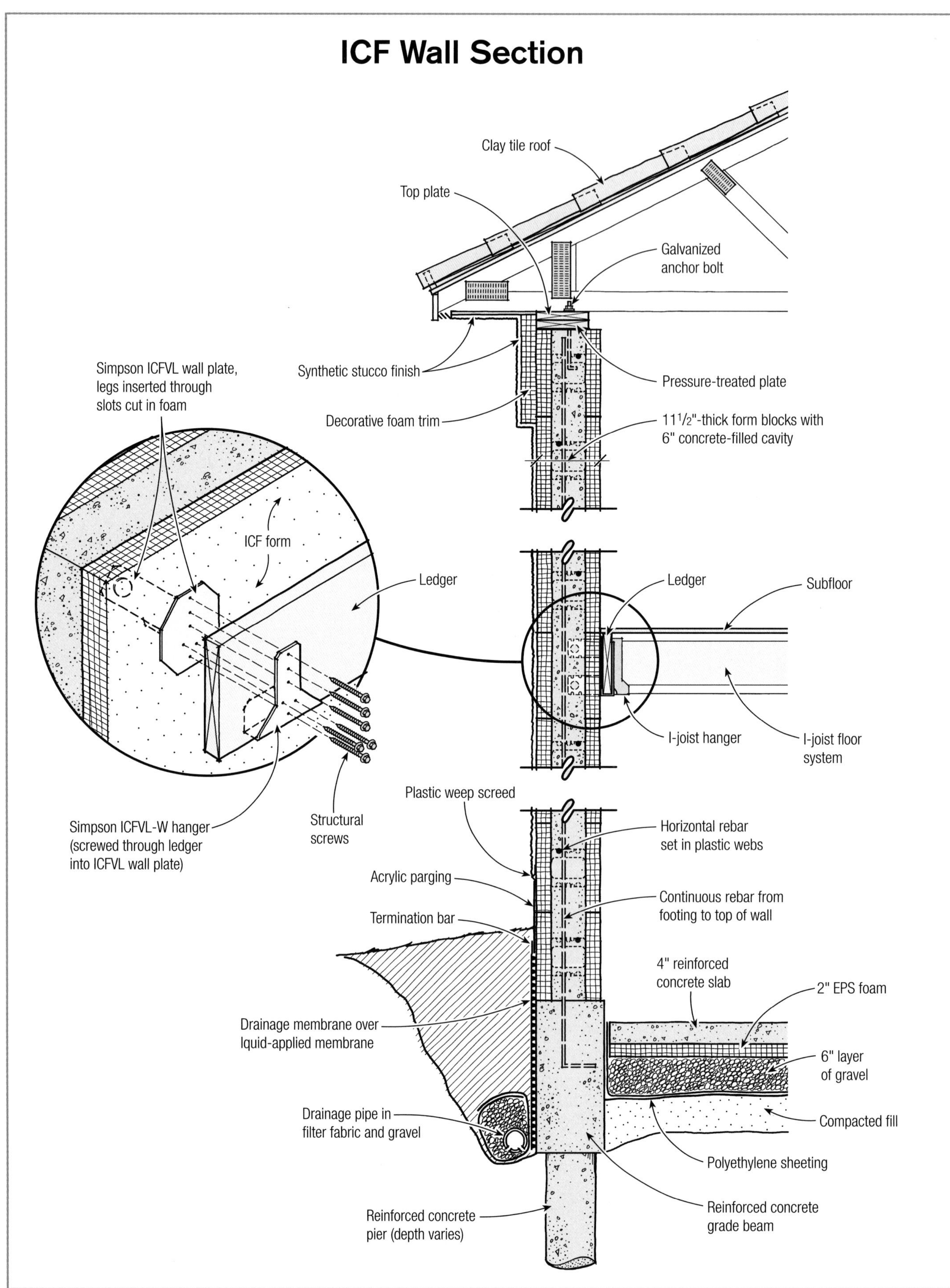
ICF Wall Section
Clay tile roof
Top plate
Galvanized anchor bolt
Synthetic stucco finish
Pressure-treated plate
Simpson ICFVL wall plate, legs inserted through slots cut in foam
Decorative foam trim
11 1/2"-thick form blocks with 6" concrete-filled cavity
ICF form
Ledger
Ledger
Subfloor
I-joist hanger
I-joist floor system
Simpson ICFVL-W hanger (screwed through ledger into ICFVL wall plate)
Structural screws
Plastic weep screed
Horizontal rebar set in plastic webs
Acrylic parging
Continuous rebar from footing to top of wall
Termination bar
4" reinforced concrete slab
2" EPS foam
Drainage membrane over liquid-applied membrane
6" layer of gravel
Compacted fill
Drainage pipe in filter fabric and gravel
Polyethylene sheeting
Reinforced concrete pier (depth varies)
Reinforced concrete grade beam

would be a multiple of 48 inches so we wouldn't have to cut blocks. That almost never happens, but we can usually limit cuts to one per course (Figure 22). The problem with cuts is that you lose the tongue or groove that keys one block to the next, which leaves a weak joint that might blow out during the pour. These joints have to be reinforced, so we either glue them with canned spray foam or screw a plywood gusset to the plastic webs in the foam.

Two at once. We lay the first two courses at once, fastening the first course together with zip ties, snapping in the horizontal rebar, then stacking the second course on top and zip-tying it to the course below (Figure 23). This gives us a long run of blocks that can

Figure 22. To minimize cutting, the crew works from the corners toward the middle of the wall with full blocks and fills in the last piece. Here a carpenter trims (left) and installs (above) the last block in a course.

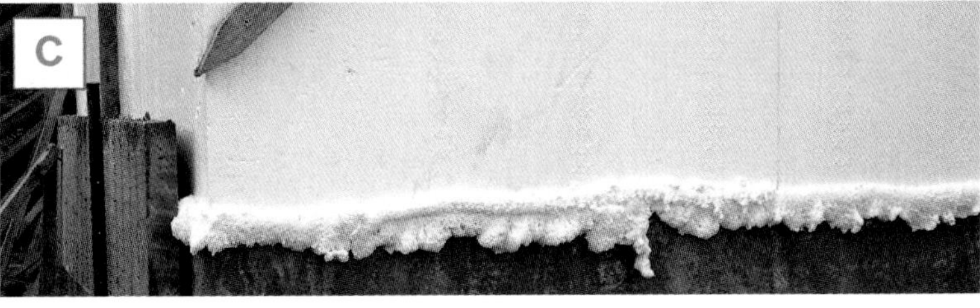

Figure 23. The author prefers to fasten the first two courses together (A), using zip ties (B). He then straightens and levels the two courses as a unit, which he glues to the footing with spray foam (C).

be positioned and leveled as a unit. We use a laser to check the wall for level, then shim or trim the bottom edge as necessary. Once the wall sits straight and level on the foundation, we glue it down with low-expansion polyurethane foam.

Each successive course keys onto the one below and is secured to it with zip ties. We install the horizontal rebar as we go, according to the plans, and every few courses we put in "form lock" — zigzag wire bracing that snaps into the plastic webs and helps straighten and stiffen the forms. When the ICFs reach the top of the vertical rebar — which starts at the footing — we splice on new pieces with tie wires so that the reinforcing is continuous to the top of the wall.

Curved walls. We considered special-ordering curved ICFs for the home's 30-foot radius walls, but for budget

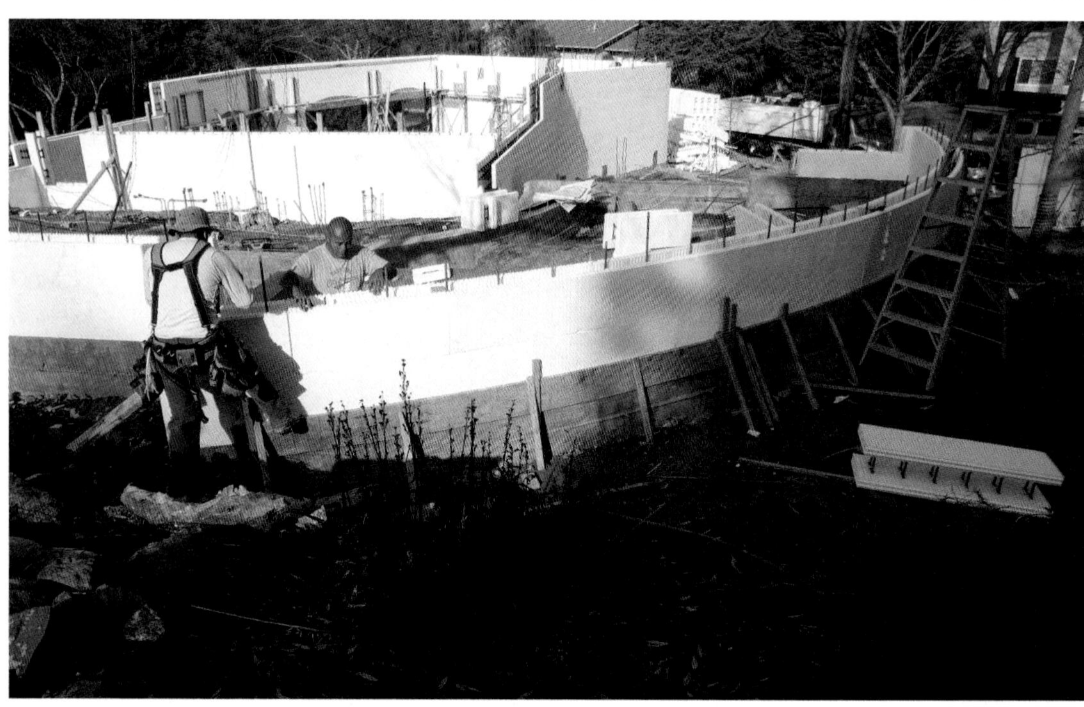

Figure 24. The crew created the curve by cutting the inside faces of the block slightly shorter than the outside faces and flexing the pieces into an arc. Kerfed 2x10 braces hold the bottom course in line with the grade beam.

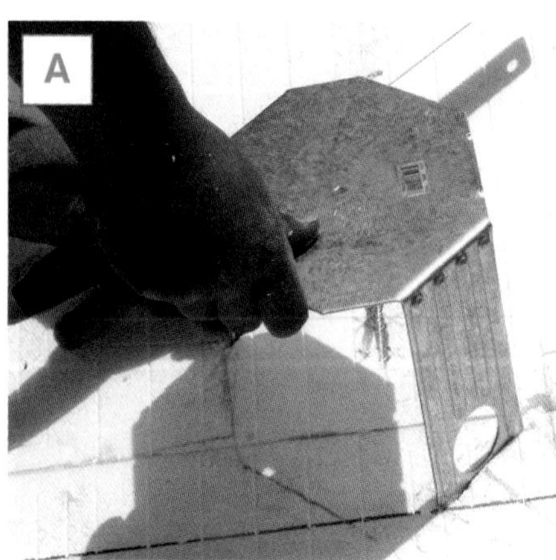

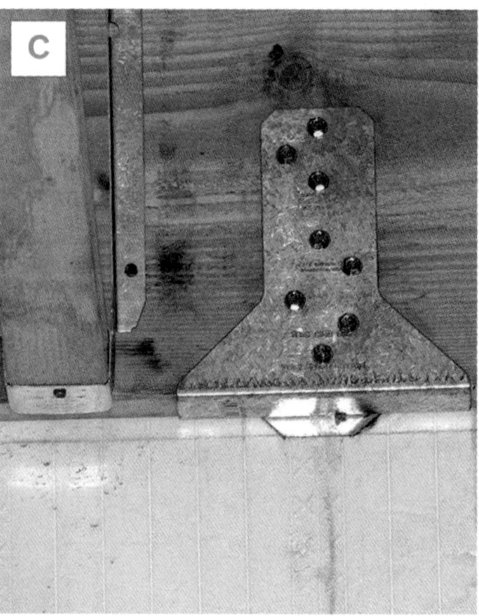

Figure 25. The upper floor hangs from ledgers attached with Simpson hardware designed for ICFs. The legs of the metal plate — punched so that they will key into the concrete — are inserted into slots in the foam (A). Then the plate is fastened with a screw so it can't fall out during the pour (B). After the concrete cures, the ledger is positioned against the wall and fastened to the plate with structural screws driven through a special hanger (C).

and schedule reasons ended up fashioning the curved blocks ourselves, from straight ones. We followed a table in the Logix manual that shows how to make various curves by shortening the inside face of standard blocks.

By flexing the blocks slightly, we were able to get them to follow the desired curve. Continuous bracing along the grade beam — kerfed 2x10s — held the bottom course in place; then each succeeding course mated with the nibs of the one below (Figure 24). Considering that they were made from straight blocks, the curves were surprisingly smooth. There were a few lumps and bumps, but nothing we couldn't fix with a belt sander.

Fastening Ledgers

Floor joists in ICF buildings have traditionally hung from ledgers fastened with cast-in anchor bolts. On this job, we saved time by using Simpson's ICF ledger-connector hardware (Figure 25). In accordance with this method, we inserted the legs of an ICFVL wall plate through slots cut in the foam; the concrete anchors the plate. To install the 2-by ledgers, we placed them against the wall plates, lapped them with ICFVL-W hangers, and drove structural screws through into the plates. Hangers for LVL ledgers are also available, while light-gauge steel ledgers can be screwed directly to the plate.

We spaced the wall plates 32 inches apart, taking care to locate them so that the ledger hangers wouldn't interfere with the joist hangers.

Door and Window Openings

If the door and window openings in this house had been rectangular, we could have used vinyl bucks. But because the heads were arched, we built wooden bucks on site (Figure 26).

Often, door and window bucks can be left in place after the pour. But the doors and windows in this house were inset — and the exterior jambs finished with stucco — so the bucks would have to be removed. To make this easier, we fastened the bucks with metal framing angles and screws (Figure 27).

For the arch-top openings in curved walls, we made the bucks straight but much thicker than the wall, to accommodate the radius (Figure 28).

Bracing and Pouring

Solid bracing is, of course, key to a successful pour, because wet concrete places a lot of pressure on the ICFs. We used the standard adjustable metal bracing designed to hold staging planks (Figure 29) and added wood bracing at those locations where the connections were the weakest — at cut blocks, for example, and at inside corners and the ends of walls. The smaller bucks were faced with solid sheets of OSB and were stiff enough to resist the force of wet concrete.

Figure 26. Carpenters plumb and brace the buck for an arch-top window (left). The buck for the garage opening is supported on a temporary stud wall; the pressure-treated side jambs will remain in place for fastening the overhead door tracks (right).

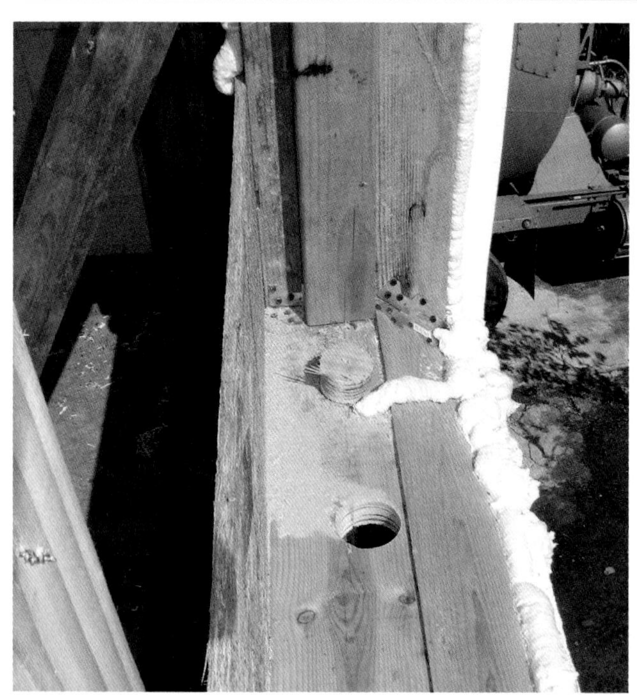

Figure 27. To make it easy to remove, this window buck was assembled from the inside with framing angles and screws. Note the sloped sill; the inspection holes allow carpenters to verify that concrete has filled the blocks below.

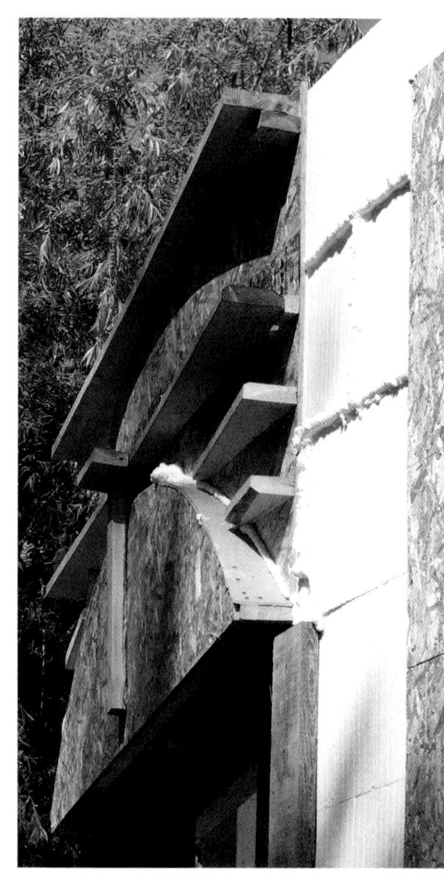

Figure 28. The arched bucks in curved walls were made extra wide to accommodate the radius.

Figure 29. In preparation for concrete, the window bucks were reinforced with additional pieces of OSB and the wall thoroughly braced.

Figure 30. The crew stacked and poured the wall in two stages -- the first came just above the main floor level. The amount of rebar in the ICFs made it impossible to use a tremie pipe to place the concrete. Instead, one worker handled the hose at the top of the wall section, and another followed behind with the vibrator.

The bucks in the larger openings required additional vertical and horizontal bracing.

We stacked and poured the walls in stages. The first stage brought the walls to just above the main floor level. After a week of curing time, we framed and sheathed the floor, and then we formed and poured the rest of the way up.

Concrete. We used a 5-inch-slump five-sack mix containing 3⁄8-inch pea gravel and 20 percent fly ash. Normally, we wouldn't drop concrete more than 3 feet, but the forms contained so much rebar the concrete more or less rolled to the bottom. There wasn't room to use a tremie pipe. To avoid blowouts, we worked our way around the perimeter — placing concrete in 3-foot lifts and vibrating as we went (Figure 30). We drilled witness holes through the bottoms of the window bucks so we could see whether the concrete had flowed underneath; if need be, we inserted a rod through the holes to move the concrete.

Plumbing and Electrical

ICF plumbing penetrations are simple: You can sleeve through the form before the pour or drill through after. Drains and vents of up to 2 inches in diameter will fit in a channel in the side of the foam form; we cut the sides of the channel with a recip saw and then rake out the foam with a pry bar.

Electrical wire is run in smaller channels, which we fill with spray foam once the wire's in place. Electrical boxes can be cut into the foam and screwed to the concrete. Logix ICFs are ribbed on the inside; we've found that if we cut through the foam and remove the concrete ribs with a cold chisel, a standard electrical box will come out flush with the drywall.

Exterior Finish

To keep the below-grade portions of the building dry, we waterproofed the foundation with Tremproof 250 GC (www.tremcosealants.com), then covered it with MiraDrain 2000 (www.carlisle-ccw.com), a polyethylene air-gap membrane that drains water away from the wall.

Though ICF homes are often finished with lap siding, stucco is preferred in our area. With ICFs, we use the same synthetic stucco materials used with EIFS, which can be applied directly to the foam without paper and lath.

Our plastering sub applied a base coat of Parflex 304 (www.parex.com) with an embedded layer of fiberglass reinforcing mesh, followed by a second coat of the base-coat material. The top coat was Fino Alto (www.variancefinishes.com), an integrally colored acrylic plaster.

Finally, to protect any areas of exposed foam between the top of the waterproofing and the stucco, we parged with Thoroseal (www.thoroproducts.com).

Victor Rasilla *is a working supervisor for Brinton Construction in San Leandro, Calif.*

Chapter 16

SOLAR AND ALTERNATIVE ENERGY

- Practical Passive Solar
- Designing Overhangs for South Glass
- Solar Hot Water Basics
- Installing Solar Electric Power
- Builder's Guide to Geothermal Heat Pumps

Practical Passive Solar

by Bruce Torrey

As a builder of energy-efficient homes, I'm often approached by clients who want some form of solar energy at work in their new home or addition. A new house we recently designed and built had the two key components of a successful solar project: a great site and an enthusiastic client.

Active solar systems — which typically involve roof-mounted panels and related equipment — have been making great advances of late and are looking more attractive to a broader spectrum of homeowners. However, at my company we believe that passive solar design considerations should be applied to a design first, before expanding to active solar installations, which can always be a future option.

New window technologies have made passive solar design easier than ever. But it's still essential to start with a tight, well-insulated shell.

And, in fact, as the design for this particular project evolved, it became clear that a full-blown, active solar system would break the budget. We determined that a passive solar approach was the most cost-effective solution and the best fit for this home.

No Moving Parts

From an investment perspective, building to take advantage of passive solar heating is often a prudent upgrade. Many of the key components add little or no cost, since they require only simple design modifications using conventional building materials.

Ordinary windows and patio doors, for instance, can act as solar collectors. On many sites, relocating the building's footprint to a more favorable solar orientation costs nothing. The "extra" glazing needed for a house's south wall can be deducted from the north and west elevations. And open floor plans and generous natural lighting are desirable features in any home, regardless of energy-efficiency issues.

What surprises many people is that, contrary to the popular image of a solar house as tortured into awkward shapes and covered with vast arrays of glazing panels and solar collectors, any home design can be adapted to benefit from passive solar.

Indeed, we now know that glazing need not be vast, let alone sloped. And we know that greenhouse-style enclosures, curved glass roofs, and vast skylight glazing not only detract from a building's aesthetics, but tend to overheat the building during many parts of the year.

The key is to start with well-established solar design guidelines and then apply them with flexibility to meet the clients' wishes and to complement the building's architectural style.

Predicting the Solar Path

Capturing the sun's warmth through south-facing glazing is a fundamental principle of passive solar design.

Since the sun's path and angle are known throughout the seasons, we can design to optimize heat gain in cold seasons and optimize shade in hot ones. This strategy involves aligning the home's solar facade to face close to true — or solar — south, an orientation that optimizes solar gain during the winter months by allowing the low angle of the winter sun to penetrate deep into the building.

The first step with this approach is to find solar south, which varies from magnetic south by a variable number of degrees depending on your location. For more information and to find your region's correction factor — also referred to as its magnetic declination — go to the Web site www.ngdc.noaa.gov/geomagmodels/Declination.jsp and enter your zip code.

Our location in the Northeast dictates an orientation of 15 degrees west of magnetic south, or 195 degrees on a compass set to magnetic north.

To ensure ideal siting of the building and optimal placement of glazing, we turn to a design tool known as the Solar Pathfinder (www.solarpathfinder.com) (Figure 1). Using a transparent convex plastic dome, this device combines a panoramic view of the site with a sun-path diagram. Anything that blocks sunlight — trees, buildings, and the like — is visible as reflections on the surface of the dome; the site's potential shade is thus superimposed on the sun-path diagram. The diagram itself is calibrated to give solar data for every hour of daylight, 365 days a year.

With this information, we can plan building elevations and window placement for maximum winter gains and also decide which deciduous trees to leave for summer shade (Figure 2).

Vertical glazing preferred. The best solar designs strike a balance between aesthetics and solar performance. Achieving this balance requires a careful consideration of both the optimal amount and placement of glazing and the proper ratio of glass to wall and floor space.

Vertical glazing works best because it effectively captures the low-angled winter sun while rejecting much of the high-angled summer sun (Figure 3).

Skylights, roof glass, and sloped greenhouse-style glazing, on the other hand, should be avoided; they can lead to excessive summer heat gain.

Stationary glass is okay, but operable doors and windows are preferable, since they allow ventilation during summer months.

Low-E Glazing

Where I work, in New England, the standard residential window has low-E double glazing, which serves well in passive solar applications. However, it's worth noting that what is sold as "standard" low-E has changed over time and varies from one region to another. Distributors and retailers typically stock windows with the glass that is recommended for their region — low solar gain in hot climates and higher solar gain and lower U-values in cold climates.

Figure 1. Once aligned to solar south, the Solar Pathfinder presents a panoramic view of the site with shading (trees, hills, buildings, and so on) superimposed on a diagram of the sun's average track across the sky throughout the year. Numbers printed along the sun-path arcs give a percentage value of "available sunshine" in half-hour increments. Unshaded numbers can be added to give the total solar energy available for the site on a daily and monthly basis. By comparing the data to regional solar radiation figures published by the National Renewable Energy Laboratory (www.nrel.gov), users can perform an accurate solar site analysis.

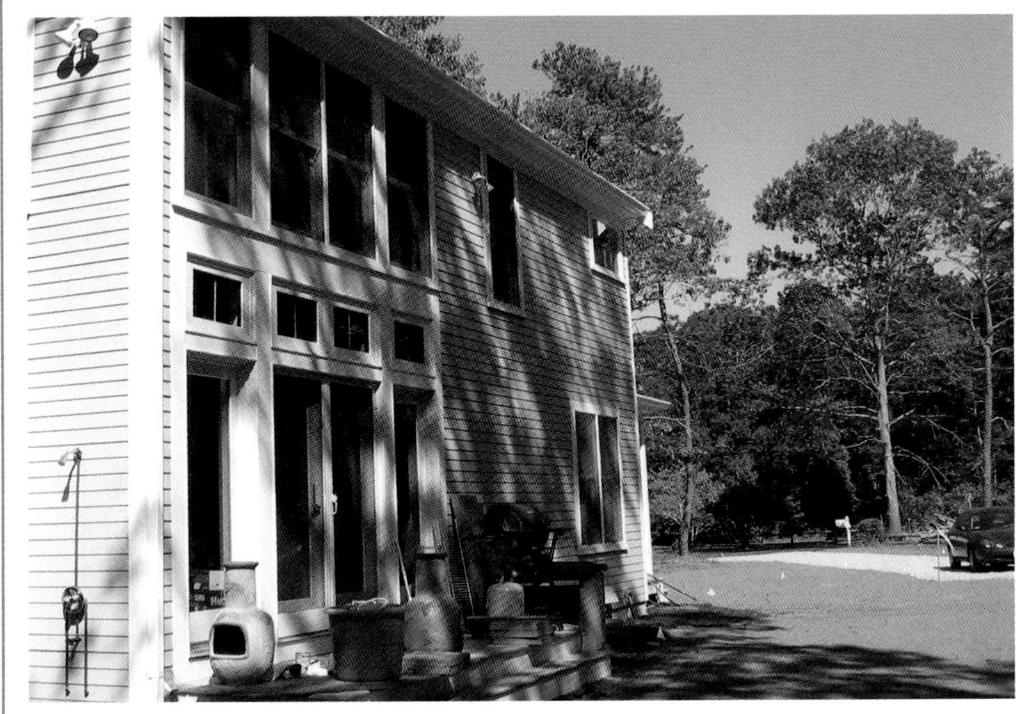

Figure 2. Well-placed deciduous trees can provide good summer shading while allowing much of the winter sun to penetrate. Selective pruning can maximize winter sunshine.

A lot of the windows being shipped now are marketed as "spectrally selective" low-E, which has high R-values but relatively low solar-transmittance values (SHGC — solar heat gain coefficient — of around .25 as opposed to .4 to .6 for "standard" low-E). These units minimize heat loss and reduce overheating problems, but they aren't great for passive solar gain because they reject solar radiation. (For good general information about windows and energy performance, visit the Web sites www.efficientwindows.org and www.nfrc.org and see "Selecting High-Performance Windows," page 152).

Different glass coatings affect solar-transmittance and U-factors to varying degrees, but they always make the solar-gain value lower than that of noncoated glass. In a passive solar application, the main advantage of low-E glass is its resistance to heat loss on cloudy days and after the sun goes down. If you're aiming for optimal passive solar design, with maximum heat gain as the goal, you may want to consider using noncoated double- or triple-pane glazing instead of low-E coatings, along with some form of active insulating shade or shutter to block nighttime heat loss through the windows.

If your clients don't want to bother with insulating shades, however, the latest glazing technologies can help. Glazing manufacturers now offer "spectrally selective" window glass with a wide variety of optical properties, some suited best to hot climates and others to colder climates. For passive solar applications, look for a SHGC of at least .60 and U-factor of .30 or less. This combines excellent solar gain with a high insulating value. For example, glazing manufacturer Cardinal Glass (www.cardinalcorp.com) produces high-solar-gain LoE-179 glazing with a SHGC of .70 combined with a U-factor of .28. Locating these products in your local market may require a bit of research and special ordering, but this may be worth the effort in comfort and energy savings.

Window placement. Typically, site conditions, landscape views, ventilation needs, and client preferences all play a role in dictating window placement. For optimal solar performance, the south-facing glass area should total between 7 and 12 percent of the total finished floor area. A "sun-tempered" house with about 7 percent south glazing does not generally require additional thermal mass. A passive solar house with south glazing in excess of 7 percent requires adding thermal mass to absorb the excess solar heat on sunny days to keep the building from overheating. The thermal mass releases its stored heat to the room later in the day as temperatures drop.

While thermal mass reduces temperature swings in the interior space, it can also have a downside: A high-mass home in New England can be pretty uncomfortable if the mass is allowed to chill after a few days of cloudy weather and low thermostat settings. Then the homeowner will experience radiant cooling (which

Figure 3. Vertical glazing allows the low-angle winter sun to penetrate deep into a house while mostly excluding the high summer sun, thereby avoiding overheating during the summer (above and right). Sloped glazing, by contrast, allows year-round penetration and can create uncomfortable overheating during the nonwinter months.

feels like standing next to a big cold rock) until the mass is brought up to comfortable temperatures, a process that can take a long time. The best defense against this experience is the backup heating system and a set-it-and-forget-it thermostat mindset — that is, set the thermostat at, say, 68°F, and then leave it alone.

Ideally, north-, east-, and west-facing glazing should each total less than 4 percent of the finished floor area. But when a desirable view lies in any of these nonsoutherly directions, natural or mechanical shade and insulating blinds can add some flexibility to those guidelines. Shading is most relevant with west-facing glass, a common source of overheating in summer months. East-facing glass doesn't present a problem in New England, but this may not be the case in warmer climates. With north-facing glass, the problem is usually heat loss, not shading.

Our clients' preference for an early start in the mornings called for east-facing bedroom and kitchen windows to jump-start their day. We located the open-space family room, used primarily during the day, on the south side of the house, where it could benefit from the prime solar-gain hours between 10 a.m. and 2 p.m. And we located the garage and storage areas on the home's north side, where they'd help buffer the house against winter winds.

Shading. Shading can be an important way to prevent overheating, particularly in homes with large expanses of west-facing glass. But in my experience, configuring building overhangs to provide shade is often impractical. I once asked an architect to design an overhang for a westerly facade, where the late afternoon sun would pour in during the summer months. He estimated that we'd need an overhang that was about 12 feet deep.

In this project, the practical answer was as simple as installing and using window blinds. However, if a plan requires a lot of exposed west-facing glass, then "solar control" or heat-reflecting glass with a low SHGC — plus shades — might be required to prevent overheating.

Shading vertical south-facing windows with fixed overhangs is easier, due to the high angle of the midday sun during the summer months). Doing so is usually unnecessary, though; little of that high summer sun enters the building anyway. Operable windows can reduce the need for shade on the south facade even further. However, for large expanses of south glass where summertime glare or overheating might be an issue, shading with overhangs is recommended (see "Designing Overhangs for South Glass," page 366).

Conservation First

All successful passive solar homes start with a tight, well-insulated building shell. Higher R-values and airtight shell details, along with advances in low-E glazing materials, combine to make the passive solar concept a practical reality, with today's designs easily

Figure 4. The author blows dense-pack cellulose insulation into the 2x6 wall cavities at about 3.5 pounds per cubic foot, yielding a nominal R-20. Adding a 1-inch layer of polystyrene foam board on the interior, taped at seams, blocks air leakage, slows vapor transmission, and adds R-value while addressing thermal bridging through the wood framing (above and right).

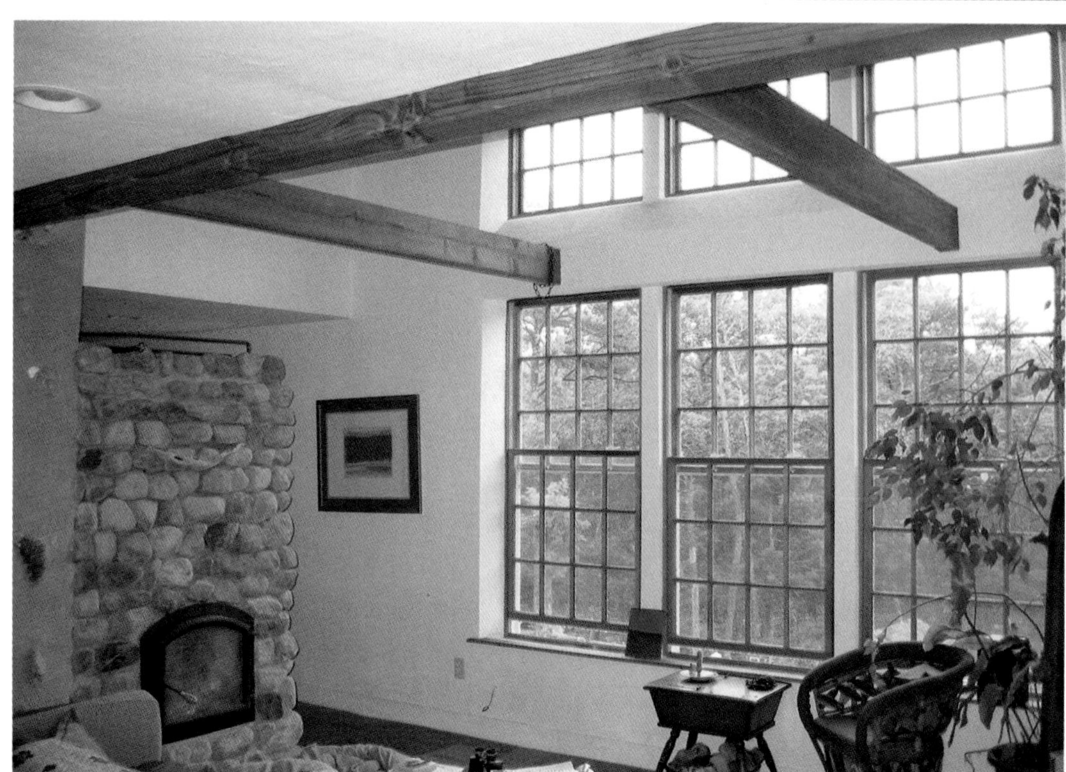

Figure 5. The stone facing on this fireplace wall receives direct winter sunlight and thus serves double-duty as direct thermal mass. Out of direct sunshine, dense masonry materials serve as indirect mass, storing daytime solar energy and releasing it at night as indoor temperatures drop.

outperforming earlier solar homes.

Our standard insulation package — a combination of blown cellulose and airtight rigid-foam insulation — creates a high-performance thermal shell. By using dense-pack cellulose and a 1-inch layer of taped foam board under the drywall, we achieve a nominal value of R-24 in the 2x6 wall cavities (Figure 4). Ceiling values — again, using blown cellulose — are around R-45, and the floor system averages R-22, thanks to fiberglass batts and an application of sprayed foam around rim joists.

Simple Solar Storage

As mentioned previously, adding thermal mass for heat storage is an essential element in passive solar homes with south glass in excess of 7 percent of the total floor area. Solar heat gains are absorbed by the mass during sunny days and released after sunset to help maintain comfort levels. Strategic thermal mass also helps temper the rate of heat gain, helping to prevent overheating. A wide range of materials can be used to absorb both direct and indirect solar energy during the day, including interior masonry walls; poured concrete slabs; and stone, ceramic tile, or brick on floors and walls (Figure 5).

Mass thickness. Generally, the denser the material, the better its thermal-storage properties. Thermal mass works best in thicknesses of 2 to 4 inches, spread out over as large an area as possible. Mass thicker than about 4 inches tends not to absorb or release heat readily enough to be effective, so only the outer 2 to 4 inches should be counted as thermal mass. Note that light-colored mass may reflect, rather than absorb, portions of the solar radiation striking the surface. Stick to darker shades for the best heat absorption in direct-gain — mostly floor — areas.

Direct versus indirect mass. The most effective thermal mass is located to receive direct sunlight. Of course, furniture has to be considered in a floor plan, and furniture blocks direct solar gain. However, thermal mass located out of direct sunlight — called indirect mass — also provides energy-storage benefits, which allows for great design flexibility. By using a mix of materials on various surfaces and locations, you can effectively spread the thermal mass around to accommodate a furnished passive solar home.

Glass-to-mass ratios and distribution. The ratio of south-facing glass to thermal mass areas has to be considered during the design phase.

The "ideal" ratio of thermal mass to glazing varies by climate. According to the guides we used in the design phase, for every square foot of south-facing, direct-gain glazing in excess of 7 percent of the overall floor area, you need about 5.5 square feet of high-mass floor space in direct sunlight. If not enough high-mass floor is in direct sunlight, other high-mass floor areas as well as walls and ceilings can serve as thermal mass. Recommended ratios of window area to mass are 1:40 for floors not in direct sunlight and 1:8 for walls and ceilings in line-of-sight with sunlit surfaces.

(Our main design guide, *Passive Solar Design Strategies*, is no longer published, but most of its content can be found in the Sustainable Buildings Industry Council's newly updated publication *Green Building Guidelines: Meeting the Demand for Low-Energy, Resource-Efficient Homes*, available at www.sbicouncil.org.)

The 2,000-square-foot house shown on these pages happened to have 200 square feet of south-facing glass, equal to 10 percent of the floor area. This put us over the ideal glazing ratio of 7 percent of total floor area by 60 square feet:

2,000 sq.ft. x 7% = 140 sq.ft.
200 sq.ft. - 140 sq.ft. = 60 sq.ft.

So, to avoid potential overheating on sunny days, we needed to add thermal mass to absorb the gain. For every square foot of south-facing glass exceeding 7 percent of the home's overall square footage, another 5½ square feet of direct-gain thermal mass needs to be provided. This meant we needed to add 330 square feet (60 x 5.5 = 330) of direct-gain thermal mass.

We opted to install a concrete "thin slab" — 1½ inches of poured concrete over wood framing as a base for a ½-inch-thick ceramic tile floor. To handle the dead load of the concrete, we upgraded the floor framing and moved the door headers up 2 inches to accommodate the extra floor thickness.

Since the owners wanted an open floor plan, most of this thermal-mass floor was directly exposed to the sun during the peak winter solar hours.

Because of the vagaries of furniture placement and actual "direct sunlight" in the room, it's hard to get exact in defining "direct gain," but we calculated the direct-gain value of the family room floor area at 275 square feet, taking care of about 50 square feet of the south-facing glass (50 x 5.5 = 275). This still left us about 10 square feet shy of the ideal ratio, so to achieve the total thermal mass requirement, we installed a ½-inch layer of cement backerboard behind the drywall on an interior partition that received direct winter sun.

This is a good example of the flexibility inherent in passive solar design. You don't have to be slavishly precise with these ratios, and you can mix and match direct and indirect thermal mass to achieve the general levels required.

However, remember that rules of thumb are just general guidelines and may need to be tweaked for different climate zones. Also, with the wide range of glazing types now available, the old rules may not always apply. To be safe, when the south glass area in your design exceeds seven percent of the total floor area, it's a good idea to have an experienced solar designer review your plans to make sure that your design will provide the expected comfort and energy savings.

Growing Solar Demand

Against a backdrop of rising energy prices and growing consumer demand for increased comfort, solar strategies really start to make sense. In this home, we knew the passive solar features wouldn't supply all of the home's heating needs. Sunless days and heat loss through the glass at night will always compromise passive-solar performance. However, the house's upgraded insulation and airtightness helped reduce the heating load to such an extent that we could meet the home's backup heating needs with a conventional high-efficiency water heater.

Basking in the radiant warmth of the sun during those cold winter months, with the thermostat turned down, is an appealing concept for potential clients. Suggesting they take advantage of these benefits is an easy sale and allows us to pursue the type of project that separates us from the competition.

***Bruce Torrey** is a consultant with Building Diagnostics in East Sandwich, Mass.*

Designing Overhangs for South Glass

by Jerry Germer

The intersection of a roof and wall is an area where seemingly minor design decisions can have a much larger effect on a home's feel and function. At a bare minimum, an overhang must be substantial enough to prevent rain and melting snow from soaking the siding, especially at the eaves. But from the standpoint of homeowner comfort, the most important characteristic of a well-designed overhang is the ability to control the amount of sunlight and solar heat that enter south-facing windows.

Sunlight and Shadow

Most houses benefit from sunlight in the cold winter months. Any heat gained from the sun cuts fuel bills while the natural light lifts spirits on short winter days. But while an abundance of south-facing glass may look great from the outside, it can be tough to live with. If the overhang doesn't provide sufficient shade, the free heat that is so welcome in January can turn an interior into a glare-filled hotbox in July.

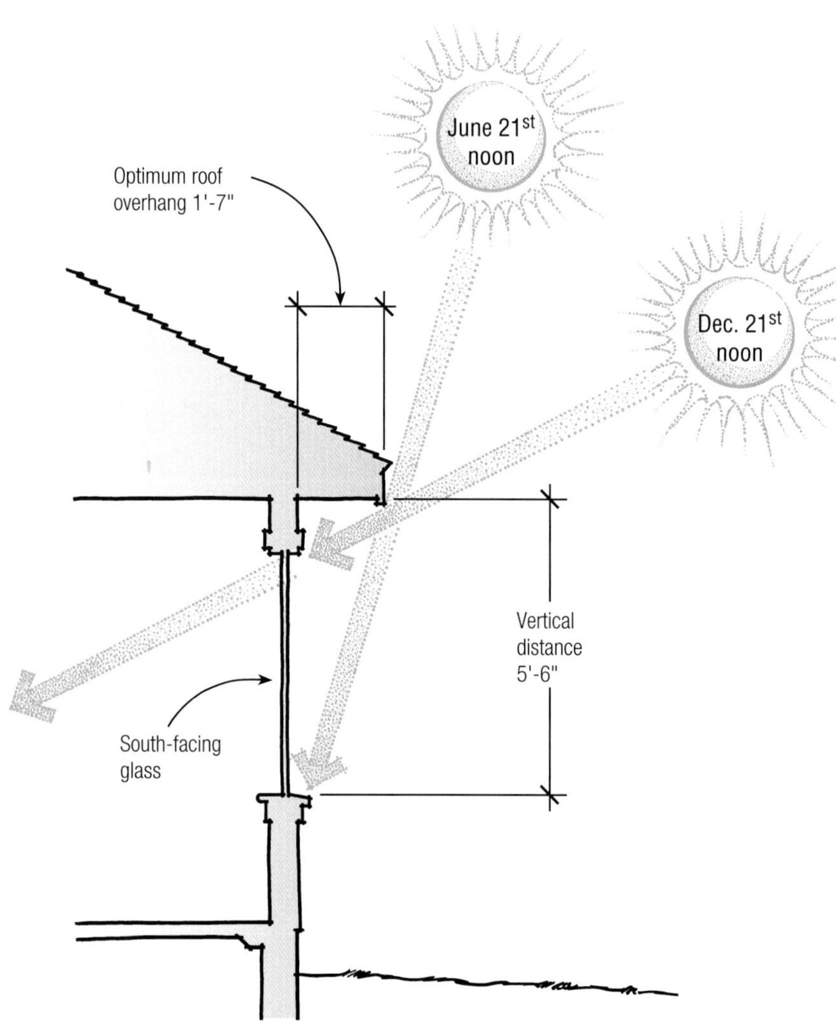

Figure 6. Multiplying the vertical distance from a south-facing windowsill to the roof overhang by the appropriate "overhang factor" provides a width that combines summer shading with maximum winter sun. In this case, on a site at latitude 40°, the window gets an overhang of 1 foot 7 inches through this calculation: 5.5 feet (5 feet 6 inches) x 0.29 = 1.6 feet.

Overhangs by the Numbers

Several variables enter into the seasonally varying amount of shade an overhang provides, and sizing it by guesswork can yield some unpleasant surprises. But fortunately, it's easy to calculate the optimum overhang extension for your area and your windows with the information contained in the table below:

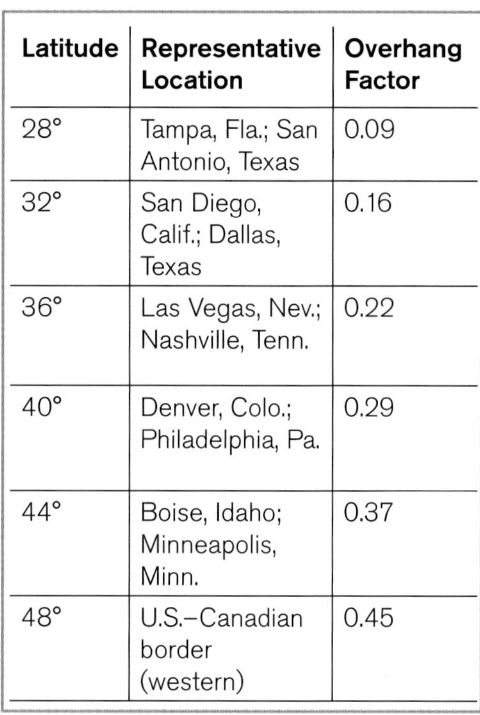

Latitude	Representative Location	Overhang Factor
28°	Tampa, Fla.; San Antonio, Texas	0.09
32°	San Diego, Calif.; Dallas, Texas	0.16
36°	Las Vegas, Nev.; Nashville, Tenn.	0.22
40°	Denver, Colo.; Philadelphia, Pa.	0.29
44°	Boise, Idaho; Minneapolis, Minn.	0.37
48°	U.S.–Canadian border (western)	0.45

As illustrated in Figure 6, simply select the appropriate "overhang factor" for your latitude and multiply it by the vertical distance between the windowsill and the lowest point on the overhang. The resulting dimension is the overhang width that will provide complete noontime shade on the longest day of summer, and

Roof Overhang Options

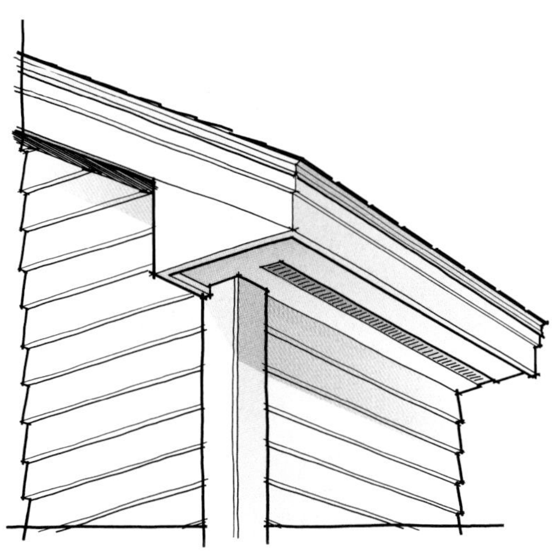

This pared-down version of the ornate cornice returns common on older homes works best where a relatively narrow overhang is called for.

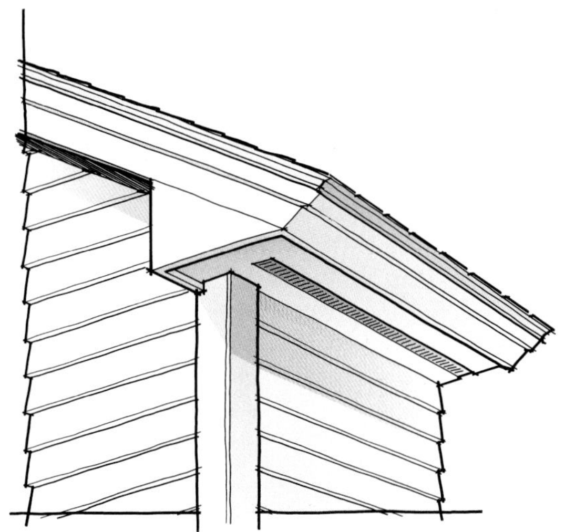

Replacing the flat eaves fascia with a sloping one gives a more contemporary look that 's appropriate where more shading is needed.

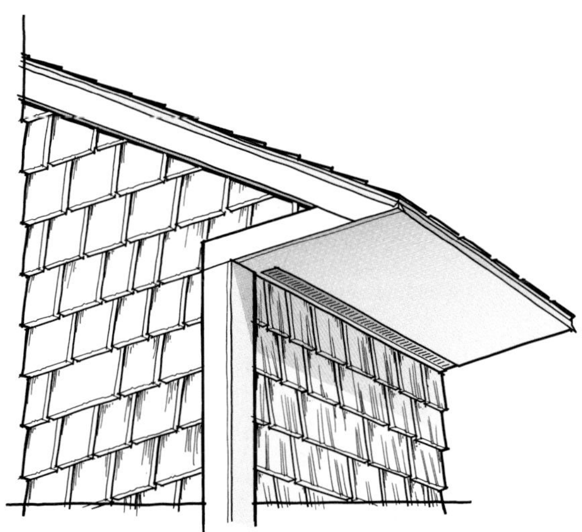

Do away with the eaves fascia board altogether for a modern approach that looks best with a steep roof and an overhang of 30 inches or more.

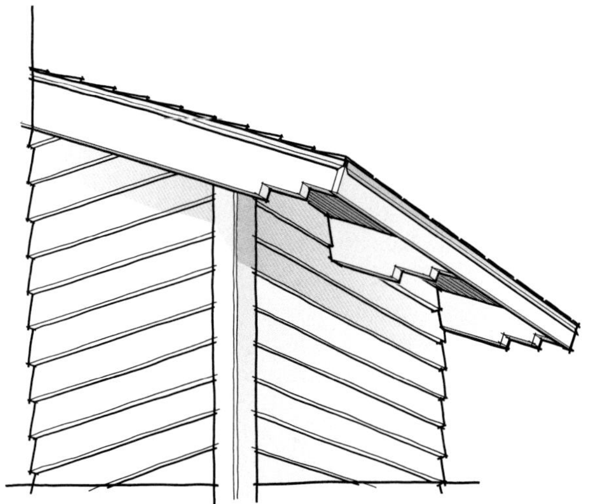

Another option is to leave rafter tails exposed and cut them into ornamental profiles, as in many bungalows and Arts and Crafts houses from the early 1900s.

full sunlight on the shortest day of winter.

If there's a lot of glass low on the wall, the required overhang may be several feet wide, making it a prominent exterior design element as well. That's another issue, and one that can be addressed in any number of ways. The drawings above show some designs that may work well when a broad overhang is needed.

***Jerry Germer** is an architect and freelance writer in Marlborough, N.H.*

Solar Hot Water Basics

by Gary Gerber

My company has been designing and installing alternative energy systems since 1975; to date, we've installed more than 1,000 solar water heating systems. Lately, as energy prices rise at an ever-accelerating rate, we've seen renewed interest in solar hot water.

A simple solar hot-water system can be installed for as little as $4,000, while a larger and more complicated freeze-protected system can cost as much as $10,000. Thanks to a variety of tax credits, subsidies, and rebates, the customer's cost is often well below the sticker price. A listing of all local, state, federal, and utility-based programs can be found at www.dsireusa.org.

In areas where natural-gas water heaters are the norm, the payback period for a residential solar water heating system will be 9 to 12 years with the $2,000 federal tax credit in place at the time this was written. Because a well-designed system will last 20 to 30 years, it should pay for itself two to three times over. If the system saves $250 worth of natural gas the first year and gas prices escalate 5 percent per year, then it will save almost $17,000 over 30 years. If the homeowner is currently using an electric water heater, the savings may top $40,000.

On the environmental side, heating water with the sun will typically reduce a home's greenhouse gas emissions by 18 tons over the life of the system. With an extra 60 to 120 gallons of hot water at their disposal, homeowners can take long, guilt-free showers. We often equip our solar hot-water systems with valves that allow the customer to completely shut off the backup heater and use only solar-heated water in the summer.

For reliable, long-term performance, it's important to match the design to the climate and to work with an experienced solar installer.

Solar Water Heating Basics

All solar water heating systems contain collection, storage, and transfer components; some systems combine all three into a single element. Most systems are designed to preheat water that goes to a backup heater — typically a conventional gas or electric water heater. A tankless heater will also work as a backup, as long as it is designed to accept hot-water input (not all of them are).

Although there are some systems in which the preheated water flows directly to the backup, it's more common for the preheated water to be stored in a separate storage tank upstream from the backup. In hot, sunny weather, the backup is rarely if ever needed, but during cloudy periods it may have to provide virtually all the domestic hot water.

Collection. The most visible part of any solar hot-water system is the collector. There are three main types of collectors, but all basically consist of a black collecting surface that transfers heat to a fluid. The collecting surface is typically enclosed in an insulated aluminum box with clear glazing to trap the heat.

A flat-plate collector — which is about 3 inches thick — contains a grid of copper tubing attached to an aluminum or copper plate (Figure 7). Both components have a black surface coating; when sunlight hits the plate, heat is conducted to the fluid inside the tubing. Sensors measure the temperature in the collector, and when it's hotter than the fluid in the system's storage tank, an electronic controller activates a pump to move the heated fluid to the tank. The uninstalled cost of a 4-by-8-foot flat-plate collector is approximately $750 to $1,000.

An evacuated tube collector is similar to a flat-plate collector except that the heat-absorbing tubes are housed in a series of evacuated glass cylinders. The vacuum insulates against heat loss in the same way that a thermos bottle does. Evacuated tube collectors are extremely efficient but cost about twice as much as conventional flat-plate collectors.

In an integral collector storage — or ICS — unit,

Figure 7. Flat-plate collectors (left) range in size from 3 by 6 feet to 4 by 12 feet and are light enough to be carried by hand (right). Because the tubing inside is of small diameter, even a large collector might contain only a gallon or two of fluid.

Figure 8. Integral collector storage units (also called ICSs or "batch heaters") contain 4-inch-diameter pipes in which water is heated and stored (A). Because of their weight, they are typically craned into place (B). Potable water enters through a pipe at the lower end, is heated by the sun, and exits through the upper end (C) when a hot-water tap is turned on.

water is heated and stored in a series of interconnecting tubes in a roof-mounted box. Sometimes called batch heaters, ICS systems are simple and inexpensive because they require no pumps or controls. However, since they store water in an exposed location, they are subject to high heat loss and freezing (Figure 8). A 42-gallon ICS unit costs about $2,100 uninstalled.

Storage. Solar energy is available only for the 6 to 10

Figure 9. An installer plumbs an 80-gallon storage tank for a pumped system (left). The tank has taps for supply and return lines to and from the collector, plus a cold-water supply inlet and a hot-water outlet to the home (above).

Integral Collector Storage (ICS) System

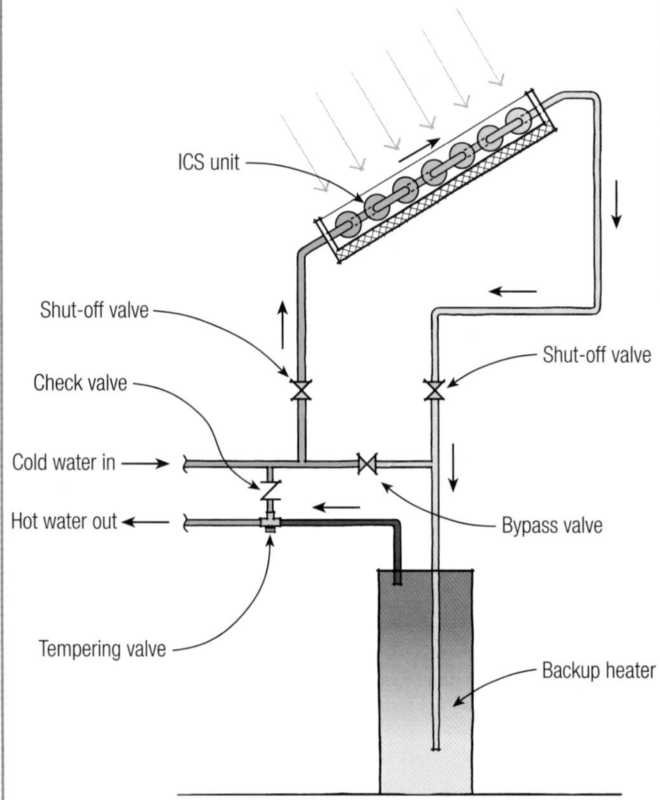

Figure 10. Since ICS heaters both heat and store water in the rooftop collector, they can be quite heavy, requiring reinforced roof framing. They are not well suited for cold climates.

hours that the sun is out, so heated water must be stored for later use. While ICS systems store hot water right in the collector, most other systems keep it in a separate storage tank located upstream from the backup heater. Because the tank has to hold an entire day's worth of hot water, it is larger than a conventional heater.

There are some systems that send solar-heated water directly to the backup, but I'm not a fan of doing this with a conventional backup heater. Because it's too small to hold an entire day's worth of water, this kind of heater will short-cycle and heat the water before the sun has a chance to do its job.

In pumped systems, storage takes place in a pressurized steel tank that resembles an electric hot-water heater. Usually located near the backup heater, this storage tank connects to the collectors with copper pipes (Figure 9).

ICS and thermosiphon systems are pumpless. Water moves through the ICS unit but does not circulate within it. Within thermosiphon systems, which rely on the principle that hot water rises, water circulates between the collector and a tank above.

Transfer. Solar hot-water systems can be categorized according to their method of heat transfer and freeze protection. In open-loop — or direct — systems, potable water flows through the collector and is heated there. In closed-loop — or indirect — systems, the liquid in the collector is isolated from the potable water and transfers heat to it with a heat exchanger next to or inside the storage tank.

Closed-loop systems provide the best freeze protection because the liquid in the collector is chemically or mechanically protected from freezing. Open-loop systems, on the other hand, are subject to freezing

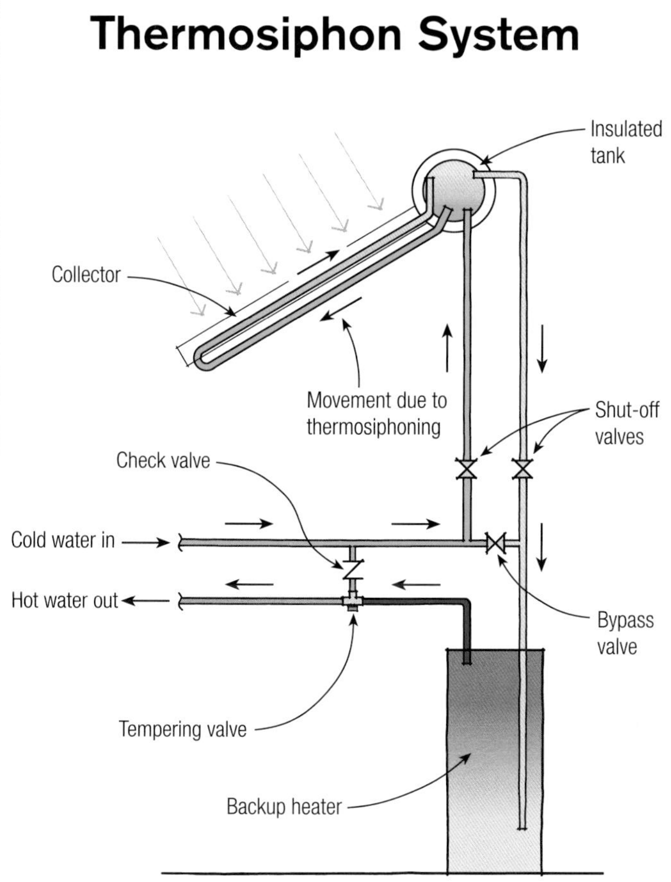

Thermosiphon System

Insulated tank
Collector
Movement due to thermosiphoning
Shut-off valves
Check valve
Cold water in
Hot water out
Bypass valve
Tempering valve
Backup heater

Figure 11. Thermosiphon units rely on convection to move hot water from the collector to the storage tank, which is mounted right above the collector. As hot water rises into the storage tank, cool replacement water enters at the bottom of the collector.

Figure 12. The author's crew always installs a freeze drip valve on the outlet side of the collectors on open-loop systems. If the temperature drops below 35°F, the valve drains enough water from the collectors to bring warm replacement water up from the house.

because the collector contains potable water. While it's possible to provide some freeze protection to open-loop systems, I don't recommend installing them in climate zones where there are hard freezes more than once every five years.

On the following pages, I'll describe the most common system designs, ranging from simpler passive systems to more complex active systems.

Integral Collector Storage

In an ICS system, potable cold water is piped into a roof-mounted unit and preheated by the sun on its way to the backup heater. Water moves through this system only when a hot-water tap is opened (Figure 10). An ICS system is simple and relatively inexpensive, but a lot of heat can be lost through the glass, so the backup has to run if the client wants hot water first thing in the morning.

Early manufacturers of ICS systems simply placed a single bulk storage tank within a glass-covered insulated enclosure aimed at the sun. Newer designs typically consist of an interconnected series of 4-inch-diameter copper tubes in an 8-inch-deep insulated box with glazing on top.

With a capacity ranging from 20 to 50 gallons, these collectors can be quite heavy. They are also subject to freezing, because the water is stored on the roof.

Thermosiphon Systems

Like an ICS system, a thermosiphon system has no pump, but it's more efficient because it separates heating and storage functions. When sunlight hits the collector, the liquid inside heats up and becomes buoyant, then flows up to the storage tank, which is located above the collector. It's replaced by cooler liquid that flows down from a separate line on the bottom of the storage tank (Figure 11). While a pump would certainly speed up the recirculation process, the convective flow is more than adequate to move the entire contents of the tank through the collector several times per day in sunny weather.

Thermosiphon systems are available in both open-loop and closed-loop configurations. In the open-loop version, the collector contains potable water, whereas the closed-loop version contains a glycol mix that flows to a heat exchanger surrounding the tank.

Two mechanisms provide freeze protection in an open-loop thermosiphon system. Water gets lighter just before it turns to ice, creating a "reverse thermosiphon" that pulls warm water down from the tank. I don't rely on this phenomenon alone, however; we also install a freeze drip valve, which opens when the collector temperature reaches 35°F (Figure 12). This

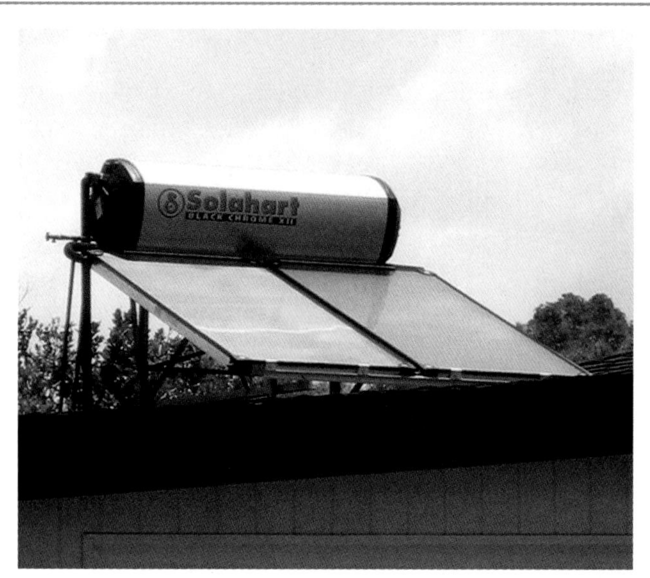

Figure 13. Because it's located in a warm climate, this thermosiphon unit contains potable water. Closed-loop thermosiphon systems containing glycol are also available for areas where freezing temperatures are common.

bleeds water from the collector and brings warm replacement water from the tank. Normally, the freeze valve won't open unless the primary protection fails.

Since they don't involve any pumps or controllers, thermosiphon systems are simple and extremely reliable. But, because the tank is outside, they have low flow rates and high storage losses, making them less efficient than pumped systems. Also, the tank in these systems is typically mounted on the roof, which means there are aesthetic and structural issues to deal with, too (Figure 13).

Open-Loop Recirculation

In an open-loop recirculation system, pressurized potable water is actively pumped between the collectors mounted on the roof and a storage tank installed inside the house (Figure 14). Heat sensors wired to an electronic controller activate the electric recirculating pump — typically whenever the collectors are 5°F warmer than the tank. This "differential" control causes the pump to run continuously as long as the sun is out (Figure 15).

If the weather gets cold enough, the collector could freeze and burst, so when the controller senses an imminent freeze, the pump comes on and brings warm water up from the indoor tank. It shuts off once the collectors reach 40°F. While this is a simple

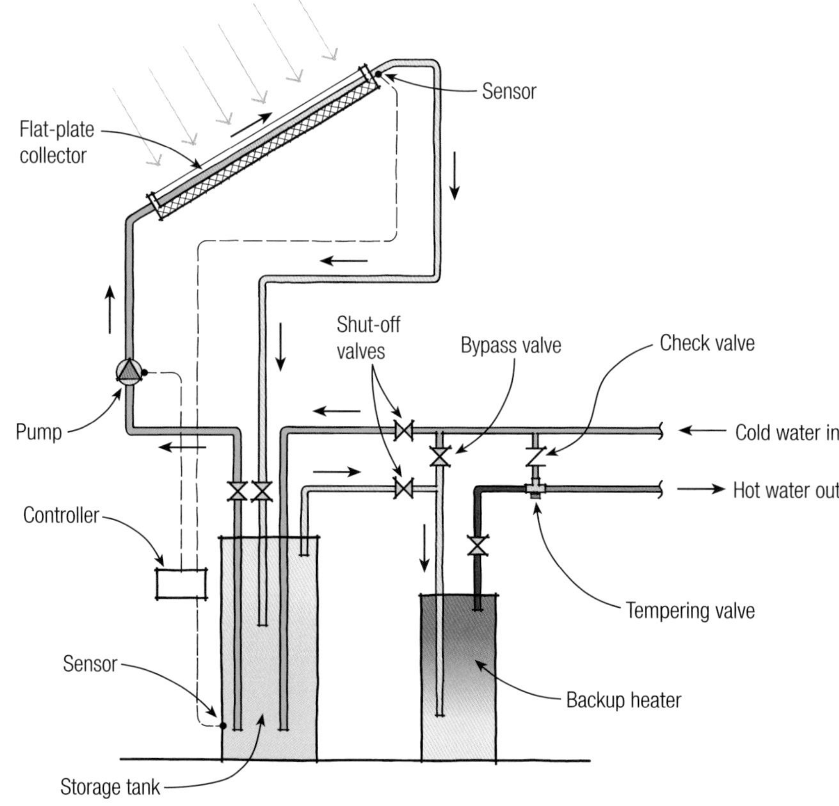

Figure 14. In an open-loop recirculating system, a sensor-activated pump moves water between the collector and the storage tank whenever the collector's temperature is warmer than the tank's. When the temperature drops, the sensor activates the pump to bring warm water from the tank back into the collector to protect against freezing.

method of freeze protection, it's not particularly energy efficient, and there are several ways it might fail: Power may go out, the pump can stop working, or a sensor or controller might malfunction. So, again, we always install a freeze drip valve just in case.

Although more expensive than such passive systems as thermosiphon and ICS, open-loop recirculation costs less than other types of pumped systems.

Closed-Loop Antifreeze System

A closed-loop antifreeze system is designed for areas with moderate to frequent freezing. These systems resemble pumped open-loop systems, except they have additional components such as a heat exchanger, two independent sets of pipes, and sometimes a second circulating pump. One pump circulates antifreeze between the collectors and a heat exchanger, while the other circulates potable water between the heat exchanger and the storage tank (Figure 16).

A typical heat exchanger consists of a pair of concentric copper pipes. Liquid from the collectors flows through one pipe and potable water flows through the other. The liquids don't mix, but heat transfers easily though the conductive wall of the inner pipe. It's also possible to exchange heat by running heated fluid through a coil inside the storage tank or backup heater, but an external heat exchanger is usually less expensive and easier to repair.

Because the liquid in the collectors contains a mixture of propylene glycol and water, it won't freeze. Unlike the ethylene glycol used in automobile radiators, this antifreeze is a nontoxic food-grade additive, so if a leak in the heat exchanger did occur, the worst that would happen to the homeowner is that the water might taste sweet. Good-quality antifreeze in a well-designed system should last at least 10 years. But because antifreeze can degrade and become acidic enough to damage the system, it should be periodically replaced.

This type of system is virtually immune to freezing, but the heat exchanger, additional pump, and antifreeze increase the cost of the system.

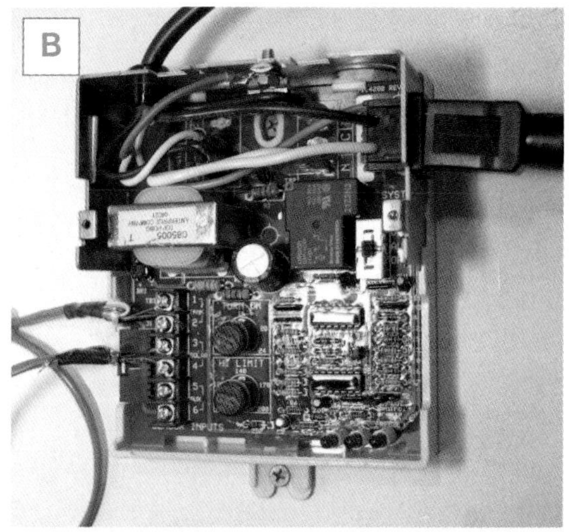

Figure 15. An installer inserts a heat sensor into a flat-plate collector (A); this sensor and another one on the storage tank connect to an electronic controller (B) that activates the pump (top center in photo C) whenever the collector is 5°F hotter than the tank.

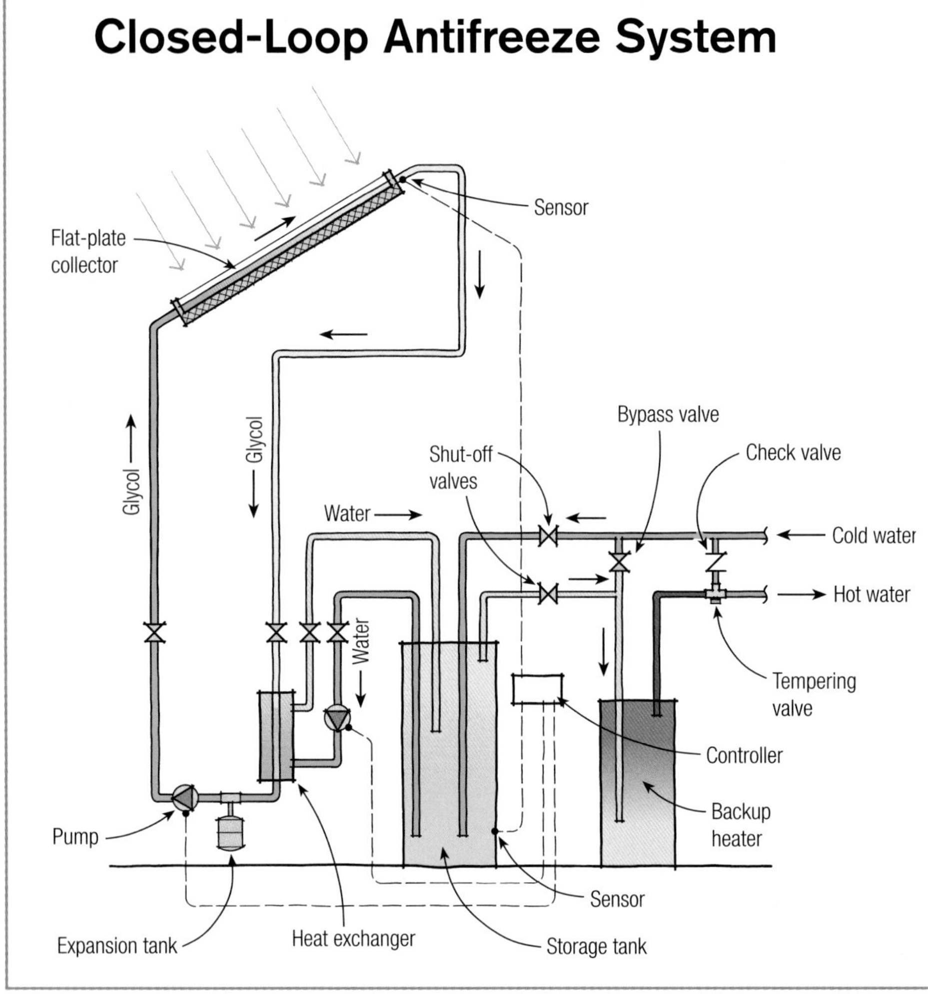

Figure 16. Designed for cold climates, closed-loop antifreeze systems use glycol to protect the collector. This requires a heat exchanger to transfer heat to the potable water, and a second pump to circulate domestic water between the heat exchanger and storage tank.

Drain-Back System

A drain-back system is a closed-loop system that relies on a pump to lift distilled water from a nonpressurized indoor reservoir and move it through the collector. When the outdoor temperature is high enough and the collector is warmer than the reservoir, the pump comes on and circulates water between the reservoir and collector. When the pump is off, gravity causes the water to drain out of the collectors and into the reservoir below. The controller won't activate the pump when the outdoor temperature is close to freezing; this keeps water out of the collector, which protects the system (Figure 17).

Solar-heated water is stored in the reservoir and transferred to the potable water with an internal or external heat exchanger. In some designs, a second pump moves water between the heat exchanger and the storage tank. In others, the reservoir is the tank, so there's no need for a second pump.

Drain-back systems provide trouble-free, reliable freeze protection because the closed side of the loop contains distilled water, which, unlike glycol, doesn't require periodic replacement. On the other hand, drain-back systems require greater pump power to lift fluid to the collectors.

Designing the System

Because there are bound to be periods when the sun doesn't shine for several days in a row, there's no point in trying to design a solar water heating system that provides 100 percent of the total yearly hot-water demand. We typically aim for 60 to 80 percent capacity, with the backup heater providing the rest.

As a rule of thumb, we assume that each person in a household uses 20 gallons of hot water per day, so a family of four would need an 80-gallon storage tank. In our mild San Francisco Bay area climate, 1 square foot of collector will produce about 1.5 gallons of hot water per day, so a system with an 80-gallon tank requires 53 square feet of collector. Since collectors aren't available in that size, we would install two 4-by-8-foot collectors (Figure 18).

The relationship between collector and tank varies by climate. In the Sun Belt, the rule of thumb is 1 square foot of collector per 2 gallons of tank capacity (daily use). In the Southeast and Mountain states, this ratio is 1-to-1.5, in the Midwest and Atlantic states it's 1-to-1, and in the Northeast and Northwest it's 1-to-.75

Orientation. It's generally best to face the collectors due south, though in some cases it's wise to account

Drain-Back System

Flat-plate collector

Sensor

Bypass valve

Shut-off valves

Check valve

Cold water in

Hot water out

Controller

Tempering valve

Pump

Backup heater

Shut-off valve

Drain-back tank partially filled with distilled water

Sensor

Heat exchanger coil

Figure 17. A drain-back system uses distilled water as the collector fluid, pumped from a nonpressurized indoor holding tank. The circulator pump runs continuously while heating conditions are good, then shuts off when the temperature drops, allowing the water in the collector to drain back to the tank, thereby preventing freeze damage.

Figure 18. A pumped system typically contains more than one flat-plate collector (left). To allow for easy installation and repair, the author joins the collectors with unions (above).

Figure 19. When this system is up and running, the gauges (A) will show how much heat the water gains as it passes through the collectors. Because the water may become too hot to safely use, the author always installs a tempering valve to prevent scalding (B). A pressure-relief valve (in the center of photo C) opens if the collector itself gets too hot; the cylindrical valve at the top automatically bleeds air from the system.

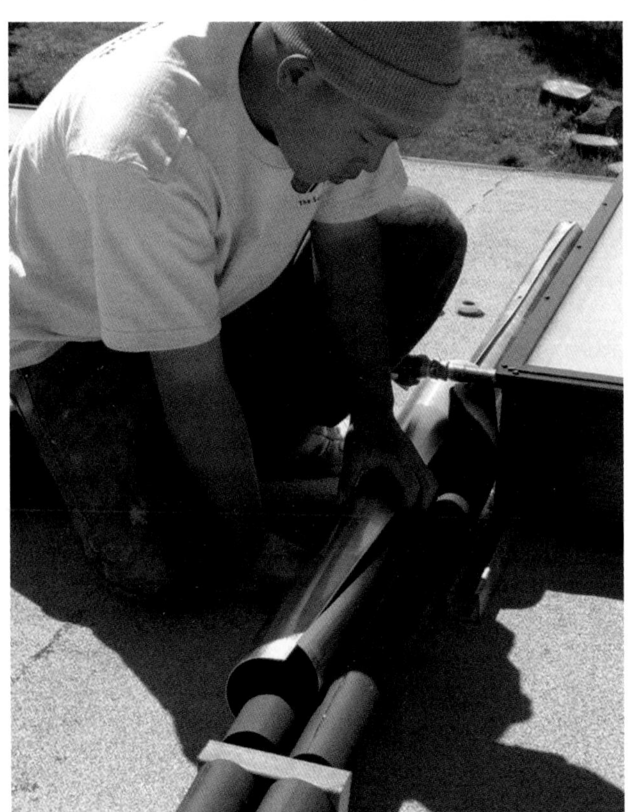

Figure 20. The author's crew insulates every pipe that contains hot or warm water. Here, an installer protects the neoprene insulation with an aluminum jacket.

for local weather patterns. For example, in the San Francisco Bay area there are a lot of overcast mornings, so we prefer to orient collectors slightly more to the west.

For optimal annual collection, collectors should not face straight up, but should be tilted above horizontal to an angle 5 to 10 degrees higher than the latitude at which they are located. Our latitude is 38 degrees, so ideally the collectors would be tilted 43 to 48 degrees. The steeper angle makes for better wintertime solar collection, when the sun is lower in the sky. In cases where aesthetic concerns trump efficiency, we'll install the collectors at the same pitch as the roof.

Temperature rise. When an actively pumped system has been properly sized, each exchange of water will increase the temperature in the storage tank 10°F. On an average day, there might be eight exchanges, creating a total temperature rise of 80°F; in hot, sunny weather it could be more. Our systems routinely reach 180°F in the summer, especially when water usage is low. This water would be too hot to use safely, so to prevent scalding we install a tempering valve downstream from the backup heater.

Excessive pressure can build up in the collectors if they get too hot, so as a matter of course we install a pressure-relief valve on the pipe where fluid exits the collector or group of collectors. A closed-loop system will have a pressure-relief valve on the roof and, if the loop contains glycol, an expansion tank in the building (Figure 19).

Solar Orphans

In the early 1980s, hefty tax credits and high energy prices led to a boom in the installation of solar water heaters. A lot of people entered the business and installed all kinds of equipment, then went under after the tax credits expired and energy prices fell in 1986.

Whereas some of these systems were quite good, others were experimental, and with so many solar companies out of business, there were few qualified people around to maintain and repair them. As a result, many of the older systems failed and gave a black eye to a legitimate technology. Our company runs into these orphaned systems all the time; some are still going strong while others have been "broken" for many years.

Bad advice. When homeowners move into a house with a nonfunctioning system, they're almost always advised to tear it out. Unfortunately, most of the people giving this advice — plumbers, roofers, and GCs — don't know anything about solar water heating.

An experienced solar hot-water installer can tell you which systems should be torn out and which can be repaired. If the system was built with high-quality components and the collectors have never frozen, there's a reasonable chance it can be saved.

Old solar systems, like the one on this original wood roof, may no longer be operable but can often be put back into service for a reasonable cost.

Inexpensive repairs. Our repair crews have revived any number of systems by making a few inexpensive repairs. Sometimes it's a matter of spending $450 (including labor) to replace a pump. A leaking storage tank can be replaced for just over $1,000, which may seem like a lot, but it's a small price to pay to repair a system that would cost $6,000 new.

The most common problem with a pumped system is a failed sensor or loose wire. These repairs may cost only $100, but most plumbers don't know how to make them.

Sometimes the problem is simply that the homeowner doesn't know how to turn on the system.
—G. G.

Installation

The lines to the roof are usually ¾-inch copper. We don't use PEX because in California it's illegal to use it for potable water — plus the high temperatures found in the closed loop of a glycol system could easily be too hot for it.

On new work, we run the lines up through the house. Because we work in a mild climate, on retrofits we usually run pipes down the exterior of the house. We insulate all the pipes that carry hot or recirculated liquid with ¾-inch neoprene, which handles high temperatures better than plastic foam insulation does. Without UV protection, the sun will destroy this insulation in less than five years, so we jacket it with aluminum (Figure 20).

Another option is to protect the insulation with a painted coating, but a metal jacket looks better.

Structural issues. To install the collectors, we use the same mounting hardware we use to install the roof-mounted portions of a photovoltaic system (see "Installing Solar Electric Power," next page). The best approach is to install post mounts before the roofing material goes on, but it's also possible to retrofit various mounting brackets over the shingles.

Weight is rarely a concern with flat-plate collectors, the largest of which weigh less than 175 pounds even when full of water. But a full ICS unit might weigh 500 pounds, and the system might require more than one unit. In such a case, it's important to find out if the roof can carry the load.

Power needs. Most pumps will run on less than one amp of electricity, so inspectors often allow us to tie into an existing circuit or share a circuit with another load in new construction. A few inspectors require us to install a separate circuit. In some jurisdictions, it's legal to plug pumps and controllers into wall receptacles, which we do whenever possible to reduce wiring costs.

Gary Gerber is the owner of Sun Light & Power in Berkeley, Calif. He has been in the solar business since 1975.

Installing Solar Electric Power

by Gary Gerber

Since its invention nearly 50 years ago, solar electric power has been a reliable but relatively expensive technology. Now, however, the cost to produce electricity from sunlight is coming down. Climbing utility rates, combined with the rebates that some states offer, are making photovoltaic (PV) power systems cost-effective in many parts of the country.

In 1975 I started a company in Northern California that specialized in solar thermal hot-water systems. While we still install those systems, the bulk of our business these days comes from designing and installing PV energy systems for residential, commercial, and municipal clients. Sum total, we've installed over a megawatt (one million watts) of solar energy capacity.

In this article, I'll explain how PV power systems are designed and installed, so that contractors know what to expect when a client decides to buy one.

What Customers Want

Clients have different reasons for wanting to install PV power. For some, it's a way to act on environmental values or to become self-sufficient. Others look at the rising energy costs and believe that, in the long run, it will be cheaper to produce their own power.

Financial incentives. Many states, local governments, and utilities provide rebates and tax breaks to property owners who purchase PV systems. A typical 4,000-watt residential system costs about $8.40 per watt without a rebate. The current rebate in California brings this down to $5.60 per watt. For a database of state, federal, and utility-based incentive programs, go to www.dsireusa.org.

Figure 21. Here, an installer bolts a mounting rail to the roof. Modules usually sit on top of rails, but with this low-profile rack they will drop between rails and be a couple of inches closer to the roof than is typical.

A PV system can deliver 30 years of reliable serivce if it's well-engineered and installed properly to avoid roof leaks.

Service life. The systems we install are designed for a 30-year service life. For the customer, it's like paying up-front for 30 years' worth of electricity. We can design the system to offset all or part of the client's electricity needs. Most customers opt to entirely eliminate their utility bills.

Solar modules come with 20- to 25-year warranties stating that the module will still produce 80 percent of its rated output at the end of the warranty period. In fact, the module will continue to function indefinitely, but the output will drop over time. Power inverters typically require one major service or replacement during the life of the system.

Common Misconceptions

Many people are confused about what solar can and can't do. One misconception is that solar modules must be installed on racks that project way off the roof (Figure 21). Solar modules do perform better when oriented perpendicular to the sun's path, but they definitely look better when installed flush to the roof. This reduces output, but can be offset by using money that would have gone into the rack to increase the number of modules.

Battery backup. Another misconception involves

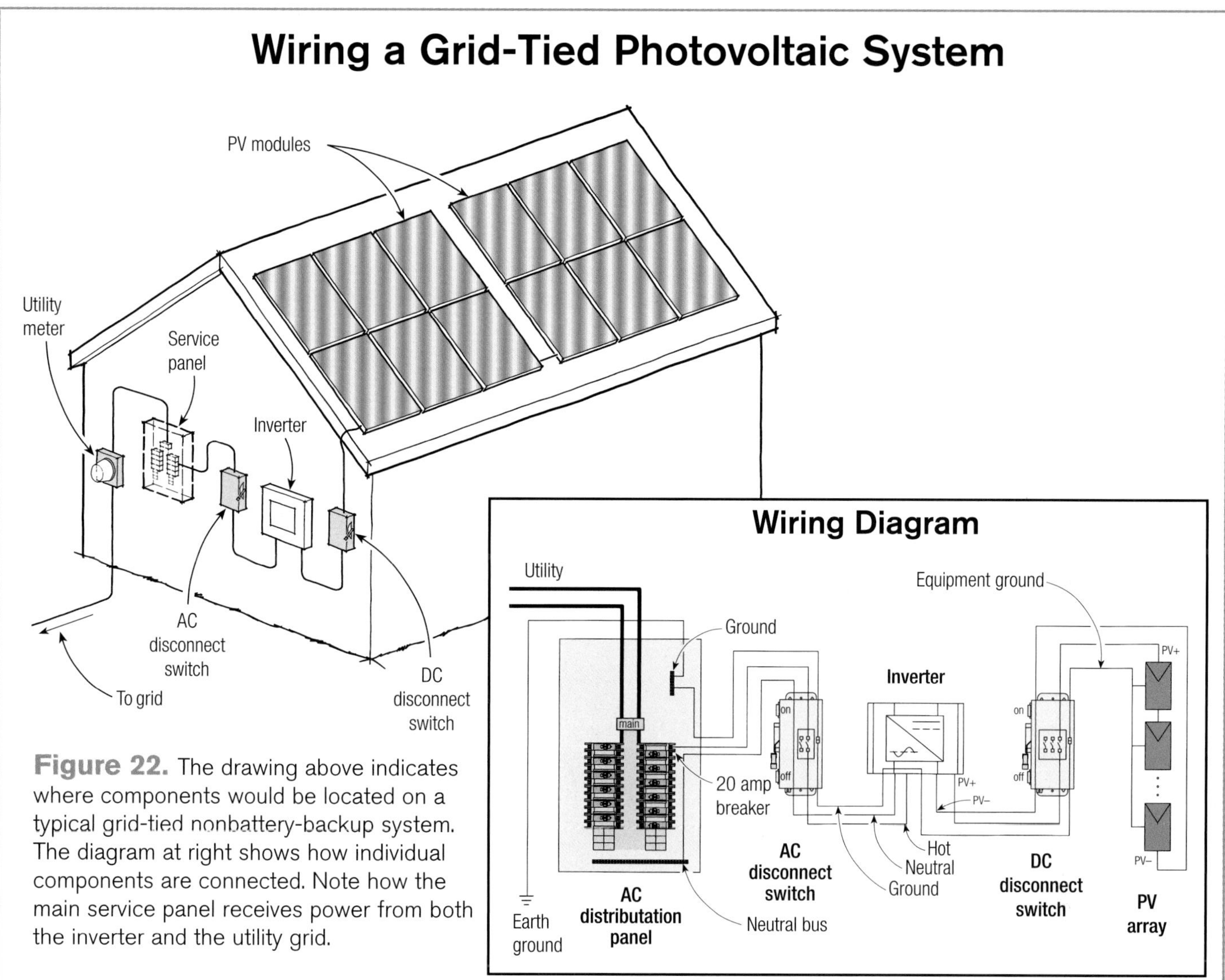

Figure 22. The drawing above indicates where components would be located on a typical grid-tied nonbattery-backup system. The diagram at right shows how individual components are connected. Note how the main service panel receives power from both the inverter and the utility grid.

what happens at night or when the electrical grid is down. There are two types of solar electric systems: grid-tied systems without battery backup and stand-alone systems that may or may not be tied to the grid but have battery backup. If the utility grid is reliable, we recommend against the added cost and complexity of a battery-backup system. The only time we recommend batteries is when the customer absolutely requires uninterruptible power or is in an area where a grid connection isn't feasible.

Nonbattery grid-tied systems will not provide power when the grid goes down. For safety reasons, the inverter in a nonbattery grid-tied system automatically shuts down when the grid is out, thus preventing electricity from backfeeding into power lines and injuring linemen who are making repairs.

Net metering. In most states, net metering legislation allows individuals to feed excess solar energy into the grid. The utility meter spins backward when clients are putting electricity in and forward when they are taking it out. In a case like this, where there is no need to store energy, the customer can install a less expensive grid-tie-only system.

Some customers believe the utility will pay them if they put in more power than they take out. Unfortunately, utilities will not pay for unused credit. The best a customer can do is pay nothing for electricity used. As a result, there is no financial incentive to design a system that produces more power than the client needs.

System Components

The most visible components of a standard grid-tied PV system are the solar electric modules; these roof-mounted devices convert sunlight to electricity. The modules produce DC power, which passes through a DC-rated disconnect switch on its way to a power inverter. The inverter converts the DC power to AC and sends it to the main breaker box via an AC-rated disconnect and standard circuit breakers (Figure 22). Battery-backup systems require additional components, including controllers, power centers, solar subpanels, and batteries.

Solar modules. Most people refer to individual solar

modules as "panels," but, technically, a panel is a group of modules that are wired together. The roof-mounted portion of the system is called an array.

Solar modules are produced by a number of manufacturers and come in many sizes and shapes. Right now, our best-selling model is a particularly efficient 185-watt unit from Sharp. It weighs 37 pounds, measures 62 inches by 32 inches, and is 2 inches thick. The edges are framed in aluminum and the face is covered with tempered glass.

Strings. Modules are ganged together on the roof and wired in series. Each group of series-wired modules is called a string, and often there is more than one string per inverter. A typical residential system might contain 21 185-watt modules in three strings of seven.

Most solar modules produce either 12 or 24 volts. Higher voltage does not equate to more power, however, because a 12-volt unit operates at higher amperage than a 24-volt unit of equal wattage. Other things being equal, output is determined by the number and type of modules. The modules usually account for 75 percent of the total cost of a PV system.

Installation Environment

The installation site will dictate the overall size of the system. Considerations include roof orientation, shading, available roof space, aesthetic concerns, and the capacity of the existing service panel.

Life span of roof. Solar modules usually have to be removed to reroof a building. Fortunately, the 30-year design life of a solar energy system is similar to the service life of most roofing products. It makes sense to synchronize reroofing with the installation of PV modules. We recommend reroofing the building if there are obvious signs of wear and tear or if the roof has less than six years of service left.

Location. It's extremely important to avoid placing modules where they could be shaded by trees, power lines, and other obstructions. Ideally, modules would face due south. In some cases, though, it's possible to install them facing slightly east or west; the drop-off in production is not always that great.

In this area, an array could be oriented to the southwest and still produce 90 percent of what it would produce if it faced due south. An easterly orientation would be a poor choice here because we get a lot of morning fog.

Mounting Schemes

Solar modules can be installed on nearly any type and pitch of roof. They are usually attached to racks — metal rails supported a few inches above the roof's surface by mounts that are bolted to the rafters (Figure 23).

New construction and reroofs. It's easiest to install mounts on new construction or on a roof that has been stripped; this way, we can fasten them without having to worry about leaks. On these jobs, we put post mounts on the sheathing and lag them to the rafters. We then flash the posts with the same flashings used on plumbing vents. This obviously produces more penetrations than usual, but the roofer should be able to warranty his work, because everything is properly flashed.

Tile. On tile roofs, we use an aluminum mounting channel called a Tile Trac (Professional Solar Products, www.prosolar.com). The channel bolts to the deck and a threaded post extends up and passes through a ⅜-inch hole in one of the tiles. This penetration is caulked and, because it's high on the tile and covered by a module, it doesn't leak.

Existing roofs. Retrofits are trickier. On tile roofs, tiles must be removed and reinstalled over the mounts. On flat roofs, some of the membrane must be removed and patched back in.

We install many systems over existing composition shingle roofs. The preferred method is to fasten mounts through the shingles. Tile Trac works well for this application. It comes in 8-inch sections, which we install up the slope on a thick bed of sealant (Figure 24). We've put a lot of effort into finding appropriate products for this application and have settled on tripolymer sealants like Geocel 2300 (www.geocelusa.com) because they are durable, adhere well, and are compatible with asphalt shingles. As an added precau-

Figure 23. Post mounts are designed for new construction and should be installed, flashed, and shingled over before the rails and modules go on. Rails and modules are already attached to the mounts upslope and will soon be bolted to the mounts at left in this photo.

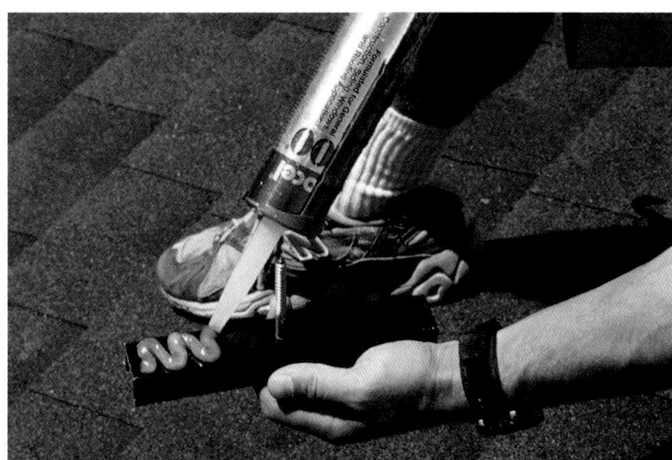

Figure 24. It's common to retrofit systems to buildings with existing shingle roofs. In the photo, above, an installer caulks the back of a Tile Trac mounting bracket before bolting it through the shingles to the rafter below. Metal flashings (right) are installed upslope to divert rainwater from the penetration.

tion, we divert water from the penetration by installing a piece of step flashing just upslope.

On retrofits, it's important to avoid drilling unnecessary holes through the roof. It's easy to locate rafters when the tails are exposed, but when they aren't, we go into the attic and drill a pilot hole next to the rafter where the first mount will be located (Figure 25). We leave the bit sticking up and locate other mounts by measuring off it. Rafters may not be evenly spaced, so we always check the layout from inside.

Loads. The local building department will want to know how much load the solar array adds to the roof. It's typically 4 pounds per square foot. We've had some success convincing concerned inspectors and engineers that the added load on the existing structure is okay because no one can walk on an area that's covered with modules. Also, it doesn't snow in our part of the country, so offsetting the local requirement for 20 pounds of live load with 4 pounds of dead load is usually a no-brainer.

Hardware. Our systems are designed to last 30 years, so it's important to use hardware that will not corrode or react. All of the components on the roof are made from aluminum or stainless steel, including the lags that secure mounts to the roof and the nuts, bolts, and washers that hold the other parts together. We've come across corrosion problems that occurred when competitors combined aluminum, copper, and galvanized steel in the same installation.

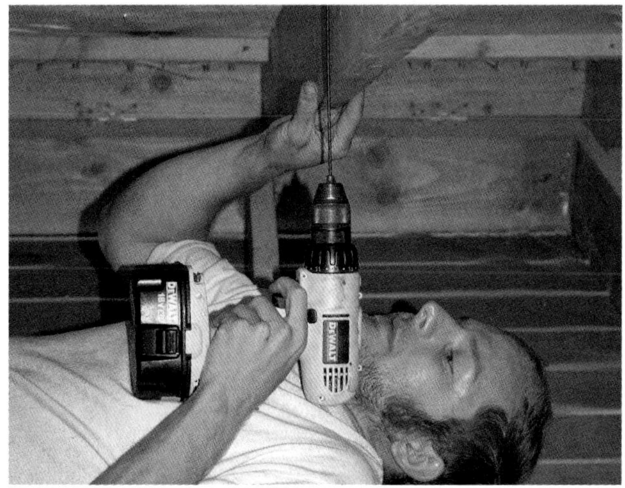

Figure 25. An installer locates the first roof mount by drilling a pilot hole next to a rafter. Other rafters are located from above by measuring off the protruding bit. To prevent leaks, the installer fills the hole with sealant and covers it with the mount.

Wiring

Whenever possible, we rough in home-run wiring from the roof to the inverter location while the studs are still open. On retrofits, we typically penetrate the roof eaves (Figure 26) and run conduit down the outside of the building. We always make sure that the owner signs off on the location of the conduit.

Once the conduit is installed, the solar crew pulls home-run wiring from the module locations to the DC disconnect. Typically, it's 10-gauge or 12-gauge outdoor-rated stranded wire.

Connecting the modules. We fasten the modules side by side on the rack and wire them together in

Figure 26. The crew uses a standard roof flashing with a self-sealing collar to waterproof the opening where electrical conduit penetrates the roof.

Figure 27. On a series-connected system, adjoining modules are connected positive to negative in much the same way as batteries in a flashlight.

Figure 28. Modules should be grounded to each other and to the rack with a continuous ground wire. On this project, the installer is using a length of tinned copper braid to ground the array.

Figure 29. This job was new construction, so the wires from the roof came down inside. The DC disconnect is usually outdoors, but on this project it's in the crawlspace on the other side of the wall from the inverter. Note the home-run wiring on the neutral and ground.

series (Figure 27). Each module has a positive and negative wire: The positive from one module connects to the negative on its neighbor. We used to hard-wire between connection boxes on the backs of modules; now we connect them using wires equipped with a waterproof quick-connect device.

Grounding. Grounding is extremely important and is something every inspector is familiar with. Section 690 of the NEC (which deals specifically with solar power) requires all modules and metal racks to be bonded to the house grounding system. It also requires a ground-fault interrupt for roof-mounted systems. Instead of using separate wires to daisy-chain the modules together, we ground them to each other and to the rack with a continuous copper wire (Figure 28). We may need to add a GFCI, but one is usually built into the inverter.

Once the modules are connected, there will be a leftover wire at each end of the string, one positive and one negative. We connect these wires plus the ground to the wires from the inverter.

DC disconnect. By code, a PV power system must have an adequately rated disconnect switch so the inverter can be isolated from modules for servicing (Figure 29). The disconnect can be located anywhere, as long as it conforms to NEC regulations with respect to accessibility and maximum height. Manual disconnects must be mounted in such a way that the midpoint of the handle in its highest position is no more than 78 inches from the ground.

The positive wire from the modules lands on a terminal in the disconnect. We run the negative straight through to the inverter, because the fewer connections there, the fewer problems there are likely to be

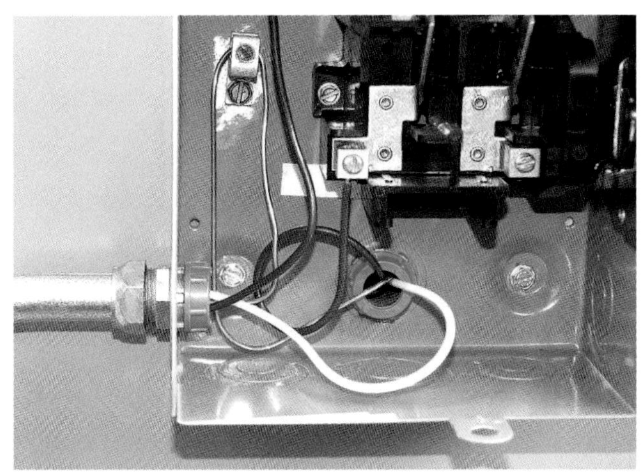

Figure 30. Each additional connection increases the risk for problems. The hot wire lands on the terminal of this disconnect, but the neutral and ground run straight through without being cut.

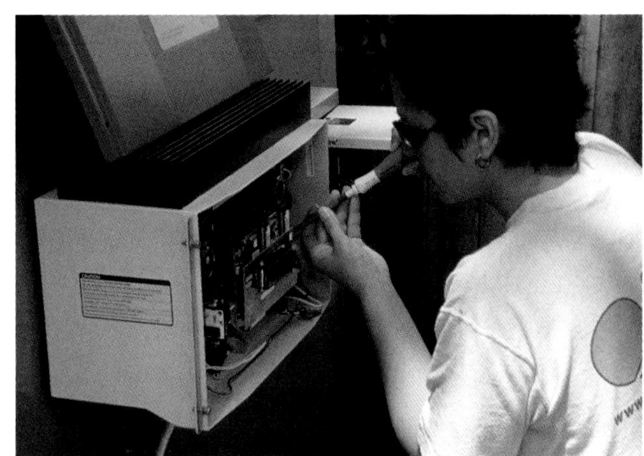

Figure 31. The inverter converts DC power from the modules to AC household current. It's a sophisticated piece of control equipment that is the brain of a grid-tie system. The fins on top of the case are for cooling.

Figure 32. It's sometimes more economical to install two smaller inverters than to go to the next larger size.

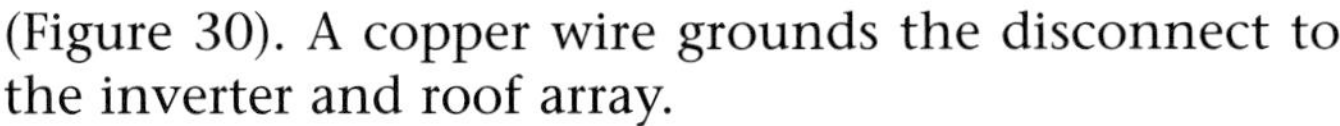

(Figure 30). A copper wire grounds the disconnect to the inverter and roof array.

Inverter

A series-connected string of modules produces high-voltage DC power, which must be run through an inverter to convert it to 120-volt AC (Figure 31). One of the more common inverters we install is rated for 2,500 watts, but inverters are also available for both bigger and smaller systems (Figure 32).

Most inverters can be mounted indoors or out. They often generate an appreciable amount of heat and make subtle humming noises during heavy operation. For these reasons, the inverter should be mounted in a well-ventilated area, out of direct sunlight, and away from walls adjoining living areas that get a lot of daytime use.

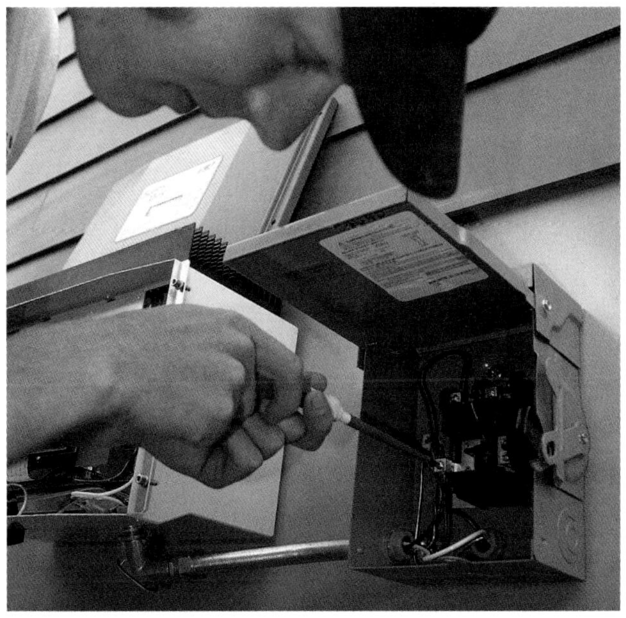

Figure 33. The inverter produces 120-volt AC power, which passes through an AC disconnect on its way to the main service panel. The hole through the lever is for a padlock to lock out the system.

AC disconnect. Our local utility requires a lockable AC-rated disconnect between the inverter and main service panel. It's there to isolate the PV system from the utility. Although it seldom does so, the utility has the right to shut off and lock out the PV system at this disconnect to prevent power from backfeeding into the grid. For this reason, the AC disconnect must be outdoors and within 10 feet of the main service panel (Figure 33).

Sizing a Photovoltaic System

The first thing the solar contractor needs to do is assess the clients' energy goals. Do the clients want to produce 30 percent, 50 percent, or 100 percent of the power they use? Do they plan to add on to the building or change something about the way it's used? Once we know what the clients want, we estimate how much energy the system will need to produce.

Historical versus projected usage. The simplest and most accurate method is to look at past utility bills and add up the number of kilowatt-hours (kWh) used per year. Divide this number by 365 and you have the average daily power consumption. The chart below contains sample data from one of our customers.

If there isn't any historical data, as happens in new construction, we sit down with the customers and list all the loads that are likely to occur. The list includes information such as the appliances they own, the number of hours per day they are at home, and how often they use air conditioning or heat. This method is most common in off-grid situations.

Month	kWh
January	310
February	298
March	305
April	370
May	365
June	410
July	487
August	500
September	480
October	370
November	350
December	300
Yearly Total	4,545
Average kWh/day	4,545÷365 = 12.45

The historical method is most accurate because it's based on real data from the actual client. Data from previous occupants or information gained before the completion of a major remodel can lead to inaccurate load assessments.

Calculations. Knowing the average daily consumption, we can roughly size the system based on the number of sun-hours per day where the building is located. In California, the yearly average is four to five hours of sun per day. In New England, it might be only three to four hours per day. The rough calculation for a system in San Francisco is as follows:

12.45 kWh per day ÷ 5 sun-hours per day = 2.49 kW AC system size

We perform the final calculation with an online design tool called PVWatts (www.nrel.gov/rredc/pvwatts/grid.html). PVWatts uses test data from actual systems to accurately project output based on such local conditions as weather and the orientation of modules on the roof. In my area, a 2.49 kW system with a true southern orientation and an 18-degree (4/12) slope will produce 4,441 kWh per year. Because the client needs 4,545 kWh of electricity per year, a 2.49 kW system will be undersized. According to PVWatts, a 2.55 kW system will produce 4,548 kWh, which is just about right.

Main Service Panel

The solar electric system is usually connected to the grid through the main service panel. AC power comes from the inverter, passes through a circuit breaker, and lands on the bus bar in the panel.

The electrical sub should talk to the solar sub to make sure there is room for an extra breaker in the service panel and that the bus bar is rated to accept the amount of power that comes from the grid plus additional power from the PV system. The existing service panel may be inadequate, in which case it will have to be upgraded or replaced before the PV system can be connected.

Tie-downs. By code, breakers that backfeed panels must be tied down to prevent them from coming free. A few municipalities enforce this provision, but we've convinced many that it's unnecessary, since all grid-tied inverters automatically disconnect from the grid when the grid goes out. This comes up because most residential systems are tied to the bus bar by 15-amp or 20-amp breakers, a size not normally available with tie-downs. Breakers can be adapted for tie-downs, but it's awkward to do.

Gary Gerber *is the owner of Sun Light & Power, Berkeley, Calif. He has been in the solar business since 1975.*

Builder's Guide to Geothermal Heat Pumps

by Bruce Harley

I'm standing in a cramped attic in a one-year-old house, trying to discover the problem with the ground-source heat pump in front of me. As an engineer who tests dozens of heat pumps each year, I often get called in to troubleshoot problems no one else is able to solve.

Within a few minutes, I determine that one of the two compressors in this two-speed heat pump has shut down. I also discover that the return duct is undersized, causing extremely low air flow, and the supply duct to one particularly cold room is losing more than half its air through leaks into the attic.

These discoveries explain the problems the homeowners recited to me over the phone. It began with the heat pump contractor who installed the unit in an uninsulated attic, contrary to the manufacturer's recommendations. After the water coil on the heat pump froze, flooding the garage ceiling, the contractor cut a small hole in the supply duct to try to warm up the attic, and attempted to repair the leak. He didn't realize, however, that the repair blocked the water flow through the coil, which soon caused the compressor to shut down.

In the meantime, the owners insulated the attic area to prevent future freeze-ups, but they were surprised to see that their electric bills skyrocketed. After several months of high utility bills, they again called the contractor, who came and pulled the fuse on the electric backup heat. But he didn't notice the shut-down compressor which, by failing to produce any heat, had been the reason the electric heat was kicking in.

Of course, with the resistance heat turned off, the upstairs zone was now too cold. So just a week before I arrived, the desperate owners had called in a different contractor, who taped up the hole in the supply duct and turned the resistance heat back on. But he also failed to notice that half the machine was shut down.

This case is not typical of heat pump installations, but it does illustrate how an inadequate understanding of how heat pumps work can make simple problems worse. If you're planning your first heat pump installation, it's important to have a good understanding of geothermal principles, because these systems are less forgiving of certain installation errors than conventional hvac systems.

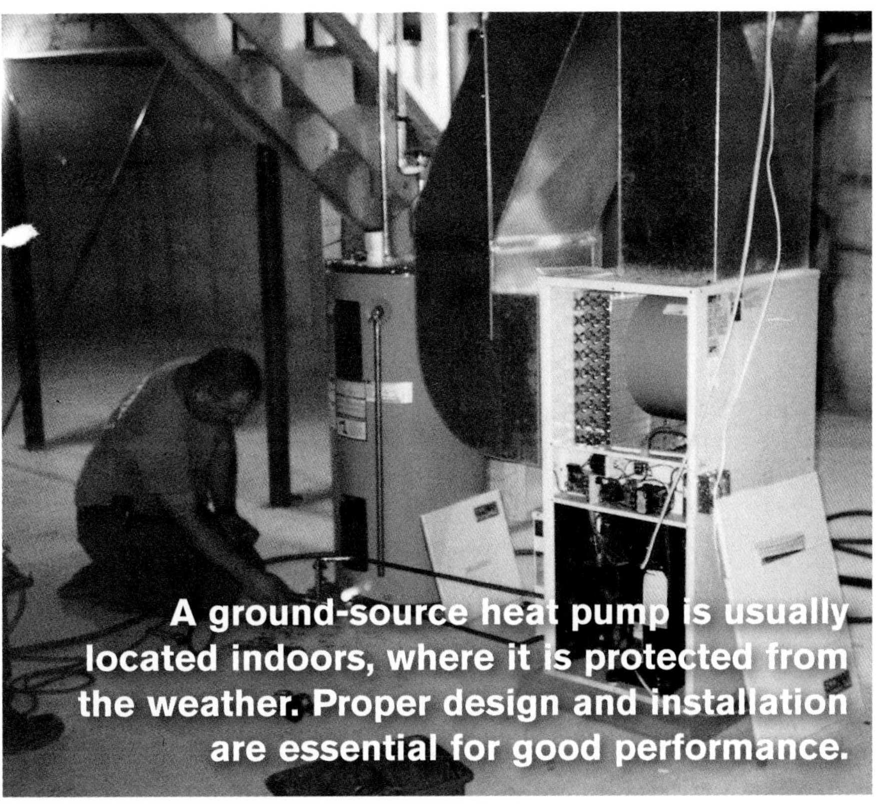

A ground-source heat pump is usually located indoors, where it is protected from the weather. Proper design and installation are essential for good performance.

Heat Pump Basics

A heat pump is basically an air conditioner that can be reversed. In the summer, it moves heat out of the house to provide air conditioning, and in the winter it moves heat into the house to provide heating. Air-source heat pumps use an outdoor coil, just like the coil in a standard central air conditioner, to move heat to or from the outdoor air. A geothermal heat pump uses a water well or a buried loop of pipe to extract heat from the soil to heat a building and to deliver heat back to the ground for cooling. Because the ground is so much warmer than outdoor air in winter, and so much cooler in the summer, geothermal systems are much more efficient than standard heat pumps and air conditioners. Geothermal systems that use a buried loop are called "closed-loop" systems, and those that use well water are referred to as "open loop" (Figure 34).

The cost of the ground loop makes a geothermal system more expensive to install than an air-source heat pump or a standard furnace with central air conditioning. However, the investment can pay for itself in lower utility bills (see "Geothermal Economics," page 388).

Closed-Loop Systems

A closed loop consists of buried polyethylene or polybutylene pipe containing water or antifreeze solution,

Geothermal Options

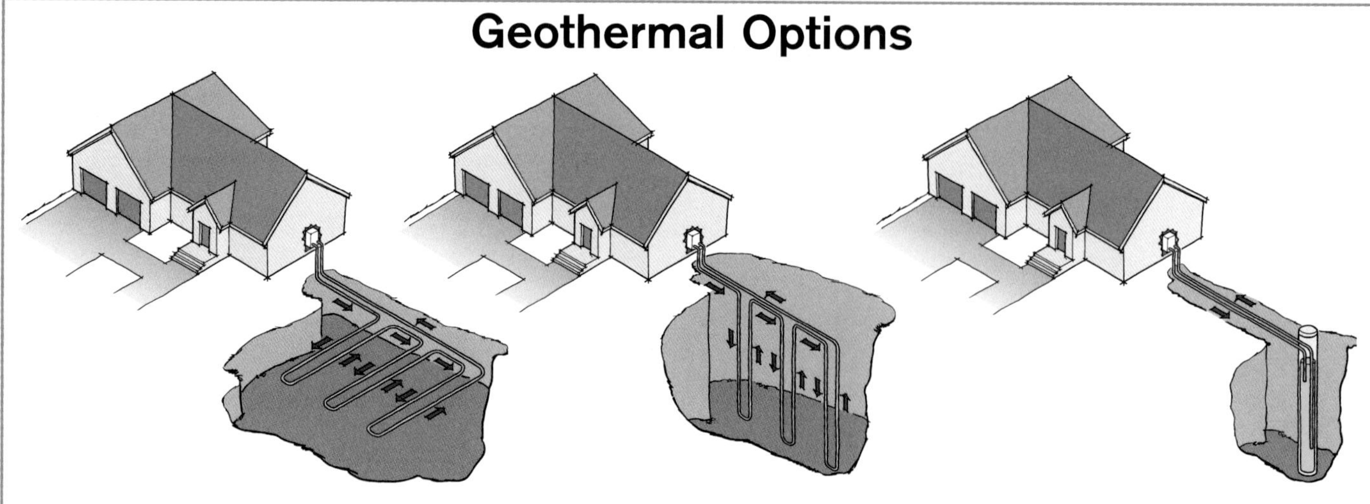

Figure 34. The three most common types of geothermal loops are horizontal closed loops, installed in trenches (left); vertical closed loops, installed in bore holes (center); and open loops, which use well water (right).

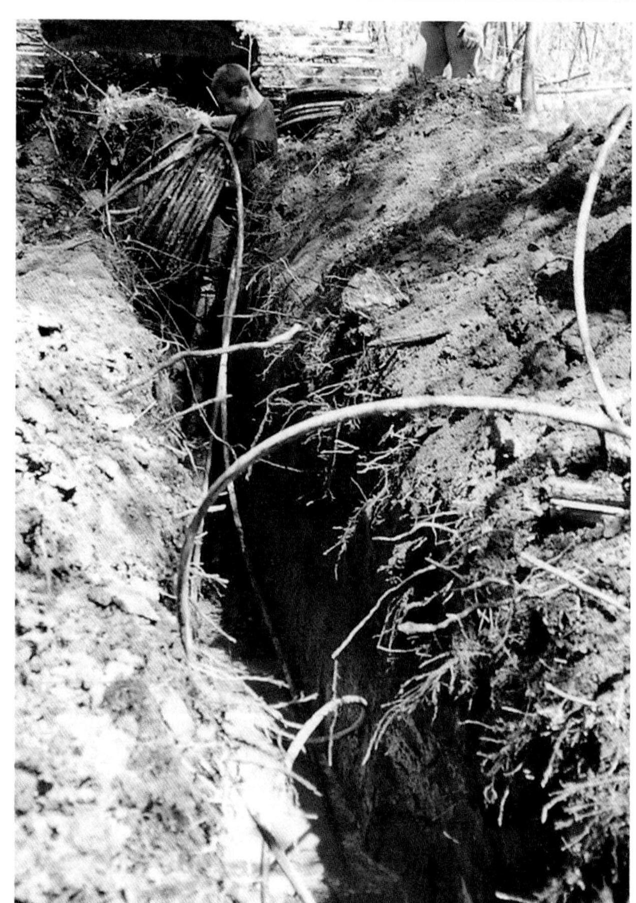

Figure 35. After a backhoe digs a 5-foot-deep trench, two parallel polyethylene pipes are laid for one section of a horizontal ground loop.

which is circulated by means of a small pump. It can be either a horizontal ground loop, installed in a trench or excavated area (Figure 35), or a vertical ground loop, installed in a drilled bore hole (Figure 36). Each bore hole in a vertical loop receives a U-shaped length of pipe, which is grouted in place (Figure 37).

Closed-loop systems are usually more expensive to install than open-loop systems. Pumping costs are lower, however, because there is no need to raise deep well water. A new type of closed-loop system achieves very high efficiencies with smaller ground loops by using copper piping instead of plastic and by circulating refrigerant directly from the ground loop to the heat pump (see "Direct-Exchange Systems Push

Figure 36. A well driller prepares to dig the bore holes for a vertical ground loop. On this job there were four 200-foot bore holes, each containing 400 feet of polyethylene pipe.

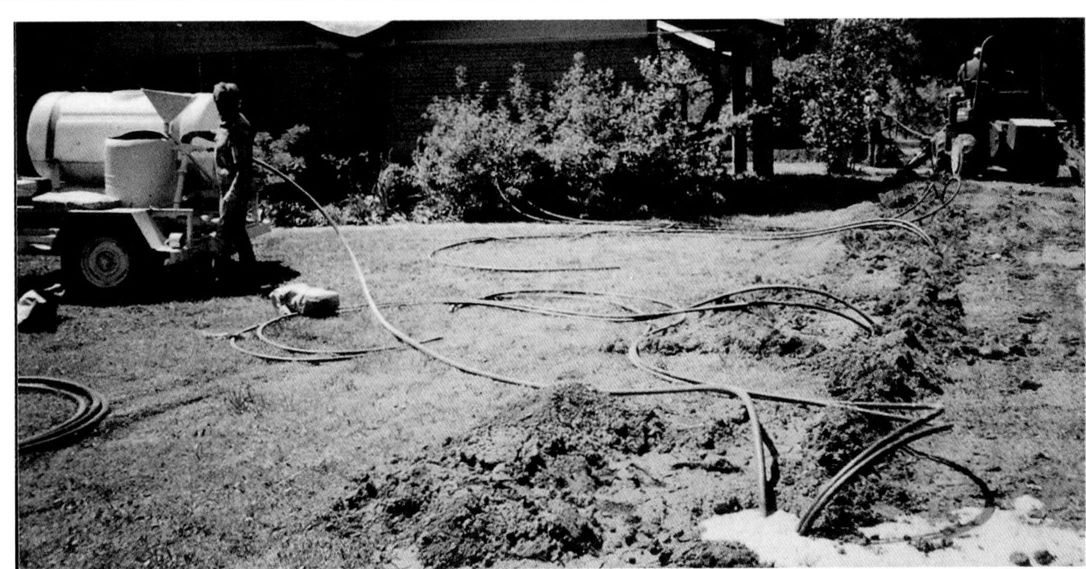

Figure 37. Each of the four bore holes for this vertical loop installation was grouted after the pipes were installed. The grout improves the thermal conductivity between the soil and the loop.

the Limits," page 390).

The following details are critical when installing a closed-loop system:

Proper loop sizing. If a loop is too small, it can cause severe efficiency problems, and there's no way to fix it once it's buried. It's better to have a loop that's slightly oversized. But if loop sizing is too generous, the installation gets expensive fast. Be sure that your installer has support from the heat pump manufacturer or plenty of local experience in loop sizing, and be sure the designer takes the local soil conditions into account.

Closed-loop systems typically vary from 100 to 150 feet of trench or bore hole per ton of heat-pump capacity, which accommodates 200 to 300 feet of pipe (assuming two pipes, one feed and one return). Be wary of any closed loop with less than 200 feet of pipe per ton. (One ton is 12,000 Btu/hour in heat or AC output.) Some configurations, like 4- or 6-pipe trenches, or "slinky" loops with extended spirals, use shorter trenches but much more pipe (Figure 38).

Pipe diameter is critical to proper loop design and must be calculated by a qualified designer. Substituting a smaller or larger pipe diameter can lead to poor performance (Figure 39).

Connection method. Any underground connections must be heat-fused — never glued or mechanically fastened (Figure 40). Pipe connections should be pressure-tested before backfilling.

Backfill material. Be sure loop trenches are backfilled with material that is free of sharp rocks that could cut the pipes.

Loop flushing. Loops must be flushed with a high-powered water pump to clean out air bubbles and any contaminants. If the flushing pump is too small, it will be unable to remove all the air bubbles, especially in a slinky installation.

Figure 38. This closed-loop system uses "slinky" coils, installed horizontally in a wide excavation. The ground loop is being backfilled with clean material.

Open-Loop Systems

Open-loop installations take water directly from a well or other source. There are three types of open-loop systems: "pump and dump," two-well, and standing-column.

In a pump-and-dump system, water is pumped out of a well, run through the heat pump, and then disposed of. This only works if there is an acceptable

Geothermal Economics

The cost of the ground loop makes a geothermal system more expensive to install than an air-source heat pump or a standard furnace with central air. The extra cost, compared with a high-efficiency furnace and central air conditioning, can vary from $2,000 to $15,000 per house, depending on many of the factors described below. In many cases, the extra cost can be recovered in lower utility bills. The details vary by locale, but here are some general factors that affect the payback period.

- ***Electricity prices***. Low electric rates favor geothermal heating systems. In areas of the country with higher electric rates, such as New England, oil or gas heating may be cheaper than geothermal heating. However, geothermal cooling will always be cheaper to operate than standard air conditioning, and higher electric rates will just speed up the payback.
- ***Cooling loads***. Homes in climates with low annual air conditioning loads have less available savings from which to pay back the initial investment.
- ***Cost of other heating fuel**s*. The higher the cost of oil, natural gas, or propane, the more likely that geothermal will be competitive.
- ***Availability of rebates***. In some parts of the country, utility rebates reduce the up-front cost. If the rebates are generous, they may reduce the payback time to zero.
- ***House size***. Larger homes have bigger budgets to absorb the initial cost, and higher annual heating and cooling loads to speed up payback times.
- ***Availability of installers***. The cost of installing a ground loop varies considerably, depending on the local availability of experienced installers.
- ***Ease of excavation***. The cost of a closed-loop system will be lower in soil that can be easily excavated with a trencher. For an open-loop system, a ready supply of groundwater can result in lower well-drilling costs.

These guidelines are by no means hard and fast rules; in New England, where I live, most of these factors are not favorable to geothermal, and yet I've seen many sensible and cost-effective installations there.

place to drain the water. Conservation authorities can be wary of pump-and-dump systems, but I've seen outflows dumped acceptably into ponds, streams, drywells, and even into a municipal sewer system. Just be sure to ask first, before you get into trouble.

Two-well systems pump water from one well through the heat pump, then back into another nearby well. There are standards for the minimum distance between the wells. These systems are less common than single-well systems, because the extra drilling can be expensive.

Standing-column systems use a single well, often the same well used for the domestic water supply. The

Figure 39. This polyethylene pipe has been prepared for lowering into a bore hole for a vertical ground loop. The U-fitting will sit in the bottom of the bore hole.

Figure 40. Heat-fusion is used to join the polyethylene pipe of a closed-loop ground-source heat pump. When properly made, such joints are said to be stronger than the pipe itself.

water for the heat pump is pumped out near the bottom of the well and returned back near the top of the well, but below the surface of the water. As a rule of thumb, a standing-column system requires a minimum of 60 feet of vertical separation per ton of heat pump capacity between the submersible pump and the return discharge.

Although a standing-column system uses 3 gallons per minute of well water per ton of heat pump capacity, the actual flow or yield from the well can be less, because all or most of the water is pumped back into the well. It helps if the static water level (the top of the water column) is relatively close to the surface — ideally, within 30 feet of grade. Lower static water levels require more power to pump the water through the system and, therefore, result in less efficient performance.

Carefully consider the following issues before putting in an open-loop system:

Pump sizing. I have tested many open-loop systems that cost the owners 50 to 100 percent more to run than expected because of oversized well pumps. The big, 240-volt beasts used to pressurize domestic water systems use two to four times as much power as a small circulator, which is all that's needed to move fluid in a closed loop. The pump size should be carefully engineered; don't let a well driller talk you into a larger pump, just to be "safe."

Flow rate. Flow rate through the heat pump is usually controlled by a ball valve or a flow regulator. If the flow is too high, it can damage the heat exchanger and will also cost more to run. However, low flows can reduce output. Heat pumps with two-speed compressors are designed to run on low speed, when there isn't much demand for heating or cooling, to save power. These systems need separate flow control for low speed; if the water flow isn't matched to the lower speed, it may cost even more to operate at low speed than at high speed.

Operating pressure. It can be tricky to design an open-loop system that shares a well with domestic water, because the domestic water system needs a higher water pressure than the heat pump, which needs only 15 to 20 psi to operate. Don't give in to the temptation to oversize the submersible pump just to satisfy the need for high pressure for the domestic water supply. A better solution is to add a second pump (an indoor jet pump) and a separate pressure tank just for the domestic supply.

Bleed water dumping. Standing-column wells may need a bleed control that senses the incoming water temperature. This control diverts a small amount of the flow away from the return pipe when the well gets too cold. As with a pump-and-dump system, you need an acceptable place to dispose of this water; but since the amount of water is less (only about 10 percent of the flow through the machine), it's much easier to deal with.

Installation Requirements

Regardless of loop type, every geothermal installation requires a tightly built house, well-installed ductwork, and coordination between the various subcontractors.

Build a tight shell. Never put a geothermal system into a home that isn't well insulated and tight. Because of the high initial cost of geothermal equipment, it's almost always cheaper to upgrade the building envelope with extra insulation, better windows, and air-sealing work than it is to install a larger heat pump. Explain the energy details of the building to the hvac contractor, so he can perform accurate heating and cooling load calculations.

Insist on high-quality ductwork. Heat pumps are not sized to provide the excess capacity that would be necessary to make up for undersized or leaky ductwork (Figure 41). I've seen poorly installed ductwork that

continued on page 392

Figure 41. This branch duct jumps under a beam and across a joist bay, creating friction losses and reducing air flow. Plan the location of duct runs before framing begins, to avoid complicated ducts like this one.

Direct-Exchange Systems Push the Limits

by John Vastyan

After extensive research, the New Hampshire homeowners decided to install a geothermal heating and cooling system in their new coastal home. The type of system they chose — called direct exchange — is at the cutting edge of ground-source technology and is currently offered by two leading geothermal companies, Earthlinked Technologies (www.earthlinked.com) and American Geothermal (www.amgeo.com).

A direct-exchange heat pump is notably different from the typical water-source geothermal system, which exchanges the earth's thermal energy through water distributed in vast networks of plastic tubing. Direct-exchange technology accomplishes thermal transfer at much higher operational efficiencies because it eliminates one complete heat-exchange process. Also, because direct-exchange uses a much smaller earth loop (or "geo field"), it requires much less disruption of the property, making it ideal for retrofits (see Figure A).

The installation contractor, Air Brokers Hvac, in Branson, Mo., has installed various types of geo systems, but the company prefers direct-exchange technology because of the higher efficiency it delivers and the greater flexibility it can offer for installation of the earth loops. "The newer technology extracts heat with little disruption to the surrounding landscape and at such high operating efficiencies that it makes payback on the investment faster than ever before," says company owner Gemma Tiller.

Installed costs are about the same for direct-exchange and water-source systems, although both are several thousand

Figure A. Because direct-exchange technology is so efficient at collecting the heat of the earth, installations are possible even on retrofits with small lots. While trenches or pits are less expensive, drilling — either vertically or at an angle — makes it possible to work around ledge or in tight quarters.

Figure B. Rather than PEX tubing used in conventional geothermal heating, direct-exchange systems use copper for a highly efficient heat transfer (top). Normally, the copper is protected by sand, which is installed in a slurry to ensure good coverage and optimum heat transfer (above). In areas where excessive groundwater might pipe away the sand, a special grout is used instead. *Note*: In some cases, corrosive soils may prevent installation.

Table 1. Typical Heating & Cooling Costs of Geothermal Systems

System description	Total heating cost	Total cooling cost	Water heating cost	Total operating cost	Average monthly cost
Direct-exchange geothermal	$463	$135	$225	$823	$69
Closed-loop, water-source geothermal	$602	$156	$512	$1,270	$106
Air source, 12 SEER HP	$737	$193	$512	$1,441	$120
12 SEER AC w/80% natural-gas furnace	$1,301	$193	$515	$2,009	$167

Note: The test case shown is for a typically insulated 2,436-square-foot new home with a family of three in Chicago, which has cold winters and hot, muggy summers. The cooling load is 24,717 Btu/hr and the heating load is 43,668 Btu/hr. The example assumes $.09 per kWh for electricity, $1.30 per therm for natural gas. Domestic hot-water design assumes a 60-gallon tank with 50°F entering water temperature and a tank temperature of 125°F. This data comes from Audit, by Elite, a widely used professional energy-analysis software.

dollars more than a conventional air-to-air heat pump. With direct-exchange systems, however, small-diameter drilling for a geo field can achieve near "surgical" insertion of the ground loops, accomplishing the task quickly and with much less disturbance to the surroundings.

How Direct Exchange Works

Typical water-source geothermal systems rely on plastic piping to transfer a water-antifreeze solution through a plastic loop and an intermediate heat exchanger, where efficiency is lost.

By contrast, direct-exchange technology circulates refrigerant through highly conductive copper earth loops that are inserted into small-diameter bore holes of 50- to 100-foot depths, then embedded in sand or a protective thermal grout that enables direct transfer of energy with the earth (Figure B).

The refrigerant moves directly from the geo field to the unit's compressor with no stops or intermediate heat exchangers required, enabling super-efficient transfer of thermal energy. Only a small amount of electricity is needed to power the system's compressor.

The direct-exchange systems can produce efficiencies in the 400 percent range, compared with 250 to 350 percent for typical water-source systems (see Table 1).

Evaluating the Site

Depending on the site, the hvac contractor will choose a vertical, horizontal, or diagonal earth-loop installation. Horizontal earth-loops are the least expensive to install, chiefly because excavating and backfilling are less expensive than drilling. But in areas where rock layers obstruct excavation, it may be necessary to drill holes for the diagonal and vertical applications. Drilling is also a viable option on small lots.

Both Earthlinked and American Geo recommend that soils be tested for high concentrations of acids, chlorides, hydrogen sulfide, sulfates, and ammonia, all of which should be avoided because of the potential for copper corrosion. Earthlinked recommends that soil samples be taken with a coring tube, specifically the LaMotte model 1016 (www.lamotte.com). Your local soils engineering firm should be familiar with these tests.

Also, locations with a pH higher than 11 or lower than 6 and coastal areas with brackish water marshes, saltwater intrusion, or acidic peat bogs should be avoided unless cathodic protection is provided for the copper piping. Earthlinked offers a cathodic protection system; it emits a small, self-adjusting electric current that prohibits corrosion.

Equipment Installation

Once the earth loop is in, installation of a ground-source heat pump is very similar to an air-source installation. Since geothermal condensing units don't require air circulation, as do typical air-source systems, they may be installed in a basement or utility room.

Typically, a geothermal system will provide service for 25 to 30 years, which is twice the life expectancy of air-source heat pumps. This is because the stable heat source prevents thermal stresses to the compressor, and the enclosed unit is out of the weather.

John Vastyan *is a freelance journalist in Manheim, Pa., who specializes in the plumbing, mechanical, radiant heat, and geothermal industries.*

continued from page 389

puts more heating or cooling air into the attic or garage than into some rooms. Be sure your installer seals all duct connections with mastic, not duct tape, and insulates the ducts thoroughly (Figure 42).

Plan ahead. Work with the hvac contractor to allow space for the ductwork in the building design. If possible, keep ducts out of the attic. If ducts must be installed in an attic, be sure they are well sealed and run low to the ceiling. Then cover the ductwork with loose-fill insulation to achieve a higher R-value than you would get with typical duct wrap.

Make communication between subcontractors a high priority. In some heat pump installations, up to four different subcontractors are involved (the excavator, the well driller, the electrician, and the hvac contractor). With this many subs, there are plenty of opportunities for miscommunication.

Design & Testing

You may be wondering, "Do I need to be a heat-pump expert to put one in a house I'm building?" No, you don't need to be an expert — but you should know enough to ask a potential hvac subcontractor the right questions:

Are you planning to do a complete heating and cooling load calculation? The Air Conditioning Contractors of America (ACCA) Manual J — Residential Load Calculation is the industry standard. Several software programs are available to help speed up load calculations. Good practice requires the contractor to measure wall, ceiling, floor, and window areas; to include insulation levels and window performance data; and to look at the house's compass orientation, since this affects cooling loads dramatically. Verify that the subcontractor is performing calculations for each room, not the whole building. With gas or oil heat, you can be sloppy in estimating heating requirements, because a larger furnace costs only a few hundred dollars more. But with a heat pump, one size too big can cost thousands. On the other hand, if your installer undersizes the unit, the house may require so much electric resistance heat to make up the difference that your customer will end up with an outrageous electric bill.

Figure 42. The ductwork for this heat-pump installation has been carefully insulated.

What about the duct design? Your hvac sub should base the duct design on ACCA's Manual D — Residential Duct Systems. Avoid flex duct, which is easily punctured and tends to develop sags and kinks.

How about factory support? Make sure that the manufacturer of the equipment has a rep who offers good support and that your hvac sub isn't afraid to use it. If possible, find a contractor who has attended a factory-authorized training program on geothermal installations.

What type of startup testing do you perform? When the system is in place, your contractor should do more than plug it in and see if it works. The minimum required tests include: water flow rate, temperature change across the water coil, temperature across the air stream, and the air pressures ("static pressures") in the main supply and return ducts. Such tests only take a few minutes. If all these values aren't within factory limits, something is probably wrong — and if so, all of the tests will need to be repeated after the problem is fixed.

Never use a contractor who doesn't have a substantial amount of experience with geothermal systems. You can look at a previous job to see if he thoroughly sealed the duct connections with mastic; used smooth, rounded fittings and direct duct runs rather than long, twisted runs with many abrupt transitions; and minimized use of flex duct.

Any installer with a good track record should be able to supply the names of several happy customers who will tell you that their house is comfortable and their electric bills are low. If you can find the right sub, you should be well on your way to providing a comfortable, efficient, and trouble-free geothermal system for your customers.

Bruce Harley *is engineering project manager at Conservation Services Group, which administers energy efficiency programs for U.S. utilities.*

K

L

M